WORLD TRADE ORGANIZATION

Dispute Settlement Reports

2000

Volume XI

Pages 5119-5719

CAMBRIDGE
UNIVERSITY PRESS

PUBLISHED BY THE PRESS SYNDICATE OF THE UNIVERSITY OF CAMBRIDGE
The Pitt Building, Trumpington Street, Cambridge, United Kingdom

CAMBRIDGE UNIVERSITY PRESS
The Edinburgh Building, Cambridge CB2 2RU, UK
40 West 20th Street, New York, NY 10011–4211, USA
477 Williamstown Road, Port Melbourne, VIC 3207, Australia
Ruiz de Alarcón 13, 28014 Madrid, Spain
Dock House, The Waterfront, Cape Town 8001, South Africa

http://www.cambridge.org

Printed in the United Kingdom at the University Press, Cambridge

French edition and Spanish edition paperbacks of this title are both available directly from WTO Publications, World Trade Organization, Centre William Rappard, 154 rue de Lausanne, CH-1211 Geneva 21, Switzerland http://www.wto.org

ISBN 0 521 82857 0 hardback

THE WTO DISPUTE SETTLEMENT REPORTS

The *Dispute Settlement Reports* of the World Trade Organization (the "WTO") include panel and Appellate Body reports, as well as arbitration awards, in disputes concerning the rights and obligations of WTO Members under the provisions of the *Marrakesh Agreement Establishing the World Trade Organization.* The *Dispute Settlement Reports* are available in English, French and Spanish. Starting with 1999, the first volume of each year contains a cumulative index of published disputes.

This volume may be cited as DSR 2000:XI

TABLE OF CONTENTS

CANADA - TERM OF PATENT PROTECTION

Report of the Panel

WT/DS170/R

Adopted by the Dispute Settlement Body on 12 October 2000 as Upheld by the Appellate Body Report

TABLE OF CONTENTS

I. INTRODUCTION

1.1 On 6 May 1999, the United States requested consultations with Canada pursuant to Article 4 of the *Understanding on Rules and Procedures Governing the Settlement of Disputes* (the "*DSU*") and, to the extent that it incorporates by reference Article XXII of the General Agreement on Tariffs and Trade 1994, Article 64 of the *Agreement on Trade-Related Aspects of Intellectual Property Rights* (the "Agreement", "*TRIPS*" or the "*TRIPS Agreement*") regarding the term of protection granted to patents that were filed before 1 October 1989 in Canada.[1] The United States and Canada held consultations on 11 June 1999 in Geneva but failed to reach a mutually satisfactory solution to the dispute.

1.2 In a communication dated 15 July 1999, the United States requested the Dispute Settlement Body (the "DSB") to establish a panel under Article 6.2 of the *DSU*.[2] Specifically, the United States alleged that the *TRIPS Agreement* requires Members to grant a minimum term of protection to all patents existing as of the date of application of the Agreement and that Canada has been obligated to apply the provisions of the *TRIPS Agreement* since 1 January 1996. The United States alleged that Canada's *Patent Act* provides that the term granted to patents issued on the basis of applications filed before 1 October 1989 is 17 years from the date on which the patent is issued and that granting of such term of protection is inconsistent with Canada's obligations under Articles 33 and 70 of the *TRIPS Agreement*.

1.3 At its meeting on 22 September 1999, the DSB established a Panel in accordance with Article 6 of the *DSU* with the following standard terms of reference:

> "To examine, in light of the relevant provisions of the covered agreements cited by the United States in document WT/DS170/2, the matter referred to the DSB by the United States in that document and to make such findings as will assist the DSB in making the recommendations or in giving the rulings provided for in those agreements."[3]

1.4 On 13 October 1999, the United States made a request, pursuant to paragraph 7 of Article 8 of the DSU, to the Director-General to determine the composition of the Panel. On 22 October 1999, the Director-General composed the Panel as follows:

Chairman: Mr. Stuart Harbinson

Members: Mr. Sergio Escudero

Mr. Alberto Heimler

1 WT/DS170/1; IP/D17, 10 May 1999.

2 WT/DS170/2, 15 July 1999.

3 WT/DS170/3, 25 October 1999.

1.5 On 22 October 1999, the United States submitted a request for expedited consideration of the dispute under Article 4.9 of the *DSU* on the grounds that premature expiration of patents during the dispute settlement procedure caused irreparable harm to the patent owners. It referred to the alleged simplicity of the issues in dispute, the absence of third parties and other circumstances. At the organizational meeting held on 25 October 1999, the United States offered to file its first submission immediately and requested that Canada be required to file its first submission two weeks thereafter. Canada opposed this request. The Panel indicated that due to other demands on its members' time, it could not accelerate the timetable prior to the first substantive meeting. In response, the United States proposed that each party file both first and rebuttal submissions prior to the first substantive meeting in order to expedite the proceedings. After the meeting, Canada opposed this proposal on the basis that it would not give the parties adequate time to prepare their submissions properly, although it did not object to a timetable which followed the minimum periods suggested in Appendix 3 to the *DSU*. On 29 October 1999 the Panel fixed its timetable based on those minimum periods and undertook to make every effort to issue its report as soon as possible after the second substantive meeting.

1.6 The first substantive meeting of the Panel with the parties took place on 20 December 1999 and the second substantive meeting with the parties took place on 25 January 2000.

1.7 The Panel issued its interim report to the parties on 3 March 2000. On 10 March 2000, both parties submitted written requests for the Panel to review precise aspects of the interim report. On 15 March 2000, Canada submitted a reply to the request submitted by the United States. No further meeting with the Panel was requested.

1.8 The Panel submitted its final report to the parties on 31 March 2000.

II. FACTUAL ASPECTS

2.1 The measure in dispute is Section 45 of Canada's *Patent Act*[4] which the United States claims is in violation of Articles 33 and 70 of the *TRIPS Agreement*. For the purpose of the context of this dispute, Sections 44 and 45 of Canada's *Patent Act* are reproduced:

> "44. Subject to section 46[5], where an application for a patent is filed under this Act on or after October 1, 1989, the term limited for the duration of the patent is twenty years from the filing date.

---

4 Canadian *Patent Act*, R.S.C., ch. P-4, Section 45 (1985).

5 Section 46 states:

> "(1) A patentee of a patent issued by the Patent Office under this Act after the coming into force of this section shall, to maintain the rights accorded by the patent, pay to the Commissioner such fees, in respect of such periods, as may be prescribed.
>
> (2) Where the fees payable under subsection (1) are not paid within the time provided by the regulations, the term limited for the duration of the patent shall be deemed to have expired at the end of that time."

> 45. Subject to section 46, the term limited for the duration of every patent issued under this Act on the basis of an application filed before October 1, 1989 is seventeen years from the date on which the patent is issued."

2.2 The substance of Section 45 was, together with a large number of other proposed amendments to the *Patent Act*, first introduced in Parliament on 6 November 1986 in Bill C-22. Although still more commonly referred to as Bill C-22, the Bill was enacted and became law under the title of *An Act to amend the Patent Act and to provide for certain matters in relation thereto*[6] (variously referred to as "Bill C-22" or the "Bill") on 17 November 1987.

2.3 However, for a variety of reasons associated with the need to devise and draft complementary regulations, to attend to other transitional issues as well as to give the intellectual property community time to adjust to the new system, most of the "modernizing" amendments, including the amendments relating to the term of protection, were not brought into force until 1 October 1989.

2.4 The reference in Sections 44 and 45 to a threshold application date served some of the transitional purposes required to effect the change from a system using a "seventeen year from grant" term to another using a "twenty year from filing" term. It did not, however, provide a mechanism for converting from one system to the other. In light of this fact, Bill C-22 included an additional transitional provision that specified the law that would apply to pre-threshold date applications. The rule was set out in Section 27 of the Bill and provided that:

> "27. Applications for patents filed before the coming into force of the provisions of this Act referred to in subsection 33(1) [which included the seventeen year term provision] shall be dealt with and disposed of in accordance with the *Patent Act* as it read immediately before the coming into force of those provisions."[7]

2.5 The law applicable to such applications is generally referred to as the "Old Act". Patents granted on the basis of applications filed before 1 October 1989, whose term is provided for in Section 45, are referred to as "Old Act patents". Patents granted on the basis of applications filed on or after 1 October 1989, whose term is provided for in Section 44, are referred to as "New Act patents".

2.6 During the consultations and proceedings, Canada provided statistics from its Patent Office which the United States did not contest. An examination of the records of the Canadian Patent Office relating to patents issued against applications filed prior to 1 October 1989 and that still existed when the *TRIPS Agreement* took effect in Canada indicates that, as of 1 October 1996[8], 142,494 or just over 60 per cent of the Old Act patents then in existence (236,431) had terms that would not, assuming

---

[6] S.C. 1987, ch. 41, ss. 46, 47. Reproduced in relevant part in Canada Exhibit 3.

[7] Canada Exhibit 3. Clause 27 of the Bill became Section 27 when enacted as part of the amending Act.

[8] For reasons related to application filing date data entry problems, the date used for the examination was actually 1 October 1996. However, given the number of patents issued in Canada on an annual basis, Canada is satisfied that the 1 October 1996 statistics are a reliable surrogate for the statistics that would have been applicable on 1 January 1996 had the data been available. See Canada Exhibit 8, paras. 13 and 15.

that annual maintenance fees were paid, expire until, or until well after, the expiry of the 20-year period following their application dates. In a very large number of these cases, the expiry dates will be two to five years after the expiry of the 20-year period.

2.7 As of 1 October 1996, 93,937 or just under 40 per cent of the Old Act patents then in existence had terms that would, assuming the payment of annual maintenance fees, expire in less than the 20-year period measured from their application dates. In 84 per cent of these cases, the patent would expire in the course of the nineteenth year following the application date. In these "nineteenth" year expiry cases, 52 per cent would expire in the last half of the year, while the remaining 32 per cent would expire in the first half.

2.8 A supplementary examination of the records of the Patent Office, but one conducted in relation to Old Act patents which would still be in force on 1 January 2000, revealed a similar result. Thus, of the 169,966 Old Act patents that would, subject to the continued payment of annual maintenance fees, then still be in existence, 103,030 or just over 60 per cent will not expire until, or until well after, the expiry of the 20-year period following their respective application dates.

2.9 Correlatively, 66,936 or just under 40 per cent of the Old Act patents still in force on 1 January 2000 will, again subject to the payment of the annual maintenance fees, expire in less than 20 years measured from their respective application dates. In 77 per cent of these cases, the patent will expire in the course of the nineteenth year following the application date. In these "nineteenth" year expiry cases, 55 per cent will expire in the last half of the year, while the remaining 22 per cent will expire in the first half.

2.10 An examination of the records of the Canadian Patent Office relating to applications filed in Canada on or after 1 October 1989 reveals that, as of 1 November 1999, there have been 285,678 New Act applications filed since the New Act came into force. Of these New Act applications, 125,406 (approximately 43 per cent) have, since filing, requested examination. On average the period between the date of filing and the date of the request for examination for these 125,406 applications has been 27½ months.

2.11 The same exercise, when focussed on patents that have actually been issued against New Act applications, reveals that 40,847 New Act patents have been issued by the Patent Office since the coming into force date of the New Act on 1 October 1989. The average pendency period, namely the period between the application filing date and the date of grant, for this subset of New Act applications which have been processed through to grant has been approximately 60 months, or five years.[9]

---

[9] The 60-month total has three components. Its first component involves the period of time between the filing date and the date on which the applicant makes the request and pays the fee for "examination". On average the delay between these two dates has, over the last ten years, been approximately 15 months. Subject to the applicant asking that its application be advanced in the queue and the payment of maintenance fees, the second component involves the time spent waiting in the queue for an available examiner. Over the last ten years, the queue has averaged approximately 24 months. The last component involves the time spent in "examination" itself this period has averaged approximately 20 months.

III. FINDINGS AND RECOMMENDATIONS REQUESTED

3.1 The United States requests that, since a large number of existing Old Act patents expire before 20 years from the date of filing, the Panel find that Canada is in violation of Articles 33 and 70 of the *TRIPS Agreement* and recommend that Canada bring its measures into conformity with its obligations under the *TRIPS Agreement.*
3.2 Canada requests that the Panel find that:

(i) the term of patent protection available under Section 45 of Canada's *Patent Act* is equivalent or superior to, and is consistent and in conformity with, the term of patent protection described by Article 33;

(ii) the minimum term of protection described by Article 33 is and has been available, without exception, under the Canadian law and practice relating to Old Act patents;

(iii) by virtue of paragraph 1 of Article 70, Article 33 does not have retroactive application to patents granted by the Commissioner of Patents prior to 1 January 1996; and,

on the basis of those findings, conclude that Section 45 of Canada's *Patent Act* conforms with its obligations under the *TRIPS Agreement.*

IV. ARGUMENTS OF THE PARTIES

4.1 The arguments of the parties are provided for in their submissions to the Panel (see Attachments 1.1 through 1.7 for the United States and 2.1 through 2.6 for Canada).

V. INTERIM REVIEW

5.1 On 10 March 2000, the United States and Canada requested the Panel to review, in accordance with Article 15.2 of the *DSU*, certain aspects of the interim report that had been transmitted to the parties on 3 March 2000. The United States did not request an Interim Review meeting but reserved the right to make comments on any changes suggested by Canada. Canada requested that it be provided with an opportunity to make written comments on changes proposed by the United States and that in the event such an opportunity to respond in writing not be provided, it reserved its right to request a further meeting with the Panel to discuss the matter at issue.
5.2 We reviewed the comments and arguments presented by the parties and finalized our report, incorporating those comments that we considered justified. To this end, we made a change to paragraph 6.63 to characterize more accurately Canada's argument and paragraph 6.105 to reflect more accurately the relevant Canadian provision. We also made minor typographical and syntactical corrections.
5.3 The United States submits that our finding contained in footnote 48 that actions of six developed country Members to amend their laws to comply with Article 33 of the *TRIPS Agreement* do not constitute "subsequent practice" is incorrect because only seven developed country Members needed to change their laws to provide a term of protection that does not end before 20 years from the date of filing. According to the United States, of those seven Members, six amended their laws and

Canada is the sole exception. The United States reiterates that "other WTO Members did not amend their law for the simple reason that they were already in compliance". The United States argues that, since Canada did not contest these facts, they sufficiently establish "subsequent practice" in the application of the *TRIPS Agreement*.

5.4 Canada agrees with our conclusion but for different reasons. Canada notes that each Member referred to by the United States had a term of protection different from those of Canada. Canada contends that each instance of amendment was an isolated act of the Member responding to the particular factual circumstances prevailing in its own jurisdiction and that the fact that several Members determined that they had a similar, but distinct, need to amend their laws does not change the "isolated act" character of their various legislative responses to the problem. Canada states that several Members doing similar things for dissimilar reasons does not constitute a "practice". Therefore, Canada argues that the fact that other Members amended their laws to comply with Article 33 obligations has no evidentiary relevance or value in making an analogous determination in respect of Canada's term of protection provisions or its alleged need to amend them. Canada adds that the fact that it did not contest the "facts" of amendment and non-amendment says nothing about Canada's position in respect of the conclusion that the United States seeks to draw from the "facts".

5.5 We wish first to emphasize that we did not make a finding that there is no "subsequent practice". Rather, we stated in footnote 48 that there is insufficient evidence before us to make a determination as to whether there is a "concordant, common and consistent" sequence of acts to sufficiently establish a "discernable pattern implying the agreement of the parties" in respect of making available a term of protection as required by Article 33 of the *TRIPS Agreement* on the basis of the practice of only six Members. However, upon further consideration of this matter, we do not consider it necessary to make a finding as to whether there is "subsequent practice" to determine the requirement under Article 33 of the *TRIPS Agreement* and to ascertain whether Section 45 of Canada's *Patent Act* is in conformity with Article 33. We have therefore made the necessary changes in footnote 48 to reflect our view.

VI. FINDINGS

A. *Preliminary Matters*

1. *Issues to be Addressed by the Panel*

6.1 In this section, we briefly summarize our understanding of each party's claims and defences.

6.2 The United States challenges Section 45 of Canada's *Patent Act* on the basis that the patent protection term of 17 years from the date of grant for those patent applications that were filed before 1 October 1989 often ends before 20 years from the date of filing. The United States argues that pursuant to Articles 33 and 70.2 of the *TRIPS Agreement*, Canada was obligated to make available a term of protection that does not end before 20 years from the date of filing to all inventions which enjoyed patent protection on 1 January 1996, including those protected by Old Act patents, since inventions enjoying protection under Old Act patents were existing "subject matter" which were protected on the date of application of the *TRIPS Agreement*.

6.3 Canada argues that Section 45 of its *Patent Act* is in conformity with Article 33 of the *TRIPS Agreement*. Canada supports its view that Section 45 is in conformity with Article 33 on the ground that the term of the "exclusive privilege and property rights" available under Section 45 is equivalent or superior to the "exclusive privilege and property rights" conferred by a patent in which the term of protection does not end before 20 years from the date of filing. Canada adds that Section 45 does not require that the term of protection end before the expiry of 20 years from the date of filing.

6.4 In addition, Canada argues that Section 45 did make "available" a term of protection that does not end before 20 years from the date of filing. Canada points out that Old Act applicants could resort to informal or statutory delays to slow down the patent prosecution process so as to obtain a term of protection that does not end before 20 years from the date of filing and that such requests were never denied although the patent examiner and Commissioner of Patents had the discretion not to grant the requested delays.

6.5 Independently from its arguments concerning equivalence and availability, Canada initially argued that since Old Act patents were granted pursuant to an administrative "act" of the Commissioner of Patents, Canada was not required to provide *TRIPS* obligations pursuant to Article 70.1. Canada later states that its interpretation of Article 70.1 to exclude Old Act patents from the obligations under Article 33 did not mean that other obligations such as those set out in Articles 28 and 31(h) of the *TRIPS Agreement* did not apply to patentable "subject matter" as the term is used in Article 70.2.

6.6 We deduce from the arguments of the parties that this dispute only concerns those Canadian patents that fulfil all of the following criteria:

(i) patents for which applications were filed before 1 October 1989;

(ii) Old Act patents which were granted less than three years after the date of filing the application. This necessarily excludes all Old Act patents granted after 1 October 1992; and

(iii) Old Act patents which were in force on 1 January 1996, the date of application of the *TRIPS Agreement* in Canada, and which are still in force. This necessarily excludes all patents granted before 1 January 1979, as their maximum 17-year term would have expired.

This dispute does not concern Old Act applications pending on the date of application of the *TRIPS Agreement* in Canada as these would not fulfil criterion (b).

6.7 Based on the claims and defences raised by the parties, we will address the substantive issues in the following order:

(i) first, we will consider whether there is an obligation to apply the rules of the *TRIPS Agreement* to inventions protected by Old Act patents. This first hinges on the question whether existing "subject matter...which is protected", as the expression is used in Article 70.2 of the *TRIPS Agreement*, includes inventions protected by Old Act patents that were in force on the date of application of the *TRIPS Agreement* in Canada. Subsequently, we evaluate Canada's argument that Article 70.1, not Article 70.2, is the relevant provision and, even if Article 70.2 does generally apply, that Canada is not required to apply the obligation set out in Article 33 to such Old Act patents; and

(ii) we will then consider whether Section 45 of Canada's *Patent Act* is in conformity with Article 33 of the *TRIPS Agreement* and evaluate Canada's arguments that it is in conformity, first on the basis that the terms of "effective" protection or "exclusive privilege and property rights" made available under Section 45 is equivalent or superior to the term of protection available under Article 33, and second on the basis that it makes "available" a term of protection that does not end before 20 years from the date of filing.

2. *Burden of Proof*

6.8 Before reviewing the substantive issues, we need to address the issue of burden of proof, as Canada argued that the United States was required to establish a *prima facie* case that Article 70.2 applied to the "acts" of filing an application and issuing patents that occurred before the date of application of the *TRIPS Agreement.*[10]

6.9 The Appellate Body stated in *United States—Measures Affecting Imports of Woven Wool Shirts and Blouses from India* that:

> "...the burden of proof rests upon the party, whether complaining or defending, who asserts the affirmative of a particular claim or defence. If that party adduces evidence sufficient to raise a presumption that what is claimed is true, the burden then shifts to the other party, who will fail unless it adduces sufficient evidence to rebut the presumption."[11]

6.10 Pursuant to the rule established by the Appellate Body, the initial burden lies with the United States to establish a *prima facie* case of inconsistency with a particular provision of the *TRIPS Agreement* by adducing sufficient evidence to raise a presumption that its claims are true. Upon establishing a *prima facie* case of inconsistency, the burden shifts to Canada which must refute the claim of inconsistency. Our analysis of the issues before us is based on this approach.

6.11 Canada also refers to Article 28 of the *Vienna Convention on the Law of Treaties* (the "*Vienna Convention*")[12] under which there is a codified presumption against the retroactive application of treaty obligations which applies "unless a different intention appears from the treaty or is otherwise established". Canada contends that the United States has the burden of proving such a different intention with respect to its interpretation of Article 70. Canada's contention first requires a finding that Article 70 has retroactive application, which we will consider below.

---

[10] Canada's First Submission, para. 128; Canada's Response to Panel Question 23.

[11] Appellate Body Report, *United States - Measure Affecting Imports of Woven Wool Shirts and Blouses from India*, WT/DS33/AB/R, adopted 23 May 1997, DSR 1997:I, 323, at 335.

[12] *Vienna Convention on the Law of Treaties*, done at Vienna, 23 May 1969, 1155 U.N.T.S. 331; (1969) 8 International Legal Materials 679.

3. *Rules of Interpretation*

6.12 Along with agreements governing trade in goods and services, protection of intellectual property rights as encapsulated in the *TRIPS Agreement* constitutes an integral part of the *Marrakesh Agreement Establishing the World Trade Organization* (the "WTO Agreement"). As such, the *TRIPS Agreement* is one of the "covered agreements" and is therefore subject to the *DSU*.[13] Article 3.2 of the *DSU* provides that panels are to clarify the provisions of "covered agreements" in accordance with customary rules of interpretation of public international law.

6.13 In *United States — Standards for Reformulated and Conventional Gasoline* ("*United States - Gasoline*"), the Appellate Body stated that the fundamental rule of treaty interpretation as set out in Articles 31 and 32 of the *Vienna Convention* had "attained the status of a rule of customary or general international law".[14] Pursuant to Article 31(1) of the *Vienna Convention*, the duty of a treaty interpreter is to determine the meaning of a term in accordance with the ordinary meaning to be given to the term in its context and in light of its object and purpose. We will apply the principles enunciated by the Appellate Body in the *United States — Gasoline* to interpret the relevant provisions of the *TRIPS Agreement* throughout the Report.

B. *Applicability of Article 70.2 of the TRIPS Agreement to Inventions Protected by Old Act Patents*

1. *Arguments of the Parties*

6.14 The **United States** construes Article 70.2 to mean that the *TRIPS Agreement* gives rise to obligations in respect of all patents existing on the date of application of the Agreement. Initially, the United States argued that the ordinary meaning of the reference in Article 70.2 to "subject matter" existing at the date of application of the Agreement was patents existing on that date but it later argued that this reference was to "inventions that can be patented", "patented inventions", "protected inventions" and "existing inventions (which may already be patented)".

6.15 The United States argues that since Article 70.2 of the *TRIPS Agreement* "gives rise to obligations in respect of all" inventions existing on 1 January 1996 which are protected on that date, Canada is obligated to apply the provisions of Article 33 to all patented inventions that existed on 1 January 1996.

---

[13] Appellate Body Report, *India - Patent Protection for Pharmaceutical and Agricultural Chemical Products* ("*India - Patents*"), WT/DS50/AB/R, adopted 16 January 1998, DSR 1998:I, 9, para. 29.

[14] Appellate Body Report, *United States - Standards for Reformulated and Conventional Gasoline* ("*United States - Gasoline*"),WT/DS2/AB/R, adopted 20 May 1996, DSR 1996:I, 3, at 16. See also Appellate Body Report, *Japan - Taxes on Alcoholic Beverages* ("*Japan - Alcoholic Beverages*"), WT/DS8/AB/R, WT/DS10/AB/R, WT/DS11/AB/R, adopted 1 November 1996, DSR 1996:I, 97, at 104; Appellate Body Report, *India - Patents, supra,* footnote 13, para. 46; Appellate Body Report, *European Communities - Customs Classification of Certain Computer Equipment*, WT/DS62/AB/R, WT/DS67/AB/R, WT/DS68/AB/R, adopted 22 June 1998, DSR 1998:V, 1851, para. 84; and Appellate Body Report, *United States - Import Prohibition of Certain Shrimp and Shrimp Products*, WT/DS58/AB/R, adopted 6 November 1998, DSR 1998:VII, 2755, para. 114.

6.16 **Canada** initially responded that Old Act patents that were granted before 1 January 1996 pursuant to an act of the Commissioner of Patents were exempt from the obligations of the *TRIPS Agreement* on the ground that Article 70.1 states that the *TRIPS Agreement* "does not give rise to obligations in respect of acts which occurred before the date of application of the Agreement for the Member in question."

6.17 According to Canada, the word "acts" as used in Article 70.1 is not qualified as referring to any particular type of class of act and therefore does not have a "limited or qualified meaning". In contrast, Canada notes that Articles 26.1, 28.1(a) and (b), 36, 41.1 and 70.4 qualify the use of the word "acts" and refers to a secondary source that states that Article 70.1 expresses the rule of non-retroactivity with respect to acts that occurred before the *TRIPS* application date. Canada concludes therefore that the term "acts" includes acts of issuance by patent authorities and also the act of filing an application.

6.18 Canada argues that the only limitation contained in the word "acts" as used in Article 70.1 is the temporal element and that the "acts" of filing an application and granting a patent for a fixed term are complete when they are made and therefore are not subject to the Agreement because they occurred before the date of application of the *TRIPS Agreement.*

6.19 Canada argues that Article 33 is to be applied prospectively to acts of grant that occurred on or after 1 January 1996 and not retroactively to "acts" of filing or grant that occurred before that date.

6.20 In response to Canada's defence that Section 45 of its *Patent Act* is excluded from the application of Articles 33 and 70.2 by the operation of Article 70.1, the **United States** agrees with Canada's interpretation of the word "acts" in Article 70.1, accepting that it could apply to both infringing acts of third parties and administrative acts of Member governments so that acts of issuing patents before 1996 are excluded from the operation of the *TRIPS Agreement*. However, the United States disagrees with Canada's view that Article 70.1 is applicable to patents in force on the date of application of the *TRIPS Agreement*, arguing that Article 70.1 has no relevance and that the inventions under protection of those patents are covered by Article 70.2. The United States emphasizes that its interpretation of Article 70.1 and 70.2 has the advantage of avoiding any conflict between them and gives them both meaning.

6.21 The United States argues that the "acts" of Canada's Patent Office prior to 1996 are not at issue. It submits that the violation is unrelated to any pre-1996 "act" but is related only to the subject matter (protected inventions) that existed on 1 January 1996. The United States argues that the rule in Article 70.1 that pre-1996 acts are not subject to the obligations in the Agreement does not imply that subject matter existing on 1 January 1996 is also not subject to the obligations of the Agreement. According to the United States, Article 70.1 does not prevent the prospective application of *TRIPS* standards, including the standard governing the term of protection, to existing subject matter as mandated by Article 70.2.

6.22 The United States also supports its interpretation of Article 70.1 on the basis that if Article 70.1 were to mean that the *TRIPS Agreement* did not apply to existing subject matter which derived from an act prior to the application of the *TRIPS Agreement*, it would render meaningless or redundant paragraphs 3, 4, 5, and 6 of Article 70 and would exclude all intellectual property rights that existed before 1996 from the operation of the *TRIPS Agreement*. The United States argues that such interpretation would undermine its effect and is not borne out by the subsequent practice of Members or the negotiating history of the Agreement.

6.23 **Canada** argues that the introductory phrase of Article 70.2 "[e]xcept as otherwise provided for in this Agreement" requires that, whatever its meaning, it is "trumped" by Article 70.1 and cannot render Old Act patents subject to the Agreement. It argues that the phrase is not limited to other provisions of Article 70.2 itself, but refers to the whole Agreement. It argues that to interpret it otherwise would be to subtract these words from the Agreement, in violation of rules of treaty interpretation in Article 31 of the *Vienna Convention* and WTO jurisprudence.

6.24 Canada relies on the argument that Article 28 of the *Vienna Convention* introduces a presumption against retroactivity "unless a different intention appears from the treaty or is otherwise established". It argued first that there is no different intention expressed in the *TRIPS Agreement* but later accepted that Article 70.2 expresses such a contrary intention, although in its view this is subject to an overriding exception in the introductory phrase. Canada argues that the United States, as the complainant, has the burden of establishing *prima facie* that Articles 33 and 70.2 apply to Old Act patents and that Article 70.1 is not applicable to Section 45 patents.

6.25 The **United States** disagrees with Canada's interpretation of the introductory phrase in Article 70.2 "[e]xcept as otherwise provided for in this Agreement", and argues that it has no bearing on the legal issues involved in this case. It argues that if this phrase produced the result that Article 70.1 applied to patents in force on the date of application of the *TRIPS Agreement* to the exclusion of Article 70.2, it would essentially read Article 70.2 out of the *TRIPS Agreement*. It argues that the introductory phrase refers, *inter alia*, to the second half of Article 70.2, which deals with copyright and related rights, which have no bearing on this case.

6.26 In response to the United States' claim that *TRIPS* obligations apply to inventions protected by Old Act patents, **Canada** argues that the obligation in respect of Article 33 of the *TRIPS Agreement* applies to a patent but not to "subject matter". In Canada's view, a "patent" is the "vehicle of protection", "a legal device through which the State protects an invention [and] not subject matter within the ordinary meaning of Article 70.2." The expression "subject matter", according to Canada, is the object of the protection, e.g. work, mark, design, invention, layout-design or geographical indication. In Canada's view, such distinction is reflected in Article 27 which defines what "subject matter" is "patentable" or "protectable"; Article 28 which defines the rights to be conferred and protected by a patent; Article 29 which defines an applicant's obligation to disclose its invention as part of the patent bargain; and Article 33 which defines a variable term of protection during which the rights conferred will endure. According to Canada, the distinction between "subject matter" and "patent" operates to detach the term of protection given by the "act" of the issuance of the patent from the exclusive and other rights conferred by the "patent" itself.

6.27 Canada argues that the Article 33 obligation in respect of the term of protection is related to the act of filing a patent application and the act of granting a patent. According to Canada, the act of filing is the trigger which sets the expiry date for the term of protection. However, Canada notes, there can be no term of protection unless a patent is in fact granted because there is no basis for the protection of the invention unless and until the patent is granted. Canada maintains that the commencement of the term of protection is triggered by the act of grant. Canada states that both the commencement and expiry of the term of protection depend upon the occurrence of these two successive and related acts. Canada concludes that the obligation in Article 33 is an obligation in respect of "acts" and that Article 70.1 states that the *TRIPS Agreement* does not give rise to obligations in respect of "acts" which occurred before 1 January 1996.

6.28 Canada argues that the act of filing a patent application and the administrative act of granting a patent were essential to initiate a term of protection under Article 33 and that Article 33 obligation does not apply retroactively to Old Act patents because the word "acts" in Article 70.1 covers the act of filing an application and the administrative act of grant of a patent. Canada argues that, unlike Article 33 which is temporal in nature because of its linkage of both the commencement and the expiry dates of the term of protection with the acts of filing and granting, the obligation in Article 28 does not depend upon the occurrence of any act. According to Canada, the operation of Article 28 depends solely upon a patent being in existence.

6.29 The **United States** notes that Canada acknowledges that pre-1996 acts do not preclude the application of the obligations in Articles 27.1, 28 and 31(h) to existing subject matter. The United States asserts that Canada is unable to explain why the *TRIPS* obligation involving the term of protection may be properly excluded under Article 70.1 while other obligations, such as the provision of exclusive rights in Article 28, are not.

6.30 The United States contends that obligations in Articles 27, 28 and 31 of the *TRIPS Agreement* cannot be distinguished in this regard from the obligation in Article 33. The United States claims that under Article 70.2, Canada must apply all *TRIPS* obligations to all inventions that were protected on 1 January 1996.

2. *Evaluation by the Panel*

6.31 We consider in this section the respective merits of:

(a) the United States' claim that the phrase existing "subject matter...which is protected", as used in Article 70.2, includes inventions protected by Old Act patents on 1 January 1996; and

(b) Canada's arguments that:

(i) Article 70.2 of the *TRIPS Agreement* is not applicable in this dispute on the basis of the meaning of the word "acts" contained in Article 70.1 and the introductory phrase "[e]xcept as otherwise provided for in this Agreement" contained in Article 70.2. We then consider the merit of this argument in light of the principle of effective treaty interpretation; and

(ii) Article 70.2, even if it were applicable to inventions protected by Old Act patents on 1 January 1996, does not require Members to apply the obligation of Article 33 of the *TRIPS Agreement* in relation to those patents.

(a) Consideration of the United States' Claim that "Subject Matter...which is Protected" in Article 70.2 is Applicable to Inventions which Enjoy Protection on 1 January 1996

6.32 The United States argued that the plain language of Article 70.2 requires Canada to apply the obligations of the *TRIPS Agreement* to all patented inventions that existed on 1 January 1996.[15] Article 70.2 states in relevant part:

> "Except as otherwise provided for in this Agreement, this Agreement gives rise to obligations in respect of all *subject matter existing at the date of application of this Agreement* for the Member in question, and which is *protected* in that Member on the said date, or which meets or comes subsequently to meet the criteria for protection under the terms of this Agreement. ..." (emphasis added)

6.33 Article 70.2 gives rise to obligations under the *TRIPS Agreement* in respect of all "subject matter" existing on the date of application of the Agreement, provided that the "subject matter" is "protected" on that date or meets or comes to meet the criteria for protection under the *TRIPS Agreement*. We note that in Article 70.2 the word "subject matter" is followed by the word "protected" to read "subject matter...which is protected". Although the term "subject matter" is not defined in the Agreement, it is used in various subheadings and provisions of Sections 1 through 7 of Part II of the *TRIPS Agreement* and is either preceded or followed by the word "protected" or variations thereof, i.e. "protectable", "protection", to describe the "subject matter" that can or is to be "protected".

6.34 As it is undisputed that this case involves patents, the relevant provisions are contained in Section 5 of Part II of the *TRIPS Agreement*. The subheading of Article 27 is "Patentable *Subject Matter*" and paragraph 1 of Article 27 provides that the "subject matter" of this Section is "inventions". The ordinary meaning of "subject matter", which is "the topic dealt with or the subject represented in a debate, exposition, or work of art",[16] and the language "*patents* shall be available for any *inventions*" in Article 27.1 of the *TRIPS Agreement* support the view that "subject matter" in relation to patents is "inventions".

6.35 When we examine the "protection" available to inventions, Article 27, read as a whole, supports the view that inventions are the relevant subject matter; novelty, inventive step and usefulness are the requirements for their "protection"; and patents are a relevant form of "protection". This view is confirmed contextually by other provisions in Part II of the *TRIPS Agreement* that deal with other "subject matter". For example, "Protectable Subject Matter" is the subheading of Article 15, which provides, *inter alia*, that any distinctive sign is capable of constituting a trademark. This indicates that signs are the relevant subject matter, distinctiveness is the basic requirement for their protection and trademarks a relevant form of protection. Other types of what we call "material" for the purpose of this analysis are described as "protected" or attracting "protection", i.e., "Protection of Geographical Indications"

[15] Response of the United States to Panel Question 7; Second Oral Statement of the United States, para. 18.

[16] *The New Oxford Dictionary of English*, (Oxford University Press, 1998), p. 1849.

in subheading of Article 22, "protected design" and "protected industrial designs" in paragraphs 1 and 2 of Article 26, which is consistent with a view that these types of "material" are specific categories of subject matter. The word "protection" is qualified by a specific intellectual property right in the phrase "copyright protection" in Article 9.2, which provides that it "shall extend to expressions", indicating that the intellectual property right is the form of protection and is consistent with a view that "expressions" refer to literary and artistic works which are the relevant category of subject matter. Indeed, the whole purpose of Part II of the *TRIPS Agreement* is to describe categories of "material", specify requirements of each which, if met, will entitle it to the conferral of the protection in the form of a particular intellectual property right and then to specify those rights and their duration.

6.36 In view of the above, we find that the term "subject matter" refers to particular "material", including literary and artistic works, signs, geographical indications, industrial designs, inventions, layout-designs of integrated circuits and undisclosed information, which, if they meet the relevant requirements set out in Part II of the Agreement, will attract protection in the form of the corresponding intellectual property rights which are set out in Sections 1 to 7 of Part II of the *TRIPS Agreement*. We therefore find that the reference to "subject matter...which is protected" on the date of application of the *TRIPS Agreement* in Article 70.2 includes "inventions" that were under patent protection in Canada on 1 January 1996. We also find that the United States has established a *prima facie* case that Article 70.2 is applicable to inventions protected by Old Act patents.[17]

(b) Consideration of Canada's Arguments

6.37 In light of our preliminary finding set out in paragraph 6.36, we now consider Canada's arguments that run counter to that finding.

(i) The Argument that Article 70.2 is Set Aside by Article 70.1

6.38 There are two elements to Canada's argument that Article 70.2 is set aside by Article 70.1. The first is based on Canada's interpretation of the word "acts" as it is used in Article 70.1 and the second is based on the application of the introductory phrase "[e]xcept as otherwise provided" contained in Article 70.2. We will consider these in turn and then apply the principle of effective treaty interpretation to Canada's argument.

---

[17] The United States pointed out that "subject matter" refers to the matter that is or can be entitled to intellectual property protection, such as "broadcasts that can be copyrighted, signs that can be trademarked and inventions that can be patented." The United States emphasized that its complaint is not based on any pre-1996 "act" but is "related only to subject matter (protected inventions) that existed on [1 January 1996]". Accordingly, the United States noted that Article 70.1 is not relevant in this dispute and that the irrelevance of Article 70.1 to the specific facts of this dispute did not render Article 70.1 meaningless. It stated that construing the first para. of Article 70 as a provision that is "otherwise provided for in this Agreement" has the effect of reading the second para. of that Article out of the *TRIPS Agreement* and produced the speaking note of the chairman of the 10 + 10 meeting which suggested that the introductory phrase in Article 70.2 was intended to apply to the second sentence of Article 70.2 (see U.S. Exhibit 11).

The meaning of "acts" as it is used in Article 70.1

6.39 We note that Canada initially argued that Old Act patents which were granted pursuant to the administrative "act" of the Commissioner of Patents before 1 January 1996 are exempt from the obligations of the *TRIPS Agreement* by virtue of the non-retroactivity rule set out in Article 70.1.[18] Canada relied on the fact that patents, unlike the subject matter of protection, flow from two "acts" - the "act" of filing an application and the "act" of issuing the patent by the Commissioner of Patents - both of which, in respect of Old Act patents, occurred before the date of application of the *TRIPS Agreement* and which were therefore covered by Article 70.1.[19] The United States also stated that the term "acts" can include the "act" of granting a patent but argued that these acts, where they occurred before 1996, are not subject to the obligations of the *TRIPS Agreement.*[20]

6.40 The word "acts", the ordinary meaning of which is "things done",[21] as used in Article 70.1, may encompass acts of third parties such as acts of unfair competition;[22] acts of infringement, potential infringement or unauthorized use;[23] acts not requiring the authorization of the right holder;[24] or an act of a right holder in relation to provisional measures.[25] On a broader view, "acts" may also refer to the acts of competent authorities of Members as reflected in Article 58 of the *TRIPS Agreement.*

6.41 However, for the purpose of this dispute, we do not consider it necessary to decide whether this broader view of the meaning of the word "acts" is correct, because even if, *arguendo*, "acts" as used in Article 70.1 include the administrative act of granting a patent by the Commissioner of Patents, they would still be distinct from the "subject matter...which is protected" as used in Article 70.2 which we have defined in paragraph 6.36 as inventions protected by Old Act patents on the date of application of the *TRIPS Agreement*. Even though Article 70.1 may exclude the administrative act of granting a patent prior to 1 January 1996 from the coverage of the *TRIPS Agreement*, we cannot conclude on the basis of that fact that the non-retroactivity rule of Article 70.1 governs inventions protected by Old Act patents that existed on 1 January 1996 because the administrative act of granting a patent results in the protection of the underlying "subject matter" and this protection granted to the "subject matter" is ongoing and can continue past 1 January 1996. To the extent that such protection does so continue past 1 January 1996 in Canada, it is a situation which has not ceased to exist[26] by the date of application of the *TRIPS Agreement* and which is therefore subject to the obligations of the Agreement from that date. Acts to apply the *TRIPS Agreement* after that date to such situations are not "acts" which occurred before the date of application of the Agreement for the Member in question and therefore not covered by Article 70.1.

---

18 Canada's First Submission, para. 5(d).

19 Canada's Response to Panel Question 6(c).

20 Rebuttal Submission of the United States, para. 25.

21 *Webster's New World Dictionary*, (The World Publishing Company, 1976), p.13.

22 Article 22.2 of the *TRIPS Agreement.*

23 Articles 26.1, 28.1(a) and (b), 36, 41 and 70.4 of the *TRIPS Agreement.*

24 Article 37 of the *TRIPS Agreement.*

25 Article 50.7 of the *TRIPS Agreement.*

26 Article 28 of the *Vienna Convention.*

6.42 For the reasons set out above, we confirm our preliminary finding in paragraph 6.36 that Article 70.2, not Article 70.1, is applicable to inventions protected by Old Act patents on 1 January 1996. We also find that the United States has established a *prima facie* case that the ongoing protection of the inventions protected by Old Act patents is a situation that did not cease to exist prior to entry into force of the *TRIPS Agreement* within the meaning of Article 28 of the *Vienna Convention.*

The meaning of "[e]xcept as otherwise provided" as used in Article 70.2

6.43 Canada also argued that Article 70.2 is not applicable because paragraph 1 of Article 70 is "a proviso 'otherwise set out in the Agreement'" which prevails over paragraph 2 of Article 70 on which the United States relies to establish the application of Article 33 to Section 45 patents.[27] Canada claimed that even though patentable subject matter is defined as inventions that meet or are capable of meeting the criteria set out in Article 27, and that those inventions which existed on the date of application of the *TRIPS Agreement* were entitled to the benefit of the obligations under the Agreement, this was subject to the qualification contained in the introductory phrase in Article 70.2 "except as otherwise provided" in the Agreement, which referred to Article 70.1 and set aside Article 70.2 in this dispute.

6.44 The introductory phrase "[e]xcept as otherwise provided for in this Agreement" qualifies Article 70.2 and the exception is only relevant where there is another provision that is inconsistent with the first sentence, in which event the other provision would prevail. Because we consider that the word "acts" and the term "subject matter" are different concepts with disparate meanings and the term "acts" as used in Article 70.1 refers only to discrete acts which predate the date of application of the *TRIPS Agreement* and not to subsequent acts to apply the Agreement, including to situations that have not ceased to exist on that date, there is no inconsistency between paragraphs 1 and 2 of Article 70. Article 70.1 therefore does not fall within the exception and does not set aside Article 70.2.

6.45 This interpretation has the benefit of avoiding any conflict between paragraphs 1 and 2 of Article 70, which is consistent with the concept of presumption against conflict as it exists in public international law.[28]

6.46 Our interpretation is also confirmed by the negotiating history. When the introductory phrase was being discussed during the *TRIPS* negotiations, the Chairman of the Negotiating Group stated:

> "In the first line [of Article 70.2], the initial phrase would be amended to read 'Except as otherwise provided for in this Agreement...' This

---

[27] Canada's First Submission, para. 126; Canada's Response to Panel Question 7.

[28] The Panel in *Indonesia - Certain Measures Affecting the Automobile Industry* stated: "...we recall first that in public international law there is a presumption against conflict. [footnote deleted] This presumption is especially relevant in the WTO context since all WTO agreements, including GATT 1994 which was modified by Understandings when judged necessary, were negotiated at the same time, by the same Members and in the same forum." Panel Report, *Indonesia - Certain Measures Affecting the Automobile Industry*, WT/DS54/R, WT/DS55/R, WT/DS59/R, WT/DS64/R, adopted 23 July 1998, DSR 1998:VI, 2201, para. 14.28.

would make it clear that, for example, Article 18 of Berne applies by virtue of Article 9.1."[29]

6.47 For the reasons given above, we do not agree that the introductory phrase "[e]xcept as otherwise provided for in this Agreement" in Article 70.2 can be construed to refer to paragraph 1 of Article 70.

Effective interpretation

6.48 We note that if we were to accept Canada's argument that patents granted prior to 1 January 1996 are not subject to the obligations in the *TRIPS Agreement* or that Article 70.1 is a provision "otherwise provided for in this Agreement", drafters of the *TRIPS Agreement* would not have needed to delineate the nature of obligations of Members with respect to "all subject matter existing at the date of application of this Agreement" in Article 70.2. Canada's argument would reduce paragraph 6 of Article 70 to redundancy or inutility. There would be no need to state in paragraph 6 that Members are not required to apply rules concerning compulsory licensing to compulsory licences granted before the date the Agreement became known. In addition, to the extent that Article 70.1 is construed to mean that a Member had no *TRIPS* obligations with respect to intellectual property for which the act of filing an application occurred prior to 1 January 1996, Article 70.7, which permits pending applications for protection to be amended to take into account enhanced protection, would be reduced to inutility.

6.49 Interpretation of treaty language that reduces certain provisions to redundancy or inutility is contrary to the principle of effective interpretation.[30] The Appellate Body stated in *United States —Gasoline* that "[o]ne of the corollaries of the 'general rule of interpretation' in the *Vienna Convention* is that interpretation must give meaning and effect to all the terms of the treaty. An interpreter is not free to adopt a reading that would result in reducing whole clauses or paragraphs of a treaty to redundancy or inutility".[31]

---

[29] 10 + 10 Meeting, Speaking Note for the Chairman (16 December 1991) which was circulated to all Members and is reproduced in U.S. Exhibit 11.

[30] The principle of effective interpretation or "l'effet utile" or in latin *ut res magis valeat quam pereat* reflects the general rule of interpretation which requires that a treaty be interpreted to give meaning and effect to all the terms of the treaty. For instance, one provision should not be given an interpretation that will result in nullifying the effect of another provision of the same treaty. For a discussion of this principle, see *Yearbook of the International Law Commission*, 1966, Vol. II A/CN.4/SER.A/1966/Add.1 p. 219 and following. See also *e.g., Corfu Channel* Case (1949) *I.C.J. Reports*, p. 24 (International Court of Justice); Territorial Dispute Case (Libyan Arab Jamahiriya v. Chad) (1994) *I.C.J. Reports*, p. 23 (International Court of Justice); and *Oppenheim's International Law* (9th ed., Jennings and Watts eds., 1992), Vol. 1, 1280-1281. See also the statement of the Appellate Body in *United States - Gasoline, supra,* footnote 14, at 21 ("An interpreter is not free to adopt a reading that would result in reducing whole clauses or paras. of a treaty to redundancy or inutility") and the Appellate Body Report on *Japan - Alcoholic Beverages, supra,* footnote 14, at 106. See also the Panel Report on *Korea - Definitive Safeguard Measure on Imports of Certain Dairy Products*, WT/DS98/R, adopted 12 January 2000, DSR 2000:I, 49, para. 7.37.

[31] Appellate Body Report, *United States - Gasoline, supra,* footnote 14, at 21. See also Appellate Body Report, *Japan - Alcoholic Beverages, supra,* footnote 14, at 106; Appellate Body Report, *Canada - Measures Affecting the Importation of Milk and the Exportation of Dairy Products ("Canada - Dairy")*, WT/DS103/AB/R, WT/DS113/AB/R, adopted 27 October 1999, DSR 1999:V,

6.50 Our interpretation that Article 70.1 does not fall within the introductory phrase "[e]xcept as otherwise provided for in this Agreement" does not reduce that phrase to inutility. In our view, the reference in the introductory phrase in Article 70.2 includes the second sentence of paragraph 2 and paragraphs 4 and 6 of Article 70.

6.51 For all of the reasons given above, we confirm our preliminary finding set out in paragraph 6.36.

(ii) The Argument that Article 70.2 does not Include the Obligation under Article 33

6.52 Canada also argued that, even if Article 70.2 were construed to cover existing patents, it would do so in respect of the scope of patent rights set out in Article 28 and the obligation in Article 31(h), but not the obligation to make available the term of protection provided under Article 33. This argument is based on the notion that, unlike the rights conferred by a patent which are in respect of the invention (subject matter), the term of protection is an "integral part" of the act of grant and thus subject to the provision in Article 70.1.[32] However, we cannot discern any merit or justification in the *TRIPS Agreement* for this distinction. No evidence has been advanced which would explain why the administrative "act" of grant of a patent, which confers protection on inventions, would preclude the application of the term of protection contained in Article 33 to existing patents but not the exclusive rights set forth in Article 28 and other matters set out in Section 5 of Part II of the Agreement.

6.53 In our view, Members are required to comply with all the relevant obligations set out in the *TRIPS Agreement*, including those in Section 5 of Part II, which require Members to provide patent protection for a term consistent with the requirement set out in Article 33 in respect of existing "subject matter...which is protected" on the date of application of the *TRIPS Agreement*, or which meets or comes to meet the criteria for protection. Neither the textual nor the contextual reading of Section 5 of Part II supports the notion that one obligation can be detached from the patent issued to the right holder or that Members need not comply with all relevant *TRIPS* obligations in relation to them. Holders of patents valid on the date of application of the *TRIPS Agreement* are entitled to protection of all of the rights set out in the Agreement for a term consistent with the requirement in Article 33.

6.54 Our interpretation is confirmed by footnote 3 to the *TRIPS Agreement*,[33] which forms part of the overall context of Article 70.2. The language contained in footnote 3 suggests that protection afforded to right holders of intellectual property is comprehensive and does not state or imply that certain rights or obligations can be detached and considered in isolation. In particular and germane to this dispute, the expression "matters affecting the...scope" of intellectual property rights refers, *inter alia*, to the term of protection and confirms that the term of protection (of a patent

2057, para. 133; and Appellate Body Report, *Argentina - Safeguard Measures on Imports of Footwear*, WT/DS121/AB/R, adopted 12 January 2000, DSR 2000:I, 515, para. 88.

[32] Canada's Response to Panel Questions 36 and 37.

[33] We note that footnote 3 describes "protection" "for the purposes of Articles 3 and 4" of the *TRIPS Agreement*. However, we are of the view that the footnote can serve as context in interpreting protection to be provided for intellectual property rights.

among other intellectual property rights) is to be protected together with the exclusive rights within the scope of a patent as set out in Article 28.

6.55 For the reasons set out above, we find that Canada is required to apply the obligation under Article 33 to inventions protected by Old Act patents on 1 January 1996 and confirm our preliminary finding set out at paragraph 6.36.

3. Overall Conclusion with Respect to Article 70

6.56 We find that the United States established a *prima facie* case that Article 70.2 applied to inventions protected by Old Act patents in force on 1 January 1996 and therefore required developed country Members to apply the relevant obligations under the *TRIPS Agreement* as of that date to those inventions. For the reasons set out above, we reject Canada's argument that the non-retroactivity rule embodied in Article 70.1 is the provision applicable to inventions protected by Old Act patents in force on the date of application of the Agreement on the basis that those patents were granted pursuant to an "administrative act" of the Commissioner of Patents. For this reason, Article 70.1 does not override Article 70.2 despite the introductory phrase "except as otherwise provided for in this Agreement". We also reject Canada's argument that Article 70.2 does not require Members to apply the obligations of Article 33 to inventions protected by Old Act patents. In so doing, we confirm our finding that, within the context of this dispute, "subject matter" refers to inventions that meet the requirements for patentability set out in Article 27.1 and that patents constitute one form of protection of those inventions, with the result that the term "subject matter...which is protected" as used in Article 70.2 includes inventions which are protected by patents, i.e., patented inventions. In view of that finding, Canada was required to apply the relevant obligations of the *TRIPS Agreement*, including those set out in Section 5 of Part II of the Agreement, which contains Article 33, to inventions protected by Old Act patents that were in force on 1 January 1996.

C. Conformity of Section 45 of Canada's Patent Act with Article 33 of the TRIPS Agreement

6.57 In this section, we consider whether Section 45 of Canada's *Patent Act* is in conformity with Article 33 of the *TRIPS Agreement*. Before evaluating the conformity of Section 45 with Article 33, the principal arguments made by the parties are set forth below.

1. Arguments of the Parties

6.58 The **United States** argues that the *TRIPS Agreement* requires that Canada grant a term of protection for patents that runs at least until 20 years after the filing date. The United States contends that the plain meaning of Article 33 indicates that the term of protection set forth in Article 33 is a minimum term and that this interpretation is supported contextually by Article 1.1 of the *TRIPS Agreement*, which states that "Members may, but shall not be obliged to, implement...more extensive protection than is required by this Agreement". With respect to those patents that were filed before 1 October 1989 and granted in less than three years by the Canadian Commissioner of Patents and in existence as of the *TRIPS* application date, the United States claims that Canada is in violation of Articles 33 and 70.2 because the protection term of 17 years from the date of grant provided by Section 45 of Canada's *Patent Act* often ends before a term of 20 years from the date of filing.

6.59 It is the United States' contention that Canada is in violation of the *TRIPS Agreement* with respect to each and every patent for which the term of protection is less than 20 years as of the filing date. For those patents that were issued in exactly three years, the United States notes that there is no difference between the term provided by Canada and the term required by the *TRIPS Agreement*. If a patent took longer than three years to be granted, the United States notes that the term of protection would actually be longer than required.

6.60 Referring to the figures set out in paragraph 2.10, the United States notes that, as of 1 January 2000, 66,936 Old Act patents would expire sooner than would be the case if Canada had provided a term of 20 years from filing. The United States contends that historically, 50 per cent (50%) of patent applications filed in Canada are from U.S. applicants. Thus, the United States estimates that well over 33,000 U.S. patent holders are currently holding patents with a term less than that required under the *TRIPS Agreement*.

6.61 The United States notes that under the *Vienna Convention*, "any subsequent practice" in the application of an Agreement may also establish "the agreement of the parties regarding its interpretation". In this case, according to the United States, state practice of other developed country WTO Members in applying Articles 33 and 70 of the *TRIPS Agreement* demonstrates the term of patent protection that other Members have viewed as legally required by the *TRIPS Agreement*. In this regard, the United States notes that, in addition to itself, Australia, Germany, Greece, New Zealand and Portugal have revised their laws to conform to the 20-year, as of the filing date, protection term.

6.62 **Canada** rebuts that Section 45 of Canada's *Patent Act* provides patent right holders an "effective" protection for the "exclusive privilege and property rights" that are "equivalent or superior" to the term of "exclusive privilege and property rights" provided by Article 33 of the *TRIPS Agreement*.

6.63 Canada claims that Article 33 does not provide for a minimum of 20 full years of protection for the "exclusive privilege and property rights" because the term referred to in Article 33 will be eroded by the operation of reasonable procedures which are prerequisites to the grant of a patent. According to Canada, the period of time between the date of filing and the grant of a patent will vary. Canada states that Article 62.2 recognizes that the period referred to in Article 33 will be curtailed by reasonable procedures that are prerequisite to the granting of a patent.

6.64 Canada argues that where in the normal course it takes, as it currently does in Canada in respect of New Act patents, five years to complete the examination process for a patent whose term is related to its application filing date, the period of exclusivity will be reduced accordingly. Since the five year examination period is the normal or average examination period, it must, in Canada's submission, be viewed as being "a reasonable period which avoids any unwarranted curtailment of the period of protection".

6.65 Canada argues that in cases where the term of protection is measured from the date of filing, the period during which a successful applicant will enjoy the exclusive privilege and property right conferred by a patent once issued will, in the normal course, be 15 years. Canada adds that it may provide either more or less protection depending on the length of the examination process in any particular case.

Canada points out that under Section 45, on the other hand, a successful applicant will enjoy 17 years of constant protection for the "exclusive privilege and property rights" conferred by a patent.

6.66 Canada then claims that since the term of the "effective" protection for the exclusive rights conferred by Section 45 is routinely two years longer than the "normal or average" period of "effective" protection provided by the joint operation of Articles 33 and 62 of the *TRIPS Agreement*, Article 33 and Section 45 can be said to be substantively or "effectively" equivalent and therefore Section 45 is consistent with the minimum standard prescribed by the *TRIPS Agreement*.

6.67 Canada submits that because both Section 45 and Article 33 provide an equivalent period of "effective" protection, it acted within the scope of the freedom afforded to Members under Article 1.1 which permits Members "to determine the appropriate method of implementing the provisions of [the] Agreement within their own legal system and practice".

6.68 The **United States** argues that Canada's equivalence argument is flawed in that it relies on the "normal or average" period of "effective" protection or "exclusive privilege and property rights". The United States notes that Canada uses the averaging methodology in two ways. First, it claims that since five years is the "normal or average" pendency period for New Act patent applications, the effective term of protection under a regime of 20 years from filing would "normally" be an "average" of 15 years, which is less than the 17-year period provided under the Old Act. The United States points out that Canada also uses the averaging methodology to make the opposite comparison, i.e., to assert that the "average" two to four year pendency period for its Old Act patents makes these patents "equivalent to and in fact...longer than the normal or average" period of "effective" protection required by the *TRIPS Agreement*. The United States contends that Canada's reliance, however, on average pendency periods of Old Act and New Act patents inevitably means that its analysis fails to take into account those patents with pendency periods outside the average. The United States maintains that the important element is that every Old Act patent that was pending for less than three years before being issued by Canada has a term that ends before a period of 20 years from the date of filing.

6.69 The United States argues that although the application of Section 45 has in fact caused harm to U.S. right holders, the United States observes that the mere potential of the provision to result in the denial of a *TRIPS*-level patent term is sufficient to establish a violation of Articles 33 and 70. Furthermore, the United States notes that in light of Canada's failure to properly implement these provisions, proof of actual trade damage is not required and nullification or impairment is presumed. Finally, the United States contends that it is irrelevant whether, under certain conditions, Section 45 might result in the grant of a term of protection to certain right holders that is longer than required under the *TRIPS Agreement*. The United States argues that Canada cannot rely upon its *TRIPS*-plus level treatment of some patentees to justify its denial of *TRIPS*-level treatment to other patentees.

6.70 **Canada** states that it is not arguing that when allegedly term-deficient Old Act patents are added together with those having surplus term and are then appropriately divided, the resulting average term is greater than the term referred to in Article 33 and is, therefore, consistent with the *TRIPS* standard. Canada also claims that it is not arguing that the "more favourable treatment" accorded to surplus term compensates for the alleged deficiency in the term granted to so-called "term-deficient" Old Act patents.

6.71 Canada claims that Section 45 of its *Patent Act* does not prescribe that the term of protection shall end before the expiration of the 20-year period from the date of filing. Canada argues that a term of protection of at least equal to (and frequently in excess of) a period of 20 years from the date of filing was "available" under Section 45, without either exceptions or discrimination, to any Old Act applicant who wished to count and obtain a term of protection on that basis. Therefore, in Canada's view, Section 45 is consistent with Article 33 of the *TRIPS Agreement.*

6.72 Canada points out that over 60 per cent of Old Act applicants obtained or will obtain terms of protection that are equal or superior to the *TRIPS* mandated term of protection of 20 years from the date of filing. The other 40 per cent chose not to take advantage of the delays available to ensure a term of protection that would end before the expiration of a period of 20 years from the date of filing. However, Article 33 only requires that a protection term of 20 years be "available". Canada concludes that since there is nothing in the Canadian "availability" measures which discriminates between applicants or applications, what was obtained in respect of 60 per cent of the Old Act applications was "available" for 100 per cent of the Old Act applications.

6.73 Canada argues that the longevity of patent protection can be strategically controlled by the applicant so as to obtain a patent protection term of 20 years from the date of filing by means of delaying the patent prosecution process.[34] Canada points out that under Section 30 of the Old Act, an applicant can delay the patent prosecution process by up to 42 months. Section 73 provides an additional 12 months of delay. When the delays available under Sections 30 and 73 are added to the 17-year term of protection for patents, the total term of protection available is

---

[34] Canada states in para. 37 of its First Submission:

"Many means exist that allow an applicant to slow down the prosecution of an old Act application. These include the following:

(i) An applicant can achieve a delay in processing simply by asking the patent examiner. In my personal experience, I am unaware of any such request being refused.

(ii) One simple means for delaying an application is for an applicant to wait until the end of each time limit imposed upon the applicant to take a specified action. For example, an applicant can wait until the end of the six month period for responding to each report issued by the examiner and until the end of the six month period for paying the final fee due before a patent is granted.

(iii) An applicant can also choose to not respond to an examiner's report within the six month period following issuance of the report. This has the consequence that the application will be treated as abandoned; however, an abandoned application can be reinstated within twelve months.

(iv) An applicant can further choose to not pay the final fee within the six month period following the Office notice requiring payment. This has the consequence that the application will be treated as forfeited; however, a forfeited application can be restored within six months.

(v) Prior to October 1, 1996, there was a provision in the Patent Rules that permitted an applicant, upon payment of a fee, to postpone the date of issue of a patent by up to 10 weeks."

21.5 years from the date of filing, in addition to other delays that may occur in the examination process.

6.74 Canada argues a patent protection term of 20 years from the date of filing was available universally and that Article 33 does not require a Member to impose a patent protection term of 20 years from the date of filing against the revealed preference of the applicant.

6.75 In Canada's view, it acted within the scope of the freedom afforded to Members under Article 1.1 of the *TRIPS Agreement* "to determine the appropriate method of implementing the provisions of this Agreement within their own legal system and practice". Consistent with the legal test established under the *India—Patents*, Canada argues that its "means" of availability of the *TRIPS* mandated patent protection term of 20 years from the date of filing was provided on a "sound legal basis".

6.76 The **United States** responds that the Canadian law provides no sound legal basis for patent applicants that filed applications before 1 October 1989, to obtain a term of protection that did not end before a period of 20 years from the filing date. It asserts that neither of the provisions of law cited by Canada - Sections 30 and 73 of the Old Act - provided such a basis.

6.77 The United States argues that an Old Act applicant could obtain a term of 20 years from filing by actually abandoning its patent application not once, but twice. Then, the United States notes, after twice abandoning its application for a maximum period of time, and having it reinstated, the applicant could forfeit that application, wait a maximum period of time, and then reinstate it a third time.

6.78 The United States points out that Section 30(2) of the Old Act provides that the reinstatement of an abandoned patent application would only be permitted if a delay "was not reasonably avoidable".[35] It argues that, far from providing a legally guaranteed right to delay a patent application, Canadian law explicitly prohibits use of the abandonment and reinstatement procedure described by Canada where a delay was reasonably avoidable.

6.79 The United States asserts that Canada essentially argues that its patent examiners routinely ignore the mandatory provisions of Section 30(2), asserting that its Commissioner of Patents is unaware of reinstatement ever having been refused.[36] However, the United States notes, regardless of the practices of Canada's patent examiners, Section 30(2) unambiguously requires that reinstatement be denied where delays were reasonably avoidable.

6.80 The United States suggests that Canada's arguments are similar to those rejected by the Panel and Appellate Body in *India - Patents*.[37] The United States notes that, in that dispute, India argued that certain "administrative instructions" provided a "sound legal basis to preserve novelty of inventions and priority of applications as of the relevant filing and priority dates," despite provisions of India's Patents Act that required the Patents Controller to reject such applications.[38] The United States points

---

[35] Canadian *Patent Act*, R.S.C., ch. P-4, § 30(2) (1985). Reproduced in relevant part in Canada Exhibit 16.

[36] Canada's First Oral Statement, para. 47.

[37] Appellate Body Report, *India - Patents*, *supra*, footnote 13.

[38] *Ibid.*, paras. 67-71.

out that the Appellate Body looked specifically at the provisions of India's Patents Act, and decided:

> "We agree with the Panel that these provisions of the Patents Act are mandatory. And, like the Panel, we are not persuaded that India's 'administrative instructions' would prevail over the contradictory mandatory provisions of the Patents Act."[39]

6.81 The United States argues that Section 30(2) of the Old Act is mandatory in that abandoned applications can be reinstated only where the delay was "not reasonably avoidable." Thus, it argues, the procedure pursuant to which Canada argues that 20-year patent terms were available is prohibited by the very statute on which Canada bases its argument.

2. *Evaluation by the Panel*

6.82 In this section of the Report, we examine the obligation set out in Article 33 of the *TRIPS Agreement* to ascertain whether Section 45 of Canada's *Patent Act* is in conformity with Article 33. We then consider whether the text or context of Article 33 allows Canada to use the concept of "effective" protection or "exclusive privilege and property rights" to argue that there is an equivalence of term of protection made available by Section 45 and Article 33. We also evaluate Canada's use of the average pendency period of the New Act and Old Act patents in support of its argument that the term of protection made available under Section 45 is equivalent or superior to the term of protection made available by Article 33. We then examine whether Section 45 makes "available", as that term is used in Article 33, a term of protection that does not end before 20 years from the date of filing.

(a) Consideration of the United States' Claim in Relation to Article 33

6.83 The United States argued that Article 33 of the *TRIPS Agreement* requires Canada to provide a minimum term of protection that "shall not end before the expiration of...twenty years counted from the date of filing" for all Old Act patents. It is the United States' contention that the 17-year term of protection measured as of the date of grant is inconsistent with Article 33 on the ground that Old Act patents often expire before 20 years from the date of filing.

6.84 Article 33 of the *TRIPS Agreement* states:

> "The term of protection available shall not end before the expiration of a period of twenty years counted from the filing date."

6.85 The language provided in Article 33 requires Members to make available a "term of protection" for patents that does not end before 20 years from the date of filing. The use of the term "shall not end *before*" suggests that the 20-year period as of the filing date is a minimum term of protection for patents to be made available by Members. Such interpretation of Article 33 is supported by the minimum standard language governing the term of protection for copyright, trademarks, industrial designs, and layout-designs of integrated circuits which provide that the term of pro-

---

[39] *Ibid.*, para. 69.

tection is to be "*no less* than 50 years",[40] "*no less* than seven years",[41] "*at least* ten years"[42] and "shall not end *before* the expiration of a period of 10 years counted from the date of filing an application for registration",[43] respectively.

6.86 Interpretation of Article 33 as a minimum standard for the expiry of the available term of protection ("minimum standard") is also borne out by Article 1.1 of the *TRIPS Agreement* which forms part of the context of Article 33. Article 1.1 provides:

> "Members shall give effect to the provisions of this Agreement. Members *may, but shall not be obliged to, implement in their law more extensive protection than is required by this Agreement*, provided that such protection does not contravene the provisions of this Agreement. ... " (emphasis added)

6.87 Article 1.1 confirms that the *TRIPS Agreement* is a minimum standards agreement in respect of intellectual property rights. Under Article 1.1, Members may, but are not obligated to, implement a more stringent standard for the protection of intellectual property rights so long as such measures do not contravene any of the provisions of the *TRIPS Agreement*. The textual reading of Article 1.1 suggests that Members are to "give effect" to, *inter alia*, Article 33 which obligates Members to make available a term of protection for patents that does not end before 20 years from the date of filing.

6.88 By making available a term of protection that runs 17 years from the date of grant for those patents that were filed before 1 October 1989, Section 45 of Canada's *Patent Act,* on its face, does not meet the minimum standard of Article 33 in all cases. This is confirmed by the figures presented by Canada which show that there were still extant, as of 1 January 2000, approximately 66,936 Old Act patents, representing approximately 40 per cent of the total 169,966 Old Act patents, that would expire before 20 years from the date of filing.[44] It is irrelevant that a "very large number of" Old Act patents, representing 60 per cent of all Old Act patents, exceeded the protection term of 20 years from the date of filing by two to five years[45] and that 84 per cent of Old Act patents expire in the course of the nineteenth year following the application date[46] because the minimum standard for the term of protection under Article 33 is 20 years from the date of filing and we agree with the United States that, pursuant to this minimum standard for term of protection, even if

---

[40] Article 12 of the *TRIPS Agreement* provides that "[w]henever the term of protection of a work, other than a photographic work or a work of applied art, is calculated on a basis other than the life of a natural person, such term shall be no less than 50 years from the end of the calendar year of authorized publication. ..."

[41] Article 18 of the *TRIPS Agreement* provides that "[i]nitial registration, and each renewal of registration, of a trademark shall be for a term of no less than seven years."

[42] Article 26.3 of the *TRIPS Agreement*, in relation to industrial designs, provides that "[t]he duration of protection available shall amount to at least 10 years."

[43] Article 38 of the *TRIPS Agreement*, in relation to layout-designs of integrated circuits, provides in para. 1 that in some cases the term of protection "shall not end before the expiration of a period of 10 years" counted from a particular date and para. 2 provides that in other cases layout-designs "shall be protected for a term of no less than 10 years" from a particular date.

[44] Canada's First Submission, para. 45.

[45] *Ibid.*, para. 42.

[46] *Ibid.*, para. 43.

there is only one patent that has a term of protection that ends before 20 years from the date of filing, Section 45 would be considered inconsistent with Article 33.[47]

6.89 As Article 33 obligates Members to make available a minimum term of protection that does not end before 20 years from the date of filing and the foregoing statistical figures showing that there are as many as 66,936 Old Act patents that existed as of the *TRIPS* application date, and were still in existence on 1 January 2000, that would expire before 20 years from the date of filing despite payment of all maintenance fees, we find on a preliminary basis that Section 45 is inconsistent with Article 33 of the *TRIPS Agreement.*[48]

(b) Consideration of Canada's Equivalence Argument

(i) The Term of "Effective" Protection or "Exclusive Privilege and Property Rights"

6.90 Canada advanced the argument that Section 45 is in conformity and harmonious with Article 33 on the basis that 17 years of "effective" protection for the "exclusive privilege and property rights" conferred by Old Act patents are "equivalent or superior" to the term of "exclusive privilege and property rights" provided by Article 33 of the *TRIPS Agreement.*[49] Canada made such assertion based on the fact that the

---

47 The United States referred to a well-known antidepressant drug as evidence of a patent that expired before 20 years from the date of filing. The United States pointed out that the Canadian patent for that drug expired in August 1999 under the term of protection provided by Section 45 whereas it would not have expired until October 2000 if the term of protection ran until 20 years from the date of filing as required by Article 33 of the *TRIPS Agreement.* See U.S. Exhibit 2.

48 The United States argued that Article 31(3)(b) of the *Vienna Convention* allows treaty interpreters to take into account "subsequent practice" to "establish the agreement of the parties regarding its interpretation" and referred to six developed country Members, including itself, that amended their laws to implement the *TRIPS Agreement.* In connection with "subsequent practice", the Appellate Body stated in *Japan - Alcoholic Beverages, supra*, footnote 14, at 106, that "the essence of subsequent practice in interpreting a treaty has been recognized as a 'concordant, common and consistent' sequence of acts…which is sufficient to establish a discernable pattern implying the agreement of the parties regarding its interpretation." For the purpose of this dispute, we do not consider it necessary to make a finding as to whether there is "subsequent practice" to determine the requirement under Article 33 of the *TRIPS Agreement* and to ascertain whether Section 45 of Canada's *Patent Act* is in conformity with Article 33.

49 We note Canada's argument that the parties to the North American Free Trade Agreement ("NAFTA") accepted the substantive equivalence of the protection offered by two types of protection term. The relevant NAFTA provision cited by Canada states that "[e]ach party shall provide a term of protection for patents of at least twenty years from the date of filing or seventeen years from the date of grant." We do not consider that the NAFTA provision means that Section 45 of the Canadian *Patent Act* and Article 33 of the *TRIPS Agreement* have substantive equivalence of protection. In this regard, we note that the Panel in *United States - Restrictions on Imports of Tuna*, GATT Doc. DS29/R, 20 May 1994 (unadopted), stated, in relation to Article 31.3(a) of the *Vienna Convention*, the following:

> "The Panel recalled that the Vienna Convention provides for a general rule of interpretation (Article 31) and a supplementary means of interpretation (Article 32). The Panel first examined whether, under the *general* rule of interpretation of the Vienna Convention, the treaties referred to might be taken into account for the purposes of interpreting the General Agreement. The general rule provides that "any subsequent agreement between the parties regarding the interpretation of the treaty

time-period between the filing date and issuance of patent necessarily erodes the term of patent protection in cases where, as in Article 33, the protection period is measured as of the filing date.[50] Since the time-period between the filing date and issuance of patent is on average five years in Canada, it was Canada's contention that a patent right holder will receive only 15 years of "exclusive privilege and property rights" under a system that grants a 20-year protection term as of the filing date whereas Section 45 provides a successful patent applicant with 17 years of constant protection for the "exclusive privilege and property rights".

6.91 Canada claimed that since the time-period between the filing date and patent issuance date varies, the patent term of protection as contemplated by Article 33 is not a fixed minimum period of 20 years but "a variable period of less than 20 years".[51] Canada stated that the *TRIPS* negotiators were aware that the period of protection would be "a variable period of less than 20 years" based on the fact that Article 62.2 requires procedures for the grant or registration of intellectual property rights take place "within a reasonable period of time so as to avoid unwarranted curtailment of the period of protection."

6.92 There is no textual or contextual support for Canada's interpretation that Article 33 of the *TRIPS Agreement* requires Members to provide patent right holders with a term of "effective" protection or "exclusive privilege and property rights". The plain language of Article 33 states that the "term of protection available shall not end before the expiration of a period of twenty years counted from the filing date." To construe the language provided in Article 33 to mean a term of "effective" protection or "exclusive privilege and property rights" would require the treaty interpreter to read into the text words that are not there[52] and would be, as noted by the Appellate Body in *Japan - Alcoholic Beverages*,[53] contrary to the rule that "inter-

or the application of its provisions" is one of the elements relevant to the interpretation of a treaty. However the Panel observed that the agreements cited by the parties to the dispute were bilateral or plurilateral agreements that were not concluded among the contracting parties to the General Agreement, and that they did not apply to the interpretation of the General Agreement or the application of its provisions. Indeed, many of the treaties referred to could not have done so, since they were concluded prior to the negotiation of the General Agreement. The Panel also observed that under the general rule of interpretation in the Vienna Convention account should be taken of "any subsequent practice in the application of the treaty which established the agreement of the parties regarding its interpretation." However, the Panel noted that practice under the bilateral and plurilateral treaties cited could not be taken as practice under the General Agreement, and therefore could not affect the interpretation of it. The Panel therefore found that under the general rule contained in Article 31 of the Vienna Convention, these treaties were not relevant as a primary means of interpretation of the text of the General Agreement."

50 Canada's First Submission, para. 74; Canada's Response to Panel Question 21.

51 Canada's First Oral Statement, para. 17; Canada's Second Oral Statement, para. 16.

52 Appellate Body Report, *India - Quantitative Restrictions on Imports of Agricultural, Textile and Industrial Products*, WT/DS90/AB/R, adopted 22 September 1999, DSR 1999:IV,1763, para. 94; Appellate Body Report, *EC - Measures Concerning Meat and Meat Products (Hormones)*, WT/DS26/AB/R, WT/DS48/AB/R, adopted 13 February 1998, DSR 1998:I, 135, para. 181.

53 Appellate Body Report, *Japan - Alcoholic Beverages , supra,* footnote 14, at 105.

pretation must be based above all upon the text of the treaty".[54] Canada's interpretation would engender unreasonable results that would allow a term of protection for patents that ends before 20 years from the date of filing to be in conformity with Article 33.

6.93 Canada also argues that it could maintain its Old Act term of protection of 17 years from the date of grant in implementing the *TRIPS Agreement* based on the freedom afforded to each Member by Article 1.1 "to determine the appropriate method of implementing the provisions of [the] Agreement within their own legal system and practice." Canada makes this argument because, in its view, the relevant "provisions of [the] Agreement" in this case only require a variable period of effective protection, which can be ascertained through a combined interpretation of Articles 33 and 62.2, and which overrides obligations concerning the dates of commencement or expiry.

6.94 We take a different view. Article 33 contains an obligation concerning the earliest available date of expiry of patents, and Article 62.2 contains a separate obligation prohibiting acquisition procedures which lead to unwarranted curtailment of the period of protection. We recognize that some curtailment is permitted by the text of these two provisions. However, Article 1.1 gives Members the freedom to determine the appropriate method of implementing those two specific requirements, but not to ignore either requirement in order to implement another putative obligation concerning the length of effective protection.

6.95 Furthermore, Article 62.2 does not support Canada's argument that its obligation is to make available a term of protection equivalent in overall length to a variable term of real or effective protection under the 20 years from the date of filing "formula". Paragraph 2 of Article 62 only deals with the "acquisition" of an intellectual property right and procedures for "grant or registration", which all refer to the commencement of the available period of protection and not to its expiry date. It recognizes some curtailment of the term of protection may occur due to a later commencement date, but not a reduction at any other point in that period, including its expiry. This applies *a fortiori* in light of the express requirement in Article 33 concerning the date of expiry. Canada also referred to paragraphs 1 and 4 of Article 62 which provide for procedures that can terminate protection of particular inventions, through default in payment of maintenance fees, revocation and cancellation, prior to expiry of the available term.[55] As such, those are precisely the procedures that are implied by the use in Article 33 of the word "available" and which are to be discounted in evaluation of the available term of protection. We therefore find that Canada's defence based on "equivalence" of terms has not displaced our finding that Section 45 is inconsistent with Article 33.

---

[54] [footnote original] *Territorial Dispute (Libyan Arab Jamahiriya/Chad), Judgment*, (1994) *I.C.J. Reports*, p. 6 at 20; *Maritime Delimitation and Territorial Questions between Qatar and Bahrain, Jurisdiction and Admissibility, Judgment*, (1995) *I.C.J. Reports*, p. 6 at 18.

[55] Canada's Response to Panel Question 29.

(ii) "Normal or Average" Pendency Period

6.96 Canada referred to the "average" pendency period for New Act patents in support of its argument that the "effective" period of protection made available by Section 45 is equivalent or superior to the term of protection made available by Article 33 of the *TRIPS Agreement*.[56] We appreciate that this, together with the factors mentioned by both parties in their respective replies to question 1 from the panel, may assist us in the interpretation of the phrase "unwarranted curtailment" of the term of protection in Article 62.2. However, in view of our findings in paragraphs 6.94 and 6.95, we do not need to decide what would constitute such an "unwarranted curtailment".

6.97 We note that Canada referred to statistics as to the average length of pendency periods of Old Act patents, which we have quoted at paragraphs 2.6 to 2.11 of this Report, according to which approximately 60 per cent of Old Act patents and patent applications both at 1 October 1996 and again at 1 November 1999 had an available term expiring later than required by Article 33, while approximately 40 per cent did not. We also note that Canada emphasized that it did not argue that Section 45 was consistent with Article 33 of the *TRIPS Agreement* on the basis that an overall average of the terms of protection of Old Act patents and patent applications in force on the date of application of the *TRIPS Agreement* met the minimum standard of Article 33.[57] Nevertheless, we find it useful in the following paragraphs to dispel any notion that average figures can be used to maintain the equivalence argument, especially in view of the fact that Canada relies on the average pendency period of New Act patents to support its argument that the term of protection available under Section 45 is equivalent or superior to the term of protection made available in Article 33 and further in light of the fact that Canada uses the average pendency period of two to four years of Old Act patents to make the same claim in relation to Article 33.

6.98 We are mindful that the Panel in *United States - Section 337 of the Tariff Act of 1930* rejected "any notion of balancing more favourable treatment…against less favourable treatment" and its statement that more favourable treatment is only relevant to the extent that it always offsets differential treatment causing less favourable treatment.[58] Specifically, the Panel:

> "…rejected any notion of balancing more favourable treatment of some imported products against less favourable treatment of other imported products. If this notion were accepted, it would entitle a contracting party to derogate from the no less favourable treatment obligation in one case, or indeed in respect of one contracting party, on the ground that it accords more favourable treatment in some other case, or to another contracting party. Such an interpretation would lead to great uncertainty about the conditions of competition between

[56] Canada's First Submission, paras. 78 and 81; Canada's First Oral Statement, paras. 22 and 26.

[57] Canada's Response to Panel Question 21.

[58] *United States - Section 337 of the Tariff Act of 1930*, BISD 36S/345, adopted 7 November 1989, paras. 5.14 and 5.16 ("*United States - Section 337*").

imported and domestic products and thus defeat the purposes of Article III."[59]

6.99 Disparate pendency periods exist among patents because the examination period required to review the criteria set forth in Article 27.1 for patentability varies from one field of technology to another. This variance also exists in Canada where the patent authority "normally took...two to four years to complete the examination process."[60] Based on simple arithmetic, if an Old Act patent took two years to issue, its term of protection measured as of the date of filing would end 19 years, as opposed to 20, from the date of filing, which is the earliest available expiry date required by Article 33. To meet the standard enunciated in *United States - Section 337*, *all* Old Act patents would have to have a term of protection that did not end before 20 years from the date of filing. It cannot be assumed that all Old Act patents had a pendency period of three years or longer and therefore a term of protection that did not end before 20 years from the date of filing because an *average* figure of two to four years necessarily embraces shorter periods which result in patents with a term of protection that ends before 20 years from the date of filing. In fact, the parties agree that many Old Act patents, including many still in force, will expire before 20 years from the date of filing.[61]

6.100 Thus, even if Article 33 could be construed to allow Members to make available a term of "effective" patent protection or "exclusive privilege and property rights", we do not find tenable any argument that Section 45 made available a term equivalent or superior to the available term of protection mandated by Article 33 on the basis of an average pendency period and resultant expiry date of protection made available by Section 45. In relation to the equivalence argument, we find that the term of protection under Section 45 is inconsistent with the minimum standard of Article 33 of the *TRIPS Agreement* because, within the calculation of the average period of effective protection, there are Old Act patents with a term of protection that ends before 20 years from the date of filing.

(c) Consideration of Canada's "Availability" Argument

6.101 In determining whether Canada made available a term of protection that does not end before 20 years from the date of filing, we first examine the ordinary meaning of the word "available" in its context. We then consider whether the suggested delays result in "unwarranted curtailment" under Article 62.2 and constitute "unnecessarily complicated or costly" procedures under Article 41.2 which is incorporated by reference in Article 62.4. Subsequently, we evaluate the merit of Canada's argument that a term of protection that does not end before 20 years from the date of filing was available prior to the date of entry into force of the *TRIPS Agreement* in Canada.

[59] *United States - Section 337*, para. 5.14.
[60] Canada's First Submission, para. 72.
[61] See paras. 2.8 and 2.10.

(i) Whether a Term of Protection that does not End before 20 Years from the Date of Filing Was "Available" under Section 45 of Canada's Patent Act

6.102 As a treaty interpreter's obligation is to first interpret the text based on its ordinary meaning within its context and object and purpose, the ordinary meaning of the word "available" as it is used in Article 33 is first considered. *Black's Law Dictionary* defines the word "available" as "having sufficient force or efficacy; effectual; valid"[62] and the word "valid" in turn means "having legal strength or force...incapable of being rightfully overthrown or set aside."[63] The dictionary meaning of the word "available" would suggest that patent right holders are entitled, as a matter of *right*, to a term of protection that does not end before 20 years from the date of filing.

6.103 We first note Canada's explanation that a patent applicant could obtain informal delays by simply asking the examiner to "retard the position of a particular application in the queue of those applications waiting examination."[64] These informal delays, according to Canada, were granted at the discretion of the patent examiner[65] without exception. Based on Canada's argument, a patent applicant would be required to resort to delay tactics to obtain the *TRIPS* mandated term of protection that does not end before 20 years from the date of filing. Although Canada stated that such delay requests have never been refused, it is apparent that the patent examiner had the discretionary authority to grant or not grant the necessary delay so as to allow a patent applicant to prolong the term of patent protection that does not end before 20 years from the date of filing. In short, these informal delays were not granted to Old Act patent applicants as a matter of right.

6.104 Canada argued that, as an alternative to informally asking for delays from a patent examiner, there are statutorily mandated delays which a patent applicant can use to obtain a protection term of 20 years from the date of filing.[66] According to Canada, Section 30(1) provides for 12 months to complete an application after filing and six months to prosecute the application after a notice that an examiner has taken action. An application is deemed abandoned if these two deadlines are not met. Section 30(2) allowed an applicant a further delay by providing a period of 12 months to have an abandoned application reinstated. When 12 months for completing an application, another 12 months for reinstatement in the event of failure to complete an application within the time-limit, six months for the prosecution of the application and a further 12 months for reinstatement of the application in case of failure to prosecute within the six-month period are added, the total period of delay is 42 months, or 3.5 years.

6.105 A second statutory delay is available under Section 73 of the Old Act. That section provides a period of up to six months to pay the prescribed fees in a notice of

62 *Black's Law Dictionary* (West Publishing Co., 1979), p. 123.
63 *Ibid.*, p. 1390.
64 Canada's Response to Panel Question 31(a).
65 *Ibid.* 31(b).
66 Canada's First Oral Statement, para. 42.

allowance on penalty of forfeiture. A forfeited application can, on the payment of prescribed fees, be restored within six months of an initial act of default in timely payment. Thus, another year of delay is available from the date of filing. When the delays available under Sections 30 and 70 are added to the 17-year term of protection for patents, the total delay amounts to a statutorily available term of 21.5 years from the date of filing. The total period of delay of 54 months does not include the time required for a patent examiner to complete the examination of the application and additional delays that may result from request for further information.

6.106 Based on the statutory delays under Sections 30(2) and 73, a patent applicant would actually have to abandon his application, reinstate the abandoned application and then again forfeit the application and then reinstate it again for the third time to obtain the *TRIPS* mandated term of protection that does not end before 20 years from the date of filing. Since the patent applicant cannot know the time-period required for the examination of the patent application by an examiner, the applicant cannot be certain about how many times the application would have to be abandoned to obtain a term of protection that does not end before 20 years from the date of filing.

6.107 It is apparent from the statutory text that the power to reinstate an abandoned application under Section 30(2) was only available where the applicant's failure to meet the deadlines of the Old Act "were not reasonably avoidable". Canada admits that the Commissioner of Patents could have refused to reinstate an application where an applicant revealed that his motive in not meeting the deadlines of the Old Act was to delay issuance of the patent to obtain a term expiring 20 years from the date of filing. Such an applicant was therefore effectively required to conceal his motive and to state another explanation for his failure to meet the deadlines in order to be entitled to reinstatement of the application. Nonetheless, Canada stated that no such request for reinstatement was ever refused.

6.108 The use of the word "may" in the statutory text of Section 73 indicates that the Commissioner of Patents had a discretion to reinstate forfeited applications, which he could refuse to exercise in certain circumstances.[67]

6.109 We find that the discretionary nature of both a patent examiner's authority to grant informal delays as well as the Commissioner's power to grant statutory delays so as to allow patent applicants to obtain a term of protection that does not end before 20 years from the date of filing does not make available, as a matter of right, to patent applicants a term of protection required by Article 33.

6.110 In addition to the interpretation that patent right holders are entitled to the term of protection for patents that does not end before 20 years from the date of filing under Article 33 of the *TRIPS Agreement*, we note that the respective use and omission of the word "available" in other provisions on terms of protection throughout the Agreement provides a plausible contextual explanation for its use in Article 33. In our view, the word "available" in Article 33 probably reflects the fact that patent right holders must pay fees from time to time to maintain the term of protection and that patent authorities are to make those terms "available" to patent right holders who exercise their right to maintain the exclusive rights conferred by the patent. Such

[67] We deal with Canada's argument that there was no real discretion under Section 73 at para. 6.118.

interpretation is supported by Article 26 of the *TRIPS Agreement*, which governs the term of protection of industrial designs, and which uses the word "available" to reflect the fact that right holders of industrial designs in some Members must pay maintenance fees to maintain the term of protection whereas "available" is not used in Article 18 in connection with the term of protection of trademarks because the seven-year term of protection refers to the initial term of registration during which time there is no need for the right holder of a trademark to pay fees to renew or maintain the protection term. Article 38.1 concerning the term of protection in respect of layout-designs requiring registration does not contain the word "available" because the ten-year protection term does not require right holders to renew or maintain the protection term during that ten-year period. Similarly, the word "available" is not used in respect of terms of protection governing copyright and related rights and layout-designs not requiring registration as a condition for protection because there are no formal requirements to obtain protection.

6.111 In light of the various reasons set out above, we confirm our finding that a term of protection that does not end before 20 years from the date of filing is not available under Section 45 of Canada's *Patent Act* and is therefore inconsistent with Article 33 of the *TRIPS Agreement*.

(ii) Whether Resorting to Informal and Statutory Delays is Consistent with Article 62

6.112 In light of the fact that Canada argued that a patent term of 17 years from grant could be considered consistent with Article 33 in view of the provisions on acquisition and maintenance procedures contained in Part IV of the *TRIPS Agreement* that enable a certain amount of delay in granting rights, we are of the view that the procedures on which Canada relies should also be assessed in relation to Part IV of the *TRIPS Agreement* which applies to patents granted after the date of application of the Agreement for the Member in question.

6.113 In addition to lacking textual support and imputing words and concepts that were not intended, requiring applicants to resort to the suggested delays to obtain a term of protection that does not end before 20 years from the date of filing also defeats the notion of promoting prompt and diligent prosecution and examination of patents as encapsulated in Articles 33, 62.1 and 62.4.

6.114 Article 62.1 provides:

> "Members may require, as a condition of the acquisition or maintenance of the intellectual property rights provided for under Sections 2 through 6 of Part II, compliance with *reasonable procedures* and formalities. Such procedures and formalities shall be consistent with the provisions of this Agreement." (emphasis added)

6.115 While it may be true in many cases that an applicant can procure a term of protection that does not end until 20 years from the date of filing by resorting to procedural delays, the types of procedural delays Canada described do not seem to constitute reasonable procedures because they are not tied to valid reasons required to ensure a proper examination but are rather purely related to artificially fulfilling the requirement of Article 33. In our view, requiring applicants to resort to delays such as abandonment, reinstatement, non-payment of fees and non-response to a patent examiner's report for the purpose of simply obtaining a term of protection that does not end before 20 years from the date of filing would constitute unreasonable procedures that are inconsistent with Canada's obligation under Article 62.1.

6.116 Turning to Article 62.4, we note that it provides:

> "Procedures concerning the acquisition or maintenance of intellectual property rights...shall be governed by the general principles set out in paragraphs 2 and 3 of Article 41."

Paragraph 2 of Article 41 provides:

> "Procedures concerning the enforcement of intellectual property rights shall be fair and equitable. They shall not be *unnecessarily complicated or costly*, or entail unreasonable time-limits or *unwarranted delays*." (emphasis added)

6.117 In our view, requiring applicants to resort to delays such as abandonment, reinstatement, non-payment of fees and non-response to a patent examiner's report would be inconsistent with the general principle that procedures not be unnecessarily complicated as expressed in Article 41.2 and applied to acquisition procedures by Article 62.4. By their very nature, the delays, which are not tied to any valid reason related to the examination and grant process, would be inconsistent with the general principle that procedures not entail "unwarranted delays" as expressed in Article 41.2 and applied to acquisition procedures by Article 62.4.

6.118 We noted in paragraphs 6.107 and 6.108 above that the Commissioner's powers to reinstate and restore applications under Section 30(2) and Section 73 were discretionary at all material times and not available as a matter of right to patent applicants. Canada argued, however, that despite the use of the word "may" in Section 73, the payment of the necessary fee enabled the applicant to obtain reinstatement of his patent application as a matter of right. In other words, had the Commissioner exercised his discretion to refuse an application for reinstatement, an applicant would have been required to pay an additional fee and pursue legal proceedings against the Commissioner in a court of law in order for a term of protection expiring 20 years from the date of filing the application to be available. We find potential requirements that an applicant commence proceedings for a writ of mandamus and pay additional fees to be in breach of the general principle that procedures not be "unnecessarily complicated or costly" as expressed in Article 41.2 and applied to acquisition procedures by Article 62.4.

6.119 A patent applicant should not be expected to resort to procedural tactics that produce results inconsistent with Article 62.1 and 62.4 in order to ensure its rights pursuant to Article 33. As such, these procedures cannot be relied upon in order to defend a claim of violation of another Article of the Agreement.

(iii) Whether a Term of Protection that does not End before 20 Years from the Date of Filing can be Made "Available" in Accordance with Article 33 Prior to the Date of Application of the TRIPS Agreement

6.120 It is agreed that this dispute only concerns patents which were granted prior to 1 October 1992 as any Old Act patents granted later would be entitled to a longer term of protection than the *TRIPS Agreement* requires (see paragraph 6.6 above). Given that Canada's argument that the requisite patent term was "available" hinges on procedures prior to the grant of a patent, it is apparent that the alleged availability is referable to the options available to patent applicants prior to 1 October 1992, i.e., prior to the entry into force of the *TRIPS Agreement*. Canada takes the view that, where Article 33 was applicable to inventions under protection in developed country Members on 1 January 1996, it would be "sufficient if the term [of protection] was available at the time the application was filed".[68] We do not agree with this view. According to Article 65.1, Canada became obligated to apply Article 33 on 1 January 1996. In our view, no Member can implement an obligation by reference to a state of affairs which ceased to exist in respect of Old Act patents at the time the obligation to make available a term of protection that does not end before 20 years from the date of filing became applicable. Consequently, the alleged availability in Canada prior to 1 October 1992 of a term of protection that complied with the requirement described in Article 33 is insufficient to discharge Canada's obligation to implement Article 33 from 1 January 1996.

6.121 In the same way, even though Old Act patent applicants prior to 1 October 1992 were able to obtain a patent term that expired 20 years or more after the date of filing on the basis of informal delays in the patent prosecution process, and the statutory procedures of reinstatement and restoration, they could not have known that they were entitled to have such a term of protection made available to them because the *TRIPS Agreement* had not yet entered into force or even been finalized. Therefore, the decision of many of those patent applicants not to seek these delays was made without that knowledge, and cannot be characterized as a choice to forego the right to a term of protection expiring later than is required by the *TRIPS Agreement*.

VII. CONCLUSIONS AND RECOMMENDATION

7.1 In light of the findings above, we conclude that:

(i) the reference to "subject matter...which is protected" on the date of application of the *TRIPS Agreement* in Article 70.2 includes inventions that are currently protected by patents in accordance with Section 45 and that were protected by patent on 1 January 1996, and this is not affected by Article 70.1; and

(ii) Section 45 of Canada's *Patent Act* does not make available a term of protection that does not end before 20 years from the date of filing as mandated by Article 33.

7.2 The Panel therefore recommends that the Dispute Settlement Body request Canada to bring its measures into conformity with its obligations under the WTO Agreement.

[68] Canada's Response to Panel Question 33.

ATTACHMENT 1: UNITED STATES' SUBMISSIONS

ATTACHMENT 1.1

FIRST SUBMISSION OF THE UNITED STATES
(18 November 1999)

I. INTRODUCTION

1. This case is an exceedingly simple one. Articles 33 and 70 of the WTO Agreement on Trade-Related Aspects of Intellectual Property Rights (TRIPS Agreement) require all WTO members to provide a patent term of at least twenty years from the date of filing of the patent application. For a large group of patents, Canada applies a term that in many cases is shorter - calculated as seventeen years from the date that a patent is issued. A term of seventeen years from issuance is not the same as a term of twenty years from filing. For patent applications that are pending for less than three years before being issued, the seventeen year term is shorter. Thus, with respect to a large number of existing patents, Canada is in violation of the TRIPS Agreement because of its failure to provide an adequate patent term.

II. FACTUAL BACKGROUND

2. The facts of this case are straight-forward and uncontested. The Canadian Patent Act provides that the term of patents based on applications filed before October 1, 1989, is seventeen years from the date that the patent is issued. For patents based on applications filed on or after that date, the term is the TRIPS-minimum of twenty years from the filing date. Sections 44 and 45 of the Canadian Patent Act are unambiguous, and provide as follows:

> 44. Subject to section 46, where an application for a patent is filed under this Act on or after October 1, 1989, the term limited for the duration of the patent is twenty years from the filing date.
>
> 45. Subject to section 46, the term limited for *the duration of every patent issued under this Act on the basis of an application filed before October 1, 1989 is seventeen years* from the date on which the patent is issued.[1]

3. In general, the extent to which a patent term of seventeen years from issuance may be shorter than the TRIPS-required term of twenty years from filing varies from patent to patent. The gap depends entirely on the time that elapsed between the date of filing of a particular patent application and the date of issuance of the patent. As a matter of simple arithmetic, for *any* patent that was issued in less than three years from its date of filing, Canada's term of seventeen years from issuance is shorter than the TRIPS-mandated term of twenty years from filing. Canada is in violation of the TRIPS Agreement with respect

[1] Canadian Patent Act, R.S.C., ch. P-4, §§ 44- 45 (1985) (Can.) (emphasis added) (Article 46 of the Canadian Patent Act, cross-referenced in the quoted articles, concerns the payment of maintenance fees for a patent).

to each and every one of these patents. If a patent takes exactly three years to be issued, there is no practical difference between the term provided by Canada and the term required by the TRIPS Agreement. If a patent took longer than three years to be issued, the seventeen-year term would actually be longer than required.

4. During the consultations in this case, Canadian officials responded to written questions submitted by the United States and provided estimates of the number of patents affected by the provisions of the Canadian Patent Act at issue.[2] According to Canada, 169,966 patents were still in existence in June 1999 for which Canada provides a term of seventeen years from grant. Of these 169,966 existing patents with a term of seventeen years from grant, Canada estimated that 66,936 - or 39.4% of them - expire sooner than would be the case if Canada had provided a term of twenty years from filing. Historically, fifty percent (50%) of patent applications filed in Canada are from U.S. applicants. Thus, it appears that well over 33,000 U.S. patent holders are currently holding patents with a term less than that required under the TRIPS Agreement.

5. Indeed, for some U.S. right holders, Canada's delay in implementing its TRIPS obligations has already caused tremendous harm. As one example, a major pharmaceutical patent owned by Pfizer Inc on its anti-depressant drug "ZOLOFT" (sertraline hydrochloride) expired in August 1999, at the end of its term of seventeen years from issuance. Under a TRIPS-level term of twenty years from the date of filing, Pfizer's Canadian patent for ZOLOFT should not have expired until October 2000, fourteen months later.[3]

6. The patents affected by the inadequate Canadian patent term cover inventions in all fields of technology. Due to the significance of patent protection to the pharmaceutical industry, Canada's TRIPS violation has a particularly severe impact on the companies in this area. However, the thousands of patents affected by the Canadian deficiency cover inventions in fields as diverse as automotive technology, telecommunications, plastics, and computer- related technologies.[4]

7. Representatives of the Government of Canada have publicly acknowledged that Canada is obligated under the WTO to provide a term of at least twenty years from the date of filing for all patents. In a 1997 presentation to the Canadian House of Commons Standing Committee on Industry that was reviewing amendments to the Patent Act, Canada's Minister of Industry, the Honourable John Manley, stated that "We must give *all* patentees, pharmaceutical or otherwise, a minimum 20 year patent term."[5]

III. PROCEDURAL BACKGROUND

8. The United States requested consultations in this case on May 6, 1999. The United States provided written questions to Canada on May 21, 1999. Consultations were held on June 11, 1999. These consultations focused on Canada's answers to the U.S. questions and the legal issue that is set forth in this submission. The consultations did not result in a resolution of the dispute. The United States first requested the establishment of

---

[2] U.S. Questions to Canada, May 21, 1999 (US-Exhibit 1).

[3] Letter from Ian C. Read, Senior Vice President, Pfizer Pharmaceuticals, to Geralyn S. Ritter, Office of the U.S. Trade Representative (Oct. 15, 1999) (Exhibit US-2).

[4] Sample affected patents corresponding to the cited areas of technology are attached. (Exhibit US-3).

[5] Speaking Notes for the Honourable John Manley, Minister of Industry, to the House of Commons Standing Committee on Industry, Review of Bill C-91, 7 (Feb. 17, 1997) (available on Industry Canada web site, *www.ic.gc.ca*) (emphasis added) (Exhibit US-4).

a dispute settlement panel at the meeting of the Dispute Settlement Body on July 26, 1999. This Panel was established on September 22, 1999. The Panel was composed on October 22, 1999.

IV. LEGAL ANALYSIS

9. Article 33 of the TRIPS Agreement describes the required term of patent protection under the Agreement. Article 70 governs the treatment of subject matter existing on the date of application of the TRIPS Agreement. By providing a term of protection for many existing patents of lesser duration than required under Article 33, Canada is in violation of both of these provisions. An analysis of the text, context and object and purpose of Articles 33 and 70 supports this conclusion.[6]

10. Article 33 of the TRIPS Agreement is entitled "Term of Protection," and provides that "The term of protection available shall not end before the expiration of a period of twenty years counted from the filing date." By its plain terms, this Article obligates all WTO Members to grant a term of protection for patents that runs at least until twenty years after the filing date of the underlying application. The phrasing of the provision - "shall not end before" - also indicates that the twenty year term is a minimum term, rather than a maximum term, and that patent terms longer than twenty years from the date of filing are wholly consistent with the Agreement.

11. Article 70 of the Agreement is entitled "Existing Subject Matter," and contains a number of transitional provisions. Article 70.2 specifically applies to "subject matter existing at the date of the application of the Agreement," and provides in relevant part as follows:

> Except as otherwise provided for in this Agreement, this Agreement gives rise to obligations in respect of all subject matter existing at the date of application of this Agreement for the Member in question, and which is protected in that Member on the said date, or which meets or comes subsequently to meet the criteria for protection under the terms of this Agreement. ...

Read in accordance with its ordinary meaning, Article 70 means that the TRIPS Agreement gives rise to obligations - including the obligation to grant a patent term of at least twenty years from the date of filing - in respect of all patents ("subject matter") existing on January 1, 1996, the date of application of the TRIPS Agreement to developed country Members of the WTO.[7]

12. The context, object and purpose of Articles 33 and 70.2 are consistent with the plain meaning of the terms of these Articles, and certainly do not contradict it. The TRIPS Agreement establishes minimum standards of protection of intellectual property rights. Article 1.1 provides that "Members may, but shall not be obliged to, implement in their

[6] As the Appellate Body stated in *India - Patent Protection for Pharmaceuticals and Agricultural Chemical Products*, WT/DS50/AB/R, adopted 16 January 1998, DSR 1998:I, 9, para. 43, the obligations of the TRIPS Agreement should be analyzed in accordance with Article 31 of the Vienna Convention. *Cf.* Appellate Body Report, *United States - Standards for Reformulated and Conventional Gasoline*, WT/DS2/AB/R, adopted 20 May 1996, DSR 1996:I, 3 at 15 (adopted May 20, 1996). Article 31 of the Vienna Convention provides in part, "A treaty shall be interpreted in good faith in accordance with the ordinary meaning to be given to the terms of the treaty in their context and in the light of its object and purpose."

[7] TRIPS, art. 65.

law more extensive protection than is required by this Agreement, provided that such protection does not contravene the provisions of this Agreement." Thus, WTO Members do not have the option of providing sub-standard protection in one area so long as they "compensate" by providing TRIPS-plus protection in another area.

13. Under Section 45 of the Canadian Patent Act, the term granted to patents issued on the basis of applications filed before October 1, 1989, is seventeen years from the date on which the patent is issued. For such patents that were issued in less than three years, the seventeen year term provided under Section 45 is shorter than the TRIPS-mandated term of twenty years from the date of filing. Thus, Canada is in violation of its TRIPS obligations under Articles 33 and 70.2 with respect to all patents filed before October 1, 1989, that took less than three years to issue, and that were still in existence on January 1, 1996.

14. The potential for Section 45 of the Canadian Patent Act to result in the grant of a sub-twenty year term is clear from the text of the statute. Although the application of this provision has in fact caused harm to U.S. right holders, the United States observes that the mere potential of the provision to result in the denial of a TRIPS-level patent term is sufficient to establish a violation of Articles 33 and 70.[8] Furthermore, in light of Canada's failure to properly implement these provisions, proof of actual trade damage is not required and nullification or impairment is presumed.[9] Finally, it is irrelevant whether, under certain conditions, Section 45 might result in the grant of a term of protection to certain right holders that is longer than required under TRIPS. Canada cannot rely upon its TRIPS-plus level treatment of some patentees to justify its denial of TRIPS-level treatment to other patentees.[10]

15. Under the Vienna Convention, "any subsequent practice" in the application of an Agreement may also establish "the agreement of the parties regarding its interpretation."[11] In this case, State practice of other developed-country WTO Members in applying Articles 33 and 70 of the TRIPS Agreement demonstrates the term of patent protection that other Members have viewed as legally required by the TRIPS Agreement.

16. In the United States, prior to the TRIPS Agreement, the term of a patent under U.S. law was seventeen years from the date of grant. To implement TRIPS, however, the United States amended its law to provide a term of seventeen years from the date of grant of the patent or twenty years from the effective filing date of the patent, whichever term is longer, for all patents in force (or that resulted from an application filed before) the date six months after the enactment of the U.S. implementing legislation.[12]

17. Other WTO members have also amended their laws to comply with these TRIPS provisions. In a 1994 amendment to its Patent Act, Australia increased its standard patent

---

[8] See United States - Section 337 of the Tariff Act of 1930, BISD 36S/386, para. 5.13 (adopted Nov. 7, 1989).

[9] See Dispute Settlement Understanding, art. 3.8.

[10] See Section 337, at para. 5.14; see also TRIPS, art. 1.1.

[11] Vienna Convention, art. 31(3)(b).

[12] Uruguay Round Agreements Act ("URAA"), Pub. L. No. 103-465, § 532(a) (1994) (codified at 35 U.S.C. § 154); *see also* Statement of Administrative Action, 334 (1994) ("A further change in U.S. law incident to the change in how patent term is measured is required by virtue of the operation of Article 33, 70.2 and 70.4 of the TRIPS Agreement. Specifically, section 532(a) of the implementing bill amends section 154 to provide that the term of a patent in force on, or that results from an application filed before the date that is six months after the date of enactment of the URAA [Dec. 8, 1994] will be the greater of 17 years from the date of patent grant or 20 years from the date of filing of the application leading to the patent.") (Exhibit US-5).

term from sixteen years from the date of filing to twenty years from the date of filing, effective July 1, 1995.[13] Moreover, Australia applied the twenty-year term not just to patents filed after the effective date, but also to all patents in force on the effective date. Similarly, Germany, Greece and New Zealand also amended their laws to implement the TRIPS obligation regarding a twenty year term for all existing patents.[14]

18. Portugal provides another example of correct - if belated - compliance with Articles 33 and 70. The United States requested dispute settlement consultations with Portugal under the WTO Dispute Settlement Understanding on April 30, 1996, regarding Portugal's failure to apply the provisions of Article 33 of TRIPS to all patents that were in force on January 1, 1996, and to all patents that were granted based on applications that were pending on January 1, 1996. On August 23, 1996, Portugal issued Decree-Law 141/96 confirming that all patents that were in force on January 1, 1996, and all patents granted after that date based on applications that were pending on January 1, 1996, will receive a term of protection that lasts either fifteen years from the date of grant of the patent or twenty years from the effective filing date of the patent, whichever term is longer.[15]

V. CONCLUSION

19. The plain text of Articles 33 and 70 of the TRIPS Agreement requires Canada to grant a minimum patent term of twenty years from the date of filing to all existing patents. With respect to a large number of existing patents, Canada applies a shorter term. For these reasons, the United States respectfully requests the Panel to find that Canada is in violation of Articles 33 and 70 of the TRIPS Agreement, and to recommend that Canada bring its measures into conformity with its obligations under the TRIPS Agreement.

---

[13] Patents (World Trade Organization Amendments) Act 1994, No. 154 of 1994, §§ 3-7 (Aust.) (Exhibit US-6).

[14] Law on the Extension of Industrial Property Rights, art. 6a (1995) (amended German law to extend term from 18 to 20 years for all East German patents that had not expired on December 31, 1995) (Germ.) (Exhibit US-7); Law No. 2359, art. 1 (15 November 1995) (Greece) (Exhibit US-8); Act to Amend the Patents Act 1953, Law No. 122, art. 18 (1994) (N.Z.) (Exhibit US-9).

[15] On October 3, 1996, the United States and Portugal notified the Dispute Settlement Body that this case had been resolved. WT/DS37/2, IP/D/3/Add.1 (8 Oct. 1996) (Exhibit US-10).

ATTACHMENT 1.2

ORAL STATEMENT OF THE UNITED STATES AT THE FIRST MEETING WITH THE PANEL

(20 December 1999)

1. Mr. Chairman, members of the Panel, it is an honor to appear before you to present the position of the United States in this important case. This case is extremely significant to U.S. patent holders, and presents important TRIPS issues. We very much appreciate the willingness of the members of the Panel to participate in hearing it. As you indicated in your statement Mr. Chairman, the Panel has read the first submission of the United States in this matter so I do not intend to repeat all of the arguments set forth in that submission.

2. The TRIPS provisions at issue in this case, Articles 33 and 70.2, are not complicated. They require Canada to provide a twenty year patent term to all patent holders. Canada's first submission goes to great lengths to avoid the plain language of Articles 33 and 70.2, and divert attention from the straight-forward nature of this case. The text of the Agreement, however, cannot be ignored. Article 33, in its entirety, states that "The term of protection shall not end before the expiration of a period of twenty years counted from the filing date."

3. What Canada's first submission actually does is establish the following key facts that are not in dispute and which are determinative of a violation of TRIPS:

- First, Section 45 of the Canadian Patent Act provides for a patent term of seventeen years from the date of issuance of the Patent.
- Second, as of January 1, 2000, there will be approximately 67,000 existing Canadian patents that will expire earlier than twenty years from the filing date.[1]

4. In light of this evidence, Canada not only has not rebutted the U.S. *prima facie* case, it has confirmed the facts that establish that case.

5. In its brief, Canada appears to rely in part on an impermissible averaging methodology to argue that the term of protection provided under Section 45 is "equivalent" to a term of twenty years from filing. The two terms are not equivalent, however, because under the seventeen year term, a very large number of individual Canadian patents received a term of less than twenty years from filing.

6. Canada's arguments about equivalence are apparently also based on its having had in place a series of procedures that allegedly would have permitted patent applicants to delay the grant of their patents. As we understand Canada's argument, a patent applicant back in the late 1980's or early 90's (years before TRIPS) should have obtained a twenty year term by asking a Canadian patent examiner to delay the examination - even though the patent law and rules contained no provision entitling the applicant to such a delay - or should have manipulated the system by actually abandoning or forfeiting his application and then reinstating it.

7. An analogous argument was made by Argentina, and rejected by the Panel, in *Argentina - Measures Affecting Imports of Footwear, Textiles, Apparel and Other Items*.[2]

---

1 *See* Canada Exhibit 8, paras 19-20, and exhibits C and D to Canada Exhibit 8.

In that dispute, the Panel observed that "[a] WTO Member cannot offer as a defence to a claim of violation of a WTO agreement, that its internal system provides for a remedy to such violation to certain individuals, ... and that no violation of the WTO has therefore taken place."[3] Canada's argument here is even weaker than Argentina's, in that the right to a twenty year term under TRIPS did not even exist at the time that right holders allegedly should have manipulated the procedural rules of the Canadian patent system to obtain twenty years. Moreover, the alleged practice of patent examiners to grant informal requests to slow down their processing of a patent application appears not to have been a legal right of the patent applicant, and was not published or available in written form.

8. In addition, Canada's argument that applicants could and should have used these informal procedures to delay the date of grant of their patents would condone the very abuses which it claims justified its decision to amend its law in 1987. Canada asserts on the one hand that pre-1989 applicants should have sought delays in the application process by urging patent officers to delay the granting of their patents. Yet Canada also observes that such conduct was "manipulative" and disfavoured.

9. The United States has not argued that the term of protection required by Article 33 cannot be modified if an applicant fails to comply with reasonable procedures or formalities, such as the payment of maintenance fees. Article 62.1 authorizes Members to condition the acquisition and maintenance of intellectual property rights on compliance with reasonable procedures and formalities, but the second sentence of that paragraph specifies that the procedures and formalities must be consistent with the Agreement. Requiring that patent applicants choose between early protection for their invention and a full twenty-year term of protection cannot be considered "reasonable." Article 62 has no relevance to this case, and does not excuse Canada from fulfilling its obligations under Articles 33 and 70.2.

10. Canada's arguments with respect to Article 70.2 also fail. The text of Article 70.2 is key. A close textual analysis reveals the flaws in Canada's interpretation of this provision. Article 70.2 states that except as otherwise provided in the Agreement, TRIPS "*gives rise to obligations* in respect of *all subject matter existing at the date of application* of this Agreement." A patent is a type of subject matter. Patents that existed at the date of application of the Agreement thus fall within the scope of Article 70.2. And Article 70.2 is quite clear: the Agreement "gives rise to obligations" in respect of such patents. The substantive obligation at issue is a twenty year patent term.

11. Canada makes much of the fact that the U.S. did not discuss in its written submission the phrase "unless otherwise provided" in Article 70.2. The phrase was not discussed, however, because it has no bearing on the legal issues involved in this case, and certainly does not have the effect described by Canada of essentially reading Article 70.2 out of the TRIPS Agreement. It refers, *inter alia*, to the second half of Article 70.2, which sets forth a different rule with respect to copyright, providing that Article 18 of the Berne Convention governs the protection of existing subject matter. When this phrase was added to Article 70.2 during the TRIPS negotiations, the Chairman of the TRIPS negotiating group reported the following: "In the first line [of Article 70.2], the initial phrase would be

---

[2] Panel Report, *Argentina - Measures Affecting Imports of Footwear, Textiles, Apparel and Other Items* ("*Argentina - Textiles and Apparel*"), WT/DS56/R, adopted 22 April 1998, DSR 1998:III, 1033, paras. 6.66 - 6.69.

[3] Panel Report, *Argentina - Textiles and Apparel*, *supra*, footnote 2, footnote 198 to para. 6.68.

amended to read 'Except as otherwise provided for in this Agreement ...' This would make it clear that, for example, Article 18 of Berne applies by virtue of Article 9.1."[4]

12. The subsequent practice of WTO Members confirms the U.S. interpretation of Article 70.2. Under the Vienna Convention (Article 31(3)(b)) subsequent practice in the application of an Agreement may establish "the agreement of the parties regarding its interpretation." In our written submission, we provided examples of our own practice, as well as that of other developed countries obligated to implement TRIPS in 1996, including Australia, Germany, Greece, New Zealand, and Portugal, all of which amended their laws to ensure that the term of patents in existence and protected in their territories did not end before a period of twenty years counted from the filing date of the application.

13. Article 70.1 of TRIPS does not mandate a different result. Article 70.1 provides that the TRIPS Agreement "does not give rise to obligations in respect of acts which occurred before the date of application of the Agreement for the Member in question." The reference in Article 70.1 to "acts" refers to, *inter alia*, the acts Canada identifies in paragraph 116 of its first submission, as well as such acts as customs permitting entry of counterfeit or pirated goods prior to the date of application.

14. Let's take a concrete example: TRIPS requires that countries provide all patentees with an exclusive right of "offering for sale." Suppose a country did not provide that exclusive right back in 1993 and someone offered for sale a patented product without authorization. In 1993, it was not a violation of the patent law. Article 70.1 simply says that in implementing TRIPS, a country does not have to go back and provide a remedy against that person for his 1993 acts. The Agreement is not retroactive.

15. Canada is confusing the *prospective application* of TRIPS standards with "retroactivity." Article 70.1 does not prevent the prospective application of these standards, including the standard governing the length of patent terms, to existing subject matter as mandated by Article 70.2.

16. Furthermore, Article 70 must be read as a whole. Article 70.1 cannot be interpreted without considering its relationship with the other paragraphs of Article 70. Canada argues that patents "issued prior to January 1, 1996 ... are not subject to the obligations in the TRIPS Agreement."[5] This interpretation of Article 70.1 leaves a glaring question unanswered: If all pre-1996 patents are not subject to TRIPS, what is the meaning of Article 70.2, particularly its reference to "subject matter existing at the date of application of this Agreement . . and which is protected in that Member on the said date"? Canada gives this language no legal effect at all in violation of fundamental principles of treaty interpretation. Similarly, Canada's reading of Article 70.1 would also imply that Articles 70.3, 70.4, 70.5, and 70.6 are meaningless or wholly redundant.

17. Finally, Canada's interpretation would have far-reaching and devastating consequences for intellectual property right holders. Under this interpretation, every intellectual property right that existed before 1996 - every patent, every copyright, every trademark, every industrial design and every geographical indication - receives absolutely no protection under TRIPS. Accordingly, WTO members could today revoke for no reason all patents that were issued prior to January 1996, and remain in compliance with TRIPS. Or they could grant compulsory licenses on all pre-1996 patents without regard for any of the TRIPS conditions set out in Article 31. Such a dramatic undermining of the protection provided by the TRIPS Agreement is impossible to square with the text of Article 70, the subsequent practice of WTO members, and the negotiating history of the Agreement.

---

[4] 10 + 10 Meeting, Speaking Note for the Chairman (16 Dec. 1991).

[5] Canada First Submission, para. 113.

18. For all of these reasons, we urge this Panel to see this case for what it is, a straight-forward dispute with undisputed key facts. We respectfully request the Panel to reject Canada's attempts to obscure the real issues, and to find Canada in violation of Articles 33 and 70.2 of the TRIPS Agreement. Thank you.

ATTACHMENT 1.3

RESPONSES OF THE UNITED STATES TO WRITTEN QUESTIONS FROM THE PANEL - FIRST MEETING

(7 January 2000)

I. REPLIES OF THE UNITED STATES TO QUESTIONS FROM THE PANEL ADDRESSED TO BOTH PARTIES

Q.1 *Article 62.2 provides that Members are to ensure that the procedures for granting intellectual property rights allow granting of the right "within a reasonable period of time so as to avoid unwarranted curtailment" of the protection period.

(a) What would constitute an "unwarranted curtailment" of a patent protection term?

The meaning of "unwarranted curtailment" cannot be determined in the abstract, and reasonableness may vary by situation. Certainly delay for its own sake should not be considered reasonable.

(b) Would an average pendency period for patents of approximately five years be considered a "reasonable period of time" which avoided "unwarranted curtailment" of a protection term? Why, or why not?

An average pendency period of approximately five years may be considered unreasonable in the context of Article 62.2. Such an average pendency results in an average loss of full patent rights for approximately 1/4 of the potential term of a patent. While some loss of term due to pendency is inevitable, the loss of 1/4 of potential term may rise to the level of unreasonableness and constitute an "unwarranted curtailment of the period of protection."

Q.2 What bearing, if any, do the general principles set out in paragraph 2 of Article 41 as incorporated in Article 62.4 have on arguments put forward in this dispute concerning delays in the grant of patents?

Article 41.2 provides that procedures concerning the enforcement of intellectual property rights shall not be "unnecessarily complicated or costly, or entail unreasonable time-limits or unwarranted delays." The same standards apply to procedures concerning the acquisition of intellectual property rights. TRIPS, Article 62.4. These principles are highly relevant to Canada's defense in this case, and squarely reveal its weaknesses. One of Canada's arguments in this case appears to be that patent owners - several years before the TRIPS Agreement was completed - should have manipulated the old Act's procedures for obtaining a patent in order to delay the grant of the patent, solely for the purpose of extending the end-date of the term to which they were entitled under Canadian law. Canada thus would require patent applicants to have followed unnecessarily complicated procedures to obtain unwarranted delays in the grant of their patents, *i.e.* - avoidable delays justified for no purpose other than mere delay. Besides conflicting with Article 62.4, the imposition of such avoidable delays appears also to conflict with the very provision cited by Canada as the source of the delay, Section 30.2, which allows reinstatement of an abandoned patent application only where a delay "was not reasonably avoidable."[1]

Q.3 Why is the word "available" used in connection with the term of patent protection in Article 33 of the TRIPS Agreement but not in the provisions on the terms of protection of other intellectual property rights?

The term "available" is used in connection with the duration of protection for industrial designs in Article 26 of the TRIPS Agreement and in connection with the term of patent protection in Article 33. It is not found in the articles dealing with the term of protection for copyrighted works (Article 12) or trademarks (Article 18). Each of these provisions, however, conveys the same essential meaning and sets forth the required minimum term of protection that applies to each type of intellectual property right. Canada emphasizes the unremarkable fact that patent owners can forfeit their patent rights (and thereby shorten their term) by failing to pay maintenance fees. By the same token, trademark owners can abandon their marks and have them cancelled for non-use. Neither of these possibilities undermines the basic requirements of Article 33 (which uses the term "available") and Article 18 (which does not) to provide a certain defined minimum term of protection to right holders. Under Article 33, Canada is required to make available a term of patent protection that does not end before the expiration of a period of twenty years counted from the filing date. Under Article 70.2, that obligation is to be applied to patents that were in force on the date of application of the TRIPS Agreement for Canada. Canada does not provide a sound legal basis for such a term. Holders of a patent in force on January 1, 1996, have no legal right to a term that did not end before a date of twenty years from the date of filing. Such a term is not available under Canadian law for thousands of right holders.

Q.4 Are you aware of any WTO Member that was obliged to apply the TRIPS Agreement as of 1 January 1996 and that does not apply a patent protection term of 20 years from the date of filing to all patents, including those patents that were in force and patent applications that were pending as of 1 January 1996?

Other than Canada, the United States is not aware of any WTO Member that was obliged to apply the TRIPS Agreement as of 1 January 1996 and that does not apply a term of patent protection of twenty years from the date of filing to all patents, including those patents that were in force and patent applications that were pending as of 1 January 1996. As we noted in our first written submission, several of these countries - including the United States - had to amend their laws to apply the twenty year term to all existing patents and thereby meet their TRIPS obligation.

Q.5 Do you believe that a system in which the patent term is calculated from the date of filing creates the same incentive to file a patent application promptly as a system in which the patent term is calculated from the date of grant?

The two systems may not create exactly the same incentive to file a patent application promptly. The United States observes, however, that priority rights, in the event of other applicants for the same invention, provide the primary incentive for prompt filing in either system of term calculation.

---

1 Canadian Patent Act, R.S.C., ch. P-4, § 30.2 (1985).

Q.6 Article 28 of the Vienna Convention on the Law of Treaties 1969 reads as follows:

> **"Unless a different intention appears from the treaty or is otherwise established, its provisions do not bind a party in relation to any act or fact which took place or any situation which ceased to exist before the date of the entry into force of the treaty with respect to that party."**

(a) **Does Article 28 belong to those provisions of the Vienna Convention which are part of customary international law?**

Yes. Article 28 of the Vienna Convention is part of customary international law.

(b) **Which paragraph(s) of Article 70 refer(s) to "any act or fact which took place...before the date of the entry into force of the treaty..."?**

Article 70.1 encompasses "any act or fact which took place...before the date of the entry into force of the treaty. ..."

(c) **Which paragraph(s) of Article 70 refer(s) to "any situation which ceased to exist before the date of the entry into force of the treaty" or did not so cease to exist? Is the ongoing protection of an intellectual property right at the date of entry into force of a treaty, e.g. a patent that has been granted and which remains in force at that date, within the scope of "situation that ceased to exist"?**

To the extent that acts which occurred before TRIPS gave rise to situations which ceased to exist before TRIPS, Article 70.1 could be said to encompass such situations indirectly. The ongoing protection of an intellectual property right at the date of entry into force of a treaty, *e.g.* a patent that has been granted and which remains in force at the date, is *not* within the scope of a "situation that ceased to exist."

(d) **Assuming that the reply to question (a) is in the affirmative, does Article 70 represent a "contracting out" of this customary rule of international law or rather does it restate this rule?**

Article 70, particularly Article 70.1, merely restates this basic rule of international law. This interpretation is supported by the negotiating history of Article 70.1, the provisions of which were considered by some Members "too obvious to be necessary to mention."[2]

Q.7 Please provide an analysis of the meaning that should be attached to the various provisions of Article 70, in particular, explaining the meaning of paragraphs 2, 4 and 6 of Article 70. What is the relationship among the paragraphs of Article 70?

Article 70.2

Article 70.2 states that except as otherwise provided in the Agreement, TRIPS "*gives rise to obligations* in respect of *all subject matter existing at the date of application* of this Agreement for the Member in question, *and which is protected in that Member on the said date*, or which meets or comes subsequently to meet the criteria for pro-

[2] "10 + 10 Meeting, 16 Dec. 1991: Speaking Note for the Chairman," 4. Attached as U.S. Exhibit 11.

tection under the terms of this Agreement." In the context of this case, this provision means that Canada is obligated to apply the provisions of the TRIPS Agreement to all subject matter that existed and was still protected on January 1, 1996.

"Subject matter" in its ordinary meaning can be defined as "the ground, basis or source of something," or "the subject or theme of a book, speech, etc., a topic."[3] In the context of the TRIPS Agreement, "subject matter" is used to refer to such things as broadcasts that can be copyrighted (Article 14.3); signs that can be trademarked (Article 15.1); and inventions that can be patented (Articles 28.1, 31, and 34.1). In short, "subject matter" as used in the TRIPS Agreement generally refers to the matter that is or can be entitled to intellectual property protection. Indeed, this is exactly how Article 70.2 utilizes the term "subject matter": It states that any subject matter that is either being protected or will meet the criteria for protection at the time of the applicability of the TRIPS Agreement is subject to the Agreement.

There is no substantive difference between the U.S. and Canadian views of the term subject matter. According to Canada, subject matter under Article 70.2 means "matter that is protectable by intellectual property rights."[4] Thus, both Parties seem to agree that patented inventions are subject matter. Under the terms of Article 70.2, TRIPS "gives rise to obligations in respect of all" inventions ("subject matter") existing on January 1, 1996, "and which [are] protected in that Member on the said date." Accordingly, Canada is obligated to apply the provisions of Article 33 of TRIPS to all patented inventions (*ie.*, protected subject matter) that existed on January 1, 1996.

The second sentence of Article 70.2 sets out a different rule that governs copyright obligations with respect to existing works. It provides, *inter alia*, that such obligations "shall be solely determined under Article 18 of the Berne Convention." Article 18.1 of Berne provides that "This Convention shall apply to all works which, at the moment of its coming into force, have not yet fallen into the public domain in the country of origin through the expiry of the term of protection." According to the negotiating history of Article 70 prepared by Daniel Gervais, on which Canada relies so heavily, this provision may be called a "'relative retroactivity provision,' in that it applies to existing subject matter (*thus affecting existing arrangements*), but with some safeguards."[5]

Article 70.4

Article 70.4 allows WTO members to limit liability for infringing acts to the payment of equitable remuneration when two conditions are satisfied: (1) the acts were commenced (or a significant investment was made) before TRIPS was accepted by the WTO Member in question, and (2) the acts became infringing under TRIPS. In this way, the Agreement allows WTO Members to balance the interests of intellectual property right holders and the interests of parties that may have engaged in acts which, prior to TRIPS were perfectly legal, yet became infringing under TRIPS.

Article 70.4 thus clearly contemplates that an act in respect of an invention could "become infringing" under TRIPS. If - as Canada argues - it has no obligations whatso-

---

[3] The New Shorter Oxford English Dictionary, 3119 (1993).

[4] First Oral Presentation of Canada, para. 67.

[5] Daniel Gervais, The TRIPS Agreement: Drafting History and Analysis, 268 (1998) (parenthetical in original; emphasis added).

ever with respect to intellectual property that existed before 1996,[6] then Article 70.4 is a nullity. This cannot be correct, and flies in the face of normal principles of treaty interpretation.

Article 70.6

This paragraph of Article 70 provides that Members are not obligated to apply the compulsory licensing disciplines of Article 31 of the Agreement, or to comply with the prohibition on discrimination by field of technology, with respect to compulsory licenses granted by the government before the date on which the TRIPS Agreement became known. This provision was important to some members that had relied on compulsory licensing in the past. Without it, under Article 70.2, the TRIPS disciples in Article 31 would have applied to existing subject matter (including patentable inventions) as of 1996, and WTO Members would have had to ensure that all of their compulsory licenses were modified if necessary to comply with the requirements of Article 31. Under Canada's argument, that it has no obligations whatsoever with respect to patents that existed prior to 1996, Article 70.6 is wholly redundant.

Relationship between all of the paragraphs in Article 70

Article 70.1 provides that TRIPS "does not give rise to obligations in respect of acts which occurred before the date of application of the Agreement for the Member in question." Notably, the term used in Article 70.1 is "acts", not "subject matter." Reading Articles 70.1 and 70.2 together, it is evident that the Agreement does not give rise to obligations regarding acts that occurred before January 1, 1996, but it does give rise to obligations concerning subject matter that might have existed before January 1, 1996 (if that subject matter existed on January 1, 1996 and was protected on that date). Article 70.1 thus does not prevent the prospective application of TRIPS standards, including the standard governing the length of patent terms, to existing subject matter as mandated by Article 70.2.

Article 70.1 cannot be interpreted without considering its relationship with the other paragraphs of Article 70. Under Canada's reading advanced in its First Written Submission and First Oral Statement, Articles 70.2 and 70.4 are meaningless, and Article 70.6 is completely redundant. By contrast, under the U.S. interpretation described above and in our previous submissions, every provision of Article 70 is given effect, and the entire article is internally consistent and logical.

[6] First Written Submission of Canada, para. 113 (patents "issued prior to January 1, 1996 . . . are not subject to the obligations in the TRIPS Agreement.").

II. REPLIES TO QUESTIONS FROM THE PANEL TO THE UNITED STATES

Q.8 *The last sentence of Article 1.1 states that Members shall be free to determine the "appropriate method" of implementing the provisions of the TRIPS Agreement within their own legal system and practice. How do you construe the term "appropriate method" as used in Article 1.1 of the TRIPS Agreement?

The term "appropriate method" does not encompass a method that results in less protection than required under the Agreement. As the first part of Article 1.1 declares, "Members shall give effect to the provisions of this Agreement." The purpose of the last sentence of Article 1.1 is to make clear that Members have flexibility to implement their obligations within the context of their own domestic legal system. For example, implementing a particular TRIPS provision might require legislative changes in some WTO Members, while other Members might only have to amend their administrative regime. So long as the relevant obligation is indeed fully implemented and has a sound legal basis in a Member's legal regime, the precise method of implementation is left to the discretion of that Member.

If Canada's method of implementing a twenty-year patent term differed from that of the United States, but nevertheless provided to each and every patent applicant a sound legal basis for a minimum twenty-year term, there would be no issue under the TRIPS Agreement. Canada, however, has not provided a twenty year term by a different method; instead, for many patent holders, it has failed to provide a twenty year term at all.

Q.9 *Canada stated in paragraph 80 of its first written submission that the substantive equivalence of the two terms of protection under the old Act and the new Act appears to have been accepted by the parties to NAFTA, i.e. that NAFTA appears to recognize the substantive equivalence of the two methods of calculating the term. Please comment.

Canada is incorrect in its assessment that the separation of two different patent terms in the NAFTA text with the word "or" necessarily implies that these two terms are equivalent. The text of NAFTA Article 1709(12) does not explicitly describe the two terms as being substantively equivalent. NAFTA allows the parties to that Agreement to choose which patent term they would provide, and thereby requires a lesser degree of harmonization among the parties regarding the length of patent terms than does the TRIPS Agreement.

Second, it is significant that TRIPS does not contain the same language as the NAFTA. Indeed, given the disparate practice among the negotiating countries in the calculation of patent term prior to conclusion of the TRIPS Agreement, the fact that the negotiators agreed on a single standard in Article 33, and did not include a choice among alternative terms, is significant. As described by Daniel Gervais,

> "The question of the term of protection was a difficult subject during the negotiation, but right holders should welcome the harmonization made possible by the TRIPS Agreement. Previously, the term of protection was sometimes calculated from grant, and in other cases from filing. For reasons that included the different starting date of the calculation, the term

varied from one country to another. *The single standard chosen here is 20 years from filing*."[7]

Q.10 If a Member put in place a system in which patent applicants were in complete control of the timing of the prosecution of their applications, and they were able to ensure that the term of protection did not expire less than 20 years from the date of filing, would that be sufficient for a Member to satisfy its ongoing obligation under Article 33 even if it had a much shorter term from grant?

No. To take an extreme example, the hypothetical situation described in the question could arise in a Member with a patent term of one day from grant. In such a situation, the patent applicant would receive the exclusive rights related to a patent for only one day. The purpose of the requirements in Article 62.4 and 41.2 was to prevent such a situation. These obligations of the Agreement must be read together, not in isolation. The term of protection required to be provided in Article 33 presupposes reasonable procedures for the acquisition of patent rights, such that the requirement of a twenty year term of protection is not rendered a practical nullity.

Q.11 *How do you define the term "acts" in Article 70.1? Does the term "acts" in Article 70.1 include the administrative act of granting a patent by a patent office?

See U.S. Response to Question 7, above, regarding Article 70.1. The New Shorter Oxford English Dictionary defines the term "acts" as "a thing done; a deed."[8] This general meaning is consistent with the use of the term "acts" in other provisions of the TRIPS Agreement (*see* Articles 14, 22, 26, 28, 36, 37, 50, and 58). By its plain meaning, "acts" would include the administrative act of granting a patent by a patent office. The United States does not argue that Canada is in violation of its TRIPS obligations as a result of the failure of the Canadian Patent Office to grant to all patent holders prior to 1996 patents with a term of at least twenty years from filing. The "acts" of Canada's Patent Office prior to 1996 are not at issue. Rather, Canada's violation of the Agreement stems from its failure, since the date of application of the TRIPS Agreement, to extend the term of protection for existing patented inventions to at least twenty years from filing. This violation is unrelated to any pre-96 "act," but is related only to the subject matter (protected inventions) that existed on 1-1-96. The rule in Article 70.1, that pre-1996 acts are not subject to the obligations in the Agreement *does not imply* that subject matter existing on January 1, 1996, is also not subject to the obligations of the Agreement.

Q.12 *(follow up question) In Article 58 the word "act" is used in connection with competent authorities. Is this broader than the definition you provided?

No. *See* U.S. Response to Question 11. As stated by the U.S. representative during the first meeting of the Panel, the United States' answers at that meeting to the Panel's questions were preliminary. While the United States regrets the need to modify these answers, it retained its full rights to do so.

Q.13 *How do you define the term "subject matter" in Article 70.2?

See U.S. Response to Question 7.

---

7 Gervais, 169 (emphasis added).

8 New Shorter Oxford English Dictionary, 21.

Q.14 The Appellate Body stated in *Japan - Taxes on Alcoholic Beverages* that "the essence of subsequent practice in interpreting a treaty has been recognized as a 'concordant, common and consistent' sequence of acts...which is sufficient to establish a discernable pattern implying the agreement of the parties regarding its interpretation". Is the fact that six WTO Members, including the United States, amended their laws to provide a patent term of 20 years from the date of filing sufficient to support a claim that there was a "concordant, common and consistent sequence of acts"? In your response, please consider the matters raised in paragraphs 72 and 73 of Canada's first oral statement.

See U.S. Response to Question 4. Concordant, common and consistent acts have indeed established a discernable pattern among WTO Members obligated to apply the TRIPS Agreement as of 1 January 1996 with regard to the interpretation of Articles 33 and 70.2. As discussed in the U.S. Response to Question 4, the United States is aware of no such WTO Member (except Canada) that fails to provide a patent term of twenty years from filing for all patents in existence on January 1, 1996. At least six of these WTO Members had to amend their law to provide such a term. Other WTO Members did not amend their law for the simple reason that they were already in compliance.

In its oral statement (paragraphs 72 and 73), Canada attempts to discount such subsequent practice by arguing that the circumstances of some of the countries that amended their laws were not the same as Canada's. This point has no relevance. Regardless of what term those countries changed *from*, the key is that they all changed *to* a system that provided a minimum term of twenty years from the date of filing *for all patents existing or pending on January 1, 1996*. By contrast, under Canadian law, such a term does not apply to all patents existing or pending on January 1, 1996.

Furthermore, Canada discounts the example of Portugal, which in order to implement the TRIPS Agreement, issued Decree-Law 141/96 on August 23, 1996, to ensure that all patents will receive a term of protection that lasts either fifteen years from the date of grant or twenty years from the date of filing, whichever is longer. Canada argues that Portugal's actions are not necessarily evidence of a common understanding of the meaning of the TRIPS provisions.[9] In making this argument, Canada has apparently chosen to ignore Portugal's own words in the communication sent to the Dispute Settlement Body:

> Portugal and the United States further mutually confirm that, with respect to developed-country members, Article 70.2 of the TRIPS Agreement requires, among other things, that the provisions of Article 33 of the TRIPS Agreement be applied to all patents that were in force on 1 January 1996, and to all patents that are granted based on applications that were pending on 1 January 1996.[10]

[9] Oral Statement of Canada, para. 77.

[10] *Portugal - Patent Protection under the Industrial Property Act: Notification of a Mutually Agreed Solution*, WT/DS37/2 (8 Oct. 1996). Attached as Exhibit 10 to U.S. First Submission.

ATTACHMENT 1.4

RESPONSES OF THE UNITED STATES TO WRITTEN QUESTIONS FROM CANADA - FIRST MEETING

(7 January 2000)

Q.1 Would the United States please explain why it believes that the rule against retroactivity contained in TRIPS, Article 70.1 would not be available to Canada in respect of patents issued before the effective date of the Agreement?

See U.S. Response to Panel Questions 7, 11 and 12.

Q.2 Would the United States please explain why it believes that the rule in TRIPS, Art. 70.2, which requires retroactivity, would cover previously issued patents, since its wording only refers to "subject matter"?

See U.S. Response to Panel Question 7.

Q.3 Would the United States please describe what, if any, mandated statutory delays comparable to those in Canada's old Act were available to patent applicants under United States patent legislation as it read prior to the Uruguay Round Agreements Act?

The U.S. patent law, as it read prior to the Uruguay Round Agreements Act, did not contain any "mandated statutory delays," nor were any added by the Uruguay Round Agreements Act. The U.S. patent law, however, did and does contain provisions similar to Section 30.2 of Canada's old Act. *See* 35 U.S.C. §§ 111(4), 133 & 151. Each of these sections authorizes the Commissioner to reinstate abandoned applications if, in the case of Section 111(4), the failure to submit the required fee and oath within the prescribed period can be shown to the Commissioner's satisfaction to have been unintentional or unavoidable, and, in the case of Sections 133 and 151, the failure to prosecute the application within six months of any office action or to pay the required issue fee, respectively, can be shown to the satisfaction of the Commissioner to have been unavoidable. The provisions, therefore, did not and do not provide an applicant with any "mandated statutory delay."

Furthermore, the United States does not consider the term "mandated statutory delay" to be an accurate description of Section 30.2 or 73.2 of Canada's old Act. There appears to be nothing "mandatory" about the delay possible in the situations described in those provisions. Such delay was hardly mandated in every instance; on the contrary, delays are clearly disfavoured. Under Section 30.2, an application can be reinstated only if a delay was "not reasonably avoidable."[1]

Q.4 Where a patent holder has finally forfeited its patent as a result of its failure to pay maintenance fees during the 20-year period counted from its application filing date, is the WTO Member, upon whose territory the application was made, in compliance with its TRIPS obligations? Assuming that a patent holder has the right, consistent with the Agreement, to reduce the 20-year period by failing to pay maintenance fees after the patent has issued, why would it not also have a right, consistent

[1] Canadian Patent Act, R.S.C., ch. P-4, § 30.2 (1985).

with the Agreement to reduce the period by taking steps to expedite the examination and allowance process, before the patent had issued?

The WTO Member in the first hypothetical situation may be in compliance with its TRIPS obligations, depending, *inter alia*, on the amount of the maintenance fees and the procedures for paying them. The second question, however, misses the relevant issue in this case. The issue is not the patent holder's right to forfeit a portion of its patent term (which is undisputed), but rather the patent holder's right to a term of protection for the patent that does not end before a period of twenty years measured from the filing date. Under Canada's law, holders of valid patents on subject matter existing on January 1, 1996, are not provided with a legal right to such a term. Patent holders can hardly be said to forfeit something to which they never had a right in the first place.

ATTACHMENT 1.5

REBUTTAL SUBMISSION OF THE UNITED STATES
(14 January 2000)

TABLE OF CONTENTS

I. INTRODUCTION

1. Under Section 45 of the Canadian Patent Act, the term of protection for patent applications filed before October 1, 1989 ("Old Act patents"), is seventeen years from the date the patent is granted. The TRIPS Agreement requires that Canada grant a term of protection that does not end before a period of twenty years from filing to all patented inventions in existence on January 1, 1996. Because a term of seventeen years from filing will often end before a term of twenty years from grant, this facial inconsistency between

Section 45 and Articles 33 and 70.2 of the TRIPS Agreement warrants a finding by this Panel that Canada is in violation of its obligations under TRIPS.

2. Contrary to Canada's assertion, a patent term of seventeen years from grant is not "equivalent" to a term of protection that expires twenty years from the date of filing. Moreover, under the Canadian patent law, a term of twenty years from filing currently is not available to all owners of patents that were in existence on January 1, 1996, nor was it available on a sound legal basis to all such patent owners at the time their applications were filed in Canada. Finally, pursuant to TRIPS Article 70, the requirements of the TRIPS Agreement, including the requirement to have a term of protection that does not end before a period of twenty years from filing, are applicable to all of Canada's so-called Old Act patented inventions in existence today, regardless of whether Canada's Patent Office had previously engaged in acts inconsistent with current TRIPS obligations.

II. A TERM OF SEVENTEEN YEARS FROM GRANT IS NOT "EQUIVALENT" TO A TERM THAT EXPIRES TWENTY YEARS FROM THE DATE OF FILING

3. By Canada's own admission, approximately 67,000 Canadian patents exist today with a term that will end *before* a period of twenty years from filing.[1] On January 1, 1996, the number was even higher: approximately 94,000 patents were in existence with terms that ended before twenty years from filing.[2] These key facts alone refute Canada's first argument regarding the alleged "equivalency" of a term of seventeen years from grant and a term of twenty years from filing. For at least 94,000 patent owners, the patent term provided under Canadian law on January 1, 1996, would end before the period stipulated in TRIPS.

4. In an apparent attempt to diminish the legal significance of its admission regarding the tens of thousands of patents in existence with terms that will end before a period of twenty years from filing, Canada reads into Article 33 the concept of an "effective" period of protection, and reads out of Article 33 the literal text of the provision. In lieu of the plain language of Article 33, Canada bases its equivalency argument exclusively on what it variably calls the "effective" period of protection or the period of "exclusive privilege and property rights."[3] According to Canada, it has satisfied Article 33 because its "effective" period of protection under a term of seventeen years from grant is at least as long as the *average* "effective" period of protection under its regime of twenty years from filing (because of an average five-year pendency period for patents). Two fatal flaws exist in this equivalency argument.

A. Regardless of the Period of "Effective Protection" Provided by Canada, under Article 33, the Term of Protection shall not End before the Expiration of Twenty Years from the Filing Date

5. The text of TRIPS Article 33 does not refer to the "effective" period of protection, or the period of "exclusive privilege and property rights," but rather to the date that the

---

[1] First Submission of Canada, para. 45 (citing 66,936 such patents).

[2] *Ibid.*, para. 43 (citing 93,937 such patents).

[3] *See, e.g.*, First Submission of Canada, paras. 68 and 74; First Oral Presentation of Canada, para. 13.

term of protection is to end.[4] In violation of the Appellate Body's repeated direction to give primary significance to the words of the Agreement,[5] Canada would read the plain language of TRIPS Article 33 right out of the Agreement, and substitute the concept of "effective protection" for the existing text.

6. Canada would have this Panel find - in direct contradiction with the plain language of TRIPS Article 33 - that a system under which a term of protection may (and often does) end before a period of twenty years from filing nevertheless does not violate Article 33. There is no basis in the TRIPS Agreement for such a finding. The plain language of Article 33 must govern the resolution of this dispute.

7. In interpreting the WTO agreements, the Appellate Body and previous panels have consistently looked to the *Vienna Convention on the Law of Treaties* for guidance and clarification.[6] Article 31(1) of this Convention states:

> A treaty shall be interpreted in good faith in accordance with the ordinary meaning to be given to the terms of the treaty in their context and in the light of its object and purpose.

Thus, the text of an agreement is often the best expression of the intentions of the parties.[7] In the words of the Appellate Body, "The proper interpretation of [a provision] is, first of all, a textual interpretation."[8]

8. Canada has sought to avoid and modify the clear language of Article 33 by relying on Article 62.[9] Article 62.2 contains a separate obligation - that of ensuring that the period of protection is not unjustifiably curtailed by unreasonable procedures. Article 62.2 addresses the issue of the commencement of the term of protection, and does not address the expiration date of the period of protection. Article 33 of course must be considered in context, and that context includes Article 62.2 of TRIPS; however, Article 62.2 does not warrant attributing a meaning to Article 33 that conflicts with its explicit terms. Canada is incorrect in its assertion that, because of the average five-year pendency period of New Act patents with a term of twenty years from filing, fifteen years of "effective protection" is all that is required under Article 33. Article 33 means what it says. Under Article 33, regardless of the period of "effective protection", the term of a patent *shall not end* before a period of twenty years from its filing date.

---

[4] TRIPS Article 33 provides that "The term of protection available shall not end before the expiration of a period of twenty years counted from the filing date."

[5] *See, e.g.*, Appellate Body Report on *Japan - Taxes on Alcoholic Beverages* ("*Japan - Alcoholic Beverages*"), WT/DS8/AB/R, WT/DS10/AB/R, WT/DS11/AB/R, adopted 1 November 1996, DSR 1996:I, 97 at 104-105. *See also, e.g.*, Appellate Body report on *United States - Standards for Reformulated and Conventional Gasoline* ("*United States - Reformulated Gas*"), WT/DS2/AB/R, adopted 20 May 1996, DSR 1996;I, 3 at 15-16; Panel Report on on *United States - Standards for Reformulated and Conventional Gasoline* (" *United States - Reformulated Gas*"), WT/DS2/R, adopted May 20, 1996, DSR 1996:I, 29, para. 6.7.

[6] *See* Sources cited *supra*, note 5.

[7] Ian Brownlie, *Principles of Public International Law* (4th ed.), at 627. *See also* Appellate Body Report on *Japan - Alcoholic Beverages*, *supra*, footnote 5, at 104.

[8] Appellate Body report on *Japan - Alcoholic Beverages*, *supra*, footnote 5, at 111.

[9] First Oral Presentation of Canada, paras. 18-19.

B. *Canada's Equivalence Argument Rests on an Impermissible Averaging Methodology between Effective Periods of Protection*

9. The second fundamental flaw in Canada's equivalency argument is that it relies on the "*normal or average*" period of "effective" protection or "exclusive privilege and property rights" that Canada currently provides to New Act patentees. Throughout its First Written and Oral Statements, Canada repeatedly and explicitly justifies the period of protection under its seventeen-years-from-grant patents by comparing it to the "normal or average" period of "effective" protection under its twenty-years-from-filing patents.[10]

10. Canada uses the averaging methodology in two ways. First, it claims that since five years is the "normal or average" pendency period for New Act patent applications, the effective term of protection under a regime of twenty years from filing would "normally" be an "average" of fifteen years, which is less than the seventeen year period provided under the Old Act.[11] Canada also uses the averaging methodology to make the opposite comparison - *ie.*, to assert that the "average" two to four year pendency period for its Old Act patents makes these patents "equivalent to and in fact ... longer than the normal or average" period of "effective" protection required by the TRIPS Agreement.[12] Canada's reliance, however, on average pendency periods of Old Act and New Act patents inevitably means that its analysis fails to take into account those patents with pendency periods outside the average. *Every* Old Act patent that pended for less than three years before being issued by Canada has a term that ends before a period of twenty years from the date of filing. Canada admits this fact,[13] yet insists on using this averaging methodology to justify its claim of equivalency.

11. The United States has already noted that such averaging methodology is inappropriate. Indeed, as explained by the panel in *United States - Section 337 of the Tariff Act of 1930*:

> The Panel rejected any notion of balancing more favourable treatment of some imported products against less favourable treatment of other imported products. If this notion were accepted, it would entitle a contracting party to derogate from the no less favourable treatment obligation in one case, or indeed in respect of one contracting party, on the ground that it accords more favourable treatment in some other case, or to another contracting party. Such an interpretation would lead to great uncertainty about the conditions of competition between imported and domestic products and thus defeat the purposes of Article III.[14]

12. After the Panel in this case pointed out the inconsistency of an averaging methodology with the Panel Report in the *Section 337* case,[15] Canada appears to have shifted its

---

[10] First Submission of Canada, para. 81 ("normal or average"). *See also* First Submission of Canada, paras. 76 ("normal or average")-77; First Oral Presentation of Canada, para. 21 ("normal or average"); *and* Canada's Response to Panel Question 22, at 38-39.

[11] First Submission of Canada, paras. 76 ("normal or average") -77(noting that "any particular case" may diverge from the average), 81 ("normal or average"). *See also* First Oral Presentation of Canada, para. 21 ("normal or average"); Canada's Response to Panel Question 22, at 39.

[12] First Submission of Canada, paras. 72-73, 81. *See also* Canada's Response to Panel Question 16, at 32.

[13] First Submission of Canada, para. 64.

[14] *GATT panel report on United States - Section 337 of the Tariff Act of 1930*, BISD 36S/386 (adopted November 7, 1989), para. 5.13 ("*United States - Section 337*").

[15] Panel Question 21.

argument slightly. In its answer to the Panel's question, Canada departs from its previous references to "normal or average" pendency times, and cites only the fact that the majority of New Act patents (89%) confer a lesser period of "exclusive privilege and property rights" than patents with a term of seventeen years from grant.[16] While Canada's excessively long examination period for New Act patents is not at issue in this dispute, it can hardly provide justification for Canada's failure to provide a TRIPS-consistent term to all Old Act patentees. More importantly, this argument is still inconsistent with the principles set forth in the *Section 337* case. Under the principles of the *Section 337* report, even the "mere potential" of a measure to deny rights under the Agreement would result in a violation.[17] Far beyond having the mere potential to deny rights to patent holders under Article 33 of TRIPS, Canada's system actually has denied such rights, on January 1, 1996, to approximately 94,000 patent holders, and today denies them to almost 64,000 patent holders. These patentees cannot be dismissed as "exceptional" as Canada attempts to do in its response to the Panel's Question on this point.

III. THE RIGHT TO A TERM OF PROTECTION THAT DID NOT END PRIOR TO THE EXPIRATION OF THE TWENTY-YEAR PERIOD FROM THE FILING DATE WAS NOT "AVAILABLE" TO ALL OLD ACT PATENT APPLICANTS

13. Somewhat inconsistently with its argument that a twenty-year term of protection is actually provided to Old Act patentees, Canada also argues that such a term was at least available to them because of the possibility of manipulating the pendency periods of applications that resulted in such patents. Canada does not dispute the fact that a term of protection of twenty years from filing is not available now to all Old Act patentees. Furthermore, such a term was not available on a sound legal basis to all such patent applicants in the past. Finally, Old Act patentees cannot be said to have voluntarily chosen to forfeit their rights to a TRIPS-level term of protection during a time when TRIPS rights did not exist, and when obtaining such a term would have required many applicants to forego a portion of the early years of protection to which they were entitled under the Old Act.

A. *For Old Act Applicants, a Patent Term that did not End before Twenty Years from Filing has never been Available on a Sound Legal Basis in Canada*

14. Canadian law provides no sound legal basis for patent applicants that filed applications before October 1, 1989, to obtain a term of protection that did not end before a period of twenty years from the filing date. Neither of the provisions of law cited by Canada - Sections 30(1) and 73 of the Old Act - provided such a basis.

15. According to Canada, an Old Act applicant could obtain a term of twenty years from filing by actually abandoning its patent application not once, but twice. Then, after twice abandoning its application for a maximum period of time, and having it reinstated, the applicant could forfeit that application, wait a maximum period of time, and then reinstate it a third time. By means of such a tortured and highly non-transparent process, Can-

[16] Canada's Response to Panel Question 21, at 37.

[17] *United States - Section 337,* para. 5.14.

ada argues that it has satisfied its TRIPS obligation to provide a patent term that does not end before twenty years from filing.[18]

16. Section 30(2) of the Old Act does not provide a sound legal basis for the procedure outlined by Canada - repeatedly abandoning and reinstating a patent application for purposes of delay. Section 30(2) of the Old Act declares in no uncertain terms that the reinstatement of an abandoned patent application would only be permitted if a delay "was not reasonably avoidable."[19] Far from providing a legally guaranteed right to delay a patent application, Canadian law explicitly prohibits use of the abandonment and reinstatement procedure described by Canada where a delay was reasonably avoidable.

17. In response, Canada essentially argues that its patent examiners routinely ignore the mandatory provisions of Section 30(2), asserting that its Patent Commissioner is unaware of reinstatement ever having been refused.[20] Regardless of the practices of Canada's patent examiners, however, Section 30(2) unambiguously requires that reinstatement be denied where delays were reasonably avoidable.

18. Canada's arguments here are similar to those rejected by the Panel and Appellate Body in *India - Patent Protection for Pharmaceutical and Agricultural Chemical Products*.[21] In that dispute, India argued that certain "administrative instructions" provided a "sound legal basis to preserve novelty of inventions and priority of applications as of the relevant filing and priority dates," despite provisions of the Indian Patents Act that required the Patents Controller to reject such applications.[22] During appeal, the Appellate Body looked specifically at the provisions of India's Patents Act, and decided:

> We agree with the Panel that these provisions of the Patents Act are mandatory. And, like the Panel, we are not persuaded that India's "administrative instructions" would prevail over the contradictory mandatory provisions of the Patents Act. ...
>
> We are not persuaded by India's explanation of these seeming contradictions. Accordingly, we are not persuaded that India's "administrative instructions" would survive a legal challenge under the Patents Act. And, consequently, we are not persuaded that India's "administrative instructions" provide a sound legal basis to preserve novelty of inventions and priority of applications as of the relevant filing and priority dates.[23]

Likewise in this dispute, Section 30(2) of the Old Act is mandatory in that abandoned applications can be reinstated only where the delay was "not reasonably avoidable." Thus, the procedure pursuant to which Canada argues that twenty-year patent terms were available is prohibited by the very statute on which Canada bases its argument.

---

[18] First Oral Presentation of Canada, paras. 43-44.

[19] Canadian Patent Act, R.S.C., ch. P-4, § 30(2) (1985). Canada Exhibit 16.

[20] First Oral Presentation of Canada, para. 47. Canada then hedges by concluding that if a reinstatement was disallowed, an applicant could simply have reapplied. Canada thus states the obvious, that a patent applicant could repeatedly file and abandon a patent application forever, thereby ensuring that a patent is never granted. The availability of such a procedure, however, is of no relevance to the term of protection.

[21] Appellate Body Report, *India - Patent Protection for Pharmaceutical and Agricultural Chemical Products*, WT/DS50/AB/R, adopted January 16, 1998, DSR 1998:I, 9.

[22] *Ibid.*, paras. 67-71.

[23] *Ibid.*, paras. 69-70.

B. *Old Act Patent Applicants with Terms of less than Twenty Years from Filing did not Choose to Forfeit their Rights under TRIPS*

19. The obligations of the TRIPS Agreement became applicable to Canada on January 1, 1996, and the right under the Agreement to a period of protection that did not end before the expiration of twenty years from filing applied as of that date. Canada argues that on January 1, 1996, it did not have to extend that right to all owners of patents with terms of less than twenty years from filing, because such patentees had already forfeited their right to a TRIPS-level term of protection. A right, however, cannot be knowingly forfeited before it comes into existence.

20. Canada attempts to characterize all patent holders with TRIPS-deficient terms of protection as having made a strategic choice in favor of such deficient terms. This characterization is inaccurate. Canada provides no persuasive reasoning as to why applicants would go through the convoluted process it described (even if its availability were apparent) and suffer the additional costs involved in twice abandoning and reinstating an application, and then forfeiting and restoring the same application. Rather, Canada acknowledges the difficulty of providing a "coherent or straightforward theory" on this point.[24]

21. Furthermore, under Canada's Old Act, patent applicants whose applications would ordinarily be issued in less than three years would have had access to a TRIPS-level term of protection only if they were willing to forfeit a portion of the early years of patent protection to which they were entitled under the Old Act. In other words, under the Old Act, Canada attached conditions to the supposedly available term of twenty-years-from-filing that for many patent owners would have resulted in a lesser "effective" period of protection. For instance, a patent applicant with a two-year pendency period would be entitled under TRIPS to an "effective" period of protection of eighteen years. Whereas under Canada's Old Act, to obtain the TRIPS-level of protection, the applicant would have had to prolong the pendency period of its patent for an additional year, and thereby forfeit one year of effective protection. Many applicants would not have made this choice, and should not have had to forego any portion of the patent term merely to obtain a term that does not end before twenty years from filing.

22. Articles 41.2 and 62.4 of the Agreement provide important guidance on this issue. The highly complicated procedure described by Canada would have imposed significant unnecessary costs on many patent owners, in violation of the basic TRIPS requirement that procedures for the acquisition of patent rights not be unnecessarily complicated or costly, or entail unwarranted delays. Reading Article 33 in context with Articles 41.2 and 62.4 of the Agreement, it is apparent that Canada's alleged system of making available a term of protection of twenty years from filing is wholly inadequate to comply with its obligations.

IV. UNDER TRIPS ARTICLE 70.2, PATENTED INVENTIONS THAT EXISTED ON JANUARY 1, 1996, ARE ENTITLED TO A TERM OF PROTECTION OF AT LEAST TWENTY YEARS FROM FILING

23. The text, context, object and purpose of Article 70.1, as well as its negotiating history, and the subsequent practice of WTO Members demonstrate that pre-1996 "acts" do not absolve Members from the obligation to provide TRIPS-level intellectual property protection - including a patent term of twenty years from filing - to all subject matter ex-

[24] Canada's Response to Panel Question 24(c), at 44.

isting on January 1, 1996. The United States has previously set forth in detail its position regarding the proper interpretation of TRIPS Article 70 in paragraphs 10-17 of its First Oral Statement and its Response to Panel Questions 7 and 11-14. Rather than repeating those arguments, the United States will primarily address in this submission the new arguments raised by Canada, particularly in its response to Panel Questions 6 and 7.

A. The Exemption for Pre-1996 Acts in Article 70.1 has no Relevance to the Requirement to Apply TRIPS Obligations to Existing Subject Matter under Article 70.2.

24. It is important to note that, despite the focus during these proceedings on the definition of the terms "acts" and "subject matter" in Articles 70.1 and 70.2, the United States sees little difference between the Parties regarding these definitions. Rather, the essence of this dispute stems from the differing conclusions that the Parties draw from these definitions.

25. According to both Parties, the term "acts" can include both administrative and legislative acts of governments as well as acts of right holders and third parties. Such pre-1996 acts could include the "act" of granting a patent, revoking a patent, infringing a patent or granting a compulsory license on a patent. These acts themselves are not subject to the obligations in the TRIPS Agreement.

26. The positions of Canada and the United States differ primarily with respect to the implications of this definition of "acts." The mere fact that Canada engaged in pre-1996 acts that denied TRIPS-level protection to certain subject matter, does not mean that Canada is forever exempted from applying TRIPS obligations to such subject matter. In the context of patented inventions, the fact that Canada denied a term of twenty years from filing before TRIPS does not mean that Canada is forever exempted from the obligation to grant a TRIPS-level patent term to such inventions that existed on January 1, 1996.

27. Of course, pre-1996 legislative and administrative acts (and infringing acts by third parties) could have negatively affected the rights of patent holders, and could have been inconsistent with TRIPS-standards. Such acts themselves are not actionable under TRIPS. The subject matter to which the acts applied, however, can be eligible for TRIPS-level protection after January 1, 1996. Article 70.1 does not prevent the prospective application of TRIPS standards, including the standard governing the term of protection, to existing subject matter as mandated by Article 70.2.

28. Articles 70.1 and 70.2 are separate provisions that address distinct situations. Canada argues that the United States has interpreted TRIPS Articles 70.1 in a way that renders it "meaningless," and fails to "resolve" the "apparent conflict" between Articles 70.1 and 70.2.[25] In the view of the United States, however, there is *no* conflict - apparent or otherwise - between Article 70.1 and Article 70.2. The "conflict" between these two provisions is apparent only to Canada, and results from Canada's strained reading of those provisions. Furthermore, Article 70.1 is not at all meaningless, but merely has no relevance in the specific factual circumstances of this case. Indeed, as we have set forth in our previous submissions, it is Canada's interpretation of Article 70.1 that would render large portions of Article 70 meaningless or redundant.

29. Canada argues that there must be "compelling reasons presented by the U.S." to "override the clear language of Article 70.1."[26] The United States, however, does not seek

[25] *Ibid.*, at 25, 27.

[26] *Ibid.*, at 25 (third para.).

to "override" any language of the TRIPS Agreement, including Article 70.1. Article 70.1 is simply not relevant to this particular dispute because the United States is not challenging Canada's pre-1996 acts. Again, the irrelevance of Article 70.1 to this dispute does not imply that Article 70.1 is without meaning and we have demonstrated in detail in our submissions why our interpretation of Article 70.1 and 70.2 is logical and consistent with the text, context, object and purpose of Article 70, the negotiating history of that provision, and the subsequent practice of WTO Members.

30. In sum, the United States does not argue that Canada is in violation of its TRIPS obligations as a result of the failure of the Canadian Patent Office to grant, before 1996, patents with a term of at least twenty years from filing. The "acts" of Canada's Patent Office prior to 1996 are not at issue, and indeed, are not subject to TRIPS obligations. Rather, Canada's violation of the Agreement stems from its failure, since the date of application of the TRIPS Agreement, to provide a term of protection for existing patented inventions of at least twenty years from filing. This violation is unrelated to any pre-1996 "act," but is related only to the subject matter (protected inventions) that existed on January 1, 1996. The rule in Article 70.1 that pre-1996 acts are not subject to the obligations in the Agreement does not imply that subject matter existing on January 1, 1996, is also not subject to the obligations of the Agreement.

B. There is no Basis in TRIPS for Canada's Argument that Article 70.2 Requires Compliance with only Some, but not All, of the Obligations in the TRIPS Agreement, with Respect to Existing Subject Matter

31. In response to U.S. arguments in its Oral Statement of 20 December that Canada's interpretation of Articles 70.1 and 70.2 would render meaningless other aspects of Article 70, Canada has clarified that Article 70.2 would apply at least with respect to TRIPS rights under Articles 27.1, 28 and 31(h). For example, in response to Panel Question 7, Canada made the following statements:

> In the result Canada also understands that, *by virtue of paragraph 2 of Article 70*, subject matter which is 'novel, inventive and useful', which was invented and protected before the application date and which continued to be protected as of that date, *would be entitled to protection by the patent vehicle pursuant to Article 27.1 and to the conveyance of the exclusive benefits, even if enhanced by TRIPS, bestowed by virtue of Article 28.*[27]
>
> ** ** ** **
>
> Patentable subject matter under Article 70.2 would include the obligations set out under Article 28 to confer certain exclusive rights on a patent owner, and the right to be paid remuneration under Article 31(h) where a Member sanctioned a use unauthorized by a right holder for patentable subject matter.[28]

32. It is significant that Canada concedes that pre-1996 acts do not preclude the application of the obligations in Articles 27.1, 28 and 31(h) to existing subject matter. Thus, for example, Canada would apparently agree that if it granted a patent on an invention in 1993, and if Canadian law provided only four of the five exclusive rights outlined in Article 28, Article 70.2 would imply that Canada must grant, as of January 1, 1996, the fifth exclusive right to that patentee.

---

27 *Ibid.*, at 22 (second full para.) (emphasis supplied).

28 *Ibid.*, at 28 (first full para.).

33. Where Canada and the United States continue to differ is whether Article 70.2 requires Canada also to apply the TRIPS obligation to provide a patent term of twenty years from filing to inventions which enjoy patent protection on January 1, 1996. While Canada agrees that WTO Members are obliged by Article 70.2 to provide TRIPS protections under Articles 27.1, 28, and 31(h) to subject matter existing on January 1, 1996, Canada argues that the term of protection applicable to such subject matter is not covered by Article 70.2. Canada has not and cannot explain why the TRIPS obligation involving the term of protection may be properly excluded under Article 70.1 while other TRIPS obligations, such as the provision of exclusive rights in Article 28, are not.

34. In elaborating its theory of Article 70.2, Canada places great weight on the argument that a "patent" is not "subject matter."[29] The Parties do not appear to be in dispute that existing inventions (which may already be patented) are subject matter within the meaning of Article 70.2. Thus, Canada's distinction is without any significance in this case. Patented inventions that existed on January 1, 1996, are entitled to TRIPS-level protection. Such TRIPS-level protection includes the rights provided for in Articles 27.1, 28, and 31 of the TRIPS Agreement, as well as a term of protection that does not expire before twenty years from filing, as provided in Article 33.

V. CONCLUSION

35. Accordingly, the United States respectfully requests the Panel to find that Canada is not in compliance with Articles 33 and 70.2 of the TRIPS Agreement, and respectfully requests that the Panel recommend that Canada bring its law into conformity with these provisions.

---

[29] *Ibid.*, at 26 (second para.).

ATTACHMENT 1.6

ORAL STATEMENT OF THE UNITED STATES AT THE SECOND MEETING WITH THE PANEL

(25 January 2000)

I. INTRODUCTION

1. Mr. Chairman, Members of the Panel, Representatives of the Government of Canada, and members of the Secretariat: On behalf of the United States delegation, I would like to first thank the Panel and the Secretariat Staff for your time and continued effort in this case.

2. Despite Canada's claims to the contrary, and its attempts to make it otherwise, this case remains "an exceedingly simple one."

3. The text of TRIPS Article 33 is unequivocally clear:

> The term of protection available [for patents] shall not end before the expiration of a period of twenty years counted from the filing date.

Yet, Canada admits that the terms of protection for forty percent of its Old Act patents that are presently in existence *will end* before the expiration of a period of twenty years counted from their respective filing dates.[1] The terms of these patents are therefore inconsistent with the express obligation of Article 33.

4. The text of TRIPS Article 70.2 is equally unambiguous:

> Except as otherwise provided for in this Agreement, this Agreement gives rise to obligations in respect of *all subject matter existing at the date of application of this Agreement* for the Member in question, *and which is protected in that Member on the said date ...*

Many of Canada's Old Act patents were still valid at the time the TRIPS Agreement became applicable for Canada on January 1, 1996. This is uncontested. Thus, the "Agreement gives rise to obligations in respect of" the inventions protected by these Old Act patents. One such obligation is that of Article 33: Canada must provide terms of protection that "shall not end before the expiration of twenty years counted from the filing date" for *all* such Old Act patents.

5. And because Canada does not meet this obligation for forty percent of its existing Old Act patents, Canada is therefore in *prima facie* violation of Articles 33 and 70.2 of the TRIPS Agreement. It is really just that simple.

II. REBUTTALS TO CANADA'S ARTICLE 33 DEFENSES

Equivalency

6. Canada has offered two defenses related to Article 33 of TRIPS. First, Canada claims that even if a term of seventeen years from grant does in fact end prior to the expiration of twenty years from filing, in direct contravention of the text of Article 33, there is nevertheless no violation of Article 33 because in Canada a term of seventeen years from

---

[1] First Submission of Canada, para. 45.

grant is "substantively equivalent" to a term of twenty years from filing. There are several major flaws to this argument.

7. This argument reflects an attempt to modify the plain language of Article 33, and ignores that provision's command that the term of protection available "shall not end before the expiration of a period of twenty years counted from the filing date." Canada justifies its departure from the text of Article 33 by citing Article 62.2 to manufacture a so-called "measurement formula" for a period of "exclusive privilege and property rights."[2] The unambiguous text of Article 33 cannot be so lightly dismissed. No such "measurement formula" can justify ignoring the explicit text of Article 33 and nothing in Article 62.2 justifies Canada's failure to make available to all right holders a patent term that does not end before twenty years from filing. Under Article 33, regardless of the period of "exclusive privilege" provided by a patent, the patent term available to right holders at a minimum "*shall not end*" before a period of twenty years from filing.

8. By using Article 62.2 to attribute a meaning to Article 33 that conflicts with the latter's explicit terms, Canada fails to respect the ruling of the Appellate Body "to take adequate account of the words actually used" in a provision.[3] Canada's interpretation would render meaningless the phrase "shall not end ... " in Article 33 - a result that contradicts fundamental principles of treaty interpretation. For this reason alone, Canada's "equivalency" argument must fail.

9. In addition to ignoring the text of Article 33, Canada also employs an impermissible averaging methodology to argue that a term of seventeen years from grant is "substantively equivalent" to a term of twenty years from filing. In our Rebuttal Submission, we cited the many times that Canada references "normal or average" pendency periods for its patents.[4] These normal or average pendency periods are the basis from which Canada makes its comparison between the period of "effective protection" provided under its regime of seventeen years from grant and the period provided under a term of twenty years from filing. Canada's averaging methodology is flawed in that it (by definition) does not take into account patents whose actual pendency periods diverge significantly from the average. This methodology is flatly inconsistent with the panel decision in the *Section 337* case, a fact that Canada has yet to reconcile.[5]

10. Furthermore, Canada's methodology of comparing "effective" terms of protection based on average pendency periods would defeat the object and purpose of Article 33. Article 33 was intended to harmonize patent terms around a system of twenty years from filing.[6] Under Canada's reasoning, WTO Members need not provide a patent term of twenty years from filing, so long as they provide a term from grant that relates to the average pendency periods in their respective countries. For example, a term of seventeen years from grant would be TRIPS-consistent for countries with average pendency periods of three years or more, but not for countries with average pendency periods of less than three years. This interpretation runs directly contrary to the TRIPS negotiators' goal of achiev-

---

[2] Second Submission of Canada, para. 3.

[3] Appellate Body report on *United States - Standard for Reformulated and Conventional Gasoline*, WT/DS2/AB/R (adopted May 20, 1996), at 16.

[4] Rebuttal Submission of the United States, paras. 9 & 10.

[5] *See* GATT panel report on *United States - Section 337 of the Tariff Act of 1930*, BISD 36S/386 (adopted November 7, 1989), para. 5.13.

[6] Daniel Gervais, The TRIPS Agreement: Drafting History and Analysis, 169 (1998).

ing what Canada itself describes as the "harmonization of the term of protection among member states."[7]

Availability

11. In addition to its "equivalency" argument, Canada also claims that it is not in violation of Article 33 because a term of twenty years from filing was "available" to patent holders by means of delay tactics in patent application prosecution. By not "taking advantage of" these delay tactics, Canada argues, the applicants essentially "waived" their right to a patent term of twenty years from filing.[8] This argument too has fundamental flaws.

12. First of all, it is uncontested that all Old Act patents were based on patent applications filed prior to October 1, 1989. It is similarly uncontested that the obligation to provide a patent term of twenty years from filing did not arise for Canada until the TRIPS Agreement became applicable on January 1, 1996. Thus, it was impossible for Old Act applicants to have knowingly waived their rights under TRIPS to a term of twenty years from filing. Moreover, since certain Old Act applicants - whose patents would be granted in less than three years - would have had to forego a period of effective protection in order to obtain a term that did not end before twenty years from filing, the "choice" that Canada made available to patent applicants was hardly that contemplated by Article 33.

13. In support of its position that a patent term of twenty years from filing was available to Old Act applicants, Canada repeatedly points out that sixty percent of Old Act patents have terms that exceed twenty years from filing. This statistic, however, proves nothing about the availability of a term of twenty years from filing to *all* Old Act applicants. It is just as significant that forty percent of Old Act patents have terms that end before twenty years from filing.

14. Second, the incredibly convoluted delaying tactics described by Canada - twice abandoning an application and then reinstating it each time, and then forfeiting the application and restoring it again - have no sound legal basis. Following the Appellate Body's guidance in the *India - Patent Protection* case,[9] the United States - in paragraphs 14 to 28 of our rebuttal submission - examined the relevant provisions of the Old Act as they relate to such delay tactics. In doing so, we noted that there is no legally guaranteed right for an applicant to use such tactics to obtain a patent term of twenty years from filing. Section 30(2) of Canada's Old Act permitted the reinstatement of abandoned applications if "the failure to complete or prosecute the application within the time specified was not reasonably avoidable."[10] In other words, a patent applicant that had abandoned an application had no legal right to reinstate that application if the applicant engaged in reasonably avoidable delays. The fact that the Chairman of Canada's Patent Appeals Board is aware of no cases of delays being refused is of no legal consequence, and does not change the plain text of the Canadian law.

---

[7] First Oral Presentation of Canada, para. 55.

[8] Second Submission of Canada, para. 29.

[9] *See* Appellate Body report in *India - Patent Protection for Pharmaceutical and Agricultural Chemical Products*, WT/DS50/AB/R, adopted January 16, 1998, DSR 1998:I, 9, paras. 66, 69, and 70.

[10] Canadian Patent Act, R.S.C., ch P-4, section 30(2) (1985). Canada Exhibit 16.

15. Canada attempts to bolster its argument regarding these delay tactics by asserting that "similar rules exist under US patent legislation."[11] This comparison only highlights the weakness in Canada's argument. The U.S. patent law does contain a rule similar to Section 30(2) of Canada's Old Act. Like Canada's Section 30(2), the U.S. provision is *not* available to anyone for the asking. Rather, it provides that patent applications can be reinstated only where a delay was "unavoidable". Furthermore, under U.S. law, patent applicants need not engage in *any* delaying tactics to obtain a patent term that does not end before twenty years from filing. Rather, all applicants and current patent owners have a legal right to such a term under U.S. law - even where they chose not to repeatedly abandon and forfeit their patent applications.

16. Finally, it is interesting to note the inconsistency between Canada's argument regarding the "availability" of a twenty-year patent term with Canada's argument that such a term is actually provided under Canadian law. One might wonder why, if the two terms were indeed "equivalent," an Old Act patent applicant would have to delay the date of grant to obtain a twenty year term. The obvious answer is that a term of twenty years from filing is not in fact provided under Section 45 of the Canadian Patent Act.

III. REBUTTALS TO CANADA'S ARTICLE 70 DEFENSE

17. Canada's final defense in this case rests upon Article 70. Article 70.2, by its terms, requires WTO developed-country Members to apply the obligations of the TRIPS Agreement - all of the obligations of the TRIPS Agreement - to inventions that were patented on January 1, 1996. Article 70.1 does not diminish this requirement or provide otherwise. By contrast, Canada's interpretation of Article 70.2 of TRIPS is inconsistent with the text of that provision, its context, object and purpose, its negotiating history, as well as the subsequent practice of every other WTO developed-country Member.

18. The text of Article 70.2 is the key to its interpretation. The plain language of this provision indicates that the obligations of the TRIPS Agreement apply to all "subject matter" existing on January 1, 1996, "which is protected" on that date. An invention is subject matter. A patent is a form of intellectual property protection. In short then, Article 70.2 requires the obligations of TRIPS to be applied to existing patented inventions.

19. Canada attempts to cloud the interpretation of this straight-forward provision by placing great weight on the distinction between a patent and the subject matter protected by a patent. This distinction has no effect on the interpretation of Article 70.2. Quite simply, the TRIPS obligations must be applied to patented inventions. Along the same lines, Canada appears to argue in its Second Submission that "patented subject matter" is not "subject matter."[12] Given that Article 70.2 applies to "subject matter ... that is protected," Canada's distinction again has no significance.

20. Apart from these irrelevant semantic distinctions under Article 70.2, Canada's Article 70 defense rests on a sweeping interpretation of Article 70.1. As described in the Rebuttal Submission of the United States, Article 70.1 applies to all "acts" which occurred before the date of application of TRIPS to Canada. Such acts can be those of private parties or acts of government authorities. In our previous submissions, the United

---

[11] Second Submission of Canada, para. 33.

[12] *Ibid.*, para. 51.

States has provided numerous examples of the acts covered by Article 70.1 and the effect of that provision.[13]

21. In the context of this case, Article 70.1 means that Canada is not today in violation of the TRIPS Agreement for its failure to make available, before 1996, patent terms of twenty years from filing to all applicants. The U.S. is not arguing that Canada's physical acts of granting patents with terms of seventeen year from grant back in the early 1990's violate TRIPS. This concept may seem obvious - and indeed, to many TRIPS negotiators, it was. As noted in the U.S. Answer to Panel Question 6.d., during the TRIPS negotiations, some countries thought Article 70.1 stated a concept "too obvious" to be included in the Agreement. The negotiating history does not support Canada's position that Article 70.1 in effect represents a sweeping and complex exemption from the provisions of Article 70.2.

22. The United States' complaint before this Panel is not based on any pre-1996 act of any Canadian authority. Rather, it is based on Canada's failure, as of January 1, 1996, to apply prospectively the obligations of TRIPS to all patented subject matter that existed on January 1, 1996. Article 70.1 has no effect on this particular case, and no relevance to it.

23. More specifically, the mere fact that Canada engaged in pre-1996 acts that denied TRIPS-level protection to certain subject matter, does not mean that Canada is forever exempted from applying TRIPS obligations to such subject matter. In the context of patented inventions, Canada's failure prior to 1996 to make available to all applicants a term of twenty years from filing, does not mean that Canada is excused from the obligation to grant a TRIPS-level patent term to patented inventions that existed on January 1, 1996.

24. Canada's contrary interpretation of Article 70.1 is unsupported by the context, object and purpose of Article 70. In this regard, Canada first attempted to convince this Panel that all the obligations of TRIPS do not apply to patents granted prior to January 1, 1996. To quote Canada's First Submission: "patents issued prior to January 1, 1996 are not subject to the obligations in the TRIPS Agreement."[14] Such a far-reaching interpretation of Article 70.1 would make several of the other provisions of Article 70 redundant or meaningless. It would also completely eviscerate the protection provided by the TRIPS Agreement for thousands of existing patent holders, with the result that the legal effect and the benefits of the TRIPS Agreement would not be felt for years into the future. This was not the intent of the negotiators of the Agreement, and is not consistent with the detailed negotiations that accompanied the drafting of Articles 70.2, 70.4 and 70.6.

25. Presumably to avoid such an extreme result, Canada subsequently narrowed its argument, and now distinguishes between some of the obligations in the TRIPS Agreement that would apply to existing subject matter, and other obligations (such as patent term) that allegedly do not. There is no textual basis in Article 70.1 or 70.2 for Canada's attempt to distinguish between the obligations in TRIPS that will apply to existing subject matter. The obligations in Articles 27, 28 and 31 of TRIPS cannot be distinguished from the obligation in Article 33. Under Article 70.2, Canada must apply all TRIPS obligations to all inventions that were protected on January 1, 1996.

26. In its Second Submission, Canada attempted to support its distinction between the various obligations of TRIPS by citing little more than the fact that the obligation concerning the exclusive rights conveyed by a patent and the obligation concerning the term

[13] *E.g.*, First Oral Statement of the United States, para. 14, U.S. Response to Panel Question 11, Rebuttal Submission of the United States, para. 25.

[14] First Written Presentation of Canada, para. 113.

of a patent appear in different articles of the Agreement. This argument ignores the fact that other patent obligations also are not merged into one provision, but are set forth in separate articles. Furthermore, there is no indication that the drafters of the Agreement intended to limit the application of Article 70.2 merely by the organization of the patent obligations in TRIPS into separate articles.

Subsequent Practice

27. On a final note, the United States must re-emphasize the highly significant fact that among all WTO developed-country members (except Canada), there appears to be complete uniformity of practice regarding the interpretation of Articles 33, 70.1 and 70.2. Canada has provided no evidence rebutting the evidence provided in the U.S. First Submission on this point. On the key issue in dispute - whether a patent term of at least twenty years from filing must be available for *all* patents in force on January 1, 1996 - every other developed country member of the WTO agrees that it must. Given the importance of subsequent practice as a guide to interpretation of the treaty provisions under Article 31(3)(b) of the Vienna Convention, this consensus among other WTO members cannot be dismissed.

IV. CONCLUSION

28. For all of these reasons, the United States respectfully requests that the Panel find that Canada is in violation of its obligations under Articles 33 and 70 of the TRIPS Agreement, and recommend that Canada bring its law into compliance with these provisions.

ATTACHMENT 1.7

RESPONSES OF THE UNITED STATES TO WRITTEN QUESTIONS FROM THE PANEL - SECOND MEETING

(3 February 2000)

B. AVAILABILITY (ARTICLE 33)

Q.32 Does the TRIPS Agreement permit Members to give patent applicants a choice between either obtaining protection early, or obtaining a term of protection that expires twenty years from the filing date?

No. The Agreement mandates that the term of protection available must not end before the expiration of twenty years from the filing date. The Agreement also mandates that patents be granted "within a reasonable period of time so as to avoid unwarranted curtailment of the period of protection", and that procedures for the acquisition of patent rights may not be unnecessarily complicated or costly, or entail unwarranted delays. The text of the Agreement does not support the notion that a Member can ignore one obligation simply by fulfilling another.[1] These obligations are not "either-or" choices. A Member cannot condition its compliance with one TRIPS obligation on a patent applicant's willingness to forfeit its rights under another TRIPS provision.

Q.33 If Article 70.2 rendered Article 33 applicable to inventions under protection in developed country Members on 1 January 1996, would it require those Members to make available on that date a term of protection for existing patents that did not expire before the end of 20 years from their respective filing dates or would it be sufficient that that term was available at te time that the patent application was filed?

The text of Articles 70.2 and 33 indicates that it would not be sufficient for a WTO Member to provide a term of twenty years from filing only at the time that a patent application was filed. Essentially, such a scenario would read into Article 70.2 an exception that does not exist in the text. The terms of Article 70.2 are unqualified on this point, and require developed country Members to comply with the TRIPS obligations in respect of inventions under protection on 1 January 1996. In this case, it is undisputed that on 1 January 1996, Canada did not make available to all patent owners a term of protection that did not end before twenty years from filing. ON 1 January 1996, an Old Act patent owner whose patent would expire sooner than twenty years from filing had no recourse under Canadian law. (Moreover, notwithstanding the premise of this hypothetical question, Canada also did not make this term available on a sound legal basis for every one of its Old Act patent applicants at any time prior to 1 January 1996.)

---

[1] *See, e.g., GATT panel report on United States - Section 337 of the Tariff Act of 1930*, BISD 36S/386 (adopted November 7, 1989), para. 5.13.

Q.34 How can those applicants whose patents were granted before the date of application of the Agreement be said to have chosen to forego a later term when the TRIPS Agreement had not even been applied?

Those applicants whose patents were granted before the date of application of the Agreement *cannot* be said to have chosen to forego a later term when the TRIPS Agreement had not even been applied. To have "chosen to forego a later term" necessarily implies that Old Act applicants knowingly made the decision to waive their right to this later term prior to the granting of their patents. Logically, one cannot waive a right that did not exist. The right to a term of twenty years from filing did not (and does not) exist for Old Act applicants under Canadian law, and did not exist under the TRIPS Agreement until its date of application to Canada on 1 January 1996.

ATTACHMENT 2: CANADA'S SUBMISSIONS

ATTACHMENT 2.1

FIRST SUBMISSION OF CANADA
(2 December 1999)

TABLE OF CONTENTS

I. INTRODUCTION

1. In these proceedings the United States of America (US) challenges the conformity of the provisions of the Canadian ***Patent Act*** (Act) respecting the duration of the term of protection accorded to certain Canadian patents with the minimum standard for that term prescribed by Article 33 of the ***Agreement on Trade-Related Aspects of Intellectual Property Rights*** (variously referred to as: TRIPS, the Agreement or the TRIPS Agreement).

2. The US notes that the term of protection granted to patents issued on the basis of patent applications filed before October 1, 1989 is defined, pursuant to section 45 of the Act, to be seventeen years from the date on which such a patent is issued. On this basis the US advances the allegation that this provision of Canadian patent law is inconsistent

with Canada's obligations under the TRIPS Agreement, including but not necessarily limited to Articles 33, 65 and 70.[1]

3. The US position is based on a narrow and incomplete analysis of the relevant provisions of Canadian law and practice as well as of the relevant terms of the Agreement.

4. In reply Canada denies that there is merit in the US allegation and confirms that its patent law and practice respecting the term of protection accorded to Canadian patents issued on the basis of patent applications filed before October 1, 1989 are consistent with the obligations imposed by the TRIPS Agreement and more specifically are consistent and conform with the minimum standard required by Article 33 as well as with the transitional or application rules set out in Articles 65 and 70 of the Agreement.

5. It is Canada's submission that the provisions of section 45 of the Act are consistent, and in conformity, with the TRIPS Agreement and more specifically with the referenced Articles because:

(a) the term of the exclusive privilege and property right available under a "section 45" patent is equivalent or superior to and consistent with the term of the exclusive privilege and property right conferred by a patent where the term of protection available does not, as required by Article 33, end before the expiration of a period of twenty years counted from the filing date;

(b) in prescribing a term of protection that is measured from the date of the grant of a patent, section 45 does not provide, or otherwise require, that the term of protection conferred shall end before the expiration of the twenty year period measured from the filing date of the patent application;

(c) the events or circumstances which may operate to limit the period of the term of protection of a section 45 patent to less than twenty years measured from the filing date are events or circumstances that are within the private decision making capacity and strategic control of the applicant; and,

(d) in any event, "section 45" patents which were issued under an act of grant executed before the application date of the TRIPS Agreement are exempt from the obligations of the Agreement by virtue of the express exception set out in paragraph 1 of Article 70 and, more particularly, neither the retroactive application provisions of the Agreement set out in paragraph 2 of Article 70 nor the term of protection prescribed in Article 33 have any application to such patents.

II. FACTS

A. *Treaty Provisions*

6. Under the heading of *"Term of Protection"* Article 33 of TRIPS provides that:

> The term of protection available shall not end before the expiration of a period of twenty years counted from the filing date [of a patent application].

[1] Letter from Ambassador Rita D. Hayes of the US to Ambassador John M. Weekes of Canada; dated May 6,1999. Reproduced as Exhibit No. 1.

7. The scope of this obligation is further addressed in paragraphs 1 and 2 of Article 62. Those two paragraphs stipulate that:

> 1. Members may require, as a condition of the acquisition or maintenance of the intellectual property rights provided for under Sections 2 through 6 of Part II, compliance with reasonable procedures and formalities. Such procedures and formalities shall be consistent with the provisions of this Agreement.
>
> 2. Where the acquisition of an intellectual property right is subject to the right being granted or registered, Members shall ensure that the procedures for grant or registration, subject to compliance with the substantive conditions for acquisition of the right, permit the granting or registration of the right within a reasonable period of time so as to avoid unwarranted curtailment of the period of protection.

8. Each Member's obligation to implement the standards prescribed by the TRIPS Agreement arises by virtue of both the provisions of paragraph 4 of Article XVI of the Agreement Establishing the World Trade Organization (WTO) and the provisions of paragraph 1 of Article 1 of the TRIPS Agreement. In their material parts these two paragraphs provide, respectively, that:

> Each Member shall ensure the conformity of its laws, regulations and administrative procedures with its obligations as provided in the annexed Agreements.
>
> Members shall give effect to the provisions of this Agreement...Members shall be free to determine the appropriate method of implementing the provisions of this Agreement within their own legal system and practice.[2]

9. As a substantive annex to the Agreement Establishing the WTO the TRIPS Agreement entered into force on January 1, 1995. However, by virtue of its one year moratorium on the obligation to implement, paragraph 1 of Article 65 delayed the "date of application" for the TRIPS Agreement in Canada and other developed Member states until January 1, 1996. Specifically paragraph 1 of the Article provides that:

> Subject to the provisions of paragraphs 2, 3 and 4 [which are not relevant here], no Member shall be obliged to apply the provisions of this Agreement before the expiry of a general period of one year following the date of entry into force of the WTO Agreement.

10. The obligations both to implement and to implement by a date certain are, despite their positive expression, nevertheless subject to the caveats or special application rules which, under the heading *"Protection of Existing Subject Matter"*, are set out in Article 70.

11. Most of these special application or transitional rules are narrowly or specifically focussed and seek to address specific, anomalous or ambiguous circumstances that the treaty negotiators expected to arise on the application date of the Agreement.

12. However the rules set out in paragraphs 1 and 2 of the Article are rules of general application. The first, the paragraph 1 rule gives specific effect within the TRIPS context

[2] The Appellate Body endorsed the application of this rule respecting Member discretion in implementing their TRIPS obligations in: *India - Patent Protection For Pharmaceutical And Agricultural Chemical Products (AB-1997-5),* WT/DS50/AB/R, adopted 16 January 1998, DSR 1998:I, 9, para. 59 and following, beginning at page 22.

to the presumption of international law[3] as well as of the municipal law of many Member states against the retroactive application of new law which would affect vested property or contractual rights subsisting on the coming into force of the new law.

13. The rule against the retroactive application of its obligations is set out in the opening paragraph of Article 70 and specifies that:

> This Agreement does not give rise to obligations in respect of acts which occurred before the date of application of the Agreement for the Member in question.

14. By its own terms, the second-or the paragraph 2-rule operates subject to the other provisions of the Agreement. In its material part it provides that:

> Except as otherwise provided for in this Agreement, this Agreement gives rise to obligations in respect of all subject matter existing at the date of application of this Agreement for the Member in question, and which is protected in that Member on the said date, or which meets or comes subsequently to meet the criteria for protection under the terms of this Agreement.

B. Term of Protection Provisions in Canadian Patent Law

15. Current Canadian patent legislation contains two provisions, which originally came into force on October 1, 1989, that define the term of protection to be accorded to a successful applicant for patent protection.

16. The two provisions are distinguishable on the basis of the filing date of a patent application, by their references to different commencement dates for measuring the running of the term of protection and by their specification of different lengths of the period for which protection will continue after the happening of the commencement date.

17. Following their recent, essentially editorial, amendment by the ***Intellectual Property Law Improvement Act*** [4] of 1993, the two provisions now specify that:

> 44. Subject to section 46, where an application for a patent is filed under this Act on or after October 1, 1989, the term limited for the duration of the patent is twenty years from the filing date.
>
> 45. Subject to section 46, the term limited for the duration of every patent issued under this Act on the basis of an application filed before October 1, 1989 is seventeen years from the date on which the patent is issued.

18. Section 46 provides for the payment of annual fees-"maintenance fees"-to maintain the rights accorded by the patent once granted. It also provides that where such fees are not paid within the time prescribed, the patent shall be deemed to have expired at the end of that prescribed time. Specifically section 46 states that:

> 46.(1) A patentee of a patent issued by the Patent Office under this Act after the coming into force of this section shall, to maintain the rights accorded by the pat-

---

[3] The presumption has been codified in Article 28 of the *Vienna Convention on the Law of Treaties* which provides that:

> Unless a different intention appears from the treaty or is otherwise established, its provisions do not bind a party in relation to any act or fact which took place or any situation which ceased to exist before the date of the entry into force of the treaty with respect to that party.

[4] S.C. 1993, ch. 15, s. 42. Reproduced in relevant part as Exhibit No. 2. These amendments came into force on October 1, 1996.

ent, pay to the Commissioner such fees, in respect of such periods, as may be prescribed.

(2) Where the fees payable under subsection (1) are not paid within the time provided by the regulations, the term limited for the duration of the patent shall be deemed to have expired at the end of that time.[5]

C. *Legislative Context and History*

19. The substance of sections 44 and 45 was, together with a large number of other proposed amendments to the ***Patent Act***, first introduced in Parliament on November 6, 1986 in Bill C-22. Although still more commonly referred to as Bill C-22, the Bill was enacted and became law under the title of ***An Act to amend the Patent Act and to provide for certain matters in relation thereto***[6] (variously referred to as: Bill C-22; or, the Bill) on November 17, 1987.

20. In Bill C-22 the provisions at issue were drafted to reflect their then prospective application. Numbered as sections 46 and 47 within clause 16 of the Bill they provided that:

> 46. Subject to section 48, the term limited for the duration of every patent issued by the Patent Office under this Act the application for which patent was filed after the coming into force of this section shall be twenty years from the date of the filing of the application in Canada.
>
> 47. Subject to section 48, the term limited for the duration of every patent issued by the Patent Office under this Act the application for which patent is filed on or after August 1, 1935 and before the coming into force of this section shall be seventeen years from the date on which the patent is issued.[7]

21. Section 48 in Bill C-22 was equivalent to what, in the current version of the Act, is section 46. But for some variation in the lapsing provision in subsection (2), section 48 is substantively identical to section 46.

> 48.(1) A patentee of a patent issued by the Patent Office under this Act after the coming into force of this section shall, to maintain the rights accorded by the patent, pay to the Commissioner such fees, in respect of such periods, as may be prescribed.
>
> (2) Where the fees payable by a patentee in respect of a period prescribed for the purposes of subsection (1) are not paid before the expiration of that period, the term limited for the duration of the patent shall be deemed to have lapsed on the expiration of such further period as may be prescribed.[8]

22. Two principal rationales underlay the introduction and enactment of Bill C-22.

23. The first involved the Canadian Government's resolve to respond to international dissatisfaction with the open-ended nature of the provisions in Canadian patent legislation which allowed for the compulsory licensing of patented inventions relating to the use,

---

[5] *Ibid.*, ch. 15, s. 43. Reproduced in Exhibit No. 2.

[6] S.C. 1987, ch. 41, ss. 46, 47. Reproduced in relevant part as Exhibit No. 3.

[7] The reference to August 1, 1935 alludes to the effective date of the term of protection provision in the prior version of the ***Patent Act*** which, to harmonize the Canadian with the US term, had originally introduced the 'seventeen year from the date of grant' term into Canadian patent law. R.S.C. 1970, Ch. P-4. Section 48 introduced the seventeen year term. Reproduced in part as Exhibit 4.

[8] S.C. 1987, ch. 41, s. 48. Reproduced in Exhibit No. 3.

preparation or production of foods and medicines.[9] (Amongst other matters, the resulting amendments considerably curtailed the period during which such compulsory licences were allowed to operate.[10])

24. The second involved the Government's decisions to ratify the ***Patent Cooperation Treaty***, to switch to a "first to file" from a "first to invent" system of patent protection and, more generally, to modernize domestic patent laws, administrative procedures and practices.[11], [12]

25. While the desire to modernize the Canadian patent system was one, it was not the only, reason which lay behind the changes to the commencement date and length of the term of protection provisions of the then contemporary patent legislation. Another and important rationale for these changes reflected "the desire to prevent patent applicants from manipulating the patent application system by deliberately delaying the grant of their patent in order to delay the date of expiry...".[13]

26. In commenting on the effect of a "twenty year from filing" term in his book, ***Intellectual Property Law Copyright Patents Trade Marks,*** Professor David Vaver gives some comparative perspective to this further rationale for change when he observes that:

> The present monopoly period [twenty years from filing] is effectively less than twenty years. ... Before [1 October] 1989, patents lasted seventeen years from date of grant, which could be long after the date of application because of delays in the PO [Patent Office]. Some delays were unavoidable. Others were deliberately caused by applicants intent on prolonging their monopoly.[14]

27. The Bill C-22 amendments were introduced and published on November 6, 1986 and just over a year later became law, as noted above, on November 17, 1987. However, for a variety of reasons associated with the need to devise and draft complementary regulations, to attend to other transitional issues as well as to give the intellectual property community time to adjust to the new system, most of the "modernizing" amendments, including the amendments relating to the term of protection, were not brought into force until October 1, 1989. Thus both Government and affected parties had three years notice of the change in regime in which to make transitional arrangements.

28. The reference in sections 44 and 45 to a threshold application date clearly served some of the transitional purposes required to effect the change from a system using a "seventeen year from grant" term to another using a "twenty year from filing" term. It did not, however, provide a mechanism for converting from one system to the other.

---

[9] See, for instance, David J. French. "Patent Law Reform in Canada", *Canadian Intellectual Property Review,* Vol.4, no. 2, 337. Reproduced as Exhibit No. 5.

[10] See: Exhibit No. 3, section 41.11 set out in clause 15.

[11] Department of Consumer and Corporate Affairs, *News Release*, June 27, 1986. Reproduced as Exhibit No. 6.

[12] Roger T. Hughes et al. *Hughes and Woodley On Patents*, (Butterworths: Toronto, 1984), Loose leaf service updated as of April 1999, pages 315 to 315-5. Reproduced in relevant part as Exhibit No. 7.

[13] Affidavit of Peter J. Davies, Chairman of the Patent Appeal Board of the Canadian Patent Office, Para. 3. Reproduced in its entirety as Exhibit No. 8. Hereafter cited as: Davies affidavit.

[14] David Vaver, *Intellectual Property Law-Copyright-Patents-Trade-marks*, (Irwin Law; Concord [Ontario], 1997)at page 114, footnote 2. Reproduced in relevant part as Exhibit No. 9.

29. In this circumstance Bill C-22 included an additional transitional provision that specified the law that would apply to pre-threshold date applications. The rule was set out in section 27 of the Bill and provided that:

> 27. Applications for patents filed before the coming into force of the provisions of this Act referred to in subsection 31(1) [which included the seventeen year term provision] shall be dealt with and disposed of in accordance with the *Patent Act* as it read immediately before the coming into force of those provisions.[15]

30. The law applicable to such applications is generally referred to as the "Old Act".

D. *The Prosecution of Patent Applications in Canada*

31. In contrast to copyright and trade-mark property rights, which arise spontaneously upon either the creation of the "work", in the case of copyright, or the association in commerce of a mark with "wares", in the case of trade-marks; patent rights do not arise until the State or its agent-in Canada, the Commissioner of Patents or a patent examiner-is satisfied that the invention claimed meets the statutory criteria of being new, inventive and useful.

32. Where satisfied that an invention is new, inventive and useful, the Commissioner will confirm these qualities by granting and issuing "letters patent"[16] to the inventor (or its assignee). The Commissioner, through one of the examiners in the Patent Office, satisfies him or her self of the novelty, creativity and utility of the claims in a patent application through a process of examination and dialogue with the applicant.[17]

E. *Old Act Applications*

33. As a consequence of the transitional rule set out in section 27 of Bill C-22, section 45 or Old Act applications continue to be evaluated on a "first to invent" basis and to be examined in accordance with the other rules governing Old Act applications.[18]

34. The Old Act application process, like the new, begins with the filing of an application for the issuance of letters patent granting the applicant an exclusive privilege or property right in respect of the invention claimed in the application. Subject to the applicant withdrawing or abandoning an application, the process culminates in the performance of one of two statutory acts. Thus at the end of the process the Commissioner will act to either: refuse the application and give notice of the refusal to the applicant by registered letter (Old Act, section 40[19]); or, under his or her signature and the seal of the Patent Office, execute the grant of the patent (Old Act, section 43[20]).

---

[15] See: Exhibit No. 3, clause 27 of the Bill became section 27 when enacted as part of the amending Act.

[16] Peter D. Rosenberg. *Patent Law Fundamentals*, (Second Edition), (Clark Boardman: New York, 1989), Vol. 5 at pages 1-5/6. Reproduced in relevant part as Exhibit No. 10. And see: Harold G. Fox. *Canadian Patent Law and Practice*, (Fourth Edition), (Carswell; Toronto, 1969) at 163. Reproduced in part as Exhibit No. 11. Roger T. Hughes. Op. cit., at page 315. David Vaver. Op. cit., at page 113.

[17] Davies affidavit, para. 8.

[18] *Ibid.*, paras. 5 and 7.

[19] *Patent Act,* R.S.C. 1985, c. P.-4; c. 33 (3rd Supp.). Reproduced in relevant part in Exhibit 12.

[20] See: Exhibit 12, section 43.

35. The "dialogue" that occurs between the date of filing and the performance of either statutory act of "grant" or "refusal" would typically begin where, after having "searched" the application-meaning examining the claims against prior art literature and other matters affecting patentability, the examiner issues a report to the applicant informing it of any deficiencies in the claims or scope of the claims advanced in the application as well as of any inconsistencies in the application with the requirements of the Old Act orRules.[21] Following the issuance of the examiner's report the applicant is accorded a six month period in which to respond to any issues raised by the examination.

36. The prosecution of an Old Act application and its period of pendency before the Patent Office was, and continues to be, under the procedural control of the applicant. Thus by controlling the speed of the "dialogue" through the several means described in the quotation that follows, the applicant is able to accelerate or, as Professor Vaver notes, retard the prosecution of its application according to its own strategic interest in the timing and longevity of the protection it receives from the patenting process.[22]

37. The principal means for controlling the pace of the "dialogue" and application process have been described by the Chairman of the Patent Appeal Board of the Canadian Patent Office. The most direct of these methods is for the applicant to simply approach the examiner and ask that the examination be postponed to a later date.[23] The Chairman describes this and the other methods of influencing the pace of the prosecution process as follows:

> Many means exist that allow an applicant to slow down the prosecution of an old Act application. These include the following:
>
> i) An applicant can achieve a delay in processing simply by asking the patent examiner. In my personal experience, I am unaware of any such request being refused.
>
> ii) One simple means for delaying an application is for an applicant to wait until the end of each time limit imposed upon the applicant to take a specified action. For example, an applicant can wait until the end of the six month period for responding to each report issued by the examiner and until the end of the six-month period for paying the final fee due before a patent is granted.
>
> iii) An applicant can also choose to not respond to an examiner's report within the six month period following issuance of the report. This has the consequence that the application will be treated as abandoned; however, an abandoned application can be reinstated within twelve months.
>
> iv) An applicant can further choose to not pay the final fee within the six month period following the Office notice requiring payment. This has the consequence that the application will be treated as forfeited; however, a forfeited application can be restored within six months.
>
> v) Prior to October 1, 1996 there was a provision in the Patent Rules that permitted an applicant, upon payment of a fee, to postpone the date of issue of a patent by up to 10 weeks.
>
> In a similar manner an applicant can accelerate the prosecution of an old Act application, for example, by making a request to advance an application for exami-

---

21 Davies affidavit, para. 8.

22 *Ibid.*, paras. 3, 4 and 9.

23 *Ibid.*, subparagraph 10.i).

nation out of its routine order and paying a fee; by asking the patent examiner to speedup processing of the application; or simply by responding immediately to examiners' reports or other requirements of the Office.[24]

38. Those who Professor Vaver has described as being "intent on prolonging their monopoly" by exploiting these various opportunities to delay the processing of an Old Act application, were able to do so without prejudice to the security of their inventions.

39. The security of the invention was attributable to two features of the Old Act system. First, and in contrast to "new Act" applications which become open to public inspection no later than eighteen months after their filing dates[25], Old Act applications are only opened for public inspection once the patent issues. Second, under the Old Act "first to invent" system, disputes as to the entitlement to patent protection are resolved through conflict proceedings[26] which, on their conclusion, award the patent right to the first to invent.

40. Thus, while the application is in the Patent Office and unless disclosed by the applicant, the contents of the application, which is to say the invention, remain secret and protectable under the laws of trade secrecy for the entire period during which the application is being prosecuted. (Moreover, where thought to be advantageous, the applicant could withdraw or abandon its application and continue to rely on trade secrecy protection indefinitely because the Patent Office never discloses the contents of an Old Act application which has been withdrawn, abandoned or refused.)[27]

F. Old Act Patents - Statistics

41. An examination of the records of the Canadian Patent Office relating to patents issued against applications filed prior to October 1, 1989 and that still existed when TRIPS took effect in Canada[28] reveals that a substantial number of Old Act applications had been prosecuted pursuant to a schedule that, when viewed from the perspective of the application filing date, prolonged the duration of the period of protection available to the applicant.

42. More particularly the records show that, as of the surrogate TRIPS application date, 142,494 or just over 60 per cent of the Old Act patents then in existence (236,431) had terms that would not, assuming that annual maintenance fees are paid, expire until, or until well after, the expiry of the twenty year period following their application dates. In a very large number of these cases, the expiry dates will be 2 to 5 years after the expiry of the twenty year period.[29]

---

24 *Ibid.*, paras. 10 and 11.

25 See: Exhibit 12, section 10 and S.C. 1993, c.15, s. 28.

26 These are "contested" proceedings within the Patent Office in which competing applicants for patents respecting an invention file affidavit evidence to establish their respective "invention dates". Davies affidavit, paras. 2 and 7.

27 Davies affidavit, para. 6.

28 For reasons related to application filing date data entry problems, the date used for the examination was actually October 1, 1996. However, given the number of patents issued in Canada on an annual basis, the Patent Office is satisfied that the October 1 statistics are a reliable surrogate for the statistics that would have been applicable on January 1, 1996 had the data been available. Davies affidavit, paras. 13 and 15.

29 Davies affidavit, paras. 14 to 17.

43. The obvious corollary of the foregoing is that, as of the surrogate TRIPS application date, 93,937 or just under 40 per cent of the Old Act patents then in existence had terms that will, assuming the payment of annual maintenance fees, expire in less than the twenty year period measured from their application dates. In 84 per cent of these cases, the patent will expire in the course of the nineteenth year following the application date. (In these "nineteenth" year expiry cases, 52 per cent will expire in the last half of the year, while the remaining 32 per cent will expire in the first half.)[30]

44. A supplementary examination of the records of the Patent Office, but one conducted in relation to Old Act patents which will still be in force on January 1, 2000, reveals a foreseeably similar result. Thus of the 169,966 Old Act patents that will, subject to the continued payment of annual maintenance fees, then still be in existence, 103,030 or just over 60 per cent will not expire until, or until well after, the expiry of the twenty year period following their respective application dates.[31]

45. Correlatively, 66,936 or just under 40 per cent of the Old Act patents still in force on January 1, 2000 will, again subject to the payment of the annual maintenance fees, expire in less than a twenty year period measured from their respective application dates. In 77 per cent of these cases, the patent will expire in the course of the nineteenth year following the application date. (In these "nineteenth" year expiry cases, 55 per cent will expire in the last half of the year, while the remaining 22 per cent will expire in the first half.)[32]

G. New Act Applications

46. When Bill C-22 introduced the "first to file" system and redefined the commencement date of the term of protection it eliminated an applicant's capacity to delay the prosecution process so as to extend the period during which it could enjoy protection. In so doing it also effectively reversed any incentive or licence to delay which had been inherent in the Old Act system.

47. The incentive to delay was reversed by the facts that the new term of protection ran from the application filing date (section 44) and the application would become open to public inspection no later than eighteen months after the date of filing (section 10) irrespective of whether the patent had been "examined" and issued. The incentive to delay was further diluted by the fact that an application does not, under the New Act, enter the "examination" queue until the applicant requests "examination" and pays the associated fees (section 35). Originally the Bill C-22 ***Patent Rules*** provided that this request had to be made within seven years of the application date. The rule has since been changed to reduce the period to five years (section 96).[33]

48. The combined effect of these New Act rules is that the measurement of the term limited for the duration of the patent begins to run before the patent is issued so as to grant the applicant an exclusive privilege and property right in the invention. Accordingly, and in contrast to the Old Act system, the period during which an applicant can expect to benefit from trade secrecy and enjoy the privilege of exclusivity for the exploi-

[30] *Ibid.* 14 to 17.
[31] *Ibid.*, paras. 18 to 22.
[32] *Ibid.*, paras. 18 to 22.
[33] *Ibid.*, para. 26.

tation of its invention is being inexorably reduced throughout the entire period during which the application for protection is being prosecuted and examined.

49. The changes introduced by Bill C-22 did, however, also preserve the capacity of an applicant to exercise substantial control over the application prosecution process. It did so by virtue of two of its provisions. First, it did so by giving the applicant the freedom to determine when, within a specified period-first seven, now five years-after it had filed its application, it filed or would file its subsequent "request for examination". Second, it preserved the capacity to control by preserving the rule which, on the payment of a fee, allows an applicant to advance its position in the queue for examination.

50. In addition to preserving measures which allowed applicants to exercise substantial control over the prosecution process, Bill C-22 also introduced new rules relating to maintenance fees which, in effect, gave successful applicants, whether under the Old Act or the New, control over the expiry date of their patents.

51. The new rules respecting "maintenance fees" have this effect because they make the longevity of the patent term of the exclusive privilege and property right accorded to a patentee for its invention contingent upon the payment of annual fees which, when not paid within the prescribed time, result in the deemed expiry of the patent.

H. New Act Patents - Statistics

52. An examination of the records of the Canadian Patent Office relating to applications filed in Canada on or after October 1, 1989 reveals that, as of November 1, 1999, there have been 285,678 new Act applications filed since the new Act came into force. Of these new Act applications, 125, 406 (approximately 43 per cent) have, since filing, requested examination. On average the period between the date of filing and the date of the request for examination for these 125,406 applications has been twenty seven and one half months.

53. The same exercise, when focussed on patents that have actually issued against New Act applications, reveals that 40,847 New Act patents have been granted by the Patent Office since the coming into force date of the New Act (October 1, 1989). The average pendency period, being the period between the application filing date and the date of grant, for this subset of New Act applications which have been processed through to grant, has been approximately sixty months or five years.[34]

54. The sixty month total has three components. Its first component involves the period of time between the filing date and the date on which the applicant makes the request and pays the fee for "examination". On average the delay between these two dates has, over the last ten years, been approximately fifteen months. Subject to the applicant asking that its application be advanced in the queue and the payment of maintenance fees, the second component involves the time spent waiting in the queue for an available examiner. Over the last ten years the queue has averaged approximately twenty four months. The last component involves the time spent in "examination" itself. Arithmetic says that this period has averaged approximately twenty months.[35]

55. Thus just as an Old Act applicant could, by its own conduct, control and **prolong** the duration of its term of protection when measured from the application filing date where it so wished, under the New Act an applicant can, by its own conduct, control and

---

[34] *Ibid.*, para. 29.

[35] *Ibid.*, para. 29.

abbreviate a substantial part of the period by which the term of its exclusive privilege and property right will be reduced by the examination process.

III. POINTS IN ISSUE

56. The issue in these proceedings is whether certain Canadian patents which:

(1) were issued against applications filed before October 1, 1989;

(2) existed on January 1, 1996; still exist: and

(3) have a term of protection that, when measured from their respective application filing dates, will end before the expiration of a period of twenty years;

are consistent and in conformity with Canada's obligations under the TRIPS Agreement.

IV. SUBMISSIONS

A. *The Root Cause of the Matters in Dispute*

57. The issue in dispute arises out of the fact that section 45 of the Canadian ***Patent Act*** uses a formula for specifying the term of protection to be accorded to successful patent applicants which is different from and, for the purposes of judging its compliance with TRIPS standards, cannot be directly compared to or converted into, the formula for specifying the term employed in and prescribed by Article 33 of the TRIPS Agreement.

58. The TRIPS formula specifies that: "The term of protection available shall not end before the expiration of a period of twenty years counted from the filing date." Similarly section 44 of the Canadian ***Patent Act*** prescribes that, for patents issued on or after October 1, 1989, "the term limited for the duration of the patent is twenty years from the filing date.". If more definite than the TRIPS formula, section 44 is easily assessed against and is clearly in conformity with the standard prescribed by Article 33. It gives rise to no issues in these proceedings.

59 The section 45 formula however makes no reference to the application filing date. And that fact lies at the heart of this dispute.

60. Instead of using the filing date as the commencement date of the term during which protection shall be available, Section 45 provides that "the term limited for the duration of every patent issued...on the basis of an application filed before October 1, 1989 is seventeen years from the date on which the patent issued.".

61. The difficulty in comparing or converting the protection available under the section 45 formula with that available under the TRIPS formula arises out of the disjunction between the various steps in the patent application process.

62. Typically, there are three discrete steps in the patenting process. First, the applicant files its application with a patent office authority. Second, through a process of examination and dialogue with the applicant, the patent authority satisfies itself as to whether or not the invention is new, inventive and useful. Third, where the patent authority is satisfied that the invention is new, inventive and useful, it grants the patent; where, alternatively, it is not so satisfied, it refuses to grant the patent.

63. It is obvious that in this sequence of events the date of application and the date of grant will be separated in time. Furthermore, because of the variability of the examination process, the temporal distance between the two dates may be quite considerable. As of

November 1999, there were, for example, about 1,000 patent applications which had been filed in Canada before October 1, 1989 and against which no patent has yet issued.[36]

64. As a result of the considerable variability of the temporal separation between the application and granting dates, a patent bearing a face term of seventeen years from grant may, when measured from its application filing date, have an "alternative" term of protection that is shorter than, equal to or longer the than twenty year period referred to in Article 33.

65. The US contends that when the "alternative" term of a seventeen year from grant patent is less than twenty years, a Member's law that confers a seventeen year term from grant is not in conformity with the Article 33 standard and the Member has an obligation to amend its law to extend the term to a full twenty years from the application date so as to bring both the law and the patents at issue into conformity with the TRIPS standard.

66. Canada disagrees. It submits that there are good reasons for disputing, and denying, the validity of both:

(a) the US proposition that the terms of protection of the patents here in issue are not consistent with TRIPS; as well as

(b) the US proposition that the TRIPS Agreement requires that both the enabling law be changed and that the terms of protection of the patents at issue be extended.

B. The Term of Exclusivity Privilege under Section 45 and Article 33 is Equivalent

67. One of the reasons to deny the validity of the US propositions is that Article 33 does not stand alone within the TRIPS Agreement but must be read in conjunction with the complementary term of protection provisions in paragraph 2 of Article 62.

68. The latter provisions specify that the granting or registration procedures of Members shall not operate so as to produce an "unwarranted curtailment" of the term of protection afforded to rights holders. Accordingly, Article 33 cannot be understood as intending to provide a minimum of twenty full years of protection for the exclusive privilege and property rights which a patent confers.

69. In this light Article 33 is properly characterized as a substantive, not a merely technical, rule. This emerges clearly from the conjoint reading of: the "*Desiring*" and paragraph (b) of the first "*Recognizing*" recitals which introduce the substance of the TRIPS Agreement and respectively read

> ...taking into account the need to promote effective and adequate protection of intellectual property rights,
>
> *Recognizing* ...the need for new rules and disciplines concerning...(b) the provision of adequate standards and principles concerning the availability, scope and use of...intellectual property rights;

with the "unwarranted curtailment" language of paragraph 2 of Article 62, which in its turn and relevant part reads

> Members shall ensure that the procedures for grant or registration, ..., permit the granting or registration of the right within a reasonable period of time so as to avoid **unwarranted curtailment** of the period of protection.

[36] *Ibid.*, para. 23.

70. Consequently when evaluating the conformity of a Member's domestic law with its TRIPS obligations under Article 33 it is necessary, not merely convenient, to scrutinize the substance, "effectiveness" and "adequacy" of both the domestic law and the TRIPS obligation.

71. When the substantive, "effective" and "adequacy" content of section 45 and Article 33 is so scrutinized, it is immediately apparent that the periods of protection extended to the holders of exclusive rights under the two term of protection formulas are equivalent. And where one term is substantively or "effectively" equivalent to, or as in the case of section 45, better than the other, the two are by definition consistent with one another within the context of the reasonableness and unwarranted curtailment standards articulated in paragraph 2 of Article 62.

72. Earlier analysis has demonstrated that, when measured from the application filing date, the term of protection accorded to a section 45 patent is variable upwards from its face term of seventeen years. The variability is attributable to the fact that, at least in Canada, it normally took the patent authority two to four years to complete the examination process.[37]

73. However while the "alternate" term of protection may vary according to the length of the examination process, the seventeen year term during which a successful applicant will enjoy the exclusive privilege and property right conferred by a patent is **constant** at seventeen years.

74. In systems such as the system contemplated by TRIPS where the term of protection is related to the date of application rather than to the date of grant but where the exclusive privilege and property right that flow from the patent run from the date of grant, the period during which a successful applicant will enjoy the exclusive privilege and property right conferred by the patent is **not** constant. Consequently in practice that period will be variably **eroded** by the time required to complete the examination and granting process.

75. The fact that under the TRIPS formula the period of exclusivity will be **eroded** by the granting process is recognized by paragraph 2 of Article 62 which, in seeking to impose a reasonable limit on the degree of erosion, nevertheless sanctions the reduction in the exclusivity period when it requires that:

> ...Members shall ensure that the procedures for grant or registration, subject to compliance with the substantive conditions for acquisition of the right, permit the granting or registration of the right within a reasonable period of time so as to avoid **unwarranted curtailment** of the period of protection. (Emphasis added)

76. Where in the normal course it takes, as it currently does in Canada in respect of New Act patents, five years to complete the examination process for a patent whose term is related to its application filing date, the period of exclusivity will be reduced accordingly.[38] Since the five year examination period is the normal or average examination period, it must, in Canada's submission, be viewed as being 'a reasonable period which avoids any unwarranted curtailment of the period of protection'.

77. In the result, where, as in the case of section 44 patents, the term limited for the duration of the patent is set at twenty years from its filing date, the period during which a

[37] *Ibid.* , para. 8 and see as well the numbers of patents that have issued more than three years after their application filing dates.
[38] Davies affidavit, para. 29.

successful applicant will enjoy the exclusive privilege and property right conferred by a patent once issued will, in the normal course, be fifteen years. (It may, of course, provide either more or less protection depending on the length of the examination process in any particular case.)

78. Thus where the section 45 class of term provision provides for a guaranteed seventeen year term of substantive or "effective" protection for the exclusive rights conferred by a patent and the other, the TRIPS, class of term provision provides a variable term of substantive or "effective" protection for those rights that is normally fifteen years, the two provisions can be said to be substantively or "effectively" equivalent.

79. Canada submits that the two classes are, in both fact and practice, equivalent when measured against any of the referenced standards.

80. In this respect it bares noting, that the substantive equivalence of the protection offered by the two classes of term provision appears to have been accepted by the Parties to the North American Free Trade Agreement (NAFTA) when they agreed to, and adopted, a term of protection provision which provides that:

> Each party shall provide a term of protection for patents of at least twenty years from the date of filing or seventeen years from the date of grant. A Party may extend the term of patent protection, in appropriate cases, to compensate for delays caused by regulatory approval processes.[39]

81. Canada submits that where the constant period of substantive or "effective" protection for the exclusive rights conferred by a section 45 patent is equivalent to and in fact is routinely two years longer than the normal or average, variable period of substantive or "effective" protection resulting from the joint operation of Articles 33 and 62 of the TRIPS Agreement, the term of protection defined by section 45 can be fairly said to be, and is, consistent with the minimum standard prescribed by TRIPS.

82. Canada submits as well that since its two methods of determining the term of protection provide equivalent periods of substantive or "effective" protection, in deciding to maintain the two provisions in the course of implementing its TRIPS obligations, it acted within the scope of the freedom afforded Members under paragraph 1 of Article 1 "...to determine the appropriate method of implementing the provisions of [the] Agreement within their own legal system and practice.".

83. Canada further submits that the fact of the substantive or "effective" equivalency and consistency of its law and practice, whether under section 44 or section 45, with the standard articulated by Article 33 is, **by itself**, sufficient to dispose of the US complaint.

C. Section 45 does not now, nor did it ever, Require that the Term of Protection End Before the Expiry of a Period of Twenty Years Counted from the Filing Date

84. A further reason to deny the validity of the US propositions is based upon the non-restrictive nature of the term of protection prescribed by section 45 which in its material part provides that "the term limited for the duration of every patent issued...on the basis of an application filed before October 1, 1989 is seventeen years from the date on which the patent is issued.".

---

[39] NAFTA, Article 1709, para. 12. Reproduced as Exhibit No. 13.

85. Section 45 makes no reference to the application filing date. It therefore makes no prescription as to when the term of protection it grants may end in relation to the filing date. More particularly, section 45 does not prescribe that the term of protection shall end before the expiration of the twenty year period counted from the filing date.

86. The mere fact that section 45 does not specify that the term of protection shall not end before the expiry of the period referred to in Article 33 neither means nor implies that the section, or its substantive or "effective" content, is inconsistent with the standard prescribed by TRIPS. The Agreement neither proposes nor imposes specific forms or formula for fulfilling the substantive or "effective" obligations of Members.

87. Paragraph 1 of Article 1 confirms this where, in its last sentence it unambiguously states that: "Members shall be **free** to determine the appropriate method of implementing the provisions of this Agreement within their own legal system and **practice.**" (Emphasis added).

88. There is therefore no obligation to implement or respond to the provisions of the Agreement according to any specific or predetermined formula. Consequently it can only be the substance, "effectiveness" or "adequacy" of a Member's legal system and **practice** that will be determinative of questions of compliance or non-compliance with its obligations under the Treaty.

89. In the presence of this freedom to implement within a Member's own legal system and practice, the issue in this dispute can be reduced to whether or not section 45 makes a term of protection which "shall not end before the expiration of a period of twenty years counted from the filing date" universally available to successful applicants for patent protection.

90. The evidence of the practice relating to the administration of Old Act patent applications makes it clear that a twenty year period measured from the application filing date was and continues to be available to any applicant for a patent to which section 45 applies.

91. It is equally clear from the evidence drawn from the records of the Patent Office that as many as forty per cent of Old Act applicants chose not to take advantage of the delays available within the application process to ensure themselves a term of protection that would not end before the expiration of a period of twenty years counted from their application filing dates.

92. The obligation in Article 33 however only requires that the term be available. It does not require that it be imposed contrary to the revealed preference or strategic choice of an applicant.

93. It is material here in discussing the availability of a 'twenty year from filing' term of protection to make reference to the fact that, not only could and can an applicant, by its own conduct, control and prolong the prosecution process to extend its term of protection but it could and can as well, by its own conduct, truncate its substantive or "effective" term of protection at any time during the life of that protection, by simply refusing, or choosing not, to pay its annual maintenance fees.

94. It is similarly material to recognize that the provisions of domestic or municipal law that give rise to this unilateral power to terminate a patent term before its statutory or, more significantly in the context of these proceedings, its treaty, course has run, is a power that is recognized and condoned by paragraph 1 of Article 62 of the TRIPS Agreement. Thus, contrary to the apparent mechanistic nature of the rule in Article 33 and of the assumption underlying the US allegation of non-conformity, TRIPS contemplates that the substantive term of protection conferred on a patentee may, at the instance of the patentee, terminate at any time during the twenty year period counted from the filing date.

95. This is so by virtue of paragraph 1 of Article 62 which stipulates that:

> Members may require, as a condition of the acquisition or maintenance of the intellectual property rights provided for under Sections 2 through 6 of Part II [which includes the provisions relating to patents] compliance with reasonable procedures and formalities. Such procedures and formalities shall be consistent with the provisions of this Agreement.

96. Where a Member may adopt measures which impose conditions on the maintenance of the substantive rights conferred by a patent, Article 33 cannot be said to establish an inflexible, mechanical formula for measuring the term of protection which imposes a minimum fixed term on the longevity of the exclusive privileges and property rights conferred by a patent. If it were otherwise then Article 33 would contradict paragraph 1 of Article 62 and unwarrantably curtail the discretion which that paragraph unambiguously extends to Members.

97. There are many reasons associated with the commercial or technological value of a patent why a patentee might refuse, or choose not, to pay its annual maintenance fees and thus **unilaterally** terminate the substantive or "effective" term of protection conferred on the patentee by virtue of either an Old Act or a New Act patent before that term had run its course under either the prescription of the TRIPS Agreement or the domestic law formula of protection.

98. Similarly, there are many reasons associated with the commercial or technological value of a patent why an Old Act applicant might have preferred to have chosen, or seen a strategic advantage for itself in choosing, to obtain the exclusive private property rights conferred by a patent as soon as possible and in so doing, choosing also to forego the opportunity to obtain a term of protection that would not end before the expiry of a twenty year period measured from its application filing date.

99. This is reflected in the fact that any applicant filing before October 1989 who prosecuted its application without regard to the pace of the process would have known that, at a minimum, it would obtain full protection of its exclusive privilege and property right for the seventeen year period running from the granting date. And if they so pursued their application, they did so knowing that if they wished a longer term measured from their application filing date they could have acted to delay the prosecution of their application to achieve that result.

100. However where an applicant has made those choices it cannot later be heard to complain of its choices and seek to reverse them in order to obtain the windfall benefit of having its term of protection retroactively extended. As the United States Court of Appeal, Federal Circuit observed in a case involving circumstances that are similar to those here in issue:

> Abbott's argument that it should not be bound by the earlier filing date because it received no benefit from the divisional application is not persuasive. The district court found that Abbott chose to designate its patent as divisional in order to receive the potential benefits associated with the earlier filing date. Abbott's choice to do so cannot be disregarded simply because it subsequently found that the later filing date would be more advantageous. Abbott must accept the consequences as well as the potential benefits of the divisional status of [its] application.[40]

[40] *Abbott Laboratories v. Novopharm Limited and Geneva Pharmaceuticals,Inc.* 104 F.3d 1305 (Fed. Cir. 1997) at 1308. The trial court expressed exactly the same view. See: *Abbott Laboratories*

101. So too here.

102. The evidence drawn from the records of the Patent Office further shows that just over sixty per cent of all Old Act applicants saw and continue to see the benefit of taking advantage of the availability of terms of protection that would not end before the expiration of the twenty year period measured from their respective application filing dates.

103. The evidence of this fact becomes particularly revealing when, as appears in the bar chart graphics annexed as Exhibit E to the Davies affidavit, the duration of the term of protection statistics are organized in relation to the portfolios of Old Act patents relating to pharmaceutical inventions that are held by a variety of individual corporate patentees.

104. The chart graphics use the TRIPS twenty year from filing date standard as their "ground zero" or datum level and depict the negative and positive deviations from this standard in respect of each Old Act patent in the several portfolios. The chart graphics clearly demonstrate that the managers of the various patent portfolios managed their respective application strategies in a manner that would, in a commanding majority of cases, provide terms of protection that were and are well in excess of the minimum term prescribed by Article 33.

105. The evidence then shows that while a minority of Old Act applicants did not act to prolong the length of the term of protection they would receive when measured from the filing date, the majority did obtain terms of protection that equalled or considerably exceeded the minimum term prescribed by TRIPS.

106. This comparative evidence of choice and predominance in respect of the length of patent terms emerges more demonstrably from the statistics relating to the pharmaceutical patents held in individual corporate portfolios. In most of these instances, only the smallest minority of the patents in the portfolio carried terms which, when viewed from their respective filing dates, would end before the expiry of the twenty year period referred to in Article 33.

107. The US has not alleged and there is otherwise no evidence that shows that any Old Act applicant that sought a term of protection that was at least equal to a twenty year period measured from its application filing date, was refused a term that met the minimum Article 33 standard. All of the evidence is to the contrary. In the words of the Chairman of the Patent Appeal Board:

> An applicant can achieve a delay in processing simply by asking the patent examiner. In my personal experience, I am unaware of any such request being refused.[41]

108. On the strength of this evidence, Canada submits that its Old Act or section 45 system made the minimum twenty year from date of filing term of protection available both in law and in **practice** to every Old Act applicant. And Canada did so without exception.

109. In the result, and given the factual availability in Canadian law and **practice** of the term of protection referred to in Article 33, Canada reiterates its submission that, in deciding to maintain both the section 44 and the section 45 methods for the specification of the term of protection in the course of implementing its TRIPS obligations, it acted

v. Novopharm Limited and Geneva Pharmaceuticals, Inc., 1996 WL 131498 (N.D. Ill) at *4. Both reproduced as Exhibit No. 14.

[41] Davies affidavit, subparagraph 10.i). Mr. Davies tenure with the Canadian Patent Office exceeds 33 years (Davies affidavit, para. 1).

within the scope of the freedom afforded Members under paragraph 1 of Article 1 "...to determine the appropriate method of implementing the provisions of [the] Agreement within their own legal system and practice.".

110. In summary conclusion, here again Canada submits that the fact that the term of protection referred to in Article 33 was available under the Canadian law and practice relating to section 45 patents is, by itself, sufficient to dispose of the US complaint.

D. Article 70

111. Canada has demonstrated that the substantive or "effective" term of protection accorded by section 45 is equivalent or superior to and consistent with the substantive or "effective" term contemplated by and available under the Article 33 obligation. Canada has, as well, demonstrated that under the law and practice relating to section 45 the term of protection contemplated by Article 33 was available without exception to every Old Act applicant.

112. Canada further submits that, notwithstanding the substantive or "effective" equivalency with, and the practical availability of, the term of protection contemplated by Article 33 under Canadian law and practice, the Article 33 obligation does not apply retroactively to patents granted by the Commissioner of Patents prior to January 1, 1996.

113. Old Act patents issued prior to January 1, 1996 were granted by the administrative act of the Commissioner of Patents and are not subject to the obligations in the TRIPS Agreement by virtue of the express language of paragraph 1 of Article 70 which, for ease of reference, is reproduced here in its entirety:

> This Agreement does not give rise to obligations in respect of acts which occurred before the date of application of the Agreement for the Member in question.

114. Read in the context of paragraph 1 the word "act" is not qualified as referring to any particular type or class of act. The only limitation contained in the paragraph is the temporal one which restricts the application of the paragraph to acts which occur before the date of application of the Agreement for the Member in question.

115. In contrast to its use in paragraph 1 of Article 70, wherever the word "act" is used elsewhere in the TRIPS text, its application and meaning is specifically limited or qualified by the context of its use or modifying references which are associated with its use.

116. "Act" or "acts" is, for example, qualified in: Article 22.2(b) to refer to 'acts of unfair competition'; Articles 26.1, 28.1(a) and (b), 36, 41.1 and 70.4 to refer to acts of infringement, potential infringement or unauthorized use; Article 37 and its heading to refer to acts not requiring the authorization of the right holder; Article 50.7 to refer to acts or omissions of a right holder in relation to provisional measures; and, in Article 58 to refer to acts of competent authorities in relation to the execution of border measures.

117. It is obvious from this pattern of use that had the TRIPS negotiators intended to limit the meaning of "acts" in paragraph 1 of Article 70 to a specific meaning such as "acts of infringement" they would have done so, just as they did in Articles 26.1, 28.1(a) and (b), 36, 41.1 and 70.4. That they did not use such words of modification argues that it was deliberate and they did not intend a limited or qualified meaning.

118. There is, as the Chairman of the Negotiating Group on TRIPS notes in his forward to Daniel Gervais's book on the TRIPS Agreement[42], no authoritative negotiating history or formal record of the TRIPS negotiation available to assist those involved in the application and interpretation of the Agreement in determining the meaning or intended meaning of the Agreement. Daniel Gervais's history and analysis, however, provides a useful substitute for a more formal record of the deliberations of the negotiators.

119. In the passages of Dr. Gervais's analysis commenting on Article 70 he explains the rule in paragraph 1 of the Article in the following terms:

> The first rule is simple: **acts** (including infringing acts) that occurred before the date of application of the Agreement...to a Member do not give rise to obligations for the Member on the territory of which those acts occurred. ***This is non-retroactivity. ... There are no exceptions to the first rule in Article 70.***[43] (**Bold** emphasis in the original. ***Bold, italicized*** emphasis added.)

120. Thus both the textual evidence and expert commentary lead to the conclusion that the word "acts" as used in paragraph 1 of Article 70 has a broader meaning than the US implies in its sparsely expounded analysis.

121. The US relies solely on paragraph 2 of Article 70 to establish its allegation that Article 33 must be applied to Old Act patents which existed on the date of application of TRIPS for Canada. Paragraph 2 of Article 70 provides, in material part, that:

> **Except as otherwise provided for in this Agreement**, this Agreement gives rise to obligations in respect of all subject matter existing at the date of application of this Agreement for the Member in question, and which is protected in that Member on the said date, or which meets or comes subsequently to meet the criteria for protection under the terms of this Agreement. (Emphasis added)

122. In its self-described "exceedingly simple" analysis of this case the US has failed to take any account of the "Except as otherwise provided for in this Agreement" words which introduce paragraph 2 of Article 70. In ignoring these words, the US also fails to take any account of the rule in paragraph 1 of Article 70 which Dr. Gervais has described as a "simple" rule respecting non-retroactivity and from which he says "there are no exceptions.".

123. In the *India - Patent Protection* case, a case relied on by the US in its first written submission, the Appellate Body, citing paragraph 2 of Article 19 of the ***WTO Understanding on Rules and Procedures Governing the Settlement of Disputes (1994)*** (Understanding),[44] noted in the sentence immediately following the passage cited by the US, that in interpreting a treaty it is **not** appropriate to read into a treaty words or concepts that are not there, so as to lend meaning and context to the Agreement. In the words of the Appellate Body:

> The duty of a treaty interpreter is to examine the words of the treaty to determine the intention of the parties. This should be done in accordance with the principles

---

[42] Daniel Gervais, *The TRIPS Agreement: Drafting History and Analysis*, (Sweet & Maxwell: London, 1998). Forward by Lars Arnell page vii at page viii. See too the Preface by Gervais himself at page ix. Reproduced in pertinent part as Exhibit No. 15.

[43] Gervais, 268.

[44] Article 19, para. 2 provides that:

> In accordance with para. 2 of Article 3, in their findings and recommendations, the panel and Appellate Body **cannot add to or diminish** the rights and obligations provided in the covered agreements. (Emphasis added)

> of treaty interpretation set out in Article 31 of the *Vienna Convention*. But these principles of interpretation neither require nor condone the imputation into the treaty of words that are not there or the importation into a treaty of concepts that were not intended.[45]

124. The obvious corollary of this rule against the **adding of words and concepts** to a treaty is that 'the principles of interpretation neither require nor condone the **subtraction of words or concepts** from a treaty' simply because it suits the interpreter's purposes.

125. The idea that subtraction of words and concepts is no more acceptable than the idea of addition of words and concepts, is an idea that is not simply applicable to the Panel and Appellate Body jurisdiction to make recommendations as was the case where the Appellate Body made reference to paragraph 2 of Article 19 of the Understanding in the *India - Patent Protection* case. It is also an idea that operates, as a general rule of the Understanding, to discipline the Dispute Settlement Body itself. This general rule is set out in paragraph 2 of Article 3 which provides that:

> The dispute settlement system of the WTO is a central element in providing security and predictability to the multilateral trading system. The Members recognize that it serves to preserve the rights and obligations of Members under the covered agreements, and to clarify the existing provisions of those agreements in accordance with customary rules of interpretation of public international law. **Recommendations and rulings of the DSB cannot add to or diminish the rights and obligations provided in the covered agreements.** (Emphasis added)

126. In the presence of these rules of construction Canada notes that on its plain language paragraph 1 of Article 70 is a proviso 'otherwise set out in the Agreement' which trumps the selected passage of the application provision upon which the US relies and which immediately follows both the rule in paragraph 1 and the words of exception which introduce the provisions of paragraph 2 that the US contends are applicable to this case.

127. Canada also notes that WTO jurisprudence is unequivocal in holding that the onus lies on the complaining party to establish a *prima facie* case of non-compliance. In the *United States - Woven Wool Shirts* case the Appellate Body expressed this principle as follows:

> ...a party claiming a violation of a provision of the *WTO Agreement* by another Member must assert and prove its claim. ... India did so in this case. And, with India having done so, the onus then shifted to the United States to bring forward evidence and argument to disprove the claim. This, the United States was not able to do...[46]

128. Canada further notes that under Article 28 of the *Vienna Convention on the Law of Treaties* (Convention) there is a codified presumption against the retroactive application of treaty obligations which applies "Unless a different intention appears from the treaty or is otherwise established...". In its reliance on a selective portion of paragraph 2 of Article 70 the US has not shown any "different intention", nor has it "otherwise established" a contrary intention to the TRIPS codification of the Convention rule against the retroactive application of treaty provisions to matters that pre-date its coming into effect.

---

[45] *India - Patent Protection For Pharmaceutical And Agricultural Chemical*, *supra*, footnote 2, para. 45.

[46] *United States - Measures Affecting Imports of Woven Wool Shirts and Blouses from India*, WT/DS33/AB/R, adopted 23 May 1997, DSR 1997:I, 323, at 337.

129. It is, therefore, Canada's position that the US legal analysis supporting its allegation that the obligation in Article 33 applies to section 45 patents does not establish a *prima facie* case of non-compliance.

130. It does not do so because that analysis relies solely on a **selected part** of paragraph 2 of Article 70 and fails to take any account of either the opening subordinating phrase of that paragraph or of the scope and application of the obviously related general rule against the retroactive application of the Agreement set out in the immediately preceding provisions of paragraph 1 of Article 70.

E. Conclusion

131. In summary it is Canada's position that:

(a) the substantive or "effective" term of protection available under section 45 of the ***Patent Act*** is equivalent or superior to and consistent with the substantive or "effective" term of protection described by Articles 33 and 62 and does not therefore breach any TRIPS obligation;

(b) the minimum term of protection described by Article 33 is and has, without exception, been available under the Canadian law and practice relating to section 45 patents; and,

(c) the US has failed to establish that Article 33 has retroactive application to patents issued against applications filed prior to October 1, 1989 and granted by the Commissioner of Patents prior to January 1, 1996.

V. DISPOSITION REQUESTED

132. Canada requests that the Panel established to examine this matter and to make such findings as will assist the Dispute Settlement Body in making its recommendations or making its rulings in respect of the conformity of section 45 of the ***Patent Act*** with Canada's treaty obligations, find that:

(a) the term of patent protection available under section 45 is equivalent or superior to and is consistent and in conformity with the term of patent protection described by Article 33;

(b) the minimum term of protection described by Article 33 is and has been available, without exception, under the Canadian law and practice relating to section 45 patents;

(c) by virtue of paragraph 1 of Article 70, Article 33 does not have retroactive application to patents granted by the Commissioner of Patents prior to January 1, 1996; and,

on the basis of those findings, conclude that section 45 of Canada's ***Patent Act*** conforms with its obligations under the TRIPS Agreement.

ATTACHMENT 2.2

ORAL STATEMENT OF CANADA AT THE FIRST MEETING WITH THE PANEL

(20 December 1999)

I. INTRODUCTION

1. Mr. Chairman and members of the panel, my name is Ted Thompson and it is my privilege to present Canada's oral argument today. With me are my colleagues, Mr. Rob Sutherland-Brown and Mr. Reagan Walker who may assist me in presenting Canada's case. The other members of the Canadian delegation are: Catherine Dickson and Mark Wigmore.

II. BACKGROUND

2. On January 1, 1995, Canada and the United States as founding Members of the WTO, assumed important new treaty obligations. Canada treats these obligations seriously. Included are the obligations flowing from the Agreement on Trade Related Aspects of Intellectual Property Rights. As you know, its application date in respect to Canada was January 1, 1996. TRIPS imposes a number of new disciplines which are intended, among other things described in the recitals, to promote adequate protection of intellectual property rights. It also (in sub paragraph C of the recitals) recognised the need to take into account differences in national legal systems. Indeed, Art. 1.1 makes specific provision for this.

3. TRIPS while concerned with protecting private intellectual property rights recognises that this has to be achieved in a wider universe. And so, we find in the statements of Objectives and Principles set out in Arts. 7 and 8 that the protection and enforcement of these private rights must be achieved "in a manner conducive to social and economic welfare and to a balance of rights and obligations" and as well permitting Members to formulate laws which "promote the public interest in sectors of vital importance to their socio-economic and technological development provided the measures are consistent with the provisions of this Agreement".

4. In Canada's view, these words are not idle platitudes; they are to be given force and meaning. Interpreting an important Agreement such as TRIPS is not a mechanical exercise, rather it requires a careful examination of the rights actually intended to be protected and a balancing of those rights within the context of the agreement's explicit allowances for dissimilar legal systems and the broader interests of society.

5. I know the panel will bear these overarching considerations in mind as it considers Canada's response to the U.S. complaint that Canada's patent term protection measures are not fully compliant with the obligation articulated in Art. 33.

6. In presenting its oral argument, Canada of course relies on its first written submission which it is confident has been carefully read. To the extent Canada makes references to legal authorities or other supplementary materials, in the course of its oral presentation, they will be suitably identified in the written version of this presentation.

7. Canada will present argument on three issues. The first two are independent stand-alone arguments. They present Canada's position that the impugned measure, which we are calling for convenience a "section 45 patent", is compliant with TRIPS.

8. First, Canada states the "period of protection" when properly construed afforded by a s.45 patent is equivalent or superior to the period of protection contemplated by Art. 33.

9. Second, Canada states a period of 20 years from filing in the terms of Art. 33 was "available" to all applicants for s.45 patents without exception. This availability is demonstrable and rooted to a "sound legal basis" to use the standard approved by the Appellate Body in the India - Patent Protection case.

10. Canada's third and final argument is that the U.S. in alleging Canada's term of patent protection is non-compliant failed to establish a prima facie case that the obligation set out in Art. 33 has retroactive application to s.45 patents which exist as a result of acts which occurred before the date of application of the Agreement to Canada. Canada will also comment on the introduction of so called "subsequent practice" evidence by the U.S.

11. With your permission, I will now turn to Canada's first argument, which is elaborated, in our first written submission at paragraphs 67 to 83.

III. ARGUMENT 1

12. In considering this argument, I would ask you to consider a basic question in respect of Art. 33. That is: What is "the term of protection"?

13. The answer to this question is fundamental to resolving the issue in dispute. The U.S. would have you accept that a period of protection that does not end before 20 years from filing - means a patent is guaranteed 20 years of protection. But this in Canada's submission is clearly not the case. The Agreement does not provide for 20 years of effective patent protection.

14. The very name of this dispute, Canada - Term of *Patent* Protection, suggests this conclusion. The inviolate condition precedent to a term of protection under Art. 33 is a patent. This obvious statement has real meaning. Understanding and applying it will have a direct result on the success of Canada's first argument.

15. Art. 33 is part of Section 5 of TRIPS which is entitled - Patents. Art. 33 in turn is titled Term of Protection. The term of protection is therefore directly related to the existence of a patent.

16. A patent does not exist until it is issued. That being said, it is evident that there is a period of time between the date of filing and the issuance of a patent, which does not benefit from the Art. 33 "term of protection" because very simply, there is no patent to protect during that interregnum.

17. This period of time will vary depending on the particular circumstances. It follows that a "patent term of protection" as contemplated by Art. 33 is not as the U.S. argues a fixed minimum period of 20 years, but a variable period of less than 20 years depending on the date of issue in relation to the date of filing. This fact was observed by Prof. Vaver as noted in paragraph 26 of Canada's first written submission.

18. The negotiators were also aware of this result as is plain from Art. 62.2 which suggests process time should be completed in a reasonable time - "so as to avoid unwarranted curtailment of the period of protection".

19. It is clear from the plain language of Art. 62.2 that the period of protection is known and accepted to be curtailed by the procedures necessary for grant or registration. The term of protection must *a fortiori* be a variable period of less than 20 years measured from the filing date. In commenting on Art. 62.2, Dr. Gervais writes in his book at page 239, "Curtailment could also refer to a general diminution of the value of the protection,

however, and thus include delaying in an unwarranted ("unjustifiable") fashion the beginning of the period of protection which may affect the right holder very negatively indeed".

20. How does this variable period inscribed in Art. 33 compare with the definite period of 17 years guaranteed by s.45?

21. The Chairman of Canada's Patent Appeal Board has said in paragraph 29 of his affidavit (Exhibit 8) that in Canada the normal or average period to process a "new Act" or s.44 patent application is 60 months or 5 years. This leaves an average period of 15 years for the term of protection contemplated by Art. 33, which will vary, up or down depending on circumstances. (Here refer to Exhibit F to Davies Affidavit)

22. Under the old Act regime, there is a minimum 17 year term of protection, which follows whatever the process time is from the date of filing. The old Act term of protection is clearly equivalent. A guaranteed period of protection of 17 years measured against a variable term ranging up or down from 15 years depending on circumstances is in fact superior to the TRIPS standard.

23. It is important to recall that the ability to control the process period is very much in the hands of the applicant. I will describe this in more detail in a moment in presenting Canada's 2nd argument. However, as noted in paragraph 80 of Canada's first written submission, the U.S. appears to have recognised the equivalency of the two terms as one of the parties to NAFTA. In Art. 1709.12 of NAFTA, the parties have approved two separate terms as acceptable; namely 20 years from filing *or* disjunctively 17 years from grant. Either term is acceptable, to the U.S. under NAFTA.

24. In paragraph 81 of its first written submission, Canada summarizes its argument on this issue. It notes that the term of real or effective protection under the 20 years from filing formula is variable depending on the process time. Accordingly, it does not lend itself to a simple arithmetic or mechanical application with an axiomatic result as suggested by the U.S. in paragraph 3 of its first written submission.

25. The U.S. argues that thousands of U.S. patentees have suffered harm as a result of time deficient 17 year patents (see for example paragraphs 4,5,6 of its first written submission). Canada says that this allegation is without foundation.

26. Again, under the s.44 patent regime, Canada has demonstrated that in Canada the average or normal period of effective protection is 15 years, that is 20 years from filing less processing time, whereas s.45 patents have a fixed 17 year patent term. The U.S. argument holds that a s.45 patent holder who chose to have his patent issue in less than three years from filing is entitled as of right to a commercial windfall, because of a subsequent configuration of patent term protection it wants applied retroactively. Notwithstanding, the period of effective protection is two years longer than the normal period to be expected under the new system, the applicant is entitled to even more protection because the process time, a period that is offered no protection under Art. 33, presents an arithmetical advantage. Canada, as I understand the U.S. position, must now give effect to some notional or artificial advantage that confers no real benefit under the new system and disavows the original bargain with society without conferring any balancing benefits.

27. This, with respect, is inconsistent with the stated objects and principles of the Agreement. It is to require that someone who is receiving substantively more under the old system than normally available under the new, be given yet more. To what end? So that Pfizer to use the U.S. example can extend its term of exclusivity for 14 months and enjoy windfall sales. Someone has to pay and the additional costs will be imposed on the Canadian consumer. Competitive manufacturers who have made plans and investments based on one system of laws will have to be told we retroactively changed the rules. This can only result in marketplace disruptions even if compensation is paid. This will not

promote competition, trade, innovation, socio-economic development or the transfer and dissemination of technology. You will search in vain for such benefits flowing from the U.S. position.

28. Such a result can only flow from a narrow and selective reading of the agreement and does not achieve protection in the language of TRIPS Art. 7, " in a manner conducive to social and economic welfare and to a balance of rights and obligations".

29. Giving support to such a mechanical application of Art. 33 will serve the ends of windfall profits and undermine the broader principles of the WTO to "promote the public interest". No reasonable expectations or legitimate interests of patent holders will be prejudiced by accepting and recognising the equivalency of these two systems. A s.45 patent holder has 17 years of full effective protection. There are no accrued rights associated with these patents that would be adversely affected by refusing to adopt the gratuitous windfall position advanced by the U.S. Giving effect to the U.S. position will disrupt commercial investment and visit increased costs on Canadian consumers.

IV. ARGUMENT 2

30. Canada's second argument supplies an independent reason for denying the U.S. complaint. (It is detailed in paragraphs 84 to 110 of Canada first written submission) It is also complementary of its first argument.

31. Like the first argument, it arises from a plain reading of the language of Art. 33.

32. Art. 33 states simply "the term of protection available" shall not end ...etc.

33. Available means something capable of being used, at hand or obtainable. S.45 is of course silent about a filing date although that is what starts the process to obtain a patent. Is or was 20 years from filing available under the old Act system? Peter Davies the Chairman of Canada's Patent Appeal Board and a man of 33 years experience in the field says it was and that it was available without exception.

34. In his affidavit (Exhibit 8) at paragraph 10(i) he says an applicant can achieve a process delay simply by asking. He is unaware of a delay ever being refused. The time was there for the asking.

35. Neither s.45 nor any other law or requirement of Canada purports to limit or restrict the period of protection available to less than 20 years from filing. As a matter of Canadian law and practice it is available for the asking. It may be argued perhaps that applicants couldn't make informed choices because it wasn't an issue before 1986 when Canada tabled Bill C-22. What is true on all the evidence is that if somebody wanted to delay the issuance of their grant, they could. The time was there for the asking in almost unlimited amounts if you consider the more than 1000 s.45 patent applications, which are still pending.

36. The Appellate Body in India - Patent Protection had the opportunity to consider what standard a member must meet under Art. 1.1 of TRIPS. By way of reminder Mr. Chairman, you will recall that s.5 of India's Patent Act prohibited issuing patents for certain pharmaceutical and agricultural chemical products. India, relying on the Art. 1.1 freedom to determine the appropriate method of implementing the provisions of the Agreement within its own legal system and practice purported to meet the obligations of Art. 70.8 of TRIPS by issuing "administrative instructions" by which applications for patents in respect of the prohibited products could be filed with filing dates assigned to them.

37. At paragraph 59 of its report, the Appellate Body affirmed a Member could rely on Art. 1.1 in meeting its obligations but concluded at paragraphs 70 and 71 of the report that India's administrative instructions did not provide a sound legal basis for preserving the novelty of inventions and priority of applications as of the relevant filing dates and accordingly the measure was inconsistent with Art. 70.8(a) of TRIPS.

38. Earlier in its reasons, the Appellate Body at paragraphs 56 and 57 affirmed the legal test established in the Panel report under appeal namely that "means" employed to meet an obligation under TRIPS must provide a "sound legal basis" to protect or preserve the right or interest in question.

39. The obligation set out in Art. 33 is to make available a term of protection that does not end before 20 years measured from the filing date. As I will explain in a moment, it is Canada's position that it has provided a legal mechanism in its laws through which an applicant can obtain 20 years from filing. And therefore Canada has provided a "sound legal basis" for such a term of protection.

40. S.45 patent term protection is not described in language that is similar to the language employed in Art. 33. S.45, unlike India's Patent Act, does not purport to prohibit or limit a benefit available under TRIPS.

41. The evidence of Mr. Davies (Exhibit 8) is unequivocal that the 20 years from filing date was available and he describes how patent applicants could exercise control over the pendency period between filing and grant in paragraphs 9, 10 and 11 of his affidavit.

42. It is clear that the obligation under Art. 33 is to make the period available. It does not require a member to impose that period against the revealed preference of the applicant. Under the Patent Act and its accompanying rules, the applicant could exercise control. The applicant could do so informally, simply by asking, or alternatively the applicant could take advantage of statutorily mandated delays for perfecting applications and other essential procedural steps.

43. Consistent with the analysis in the India-Patent Protection dispute Canada submits that the time periods established by statute for an applicant to prosecute its application provides the "means" by which Canada makes the term of protection available and the fact they are statutory rights establishes the "sound legal basis". Under Canada's Patent Act, unlike the administrative instructions to India's officials, Canadian officials are not required to ignore statutory provisions, but to give effect to them. Under s.30 (1) of the old Act, which is being distributed to you now, there are two time frames established for completing certain acts under penalty of an application being deemed abandoned, the first is 12 months to complete an application after filing and the second is 6 months to prosecute the application after notice that an examiner has taken action. Under s.30 (2), an applicant is provided a period of 12 months to apply to have an abandoned application reinstated. When each of these process delays are added, together, that is; 12 months to complete the application plus where one fails to do so a further 12 months to have it reinstated plus 6 months to prosecute the application plus, where one fails to so prosecute, a further 12 months for re-instatement, it can be seen that s.30 alone permits delays of 42 months or 3.5 years available to any applicant who chooses to take advantage of the provisions. (Canada Exhibit 16)

44. A second statutory delay is found in s.73 of the old Act. That section provides a period of up to 6 months to pay the prescribed fees in a notice of allowance on penalty of forfeiture. A forfeited application may be restored within 6 months from incurrence on payment of the prescribed fees. This makes a further year of delay available from the filing date. When one adds the delays from filing available under s.30 and s.73 to the 17

year patent term protection from grant, the total amounts to a statutorily available term of 21.5 years from date of filing. Of course none of these delays take account of the time required for a patent examiner to complete an examination or the potential for multiple additional delays to provide requested information to an examiner during that process.

45. There is a difference between the delays provided in s.30 and s.73 of the old Patent Act. Under the latter section reinstatement is automatic on payment of the prescribed fees; however, under s.30 (2) the applicant must satisfy the Commissioner the reason for the delay was not reasonably avoidable. This discretion not to allow reinstatement does not undermine the "sound legal basis" of the statutory scheme for several reasons.

46. First, as we have noted in Canada's first written submission at paragraph 95, pursuant to Art. 62.1 of TRIPS, Members may require compliance with reasonable procedures to maintain intellectual property rights. That is exactly what the discretion in s.30 (2) provides.

47. Second, as Mr. Davies affidavit (Exhibit 8) affirms at paragraph 10(iii) an abandoned application can be reinstated. A search of Canadian jurisprudence reveals there has never been a challenge based on reinstatement being disallowed under s.30 (2) of the old Act. Mr. Davies has sworn he is unaware of any delay being refused. Finally, the consequence of a refusal if there ever was one is only that the process would have to be recommenced with a new application. This results in further delay, which is presumably what the applicant desired.

48. In light of the continued secrecy protection and the "first to invent" regime for resolving conflicting claims the applicant/inventor's rights are at no risk. You will recall that under the old Act, trade secrets are protected indefinitely until a patent is issued; and that conflicting claims are resolved in favour of the first to invent.

49. Accordingly, under the old Act regime, a bona fide inventor was at no risk during the period his application for patent was pending or abandoned. Applicants were vested with the right to expedite, delay or let the process proceed at its natural pace. These rights, being those of the applicant, were exercised according to their interest and not the Canadian government. Indeed, Mr. Davies at paragraph 23 of his affidavit has identified approximately 1000 old Act applications that are still pending.

50. The U.S. complaint, while it embraces all patent subject matter is driven by elements of the pharmaceutical industry. The U.S. admits as much in its first written submission at paragraphs 5 and 6 by using Pfizer Inc. as an example. Pfizer sued Canada unsuccessfully, earlier this year, in an attempt to have its "Zoloft" patent extended. Bristol-Myers Squibb has orchestrated media campaigns encouraging other s.45 patent holders to demand the type of extensions that the U.S. alleges are required by TRIPS. To date, none have been forthcoming.

51. If we examine the s.45 patent portfolios of some major drug manufacturers, the availability of terms as long or longer than twenty years from filing is manifest. Mr. Davies has appended graphic depictions of this as Exhibit E to his affidavit. I will not take you through all of them but have chosen three as illustrative, Pfizer Canada Inc., Bristol-Myers Squibb and Merck Frosst Canada (Exhibit E at page 10, 4 and 8 respectively). The graphs show the term of protection for the portfolio of s.45 patents in relation to 20 years from filing which equals 0. (Here use overhead depiction and describe)

52. Although the right to extend s.45 patents beyond 20 years from filing has not always been exercised, it is plainly apparent that it is obtainable or available if desired.

53. The U.S. has also led evidence in addition to Zoloft of ten other non-pharmaceutical s.45 patents, which according to their argument are term deficient. The ten selected patents were issued on December 28, 1998. There were in fact 500 s.45 patents

issued on that date; 77% had terms greater than 20 years from filing which in Canada's submission is further confirmatory evidence of the availability of such a term. (Canada Exhibit 17)

54. It is unambiguously the case that an applicant relying solely on statutorily mandated delays can arrange its affairs so as to obtain 20 years of protection from the filing date under the old Act regime. Those that did not received the right to their exclusive patents early and can exploit them for a full 17 years. As in the Abbott case referred to in paragraph 100 of Canada's first written submission, those who made that choice must accept both the benefits and the consequences. Pfizer, for example, through the U.S. complaint is asking the WTO to give it the full benefit of both regimes even though it had no legitimate right to both terms when it decided to have its patent issue.

55. Before turning to Canada's final argument, it is useful to consider the underlying purpose of Art. 33. Dr. Gervais at page 169 of his book, indicates the goal was to achieve harmonization of the term of protection among member states. Canada has provided the twenty year from filing formulation since 1989. Dr. Gervais also made the following observation:

> "During the negotiation, attempts were made to extend protection for certain products the marketing of which is often delayed by regulatory approval processes, notably pharmaceuticals. No such provision is included in the final version".

56. Statutory mandated delays aside, the complexity of the approval process alone caused such delays that consideration to extending the 20 year term was debated and given some recognition in Art. 62.2.

57. It is apparent that for the pharmaceutical companies who are driving this complaint it may well have required extra effort to expedite their s.45 applications in order to avoid a delayed term of protection which would not start before three years after the date of filing.

V. ARGUMENT 3, Art. 70 - (paragraphs 111 to 130 Canada's first written submission)

58. In order to found a complaint of non compliance, the U.S. must at a minimum establish a prima facie case that Art. 33 has application to s.45 patents. In Canada's submission, the U.S. has failed this threshold standard.

59. Art. 28 of the Vienna Convention is directly relevant here. It raises a presumption against the retroactive application of treaties in relation to any act or fact or situation, which ceased to exist before the date a treaty, comes into force. "Unless a different intention appears from the treaty or is otherwise established". Because of their obvious potential to negatively impact on accrued rights and interests, Canada submits that retroactive provisions, where there is any doubt as to their scope or meaning, should be construed narrowly.

60. To meet this challenge to demonstrate a treaty obligation has retroactive application, the U.S. has chosen to rely on a selective passage in Art. 70.2 without reference to is context. That is just not good enough.

61. Canada readily concedes that presenting a coherent, consistent and complete interpretative rationale for Art. 70 and each of its paragraphs is a daunting task. In light of Canada's first two arguments, it is a task this panel may not have to undertake. But that does not relieve the U.S. of its evidential burden.

62. As the Appellate Body wrote in Brazil-Desiccated Coconut:

> "Absent a contrary intention, a treaty cannot apply to acts or facts which took place, or situations which ceased to exist, before the date of entry into force". (Brazil-Measures Affecting Desiccated Coconut WT/DS22/AB/R, 21 February 1997 at page 15)

63. The legal analysis in U.S. first written submission does not even attempt to address the clear affirmation of Art. 28 of the Vienna Convention expressed in Art. 70.1. In fact, it does not acknowledge the paragraph in any way.

64. Art. 70.1 is brief and bears repeating in its complete text:

> "This Agreement does not give rise to obligations in respect of acts which occurred before the date of application of the Agreement for the member in question".

65. In Canada's submission, it is for the U.S. to demonstrate that this clear and unambiguous language has no application to s.45 patents issued before January 1, 1996. Canada notes that the act of filing an application is necessary to trigger the time period in Art. 33 and the administrative act of issuing a patent is necessary to trigger the term of patent protection that may occur in the course of that time period.

66. In paragraph 11 of its first submission, the U.S. without explanation, discussion or analysis equates patents with "subject matter". Let us consider Art 70.2 for a moment; it commences with the following words:

> "Except as otherwise provided for in this Agreement, this Agreement gives rise to obligations in respect of all subject matter existing at the date of application of this Agreement".

67. In TRIPS as is clear from the sub-heading of Art. 27 patents are not subject matter. Some subject matter is patentable; that is capable of being patented but the patent itself is not subject matter. A patent is a grant of an exclusive right for a specific period of time by a government, it is not the subject matter of that grant. The expression "subject matter" clearly refers to matter that is protectable by intellectual property rights and not the vehicle through which they are protected.

68. The U.S. theory of Art. 33 applying to s.45 patents is therefore both incomplete and misconstrued.

69. There is one further argument advanced by the U.S. that Canada will address at this time.

Argument on Subsequent Practice

70. In the U.S. first written submission at paragraph 15, it is alleged that the subsequent practice of certain WTO Members has established the general agreement of all Members with the American interpretation of TRIPS, Arts. 33 and 70.

71. Canada submits that subsequent practice is a rule of evidence and not a canon of interpretation. As Lord McNair has described, it:

> ...subsequent practice of the parties is not so much a principle of interpretation as a rule of evidence. "It is a question of the probative value of the practice of the parties as indicative of what the treaty means."[1]

---

[1] Lord McNair. *The Law of Treaties*. Oxford (Clarendon Press:1961), p. 427

72. It is necessary to examine the U.S. evidence in order to see what it proves. In Canada's submission, that evidence falls well short of establishing the agreement of all WTO Members with the American interpretation. For such an agreement to be established, evidence of a common understanding as to the application of these provisions in the same, or at least, similar, circumstances, would be required. The rule is described in the Encyclopaedia of Public International Law Vol. 2 at page 1421 in these words:

> "Subsequent practice must be more or less uniform and accepted by the parties in order to furnish a valid means of treaty interpretation."

73. In paragraph 17 of its first written submission the U.S. lists five WTO Members who allegedly amended their laws to comply with the mentioned TRIPS provisions in the same way as the US did: Australia, Germany, Greece, New Zealand and Portugal. But the circumstances in these Members was not the same, or even similar, to Canada's disputed measure.

74. Each of the first three countries mentioned had, prior to TRIPS, a term from filing system. Because that system fell short of 20 years protection, - 15 years from filing for Greece; 16 years from filing for Australia, and 18 years from filing for Germany; each of these was deficient in terms of the 20 years from filing obligation of TRIPS, Art. 33. Apparently uniquely, New Zealand established that; "S.30 (3) The term of every patent shall be 20 years from the date of the patent" (U.S. first submission Exhibit 9 page 59).

75. Canada's term from filing system was already at the level of 20 years of protection at the time the TRIPS Agreement took effect and had been at that same level ever since the relevant provisions of Bill C-22 came into force, i.e. on 1 October 1989. This fact is not in issue in this dispute.

76. The U.S. offers no evidence of the existence of a subsequent practice establishing an agreed application of the Agreement to term-from-grant patents.

77. The only WTO Member having a term-from-grant system, that is mentioned by the U.S. as agreeing with the American interpretation, is Portugal. However, it is obvious that Portugal did not amend its legislation of its own volition.

78. Whereas the other WTO Members mentioned by the U.S. all passed legislation in 1994 or 1995, in anticipation of their TRIPS obligations. Portugal did not do so until much later. And this was only because the U.S. initiated a WTO Panel proceeding against them. When a country amends its legislation and applies a provision of a treaty in order to resolve a trade dispute, it is **not** necessarily evidence of a common understanding of the meaning of the provision. Indeed, it is only the exceptional case that is settled solely on the basis that one party has decided the other was right in its position. (Canada notes, with some curiosity, that the U.S. initiated its complaint against Portugal in 1996 but has waited until 1999 to commence a similar complaint against Canada).

79. The reality is that the U.S. is alone in its interpretation of how Arts. 33 and 70 apply to term-from-grant systems. It is also the case that the U.S. has no evidence to demonstrate its legal system and practice or any of the Members it identifies are in any way similar to Canada's. The international law commentators and the WTO Appellate Body alike are agreed that a unilateral interpretation by one of the parties to a treaty does not establish a subsequent practice so as to be binding on other parties. The Appellate Body in Japan-Taxes on Alcoholic Beverages put it in the following terms:

> "...the essence of subsequent practice in interpreting a treaty has been recognized as a 'concordant, common and consistent' sequence of acts or pronouncements which is sufficient to establish a discernible pattern implying the agreement of the parties regarding its interpretation. **An isolated act is generally not sufficient to establish subsequent practice...** (emphasis added)"

80. Canada submits that the U.S. has submitted no subsequent practice evidence capable of assisting the Panel in interpreting the relevant provisions of the TRIPS Agreement.

VI. CONCLUSION

81. In summary, Canada asserts that the U.S. has failed to meet the evidentiary burden to establish that Art. 33 has application to Canada's s.45 patent regime. Even assuming Art. 33 is applicable, a term of protection as described in that paragraph has always been available under both of Canada's patent regimes. As well, the guaranteed term of protection of 17 years from grant prescribed by s.45 is equivalent to the variable term of effective protection which arises under the Art. 33 formulation.

82. That concludes Canada's first oral submission and we appreciate the close attention you have given our remarks.

ATTACHMENT 2.3

RESPONSES OF CANADA TO WRITTEN QUESTIONS FROM THE PANEL - FIRST MEETING

(7 January 2000)

I. REPLIES OF CANADA TO QUESTIONS FROM THE PANEL ADDRESSED TO BOTH PARTIES

Q.1 *Article 62.2 provides that Members are to ensure that the procedures for granting intellectual property rights allow granting of the right "within a reasonable period of time so as to avoid unwarranted curtailment" of the protection period.

(a) What would constitute an "unwarranted curtailment" of a patent protection term?

In answering this and associated questions Canada believes that it is critical to bear in mind that Article 62 of TRIPS is specifically concerned with giving the treaty's sanction to the erosion of nominal terms of protection which occur where the term begins on the application filing date but the intellectual property right at issue is subject to reasonable pre-registration or pre-granting procedures that have the effect of curtailing the actual length of the term of protection accorded to the rights holder.

The Article is therefore relevant to the term of protection accorded to patents governed by section 44 of the Canadian ***Patent Act*** (Act) but not to patents governed by section 45 of the Act. The United States of America (US), the complaining party in this dispute, has neither challenged nor otherwise put in issue, any attribute of section 44 patents or the system by which they are granted.

With these considerations in mind Canada would begin its answer to this specific question by observing that "unwarranted" means "unauthorized, unjustified" and that "curtailment" means "cut short, deprive of".[1] Taken together in the phrase "unwarranted curtailment", the two words would therefore mean: An unauthorized or unjustified cutting short of something, in this case, the period of protection associated with a patent. The phrase expresses an ordinal concept which, like the analogous ordinal concepts of "unreasonableness" and "undueness", must take its meaning from the facts and circumstances that are relevant in the context of its use. In other words "unwarranted curtailment" is a question of fact to be determined in the particular circumstances in which the curtailment occurs.

Thus to know what may constitute "unwarranted curtailment" treaty interpreters must, in the context of the "reasonable procedures and formalities that Members may require as prerequisites" for the application, approval, granting and maintenance of patents, examine the procedures and formalities in issue and decide: whether they are "authorized", in the current context, by statutory or regulatory provisions of a Member or, where they flow from administrative practices and rules, whether they are justified by the nature and purpose of the application-approval and granting processes.

---

[1] *The Concise Oxford Dictionary of Current English, Seventh Edition, (Oxford: The Claredon Press, 1982).*

In this regard treaty interpreters will need to take into account the function of the procedures at issue, the resources available to perform those functions, reasonable administrative response times to fulfill those functions, variations in demand for the applicable administrative services, the conduct and degrees of freedom given to an applicant in the prosecution of its application as well as the level of user satisfaction with the patent granting system.

It is Canada's view that in drafting paragraphs 1 and 2 of Article 62 the TRIPS negotiators understood that the patent application and examination process is a variable exercise that will depend on the simplicity or complexity of the invention claimed, the sophistication of the field of technology in which it occurs as well as on the relationship between the invention claimed and other inventions in that field of technology (prior art). They therefore also understood that the duration of the process would itself be variable and so could not be defined by, or confined to, a single, specific cardinal period of time.

Accordingly, in seeking to impose some reasonable limitation on a Member's freedom to condition the acquisition or maintenance of intellectual property rights on compliance with reasonable procedures and formalities, the TRIPS negotiators deliberately chose the flexible, ordinal standard of "unwarranted curtailment" to discipline curtailment of the period of effective protection that might be caused by delays in the application-approval and granting process which were neither authorized by law nor justified by the nature of the substance of the approval-granting process.

In the result there is no unique, universally applicable definition of what may constitute "unwarranted curtailment" of the period of protection referred to in paragraph 2 of Article 62. Accordingly, in an "authorized" system where the rules are "justified" by the nature of the patent granting process and the need of the granting authority to be satisfied in respect of the novelty, inventiveness and utility of the invention claimed, the "warrantedness" of the amount of curtailment associated with the process will always be a question of fact.

(b) Would an average pendency period for patents of approximately five years be considered a "reasonable period of time" which avoided "unwarranted curtailment" of a protection term? Why, or why not?

As noted in the answer to the question in paragraph (a), the "reasonableness" or "warrantedness" of any particular pendency period related to a particular patent application will always be a question of fact to be determined on the basis of the particular system used to process applications, the circumstances relating to the particular application, the particular invention claimed and the conduct of the applicant in the prosecution of that particular application.

In view of the foregoing, some may argue that "average pendency" periods may not be looked at for the purposes of TRIPS treaty analysis and interpretation. While this may in fact be a valid criticism where a dispute is focussed on a particular patent application, it is doubtful that it has any similar force where a dispute has a systemic focus on or, as in these proceedings, may or can be related to the particular system used to process and grant patents in respect of claims to patentability.

That said, as a general or "average" matter, in Canada's view the answer to the first of these two questions is, at least in respect of section 44 patents[2]: yes

[2] As explained in paras. 49 and 54 of Canada's First (Written) Submission New Act (section 44) applications will not proceed to examination until the applicant files a request, and pays the fee, for

In answer to the second, the "Why, or why not", of these two questions is grounded in the fact that, as suggested in paragraphs 54 and 76 of the Canada's First (Written) Submission, and given the expert resources that Canada has made available for the conduct of the patent application approval and granting process, in the normal course - a course that has been processing some 285,678 patent applications[3] over the last ten years - the average pendency period has been sixty months, or five years. Consequently, for being an average pendency period achieved by an adequately staffed, professional patent-granting organization which follows examination and granting procedures that mirror international practice standards and, like other patent granting authorities, is subject to application prosecution decisions which are in the control of applicants, Canada's five year pendency period for New Act patents must be accepted as being a "reasonable" pendency period.

As such, a five year pendency period for (New Act) patents issued pursuant to Canadian or any analogous national law must be accepted as being pendency periods that are "reasonable period[s] of time" which avoid "unwarranted curtailment of the period of protection" bestowed on successful applicants for the exclusive privileges and property rights which are conferred by a patent.

In conclusion Canada would note again, as it did when it responded orally to this question when originally posed by the Panel, that it is aware of no coherent body of evidence which suggests that the beneficiaries of the Canadian patent system are dissatisfied with the timeliness with which patent applications are processed by the Canadian granting authority.

Where the users or beneficiaries of the system are not dissatisfied with the time taken to process and grant a patent in response to an application it is difficult, if not impossible, to argue or conclude that the effective term of protection which results from the process of approval and grant has been or is being "unwarrantedly curtailed".

Q.2 What bearing, if any, do the general principles set out in paragraph 2 of Article 41 as incorporated in Article 62.4 have on arguments put forward in this dispute concerning delays in the grant of patents?

The US, the party of adverse interest in these proceedings, has not complained of or otherwise put in issue the "fairness, equity, complexity, costliness, timeliness or delay characteristics" of the procedures for the examination, approval and granting of patents in Canada. Consequently in Canada's view the principles articulated in paragraph 2 of Article 41 which, by virtue of paragraph 4 of Article 62, are to govern the "[p]rocedures concerning the acquisition and maintenance of intellectual property [in this case, patent] rights" have no direct bearing on the "arguments put forward in this dispute concerning delays in the grant of patents".

examination. This introduces a new element in the approval process which, while under the obvious control of the applicant, introduces a statutory delay in the approval process - one that has averaged 15 months for granted patents and 27 odd months for those not yet granted, which was not present in the Old Act procedure - which typically took 2 to 4 years or an average of 3 years to complete. Thus for Old Act patents Canada would be more comfortable with saying that on average, the reasonable pendency period for an Old Act application would have been 2 to 4, or, when averaged, 3 years.

[3] Affidavit of Peter J. Davies, Chairman of the Patent Appeal Board of the Canadian Patent Office, Para. 28. Reproduced in its entirety as Exhibit No. 8 to Canada's First (Written) Submission. Hereafter cited as: Davies affidavit.

In making the foregoing observation Canada does not suggest that the principles of fairness and equity articulated in paragraph 2 of Article 41 are irrelevant to Canadian or other Member entity's legal and administrative procedures governing the application for, examination, approval and granting of domestic patents. They clearly must be a part of, and relevant within, any rules-based system which is governed by the fundamental principles of the rule of law.

In this respect Canada would note that all Canadian federal law is subject to the standards of fairness, equity and non-arbitrariness articulated by the ***Canadian Charter of Rights and Freedoms***, the ***Canadian Bill of Rights*** as well as the complementary quasi-constitutional common law rules governing procedural fairness. The rules governing the application for, the examination, approval and granting of patent rights are subject to these standards and have not been successfully challenged on any of the "unfairness", "equitable" or "procedural fairness" grounds guaranteed by those constitutional laws.

The fact that there is no such evidence supports Canada's conclusion that there is no "unwarranted curtailment" of the period of protection available under section 44 of the Canadian New Act patent law and that the resulting fifteen years of patent protection offered by the New Act's "first to file" system is both reasonable and compliant with the minimum standards required by TRIPS.[4]

Since, under a "first to invent" system, the examination process takes place prior to the commencement of the period of protection accorded to the exclusive privilege and property rights conferred by a patent, the application of these principles to the "curtailment" analysis have little relevance to the amount of effective protection offered to patentees under the Old Act system governing section 45 patents. Subject to the payment of maintenance fees, the latter term, of course, remains constant at seventeen years.[5]

That said the application of those principles to a "first to file" system is, of course, critical to the exercise of judging the compliance, comparability, equivalence and consistency of a "first to file" system's effective period of protection with that provided by a "first to invent" system of patentability.

Q.3 Why is the word "available" used in connection with the term of patent protection in Article 33 of the TRIPS Agreement but not in the provisions on the terms of protection of other intellectual property rights?

In Canada's view the notion or concept of "availability" is, where not explicit as in Articles 26 (Industrial Designs) and 33 (Patents), inherent in all the "term of protection" provisions found within sections 1, 2 and 4 to 6 inclusive of Part II of the TRIPS Agreement.

Canada takes this view because, although each was, in Canada's understanding, negotiated separately, each reflects or reproduces in some measure the concepts or language used in the other term of protection provisions. Thus all of the term of protection provisions use a formula that first requires or implies the availability of a term of protection, and, second, specifies an open-ended limit on the duration or, what is perhaps a less precise measure, the ending of the term referred to.

Specifically and in the sequencing of the Agreement: the **Copyright** term provision (Article 12) provides that, "...such term shall be no less than 50 years from the end of

4 See: Paras. 76 and 77 of Canada's First (Written) Submission.

5 See: Para. 73 of Canada's First (Written) Submission.

[a variety of commencement dates]..."; the **Trademarks** provision (Article 18) provides that, "...registration...shall be for a term of no less than seven years."; there is no term provision for **Geographical Indications**; the **Industrial Designs** provision (Article 26) provides that, "The duration of protection available shall amount to at least 10 years."; the **Patents** provision (Article 33) specifies that, "The term of protection available shall not end before the expiration of a period of twenty years counted from the filing date."; last, the **Layout-Designs** provisions use two formula (paragraphs 1 and 2 of Article 38), the first specifies the term where registration is a precondition to protection and requires that "...the term...shall not end before the expiration of a period of 10 years counted from the date of filing an application for registration..." and the second specifies that, where registration is not a required prerequisite, the design "...shall be protected for a term of no less than 10 years from the date of the first commercial exploitation...".

All these provisions therefore require, assume or imply "availability" of a term of protection for the right at issue. They also require, in the course of defining the term of protection, that it be a minimum or open-ended term insofar as each provision makes use of some variant of "no less than", "at least", or "not end before".

In these circumstances what is of interest in this dispute is not the use of the word (or concept of) "available", but rather how the concepts of "availability" and "open-endedness" work in conjunction with paragraphs 1 and 2 of Article 62. The latter, as noted in paragraphs 74 to 76 of Canada's First (Written) Submission and the answers to question 1(a) and (b) above, sanction the erosion of the period of protection. They, of course, sanction erosion of the term by acknowledging the right of Members to "condition the acquisition or maintenance of intellectual property rights on compliance with reasonable procedures and formalities so long as those procedures and formalities do not result in an 'unwarranted curtailment' of the period of protection elsewhere prescribed in the Agreement".

As is clear from the face of the provision, paragraph 2 of Article 62 only applies to sanction the erosion of the term of protection otherwise specified by the Agreement where the right in issue is subject to the "right being granted or registered". The interplay between availability, open-endedness and prerequisite procedures therefore only has significance in the cases of trademarks, certain layout-designs and patents.

Where, as in the case of Trademarks and one class of layout-design, the term provision uses the "no less than" open-ended formula, the formula can only be understood as describing an absolute minimum term which will run from the date of the registration of the mark or design. Accordingly, the paragraph 2 provisions of Article 62 cannot operate to permit the erosion of the term of protection to a period that is less than the absolute minimum specified by the applicable term provision.

However, where, as in the case of the Patent and paragraph 38.1 Layout-Design provisions, the open-ended formulas provide that the term of protection "shall not end before the expiration of" a specified period of years counted from a filing date of an application and are not, therefore, referable to the date that the protection is recognized by registration or bestowed by grant, it is clear that the right only arises on registration or grant and, hence, the "effective" term that is defined by the "not ending before a specified date" formula may, without violating TRIPS, be less than the number of years referred to in the formula for describing the period during, **but not for**, which protection of the exclusive privileges and property rights must be **available**.

Thus in these latter two cases, those involving patents and paragraph 38.1 Layout-Designs, the minimum term is not an **absolute** minimum, but rather is a **variable** minimum which runs its variable course within the specified period but will vary within that period according to the time that lapses between the date of filing for recognition of the right and the date on which the right is recognized by the act of grant or registration, as the case may be.

Q.4 Are you aware of any WTO Member that was obliged to apply the TRIPS Agreement as of 1 January 1996 and that does not apply a patent protection term of 20 years from the date of filing to all patents, including those patents that were in force and patent applications that were pending as of 1 January 1996?

Canada is concerned that the question as posed, appears to suggest that, notwithstanding the Article 1.1 licence to determine the appropriate method of implementing their TRIPS obligations, Members have an obligation to "apply a patent protection term of 20 years from the date of filing".

Canada does not share this view, believing that the scope of the Article 33 obligation is limited to ensuring that "The term of protection **available** shall not end before the expiration of a period of twenty years counted from the filing date.". (Emphasis added) The concept of availability is critical to the proper interpretation of Article 33 because paragraph 2 of Article 62 clearly contemplates that rights granting and registration procedures will **curtail** any period of protection where, while the period is measured from an application filing date, the right does not arise until some subsequent time when the right claimed is either registered or granted such that the "effective" term of protection is **less** than the period referred to in the formula used to define how the term of protection is to be measured.

Against that background, Canada is aware of two WTO Member jurisdictions where the Member has not adopted, or has not exclusively adopted, a term of protection provision that explicitly uses the TRIPS reference to a "term of 20 years from the date of filing".

First, and on the evidence led by the US[6], it would appear to Canada that New Zealand law, as amended in December 1994, provides that: "The term of every patent shall be twenty years from the date of the patent." Thus although this formula may exceed the minimum required by TRIPS, it does not apply a "term of 20 years from the date of filing". Accordingly, unless subject to special definitions that are not available in the US exhibit, the quoted language would appear to include every patent issued pursuant to New Zealand law whether before or after January 1, 1996. It would thus also appear to embrace patents issued after January 1, 1996 on the basis of an application filed before that date.

Second, as noted in paragraphs 17 and 20 of Canada's First (Written) Submission, Canadian patent law contains two term of protection provisions one of which - section 44 - uses the TRIPS style formula to provide that;

> 44. Subject to section 46, where an application for a patent is filed under this Act on or after October 1, 1989, the term limited for the duration of the patent is twenty years from the filing date.

and the second of which - section 45 - provides that;

> 45. Subject to section 46, the term limited for the duration of every patent issued under this Act on the basis of an application filed before October 1, 1989 is seventeen years from the date on which the patent is issued.

[6] See: US Exhibit 9.

For the independent reasons advanced in paragraphs 57 through 83 and, subsequently, in paragraphs 84 through 110 of Canada's First (Written) Submission, Canada takes the view and submits that the term of protection prescribed by section 45 on the basis of "first to invent" patent applications filed before October 1, 1989 makes a twenty year from filing term **available** and is equivalent, comparable, consistent, harmonious and compliant with the term of protection required to be accorded to "first to file" applications by the TRIPS Agreement and as is prescribed by the undisputedly TRIPS compliant provisions of section 44 of the Canadian legislation.

Further, for the reasons referred to in the preceding paragraph Canada does not concede, as assumed by the question, that it was obliged to apply the TRIPS Agreement to provide a term of protection measured from the patent application filing date where, such of its patents that were not so measured, are **available** for a twenty year from filing term and are substantively equivalent, comparable and in harmony with the variable terms of protection that are available under the formula of protection defined by Article 33 of the Agreement.

As noted in the introduction to this answer, it is Canada's position that the obligation set out in Article 33 is an obligation to ensure that "The term of protection **available** shall not end before the expiration of a period of twenty years counted from the filing date." (Emphasis added) By virtue of the freedom conferred on Members by paragraph 1 of Article 1 "to determine the appropriate method of implementing the provisions of [the] Agreement", Members are not required to implement this or any other obligation by the adoption of any particular form of words or formula of measurement so long as, as a matter of substance, the specified term is, as it is under section 45, **available** on a "sound legal basis" under the law and practice of the implementing Member.[7]

Q.5 Do you believe that a system in which the patent term is calculated from the date of filing creates the same incentive to file a patent application promptly as a system in which the patent term is calculated from the date of grant?

Canada has discussed or adverted to the incentives inherent in both of the "first to invent" and "first to file" systems for awarding patents in paragraphs 36, 38 to 40 and 46 to 48 of its First (Written) Submission. In those paragraphs it made the point that the difference in incentive between a "first to invent" and a "first to file" system related to the speed with which the application, once filed, would be prosecuted by the applicant. The calculation of the term of protection thus is more likely to influence the speed of the prosecution of a patent application than it may influence the alacrity with which the application is itself filed.

In a "first to invent" system where the patent term of protection runs from the date of issuance of the patent and the inventor's "secret" is protected by non-disclosure and trade secrecy laws prior to grant, there is little if any systemic incentive to prosecute the application expeditiously. There may, of course, be very substantial commercial or other self-serving strategic reasons that might negative and reverse the absence of any such incentive in the application and granting system and so motivate the applicant to prosecute its application with speed.

In contrast, in a "first to file" system where the term of protection runs from the date of the filing of the application, where the amount of protection is eroded by the

[7] See: Paras. 37 to 39 of Canada's First Oral Presentation and the Appellate Body jurisprudence cited and referred to in those paras..

granting process and where the contents of the application may be required to be made publicly known well before the patent issues and so expose the invention to potentially infringing uses by third parties, the incentive to prosecute an application expeditiously would appear to be considerably stronger. However, here too there may be very compelling commercial - read financing, manufacturing, distributional and marketing - as well as regulatory - read marketing approval, reasons which may negate and reverse the incentive to prosecute an application vigorously and so make the applicant indifferent to the speed with which its application is processed.

While as a general matter it may be fair to say that the systemic incentives in the two systems operate in different directions insofar as the speed of the processing of the application may be concerned, it is less clear that the system used for the measurement of the term of protection has a similarly divergent influence on the promptness of the act of filing itself.

This may be the case because, while a "first to file" system may seem to encourage early filing so as to make the "first filer" the winner in a patent entitlement dispute with another inventor (or the patent office), if the other inventor (or the patent office) establishes that another invention constitutes "prior art" the patent is unlikely to issue to or, if issued, have any continued longevity for the benefit of, the "first to file" applicant.

In this sense the risk that may appear to be negated by a "first to file" system may be illusory. This may be so because in both the "first to file" and the "first to invent" systems the incentive to file, as opposed to prosecute, promptly is ordinarily related to the risk that someone else may "invent" the same or substantially or obviously the same subject matter and so defeat the claim to exclusivity whether through a claim to be the "first to invent" or through an assertion of lack of novelty or inventiveness notwithstanding a "first to file" date.

Undoubtedly a "first to file" system that allegedly ignores "first to invent" considerations creates some incentive to file quickly, however a prior "unfiled" invention, if it exists, will, for undermining the novelty and inventiveness criteria of the claimed invention, ordinarily operate to defeat the patentability of the "first filed" claimed invention. In view of the foregoing it would appear to be uncertain whether or not one can fairly conclude that a "first to file" system creates a greater incentive to file a patent application promptly as compared to a "first to invent" system.

Q.6 Article 28 of the Vienna Convention on the Law of Treaties 1969 reads as follows:

> **"Unless a different intention appears from the treaty or is otherwise established, its provisions do not bind a party in relation to any act or fact which took place or any situation which ceased to exist before the date of the entry into force of the treaty with respect to that party."**
>
> **(a) Does Article 28 belong to those provisions of the Vienna Convention which are part of customary international law?**

Canada believes that a strong case can be made for the proposition that Article 28 of the ***Vienna Convention on the Law of Treaties*** (the Convention) has entered into the realm of "customary international law". It bases its view on the criteria required to promote a treaty norm into a customary rule of law that are set out in *North Sea Continental Shelf (Federal Republic of Germany v. Denmark),* [1969] I.C.J. p. 4, the leading case on this issue. After sounding a cautionary note to the effect that such a conversion "...is not lightly to be regarded as having been attained"[8], the International Court of Justice went on to say that the following three criteria would be required to demonstrate that such a result had been achieved and that the treaty norm at issue had indeed matured into a customary rule of international law.

The first of these criteria requires that "...the provision concerned should, at all events potentially, be of a fundamentally norm-creating character such as could be regarded as forming the basis of a general rule of law".[9] The second requires that the norm at issue enjoy extensive and virtually uniform application in State practice so as to show a general recognition that a rule of law or legal obligation is involved.[10] Thirdly the Court suggested that, as a matter of *opinio juris*, "Not only must the acts concerned amount to settled practice, they must also be such, or be carried out in such a way, as to be evidence of a belief that this practice is rendered obligatory by the existence of a rule of law requiring it."[11]

In Canada's view the facts that: analogous rules expressing the presumption against the retroactive application of new law to subsisting vested rights and obligations exist in the municipal law of many, if not most, modern states; the rule has, as a rule of general application, been recreated within Article 70 of the TRIPS Agreement; and, that the Convention rule has, at least twice, been referred to and applied by the Appellate Body[12], all argue that the three criteria of: creating a fundamental norm; being widely endorsed by State practice; and, State practice being confirmed by statutory and international tribunal recognition, are met by the treatment accorded Article 28 of the Convention.

This conclusion is strongly supported by the additional fact that the Appellate Body has, in the Bananas case, described Article 28 as stating "a general principle of international law".[13]

(b) Which paragraph(s) of Article 70 refer(s) to "any act or fact which took place...before the date of the entry into force of the treaty..."?

Although obviously drawn directly from Article 28, Canada believes that the reference to the "date of the entry into force of the treaty" is not entirely apt in the circumstances of this case. This is so because in the TRIPS context "the date of the entry into force" being January 1, 1995[14] has a particular or special meaning and is distinct from "the date of application of the [or this] Agreement for the Member in question" being, *inter alia*, January 1, 1996 for most developed country Members. Within TRIPS, the latter date serves the function of a coming into force date for a particular or particular class of Member as opposed to the date which is elsewhere normally referred to as "the date of the entry into force".

---

8 *North Sea Continental Shelf* at para. 71. Reproduced as Exhibit No. 20

9 *Ibid.* at para. 72.

10 *Ibid.* at para. 74.

11 *Ibid.* at para. 77.

12 Appellate Body Report, *Brazil - Measures Affecting Desiccated Coconut* ("*Brazil Desiccated Coconut*"), WT/DS22/AB/R, adopted 20 March 1997, DSR 1997:I, 167 at 179. Appellate Body Report, *European Communities - Regime for Bananas* ("*EC – Bananas III*"), WT/DS27/AB/R, adopted 25 September 1997, DSR 1997:II, 591, para. 235 and following.

13 *European Communities - Regime for Bananas, supra, footnote 12,* para. 235.

14 See: Para. 1 of Article 65 and the footnote, footnote **, to that para..

The dichotomy does have significance within TRIPS because, as paragraphs 8 and 9 of Article 70 make clear, some provisions trigger obligations from the "entry into force date" while most - but not all - others use the date of application as the applicable triggering date. However, Canada has sought to avoid confusion by reading the reference as being a reference to the "date of application of the Agreement for the Member in question" and would, in this light, answer the question as follows.

Paragraph 1 explicitly refers to "acts which occurred before the date of application of the Agreement for the Member in question". As such it would, but for its reference to "the date of application" rather than the "date of entry into force", appear to restate the substance of what Article 28 of the Convention has to say about "acts which took place before the coming into force" date of a treaty.

Paragraph 2, in referring to "subject matter existing at the date of application of this Agreement for the Member in question, and which is protected in that Member on the said date", would appear to be addressed to "facts" which existed before the date of application but continued as of that date. It may not, therefore, fall within the ambit of this branch of the question.

Paragraph 3 by its reference to an intellectual property right that had entered into the public domain before "the date of application of this Agreement for the Member in question", would clearly appear to refer to "facts" which occurred before the referenced date and were not continuing as of that date. However, the paragraph could also be more accurately characterized as addressing a "situation which ceased to exist before the date of the entry into force of the treaty".

Paragraph 4, like paragraph 1, also makes explicit reference to "acts". However, it limits the universe of relevant "acts" to those that occurred "before the date of acceptance of the WTO Agreement by that Member". Given that paragraph 1 of Article XIV of the ***Final Act Embodying the Results of the Uruguay Round of Multilateral Trade Negotiations*** (Final Act) gave contracting-party Members two years from the date of the Final Act (April 15, 1994) to "accept" the Agreement, the date of acceptance may fall on either side of the date of application. In the result this provision may or may not address "acts" which occurred before the date of application of the TRIPS Agreement. (However, since the acts referred to in the paragraph are embodied in subject matter that exists on the application date, this paragraph also has a hybrid character and could also be said to apply to a "situation which had not ceased to exist" on the coming into force of the Agreement.)

Paragraph 5 refers to purchases of originals or copies of certain copyrighted materials which occurred before "the date of application of this Agreement for the Member in question". It would, therefore, appear to fall within the branch of the question which is concerned with references to "acts". However to the extent which the "works" purchased may remain in the channels of commerce, this provision too would appear to have a hybrid character and, therefore, could also refer to a "situation that continues to exist".

Paragraph 6 refers, by implication, to administrative "acts" of Member governments which granted compulsory licences to third parties without the authorization of the rights holder. However, here again as with paragraph 4, the paragraph only addresses a limited subset of such "acts" insofar as the granting "act" had to have taken place before the date on which the TRIPS Agreement became known before the Member may rely on the "grand-fathering" exception created by the paragraph to save an otherwise offending "compulsory licence". (The date the "Agreement became known" is generally accepted to be a reference to the date of the "publication" of the Dunkel text of the Agreement, that date being December 20, 1991.)

Paragraph 7 refers to applications for intellectual property right protection that were pending on "the date of application of this Agreement for the Member in question". It would, therefore, appear to address "facts - application filings - which occurred before but had not been acted upon by the date of application. In this sense, the paragraph may more accurately be described as addressing a continuing situation rather than an "act" or a "fact".

Finally, paragraphs 8 and 9 refer to "facts" - patent protection for pharmaceutical and agricultural chemical products - or perhaps "situations" that did not exist "as of the entry into force date of the WTO Agreement" in the law of the Member in question and impose certain interim obligations on such Members in respect of the products referred to. That said, because these two paragraphs in essence are concerned with the creation of new obligations, albeit of a transitional nature, they do not appear to fit well within Article 70 which is predominantly concerned with the transition rules that will govern the application of obligations specified elsewhere in the Agreement. They therefore may not be intended to make any reference to "the acts, facts or situations that have ceased to exist" which are at the heart of Article 28 of the Convention.

(c) **Which paragraph(s) of Article 70 refer(s) to "any situation which ceased to exist before the date of the entry into force of the treaty" or did not so cease to exist? Is the ongoing protection of an intellectual property right at the date of entry into force of a treaty, e.g. a patent that has been granted and which remains in force at that date, within the scope of "situation that ceased to exist"?**

The answer to the first branch of this question has already been partially canvassed by the answers to the questions in 6(b). As noted in those answers, paragraph 3, although it may be characterized as addressing "facts", is probably more clearly concerned with elaborating a clarifying transitional rule that denies the treaty's application to situations - the presence of subsisting intellectual property rights - which had ceased to exist as of the application date of the Agreement for the Member on whose territory the situation had once existed.

Similarly, but in response to the second branch of this question, a number of the provisions of Article 70 have, as noted in the answers to the questions in 6(b), a hybrid character. Thus while they may be characterized as addressing some "act" as is the case in paragraphs 4, 5 and 6, that "act" can be or is related to a "fact" or "situation" which, in intellectual property law, could have continuing significance. This relationship exists, for instance, in paragraph 4 where the "act" in question is embodied in protected subject matter which may continue to be protected after the application date and may therefore give rise to infringement liability. The same may, with appropriate technical modifications, be true in respect of the "acts" implicitly referred to in paragraphs 5 and 6.

In summary of the answers to the first two branches of this question, Canada is of the view that, with the exception of paragraph 3 of Article 70 - which itself is at least slightly ambiguous - the drafting of the paragraphs of Article 70 as well as the of the included references to the fact situations which the drafting seems to have contemplated, is sufficiently opaque or illusive to defeat clear and unambiguous characterization of any of those paragraphs as clearly belonging solely to one particular class of category of exempt subject matter referred to in Article 28 of the Convention.

In consideration of the third branch of this question Canada is of the view that patents which were, before the application date of the Agreement, issued in respect of particular subject matter that continued to exist as protected subject matter on the application date for the Member in question cannot be easily dismissed as being "within the scope of a 'situation that ceased to exist'."

Canada holds this view because, in its understanding of the TRIPS Agreement, the Agreement draws distinctions between: the vehicle which conveys an intellectual property right; the act, where an act is so required, which triggers the recognition of the right; and, the subject matter which attracts both the right and the protection that is to be made available to the right holder.

Thus, as in this dispute, Canada understands that the Agreement imposes three essential elements in respect of intellectual property rights. First it requires that a vehicle of protection - in this dispute, a patent - be available pursuant to Article 27 to protect qualified "subject matter" - in this dispute, an invention which is novel, inventive and useful. Second, it requires that protection of the rights at issue be available for the period specified by the formula prescribed by the Agreement for the definition or measurement of that period - in this dispute, the period referred to in Article 33. And, third, it requires that the subject matter shall be accorded a bundle of exclusive benefits - in this dispute, the rights set out in Article 28.

In the result Canada also understands that, by virtue of paragraph 2 of Article 70, subject matter which is "novel, inventive and useful", which was invented and protected before the application date and which continued to be protected as of that date, would be entitled to protection by the patent vehicle pursuant to Article 27.1 and to the conveyance of the exclusive benefits, even if enhanced by TRIPS, bestowed by virtue of Article 28.

Dissimilarly Canada does not understand, and it would take issue with the proposition, that the patent, as the vehicle of the pre-existing and continuing protection, is itself "existing subject-matter" within the meaning of paragraph 2 of Article 70. Unlike the subject matter of protection which is the creation of an "inventor" and subsists indefinitely, the patent, as the vehicle of protection, flows from two "acts" - the act of application and the act of grant - both of which pre-date and were fully executed before the application date of the Agreement and respectively ask for or consummate a time-limited bargain between the inventor and the State (and the third parties it represents) as of the discrete moment in time when each "act" is executed.

There is nothing in the "subject matter" language of paragraph 2 of Article 70 which suggests that the time-limited bargain consummated by the "act" of grant is a bargain that has been or was intended to be disturbed by the obligations agreed to within TRIPS. Similarly, there is nothing in the "subject matter" language of paragraph 2 of Article 70 which suggests that the saving language of paragraph 1 of Article 70 does not apply to preserve the bargain here at issue. However, there is, in contrast, language in paragraph 2 of Article 70 which strongly suggests that its "subject matter" provisions will not apply where the Agreement makes an alternative provision as it does, for pertinent example, in paragraph 1 of Article 70.

That paragraph 2 language introduces the whole of the paragraph and reads: "Except as otherwise provided for in this Agreement..." In Canada's view paragraph 1 of Article 70 provides otherwise.

(d) Assuming that the reply to question (a) is in the affirmative, does Article 70 represent a "contracting out" of this customary rule of international law or rather does it restate this rule?

As set out in the answer to question 6(a) Canada believes that a strong case can be made for the proposition that Article 28 of the Convention has matured into a "customary rule of international law".

That noted, Canada also believes that at least the first three paragraphs of Article 70 of the TRIPS Agreement recreate or restate the rule in Article 28 of the Convention and do not "contract out" of its substance. Canada has formed this belief because, in its view, in drafting Article 70 of the Agreement the TRIPS negotiators in effect unbundled the "acts, facts and situations which ceased to exist" trilogy set out in the Vienna Convention.

They did so, apparently, in order to distinguish between and provide separately for the application or transitional rules which would be applicable to each category of circumstance included in the Convention trilogy. In so doing, however, they made some modifications to the "acts, facts and situations" language of the Convention to reflect the nomenclature and substance of intellectual property law and practice. The TRIPS recasting of the Convention trilogy is set out in paragraphs 1, 2 and 3 of Article 70.

First, paragraph 1 recreates the Convention rule against the retroactive application of new rules to existing **acts** when, for TRIPS application purposes, it provides that:

This Agreement **does not give rise** to obligations in respect of **acts** which occurred before the date of application of the Agreement for the Member in question. (Emphasis added)

Second, paragraph 2 expresses a "contrary intention" to the Convention rule respecting the retroactive application of new rules to existing **facts** or factual circumstances, which the TRIPS negotiators refer to as "existing subject matter which is protected or protectable on the application date" of the Agreement. For TRIPS purposes however the contrary intention is, itself, subject to exception since, for those purposes, it provides that:

> **Except as otherwise provided** for in this Agreement, this Agreement **gives rise** to obligations in respect of **all subject matter existing** at the date of application of this Agreement for the Member in question, and which is protected in that Member on the said date, or which meets or comes subsequently to meet the criteria for protection under the terms of this Agreement. (Emphasis added)

Third, paragraph 3 recreates the Convention rule against the retroactive application of new rules to **situations which ceased to exist** before the entry into force date of the treaty. The TRIPS negotiators describe these situations as being those where intellectual property "subject matter" has fallen into the public domain (and, therefore, has ceased to be protected). Specifically and for the purposes of the TRIPS Agreement, paragraph 3 provides that:

> There shall be **no obligation to restore** protection to subject matter which on the date of application of this Agreement for the Member in question has **fallen into the public domain**. (Emphasis added)

Q.7 Please provide an analysis of the meaning that should be attached to the various provisions of Article 70, in particular, explaining the meaning of paragraphs 2, 4 and 6 of Article 70. What is the relationship among the paragraphs of Article 70?

In responding to this question Canada notes that it is the US that has chosen to rely on a selective passage of Article 70.2 to establish its claim. In Canada's view the burden of establishing the applicability of Article 33 to Canada's impugned measure is for the US. In raising Article 70 as the essential link to the applicability of Article 33 the burden to present a rational explanation of that article remains with the US. Canada's view of the appropriate analysis of the meaning that should be attached to the various provisions of Article70 will address some of the positions advanced to date by the US in its representations to the Panel.

In its first oral statement the US asserts at paragraph 16 that Canada's reading of Article 70.1 renders much of the rest of Article 70 "meaningless or wholly redundant". Canada disagrees, but even if that were the case, that does not justify reading Article 70.1 in such a way as to render it meaningless for the reasons set out in paragraphs 122 to 126 of Canada's First (Written) Submission of December 2nd,1999, which speak to the applicable rules of treaty interpretation.

It is Canada's position that to the extent Article 70 imposes obligations on Members or grants benefits to existing subject matter it should be read narrowly where there is any uncertainty as to its scope or applicability. In any event Article 70 can not be read to override the clear language of Article 70.1 in the absence of compelling reasons presented by the US.

Article 70 arises under TRIPS Part VII, Institutional Arrangements: Final Provisions. Article 70.2 is concerned with the protection of existing subject matter. In respect to patents, which is the only class of intellectual property at issue in this dispute, patentable subject matter is defined under Article 27. That article is the first of eight within TRIPS that make up Section 5: Patents.

Subject to the exceptions described in paragraphs 2 and 3 of Article 27, patents are available for any inventions, whether products or processes, which meet the qualifying criteria of "novelty, inventiveness and utility". Article 28 provides that a patent shall confer on its owner certain exclusive rights. Article 31 authorises certain uses without authorization of the right holder and in so doing refers expressly to "other use of the subject matter of a patent". Accordingly, the subject matter referred to in Article 70.2 as it relates to patentable subject matter is as defined in Article 27 and does not, as contended by the US, include a patent itself.

In Canada's view Article 70.2 is a provision which "Except as otherwise provided for in this Agreement" gives rise to obligations to all existing subject matter (inventions in this case) at the date of application of this Agreement and which is protected as of that date or which meet, or comes subsequently to meet, the criteria for protection under the terms of this Agreement.

Patentable subject matter is defined under Article 27, that is products or processes which are new, involve an inventive step and are capable of industrial application. Therefore, any invention which meets or is capable of meeting the criteria set out in Article 27 and which existed on the application date of the Agreement is entitled to the benefit of the obligations under the Agreement except, of course, as otherwise provided. The exception is not limited to exceptions which are described in Article 70.2 as argued by the US in paragraph.11 of its first oral submission. The exception expressly refers to the whole Agreement and not just paragraph 70.2. Nor does the quote cited by the US in the noted paragraph support its thesis because the example given in the quote of an exception contained in Art 70.2 is unambiguously illustrative in nature and in no way suggests exceptions are limited in the manner contended for by the US.

It is apparent that the language employed in Articles 70.1 and 2 is similar. Namely, "this Agreement does not give rise to obligations in respect of acts which occurred before the date of application of the Agreement..."and "This Agreement gives rise to obligations in respect of all subject matter existing at the date of application of this Agreement...". In Canada's submission the apparent conflict between these two paragraphs is for the US, as the party relying on the provisions, to resolve. That is the US must ensure both paragraphs have meaning and its failure to do so should result in its complaint being dismissed.

One interpretation that is open that results in Canada's section 45 patents not being subject to the Agreement is to recognise that the act of filing an application for a section 45 patent and the administrative act of issuing such a patent are essential to initiating a term of protection under Article 33. In the event that either of these acts occurred before the date of application of the Agreement no obligations in respect of the term of protection accorded to the patent arise under the Agreement.

In this respect Canada notes that by implication the US appears to accept that an administrative act is included within the scope of Article 70.1. At paragraph 13 of its first oral statement the US, submits that acts of customs officials permitting entry of counterfeit or pirated goods prior to the date of application of the Agreement are within the scope of acts not subject to obligations under the Agreement.

In Canada's view there are no legal distinctions between the administrative character of these official acts of customs and patent officials. Canada further notes that in Article 70.6 an administrative act is given express recognition as excluding the application of Article 31 for Members "where authorization for such use was granted by the government before the date this Agreement became known". This formulation in Article 70.6 is consistent with the administrative act of issuing a patent being found within the scope of Article 70.1.

This interpretation of Article 70.1, that is excluding section 45 patents from the obligation under Article 33, does not, in the words of the US, imply that other paragraphs of Article 70 are meaningless or wholly redundant. Patentable subject matter under Article 70.2 would include the obligations set out under Article 28 to confer certain exclusive rights on a patent owner, and the right to be paid remuneration under Article 31 (h) where a Member sanctioned a use unauthorised by the right holder for patentable subject matter. These examples are not intended to be exhaustive but illustrate that there is a rational resolution of the apparent conflict between paragraphs 1 and 2 of Article70 and which results in section 45 patents not being subject to Article33.

The question further asks for direct comment on the meaning of paragraphs 4 and 6 of Article 70 and which the US also claimed in its oral statement were rendered redundant by its inaccurate characterization of Canada's statement in relation to Article 70.1.

The transitional rule in Article 70.4 is clearly intended to apply in circumstances in which TRIPS requires a Member to protect subject matter that the Member did not previously protect, and has no application to the circumstances here. Article 70.2 gives rise to certain obligations in respect to the subject matter at issue but not in respect of patents. Where for example there was a field of technology not previously protected under the laws of a developed Member, and the TRIPS Agreement now requires it be protected, implementing legislation would be required to provide for the issuance of patents for existing inventions (subject matter) in that field of technology.

It may be that persons were using inventions in that field of technology prior to the application date of the Agreement. The transitional rule in Article 70.4 applies to acts which were not infringing at that time but which subsequently became infringing once, as in Canada's example, patents in the field of technology are issued in accordance with the implementing legislation.

Article 70.6 represents another exception available to Members in respect to existing subject matter. It is in effect a grand-fathering clause which protects pre-existing compulsory licences granted by the government before the date this Agreement became known.

Canada agrees with the assertion of the US in paragraph 14 of its oral statement that the Agreement is not retroactive, at least it is not in respect of concluded, pre-application date acts. This is consistent with international law as expressed in Article 28 of the Vienna Convention and Article 70.1. which provides that the Agreement has no application to "acts" which occurred prior to the application date of the Agreement.

At paragraph 17 of its oral statement the US makes the rather extravagant claim that if section 45 patents are excluded from the Agreement then all forms of intellectual property that existed prior to the application date would receive "absolutely no protection under TRIPS" and then advances *"in terrorem"* arguments that Members could revoke, for no reason at all, patents issued before January 1996 and still remain in compliance with TRIPS.

Such statements without more do little to enlighten the understanding of the obligations set out in Article 70. The scope of the word "acts" in Article70.1 as suggested by Canada does not, for example, exclude the results of creative acts from the obligations which arise under Article 70.2 as implied by the US. The act of creation within the contemplation of TRIPS results in subject matter. The product is not itself an "act". Inventing something may be an act but the resulting invention is subject matter and not an act. TRIPS obligations apply to subject matter and not acts. Article 70.1 on the other hand applies to acts but not to subject matter.

In Canada's view the relationships that exist between the various paragraphs of Article 70 broadly exceed the issues that need to be decided in this complaint. As noted in response to question 6 (d) it appears that paragraphs 1, 2 and 3 of Article 70 could be said to reflect the "acts" "facts" and "situations which ceased to exist" set out in Article 28 of the Vienna Convention.

Article 70 is concerned with the protection of existing subject matter. Paragraphs 1, 2 and 3 describe generally what obligations the Agreement does and does not give rise to. Paragraphs 4 ,5, 6 and 7 describe certain special situations of application.

Finally paragraphs 8 and 9 of Article 70 are concerned with what has come to be referred to as "mail box" provisions requiring a Member to make special provision for certain pharmaceutical and agricultural chemical products where patent protection was not available prior to the entry into force of the WTO Agreement. These latter two transitional provisions do not appear to contain any particular relationship to the other paragraphs of Article 70 beyond providing "protection for existing subject matter" which, of course, is consistent with the general purpose of the Article.

II. REPLIES TO QUESTIONS FROM the PANEL TO CANADA

Q.15 *Concerning the interpretation of "appropriate method" in Article 1.1, do you believe that, had a new Act not been implemented in Canada in 1989, the old Act would have been an appropriate method to comply with the TRIPS Agreement?

This is, clearly, a "counterfactual" speculative question. Canada's 1994 decisions relating to its implementation of its TRIPS obligations were necessarily conditioned on the state and scope of its then existing laws and practices and their degree of compliance or consistency with its then impending TRIPS Treaty obligations.

However, based on the discussion and elaboration of the legislative context and history of the 1989 amendments to Canada's patent laws which is set out in paragraphs 22 to 30 of Canada's First (Written) Submission, one might, as a matter of reasoned speculation, conclude from the reasons that led Canada to introduce those far reaching amendments in 1986 that, had it not made those amendments, it would, in the interests of modernizing its patent legislation and administrative practice and in switching to a "first to file" from a "first to invent" system, probably have, in the further interest of achieving the harmony in patenting systems desired by the TRIPS negotiators, decided to make similar amendments to its patent laws, within its TRIPS implementing legislation.

Notwithstanding this informed speculation, it is germane to note that since the protection provided to patents and patentees under the Old Act - being the legislation that would have been in force in 1994 had the 1986 amendments not been made - is, and was in 1994, substantively equivalent to the protection prescribed by the TRIPS Agreement.[15] It is similarly germane to note that under section 45 of the Old Act the term of protection **available** to patentees was, when measured from the TRIPS filing date perspective, then as it is now, more certain than and equal or superior to the variable minimum term prescribed by TRIPS.

All of which is to say that, since the equivalency and availability arguments would have been available to Canada in 1994 when it was drafting and enacting its TRIPS implementing legislation, it could then, given the Article 1.1 freedom to chose an appropriate method of implementation, have chosen not to amend its term of patent protection statutory provisions and still have fulfilled its TRIPS patent term obligations.

Q.16 *You stated that the average pendency period, described as the period between the filing date and the date of grant, is approximately 60 months or five years for those applications that were filed after 1 October 1989 and for which patents were granted. For those patents that were filed prior to 1 October 1989:

(a) please confirm that the average pendency period was two to four years (paragraph 72 of your First Submission); and

As requested Canada confirms that the average pendency period in respect of patent applications filed prior to October 1, 1989 has, historically, been two to four years as stated in paragraph 72 of its First (Written) Submission. This fact is set out in paragraph 8 of the Davies affidavit - Exhibit 8 to Canada's First (Written) Submission - and can be further confirmed by reference to Exhibit B to that affidavit.

In confirming this fact Canada would go on to note that the difference between the average pendency period under the Old Act - two to four years - and the average pendency period under the New Act - five years - is, on an average basis, explained by the provisions in the New Act which hold an application in abeyance until the applicant fulfils its obligation to file a request, and pay the fee, for examination.

As discussed in paragraphs 53 and 54 of Canada's First (Written) Submission, although applicants are given five years from their filing date in which to meet these requirements, they have, on an average basis, filed their request and paid the fee for examination fifteen months after filing their applications, in the case of patents which have issued; or, twenty seven odd months, in the case of patents that have not yet issued. The fifteen or twenty seven month periods are, roughly speaking, equal to the difference between the New Act and the Old Act pendency periods.

(b) what were the shortest and longest pendency periods for those Section 45 patents that have been granted?

By reference to the same data base used to calculate the number of patents that might have been affected by the term of protection obligations defined by Article 33, the

[15] As noted in para. 80 of Canada's First (Written) Submission, NAFTA would appear to recognize and, by recognition, endorse the equivalence here under discussion.

Chairman of the Canadian Patent Appeal Board reports that: the shortest pendency period for a section 45 patent which has been granted is: 2.76 months.

By reference to the same data, the longest pendency period for a section 45 patent which has been granted is reported as having been: 493.08 months (or 41 odd years).[16]

Q.17 *Is the term "term of protection" as used in Article 33 synonymous with a period of "exclusive privilege and property rights" as used in your First Submission? Please explain why or why not.

No. As used in reference to Article 33, (and as they would also be used in an analysis of paragraph 1 of Article 38) the two terms are not synonymous.

As explained in paragraphs 74 to 78 of Canada's First (Written) Submission and more extensively canvassed in the answer to Question 3 set out above, the two terms differ for the following reason. The term of protection referred to in Article 33 defines the period during which protection **shall be available** but during which the "exclusive privilege and property rights" conferred by a patent **may not yet exist** because, by virtue of the operation of the granting procedures sanctioned by paragraphs 1 and 2 of Article 62, the patent conferring the exclusive privilege and property rights associated with a patent once granted, **has not been granted**, notwithstanding that the period of nominal protection, as measured from the filing date of the patent application, has already begun to run.

Q.18 *In your first oral statement, you seemed to imply that in a first-to-file patent system, where four or five years elapsed before a patent was granted, the period of protection of that patent would be 16 or 15 years. However, does the period of protection run from the date of filing, rather than the date of grant, so that the period of effective protection is 20 years?

In Canada's first oral statement it did indeed say - throughout paragraphs 13 to 26 - that the effective term of protection under the combined operation of Article 33 and paragraph 2 of Article 62 would invariably be less that the period referred to in Article 33 as being the minimum period during which the term of protection must run. However, as explained in the answer to Questions 17 and 3 as well as in paragraphs 74 to 78 of Canada's First (Written) Submission, the period of "effective" protection **can only begin to run once the patent** (or other intellectual property right which is subject to prerequisite granting or registration procedures) **is in fact granted** or registered, as the case may be.

If a patent has not issued, it attracts no exclusive privilege or property right. Accordingly where the defined period of protection begins to run before the right is granted, the defined period cannot confer and does not define "a period of effective protection" for the period defined. Because of the separation in time between the date of application and date of grant, the period of "effective" protection will, as a practical matter, always be less than a period that is defined to commence before the granting, or other formal recognition, of the right.

Q.19 *(follow up to previous question). If, during the, say, five years that a patent is pending in Canada, the applicant can sell the claimed product in Canada, why would it be willing to act so as to delay the grant, given that it could be at risk if it

[16] See: E-mail message from Peter Davies, the Chairman of the Patent Appeal Board to Rob Sutherland-Brown dated January 4, 2000 and reproduced as Exhibit No. 21.

were to operate in the market prior to grant? Would it not wish to receive the grant of patent as soon as possible?

While it is indeed possible for a patent applicant to sell its invention in the market prior to the date of grant, it is unlikely that a typical applicant would do so because, as the question notes, it would risk losing its opportunity to eventually obtain or thereafter maintain the exclusive right to exploit the invention. (The fact that the absence of any exclusive right would probably have a negative effect on the price that such an applicant could obtain for its invention or the product of its invention, may also operate to discourage such pre-grant selling.)

As to the second branch of the question, Canada would note that the question will almost invariably be a question of fact. There are any number of factors which may influence an applicant's behaviour or decisions in both seeking patent protection itself and in prosecuting its application for protection once it has made the decision to do so. The applicant's decisions in this respect are very subjective and it is not therefore possible on a prospective basis to elaborate a theory or to identify any particular factor which will explain the conduct of any given applicant in making a decision to accelerate or retard the filing or prosecution of a patent application.

Some of the factors that commonly influence these decisions include: whether or not the applicant can or is ready to manufacture; where it cannot or is not, whether the applicant can licence its invention to a third party; whether the applicant has or has located the financial resources to exploit the invention; whether the applicant has or has not arranged for the marketing and/or distribution of its invention; and, where the invention or the product of the invention is regulated, whether or not it has, or can expect to obtain, marketing approval from the competent authorities.

Q.20 *You state in paragraph 72 of your First Submission that it took two to four years to complete the "examination process" for Section 45 patents and in paragraph 76 that it took five years to complete the "examination process" under the new Act. Please confirm that the term "examination process" as used in paragraphs 72 and 76 covers the period between the filing date and the date of grant. (Note that you use the term "examination" elsewhere to describe the period during which the patent office examines the patent application).

Canada confirms that in both paragraphs 72 and 76 of its First (Written) Submission it has used the phrase "examination process" as a term of art to describe the period - often referred as the pendency period - between the application filing date and the date of grant.

Canada acknowledges that it has, in several places in its submissions, used the word "examination" to describe either: the activity of the patent authority in "examining" the patentability of the claims in an application, or the period during which that activity takes place.

The different terms or references are intended to contrast the "shorter" actual or *per se* "examination" activity with the "longer" "examination process" which includes all pre-grant activities or delays, being: the period before a request for "examination" is made (New Act only); the time spent in the pending queue awaiting "examination"; the "examination" period itself; and, the delay period between the notice of approval and the actual grant.

Canada trusts that the appropriate or intended meaning of either term will be clear in the context of use and, where that is not the case, Canada would be pleased to clarify its use or intended meaning in such instances.

Q.21 It is argued that whereas the protection term in respect of patents granted under Section 45 may be longer or shorter than 20 years from filing, that this provision is consistent with Article 33 because the average term is in excess of 20 years from filing. How do you reconcile this fact with the Panel's finding in *United States—Section 337 of the Tariff Act of 1930* that "an element of more favourable treatment would only be relevant if it would always accompany and offset and element of different treatment" and its rejection of "any notion of balancing more favourable treatment...against less favourable treatment"?

This question would appear to reflect the assertions of the US[17] that Canada's arguments are based upon "an impermissible averaging methodology". This misapprehends Canada's arguments which do not rely on any such "averaging methodology". Moreover they do not assert that when allegedly term-deficient section 45 patents are added together with those having surplus term and are then appropriately divided, the resulting average term is greater than the term referred to in Article 33 and is, therefore, consistent with the TRIPS standard.

Nor do Canada's arguments assert that, for TRIPS interpretative purposes, the "more favourable treatment" accorded to surplus term section 45 patents otherwise compensates for the alleged deficiency in the term granted to so called "term-deficient" section 45 patents.

Canada's arguments as set out, respectively, in paragraphs 67 to 83 and paragraphs 84 to 110 advance two independent, albeit mutually reinforcing, propositions which: first assert the equivalency of the terms of protection available under the two filing and term measurement systems; and, second, assert the availability of the TRIPS twenty year from filing term under section 45 and other provisions of the Old Act, notwithstanding that under the Old Act the term or period of protection granted ran, by virtue of the statute, from the date of grant.

The first proposition, in summary characterization, argues that while Old Act (section 45) patents confer a guaranteed, constant seventeen years of protection for the "exclusive privilege and property rights" conferred by a patent measured from the date of the grant of the patent, New Act (unambiguously TRIPS compliant section 44) patents confer a variable period of protection for the "exclusive privilege and property rights" conferred by a patent which variable period has, in 89 per cent [18] of those instances where a section 44 patent has been issued, conferred seventeen or fewer years of protection for those "exclusive privileges and property rights". (For the purposes of this type of analysis, Canada considers that, where the term of "effective" protection under one patent granting system is variable, it is inappropriate to restrict or limit its equivalency comparison to a system using a fixed term of "effective" protection by referring only to the exceptional, upper-limit results achievable under the variable term regime.)

As noted generally elsewhere above and specifically in paragraph 77 of Canada's First (Written) Submission this curtailment from the term referred to in Article 33 occurs because the "examination process" has, under the aegis of Article 62, eroded the period of protection defined by the term measurement criteria set out in Article 33. In the result to two systems produce equivalent, comparable, harmonious and consistent terms of protection for the "exclusive privileges and property rights" that are here at issue.

---

17 See: Para. 14 of its First (Written) Submission and para. 5 of its (First) Oral Statement.

18 See: Exhibit F to Davies Affidavit.

Second, and again in summary characterization, Canada has argued that, while the section 45 patent term provision guarantees seventeen years of protection from the date of grant for the "exclusive privileges and property rights" conferred by a patent, when viewed from the perspective of the patent application filing date, it also makes a twenty year from filing date term available, without exception, to any patent applicant wishing to view and obtain protection on that basis. The second argument concludes with the proposition that, since the twenty year term from filing was available to any applicant who sought it, where an applicant did not seek to obtain the twenty year term it would itself be responsible for the deficiency and could not later complain of the deficiency.

Given the substance of these two arguments and the difference between them and what was at issue in the *Section 337* case which has been cited by the US and quoted in the question, Canada does not agree that the referenced jurisprudence has any pertinence or application to this dispute or the agreed facts from which its arises.

Q.22 *You argue that the term of protection under the old Act and the new Act are equivalent. You also argue that the United States has failed to establish a prima facie case that Article 33 has retroactive application. In order to clarify these arguments, could you indicate whether, in your view, if the old Act provided a much shorter term of protection, say 10 years from grant, such a provision would comply with the TRIPS Agreement, because the TRIPS Agreement lacked retroactive application?

In its oral response to this question Canada suggested that in order for a ten year from grant term to be equivalent to the term defined by Articles 33 and 62 of TRIPS, the granting procedures applicable to New Act patents would need to involve 10 years of delay. This, in Canada's initial view, appeared to lack balance and justification given the nature and purpose of the granting procedures.

Canada continues to hold this view. It would however elaborate on its verbal response by noting that if the term set out in section 45 were 10, not 17, years and all other provisions of both the Old and New Acts remained constant as they now are, then both the "equivalency" and the "availability" arguments and analyses would fail.

The "equivalency" argument and analysis would fail because the constant period of protection for the "exclusive privilege and property rights" offered by the hypothetical section 45 ten year guaranteed term - being ten not seventeen years - would fall far short of and clearly not exceed the normal fifteen years of "effective" protection afforded to those exclusive privileges and rights by the term of protection formula prescribed by the conjoint reading of Articles 33 and 62.

Similarly, the "availability" argument and analysis would fail because the statutory provisions which are catalogued in paragraph 43 of Canada's First Oral Presentation and which provide a "sound legal basis" for an applicant's ability to prosecute its application without any rights-defeating penalty for at least 42 months after filing its application would, when added to the guaranteed base hypothetical term of ten years from grant, only result in a total of thirteen and one half years of protection being available to an applicant. This clearly contrasts unfavourably with the twenty and one half years of protection that are available to applicants when the same calculation is made in respect of a system using a seventeen year from grant base term.)

As the Panel knows it is Canada's position that, while the US has not made out its interpretative case respecting the application of paragraph 2 of Article 70 to the application of Article 33 to Canada's section 45 patents, the US's spare analysis of, and attempt to apply, that paragraph in this dispute is irrelevant in the face of the undisputed facts that underlie the dispute. It is irrelevant or redundant for two reasons. It lacks relevance because, first, on a substantive basis, the "effective" protection available under section 45 is equivalent to the "effective" protection available under the TRIPS system of term measurement. Second, it lacks relevance, because, pursuant to an undeniably sound statutory - that is, legal - basis, a twenty year from date of application term of protection was available to any Old Act applicant that sought to measure and obtain its term of protection on that basis.

In sum, therefore, because section 45 is, for reasons of equivalency and availability, TRIPS compliant, no change in Canadian law is required. Of course, where no change in law is required (or made), there is no need to provide for or, as in this case, apply a transitional rule, such as the rule in paragraph 2 of Article 70, to regulate the transition form one set of laws to another. Where there is no need, there is irrelevance and, as in this case, redundancy.

Against this background of irrelevancy and redundancy of the application of Article 70 in these proceedings, Canada would address the Panel's hypothetical question by noting that, where both the "equivalency" and the "availability" arguments and analyses have no application, the relevancy of Article 70 would acquire life.

Were it to so spring to life and become a determinative factor, and Canada does not concede that it does or has (except in the face of the hypothetical character of the question put), then Canada would again observe, as it has at paragraphs 126 to 129 of its First (Written) Submission and paragraphs 58 to 68 of its First Oral Presentation, that, as suggested in the answers to questions 6 and 7 elaborated above: paragraph 2 of Article 70 has no application to patents *per se,* since patents are not within the meaning of the "subject matter" referred to within that paragraph; and, paragraph 2 of Article 70 being, by its own terms subject to other provisions of the Agreement, cannot and does not operate to usurp the saving provisions respecting pre-application date "acts", such as the act of filing a patent application and the subsequent act of granting the patent, that are explicitly protected by paragraph 1 of Article 70.

Q.23 You indicated in paragraph 7 of your first oral statement that your first two arguments were independent and stand-alone. Which is your principal argument and which is the alternative? Is the third argument independent of, or complementary to, the first two?

In Canada's First Oral Presentation it presented three principal arguments as well as a fourth, attacking the sufficiency of the US evidence respecting "subsequent practice". Although within the context of these proceedings the principal arguments are related, each is independent and not subordinate to another.

Nor is any one of the principal arguments alternative to the others in the sense that if one fails, then the second or third comes into play as a subsequent "fall back" argument of lesser force than any of its predecessors in a sequenced hierarchy. This is so because each establishes an independent rationale for the Panel to dismiss the US complaint.

The first two arguments, which are admittedly complementary and mutually reinforcing, rather than merely "related", advance reasons, as matters of fact and the substantive municipal law of Canada as well as of the substantive treaty law of the TRIPS Agreement, explaining why the substance of section 45 of the Canadian ***Patent Act*** is consistent with TRIPS obligations and standards. The substance of section 45 does so for two reasons.

The first reason is that, as a matter of substance, section 45 provides for equivalent "effective" protection for the "exclusive privileges and property rights" it confers as compared to the "effective" protection accorded to those privileges and rights by a patent that is issued under an undeniably TRIPS compliant system. The second is that, again as a matter of substance, the Old Act law includes provisions for ensuring that the term of protection available pursuant to section 45 is not required to end before the expiration of a period of twenty years counted from the filing date of the patent application.

The third argument advanced in Canada's First Oral Presentation presented independent argument as to why the US had failed to make out a prima facie case that the transitional rule set out in paragraph 2 of Article 70 applied to "acts" of application and grant that pre-dated the application of TRIPS for Canada.

The third argument contends that paragraph 2 of Article 70 is limited in its application to "subject matter" of intellectual property protection and thus has no application to patents and the other "vehicles" of such protection. It also contends that, since by its own terms, the paragraph is subject to the other provisions of the TRIPS Agreement, it did not, nor did the US establish that it did, have any application to "acts" that pre-dated the application of the Agreement and were, for that non-retroactive reason, saved by the substance of paragraph 1 of Article 70.

In addition to the three principal arguments, Canada's fourth argument challenges the "subsequent practice" evidence led by the US and demonstrates that that evidence was deficient because the practice referred to did not arise out of circumstances that were the same as, or even closely similar to, the circumstances that prevail in Canada in respect of the substance of the protection afforded under section 45.

Q.24 *You argue that an applicant can obtain a patent protection term of 20 years from the date of filing under Section 45 by controlling the prosecution process which is "within the private decision making capacity and strategic control" of the applicant.

(a) How could patent applicants whose applications had been examined prior to the entry into force of Bill C-22 on 17 November 1987 obtain a patent protection term of 20 years from the date of filing?

The substance of the Old Act patent rules and system had, prior to 1987 (or, perhaps more accurately, prior to 1989 when the 1986 proposed amendments were brought into force), been in place since the Old Act had last been consolidated in 1952. Therefore at any time after 1952 any applicant who had been interested in obtaining a term of protection which, when measured from the applicant's filing date, equalled or exceeded twenty years from that date could have obtained the desired term in the same manner as described in paragraph 10 of the Davies affidavit, paragraphs 36 to 38 of Canada's First (Written) Submission and paragraphs 33 to 49 of Canada's First Oral Presentation.

It may be implicit in this question that before the New Act amendments or the TRIPS obligations were law or became known, this possibility would have been irrelevant. No one would have organized their patent interests in a way that would have delayed the earliest possible grant of the patent sought. All the evidence contradicts this hypothesis.

The evidence, both that which relates to the whole universe of patent applicants and that which relates to pharmaceutical patent applicants, shows that sixty per cent of all applicants filing applications before October 1, 1989 and an overwhelming majority of pharmaceutical applicants filing applications before October 1, 1989, managed their applications or otherwise behaved so as to obtain patent terms that, when measured from the application filing date, exceeded the twenty year period counted from the applicable application filing date.

(b) What remedies, if any, would an applicant be able to invoke in case of an unauthorized use by a third party prior to the grant of a patent?

Typically speaking "first to invent" patent granting systems do not provide pre-grant remedies to those who, pre-grant, are merely "applicants" for rights that, until granted, have not come into existence. In this situation there is no exclusive right in existence which would support the concept of "unauthorized use".

Such systems do, however, typically preserve the confidentiality of the contents of the application. Accordingly, any Old Act "first to file" applicant would enjoy any remedy it would otherwise at law enjoy to protect its own commercial or inventive confidences. In the normal case such recourse would be available under the common law of trade secrecy.

(c) If a patent applicant might suffer prejudice prior to the grant of its patent, why would it not be in its best interest to obtain a speedy examination?

The risk of prejudice to a patent applicant's anticipation or expectation of obtaining a monopoly right for its invention before the grant of an anticipated patent, is always present. It is, as suggested in the answers to questions 5 and 19 without doubt one of the factors that may influence a patent applicant to accelerate either the filing or the prosecution of an application. However, as particularly noted in the answer to question 19 there are many factors at play that may reverse what appears to be an obvious motivation to obtain patent protection as soon as possible. There are however a large number of compelling reasons why a patent applicant might chose to retard its filing or its prosecution of a patent application.

Unfortunately, it has not proven easy to elaborate a coherent or straightforward theory to reliably explain, on an anticipatory basis, why or why not patent applicants may chose to behave in one manner or another or to identify one or more factors as being predominant motivators in what are, in final analysis, private, individual decisions by each applicant.

Q.25 Is it not the responsibility and obligation of the government to provide a patent term ending at least 20 years from the date of filing, especially in light of the fact that Article 33 provides that the term of patent protection available "shall" not end before the expiration of a period of twenty years counted from the filing date?

No. It is, as set out as a matter of fact in paragraph 8 of Canada's First (Written) Submission the responsibility and obligation of each Member to implement its treaty obligations. Thus, in the context of this dispute and the obligation described by Article 33, it is the responsibility and obligation of each Member to ensure that "The term of protection available [in respect of patents] shall not end before the expiration of a period of twenty years counted from the filing date [of the patent application].".

Given the freedom granted by paragraph 1 of Article 1 of TRIPS, this obligation does not extend to requiring that a Member implement its obligations in the manner suggested by the question. This is particularly the case where, as in the case of Article 33, its facial obligation is refined and modified by the provisions of paragraph 2 of Article 62 which explicitly authorize the reasonable or "warranted" curtailment of the term defined by Article 33.

In this respect and in light of the last branch of this question, Canada notes that the word "shall" in Article 33 refers to the expiry date of the patent and not to the obligation of Members to make available a term of protection that "shall not end before the expiration" of the period referred to.

Thus the obligation set out in Article 33 is not a responsibility or obligation for Members to adopt laws that force patent applicants to pursue their applications or pay their maintenance fees in a manner which is contrary to their own perceived best commercial or other interests. As the US conceded in an oral response to a question put by Canada, where a patentee determines that it is not in its continued interest, commercial or otherwise, to "maintain" its patent, it may, without jeopardising its host Member's compliance with its TRIPS obligations, cease to pay those fees and so trigger the deemed expiry of its patent before it TRIPS term has run. Similarly, it can, within statutory limits, control when its period of effective protection will commence in relation to the date it chooses to file its application.

Q.26 You refer to potential statutory delays in paragraphs 43 and 44 of your first oral statement. Are these the type of delays which are to be minimized under Article 62.2? If so, how is it reasonable to require an applicant to rely on tactics entailing exploitation of such delays to obtain a term of protection consistent with Article 33 when they are discouraged by Article 62.2 and 62.4?

In Canada's view the answer to the first branch of this question is: no. The delays permitted under Canadian patent legislation are delays that are designed to ensure that, from the users point of view, the administration of the patent-granting system is fair, equitable, non-arbitrary and does not impose the "unreasonable time-limits" referred to in paragraph 2 of Article 41.

The statutory provisions at issue are in essence rules which allow an applicant for a benefit granted by the State to pursue its application and arrange its affairs in relation to that application in accordance with its own best interests, perceived or real.

From this "own best interest" perspective, it is important in Canada's view to bear in mind that under Canadian law any patent applicant whose perceived "own best interest" was or would be to accelerate the processing of its application has, within its own control and power, the capacity to request the acceleration of its patent application.[19]

Against the background of the foregoing Canada would suggest that there is nothing improper or untoward in allowing an applicant for a benefit to be granted by the State to take advantage of the rules governing the granting of that benefit. Governmental benefit programmes and systems are not unlike the private sector credit system. Thus, if the creditor or governmental programme allows one sixty days to settle an account or take some defined step, there is no shame, penalty or allegation of abuse that can fairly be attached where the account is not paid, or the defined step is not taken, until the sixtieth day.

Q.27 *Given that, in your first oral statement at paragraph 67, you state that "subject matter" in Article 70.2 does not refer to patents, but rather to "matter that is protectable by intellectual property rights", please explain what Article 70.2 means.

Within the context of the TRIPS Agreement "subject matter" would appear to have a "term of art" meaning as appears from its use in Articles 14.3, 15 heading, 27 heading, 28(1)(a), 28(1)(b), 31, 34, and 44. (An exceptional use occurs in paragraphs 3 and 4 of Article 40, where the phrase is used to refer to what is being discussed therein, as opposed to the work, mark, indication, industrial design, invention or layout-design that is subject to intellectual property protection.)

[19] See: Para. 11 of the Davies affidavit and para. 37 of Canada's First (Written) Submission.

For a full discussion of the meaning to be attached to "subject matter" and the operation and meaning of paragraph 2 of Article 70, please see the answers to questions 6 and 7.

Q.28 What does Article 70.2 refer to in the phrase "subject matter existing at the date of application of this Agreement for the Member in question, and which is protected in that Member on the said date". Does it include an invention under patent on the date of application of the Agreement?

In Canada's view patentable subject matter are qualifying inventions and not the patents issued to such inventions. For a full discussion of this issue and related matters please refer to the answers to questions 6 and 7.

ATTACHMENT 2.4

REBUTTAL SUBMISSION OF CANADA
(14 January 2000)

I. INTRODUCTION

1. Having considered the representations advanced by the United States of America (US) in its First Submission filed on November 18, 1999, in its Oral Statement to the Panel at its First Meeting on December 20, 1999 as well as in its Responses to Questions Posed to the Parties by the Panel and by Canada filed on January 14, 2000, Canada is confirmed in its view that the US has failed to establish a *prima facie* case that the term of protection provisions of section 45 of Canada's ***Patent Act*** (Act) do not comply with the obligations which the US contends are imposed under Article 33 by virtue of the transitional provisions of paragraph 2 of Article 70 of the ***Agreement on Trade-Related Aspects of Intellectual Property Rights*** (variously referred to as: TRIPS, the Agreement or the TRIPS Agreement).

2. Furthermore, even if the US had established a *prima facie* case that the Article 33 obligation applied to certain section 45 patents by virtue of the transitional provisions of paragraph 2 of Article 70, which Canada denies and does not concede, it has either misconstrued or simply ignored and, therefore, failed to rebut or otherwise discredit Canada's arguments respecting "equivalency" and "availability" which render the application of paragraph 2 of Article 70 irrelevant or redundant in these proceedings.

3. Briefly put those arguments[1] have, without reasoned contradiction, established that:

(a) the guaranteed seventeen years of substantive patent protection extended to the "exclusive privilege and property rights" conferred by a section 45 patent are substantively equivalent and comparable to and, therefore, consistent and harmonious with the substantive patent protection of that privilege and those rights which is conferred by the variable term of protection available under the term of protection measurement formula defined by the conjoint provisions of Article 33 and paragraph 2 of Article 62 of the TRIPS Agreement; and,

(b) the term of protection **available** under section 45 was (and is[2]), by virtue of the statutory procedures and legal practices applicable to the prosecution of Old Act patent applications, **available**, without exception and on a sound legal basis, for a term that, as specified by Article 33, would not end before the expiration of a period of twenty years counted from the application filing date, notwithstanding that the formal statutory term under

[1] The arguments are, respectively, elaborated in paras. 67 to 83 and 84 to 110 of Canada's First (Written) Submission and in paras. 12 to 29 and 30 to 59 of Canada's First Oral Presentation. They are also further amplified, where relevant, in many of Canada's Responses to Questions Posed to the Parties by the Panel.

[2] There are approximately 1,000 Old Act applications still outstanding. See: Davies Affidavit at para. 23.

the Old Act is defined to run for seventeen years measured from the date the patent was issued.

4. The balance of these rebuttal submissions will address certain arguments advanced by the US in its various submissions to the Panel and demonstrate why the US has failed to establish a *prima facie* case in support of its complaint.

II. THE FAILURE OF THE US COMPLAINT

5. The US complaint is based on two propositions:

(a) its first premise is that by virtue of Article 33 of TRIPS, all WTO Members are required to provide or grant a term of protection for patents that runs at least until twenty years after the application filing date;

(b) its second premise is that by virtue of paragraph 2 of Article 70, all patents existing at the date of application of TRIPS for the Member in question and which were protected as of that date, are entitled to a term of protection equal to the term described in Article 33.

As set forth in the paragraphs that follow and as is clear from the evolution of the US submissions and the points that have been conceded within those submissions, neither premise is accurate. Accordingly, neither sustains the US complaint.

The Failure of the First Premise - The TRIPS Term is Variable

6. In its initial articulation of this complaint the US alleged that "By its plain terms [Article 33] obligates all WTO Members to **grant** a term of protection for patents that **runs at least until twenty years after the filing date** of the underlying application". It went on to allege that "The phrasing of the provision...also indicates that the **twenty year term is a minimum term**..."[3] (**Bold face** added for emphasis)

7. It reiterated this position in the second articulation of its complaint where it stated that: "They [being Articles 33 and 70.2] require Canada to provide a twenty year patent term to all patent holders." In support of this proposition the US inaccurately quoted Article 33 as providing that: "The term of protection shall not end before the expiration of a period of twenty years counted from the filing date."[4]

8. To critical effect, this rendition of Article 33 omits the word **available** from the specification or definition of the obligation which, in its authentic version, reads: "The term of protection **available** shall not end before the expiration of a period of twenty years counted from the filing date."[5] (**Bold face** added for emphasis)

9. The US again advanced the "twenty year minimum term" hypothesis in its third articulation of its position where, in its answer to the third Question posed to both Parties by the Panel, it characterized the basic requirement of Article 33 to be "to provide a certain defined minimum term of protection to rights holders."[6]

10. As the Panel is aware, in Canada's view Article 33 cannot be read in isolation from other Articles of the Agreement and, most particularly, cannot be read in isolation from or as ignoring Article 62, paragraph 2 of which **recognizes** and **sanctions** the fact

---

3 Para. 10 of the First Submission of the United States, at page 3.

4 Para. 2 of the Oral Statement of the United States, at page 1.

5 TRIPS, Article 33.

6 Answer 3, Responses of the United States to Questions Posed to the Parties by the Panel.

that the term referred to in Article 33 will be **eroded by the operation of reasonable procedures which, *inter alia*, are prerequisite to the granting of a patent.**[7]

11. Notwithstanding the US assertion referred to above in paragraph 10 and notwithstanding that in paragraph 9 of its Oral Statement, the US contended that "Article 62 has no relevance to this case...", elsewhere in its responses to the Panel questions it now concedes that, by virtue of the operation of paragraph 2 of Article 62, "...some loss of term due to pendency is **inevitable**..."[8] (**Bold face** added for emphasis)

12. In making this concession, the US admits that Article 33 **does not require** Members "to provide a certain defined minimum term of protection to rights holders."

13. Further, where in its answer to paragraph (a) of the Panel's first question to both Parties, the US states that "The meaning of unwarranted curtailment cannot be determined in the abstract, and reasonableness may vary by situation", it concedes that not only will the term referred to in Article 33 be inevitably eroded and thus be less than that twenty year term, but also that the amount of inevitable erosion will be **variable**.

14. A Member's compliance with the Article 33 obligation cannot, therefore, be determined by a simple, arithmetic comparison.

15. The US admissions that the term referred to in Article 33 will inevitably be eroded and that the inevitable erosion will vary in accordance with the circumstances defining the reasonableness of the procedures referred to in Article 62, jointly and severally admit by necessary implication that the first premise advanced in support of the US complaint is fallacious and cannot be sustained in the face of the unequivocal clarity of the relevant provisions of the Agreement.

The Failure of the First Premise - The TRIPS Term is Available

16. The first premise of the US complaint also fails for the additional reason that it does not take account of the uncontested fact that under Canadian law and practice respecting Old Act patents, a term of protection at least equal to (and frequently in excess of) a period of twenty years counted from the filing date of an underlying patent application was (and continues to be) **available**, without either exception or discrimination, to any Old Act applicant who wished to count and obtain a term of protection on that basis.

17. As a matter of public record, just over sixty per cent of all such Old Act applicants obtained or will obtain such equal or superior terms of protection. Such terms, therefore, were (or will be), as Article 33 requires, unequivocally **available** to any applicant who chose to similarly order their affairs under section 45 and the other relevant provisions of the Old Act.

18. The US has, by necessary implication, conceded the fact of "availability" where it argues[9] that the twenty year and twenty year plus terms that have been or will be granted under section 45 do not compensate for the terms that, notwithstanding their substantive

---

[7] The US would appear to share this view since, in reference to Articles 33, 62.4 and 41.2, it states in its answer to the 10th question posed by the Panel that: "These obligations of the Agreement must be read together, not in isolation. The term of protection required to be provided in Article 33 presupposes reasonable procedures for the acquisition of patent rights, such that the requirement of a twenty year term....is not rendered a practical nullity."

[8] See: Lines 3 and 4 of the US Response to Question 1(b). See too the US response to Question 10 referred to in footnote 6. The US had previously noted this "variability", but only in relation to its analysis of the alleged term-deficiency of section 45 patents, see: Para. 3 of its First Submission.

[9] See: Para. 14 of the First Submission of the US.

equivalency with the effective patent term protection offered by the conjunctive provisions of Articles 33 and 62, did or do not meet the twenty year from filing date standard.

19. Similarly, in focussing its allegations of TRIPS non-compliance on the forty per cent of section 45 applicants who obtained a term of protection which was less than the nominal term referred to in Article 33[10], it concedes by necessary implication that the twenty year or twenty year plus term was nevertheless "available" as demonstrated by the results obtained by the remaining sixty per cent of all section 45 applicants.

20. In other words, since there is nothing in the Canadian "availability" measures which discriminates between applicants or applications, what was obtained in respect of sixty per cent of the section 45 applications was "available" for one hundred per cent of the section 45 applications.

21. Notwithstanding these admissions by necessary implication, the US has subsequently sought to impugn the propriety or TRIPS relevance of the Canadian measures which made the twenty year term from application filing date available to any Old Act applicant who sought to view and obtain its protection on that basis.[11]

22. Thus in its answer to the second question posed by the Panel to both Parties, the US is critical of the provisions of Canadian law that allowed patent applicants to delay both the commencement date and, as a result, the end date of their term of full, substantive patent protection. It condemns those measures as being "unnecessarily complicated procedures".

23. Canada disagrees. The procedures at issue are, as described in Canada's answer to the Panel's Question 26, designed to ensure that, from an applicant's point of view, the rules of the patent-granting system would, as contemplated and required by Articles 41.2 and 62.4, be >fair, equitable, non-arbitrary and free of "unreasonable time limits".

24. As admitted in the US answer to the third question posed by Canada, A...US patent law ...did and does contain provisions similar to Section 30.2 (*sic*) of Canada's Old Act. (In the description which follows, the US answer makes clear that its system also contains a rule similar to the rule in Section 73 of the Old Act but for the fact that, unlike the Canadian provisions which operate as of right, the US provisions are subject to the Commissioner's discretion.)

25. Canada has tabled the applicable procedural rules as Exhibit 16. Contrary to the allegations in paragraphs 6 and 7 of the First Oral Statement of the US, the applicable rules speak to legal rights albeit one is, like all the analogous rules in US law, subject to the discretion of the Commissioner of Patents and they have, at all material times been available in a written, published form as integral parts of the Old Act and Rules.

26. The procedural stipulations and rules, if awkwardly drafted, are simple and straightforward. At their most complicated, they require as does US law the applicant-petitioner to satisfy the Commissioner of Patents that its failure to prosecute its application within the specified time "was not reasonably avoidable". Why this requirement might be "unnecessarily complicated" for an applicant who would have first hand knowledge of the reasons why it could not complete its prosecution within the specified time, is unclear to Canada.

---

[10] See: Para. 4 of the First Submission of the US.

[11] See: Paras. 6 and 7 of the Oral Statement of the US as well as the US answer to the second question posed by the Panel to both Parties.

27. Furthermore, the US alleges, in its answer to the Panel's second question, that Canada required applicants to follow such "unnecessarily complicated procedures to obtain unwarranted delays in the grant of their patents, *i.e.* avoidable delays justified for no purpose other than mere delay."

28. Canada denies this speculative allegation. Further, contrary to the companion allegations set out in the same answer that Canada "imposed" such delays on applicants, Canada reiterates the fact that the procedural rules in question were designed to ensure fairness and equity in the granting process. As such they established rules that offered relief from the otherwise arbitrary time limits set out in the statute or regulations for the completion of certain steps in the patent application process. They were **available** to, not "**imposed**" on, applicants. It is inescapable from the face of the rules themselves that they were, at the instance that is, on the "petition" or "application" of the applicant, available to any applicant wishing to obtain the relief provided for by the rules.

29. Moreover, although designed and enacted in the interests of fairness and equity, the rules could also be used to obtain a delay in the commencement and end dates of full patent protection in the interests of practical commercial or regulatory reasons which might supplant the incentive to obtain patent protection as soon as possible.[12]

30. An excellent example of one of the reasons an applicant might wish to shift its patent protection forward in time is described by the Chairman of the 10 + 10 Meeting when he reported on the concerns some TRIPS negotiators had about "...the normal period of delay between the filing of a pharmaceutical patent application and the obtaining of approval for marketing the pharmaceutical... [being]...something over 10 years."[13]

31. Clearly, where the start and end date of the full patent protection to be conferred on a pharmaceutical invention can be moved forward in time to more closely coincide with the date of regulatory approval for the marketing of the product, the forward shift in time will reduce the erosion of the exclusive patent rights, not to mention their value, which would otherwise result from the regulatory approval process.

32. In view of the foregoing, Canada submits that neither the propriety nor the relevance of the Canadian rules and practices respecting relieving delays in the patent application prosecution process can be dismissed as being improper in or irrelevant to an analysis of the availability of a twenty year from filing date term of protection under section 45 of the Old Act. The fact that similar rules exist under US patent legislation argues that it is not open to the US to impugn their propriety. The fact that they can and did operate to make a twenty year from filing date term available under a term from grant system confirms that they are not irrelevant.

33. In the result under this, the "availability", branch of the analysis respecting the failure of the first premise of the US complaint, it can be shown to fail for two reasons. It fails first because it has, by necessary implication, admitted that a twenty year from filing date term of protection was **available** under the Canadian law and practice relating to section 45 patents.

34. It fails second because it has not established that the procedural mechanisms which ensured **availability** are improper or irrelevant either: to the assessment of Canada's compliance with its TRIPS obligations; or, to the related determination as to whether or not, under the test articulated by the Appellate Body in the *India - Patent*

[12] See: Canada's answers to Panel Questions 5 and 19.

[13] See: US Exhibit No. 11 at page 4.

Protection case[14], those mechanisms provided a "sound legal basis" for the **availability** of the term of protection here at issue.

35. In this latter regard Canada notes that in the *India - Patent Protection* case the Appellate Body endorsed a Member's Article 1.1 freedom to determine the appropriate method of implementing its TRIPS obligations within its own legal system and practice.[15] However it also went on to decide that, if implementation was by "practice" it had to have a "sound legal basis" which "would survive legal challenge".[16]

36. Canada submits that its "availability" measures, whether grounded in the formal legal rules disclosed in Exhibit 16 respecting the Old Act or in the informal practices of examiners referred to in Exhibit 8[17] that existed in the shadow of those formal rules, are consistent with this standard.

37. Canada makes this rebuttal submission on the basis that all of the delays that may have been granted pursuant to either the formal or informal rules although once, are no longer, exposed to legal challenge.

38. This is so because, first, the period roughly being October 1979 to April 1992 in which such decisions could have had any impact on the term of protection here at issue has long since expired. Second it is so because, as emerges clearly from the undisputed evidence in the Davies affidavit, no request for delay was ever refused. And, third, it is so because the procedural rules permitting challenges of such decisions, require that such challenges be filed within thirty days of the decision complained of becoming known by the party directly affected by the decision.[18]

39. In the result, it is unambiguously the case that any applicant in a position to request any of the procedural delays at issue either obtained the delay requested, or, chose not to take advantage of its position to request a delay. Consequently, there are no longer any such informal "practice" decisions that would, under the *India - Patent Protection* test, be exposed to reversal under a legal challenge.

40. There are no reported cases in respect of legal challenges brought against the Commissioner on the basis of a formal statutory decision respecting the delays here at issue.

41. In conclusion, Canada submits that, as explained in its answer to the Panel's Question 22, where the first premise of the US complaint fails whether because TRIPS does not prescribe a fixed term or whether because Canadian law complied with the TRIPS standard the second premise of the US complaint becomes irrelevant or redundant.

The Failure of the Second Premise

42. Ignoring, for the time being, its irrelevance, the second premise on which the US complaint is advanced presupposes that paragraph 2 of Article 70 applies to all patents existing at the date of application of the TRIPS Agreement for the Member in question and which were protected as of that date, and that all such patents are entitled to a term of protection equal to the term described in Article 33.

---

14 *India - Patent Protection For Pharmaceutical And Agricultural Chemical Products (AB-1997-5)*, WT/DS50/AB/R, adopted 16 January 1998, DSR 1998:I, 9 paras. 70-71.

15 *India - Patent Protection*, *supra*, footnote 14, para. 59.

16 *Ibid.*, *supra*, footnote 14, para. 70.

17 Affidavit of Peter J. Davies, Chairman of the Patent Appeal Board of the Canadian Patent Office, para. 10.

18 *Federal Court Act*, R.S.C 1985, c. F-7, subsection 18.1(2). Reproduced as Exhibit No. 22.

43. In its initial iteration of this proposition in paragraph 11 of its First Submission, the US maintained that in "its ordinary meaning" Article 70.2 gave "rise to obligations including the obligation to grant a patent term of at least twenty years from the date of filing in respect of all patents ("subject-matter") existing..." on the date of the application of the TRIPS Agreement to, *inter alia*, Canada.

44. It made no reference to any other provision of Article 70.

45. In paragraph 2 of its Oral Statement the US recast this second premise and said that: "Articles 33 and 70.2 are not complicated. They require Canada to provide a twenty year term to all patent holders."

46. It went on to explain in paragraph 10 of that Statement that the "...text of Article 70.2 is key. ... [it] states that except as otherwise provided in the Agreement, TRIPS *gives rise to obligations* in respect of *all subject matter existing at the date of application* of this Agreement." (Underlining in the original) Immediately thereafter it contended that: "A patent is a type of subject matter.". It next drew the conclusion that: "Patents that existed at the date of Application of the Agreement thus fall within the scope of Article 70.2."

The failure of the "subject matter" thesis

47. As the Panel is aware, Canada took issue[19] with the US equation of "patents", being the vehicles of protection, with "subject-matter", being the object work, mark, design, invention etc. of protection. As appears from the US answers to Panel Questions 7 and 13, it has now modified, if not resiled from, its earlier views and agrees with Canada that: "... subject matter as used in the TRIPS Agreement generally refers to the matter that is or can be entitled to intellectual property protection. Indeed, this is exactly how Article 70.2 utilizes the term subject matter."

48. While the US concludes that there is now "no substantive difference between the U.S. and Canadian views of the term subject matter", Canada does not agree with the US further proposition in which it merges the concepts of "patent", being the vehicle of protection, and "subject-matter", being the object of protection, back together again when it says that: "...both Parties seem to agree that patented inventions are subject matter."

49. Canada does not agree with this formulation for two reasons. First it involves **adding words and concepts** to the TRIPS treaty and as such is to be condemned for the reasons given in the ruling of the Appellate Body in the *India - Patent Protection* case to the effect that:

> The duty of a treaty interpreter is to examine the words of the treaty to determine the intention of the parties. This should be done in accordance with the principles of treaty interpretation set out in Article 31 of the *Vienna Convention*. But these principles of interpretation neither require nor condone the imputation into the treaty of words that are not there or the importation into a treaty of concepts that were not intended.[20]

50. Second, Canada does not agree with the formulation because, within the structure of Article 70.2, "subject-matter" and "protection" or the "vehicle of protection" are segregated to distinguish the two ideas. To merge them together introduces redundancy into the Article 70.2 text by changing the Article's reference to "...subject matter existing...and

[19] See: Paras. 66 and 67 of Canada's First (Written) Submission.

[20] *India - Patent Protection*, *supra*, footnote 14, para. 45.

which is protected..."; into *patented subject matter...which is protected* which, of course, is the equivalent of saying *protected subject matter...which is protected.*

51. The negotiator-drafters of the TRIPS Agreement could not have intended such an obvious redundancy.

52. The distinction between the concepts of "subject-matter" and "protection" or "vehicle of protection" is not insignificant. It is not insignificant because the "subject-matter" of protection may be defined by certain attributes and, when protected, attract certain rights and obligations; whereas, the "vehicle of protection" may be defined by different attributes and may attract or carry with it a different set of rights and obligations.

53. The distinction is reflected in the TRIPS patent provisions inasmuch as: Article 27 defines what "subject-matter" is "patentable" or "protectable"; Article 28 defines the rights to be conferred and protected by a patent; Article 29 defines an applicant's obligation to disclose its invention as part of the patent bargain; and, Article 33 defines a variable term of protection during which the rights conferred will endure.

54. The same distinction is reflected in the municipal patent law of Canada where: the definition of "invention" in section 2 combined with sections 27, 28.2 and 28.3 define what may be "patentable" or "protectable"; the rights conferred and to be protected are defined in section 42; sections 10 and 27 require the disclosure of the invention; while, the duration of the protection to be granted to those meeting the requirements of the Act is defined by section 44 or 45, depending on the filing date of the application.[21]

55. Thus, in the municipal law of Canada, as in the international law of TRIPS, the patent conveys or "grants" a bundle of rights, exclusive or otherwise; and the act and words of "grant" establish the term of the duration of the rights granted.[22] In other words, the term of protection flows, under the direction of the statute, from the "grant" and not from the "patent" or the "subject-matter" which it protects with exclusive privilege and property rights.

56. Were this distinction not significant, then the drafters of both the municipal law of Canada and of the international law of TRIPS would have merged or melded the term-defining provision into the rights-granting provisions, such that patents would convey or grant both the bundle of rights and the term of protection. That the drafters did not do so, speaks with persuasive authority.

57. In the presence of these structural and substantive distinctions, both the initial US position of equating "subject-matter" with "patents" and its subsequent position of re-merging the two concepts in the compound phrase "patented subject-matter" are revealed as being critical to its case. Thus its failure to sustain either its initial "equation" or its subsequent "re-merging" of the two concepts is fatal to its second premise. And, of course, to its case.

The failure of the "acts" thesis

58. At paragraph 122 of its First (Written) Submission Canada called attention to the fact, noted above at paragraph 45, that the US, in advancing its Article 70.2 premise, had failed to take any account of the non-retroactivity rule in respect of pre-application date

21 See: Exhibit No. 23.

22 See: Section 42 of the Patent Act, reproduced in Exhibit No 23; and, the words of grant used by the Canadian Patent Office which first establish the term and second describe the scope of the rights granted by the patent, reproduced as Exhibit No. 24.

"acts" set out in paragraph 1 of Article 70. In this connection it should be noted that the US has conceded that Article 28 of the Vienna Convention is part of customary international law and that Article 70.1 merely restates the treaty rule [23].

59. The US responded to this observation in paragraph 13 of its Oral Statement, saying that "Article 70.1 of TRIPS did not mandate a different result" from the TRIPS implementation conduct of other Members which it had adduced as evidence it chose to identify as "subsequent practice" evidence.[24]

60. After quoting the substance of the Article 70.1 non-retroactivity rule, the US states that it agrees with Canada that the word "acts" in the Article "refers to, *inter alia*, the acts Canada identifies in paragraph 116 of its first submission, as well as such acts as" those of customs officials administering import control policies.

61. The US then illustrates[25] its view of the operation of Article 70.1 by giving an example of where and how it would apply. From this it concludes that "Article 70.1 simply says that in implementing TRIPS, a country does not have to go back and provide a remedy against [a] person for his 1993 acts." Notwithstanding that the US agrees that "acts" refers to all the "things done" i.e. "acts" described in paragraph 116 of Canada's First (Written) Submission, the example it gives is limited to demonstrating how it would operate in respect of pre-application date acts of infringement or potential infringement.

62. The example therefore does not explain how Article 70.1 would operate in respect of the other types of "acts" at issue. Thus it says nothing about the Article's operation in respect of the "act" of a patent applicant filing an application. Similarly, it says nothing about the Article's operation in respect of the subsequent "act" of a patent authority issuing a patent.

63. Since the latter two types of "act" are the types that Canada has, in its defense of this complaint, put in issue, it is incumbent on the US to go forward with evidence or, at least, interpretive theory to explain why Article 70.1 would operate any differently from its example when or where a pre-application date administrative act of filing or grant was at issue. A failure to discharge this burden, would threaten its capacity to make out a *prima facie* case. And, of course, threaten its prospect of success in its complaint.

64. In its answer to the Panel's eleventh question the US was forced to respond to this very issue. In the course of its answer to this question, the US conceded that "By its plain meaning, "acts" would include the administrative act of granting a patent by a patent office."

---

[23] See: US answers to Questions 6(a) and (b).

[24] See: Paras. 69 to 79 of Canada's First Oral Presentation for Canada's views on the value and weight of this alleged "subsequent practice" evidence. In its answers to Panel Questions 4 and 14 the US has responded to Canada's concerns respecting the value of the evidence in question, saying that one of Canada's criticisms: "..had no relevance". Parenthetically, Canada would note that the US suggestion that Canada's points respecting the fact that several, if not most, of the Members amending their laws to implement TRIPS standards had "first to file" systems which granted terms of protection in respect of "first to file" applications which ran from the application filing date and were "arithmetically" less than the twenty year standard prescribed by TRIPS, "have no relevance" is obscure. How such unambiguous deficiencies in "first to file" terms of protection might be "of no relevance" to whether or not those Members' obvious need to amend their laws to be TRIPS compliant had any subsequent value to assessing Canada's need to amend its "first to invent, term from grant" system, is unclear to Canada.

[25] See: Para. 14 of its Oral Statement.

65. It then explained that: "The acts of Canada's Patent Office prior to 1996 are not at issue." Without saying anything about whether or not "acts" of applicants for Canadian patents were or were not at issue, the US answer went on, in an obvious reference back to its hypothesis that "subject-matter" means "patented invention", to explain that: "Canada's violation....stems from its failure, ...to extend the term of protection for existing **patented inventions** to at least twenty years from filing. This violation is unrelated to any pre-96 "act", but is related only to the subject matter (**protected inventions**) that existed on 1-1-96. (**Bold face** added for emphasis)

66. Canada submits that this theory or explanation of the US complaint is deficient. It is so for two reasons. First for the reasons set forth in paragraphs 49 to 58 of this rebuttal, Canada does not agree that a case can be made for the proposition that "subject-matter" means, or includes in its meaning, "patented or protected inventions".

67. Accordingly, the distinctions elaborated in the referenced paragraphs would operate to detach the term of protection given by the act of the grant of the patent from the exclusive and other rights conferred by the patent itself. "Acts" of grant cannot be viewed as continuing acts that attract the prospective patent-term extensions that the US alleges are due to rights holders possessed of patents that existed on the date of application of the Agreement and, in the view of the US, were "term-deficient".

68. The "act" of grant is decisive and, subject to judicial review, conclusive unlike the consequential rights it gives rise to, which continue, subject to the vagaries of maintenance fee payments, forfeiture, revocation and cancellation, for a defined but variable term. The "act" of grant is a final "act" and is no more a continuing act than life, subject to all its vagaries, is a continuing act of birth.

69. A pre-application date "act" of grant does not therefore exist, nor is it "protected", except by paragraph 1 of Article 70, on the date of application of the Agreement for the Member in whose territory the "act" took place.

70. The second reason why the US theory arguing that "acts" of grant are subject to the obligations of paragraph 2 of Article 70 respecting existing "subject-matter" is deficient is that its "patented or protected invention" theory takes no account of the fact that the "act" of grant is consequential to the "act" of filing an application.

71. In this respect it is significant that since the obligation in Article 33 is triggered by the applicant's act of filing a patent application, the obligation to provide the term of protection referred to in that Article is clearly an obligation "in respect of" the "acts" of filing a patent application or granting a patent and, therefore, falls squarely within the meaning and scope of Article 70.1.

72. Article 33 specifies that the term of protection that it requires is "counted from the filing date" of the application. The "act" of filing an application therefore is the trigger which starts the clock of protection. Like the "act" of grant, the "act" of filing an application is, within a term from filing system, a decisive, conclusive, and final act.

73. Thus just like the pre-application "act" of grant, the pre-application "act" of filing does not have a continuing existence, nor is it protected except by paragraph 1 of Article 70 on the date of application of the Agreement for the Member in whose territory the "act" of filing took place.

74. To complete this rebuttal discussion of the US second premise, Canada would first reiterate its view that where the US first premise fails, its second premise becomes irrelevant.

75. Canada would then note that the US has, within the context of the non-retroactivity rule of Article 70.1, made two telling admissions: first, it admits that the

word "acts" in the Article includes the "acts" of officials in the Patent Office granting patents; and second, it admits that a pre-1996 "act" of grant would not give rise to obligations under the TRIPS Agreement. The initial version of the US= second premise fails in the face of these admissions.

76. However in admitting that "acts" of grant do not give rise to TRIPS obligations the US refocuses its complaint on the fact that Canada had not, as of January 1996, and has not since extended the terms of protection of allegedly term-deficient section 45 patents that continued to exist on and after that threshold date.

77. In refocusing its premise the US reintroduces its concept that "subject-matter", as used in Article 70.2 includes the US compound notion of "patented or protected subject-matter". In the result the refocused thesis gives rise to the same interpretive flaws that lead to the failure of the "subject-matter" thesis. Accordingly, the refocused thesis fails and it fails for the same reasons.

III. CONCLUSION

78. This case is not an "exceedingly simple" one as initially contended by the US. However, in light of the undisputed evidentiary record, the subsequent admissions, refinements and changes in the US theory, it lends itself to a simple solution. A solution which in Canada's submission, the Panel is obliged to adopt. That solution is to find: that there is no case to answer.

79. As demonstrated above, the US now accepts that Article 33 of TRIPS, like its own implementing legislation, establishes a variable period of patent protection "beginning on the date the patent issues and ending 20 years from the date on which the application for the patent was filed".[26]

80. Canada has also demonstrated that the normal period of patent protection in Canada under its comparable, TRIPS-compliant section 44 patent term regime is 15 years, while its section 45 patent term regime confers a fixed term of 17 years. This in Canada's submission is, as a matter of fact, equivalent or superior to the variable term obligation agreed to in Articles 33 and 62 of TRIPS.

81. Similarly, the US has conceded that sixty per cent of all section 45 patent applicants obtained a period of patent protection in excess of twenty years measured from the date of filing of their patent applications. The evidence that any applicant could take advantage of the various formal and informal delays provided under Canadian law and practice is uncontested.

82. There is no evidence that any Canadian law purported to restrict or limit the term of patent protection measured from the filing date. Indeed the evidence is to the contrary. Accordingly, the TRIPS required term as a matter of undisputed fact, was available for the asking, to any and all applicants during the period they were prosecuting their applications for patents. That "availability" is all that TRIPS Article 33 requires.

83. Finally, the US has conceded that "acts" as used in TRIPS Article 70.1 includes the act of granting a patent by a patent office. Issuing a patent for a fixed term is a final act. As demonstrated, section 45 patents are issued by the Commissioner of Patents on a specified date and are issued "for a term which expires seventeen years from the date on

---

[26] United States Code Title 35 s 154 (2). Reproduced as Exhibit No. 25.

which the patent is granted and issues in Canada".[27] The patent itself, once granted, is the vehicle which conveys the exclusive privileges and property rights associated with a patent.

84. The US has failed to establish that a "patent" is "subject-matter" within the meaning of TRIPS and yet now, in January 2000, it still argues that patented subject matter became entitled to an extended term of protection on January 1, 1996, the date of the application of TRIPS for Canada. This, notwithstanding that the "act" of grant, which the US concedes is within the scope of Article 70.1 is, on the evidence, an act of grant for a fixed term. In Canada's submission this is a final act which occurred before the application of the Agreement and, by virtue of Article 70.1, no obligations arise under the Agreement in respect of that act.

IV. DISPOSITION REQUESTED

85. Canada, therefore respectfully asks that this complaint of the US be dismissed by the Panel as being unfounded in fact, and that, the Panel find that Canada's impugned section 45 measure is, in any event and on all the evidence, compliant with its TRIPS obligations.

---

[27] See: Exhibit No. 24.

ATTACHMENT 2.5

ORAL STATEMENT OF CANADA AT THE SECOND MEETING WITH THE PANEL
(25 January 2000)

TABLE OF CONTENTS

I. INTRODUCTION

1. Canada is pleased to have this opportunity to present its rebuttal argument this morning. Canada, relies on its earlier submissions and answers to questions. It takes issue, however, with the evolving theories the US has been developing in support of its complaint which, in Canada's submission, are founded on false premises and *ad hominem* arguments. That is to say, the US case is based on what the US would prefer the TRIPS Agreement to require, rather than the actual obligations set out in the Agreement that all Members have adopted.

2. Rather than attempt a point by point critique of the US arguments, in rebuttal Canada will present five arguments in answer to the US case. We will address the scope of the obligation under Article 33 and explain why our measure is consistent both in terms of equivalence and availability. Canada will then explain why its section 45 patent term provisions are not subject to the Agreement. It will conclude by explaining that since neither patents nor terms of protection are "subject matter" within the meaning of TRIPS, they do not, where either existed on the application date of the Agreement, attract or otherwise give rise to obligations under paragraph 2 of Article 70 of the Agreement.

II. THE SCOPE OF THE OBLIGATION IN ARTICLE 33

3. The US persistently and inaccurately seeks to impose an obligation under Article 33 to provide a term of patent protection of twenty years as it did for example: in paragraph 2 of its first Oral Statement; in its answer to Question 10 of the Panel; and, in a modified, but still inaccurate form, where it posits that the Agreement requires a patent term of twenty years measured from the filing date, as it has in the first paragraphs of both its First and Second Submissions.

4. No matter how often these mischaracterizations are repeated, they cannot change or amend the actual requirement created by the words used in Article 33. The object of the Article is not a twenty year term of patent protection. Article 33 does not say that. The US case hinges on reading Article 33 as if the word **available** is not there[1]. But it is.

5. The US case hinges too on the US applying or interpreting the instrument or formula of measurement, namely, "...a period of twenty years counted from the filing date..." as if it were itself the definition of the term of patent protection. But it is not.

6. This is made manifestly clear by paragraph 2 of Article 62 which, as Canada has explained[2] and the US has conceded,[3] recognizes that the period referred to in Article 33 will be "curtailed" by reasonable procedures that are prerequisite to the granting of a patent. This fact is unambiguously confirmed by the US municipal law respecting the term of protection where it specifies that the:

> ...grant shall be for a term beginning on the date the patent issues and ending 20 years from the date on which the application for the patent was filed...[4]

7. As the Panel is aware, Article 33 in fact provides that 'the term of protection "**available**" shall not end before' the twenty year period it specifies; and, paragraph 2 of Article 62 in fact recognizes that the period referred to in Article 33 will be **curtailed** such that the substantive term of protection[5] will inevitably be less than that period.

8. In short, Article 33 requires that the "term of protection"-whatever its exact length-be **available** within the twenty year period it specifies. And that-the obligation to make the term **available**-is the only obligation or requirement of the Article.

9. As the Agreement does not, on its plain wording, impose the obligation or requirement upon which the US advances its claim, the US complaint must fail. It is not now open, in the middle of the process, to the US to formulate a fresh or different complaint. Nor should it be the role of this Panel to undertake a general inquiry into Canada's various measures respecting the term of protection to determine if they are consistent with its TRIPS obligations.

10. This is a dispute settlement proceeding respecting a defined complaint, not a general audit of Canada's compliance with its TRIPS obligations respecting the term of protection. And within that proceeding the US complaint should stand or fall on its own merit.

---

[1] See, for instance, para. 2 of the US' Oral Statement where it omits the word "available" from its quotation of Article 33. See too the subtitle of II A in the US' Rebuttal Submission and the discussion which follows where, in the course of insisting on a plain language interpretation and application of Article 33, the US avoids any reference to the word "available". (It does however quote Article 33 accurately in footnote 5 but in so doing offers no explanation of its meaning.)

[2] See: Paras. 67 to 75 of Canada's First (Written) Submission and see, too, Canada's responses to Panel Questions 1 and 3.

[3] See: the US response to Panel Question 1(b) where it states: "...some loss of term due to pendency is **inevitable**...".(**Bold face** added for emphasis)

[4] See: Canada Exhibit No. 25, being Title 35 Patents, para. 154(a)(2). Canada notes that because there will, in such a system, always be a temporal disjunction between the date of filing and the date of grant, the system guarantees that the amount of "effective" protection available will never equal the maximum 20 year period that the US suggests is required of Canadian law.

[5] As the US notes at para. 4 of its Rebuttal Submission, Canada frequently refers to the substantive term of protection as the "effective" term of protection or the term of protection for the "exclusive privilege and property rights" conferred by a patent.

III. CANADA'S "EQUIVALENCY" ARGUMENT AND EVIDENCE

11. Canada observed in its Second Submission[6] that the US has failed to confront Canada's arguments directly. Instead the US has often resorted to speculative statements[7] and to providing extreme hypothetical examples such as a patent term of 1 day from grant[8].

12. Such resort to straw dog argumentation is of no assistance in assessing the actual compliance of Canada's section 45 measure with its TRIPS obligations. In its Rebuttal Submission, the US continues to misstate and mischaracterize Canada's arguments, and to confuse the concepts of "equivalency" and "availability" and the undisputed facts which support each.[9]

13. Contrary to the suggestion in paragraph 12 of the US' Rebuttal Submission, Canada has not shifted its position in respect of the "equivalency" argument. In contrast, all Canada has done in its answer to the Panel's Question 21 is to refer to the **same** pendency statistics[10] used to calculate the average "effective" term of a section 44 patent, to make the **same**, not some 'slightly shifted' "equivalency" point.

14. That point is that, whatever the average pendency period may be, in nine cases out of ten, section 44[11] patents receive the same or less "effective" protection than section 45 patents receive. And the two systems therefore generate "equivalent" results when examined on the basis of the duration of their respective protection of the "exclusive privilege and property rights" that are conferred by a patent **once it has actually been issued**.[12]

15. Nor does Canada rely on an "impermissible averaging methodology".[13] Canada does not average trade concessions or obligations such that "on average" it meets its National Treatment obligations as was at issue in the *Section 337* case that the US cites in support of its criticisms of averaging. In any event, the legal principles in that case were derived from a text, namely Article III:4 of GATT 1994, which is completely different from the text under consideration here, namely TRIPS Article 33.

16. The US has put the compliance of Canada's section 45 **fixed-term**-from-grant system with the TRIPS Article 33 **variable-term**-from-filing system at issue. In the course of doing so, the US concedes[14] that the latter system results in a term of protection which, by virtue of the operation of the granting procedures sanctioned by Article 62 of TRIPS,

---

6 See, for instance, para. 2

7 See, for example, the US contention that 'Canada required applicants to follow an "unnecessarily complicated" procedure' elaborated, without evidence of any such requirement, in the US response to Panel Question 2. The procedures were "available" not "imposed". See also Canada's response to Panel Question 26.

8 See, for instance, the self styled "extreme" hypothesis set out in the US' response to the Panel's Question 10.

9 See: para. 10 of the US' Rebuttal Submission.

10 Affidavit of Peter J. Davies, Chairman of the Patent Appeal Board of the Canadian Patent Office, Exhibit F.

11 The US appears to accept that section 44 patents are clearly TRIPS compliant: see para. 2, Factual Background, of the First (Written) Submission of the US.

12 Canada notes that, in its Rebuttal Submission, the US has not taken up Canada's invitation, extended during the course of the first meeting with the Panel, to put its own pendency statistics in evidence in these proceedings.

13 See: Para. 5 of the Oral Statement of the US and the subtitle to Section II B of its Rebuttal Submission.

14 See: The US response to the Panel's Questions 1(a) and (b).

is **inevitably and variably** less than the twenty year period referred to in Article 33. In this 'apples and oranges' circumstance the US offers no theory of how the two methods of establishing the term of protection may be analytically compared to one another. Its case requires that it do so.

17. Canada, in contrast, presents a defence which comprises of analysing and comparing the period of "effective" protection available under the two systems. This is a logical, entirely reasonable, TRIPS-consistent approach to the issue. It is so because, as clearly set out in the recitals "...[E]ffective and adequate protection of intellectual property rights..." are the ultimate objectives of the TRIPS Agreement.[15] Canada made this point in paragraph 69 of it First Submission. The US has never challenged it.

18. In the course of making its analysis Canada had several options for comparing terms of "effective" protection. It could, for example, have chosen to look at the lower extreme of the variable TRIPS system-the one day term suggested by the US[16]. Similarly it could have looked at the upper limit of the variable system-the full twenty year term that the US concedes will never occur.[17] As noted in its response to the Panel's Question 21, Canada does not believe that it is analytically appropriate to make comparisons based on extreme, or exceptional, results that may only be achieved in unlikely or impossible circumstances.

19. Canada therefore turned to look at alternative analytical techniques or tools for judging the equivalency between the fixed-term-from-grant and the variable-term-from-filing systems. Given that a fixed-term-from-grant system always defines a term of "effective" protection, Canada's inquiry focussed on techniques or tools that could measure the "effective" protection available under variable term systems. Therefore, it looked at the "mean" "effective" term in a variable system. It looked at the "modal" "effective" term in a variable system. It looked at the "average" "effective" term in a variable system. And it looked at the "probable" "effective" term in the variable system.

20. The first three tools all produced similar results and showed a "normal" pendency period of approximately five years resulting, of course, in an "effective" term of protection of approximately fifteen years. The fourth tool showed, as noted in paragraph 14 of this submission, that in nine cases out of ten, a section 44 applicant obtained an "effective" term of seventeen years or less.

21. Thus all of these analytical techniques point to the same conclusion: where the "normal" term of "effective" protection available under a **variable-term** system is, on a statistically sound basis, equal to or less than the "effective" protection guaranteed under a **fixed-term** system, the two systems can fairly be said to be, and are, equivalent in providing the "...effective and adequate protection of intellectual property rights..."[18]-in this case, patent rights-that are at the heart of the TRIPS Agreement.

22. Notwithstanding the confusing characterizations put forward in paragraphs 6 and 7 of the US' Oral Statement, Canada has argued consistently that the **fixed and guaranteed term** of protection provided to section 45 patents is equivalent or superior to the **variable term** which results from the operation of Articles 33 and 62 and which is normally shorter and, on average, has been 15 years in Canada.

---

[15] See: the opening or "Desiring" recital to the Agreement.

[16] See: the US response to Panel Question 10.

[17] See: the US response to Panel Question 1(b) and its "...some loss of term due to pendency is inevitable..." statement.

[18] TRIPS, the opening, or "Desiring", recital to the Agreement.

23. US municipal legislation supports this reasoning. Canada's Exhibit 25 reproduces the patent term provisions of the current US Title 35 Patent legislation. As also quoted above[19] the provisions stipulate that:

> ...such grant shall be for a term beginning on the date the patent issues and ending 20 years from the date on which the application for the patent was filed in the United States.

24. To maintain its argument, the US must deny its own law. The period of "patent protection" or, as Canada also refers to it, the period of "effective protection" does not start until the patent issues and it inevitably runs for a variable period that is shorter than the twenty years referred to in the US legislation. Of course, this result might change if the variable-term system in place in the US, were made subject to some legislative amendment that reduced the variability of its current system.

25. Given the substance of the US complaint and its chronology, it was with some surprise that Canada recently learned that the US Title 35 patent legislation had been amended by the enactment of the ***Intellectual Property and Communications Omnibus Reform Act of 1999*** (S. 1948) in November 1999. The reform proposals appear to have come before the House of Representatives in March 1999 and subsequently, before the Senate in November 1999. In the result the amending proposals were both debated and passed into law during the pendency of this complaint. The Panel will recall from the record of these proceedings that the US Ambassador formally requested consultations on May 6, 1999.

26. As the amendments are not currently before the Panel, Canada would now put them in evidence as Exhibit No. 26. In their material part the amendments appear as Subtitle D of Title IV of the amending Act and may be cited as the: ***Patent Term Guarantee Act of 1999*** (Term Guarantee Act).[20]

27. The purpose of the Term Guarantee Act is, in the synopsis given by the US Patent and Trademark Office, to ensure that: "Diligent applicants are **guaranteed a minimum 17-year patent term.**".[21] (**Bold face** added for emphasis) A Member of the US House of Representatives, Dana Rohrabacher, expressed the same view in respect of the purpose of the amending legislation, reporting that it was enacted "...to assure a **minimum patent term of 17 years** from the date a patent is **granted.**"[22] (**Bold face** added for emphasis).

28. The parallels between these descriptions of the effect and purpose of the Term Guarantee Act with the US, Mexican and Canadian NAFTA commitments as well as with Canada's section 45 regime are striking.

29. Two provisions of Subtitle D merit particular consideration. The first concerns subparagraph 4402(b)(1)(B). It provides and **guarantees** that, subject to certain prescribed conditions, if, in the face of failures or delays in the Patent and Trademark Office, a patent does not issue within 3 years of the actual filing date, the term shall be extended one day for each day of delay beyond that three year period. In other words, this new US

[19] At para. 6 of this submission, and see: Exhibit No. 25.

[20] *Intellectual Property and Communications Omnibus Reform Act of 1999* (S. 1948), Subtitle D-Patent Term Guarantee. Reproduced as Exhibit No. 26.

[21] PTO Pulse -January 2000, *American Inventors Protection Act of 1999 is Law*, at page 2. Reproduced as Exhibit No. 27. (Note that 'guaranteed minimum term' appears to be 'code' for "effective" term.)

[22] Dana Rohrabacher, *Summary of Patent Reform Legislation*, at page 1. Reproduced as Exhibit No. 28.

legislation provides that **there is a guaranteed term of "effective" protection for 17 years from the date of grant.**

30. The second provision concerns the exception to the guarantee set out in clause 4402(b)(1)(B)(iii). It is of particular note because it expressly excludes from the calculation of the guarantee period, any processing delays requested by the applicant. Canada believes this provision to be noteworthy because the US has argued that the average pendency period of 5 years under Canada's section 44 regime is too long and unwarranted.[23]

31. However when, in this latter respect, one deducts the delays that occur because of the failure of an applicant to request "examination" on an immediate basis, as the Rules described in Canada's evidence[24] respecting section 44 applications would encourage, the approximate total delay at issue is the same 3 year delay that is sanctioned by the US in its new law as being "a reasonable period of time [which avoids] unwarranted curtailment of the period of protection.".[25]

32. Succinctly put, the Patent Term Guarantee Act enacts a new term of protection regime which limits the erosion of the "effective" term of protection under the US 20 years-from-filing regime to 17 years. This is, of course, the identical "effective" term of protection that is guaranteed under Canada's section 45 regime.

33. Canada believes that it is pertinent to recall that the US conceded in its response to the Panel's Question 8 that the effect of Article 1.1 is to require **substantive** compliance with the relevant obligations of the TRIPS treaty and that the **form** of compliance is not determinative of a compliance issue.

34. The US' implementing legislation in consequence of TRIPS and its patent term guarantee amending legislation confirm that the US recognises, and accepts in its municipal law and policy, that 17 years of patent protection is substantially equivalent or superior[26] to the variable term of "effective" patent protection which, under the TRIPS term formula, is inevitably shorter than the twenty year period it (and other municipal laws) refer to.

35. Thus while conceding that **substance** is more important than **form**, the US, in direct contradiction to this admission, is asking this Panel to **disregard the substantive compliance** of Canada's measure and to **denounce it as deficient in form**.

36. In the face of this request, and taking into account the TRIPS Agreement's broad and underlying objective of 'promoting the **effective and adequate** protection of intellectual property rights'[27], the comments of Representative Rohrabacher respecting the rationale underlying the ***Patent Term Guarantee Act of 1999*** deserve close attention within the context of these proceedings. Those comments were:

---

[23] The 1997 and 1998 Annual Reports of the EPO (European Patent Office) indicate that EPO's average processing time for applications which resulted in a patent during 1996 was 46.9 months, rose to 50.2 months in 1997 and in 1998 decreased to 44.7 months. It would appear that this period begins when an applicant requests examination and consequently EPO response times are of the same order of magnitude as Canada's.

[24] Davies Affidavit, paras. 26 to 29.

[25] The quoted words, with necessary grammatical adjustment, are, of course, drawn from para. 2 of Article 62.

[26] It is equal or superior because it establishes a floor, beneath which the variable term may not fall (except when the delays are caused by the applicant).

[27] TRIPS, the opening, or "Desiring", recital to the Agreement.

> As everyone is aware, the current law governing patent term is 20 years from the date of file *(sic)*. Patents applied for after June 8, 1995, when the provision eliminating the 17-years-from-grant guarantee took effect, have been losing precious time under the law. Before the enactment of S. 1948, these inventors could no longer rely on a guaranteed term of protection. In some cases, several years of **effective post-grant protection** could have been lost due to Patent and Trademark Office (PTO) administrative delay. (**Bold face** added for emphasis)

Ultimately, if the PTO does not issue a patent within 3 years from the date of original file, the patent term will be compensated day-for-day until the patent issues, ...

> This approach, ... effectively gives back to the non-dilatory patent holder what I have fought for - the right to a guaranteed 17 year patent term.[28]

37. In providing 17 years of guaranteed patent protection, Canada's measure is not only consistent with and equivalent to the substantive requirement of Article 33 when read in conjunction with Article 62, it is also consistent with the complainant's own law and policy as expressed in US municipal law.

IV. CANADA'S "AVAILABILITY" ARGUMENT AND EVIDENCE

38. The US has also misstated and mischaracterized Canada's argument in respect of the "availability" of a term of patent protection that "shall not end before the expiration of a period of twenty years counted from the filing date.". In this respect Canada has stated that "section 45 does not provide, or otherwise require, that the term of protection conferred shall end before the expiration of the twenty year period measured from the filing date of the patent application".[29] The US has never contradicted this statement.

39. As Canada has already observed, the US argument and description of the requirement imposed by Article 33 reads out the word "**available**". The US also relies on inconsistent propositions of law; for example, it has, in developing its Article 70 argument, denied that the Agreement is retroactive.[30] However, in impugning Canada's availability argument, the US argues, at paragraph 13 of its Rebuttal Submission, that Old Act patentees cannot be said to have waived a TRIPS-level term of protection before it existed. This argument not only misrepresents Canada's position, it lacks logical consistency with the US' other arguments.

40. It is obvious that prior to the 1989 changes in Canada's municipal law or the negotiation of TRIPS, patent applicants would not be directing their minds to a "twenty year from filing" time frame. In Canada's view that is beside the point.

41. As Canada observed in paragraphs 31 and 32 of its Second Submission in reference to US Exhibit 11, the normal period of delay between filing a patent application and obtaining regulatory approval for pharmaceuticals typically took 10 years. In these cir-

[28] Exhibit No. 28, Subtitle D - Patent Term Guarantee Act of 1999, para. 2 and parts of paras. 3 and 4.

[29] Subparagraph 5(b), of Canada's First (Written) Submission.

[30] Para. 14 of the Oral Statement of the US.

cumstances, and as Canada's explanation clearly demonstrates, the applicant for a patent would have a clear motive to delay the process time so that the start of the period of patent protection would more closely match the time from which it was 'licensed'-received marketing approval-to market the product. Such conduct has nothing to do with a future right or benefit that may flow from TRIPS.

42. The evidence is undisputed that anyone who wanted to delay the issuance of their patent could do so and, within the existing law and practice of Canada, terms of 20 years of patent protection measured from the filing date were available without exception.

43. In Canada's submission, it is not necessary that every applicant made a conscious choice in respect to an unknowable, future 'minimum' term formulation. The substance of the Article 33 requirement is that the term be "**available**". On all the evidence it was, and is. Anyone who saw an advantage in delaying the issuing date of their patent in relation to the filing date could do so, and **did.**

44. Canada will not take up more of the Panel's time by reiterating all of its arguments in relation to availability. They are fully developed in Canada's earlier Submissions and Responses to Panel Questions.[31] Canada will, however, take this opportunity to further respond to the US argument that Canada's Old Act law and practice did not provide a "sound legal basis" for the availability of a twenty year from filing date term.

45. The Panel will recall that, as Exhibit 16, Canada filed evidence of the statutory basis for demonstrating that there is a right, under the combined effect of subsection 30(2) and section 73 of Canada's Old Act regime, to 42 months of delays between the time of filing and issuance. These delays are directly related to essential steps in the processing of an Old Act patent application. They are not dependant on particular circumstances which may give rise to additional delays provided by statute[32] in any given case. Nor are they dependent on the other, informal delays described by Mr. Davies in his affidavit.[33]

46. Nor, as noted in paragraph 44 of Canada's First Oral Presentation, does this showing of the existence of a statutory basis for obtaining a delay in the prosecution of an application, take into account the effect on "availability" that the actual examination time would have on the duration of the term of protection if it were to be assessed against the filing date.

47. The US, in its Rebuttal Submission under section III A, treats the delays under section 30(2) and section 73 as the **only** delays that were available to prolong the fixed seventeen year term, when the latter was measured from the application filing date. As Canada has just explained, this is wrong.

48. The US also seeks to establish that these statutory provisions are unduly complex and somehow abusive. Canada denies this and would refer you to the discussion in paragraphs 10 to 13 in its Second Submission.

49. In this respect Canada recalls that in answer to its third question, the US admits that its own patent legislation "does and did contain provisions similar to Section 30.2 (sic) of Canada's old Act". As Exhibit No. 28 demonstrates, these US statutory opportuni-

---

[31] See: Paras. 84 to 110 of Canada's First (Written) Submission; paras. 30 to 57 of Canada's first Oral Presentation; and, Canada's response to Panel Question 3.

[32] Such other delays would include, for example, requests from a patent examiner for information additional to that already found in the application. Under the statute the applicant has six months to respond to such requests.

[33] Davies Affidavit, para. 10.

ties for delay would, as in Canada, be additional to the everyday internal delays which occur within the US Patent and Trademark Office.

50. Canada has demonstrated with uncontradicted evidence that everyone without exception was able to delay the issuance of its patent to a time later than 3 years after the application was filed. No one who chose to take advantage of those delays is subject to a court or any other body interfering with its patent term as a result of the administrative actions taken to effect those delays.[34]

51. Thus Canada has also demonstrated that its laws and practices permitting administrative delays that had the effect of extending the term of protection (when measured from an application filing date) had a 'sound basis in law' as required by the test set out in the *India - Patent Protection* case.[35] The US, in contrast, has failed to disprove the "sound legal basis" underlying these Canadian laws and practices.

52. The Panel will also recall that Canada anticipated and addressed the issue that some of the delays under section 30(2) were discretionary in its first Oral Presentation at paragraph 45 to 49. Not only are discretionary limitations expressly authorised under TRIPS Article 62.1, but we are concerned here, in contrast to the prospective issues in the *India - Patent Protection* case, exclusively with historical fact.

53. There is, in addition, no evidence that someone who was granted a delay had its patent term subsequently shortened or otherwise interfered with on judicial or other competent authority review. Nor is there any evidence that someone who sought to delay the issuance of a patent, for whatever their private interest may have been, was ever denied the delay requested.

54. As a matter of uncontested fact the period of twenty years from filing was available to every applicant throughout the period during which their application was pending. There is no evidence which can sustain or support a contrary finding.

55. The evidence is undisputed that anyone who wanted a delay obtained it, because it was available, without exception, to anyone who made such a request. Any applicant could within Canada's existing legal system and practice exercise control over when its patent issued in relation to the application filing date. The twenty year and twenty year plus terms of protection which, when measured from their respective filing dates, were accorded to some 150,000 Old Act patents, and this coupled with the total absence of any evidence that a request to delay or postpone the issuance of a patent was ever refused, is uncontradictable evidence of availability.[36]

56. History is history. In these proceedings the US seeks to unmake it-on the basis of speculative assertion and theory. Not on the basis of evidence.

V. ARTICLE 70

57. Canada has previously argued that the transitional rules set out in Article 70 are irrelevant because Canada's pre-existing section 45 patent regime is fully compliant with the TRIPS Agreement. Since Canada's section 45 patent term of protection is equivalent

---

[34] See: Paras. 34 to 41 of Canada's Second Submission.

[35] *India - Patent Protection For Pharmaceutical And Agricultural Chemical Products (AB-1997-5)*, WT/DS50/AB/R, adopted 16 January 1998, DSR 1998:I, 9 and see discussion of this issue at para. 36 and following of Canada's first Oral Presentation and at paras. 35 to 41 of Canada's Second Submission.

[36] Davies Affidavit, para. 15.

to the TRIPS variable standard, and since a term of protection of 20 years measured from the filing date was always available; the TRIPS transitional rules are not engaged.

58. The US as the complaining party must not only establish that Canada's impugned measure does not comply with the requirement in Article 33, it must also establish that section 45 patents are subject to Article 33. In Canada's submission, the US submissions have failed on all counts.

59. Article 70.1 provides that the Agreement, which of course includes Article 33, does not give rise to obligations in respect of "acts" which occurred before the date of application of the Agreement. The US has conceded in response to the Panel's question 11 that "By its plain meaning, 'acts' would include the administrative act of granting a patent by a patent office". The US in paragraph 25 of its Rebuttal Submission appears to further concede that the "act" of filing an application by a right holder is also within the scope of Article 70.1.

60. Canada has produced as Exhibit 24 copies of Canadian Patent certificates for both the section 45 and section 44 regimes. It is clear from the 'language of grant' used that the administrative act of granting a patent includes, as an integral component of that act, a temporal limitation.

61. Thus in respect to a section 45 patent, the patent grants to the owner "for a term which expires seventeen years from the date on which the patent is granted and issued in Canada" certain exclusive rights and privileges in respect of the invention. The certificate is then dated over an official signature. The certificate of grant is therefore conclusive of both the existence of the patent and the duration of its term.

62. The result is that the TRIPS Agreement does not give rise to any obligations in respect of those "acts" which occurred before the implementation date. This does not mean that the Agreement does not have application to the "subject matter" which those patents protect.[37] By force of Article 70.2, it clearly does "Except as otherwise provided in the Agreement". There is, however, such an express "otherwise" proviso for "acts" under Article 70.1. There is no similar proviso for the rights and privileges that flow from the patent and are attached to the invention or the "subject matter" of patent protection.

63. In paragraph 27 of its Rebuttal Submission, the US again seeks to rely on contradictory and inconsistent reasoning. The US has said unequivocally that the Agreement is not retroactive (see paragraph 14 First Oral Statement). Now, however, it argues that pre-1996 administrative acts are exempt, but only until January 1, 1996 at which time they become subject to what the US characterizes as the prospective[38] application of TRIPS standards. That is, in the US view, pre-application date "acts" are exempt until the application date. Thereafter they become subject to the Agreement. This empty distinction is disingenuous. The "acts" of filing an application and of granting a patent for a fixed term are complete when they are made and, therefore, are not subject to the Agreement.

[37] Contrary to the US criticism of Canada's para. 113 (first submission), the US now acknowledges that Canada is not making the unequivocal statement that the agreement has no application to pre-1996 patents: paras. 31 and 32 US Rebuttal Submission.

[38] See: para. 15 of the US Oral Statement.

VI. SUBJECT MATTER

64. Consistent with their reconstruction of the substance of Article 28 of the *Vienna Convention on the Law of Treaties*[39], the TRIPS negotiators clearly intended to confirm, not contract out of, the Article 28 Convention rule against the retroactive application of treaties to pre-treaty acts, facts and no longer existing situations, **except as they otherwise provided**.

65. They did this to a limited extent in paragraph 2 of Article 70 where they stipulated that the TRIPS Agreement would, "Except as otherwise provided for in this Agreement", have a limited retrospective application, and give

> ...rise to obligations in respect of all subject matter existing at the date of application of this Agreement...and which is protected...on the said date, or which meets or comes subsequently to meet the criteria for protection under the terms of this Agreement...

66. Paragraph 2 of Article 70 is concerned with obligations in respect of "subject matter". Canada and the US do not agree on the contextual scope of the expression "subject matter". Canada says that granting a term of patent protection is an integral part of the act of issuing a Canadian patent. Moreover, a term of patent protection is an obligation in respect of the life of the patent. A patent term is not an obligation in respect of subject matter.

67. The US position is more transitory and uncertain. The initial position of the US assumed that patents were "subject matter" and since they were "subject matter", the Article 70.2 rule applied unambiguously.[40] In its subsequent Oral Statement the US restated this assumption affirmatively, where, after quoting the substance of Article 70.2, it asserted that: "A patent is a type of subject matter.". Given this assertion, here again the Article 70.2 rule was said by the US to apply, unambiguously.[41]

68. Canada denied the validity of the US assertion that patents were "subject matter" within the meaning of TRIPS, noting that it was clear from the textual and contextual use of the phrase "subject matter" in the treaty that it meant the **matter**; that is, the 'work', 'mark', 'geographical indication', 'industrial design', 'invention' or 'layout-design', that attracts the exclusive intellectual property rights which serve to protect it.[42]

69. Subsequently[43] the US resiled fully from its two opening positions to agree with Canada that:

> ...'subject matter' as used in the TRIPS Agreement generally refers to the matter that is or can be entitled to intellectual property protection. Indeed, this is exactly how Article 70.2 utilizes the term 'subject matter'.[44]

---

[39] See: Canada's response to Panel Question 6(d).

[40] See: Para. 11 of the first Submission of the US, where it states that "...TRIPS...gives rise to obligations...in respect of all patents ("subject matter") existing...".

[41] See: Para. 10 of the Oral Statement of the US.

[42] See: Paras. 66 and 67 of Canada's first Oral Presentation, paras. 48 to 58 of Canada's Second Submission as well as its answers to Panel Questions 6,7 and 27.

[43] See: the US responses to Panel Questions 7 and 13.

[44] Canada assumes the use of the word "generally" is a reference to the fact, noted in Canada's answer to Panel Question 27, that in Articles 40.3 and 40.4 "subject matter" is used to refer to the

70. However, having so resiled from its initial position, the US next attempted to bring the concepts of both "patent" and "term of protection" back within the ambit of "subject matter" and, therefore, of Article 70.2 by the use of a variety of compound terms, such as patented inventions[45], or expanded phrasings or explanations such as those used in paragraphs 24 to 30 of the Rebuttal Submission of the US.

71. As argued in paragraphs 48 to 58 of Canada's Second Submission, to read words like "patentable" or "protected" into "subject matter" does violence to Article 70.2 as well as to the term "subject matter" itself. Such words when used in relation to "subject matter" are adjectival only. They do not transform the thing itself.

72. Similarly, the resort to extended phrasings or explanations such as those used in paragraph 26 of the US' Rebuttal Submission, saying that there is, under paragraph 2 of Article 70, an "...obligation to a grant a TRIPS-level patent term to such inventions that existed on January 1, 1996.", exceed the plain meaning of the words used in both of paragraph 2 of Article 70 and Article 33.

73. The US now asserts that obligations in respect of subject matter, must be read as obligations in respect of patentable subject matter and this would therefore include the Article 33 obligation for a term of protection. Reading in words is impermissible and reading in "patentable" into Article 70.2 creates redundancies as Canada previously argued.[46]

74. Clearly, a patent, which is the legal device through which the State protects an invention, is not subject matter within the ordinary meaning of Article 70.2. Consequently, the obligations referred to in that Article do not apply to patents themselves, once issued, and would therefore not include Article 33.

VII. CONCLUSION

75. Canada believes that this, contrary to the US characterization, is a complex case. It is full of subtlety and nuance. It raises important questions of the relationship between form and substance. Of course, it is, more particularly, a case about the meaning and scope of Article 33. And, depending on the answers to those two issues, it is perhaps also a case about the meaning and scope of paragraphs 1 and 2 of Article 70.

The context of this dispute

76. The commercial stakes at issue are undeniably large. The US has made this very clear. It has said that Canada's alleged non-compliance with its TRIPS obligations have "caused tremendous harm"[47]. And that this harm has been particularly severe for the pharmaceutical industry.

77. In its subsequent submissions the US has not pursued this aspect of its case. There is, however, no doubt that windfall monopoly profits would accrue to the pharmaceutical industry from extensions to the terms of protection that were granted by the Commis-

matters under discussion elsewhere in the Article rather than to matters that may be the objects of intellectual property protection.

45 See, for example the discussion of this issue in the US response to Panel Question 7. See also the discussion of the issue in paras. 48 to 58 of Canada's Second Submission.

46 See Canada's Second Submission paras. 50 to 52.

47 See: paras. 5 and 6 of the First (Written) Submission of the US.

sioner of Patents against applications which were filed in Canada prior to October 1, 1989. And that those windfall monopoly profits would be substantial.

78. Irrespective of quantum, there is an issue of equity that arises against those who, in the past, made an economic choice to exploit their section 45 patent terms in one way and now seek to vary the terms of their bargain with society. They wish now to exploit the new TRIPS term of protection regime for their private advantage and against the broader interest of society. This breaches two Article 7 objectives. It breaches the objective that intellectual property rights should contribute to the mutual advantage of its producers and of its users. And it breaches the objective that the intellectual property rules should contribute "to a balance of rights and obligations".

79. Thus the pith and substance of the US position is that it is attempting to obtain relief from the World Trade Organization that, as the Abbott case[48] demonstrates, would not be available under its own municipal law because of the inequity of the relief sought.

Summary of Canada's Case

80. Against this background, Canada would like to thank the Panel for its close attention. Interpreting the relevant provisions of the TRIPS Agreement is seldom, if ever, an easy task. In this regard it has been Canada's goal throughout these proceedings to assist you in this challenge.

81. In further pursuit of this goal, Canada would sum up and reduce its submissions to their bare essentials by offering the following synopsis of its position.

The scope of the obligation in Article 33

82. First, Article 33 imposes a single requirement which is: to make a term of patent protection **available** beginning on the date the patent issues and ending 20 years from the date on which the application was filed. That is how the US has characterized the requirement in its legislation. The Article does not impose a requirement for a 20 year term of protection as contended by the US in its submissions. As the Agreement does not contain the very requirement upon which the US founds its complaint, it fails.

The "equivalency" of terms of "effective" protection

83. Second, the term of "effective" patent protection that, under the TRIPS formula, begins sometime during the course of the 20 years measured from the filing date, is **inevitably** less than 20 years. In Canada, it is normally 15 years. In the European Patent Office, it is of the same order.

84. The US, recognising the erosion of the term of protection that occurs as a result of processing delays, has recently guaranteed a minimum period of 17 years from grant, excluding from the calculation of 'compensable delay' any delays requested by the applicant. Canada's section 45 regime guarantees an equivalent term of protection to that which, by virtue of its 17 year statutory guarantee, the US deems reasonable within a 20 year from filing date system.

85. There is no room for debate here. The US cannot seriously seek, on the authority of TRIPS, to have the WTO impose a more onerous substantive requirement on Canada than it, in compliance with its own TRIPS obligations, imposes on itself.

[48] See: para. 100 of Canada's First (Written) Submission and Footnote 40 to that para..

The "availability" of a 20 year-from-filing term under section 45

86. Third, all of the evidence before you is uncontradicted. It confirms and establishes that a period of protection of twenty years from filing grounded on a sound legal foundation was, under Canada's Old Act, **available**. And, it was **available** without exception. These are the uncontested facts, there are no points of law involved. The period described in Article 33 was **available**. That is a complete answer to the US complaint.

Article 70.1 and pre-application date "acts"

87. Fourth, the US now concedes that, consistent with rule against treaty retroactivity set out in Article 28 of the *Vienna Convention on the Law of Treaties*, the acts of filing an application for a patent and the administrative act of granting a patent are within the scope of Article 70.1. These are complete and final acts all of which occurred before the date of application of the Agreement. This allows for only one answer. The Agreement, including Article 33, does not give rise to any obligations in respect of those acts.

Article 70.2 and the meaning of "subject matter"

88. Finally, the US over reads the meaning of "subject matter" within TRIPS in order to bring either "patents", or the "term of protection" obligations respecting patents, within the scope of the obligation set out in paragraph 2 of Article 70. This misconstrues both patent law and the Agreement. Neither a "patent" nor the "term of protection" is "subject matter" within the meaning of TRIPS.

89. Nor, since the "term of protection" is not "subject matter", can the Article 33 obligation respecting the "term of protection" be interpreted, as the US seems to suggest, as being "an obligation in respect of subject matter" within the meaning of paragraph 2 of Article 70. Consequently the obligation in Article 33 does not give rise to obligations under paragraph 2 of Article 70.

VIII. DISPOSITION REQUESTED

90. For all these reasons as well as the reasons set out in Canada's prior submissions and responses to Panel Questions, the US complaint fails and Canada respectfully asks that it be dismissed.

ATTACHMENT 2.6

RESPONSES OF CANADA TO WRITTEN QUESTIONS
FROM THE PANEL - SECOND MEETING
(3 February 2000)

A. EQUIVALENCE

Q.29 (Canada) Even if Canada's Old Act patent term is roughly the same *length* as the New Act term, how does it satisfy the requirement as to when the patent term should *end*? Article 62.2 only authorizes curtailment of the patent term at the beginning, not the end, and Article 33 clearly specifies a minimum end date. Does this depend on the success of the availability argument?

As Canada will demonstrate the TRIPS Agreement does not impose a specific end point for a term of patent protection that must be met in all circumstances. In this respect Canada notes that Article 62, when read as a whole, is not limited to the authorization of the "curtailment" of the patent term at the beginning of the term of protection. Article 62 also contemplates and authorizes the termination of the term of protection, **before** the expiry of the period referred to in Article 33.

In contrast to the implicit argument of the United States of America (US), Canada does not believe that the term of protection provisions of Canada's Old Act section 45 and of TRIPS' Article 33 are susceptible, on their face, to direct comparison.

Canada does not believe that the section 45 formula-which provides for a specified, fixed term of protection measured from the date of grant-can be directly compared to the Article 33 formula-which provides for a variable term measured from the application filing date-because the two provisions reference different commencement dates and specify different numbers of years during which the different amounts of protection they refer to shall be "available".

Since the two types of provision cannot be compared by simple reference to their **forms** of expression, Canada has, within its equivalency argument, sought to compare or assess the consistency of one with the other by an examination and analysis of the **substance** of the amount of protection described by the two different prescriptions of the term of protection.

As the Panel will recall from Canada's previous elaborations of its analysis, it proceeds from the basis that section 45 offers a guaranteed, fixed seventeen year term of protection for the exclusive privilege and property rights which, once granted, flow from a patent. It next observes-and the US concedes[1]-that, in view of the combined operation of Article 33 and paragraphs 1 and 2 of Article 62, the period of "effective" protection of the exclusive privilege and property rights will, under the TRIPS formula, vary.

The amount of variation will depend on the length of the Article 62.2 pendency period which, of course, delays the date of grant and so foreshortens the nominal amount of protection of the exclusive privilege and property rights available under the TRIPS formula. The amount of variation will also depend on the happening, under the authority

1 See: the US response to Question 1(b) in the questions posed by the Panel at the conclusion of its first substantive meeting with the parties (December 20, 1999).

of Articles 62.1 and 62.4, of any act of revocation, of cancellation or of default in the payment of maintenance fees. All or any of these will, of course, accelerate the expiry date of the patent in question and so truncate the amount of "effective" protection afforded to the exclusive privilege and property rights granted by a patent.

In the result, under the TRIPS formula neither the commencement date-the date of filing-nor the end date-the expiry of the twenty year period-can be said to represent a **fixed, substantive norm** of the quantum of "effective" protection offered by the scheme of the treaty. Accordingly, neither the commencement nor the end date parameters used by the Article 33 formula for determining the term of protection can be viewed as being fixed, **substantive requirements** or "benchmarks" of the "effective" protection contemplated by the treaty. They are instead elements of **form** within which **substance** is determined. Once the **substance** is determined, **form** loses any further significance in an assessment of the equivalency or consistency between one system for the measurement of the term of patent protection and the other.

As the Panel will also recall[2] in Canada the pendency period under the New Act's, undeniably TRIPS consistent, formula has, whether as an average, a mean or a modal "norm", been approximately 5 years.[3] In the result, in Canada the "normal" "effective" term of protection under its undeniably TRIPS compliant section 44 has, correspondingly, been approximately 15 years.[4]

Given this analysis and its results Canada has consistently framed it's argument as being that a fixed term of 17 years from grant was equivalent or superior to the variable term that results from the formula in Article 33. This argument is not dependant on the availability argument, although the latter is complementary of the first.

In paragraph 8 of it's Second Submission, the US asserts that Article 62.2 addresses the commencement of the term of protection and not the expiration date while Article 33 is concerned with the end of the period of protection. This assertion is unfounded and is based on an incomplete contextual analysis.

Article 33 addresses the commencement-being, the filing date-and the end-being twenty years from the filing date-of a period during which a patent will provide protection after the patent issues. Moreover, as noted above Articles 62.1 and 62.4 address TRIPS sanctioned actions which operate to deprive the Article 33 end date of any fixed meaning. Accordingly the provisions of Article 62 operate to reduce the dates referred to in Article

---

2 See: paras. 53 and 54 of Canada's First (Written) Submission, the Davies Affidavit, para. 29 and Exhibit F thereto, paras. 21 to 26 of Canada's First Oral Presentation as well as the discussion in paras. 17 to 21 of Canada's Second Oral Presentation.

3 The five year pendency period compares favourably with the experience in the European Patent Office (EPO). See para. 30 of Canada's Second Oral Presentation and footnote 23 to that para.. This pendency period would also appear to compare favourably with the US experience under its TRIPS compliant legislation since the US has been motivated to enact a ***Patent Term Guarantee Act*** that compensates successful applicants for delays in the grant of their patents that have exceeded three years. See: paras. 25 to 37 of Canada's Second Oral Presentation and Exhibit No. 26.

4 Canada has not presented any evidence in respect of the "normal" amount of "effective" protection that may be lost as a result of acts of revocation, cancellation or default of maintenance obligations because neither the TRIPS scheme-in place for about 4 years-nor its municipal counterparts-in place in Canada for about 10 years-have been in place for long enough to generate a reliable indication of the amount of term truncation that may be expected to occur. The doubtful reliability is enhanced by the fact that, *a priori*, acts of default are most likely to occur at the end of the nominal TRIPS term rather than in the early years of protection.

33 to matters of the **form of determining, not defining**, the amount of "effective" protection available under the Article.

Article 62 by its plain language is concerned with both the acquisition and maintenance of intellectual property rights as stated in it's title. Article 62.2 addresses unwarranted curtailment by procedures associated with obtaining the right; while Articles 62.1 and 62.4 address matters relating to the acquisition, maintenance and revocation of "effective" protection.

Canada recalls that in answer to Canada's Question 4 following the first substantive meeting of the parties with the Panel, the US conceded that a patent owner could forfeit it's patent by failing to pay maintenance fees at any time during the 20 year period counted from the filing date. The rationale for this admission is clear. A patent is a private right which the owner can, within certain legal limitations[5], exploit or abandon as the owner chooses.

US municipal law accurately describes the TRIPS term of patent protection as a term beginning on the date the patent issues and, subject to the fulfilment of maintenance obligations, ending 20 years from the filing date. The term of protection which must be made available occurs within a twenty year time frame but is, as the US concedes[6], inevitably less, whether by erosion of the commencement date or whether by truncation of the expiry date. There is nothing in the Agreement that requires a patent owner to either choose or accept a patent for an irrevocable period of time. A patent is a privilege, obtained on the application of and largely at a time controlled by the applicant, to be exploited as the grantee chooses. It is not a burden which the grantee must take up and discharge at the behest of and for a period prescribed by the grantor, irrespective of the grantee's interests-whatever they may be.

Against this background, a Member's obligation under Article 33 is to make a period of protection "available" which, subject to acts of revocation, cancellation and of default in maintenance obligations, does not end before twenty years from the filing date. That is the **form** or standard of measurement for the protection to be afforded. It is **not** a definition of the **substance** of the protection which is actually to be **realized** under the TRIPS obligation and against which a Member's compliance is to be considered.

The substantive period of patent protection only arises after a patent issues and may, by either an act of revocation (or cancellation) by the granting authority or an act of default by the grantee, end at any time before the running of the term set out in Article 33. The US has conceded[7] that Article 1.1 allows that, within a Member's legal system or practice, a Member is free to determine the method of achieving **substantive compliance** with its TRIPS obligations and is not limited by **matters of form**.

Canada has demonstrated that in Canada and Europe[8] the normal pendency period for the processing of an application is approximately five years, resulting in approximately 15 years of substantive or "effective" protection. This is less "effective" protection than the 17 years guaranteed by a section 45 patent.[9]

---

[5] See, for example, Articles 29, 30, 31 and 40.

[6] See, the US response to the Panel's December 20, 1999 Question 1.

[7] See: the US response to the Panel's December 20 1999 Question 8.

[8] See: para. 30 of Canada's Second Oral Submission and footnote 23 to that para. respecting the EPO's average response times in respect of EPO patent applications.

[9] This too is less than the seventeen years of protection from grant recently guaranteed by the US' new ***Patent Term Guarantee Act of 1999.***

As the fourth Recital to the TRIPS Agreement acknowledges "intellectual property rights are private rights", thus a patent owner is free in the exercise of it's private property rights to terminate its "effective" term of protection prematurely without any negative impact on the grantor Member's level of compliance with its TRIPS obligations.[10] Similarly, in the prosecution of its application for patent privileges, an applicant is, within certain limits, free to choose when the privileges will be granted and so give life to the benefits of patent protection. Thus the substantive benefit of 17 years under section 45 is at least equivalent to the substantive, but variable, period of normally 15 years available under the TRIPS formula, no matter when it might occur in respect of the defined, nominal period which falls within the parameters set out in Article 33.

The period of "effective" patent protection is substantively equivalent and not dependant on a specific end date as described in Article 33, particularly as that period may be modified by the operation of the activities referred to in Articles 62.1, 62.2 and 62.4. Article 1.1 suggests that if the substantive obligation is met by a member's legal system and practice, that is sufficient. As the US put it in answer to the Panel's Question 8 of December 20, 1999:

> So long as the relevant obligation [to provide a **patent** term of protection] is indeed fully implemented and has a sound legal basis in a Member's legal regime, the precise method of implementation [17 years from grant term versus a variable 15 year from filing term] is left to the Member.

Canada's section 45 regime does not specify an end date in relation to the application filing date. Canada's law and practice does not, therefore, require the period to end before the expiry of any particular period measured from the filing date. Accordingly, an applicant acting in it's own private interest is free to expedite or delay the issuance of it's patent in the same way it is free, once possessed of a patent, to abandon or forfeit it's patent and its patent rights whenever it chooses. In other words the commencement and end date benchmarks of the TRIPS formula for determining the term of protection circumscribe the limits of, but do not define, the minimum quantum of the "effective" term of protection that the Agreement requires its Members to provide to successful applicants for the patent privilege.

In Canada's First Oral Presentation[11], it observed that the inviolate condition precedent to a term of protection is a patent. It is Canada's view that Article 33 reflects the TRIPS objective of the need "to promote **effective** and adequate protection of intellectual property rights".[12] (**Bold face** added for emphasis) The substantive concern of Article 33 is not the end date, which a patent owner can end early if it chooses, but rather the effective term of protection. Substantively, 17 years from grant provides more "effective" protection than a 20 year from filing regime. The US understanding and acceptance of this fact is reflected in it's new ***Patent Term Guarantee Act of 1999.***[13]

Accordingly, since within Canada's "equivalency" argument the TRIPS end date only has significance for the purposes of determining the amount of "effective" protection offered by the Article 33 formula, it loses any further significance in the consistency

---

[10] This point has been conceded by the US in its response to Canada's Question 4 posed following the first substantive meeting of the parties with the Panel.

[11] See: paras. 12 to 14 of the written version of that Presentation.

[12] TRIPS, the first or "desiring" recital to the Agreement.

[13] See: paras. 25 to 37 of Canada's Second Oral Presentation and the associated exhibit, Exhibit No. 26.

analysis and is 'spent' once that analysis is complete.[14] In this sense the "equivalency" argument is sustainable on its own merit and is not dependant on the success of Canada's "availability" argument.

However, as noted above, the "availability" argument is complementary to the "equivalency" argument. Under Canada's section 45 patent regime, the period of twenty years from filing, although not expressly identified by statutory reference was nevertheless "available" to any section 45 applicant who wished to view, measure, **seek** and **obtain** its term of protection on that basis.

Accordingly, if the end date prescription in Article 33 has, contrary to Canada's view and analysis, any residual substantive content such that the Article 33 termination standard might be seen to defeat substantive equivalency, then the fact that the twenty year term from filing was unambiguously available under Canadian law and practice would operate to reinforce the "substantively equivalent" argument as a complete and unrefuted answer to the US complaint.

B. AVAILABILITY (ARTICLE 33)

Q.30 (Canada) Are the powers under Canada's *Patent Act* to reinstate and restore patent applications discretionary and not automatic? Is the Canadian Patent Office obliged to reinstate or restore applications which have been abandoned or forfeited simply to procure a delay in the term of protection?

There are two discrete elements to this question. Both invite two answers: one technical; one contextual. The first technical answer is that under the Old Act some of the statutory powers to reinstate and restore patent applications were discretionary, some were automatic.

The section 73 remedy was automatic insofar as the relief was available as of right to an applicant who paid the necessary fee. In this sense the "powers" were not really "powers". Instead they were, notwithstanding the statutory use of the permissive word "may", more akin to duties of the Commissioner of Patents. As such the duty to grant relief could, on proof of the payment of the fee, be enforced in the courts by an applicant through the service of a writ of mandamus. There was, therefore, no administrative discretion at play.

The powers of relief under subsection 30(2) were discretionary insofar as, beyond the payment of a fee, they were only exercisable where the applicant-petitioner was able to satisfy the Commissioner that the applicant's failure to meet the deadlines of the Old Act were "not reasonably avoidable".

However, the quasi-constitutional rules of natural justice, which the courts will apply to the exercise of discretionary authority by administrative officials, require that the exercise of discretion not be unreasonably denied. Among others standards, the courts will, in applying the rules of natural justice, require that discretion be exercised in good faith, be exercised without discrimination, be exercised taking into account the purpose of the legislation granting the discretion and be exercised without reference to irrelevant or

[14] In simplistic arithmetic form the analysis says that: twenty years from filing less the pre-granting pendency period and less any period arising from acts of revocation or default in maintenance obligations equals the term of "effective" protection.

other improper considerations unrelated to the purposes or criteria of the statute granting the authority.

Thus the discretionary authority created by subsection 30(2) does not impose a serious impediment to or burden on any applicant who, knowing the circumstances of its own delay, may offer the explanation implicitly required by the statute and so deprive the Commissioner of the capacity to refuse the relief requested. In sum, although discretion exists it is not a discretion that may be exercised frivolously to deny relief where the delay involved resulted from some reasonable circumstance. In the world of patent applications there are myriad factors that may exist to impede an applicant's capacity to proceed as expeditiously as the statute, in its arbitrary, general-rule-writing fashion, contemplates.

In respect of the second element of the question asked, the technical answer is that the statutory criteria that frame and limit the exercise of the discretion referred to in subsection 30(2) make no reference to the motive of an applicant seeking to have the discretion exercised in its favour. The test for the exercise of discretion is "not reasonably avoidable".

In this circumstance, were an applicant to say "I merely wish to delay the issuance of the patent in question in order to obtain a twenty term from my filing date." the Commissioner could, had the situation ever arisen, have been entitled to refuse the relief requested since the applicant, in revealing its motive, would not have shown that its failure to meet the deadlines of the application process was "not reasonably avoidable".

However, were the applicant able to say-as the evidence clearly suggests-that, irrespective of its underlying motive, "I was unable to meet the statutory delays because of" some reason related to the timely completion of its application, then the Commissioner would have no authority to look behind that reason to examine the motive of the applicant and refuse relief requested on the basis of "motive".

The contextual answer begins with the observation that the US complaint is only addressed to those Canadian patents where the application was filed before October 1, 1989-that is before section 44 came into effect-and which were granted before October 1, 1992.

The question posed by the Panel concerning the discretion to re-instate assumes that there may be circumstances where a discretion could be exercised to deny an applicant access to a term of protection equal to the period referred to in Article 33.

There is no evidence that anybody who requested the reinstatement of their patent application was ever refused that reinstatement by the Commissioner. A search of Canadian jurisprudence has revealed that no patent applicant has ever sought judicial review of an administrative decision to deny the reinstatement of a section 45 patent application.

Peter Davies, the Chairman of the Canadian Patent Appeal Board, has sworn that, in 33 years of experience, he is unaware of any situation where an informal request for a delay was refused. The evidence is that informal delays were granted without any necessity for the applicant to resort to the statutory provisions of subsection 30(2) of the Old Act.

As noted above, the statutory delay under section 73 of the Old Act was available automatically on payment of the required fee. The subsection 30(2) discretionary power to refuse reinstatement was never used. The section was ultimately repealed as being redundant. The reinstatement provision now forms part of the procedures under section 73 of the current Act and there is no discretion to refuse reinstatement so long as the applicant seeking reinstatement pays the appropriate administrative fee.[15]

In all these circumstances the existence of a discretionary power in the past has had no impact on any patent applicant. The evidence is uncontested. It shows that no applicant who sought a delay or who utilized the various statutory devices available in order to postpone the issuance of its patent was ever hindered in its achievement of that goal in any way. Neither the existence nor the exercise of the discretionary power in subsection 30(2) ever adversely affected any applicant. Moreover, no one since October 1, 1992 could have been, or will be, affected by the existence or exercise of such powers because all patents issued after that date provide, or will provide, at least twenty years of term when viewed from the perspective of their application filing dates.

In these circumstances, whether or not the Canadian Patent Office was obliged to re-instate or restore applications which had been or were deemed to have been abandoned or forfeited simply to procure a delay in the issuance of a patent, is moot. The uncontested fact is that it did so in every case. And it did so without exception.

As Canada has argued in its First Oral Presentation at paragraph 46, the discretion in subsection 30(2) to refuse reinstatement where the applicant has failed to satisfy the Commissioner that the reason for its delay was "not reasonably avoidable", although never exercised, is a reasonable formality for the maintenance of intellectual property rights within the meaning of Article 62 and as Canada also argued in that and the following paragraphs the existence of the discretion at issue posed absolutely no risk to a patent applicant's right to seek patent protection for its invention.

Q.31 (Canada) Paragraph 37 of your First Submission states that an Old Act applicant could "slow down the prosecution" of an application "by simply asking the patent examiner" and paragraph 42 of your First Oral Statement states that "the applicant could do so informally, simply by asking, or alternatively the applicant could take advantage of statutorily mandated delays for perfecting applications and other essential procedural steps." In addition to the delays provided under Section 30(1) and (2) and Section 73 of the Old Act:

(a) What type of delay can an Old Act applicant ask the patent examiner for?

Beyond the formal delays available through the abandonment/forfeiture and reinstatement procedures permitted by the statute and the regulatory delay of the final issuance referred to in subparagraph 10 v) of the Davies Affidavit[16], the "informal" delays referred in the question and in the Canadian materials referenced by the question were, just as described, "informal". That is to say that they were not a delay of any particular or defined "type" or "class" of delay.

---

[15] Subsection 73(3) of the current Act now reads:

> (3) An application deemed to be abandoned under this section shall be reinstated if the applicant (a) makes a request for reinstatement to the Commissioner within the prescribed period; (b) takes the action that should have been taken in order to avoid the abandonment; and (c) pays the prescribed fee before the expiration of the prescribed period.

[16] Affidavit of Peter J. Davies, Chairman of the Patent Appeal Board of the Canadian Patent Office. Reproduced in its entirety as Exhibit No. 8. Hereafter cited as: Davies affidavit.

As the Davies affidavit makes clear, where an applicant may have had an interest in postponing the issuance of its patent as, for instance, was often the case with a pharmaceutical applicant seeking a closer confluence between its patent term and its marketing approval, it simply needed to approach the examiner and ask him or her to retard the position of a particular application in the queue of those applications awaiting examination.

Since the patent granting authority and its examiners are typically only interested in getting a targeted amount of work done within a targeted time frame, they have little interest in whether the targets are met by examining any particular application at any particular time. Consequently, they have neither a private nor a rule-based reason not to behave in a fashion that accommodates the private timing interests of an applicant.

However, while there may not be any rule categorizing "types" or "classes" of delay, there were several common types of circumstance in which an applicant might approach an examiner to request the postponement of the examination of its application. One such situation was where the applicant had an interest in a "co-pending" application, and wished to ensure that the two related patents would issue on the same date. Another was where the applicant was in the process of preparing to file a "divisional" application for a previously filed application and wished to delay the issuance of the patent against the previous application because one may not divide-"divisionalize"-an issued patent. A third involves the situation where the applicant is preparing a voluntary amendment to its claim and so wishes to forestall the examiner from writing an unnecessary report (to which the applicant would, of course, need to respond).

(b) What is the duration of the delay that a patent examiner is authorized to allow an Old Act applicant?

As noted in the answer to paragraph (a) of this question, the delays or postponements described in the Davies affidavit, were informal delays or postponements and as such they were neither authorized nor unauthorized. They were agreed to by examiners as a matter of professional discretion, courtesy and client service.

In these circumstances the delays or postponements involved could have been for a relatively short period or for a longer period of several years. It was not uncommon, for instance, for applicants for pharmaceutical product or process patents to seek postponements of several, sometimes as many as six or seven, years duration so that the term of their exclusive marketing rights under the patent would not be reduced and 'wasted' while the pharmaceutical product in question was waiting for marketing approvals from the competent health and safety authorities.

That said, it is important to understand that while examiners enjoy a certain amount of professional discretion in the exercise of their duties, the length of the delay they might be prepared to entertain as a matter of discretion and courtesy would be subject to, or influenced by, the reason advanced by the applicant in support of its request.

Thus, for example, if an applicant requested a delay to amend its original claims or to file a "divisional" application, the time reasonably required to do either of those things would clearly serve to set limits on the length of the delay or postponement that the examiner might tolerate. The tolerance of examiners would also have been disciplined by the productivity standards or expectations of their immediate supervisors as well as of the institutional expectations of the authority in which they work.

(c) On what grounds can the patent examiner refuse such a request?

An informal request for postponement, like the informal agreement to postpone, is an "informal" matter. As such an informal request for delay, like the informal agreement to permit a delay, is not bound by any formal rules defining what is "acceptable" and what is "not acceptable".

However, the informal postponements available under Canadian administrative practice existed in the shadow of the formal procedures available to procure formal postponements or delays in the granting process.

Accordingly, just as the Commissioner may not unreasonably refuse to exercise his or her formal, statutory discretion to reinstate an application in favour of an applicant who offers some reasonable explanation of why its delay was "not reasonably avoidable", examiners would not, under the discipline of the rules of natural justice and the doctrine of reasonable or legitimate expectations[17], be able to lightly refuse a reasonable request for a postponement of the issuance of a particular patent.

In this latter respect Canada would refer back to the examples justifying postponements that are described in the answer to paragraph (b) of this question, and suggest that they offer some guidance as to when an examiner might refuse to exercise his or her professional discretion to grant a postponement or a postponement for the time requested.

Since the examples of justified postponement are linked to the reason for, and the reasonableness of, the requested postponement, it would, in the absence of any formal rule, be reasonable to conclude that examiners would refuse requests which were "unreasonable".

Q.32 (Both parties) Does the TRIPS Agreement permit Members to give patent applicants a choice between either obtaining protection early, or obtaining a term of protection that expires twenty years from the filing date?

Yes, in theory. Although it is not clear on its face that the TRIPS Agreement actually provides for the bipolar choice described by the question. However, the Agreement certainly does not prevent a Member from making such a choice available.

The obligation in Article 33 is straightforward. It requires Members to provide that "The term of protection available shall not end before the expiration of a period of twenty years counted from the filing date." Once a Member has, consistent with its Article 1.1 rights and obligations, adopted laws or practices that make the term referred to "available" on a sound legal basis, neither Article 33 nor any other TRIPS obligation prevents a Member from also making alternative terms of protection available to such applicants who might, for their own private commercial or other strategic interests, wish to obtain patent protection on a different basis than that referred to by Articles 33 and 62.

In this respect it is useful to recall, as the recitals to the Agreement plainly recognize, that "intellectual property rights are private rights."[18] It is similarly useful to recall that the US has conceded[19] that, as an incidence of the private nature of patent rights,

---

[17] The doctrine of reasonable or legitimate expectations holds that the legislative and executive branches of government may not deny an applicant the benefit of some procedure or process where the procedure or process has, as a matter of practice, previously been available to applicants in analogous circumstances. It is usually viewed as being an extension of the rules of natural justice and procedural fairness. See: ***Reference re Canada Assistance Plan (British Columbia), 1991 2 S.C..R..525; (1991) 83 D.L.R. (4th) 297.*** (Supreme Court of Canada)

[18] TRIPS, third "recognizing" recital.

[19] See the US response to Canada's Question 4 as posed during the first substantive meeting of the Parties with the Panel (December 20, 1999).

patent owners have the right to alienate, abandon or forfeit their exclusive patents rights on whatever terms they find acceptable.

It follows from the foregoing that: since TRIPS does not prohibit Members from offering alternative terms of protection to patent applicants so long as the latter have a right to obtain the term referred to in Article 33; and, since, applicants and patentees are free to deal with their private property rights as they choose, a Member could, without breaching its TRIPS obligations, offer an alternative term of protection formula which would provide greater certainty of protection to the applicant by expediting the granting process and specifying a fixed term of protection that would, while offering a substantively equivalent amount of "effective" protection, end on a date that would occur before the date referred to in Article 33.

In such a scheme the applicant's part of the bargain would, of course, be that it agrees, in the exercise of its private property rights, to forfeit or abandon its right to obtain a term of uncertain duration that would, nevertheless, not end before the expiration of the twenty year period counted from its application filing date.

In sum the alternative scheme would offer patent applicants the hypothetical choice set out in the question. That is to say that the alternative would give applicants a choice between the variable term of protection provided for by the TRIPS formula and a more certain period of protection that would be available on an accelerated basis but would require the applicant to forego the right to a term that did not end before the date referred to in Article 33.

Q.33 (Both parties) If Article 70.2 rendered Article 33 applicable to inventions under protection in developed country Members on 1 January 1996, would it require those Members to make available on that date a term of protection for existing patents that did not expire before the end of 20 years from their respective filing dates or would it be sufficient that that term was available at the time that the patent application was filed?

In the circumstance assumed by the question, it would be sufficient if the term was available at the time the application was filed. Indeed, as Canada has argued, the unchallenged facts that the period was indeed available at the time applications were filed for section 45 patents is a complete answer to the US case in any circumstances. Canada of course has argued that Article 70.2 does not render Article 33 applicable to section 45 patents on two grounds.

First, no obligations arise under the Agreement in respect of an act of filing an application or an act of issuing a patent for a fixed term where those acts occurred before January 1, 1996, being the date of application of the Agreement for developed country Members. Second, a patent is not "subject matter" within the meaning of the TRIPS Agreement[20] and consequently an obligation in respect of the **term of a patent** cannot be an obligation in respect of "**subject matter**".

The burden is on the US to establish that the non-retroactivity rule in Article 70.1 does not apply so as to take those "acts" outside the scope of Article 70.2 upon which, of course, its argument relies. It has not discharged this burden. Moreover, the US has not

[20] The US has conceded that a "patent" is not "subject matter" within the meaning of the Agreement, see the US response to the Panel's December 20, 1999 Question 7. The US has also agreed with Canada that "subject matter" refers to the object of protection, that is the work, mark, indication, industrial design, invention or layout-design that attracts protection.

addressed, let alone refuted, Canada's submission that the obligation under Article 33 is triggered by the act of filing an application and is confirmed by the act of issuing a patent and that the Article is, therefore, an obligation in respect of those Article 70.1 "acts". The US admits[21] that both these "acts" are, where they occurred prior to January 1, 1996, within the scope of Article 70.1. Consequently, the US admits that neither "act" gives rise to obligations under the Agreement. However, the US goes on in the face of the plain language of Article 70.1 to argue, without reason or logic, that, nevertheless, the Agreement gives rise to obligations in respect of the patent term that is an integral[22] element and feature of those pre-application date "acts".

Q.34 (Both parties) How can those applicants whose patents were granted before the date of application of the Agreement be said to have chosen to forego a later term when the TRIPS Agreement had not even been applied?

Canada has addressed this question in it's prior submissions and answers to questions.[23] The issue is not whether a particular TRIPS formula was known years before it was negotiated, obviously it was not.

Section 45 patent applicants knew that when a patent issued it was guaranteed 17 years of "effective" protection. Those applicants also knew that Canada's law and practice permitted the applicant to take advantage of formal rules and informal administrative practices to control the issuing date of the patent such that it would issue either at an earlier or later time than normal. On the evidence before the Panel applicants clearly exercised this control in pursuit of their own choices as determined by their own private interests.

Canada's published laws and regulations, which applicants are deemed or presumed by law to know, provided for delays in excess of 42 months. When these formal delays are combined with the other opportunities for formal statutory or informal administrative delays described in Canada's Exhibit 8, there is no question but that periods of protection of twenty years or more were, when measured from the application filing date, available. The uncontradicted evidence is that more than 150,000 applicants succeeded in obtaining terms of protection that, when measured from the application filing date, were equal to or longer than twenty years. The uncontradicted evidence also shows that no one who desired a similar term was ever denied it.

---

[21] See the US response to the Panel's December 20, 1999 Question 11 and para. 25 of its Rebuttal Submission.

[22] See para. 56 of Canada's Second (Written) Submission, para. 60 of Canada's Second Oral Presentation and Exhibit No. 24.

[23] See for example paras. 97 to 101 of Canada's First (Written) Submission, Canada's response to the Panel's December 20, 1999 Question 24(a) and paras. 39 to 41 of Canada's Second Oral Presentation.

C. EXISTING SUBJECT-MATTER (ARTICLE 70)

Q.35 (Canada) Do you argue that Article 70.2 does not apply to inventions under protection of Old Act patents at all because of the words "Except as otherwise provided for in this Agreement...", or do you argue that it applies to them in some respects, or do you argue both as alternatives?

Canada argues that, by virtue of Article 70.2, some of the obligations under the Agreement apply to and are in respect of "subject matter" recognized by and protected under the Old Act. Canada also argues that Article 70.2 does not apply to all of the obligations of the Agreement respecting patents.

More particularly, Canada argues that the obligation under Article 33 does not fall within the scope of the obligations that are referred to in Article 70.2. Article 70.2 does not apply to the Article 33 obligation both because of its own deference to the "otherwise provided" prescriptions of Article 70.1 and because Article 33 is not an obligation in respect of the "subject matter" referred to in Article 70.2.

In this latter respect, an obligation in respect of the act of applying for or the act of issuing a patent which occurred prior to January 1, 1996 is not within the scope of Article 70.2 because Article 70.1 expressly provides otherwise. A patent term is granted as an integral element of, and attaches to, the patent itself. A patent is not "subject matter" within the meaning of TRIPS. The US concedes this fact.[24] Accordingly Article 33, which sets out the TRIPS obligation respecting the term of protection to be attached to a patent, cannot be an obligation in respect of "subject matter" as that term is used and understood within the Agreement.

Q.36 (Canada) If you argue that Article 70.2 applies to inventions under protection of Old Act patents in some respects, do you argue that it only applies to rights conferred in relation to inventions but not to the term of protection? If so, why?

Yes. As explained in the answer to questions 5 and 7, the obligation respecting the term of protection that is set out in Article 33 is an obligation that is in respect of two acts, namely: the act of filing a patent application; and, the act of granting a patent.

The act of filing is the trigger which, subject to acts of revocation, cancellation and default in maintenance obligations, sets the expiry date for the term of protection. However, there can be no term of protection unless a patent is in fact granted because there is no basis for the protection of the invention unless and until the patent is actually granted. Therefore, the commencement of the term of protection is triggered by the act of grant. Accordingly, both the commencement and the expiry of the term of protection depend upon the occurrence of these two successive and related acts.

The obligation in Article 33 is clearly an obligation in respect of "acts" and Article 70.1, which confirms or reproduces the rule against non-retroactivity set out in Article 28 of the *Vienna Convention on the Law of Treaties* (Vienna Convention), states, in unequivocal terms and without exception, that TRIPS does not give rise to obligations in respect of "acts" which occurred before 1 January 1996.

The wording of the obligation described in Article 33 reinforces this conclusion. The concept of making something "available" which is central to the obligation described in Article 33 clearly indicates an intention that the obligation is to be applied prospec-

[24] See the US responses to the Panel's December 20, 1999 Questions 7 and 13.

tively in respect of future acts and not retrospectively or retroactively in respect of past acts. Were it otherwise the Agreement would be retroactive in respect of this obligation and the US has clearly indicated that, in the case of the Article 70.2 obligation, the Agreement is not retroactive.[25]

Tellingly, the US has regularly used the word "prospectively" in respect of the application of TRIPS obligations throughout the material that it has filed with the Panel.[26] The word prospective means, "in the future", as distinguished from "retrospectively" or "retroactively". Canada agrees. Article 33 is to be applied prospectively to acts of grant that occurred on or after 1 January 1996 and not, by virtue of the direction of Article 70.1, retroactively to "acts" of filing or grant that occurred before that date.

Canada assumes that the reference in Question 8 to "rights conferred in relation to inventions" refers to the rights described in Article 28. Article 28 provides that a patent shall confer on its owner certain exclusive rights. Unlike the obligation in Article 33, which is principally temporal in nature because of its linkage of both the commencement and the expiry dates of the term of protection with, as the case may be, the acts of filing and granting, the obligation in Article 28 does not depend upon the occurrence of any act.

The operation of Article 28 depends solely upon a patent being in existence, and would apply to any patent, whether Old Act or New Act, regardless of when issued. As Canada pointed out in paragraph 68 of its Second Submission, these rights are conferred by the patent itself. As is clear from the language of Article 28, they arise by virtue of the fact that the patent exists.

It is significant that the drafters of the TRIPS Agreement dealt with the rights that attach to a patent (Article 28) and the term of protection (Article 33) in two spatially and connotatively separate as well as distinctively worded provisions. Article 28 states unequivocally that a **patent** shall confer the exclusive rights enumerated therein. Such rights do not include a right to a the term of protection. (Article 33, of course, sets out the formula for determining the term of protection and establishes the obligation that the term, as thereby circumscribed, shall be made "available" by Members.)

The time at which the rights must be made available is clearly at the time that the act of grant occurs because the rights flow from the patent itself as opposed to the act of grant. However, aside from the fact that both the commencement and the expiry of the term of protection described in Article 33 depend, respectively, upon the occurrence of the acts of grant and filing, Members cannot, simply because the rights arise as of the date of grant, be expected to make available terms of protection in respect of acts of grant that have already occurred.

Had the TRIPS drafters intended this retroactive result, the term of protection would have been included in Article 28 as a right "conferred" by a patent and the rule against retroactivity in Article 70.1 would have been expressly overruled by the association of the term of protection with the other rights conferred by the patent as opposed to its existing association within the Agreement with the acts of filing and granting.

Alternatively and more directly, the drafters could have taken two other approaches to the issue. First they could have adopted a provision, like the Article 70.6 provision, which would have explicitly made the Article 33 obligation retroactive to a time

[25] See paras. 14 and 15 of the Oral Statement of the US.

[26] The most recent reference is to be found in its Oral (Rebuttal) Statement at para. 22 and see too para. 15 of its (first) Oral Statement.

before the coming into effect of the treaty, notwithstanding that, when granted, the term granted was in accordance with the then prevailing municipal law. Second, they could have written Article 70.2 to say that 'except as otherwise provided by the Agreement, TRIPS would give rise to obligations in respect of "subject matter" and "terms of protection" existing at the application date'

Given their creation of and agreement to the retroactive rule respecting compulsory licences, the fact that the TRIPS negotiators did neither in respect of the term of protection obligation is telling evidence of their intentions. They clearly understood how to make an obligation retroactive, and they clearly did not do so in respect of Article 33.

Q.37 (Canada) Why is the term of protection an "integral part" of the act of grant but the scope of the rights is not?

The term of protection is an "integral part" of the act of grant because the term of protection is made (to use the word in Article 33) "available" to a patent owner when the act of grant occurs, and the commencement of the term of protection is triggered by the act of grant.

Since the term of protection is an "integral part" of the act of grant in the sense just described, the obligation in Article 33 is an obligation in respect of the act of granting a patent (as well as the act of filing a patent application) and, thus, subject to the non-retroactivity rule in Article 70.1. The other rights referred to in the question are those described in Article 28. As stated in the response to Question 8, Article 28 is structured completely differently from the term of protection provision in Article 33. It is clear from the wording of Article 28 that the rights referred to there are conferred by the patent and unlike the term of protection, these rights are in respect of the invention (subject matter) and are not dependent on or derived from the happening of the act of grant or any other act.

Q.38 (Canada) You stated that if Article 70.2 would have applied to Article 33 the extension of a patent would lead to windfall profits, and that such windfall profits are contrary to the philosophy of the Agreement. Does the application of Article 70.2 to other obligations with respect to subject-matter already protected give rise to windfall profits as well?

In theory, if the exclusive rights granted by a Member did not include all the exclusive rights described in Article 28 as of the application date of the Agreement, the value of the patent would be enhanced. However, unlike prior acts which are expressly excluded by Article 70.1, the negotiators used clear language in Article 70.2, in respect of subject matter, as they did in Article 70.6, in respect of Article 31, to override the legal presumption against the retroactive application of an Agreement.

As noted in Canada's response to Question 6(c)[27] posed by the Panel following the first substantive meeting with the Panel, the act of grant consummates the time-limited bargain between the patent owner and society under which the patent owner discloses the invention in return for a limited period of exclusivity. The time limitation of the exclusivity is critical to the bargain, both for the patent owner and for society. Had the TRIPS drafters intended that this critical term of the bargain be re-written, they were required by Article 28 of the Vienna Convention to have so provided in unequivocal terms. Rather than doing this, the TRIPS drafters affirmed the non-retroactivity rule in Article 28 of the

[27] See the second last para. of that response.

Vienna Convention through the inclusion of Article 70.1, from which it is clear that the TRIPS drafters did not intend that the time limitation be altered in respect of such bargains (consummated through the act of grant) entered into before 1 January 1996.

The U.S. complaint only affects some patents applied for before October 1, 1989 and that were granted before October 1, 1992. These will be referred to as the "affected patents".[28] Canada's rules respecting the bargain on time limitation at each of these times (October 1, 1989 and October 1, 1992) was fully consistent with Canada's then-existing international obligations.

The TRIPS Agreement was not even known at the time that these patent owners decided to initiate the process of concluding their proposed bargains by filing patent applications. By October 1, 1992, the proposed provisions of the TRIPS Agreement were known (through the release of the Dunkel Draft on December 20, 1991) but the patent owners whose patents were issued after the release of the Dunkel Draft had no reason for believing that the TRIPS Agreement would ever come into effect.

These patent owners disclosed their inventions under the rules that existed at the time that their time-limited bargains were consummated. As has been argued by Canada throughout, these patent owners disclosed their inventions under rules that (unlike the TRIPS rule) *guaranteed* a term of effective protection of seventeen years from grant. If the Panel finds that Article 70.2 applies so as to require an extension of the terms of affected patents, the patent owners in question will receive a pure windfall in having their bargains unilaterally re-written with nothing having been given or nothing being required to be given in exchange, to the detriment of the Canadian users of technological knowledge and so too, to the detriment of the Canadian consumer at large.

Such a result would clearly be contrary to the spirit of the statement of objectives in Article 7 of the Agreement which speaks severally of the importance of protecting and enforcing intellectual property rights as contributing to a "...balance of rights and obligations...", of contributing to "... the mutual advantage of producers and users of technological knowledge..." and of being "...conducive to social and economic welfare".

Canada assumes that the reference to "other obligations in this Question with respect to subject matter already protected" is intended to refer primarily to the rights conferred by a patent and acquired pursuant to Article 28. As noted in the response to Question 8, Article 28 is drafted in a manner such that the rights described therein are conferred by, and therefore attach to, the patent. Canada conferred the rights described in Article 28 under both the Old Act and the New Act, so the application of Article 28 to the affected patents cannot in fact result in any windfall to the affected patent owners.

In any event, the concept of exclusivity lies at the heart of any patent regime. While the application of Article 28 to patents issued before 1 January 1996 in a patent regime of a member that provided less than the full range of rights described in Article 28 might clarify and even expand upon the rights and therefore the profits of an owner of a pre-1996 patent, that owner would already have been enjoying a substantial degree of exclusivity and could hardly be said to have received a windfall of the magnitude that would flow from the wholesale extension of a predetermined patent term that is at issue in these proceedings.

[28] Any Old Act patent granted on or after October 1, 1992 received (or if the application is still pending will receive) a term of protection equal to or in excess of TRIPS obligations.

Further and again in any event, the principal TRIPS obligation to which the TRIPS drafters ascribed any real retroactive significance was the obligation respecting the termination of the then lawful compulsory licenses which, by virtue of the demonstrably retroactive provisions of Article 70.6, gave effect to the obligation in Article 31 some four years before the Agreement actually came into effect for developed country Members. The fact that the TRIPS drafters did not include a similar rule respecting time-limited bargains consummated through acts of grant occurring before 1 January 1996 clearly indicates that they did not intend that such bargains be disturbed.

The issue of equity impacts on the entire US case. The US demands that Article 33 and 70.2 be interpreted in a manner that would re-open the bargains with all patent owners whose patents were issued with terms of protection that were less than 20 years measured from the application date. And that those terms be extended resulting in windfall profits of tens and perhaps hundreds of millions of dollars to individual patent owners at the expense of Canadian consumers. And those gratuitous extensions of terms of "effective" protection would do so without any reciprocal benefits for Canadian society.

As previously observed, if the TRIPS negotiators had intended such far reaching and extraordinary results, they were required by Article 28 of the Vienna Convention to use unequivocal language or unequivocal descriptions of circumstance such as that or those to be found in Article 70.6. In marked contrast the TRIPS drafters, through Article 70.1, expressly reaffirmed the non-retroactivity rule which is a general principle of international law and has been specifically recognized as such by the Appellate Body in *European Communities - Regime for Bananas.*[29]

[29] Appellate Body Report, *European Communities - Regime for the Importation, Sale and Distribution of Bananas ("EC – Bananas III")*, WT/DS27/AB/R, adopted 27 September 1997, DSR 1997:II, 591, para. 235.

GUATEMALA - DEFINITIVE ANTI-DUMPING MEASURES ON GREY PORTLAND CEMENT FROM MEXICO

Report of the Panel
WT/DS156/R

Adopted by the Dispute Settlement Body on 17 November 2000

TABLE OF CONTENTS

Page

I. INTRODUCTION

A. Background

1.1 On 5 January 1999, Mexico requested consultations with Guatemala under Article 4 of the Understanding on Rules and Procedures Governing the Settlement of Disputes ("DSU") and Article 17.3 of the Agreement on Implementation of Article VI of the General Agreement on Tariffs and Trade 1994 ("AD Agreement") regarding the definitive anti-dumping measure imposed by Guatemala on imports of Portland cement from Cooperativa Manufacturera de Cemento Portland la Cruz Azul, SCL, of Mexico ("Cruz Azul"), as well as the actions that preceded it (WT/DS156/1).

1.2 Mexico and Guatemala held one-day consultations on 23 February 1999, but failed to reach a mutually satisfactory solution.

B. Establishment and Composition of the Panel

1.3 On 26 July 1999, pursuant to Article 17.4 of the AD Agreement and Article 6.2 of the DSU, Mexico requested the establishment of a panel to examine the consistency of Guatemala's definitive anti-dumping measure on imports of Portland cement from Mexico, as well as the actions that preceded it, with Guatemala's obligations under the Agreement Establishing the World Trade Organization ("WTO Agreement"), in particular those contained in the AD Agreement (WT/DS156/2 and WT/DS156/2/Corr.1).

1.4 At the meeting of the Dispute Settlement Body ("DSB") on 26 July 1999, Guatemala stated that it could not join the consensus to establish a panel until certain domestic procedures concerning the investigation had been completed. The DSB agreed to revert to this matter at a later date.

1.5 At its meeting on 22 September 1999, the DSB established a panel in accordance with Article 6 of the DSU with standard terms of reference. The terms of reference were:

> "To examine, in the light of the relevant provisions of the covered agreements cited by Mexico in documents WT/DS/156/2 and WT/DS/156/2/Corr.1, the matter referred to the DSB by Mexico in that document and to make such findings as will assist the DSB in

making the recommendations or in giving the rulings provided for in those agreements".

1.6 Ecuador, El Salvador, the European Communities, Honduras and the United States reserved their rights to participate in the Panel proceedings as third parties.

1.7 On 12 October 1999, Mexico requested the Director-General to determine the composition of the Panel, pursuant to Article 8.7 of the DSU. The Director-General composed the following Panel:

Chairman:	Mr. Johan Human
Members:	Mr. Antonio Buencamino
	Mr. Oscar Hernández

C. *Panel Proceedings*

1.8 The Panel met with the parties on 15-16 February 2000 and 12-13 April 2000.

II. FACTUAL ASPECTS

2.1 This dispute concerns the definitive anti-dumping measure imposed by Guatemala's Ministry of Economy ("Ministry"), as well as the actions that preceded it, in particular the anti-dumping investigation against imports of grey Portland cement from Cruz Azul, a Mexican producer. Cementos Progreso SA ("Cementos Progreso"), the only cement producer in Guatemala, filed a request for an anti-dumping investigation on 21 September 1995 and a supplementary request on 9 October 1995. On 11 January 1996, based on these requests, the Ministry published a notice of initiation of an anti-dumping investigation regarding allegedly dumped imports of grey Portland cement from Cruz Azul of Mexico. The Ministry notified the Government of Mexico of the initiation of the investigation on 22 January 1996. The Ministry requested certain import data from Guatemala's Directorate-General of Customs by letter dated 23 January 1996. On 26 January 1996, the Ministry transmitted questionnaires to interested parties, including Cruz Azul and Cementos Progreso, with a response originally due on 11 March 1996. In answer to Cruz Azul's request, the Ministry extended the deadline for submission of the questionnaire responses until 17 May 1996. Cruz Azul filed a response on 13 May 1996. On 16 August 1996, and with effect from 28 August 1996, Guatemala imposed a provisional anti-dumping duty of 38.72% on imports of type I (PM) grey Portland cement from Cruz Azul of Mexico. The provisional duty was imposed on the basis of a preliminary affirmative determination of dumping and consequent threat of injury. That provisional duty expired on 28 December 1996.

2.2 The original investigation period set forth in the published notice of initiation ran from 1 June 1995 to 30 November 1995. On 4 October 1996, the Ministry extended the investigation period to include the period 1 December 1995 to 31 May 1996. On 14 October 1996, the Ministry issued supplemental questionnaires to Cruz Azul and Cementos Progreso, requesting that Cruz Azul provide cost data and other information for the extended investigation period.

2.3 A verification visit was scheduled to take place from 3 - 6 December 1996. This verification visit was cancelled by the Ministry shortly after it commenced on 3

December 1996, in the face of Cruz Azul's refusal to accept named non-governmental experts.

2.4 On 17 January 1997, Guatemala imposed a definitive anti-dumping duty of 89.54% on imports of grey Portland cement from Cruz Azul of Mexico. The definitive measure was imposed on the basis of a determination of dumping and consequent injury.

III. FINDINGS AND RECOMMENDATIONS REQUESTED BY THE PARTIES

A. *Mexico*

3.1 **Mexico** has requested the Panel to find and recommend that:

(a) the initiation of the investigation by the Ministry of the Economy of Guatemala is inconsistent with Articles 1, 2, 3, 5 and 12 of the AD Agreement;

(b) Guatemala violated Article 6.1.3 of the AD Agreement by failing to provide Cruz Azul and the Government of Mexico with the full text of the application as soon as it initiated the investigation;

(c) the provisional anti-dumping measure was imposed in violation of Articles 1, 7, 12 and 18 of the AD Agreement;

(d) Guatemala committed the following procedural violations:

1. Guatemala did not set a specific period for the gathering, submission and consideration of evidence and did not determine a time limit for the admission and receipt of evidence, in violation of Article 6.1 and 6.2 of the AD Agreement.
2. Guatemala did not give Cruz Azul the opportunity to examine the evidence used by the Ministry of the Economy in the course of the investigation, thus violating Article 6.1.2, 6.2 and 6.4 of the AD Agreement.
3. Guatemala did not satisfy itself as to the accuracy of the information provided by Cementos Progreso that formed the basis for its conclusions throughout the various stages of the investigation, failing to comply with its obligations under Article 6.6 of the AD Agreement.
4. Guatemala extended the investigation period in the ninth month after initiation of the investigation without giving the grounds for the extension, thus violating Article 6.1 and 6.2 and paragraph 1 of Annex II to the AD Agreement.
5. Guatemala improperly asked Cruz Azul to provide information on production costs corresponding to both investigation periods - the original period and the extended period - in violation of Article 2.1 and 2.2 of the AD Agreement.
6. Guatemala sought to conduct an on-the-spot investigation without having obtained the express consent of the firm, in violation of several obligations and requirements in Article

6.7, and paragraphs 2, 3, 7 and 8 of Annex I to the AD Agreement.

7. Guatemala rejected the technical accounting evidence furnished by Cruz Azul on the normal value and the export price during the original investigation period, in violation of Article 6.1, 6.2 and 6.8 and paragraphs 5 and 6 of Annex II to the AD Agreement.

8. Guatemala admitted confidential information from Cementos Progreso without a public version thereof, did not give the reasons for which it deemed the information confidential and did not promptly give Cruz Azul the documentation provided by Cementos Progreso, in violation of Article 6.1, 6.2, 6.3 and 6.5 of the AD Agreement.

9. Guatemala did not promptly inform Cruz Azul of the essential facts taken into account for the imposition of the definitive anti-dumping measure, thus violating its right of defence provided under Article 6.1, 6.2 and 6.9 of the AD Agreement.

10. during the final stage of the investigation, Guatemala changed the determination of threat of material injury made at the initiation of the investigation and when imposing the provisional measure into a determination of material injury. This was done without giving Cruz Azul any opportunity to defend itself or present relevant evidence, in violation of Article 6.1 and 6.2 of the AD Agreement.

(e) the definitive anti-dumping measure was imposed in violation of Articles 1, 2, 3, 9, 12 and 18 of the AD Agreement and Article VI of the GATT 1994;

(f) the Guatemalan authority did not adequately establish the elements of fact and law put forward in the investigation and did not make an unbiased and objective evaluation of them;

(g) where applicable, Guatemala made impermissible interpretations of the AD Agreement and imposed the definitive anti-dumping measure, as well as the action that preceded it, including the provisional measure, on the basis of these impermissible interpretations.

Consequently, on the basis of Article 19.1 of the AD Agreement, Mexico respectfully requests that the Panel:

(a) recommend that Guatemala bring its measure into conformity with the GATT 1994 and the AD Agreement;

(b) suggest that Guatemala revoke the anti-dumping measure adopted against imports of Mexican cement and refund the anti-dumping duties collected.

B. Guatemala

3.2 **Guatemala** has requested the Panel to make the following rulings:

1. *As a Preliminary Matter the Panel is Without Jurisdiction to Consider this Dispute*

3.3 Guatemala respectfully requests the Panel to find that:

- the Panel is not properly composed, because it includes one of the members of the previous panel which examined the case *Guatemala - Cement I*, a fact which compromises the impartiality of the Panel established to examine this dispute, and rule that this Panel has no jurisdiction to consider the present case;
- the Panel lacks jurisdiction to consider Mexico's complaints concerning the provisional measure, because Mexico did not request consultations in respect of that measure and because in its first submission, Mexico does not prove, as required by Article 17.4 of the Anti-Dumping Agreement, that the said measure has had an enduring significant impact;
- in the alternate, the Panel lacks the jurisdiction to consider Mexico's complaints concerning the provisional measure because the said provisional measure never had a significant impact on Mexico's overall trade interests;
- in view of the findings of the Appellate Body in *Guatemala - Cement I*, the report of the Panel in that case has no value as a precedent and lacks legal value to be invoked by Mexico as a basis for its allegations, and that the Panel should therefore reject those of Mexico's arguments that are based on the said report. Similarly, the Panel should refrain from using the report in the *Guatemala - Cement I* case to substantiate such conclusions and recommendations as it reaches after analysing the present case.

3.4 Guatemala requests the Panel to rule on the preliminary objections separately and before examining the substantive arguments of the parties.

2. *The Substantive Claims of Mexico Should Be Rejected*

3.5 If, notwithstanding the solid factual foundations and legal underpinning of Guatemala's preliminary objections, the Panel should decide to proceed to consider the merits of the case, Guatemala requests that the Panel reject Mexico's arguments and petitions and find that:

- Guatemala's definitive anti-dumping measure and the actions that preceded it are fully consistent with the GATT 1994 and the Anti-Dumping Agreement;
- all other aspects of Guatemala's anti-dumping investigation are fully consistent with GATT 1994 and the Anti-Dumping Agreement and, specifically that:
    - Guatemala initiated its investigation in conformity with Article 5 of the Anti-Dumping Agreement;
    - all aspects of the notification of initiation were in compliance with Articles 5, 6 and 12 of the Anti-Dumping Agreement;

- Guatemala imposed the provisional measure in conformity with the Anti-Dumping Agreement;
- Guatemala formulated the final affirmative determination in conformity with the Anti-Dumping Agreement.

3.6 If, notwithstanding the solid factual foundations and legal underpinnings of Guatemala's position, the Panel were to decide that in conducting its investigation Guatemala committed procedural or technical errors, Guatemala requests the Panel to find:

- any procedural or technical error that Guatemala may have committed is harmless or was acquiesced in by Mexico;
- Guatemala has rebutted the presumption of nullification or impairment referred to in Article 3.8 of the DSU.

3.7 In the alternative Guatemala requests the Panel to find that any technical error that it may have committed is insufficient to justify the formulation of a recommendation by the Panel under Article 19.1 of the DSU.

3.8 In the further alternative, Guatemala requests that, regardless of what is decided in the present case, the Panel rejects Mexico's request that the Panel should suggest that Guatemala revoke the definitive anti-dumping measure or refund the anti-dumping duties collected.

IV. PRELIMINARY OBJECTIONS

4.1 **Guatemala** raises a number of preliminary objections in support of its argument that the Panel was without jurisdiction to consider the present dispute. The submissions of Guatemala and Mexico on these preliminary objections, presented *verbatim*, are as follows:

A. *The Panel Was Improperly Composed and is Not Competent to Examine the Matter Before It*

1. *Submissions of Guatemala*

4.2 **Guatemala's** first preliminary objection is that the Panel was improperly composed, and hence was not competent to examine the matter referred by Mexico to the DSB. Guatemala's arguments in this regard were are as follows:

4.3 Guatemala objected to the appointment of any members who had served on the panel in the previous dispute, because having examined Mexico's first complaint, without the competence to do so, they would have preconceived positions. Specifically, it must be borne in mind that the first dispute involved the examination of claims relating to the violation of Article 5.3 and 5.5 which will be examined once again in this case. Guatemala would like to state clearly for the record that it does not question or dispute the integrity or qualifications of the panellist appointed in the first dispute and reappointed to serve on the Panel in this dispute. However, it would be virtually impossible for him or any other person not to take account of the opinions of those who served with him and of the discussions held and the decisions taken in the previous dispute in which he participated, above all if we bear in mind that panel decisions are collegiate and do not reflect the position of any individual member in particular. Thus, the inclusion of a member who served on the previous

Panel would seem to deprive this Panel of its independence and to render it unsuitable.

4.4 This is considered to be the first time under the DSU that a panel report has been reversed because the panel did not have the mandate to examine the complaints, that a complaining Member has brought a second dispute settlement case involving some of the complaints submitted in the first case, and that the Director-General has been asked to appoint a new panel under Article 8.7. Guatemala considers that in such situations, the DSU *does not* permit the Director-General to reappoint the members of the previous panel.

4.5 *First*, the DSU does not empower the Appellate Body to refer the dispute back to the panel whose conclusion was reversed. As recognized by the Appellate Body in paragraph 89 of its report, Mexico's only option in the face of the reversal of conclusions in *Guatemala - Cement I* was to pursue "another dispute settlement complaint" under the provisions of Article 17 of the AD Agreement and of the DSU.

4.6 *Second*, neither Article 17 nor the DSU provides for the reappointment of members that served in a previous dispute concerning the same anti-dumping investigation. This is particularly important when one of the parties (in this case Guatemala) objects to such a course.

4.7 *Third*, Article 8.2 of the DSU stipulates that "Panel members should be selected with a view to ensuring the *independence* of the members ... ."[1] Although the DSU does not define the word "independence", Article 3.2 stipulates that panels must interpret the DSU and the "covered agreements" in accordance with customary rules of interpretation of public international law. In the case *United States - Standards for Reformulated and Conventional Gasoline* (hereinafter *Reformulated Gasoline),* the Appellate Body concluded that the fundamental rule of treaty interpretation contained in Article 31(1) of the Vienna Convention on the Law of Treaties (the *Vienna Convention)* "has attained the status of a rule of customary or general international law". [2] Article 31(1) of the *Vienna Convention* states that the words of a treaty constitute a point of departure in the process of interpretation. Thus, the words of a treaty must be interpreted in their "ordinary meaning", taking account of "their context" (i.e. other provisions of the same treaty) and the "object and purpose" of the treaty.[3] The ordinary meaning of the term "independence" is "quality or condition of being independent", and the ordinary meaning of the term "independent" is "said of a person who upholds his rights or opinions without accepting external intervention."[4]

[1] DSU, Article 8.2 (emphasis added).

[2] Report of the Appellate Body, *United States - Standards for Reformulated and Conventional Gasoline*, WT/DS2/AB/R, adopted 20 May 1996, DSR 1996:I, 3, at 16.

[3] See, for example, *Competence of the General Assembly for the Admission of a State to the United Nations (second case) [1950]* ICJ Report, *8 ("The Court considers it necessary to say that the first duty of a tribunal which is called upon to interpret and apply the provisions of a treaty, is to endeavour to give effect to them in their natural and ordinary meaning in the context in which they occur.").

[4] *Diccionario de la Lengua Española,* Twenty-First Edition, page 817 (Real Academia Española, 1992). See also *The Compact Edition of the Oxford English Dictionary,* 1413 (Oxford University Press 1971). Oxford defines "independence" as "the fact of not depending on another; exemption from external control or support", *idem*, 199. See also Webster's Encyclopedic Unabridged Dictionary of the English Language (Gramercy Books, 1994).

It is obvious that a member of the Panel in *Guatemala - Cement I* will have been influenced by the other members of the Panel in respect of the claims that were already examined during that first dispute and are now to be examined again.

4.8 *Fourth*, according to Article 11 of the DSU, the panel should "make an objective assessment of the matter before it, including an *objective* assessment of the facts of the case, and the applicability of and conformity with the relevant covered agreements ...".[5] An *objective* assessment would appear to be impossible when the panel includes someone who has already formed opinions with respect to the identical complaints made in a previous case between the same parties.

4.9 *Fifth*, under Article 9 of the DSU, a single panel may be established to examine the complaints in cases involving more than one complainant, or if more than one panel is established to examine complaints related to the same matter, the same persons shall serve as panelists on each of the separate panels. In the case at issue, Mexico is the only complainant. Thus, Article 9, is not applicable.

4.10 *Sixth*, the fact that the drafters considered it necessary to include Article 9 in the DSU in order to enable the same persons to serve on different panels established to examine complaints relating to the same matter proves that this is an exception to the rule. Where there is not more than one complainant, the DSU does not authorize the same persons to serve on the different panels examining different disputes relating to the same matter.

4.11 Moreover, a fundamental principle of public international law stipulates that the decision of an international tribunal must be impartial and objective.[6] The concept of impartiality not only covers the question of whether the person taking the decision has a personal interest in the result of the dispute, but also requires that that person should come to the case "with an open mind, ready to be convinced by the arguments of the parties, and should not already have formed and expressed a view on the questions arising in the case".[7] Indeed, it is essential to the proper operation of any international dispute settlement procedure that "the parties to proceedings are satisfied that they will receive procedural justice, in the sense that their arguments will be fairly heard and impartially examined, on the basis of complete equality with each other ...".[8] "If the parties are concerned about the perceived bias of the mediator/arbitrator, then the use of different persons as the mediator and the arbitrator is appropriate."[9]

4.12 Recognizing these principles, the preamble to the Rules of Conduct for the DSU states that the operation of the DSU "would be strengthened by rules of conduct designed to maintain the integrity, impartiality and confidentiality of proceedings conducted under the DSU ...".[10] According to the principles contained in the Rules of

---

[5] DSU, Article 11 (emphasis added).

[6] See V.S. Mani, *International Adjudication: Procedural Aspects*, page 20 (M. Nijhoff 1980).

[7] See N. Singh, *The Role and Record of the International Court of Justice*, page 190 (Kluwer 1989) (in English).

[8] *Ibid.*, page 189.

[9] J. Grenig, *Alternative Dispute Resolution* § 2.47 (1997).

[10] WT/DSB/RC/1, 11 December 1996. The Working Procedures stipulate that "The deliberations of the Panel ... shall be kept confidential." (DSU, Appendix 3, para. 3.) The appointment of a person who served on a previous panel as member of a second panel to examine identical complaints would

Conduct, the impartiality of the members of the panel requires those members to approach the dispute without any preconceived positions. All of the members of the panel "shall be independent and impartial, shall avoid direct or indirect conflicts of interest ...". Moreover, "such persons shall consider *only issues raised in*, and necessary to fulfil their responsibilities *within the* dispute settlement proceeding ...".[11] The principles contained in the Rules of Conduct for the DSU would be undermined if any member of the previous panel were allowed to participate in the present panel.[12]

4.13 Consequently, with due respect, Guatemala requests that a preliminary resolution be issued to the effect that the Panel was improperly composed and does not therefore have the competence to examine the matter referred by Mexico to the DSB.

2. *Rebuttal of Mexico*

4.14 Mexico set out its position regarding Guatemala's preliminary objection regarding the competence of the Panel as follows:

4.15 In its written submission, Guatemala "requests that a preliminary resolution be issued to the effect that the Panel was improperly composed and does not therefore have the competence to examine the matter referred by Mexico to the DSB".

4.16 Mexico contends that the Panel was properly composed and had the competence to examine the matter referred by Mexico to the DSB.

4.17 In general Mexico states that Panel was established in conformity with the DSU. The Director-General, following the procedures set forth in Article 8.7 and in consultation with the Chairman of the DSB and the Chairman of the Committee on Anti-Dumping Practices, appointed the members which he considered suitable after having consulted Guatemala and Mexico.

4.18 Guatemala's preliminary objection is not clear. At certain points Guatemala asserts that it "would seem" or "would appear" that the composition of the Panel was not suitable or lacked independence (see paragraph 21 and 26 for example), while at other points (paragraph 31) it categorically asserts that the Panel was not properly composed. If Guatemala considers that the Panel or one of its members lacks independence or objectivity, it not only has to say so clearly, but it also has to provide specific facts to show that this is the case. This is too delicate a matter to rely on simple appearances or on the suppositions or suspicions of one of the parties (in this case the defendant) without supporting evidence. What is at stake is the credibility of the panels, the prestige of the members of those panels and the power of the Director-General of the WTO to appoint the members of a panel when there is no agreement between the parties.

4.19 Even supposing Guatemala were to present evidence to support its preliminary objection, the Panel is not the suitable body to examine the substance of that

give the impression that the confidential deliberations of the previous panel were being shared with the second panel.

[11] *Ibid.*, II and III.2 (emphasis added).

[12] Similarly, Article 17(2) of the Statute of the International Court of Justice stipulates that "no member may participate in the decision of any case in which he has previously taken part as agent, counsel or advocate for one of the parties, or as a member of a national or international court or of a commission of enquiry or in any other capacity." See in general S. Rosenne, *The Law and Practice of the International Court*, page 196 (1985).

objection or to rule on the subject. Under Articles VIII.1 and VIII.5 of the Rules of Conduct for the DSU (hereinafter the "Rules of Conduct") Guatemala should submit the evidence in its possession as soon as possible to the Chairman of the DSB so that he can initiate the procedure aimed at determining whether a material violation of those Rules has occurred. Guatemala should withdraw its preliminary objection before the Panel, failing which the Panel should determine that Guatemala's objection comes under the scope of the Rules of Conduct.

4.20 The reasoning behind Guatemala's preliminary objection does not make sense. To accept it would be to imply, *inter alia*, that this dispute could not be the subject of an appeal, since the Appellate Body already conducted an examination and issued a ruling beforehand in respect of the previous dispute. In other words, Mexico would have the right not to accept an appeal because the Appellate Body might lack independence and objectivity, having already ruled on the matter at issue in this dispute. The fact that the members of the Appellate Body involved could be wholly or partly different from the original members is irrelevant since as we know, all of the members of the Appellate Body are involved in all disputes under the principle of collegiality.

4.21 Sticking to the order of Guatemala's arguments, Mexico makes the following remarks:

4.22 Regarding Guatemala's first arguments, its references to the Appellate Body have nothing to do with its preliminary objection. Nobody, let alone Mexico, has argued that the composition of the Panel which is currently examining the present dispute derives from some statement by the Appellate Body in the previous case. The Appellate Body simply did not make any statement concerning the composition of the Panel in this case.

4.23 In its second argument Guatemala states that "neither Article 17 nor the DSU provides for the reappointment of members that served in a previous dispute concerning the same anti-dumping investigation". In this connection, Mexico would like to stress that Article 17 (of the Anti-Dumping Agreement) does not regulate the requirements for membership of a panel, so that it is not applicable.

4.24 As regards the DSU, the requirements for membership of a panel are contained in Article 8, in particular in paragraphs 1, 2 and 3 thereof. Thus, the persons who comply with these requirements are eligible to compose a panel. Article 8.1 of the DSU expressly stipulates that panels shall be composed, *inter alia*, of "persons who have served on ... a panel". In other words, not only is the fact of having served on a panel not an obstacle, it is an advantage.

4.25 Furthermore, it is a well-established practice in the WTO to rely on members of a panel in a previous or similar dispute. This is what has been done, for example, in the case of disputes brought under Article 21.5 of the DSU.

4.26 During the process of appointment of the members of the Panel, Mexico cited at least three cases in which the Director-General had appointed the same members who had served on a previous panel, unless they were unavailable (Mexico's communications to the Director-General and his reply to the parties are annexed hereto).[13]

[13] See *India - Patent Protection for Pharmaceutical and Agricultural Chemical Products*, WT/DS50/R, adopted 16 January 1998, DSR 1998:I, 41 (and WT/DS79/R). See also *Australia -*

This same reasoning has been applied to disputes on the subject of anti-dumping measures, for example the two disputes on *United States - Anti-Dumping Act of 1916*.[14]

4.27 Guatemala's third argument in this objection focuses on the term "independence" referred to in Article 8.2 of the DSU. According to Guatemala, the DSU does not define this word, and ultimately it is necessary to resort to the rules of treaty interpretation of the Vienna Convention.

4.28 While it is true that the DSU does not contain any definition of the word "independence", it is also true that through this reasoning, Guatemala is seeking to ignore the existence of clearly established procedures for cases in which one of the parties considers that one or several members of a panel do not comply with that requirement. As stated above, these procedures are contained in the Rules of Conduct.

4.29 Consequently, if Guatemala has any problem in this respect, it should follow the procedures set forth in the Rules of Conduct. In any case, the Panel does not have the authority to determine whether or not one or several of its members are independent, since this would be contrary to the principle that one cannot be a judge and a party at the same time.

4.30 Nor is Guatemala's interpretation of the term "independent" correct. According to the Vienna Convention, a treaty must be interpreted in accordance with the ordinary meaning to be given to the terms in their context and in the light of its object and purpose. Guatemala only referred partially to the ordinary meaning of the word "independent", ignoring the context in which it appears and the object and purpose of the DSU.

4.31 According to Guatemala, the ordinary meaning of the term independent is "said of a person who upholds his rights or opinions without accepting external intervention". However, the context and the object and purpose of the DSU clearly show that:

(a) The term "independence" in Article 8.2 refers to the independence of the members of a panel with respect to the governments and parties of the other Members of the WTO (see Article 8.9 of the DSU) and not with respect to the other members of the panel. To consider that independence refers to the other members of the panel is to imply that panel reports can contain differing views among the panel members, which has in fact never happened. As we know, panel reports are the result of the collective work of the different members and not of the work of each one of those members taken independently.

Measures Affecting Importation of Salmon, WT/DS18/R, adopted 6 November 1998, DSR 1998:VIII, 3407 in conjunction with *Australia - Measures Affecting the Importation of Salmonids*, WT/DS21, and *Argentina - Measures Affecting Imports of Footwear, Textiles, Apparel and Other Items*, WT/DS56/R, adopted 22 April 1998, DSR 1998:III, 1033 in conjunction with *Argentina - Measures Affecting Textiles, Clothing and Footwear*, WT/DS77.

[14] Panel Report, *United States – Anti-Dumping Act of 1916 – Complaint by the European Communities* ("*US – 1916 Act (EC)*"), WT/DS136/R, adopted 26 September 2000 and Panel Report, *United States – Anti-Dumping Act of 1916 – Complaint by Japan* ("*US – 1916 Act (Japan)*"), WT/DS162, adopted 26 September 2000, as upheld by the Appellate Body Report. Both cases are being examined by Johan Human, Dimitrij Grcar and Eugeniusz Piontek.

(b) The DSU does not contain any provision to the effect that the participation of a panel member in two panels would be contrary to the independence, objectivity and impartiality of that member in either of the two panels in question. On the contrary, the DSU recognizes, in Article 8.1, that the participation of a person in a panel must be seen as an advantage in terms of experience for other panels, and in the case of Article 21.5 it expressly states that a disagreement concerning implementation must be resolved "wherever possible through resort to the original panel". If the independence requirement in Article 8.2 were interpreted as Guatemala argues, Article 21.5 could not be applied, since by definition all of the members of the second panel could not be considered independent.

(c) The Members of the Appellate Body will never be independent, since they are governed by the principle of collegiality.

4.32 In view of the above considerations, under the Vienna Convention, the word "independence" cannot be given the meaning that Guatemala gives it, since this is not the ordinary meaning of the word in its context, nor does it take account of the treaty's objective and purpose.

4.33 Concerning Guatemala's fourth argument, after referring to Article 11 of the DSU, Guatemala indicates that "An objective assessment would appear to be impossible when the panel includes someone who has already formed opinions with respect to the identical complaints made in a previous case between the same parties."

4.34 Guatemala's reference to Article 11 of the DSU is inappropriate. This Article refers to the function of panels as a whole and not to the independence or lack of independence of one of their members. Assuming that one of the members holds a preconceived opinion because he had participated in a previous panel, this does not necessarily imply that the panel as a whole is no longer objective. Moreover, Guatemala is not even sure of what it affirms. It does not argue that the Panel cannot make an objective assessment, what it states is that an objective assessment "would appear to be impossible".

4.35 If Guatemala's purely speculative argument is accepted, this would imply:

(a) That opinions of the Panel member whose participation is contested by Guatemala were not objective in the previous Panel either. Conversely, if these opinions were objective in the first Panel, then they would be objective in the second Panel. As will be recalled, in paragraph 21 of its written submission, Guatemala acknowledges that it does not "question or dispute the integrity or qualifications of the panellist appointed in the first dispute", so its objection contradicts its initial statement;

(b) that not only were the opinions of the member contested by Guatemala not objective but they also prevailed over the opinions of the other members of the first Panel (including its Chairman) and, what is even more unlikely, these non-objective opinions prevailed over those of the other members of the second Panel, including its Chairman;

(c) that no person who has read the report of the Panel in the *Guatemala I* case may participate in the current proceedings because they would hold opinions regarding these complaints;

(d) that no person who has examined any matter relating to the Anti-Dumping Agreement would be objective, for the same reasons;

(e) that the complaints made under Article 21.5 do not require members of panels to be objective;

(f) that in the cases cited by Mexico when the Panel was appointed[15], the principle of objectivity was disregarded; and

(g) that this matter may not be the subject of an appeal because the Appellate Body would not be objective.

4.36 Regarding Guatemala's fifth argument, Guatemala states that Article 9 of the DSU does not apply because it refers to cases involving several complainants. Mexico agrees that there is only one complainant in this case, but this does not detract from Article 9 of the DSU as a clear example that the same persons may consider different cases without forfeiting their objectiveness or independence.

4.37 In paragraph 28 of its written submission, Guatemala states that the inclusion of Article 9 in the DSU "proves that this is an exception to the rule", without explaining why, but above all how, it is possible that such a sensitive matter as the independence of one or more members of a panel or the objectivity of the panel as a whole could be the subject of an exception to the rule. Both independence and objectivity are absolute concepts that are either applied or not applied. If Article 9 was an exception to the rule, in other words to independence and objectivity, all panels set up under this Article would also be an exception to the rule, in other words dependent and not objective.

4.38 In addition, a statement that "where there is not more than one complainant, the DSU does not authorize the same persons to serve on the different panels examining different disputes relating to the same matter" does not imply, as Guatemala suggests, that the DSU does not allow such a possibility. On the contrary, as already indicated, not only are there a number of precedents in which such action has been taken, but no provision of the DSU establishes a presumption against this and there are even provisions which specifically provide for recourse to the original panel, for example, Article 21.5.

4.39 Guatemala further states that "if the parties are concerned about the perceived bias of the mediator/arbitrator, then the use of different persons as the mediator/arbitrator is appropriate". This statement does not apply to disputes brought under the DSU. As will be recalled, Article 8.6 of the DSU provides that "the parties to this dispute shall not oppose nominations except for compelling reasons". In other words, it is not enough for there to be a perceived bias. There must be compelling reasons not to accept a candidate proposed.

4.40 In addition, according to Rule VIII.1 of the Rules of Conduct, a party must present evidence of material violation of the obligations of independence, impartial-

[15] See *India - Patent Protection for Pharmaceutical and Agricultural Chemical Products, supra*, footnote 13. See also *Australia - Measures Affecting Importation of Salmon* (WT/DS18), in conjunction with *Australia - Measures Affecting the Importation of Salmonids, supra*, footnote 13 and *Argentina - Measures Affecting Imports of Footwear, Textiles, Apparel and Other Items, supra*, footnote 13, in conjunction with *Argentina - Measures Affecting Textiles, Clothing and Footwear* (WT/DS/77).

ity or confidentiality or the obligation to avoid conflicts of interest. In other words, perception or semblance is not enough.

4.41 Lastly, nothing prevents members of the Panel from considering "only issues raised in, and necessary to fulfil their responsibilities within the dispute settlement proceeding", because this is their mandate. That mandate governs all their action, irrespective of any past experience they might have.

4.42 In view of the foregoing, Mexico requests the Panel:

(a) To find that the Panel does not have the mandate or competence to take any decision on the substance of the preliminary objection by Guatemala and should therefore continue to consider the matter raised by Mexico;

(b) to determine that, because of its nature and content, the preliminary objection by Guatemala should be rejected in accordance with the procedures laid down in the Rules of Conduct; and

(c) to ask whether Guatemala intends to apply immediately the procedures laid down in the Rules of Conduct and, if not, to enquire as to its reasons for not doing so.

B. Consideration by this Panel of Previous Panel Report

1. Submissions of Guatemala

4.43 **Guatemala** raises the further preliminary objection that because the previous panel dealing with this dispute did not have a mandate to examine the complaints brought by Mexico in these proceedings, its report is without value as a precedent to this case and should not be taken into consideration by this panel. Its arguments in this regard are as follows:

4.44 In it's first submission, Mexico speaks extensively of the Report of the Panel in *Guatemala - Cement I*. In fact, Mexico quotes that report at least 85 times. Essentially, Mexico would like this Panel to forego its obligation to make an objective assessment of the matter before it in this dispute settlement procedure as stipulated in Article 11 of the DSU, and rely on the examination conducted by the previous Panel in respect of complaints that are identical. This has clearly been Mexico's objective from the outset, when it improperly insisted that the Director-General reappoint the members of the first Panel to consider this second complaint.

4.45 However, the members of this Panel must reject Mexico's request to take up the assessment of the matter made by the first Panel. This Panel must fulfil its obligation to carry out its own objective assessment of the matter, and to that end it must completely disregard the report issued by the previous panel.

4.46 In international law it is accepted that any decision by an international body, including panels in a dispute settlement procedure, representing an excess of jurisdiction, must be considered void and without legal effect.[16] If a municipal tribunal

[16] See H. Lauterpacht, *The Legal Remedy in Case of Excess of Jurisdiction*, 9 Brit Y. B. Int'l L. page 117 (1928), and E. Lauterpacht, *The Legal Effect of the Illegal Acts of International Organizations* in CAMBRIDGE ESSAYS IN INTERNATIONAL LAW, page 88 (1965).

lacks jurisdiction, its decisions are void and without any effect.[17] In fact, a decision which has been reversed has no value as a precedent.[18]

4.47 In *Guatemala - Cement I*, the Appellate Body ruled that the Panel which examined the dispute should never have examined the complaints submitted because the matter was not properly before it. The Appellate Body reversed the report of the Panel on the grounds that it lacked jurisdiction. As a result, the report produced in *Guatemala - Cement I* has no value as a precedent, as evidence, or as guidance. Moreover, it would be extremely injurious to Guatemala, a Member which has the right to an objective examination by this Panel, if the Panel were to be guided by the reasoning of the report released in *Guatemala - Cement I*.

4.48 In the report issued in the case *Japan - Taxes on Alcoholic Beverages* (hereinafter *Japan - Taxes*) the Appellate Body confirmed that "unadopted panel reports 'have no legal status in the GATT or WTO ...'".[19] In *Argentina - Measures Affecting Imports of Footwear, Textiles, Apparel and Other Items* (hereinafter *Argentina - Footwear, Textiles and Apparel*) the Appellate Body considered that the Panel had committed an error by relying on an unadopted report.[20]

4.49 Under the GATT dispute settlement system, the legal status of unadopted panel reports was not recognized because the losing party had prevented adoption for political reasons. In the case at issue, the Report of the Panel in *Guatemala - Cement I* has no legal status and cannot constitute a valid precedent not because Guatemala prevented its adoption, but because the Appellate Body concluded that the Panel did not have the mandate to examine the complaints before it. Thus, recourse to the report issued in *Guatemala - Cement I* as useful guidance in respect of any matter being examined in the present dispute would be a violation of the decision of the Appellate Body.

4.50 Consequently, Guatemala requests that a preliminary decision be issued stating that the Panel shall not take account of the report issued in *Guatemala - Cement I*.

2. *Rebuttal of Mexico*

4.51 **Mexico's** rebuttal of Guatemala's preliminary objection against Panel consideration of the panel report issued in *Guatemala - Cement I* is as follows:

4.52 Guatemala's request was based on two premises in particular:

(a) The Panel must meet its obligation to carry out an objective assessment of the matter[21]; and

---

17 See, for example, *Rex V. Judge Pugh* [1951], page 2, K.B. 623.

18 See, for example, *League of Latin American Citizens v. Wilson*, 131 F. 3d 1297, 1305 n. 5 (9th Cir. 1997); see also *Durning v. Citibank*, 950 F 2d 1419, 1424 n. 2 (9th Cir. 1991) (decisions that have been reversed have no value as a precedent).

19 Report of the Appellate Body, *Japan - Taxes on Alcoholic Beverages*, WT/DS8/R, WT/DS10/AB/R, WT/DS11/AB/R, adopted 1 November 1996, DSR 1996:I, 97, at 108 (hereinafter *Japan - Taxes*).

20 Report of the Appellate Body, *Argentina - Measures Affecting Imports of Footwear, Textiles, Apparel and Other Items*, WT/DS56/AB/R, adopted on 22 April 1998, DSR 1998:III, 1003, para. 43.

21 *Ibid.*, paras. 32 and 33.

(b) the report of the Panel in *Guatemala-Cement I* was issued outside its jurisdiction, was not adopted and therefore has no effect as a precedent, a means of conviction or as guidance.[22]

4.53 In its oral submission at the first substantive meeting with the parties, Mexico rejected Guatemala's arguments for the following reasons:

(a) The arguments put forward are those of Mexico irrespective of whether or not they were issued by a Panel.[23]

(b) The report of the Panel in *Guatemala - Cement I* was adopted.[24]

---

[22] *Ibid.*, paras. 34-37.

[23] Oral submission by Mexico's, 15 February 2000, paras. 18 and 19, which state the following:

"18. In fact, the findings of the Panel in *Guatemala-Cement I*, were favourable to Mexico. This means that both Mexico and the Panel agree that the facts presented (i.e. Guatemala's acts and omissions during the investigation) violated the AD Agreement. It is therefore necessary to make clear that the legal reasoning explained here constitutes Mexico's position and should be taken as such.

19. Consequently, irrespective of the validity which the current Panel attributes to the previous Report, it should always be borne in mind that what is being examined here is Mexico's arguments before this Panel".

[24] *Ibid.*, paras. 20-25, which state the following:

"20. According to Articles 16.4 and 17.14, the DSB is the body empowered to adopt reports of panels and of the Appellate Body respectively. The fact that the Appellate Body reversed three of the Panel's findings does not mean that the latter's report was not adopted.

21. Guatemala holds a contradictory position regarding unadopted reports. On the one hand, it cites them when it believes this is useful and, on the other, it mentions several sources to show why this Panel should not consider the direct precedents in *Guatemala - Cement I*. The sources cited by Guatemala are not applicable to this case and are completely irrelevant and without any legal merit. Moreover, Guatemala does not take account of the rules on the adoption of reports in the DSU, which will be seen below, and gives a biased interpretation of the findings of the Appellate Body in *Japan - Taxes on Alcoholic Beverages, supra*, footnote 19. It also places on a same level the Report of a Panel (*Bananas II*) which unlike the Report in the *Guatemala - Cement I* case, was simply not adopted.

22. In order to apprehend the validity of this Report which was adopted 'as rejected by the Appellate Body', it is important to determine how the rejection affected the Report. To do so, it is necessary to turn to Article 17.6 of the DSU, which states the following: 'An appeal shall be limited to issues of law covered in the panel report and legal interpretations developed by the panel.'

23. The foregoing shows that the Appellate Body's terms of reference were limited to 'issues of law' and to 'legal interpretations' developed by the Panel. The factual elements which the parties submitted to the Panel, mainly in their written submissions and in positions stated orally, could not therefore be rejected because they do not fall within the Panel's authority. Consequently, the Panel Report is an adopted report and the adoption of the Appellate Body's Report does not in any way affect the part concerning the facts.

24. As we all know, the Panel Report in *Japan - Taxes on Alcoholic Beverages*, WT/DS8R, WT/DS10/R, WT/DS11/R, adopted 1 November 1996, DSR 1996:I, 125 contains useful guidance when determining the merits of panel reports because it recognizes that 'Adopted panel reports are an important part of the GATT *acquis*. They are often considered by subsequent panels. They create legitimate expectations among WTO Members, and, therefore, should be taken into account where they are relevant to any dispute.'

25. Following this logic, Mexico has legitimate expectations that the Panel responsible for considering the present case will take into account the facts submitted to the previous Panel and base its reasoning on these. Moreover, the *Guatemala - Cement I* Report is un-

(c) The Report of the Panel (WT/DS60/R) is an integral part of the request for the establishment of this Panel, so it forms part of the latter's terms of reference.[25]

(d) Supposing, for the sake of argument, that the Panel's report in *Guatemala - Cement I* was not adopted, it nevertheless contains useful indications that are relevant to the matter before this Panel.[26]

4.54 In order to supplement its subsidiary claims, Mexico provides some details and makes some remarks.

4.55 Firstly, it must be emphasized that the legal interpretations in the Panel's report in *Guatemala-Cement I* constitute part of Mexico's pleadings, so there can be no doubt that the Panel has to consider them. It should be recalled that, in the *Shrimps-Turtle* case, the Appellate Body determined that it was legitimate for a party to a dispute to attach the briefs by non-governmental organizations, or any portion thereof, to its own submissions.[27] If it is permitted to include the arguments of a body outside the WTO, it is equally possible for Mexico to cite the Panel's reasoning in *Guatemala*

---

doubtedly relevant to the dispute before you. Guatemala's exigency that the previous report should not be taken into account is not only groundless but is also contrary to the reasoning developed by the Appellate Body."

25 *Ibid.*, paras. 26 and 27, which state the following:

"26. This is a very simple claim: as shown below, the Report of the previous Panel was duly identified as a precedent in this case and, as Guatemala specifically recognizes, forms part of this Panel's terms of reference (footnote omitted).

27. In outlining the problem, Mexico specifically identified the report of the previous Panel and requested that this Panel: 'Examine, in the light of Article VI of the GATT 1994 and the Anti-Dumping Agreement, the matter referred to the DSB by Mexico on the basis of this request and of the direct precedents to this WTO dispute as set forth in the Report of the Panel, *Guatemala – Anti-Dumping Investigation Regarding Portland Cement from Mexico* ("*Guatemala - Cement I*"), WT/DS60/R, adopted 25 November 1998, DSR 1998:IX, 3797 and of the Appellate Body Report, *Guatemala – Anti-Dumping Investigation Regarding Portland Cement from Mexico* ("*Guatemala - Cement I*"), WT/DS60/AB/R, adopted 25 November 1998, DSR 1998:IX, 3767.

26 *Ibid.*, paras. 28-31, which state the following:

"28. Supposing, for the sake of argument, that Guatemala was right in saying that the Panel's report in *Guatemala - Cement I* was not adopted, it is nevertheless useful for this Panel to consider the reasoning followed by the previous Panel.

29. As we all know, according to the Appellate Body in *Japan - Taxes on Alcoholic Beverages* 'a panel could nevertheless find useful guidance in the reasoning of an unadopted panel report that it considered to be relevant'.

30. This reasoning was reaffirmed by the Appellate Body itself, for example, in *Argentina - Measures Affecting Imports of Footwear, Textiles, Apparel and Other Items*, supra, footnote 20.

31. Given the similarity between *Guatemala - Cement I* and the present case, it is obvious that the reasoning of the previous Panel is especially useful. It is also undeniable that, legal status notwithstanding, this Panel is empowered to consider the reasoning set out in this Report." (footnotes omitted).

27 Report of the Appellate Body in *United States - Import Prohibition of Certain Shrimp and Shrimp Products*, WT/DS58/AB/R, adopted 6 November 1998, DSR 1998:VII, 2755, para.110. The Appellate Body recognized that "the Panel acted within the scope of its authority under Articles 12 and 13 of the DSU in allowing any party to the dispute to attach the briefs by non-governmental organizations, or any portion thereof, to its own submissions."

- *Cement I* in its submission, particularly since this is a direct precedent to the present case and was identified as such in the request for the establishment of a Panel.

4.56 Secondly, it is interesting to see the way in which Guatemala has constructed the logic of its objection. In its first written submission, Guatemala intimates that Mexico wished to "incite" the Panel to act improperly using expressions such as "Mexico would like this Panel to forego its obligation to make an objective assessment of the matter"[28] or "the members of this Panel must reject Mexico's request to take up the assessment of the matter made by the first Panel".[29]

4.57 The way in which Guatemala puts forward its arguments is very simple. According to Guatemala, as Mexico cites the Panel report in *Guatemala - Cement I* "at least 85 times"[30] this means that Mexico would like the Panel to forego its obligation to make an objective assessment.

4.58 Guatemala's approach is unrealistic. If panels lose their objectivity when evaluating previous reports, then no panel which has taken action under the WTO dispute settlement mechanism (or, where applicable, under the GATT) would have made an objective assessment of the matter because they referred to reports by other panels. When considering the *Japan - Taxes* case, the Appellate Body made very clear the pertinence of panels examining reports of other panels, whether or not adopted.[31] In fact, following Guatemala's argument, it is possible to reach the conclusion that Guatemala would also like the Panel to forego an objective assessment because in its first submission it mentions the Appellate Body at least 36 times.

4.59 Suffice it to say that Mexico would like the Panel to "make an objective assessment of the facts, the applicability of the relevant covered agreements and conformity with these" and it has furnished all the elements of fact and of law available to it for this purpose, whether or not the previous Report was adopted. To follow Guatemala's logic would be tantamount to limiting Mexico's right of defence.

4.60 Thirdly, Guatemala cannot prohibit the Panel from taking into account the Report of the previous Panel.[32] In the *Shrimp-Turtle* case[33] the Appellate Body determined that "It is particularly within the province and the authority of a panel ... to ascertain the *acceptability* and *relevancy* of information or advice received, and to decide *what weight to ascribe to that information or advice*."[34]

---

[28] First submission by Guatemala, para. 32.

[29] *Ibid*., para. 33.

[30] *Ibid*., para. 32.

[31] Report of the Appellate Body in *Japan - Taxes*, *supra*, footnote 19, at 108. Referring to reports adopted by panels, the Appellate Body considered that adopted panel reports were an important part of the GATT *acquis* and recognized that "They are often considered by subsequent panels" and "should be taken into account where they are relevant to any dispute". Regarding unadopted panel reports, the Appellate Body indicated that "a panel could nevertheless find useful guidance in the reasoning of an unadopted panel report that it considered to be relevant."

[32] First submission by Guatemala, paras. 33, 35, 37 and 38.

[33] Report of the Appellate Body in *United States - Import Prohibition of Certain Shrimp and Shrimp Products* , *supra*, footnote 27.

[34] *Ibid*., para. 104. See also the Report of the Panel in *Mexico - Anti-Dumping Investigation of High Fructose Corn Syrup (HFCS) from the United States*, WT/DS132/R and Corr.1 adopted 24 February 2000, DSR 2000:III, 1345, para. 7.34; see also *United States - Imposition of Countervailing Duties on Certain Hot-Rolled Lead and Bismuth Carbon Steel Products Originating in the United Kingdom* ("*US – Lead and Bismuth II*") (under appeal), WT/DS138/R, adopted 7 June 2000,

4.61 Consequently, Mexico submits that it is not necessary to determine the status of the Report in the previous case because, irrespective of its status, the Panel is entitled to examine it and, in this particular case, it is especially relevant as a direct precedent to the case.

4.62 Mexico therefore reiterates what it stated in its request for the establishment of the Panel, namely, that the Panel should examine the matter submitted to the DSB by Mexico in the light of Article VI of the GATT 1994 and the AD Agreement, on the basis of its request, (which specifically includes the document WT/DS60/R), as well as the direct precedents to this WTO dispute as set forth in the Report of the Panel (WT(DS60/R) and of the Appellate Body (WT/DS60/AB/R).

3. *Guatemala's Response to Rebuttal Arguments of Mexico*

4.63 **Guatemala** responds to Mexico's rebuttal by asserting that since the previous panel did not have a mandate to examine the complaints brought by Mexico, its report is without value as a precedent to this case and should not be taken into consideration by this panel. The following are the arguments Guatemala advanced on this point in its second written submission:

4.64 Guatemala objects to Mexico's considering the report of the previous panel (hereinafter *Guatemala - Cement I*) as the "law" applicable to this dispute. Throughout its first written submission and during the first meeting on this case, Mexico repeatedly cited the report of the previous case as if it governed this dispute. In citing the report in the previous case, Mexico is trying the convince the Panel that it does not have to address certain questions because they have already been resolved.

4.65 Guatemala respectfully submits that no one, still less the Panel, should look to the *Guatemala - Cement I* report for useful guidance in settling the present dispute. Firstly, that Panel exceeded its jurisdiction. The Appellate Body considered that the Panel in the previous dispute should not have examined the complaints brought before it because it did not have the jurisdiction to hear the case.[35] If a subsequent panel were to ignore the findings and use the Report of the Panel in *Guatemala - Cement I* for guidance, it would be violating the ruling of the Appellate Body.

4.66 During the first meeting of the present procedure, Mexico not only insisted that the Panel use the report in *Guatemala - Cement I* as "useful guidance", but it also argued that the "legal interpretations made" in that report were "as valid and permissible as those of any other adopted panel report".[36] Mexico bases this astonishing conclusion on two premises: 1. that the Appellate Body did not reverse the conclusions of the panel report on the merits of the case; 2. that the Dispute Settlement Body (DSB) adopted the panel report.[37]

4.67 Guatemala submits that it is contrary to the law to equate the report in *Guatemala - Cement I* with the adopted report of a panel which was issued in accordance with the terms and stipulations of the WTO dispute settlement system. The latter

DSR 2000:VI, 2631, para. 6.3 and 6.6. It should be noted that these legal interpretations were not the subject of the appeal.

[35] Report of the Appellate Body, *Guatemala – Cement I*, *Supra*, footnote 25, para. 90.

[36] Oral submission by Mexico, para. 22.

[37] *Ibid.*.

reflects a ruling under the auspices of a multilateral institution, adopted by the corresponding body of that institution, while the former reflects a statement that does not come under the auspices of any multilateral institution. This distinction is at the heart of the Appellate Body's ruling: the Panel in *Guatemala - Cement I exceeded* its jurisdiction. The Panel *did not* have the mandate to do what it did. Thus, from the legal point of view, the report in *Guatemala - Cement I* does not have any more relevance than, say, an interesting book or some Article that was published on legal matters.[38]

4.68 In the recent ruling in the case *Mexico - Anti-Dumping Investigation of High Fructose Corn Syrup (HFCS) from the United States* (hereinafter *Corn Syrup*), the Panel found that the *Guatemala - Cement I* report "has no legal status".[39] Unfortunately, the Panel added that it could refer to the report "to the extent we consider it persuasive". The text suggests that the Panel treated the report in *Guatemala - Cement I* in the same way as an unadopted report. We consider this to be an error and respectfully request the Panel not to make this same error.

4.69 Equally spurious is Mexico's claim that the *Guatemala - Cement I* report comes under the Panel's terms of reference since it was mentioned in the request for the establishment of a panel. If this were the case, the result of every dispute could effectively be decided by the claimant if it were sufficiently prepared to cite favourable reports in their request for the establishment of a panel and to ignore the panel reports that were contrary to their position. Obviously, this interpretation of the Dispute Settlement Understanding (DSU) is ridiculous and unworthy of further attention by Guatemala or the Panel.

4.70 Finally, Guatemala respectfully submits that the rejection of this preliminary objection would set a bad precedent. It would motivate panels to ignore their terms of reference and settle questions that could appear important or new because even if their conclusions were reversed at the appellate stage, the ability to make their reasoning prevail would survive and be cited by future panels.

4.71 At the second substantive meeting, in its final oral submission, Mexico emphasized that Guatemala's attempts to undermine the legal reasoning in the Report of the Panel which examined the *Guatemala - Cement I* case are nothing new. What is new is that Guatemala finally recognizes that Mexico can turn to the arguments in this report[40] because this is precisely Mexico's argument. It recalled that on many occasions Mexico had indicated that the Panel's arguments were those of Mexico and consequently, the validity and relevance of the previous report are irrelevant. Everything else is superfluous.

---

38 At one point during the first hearing with the Panel, Mexico accused Guatemala of hypocrisy. The representative of Mexico said that Guatemala frequently invoked unadopted reports in support of its arguments. *Ibid.*.

39 Panel Report, *Corn Syrup*, *supra*, footnote 34, para.7.63, footnote 556.

40 Oral statement of Guatemala, para. 14.

C. *Preliminary Objection to Panel Consideration of the Provisional Measure and the Complaints Relating Thereto*

1. *Submissions of Guatemala*

4.72 **Guatemala** makes the following arguments in support of its preliminary objection that the Panel does not have the mandate to examine the provisional measure and the complaints relating thereto:

(a) Mexico did not request consultations in respect of the provisional measure

4.73 Under Article 4.4 of the DSU, all requests for consultations shall identify "the measures at issue". The request for consultations submitted by Mexico identifies the definitive anti-dumping measure, but not the provisional anti-dumping measure. Consequently, this Panel does not have the mandate to examine the provisional measure or Mexico's complaints challenging that measure. Specifically, the Panel does not have the mandate to examine the complaints contained in Mexico's first submission in Part V.B, "Imposition of the provisional anti-dumping measure violated Articles 2 and 7 of the AD Agreement and Article VI of the GATT 1994", pages 40-54.

4.74 In *Guatemala - Cement I*, the Appellate Body considered that "the consultation and dispute settlement provisions of a covered Agreement are not meant to *replace*, as a coherent system of dispute settlement for that Agreement, the rules and procedures of the DSU."[41] Thus, the provisions of Article 17 of the AD Agreement and Article 4 of the DSU must be understood as having to be applied jointly. It is only in the specific circumstance where a provision of the DSU and a special or additional provision of paragraphs 4 to 7 of Article 17 are mutually inconsistent that the provisions of Article 17 may be read to prevail over the provision of the DSU.[42] The Appellate Body therefore rejected Mexico's argument that Article 17.4 of the AD Agreement replaced Article 6.2 of the DSU and submitted that the request for the establishment of a panel must identify the anti-dumping measure at issue, as required under Article 6.2 of the DSU.

4.75 Similarly, Article 17.3 of the AD Agreement does not replace Article 4.4. of the DSU in respect of the applicable procedure for requesting consultations. In fact, Article 17.3 is not even mentioned in Annex 2 of the DSU as a special or additional provision. Thus, the request for consultations "shall be submitted in writing and shall give the reasons for the request, including identification of the measure at issue and an indication of the legal basis for the complaint".[43]

4.76 In *Guatemala - Cement I*, the Appellate Body also ruled that the "matter" consisted of two elements: the specific "measure" and the "claims" relating to it.[44] Moreover, it concluded that the word "matter" had the same meaning in paragraphs 3, 4 and 5 of Article 17 of the AD Agreement (Consultation and Dispute Settlement)

---

41 Appellate Body Report, *Guatemala – Cement I*, *supra*, footnote 25, para. 67.

42 *Ibid.*, para. 66.

43 DSU, Article 4.4.

44 Appellate Body Report, *Guatemala – Cement I*, *supra*, footnote 25, para. 76.

as it had in Article 7 of the DSU (Terms of Reference of Panels). Thus, by limiting the scope of its request for consultations to include only the definitive anti-dumping measure and the complaints relating thereto, Mexico clearly excluded from this dispute settlement procedure the provisional measure and the complaints relating to it.

4.77 Mexico's request for the establishment of a panel of 15 July 1999 recognizes that the request for consultations only identified the definitive anti-dumping measure "as well as the actions that preceded it".[45] In the request for the establishment of a panel, Mexico challenges the definitive anti-dumping measure and "the actions that preceded it, including the provisional anti-dumping measure and various matters relating to the initiation of the investigation and the anti-dumping proceeding".[46] Thus, Mexico does not challenge the provisional measure *per se*. Mexico challenges the provisional measure only as one of the actions preceding the challenge of the final measure. In other words, if we read Mexico's request for the establishment of a panel together with its request for consultations, we find that Mexico did not identify the provisional measure as a specific measure at issue, but only as one of its complaints against the final measure.

4.78 However, to the extent that it can be said that Mexico's request for the establishment of a panel did identify the provisional measure as the subject of its complaint, that request violates Article 4 of the DSU. Under Article 6 of the DSU, a Member may not request the establishment of a panel to challenge a measure in respect of which it has not requested prior consultations under Article 4 of the DSU. Article 4.3 stipulates that a Member may proceed directly to request the establishment of a panel if the other Member does not respond to the request or enter into consultations within specified periods of time. Article 4.7, for its part, stipulates that "If the consultations fail to settle a dispute" within the time-period specified therein, "the complaining party may request the establishment of a panel." Similarly, Article 6.2 requires that in its request for the establishment of a panel, the Member "indicate whether consultations were held" and "identify the specific measures at issue". Since the request for consultations submitted by Mexico did not identify the provisional measure as the specific measure at issue, that measure cannot be the subject of the dispute. Allowing Mexico to extend the scope of the *litis* to include the provisional measure would undermine the provisions of Article 4 of the DSU, which stipulates, as already mentioned, that consultations must be requested in respect of a specific measure before the request for the establishment of a panel to examine that measure can be submitted.

4.79 To permit Mexico to include the provisional measure in its complaint, as it tries to do in its first submission, would be to ignore an important stage in the dispute settlement process, in violation of Article 3.7 of the DSU which states that:

> "Before bringing a case, a Member shall exercise its judgement as to whether action under these procedures would be fruitful. The aim of the dispute settlement mechanism is to secure a positive solution to a dispute. A solution mutually acceptable to the parties to a dispute and consistent with the covered Agreements is clearly to be preferred."

---

45 WT/DS156/2, page 2.

46 *Ibid.*.

Under this Article, the parties must do their utmost to find a mutually acceptable solution. If a Member chooses not to request consultations in respect of a measure which it challenges in its first submission, as in the case at issue, a fundamental objective of the DSU is thereby completely undermined.

4.80 In *United States - Imposition of Anti-Dumping Duties on Imports of Fresh and Chilled Atlantic Salmon from Norway* (hereinafter *United States - Salmon from Norway*), the Panel found that under Article 15 of the special dispute settlement provisions contained in the Agreement on Implementation of Article VI of the General Agreement on Tariffs and Trade 1947 (Tokyo Round Anti-Dumping Code), "before a party to a dispute could request a Panel concerning a matter, the parties to the dispute had to have been given an opportunity to reach a mutually satisfactory resolution of the matter. This condition would not be meaningful unless the matter had been raised in consultations and conciliation."[47]

4.81 Guatemala recognizes that Article 7.1 of the DSU defines the terms of reference of a panel, which are normally established on the basis of the request for the establishment of a panel presented by the complainant.[48] Moreover, it recognizes that the terms of reference of a panel establish its jurisdiction.[49] However, they would not determine its jurisdiction if it were found that the request for the establishment of a panel submitted by the complainant covered a dispute that had not been the subject of a request for consultations.[50] As clearly explained in *Canada - Civilian Aircraft*, Article 4.4 of the Agreement on Subsidies and Countervailing Measures (SCM Agreement) read together with Article 4.7 of the DSU, "prevent a Member from requesting the establishment of a panel with regard to a 'dispute' on which no consultations were requested".[51] Similarly, read together, the provisions of Article 17.4 of the AD Agreement and those of Article 4.7 of the DSU prevent Mexico, in this case, from requesting the establishment of a panel on a dispute concerning Guatemala's provisional measure in respect of which it did not request consultations.[52]

4.82 Mexico's failure to identify the provisional measure (and to present the complete category of complaints regarding the provisional measure) in its request for consultations prevented the special dispute settlement rules for anti-dumping cases

47 ADP/87, adopted on 27 April 1994, para. 333.

48 Report of the Panel, *Canada - Measures Affecting the Export of Civilian Aircraft* (hereinafter *Canada - Civilian Aircraft*), WT/DS70/R, adopted 20 August 1999, DSR 1999:IV, 1443, para. 9.11.

49 *Ibid.*.

50 *Ibid.*, para. 9.12.

51 *Ibid.*.

52 Unlike in the case *Brazil - Export Financing Programme for Aircraft*, this case does not involve a situation in which the measure identified in the request for consultations (a resolution for the payment of export subsidies under PROEX) and the measure identified in the request for the establishment of a panel (regulations issued subsequently for the payment of export subsidies under PROEX) essentially involved the same practice or dispute (Appellate Body Report, *Brazil - Export Financing Programme for Aircraft*, WT/DS46/AB/R, adopted 20 August 1999, DSR 1999:III, 1161, para. 132). A provisional anti-dumping measure is clearly different and separate from a definitive anti-dumping measure, and the challenge of one of the measures may be accepted while the other may be rejected. Consequently, they constitute different "disputes".

from providing the parties an opportunity to reach a "mutually satisfactory resolution" of the dispute under Article 17.3 of the Anti-Dumping Agreement.

4.83 Thus, Guatemala requests the Panel to issue a preliminary decision to the effect that the Panel does not have a mandate to examine the provisional measure and all of the complaints referring thereto, since Mexico did not request consultations in respect of that measure.

(b) In the alternative the provisional measure does not have a "Significant Impact" in conformity with Article 17.4

(i) The requirement to prove "Significant Impact"

4.84 Article 17.4 of the Anti-Dumping Agreement refers mainly to the definitive anti-dumping measures. The provisional measures may only be challenged in certain limited situations. Specifically, a complainant may challenge a provisional measure only: (a) "when a provisional measure has a significant impact", and (b) "the Member that requested consultations considers that the measure was taken contrary to the provisions of paragraph 1 of Article 7" of the Anti-Dumping Agreement.[53]

4.85 These requirements were also contained in Article 15.3 of the Tokyo Round Anti-Dumping Code, which is the legal precedent for Article 17.4 of the Anti-Dumping Agreement.[54]

4.86 The simple wording of Article 17.4 indicates that the complainant must prove that there was a significant impact. In contrast, the complainant only needs to *consider* that the measure was taken contrary to the provisions of Article 7.1. Moreover, the use of the present tense ("has a significant impact") indicates that the provisional measure must have a current and enduring impact, and not a historical impact.

4.87 Finally, the intention of the drafters of Article 17.4 must have been that the significant impact must be proven in relation to the trade interests of the complaining party and not in relation to the exporting industry under investigation. This is due to the fact that the complainant in a dispute settlement procedure is a WTO Member and not the exporter or exporters under investigation. Since the WTO dispute settle-

---

[53] Article 7.1 reads as follows:

Provisional measures may be applied only if:

(i) an investigation has been initiated in accordance with the provisions of Article 5, a public notice has been given to that effect and interested parties have been given adequate opportunities to submit information and make comments;

(ii) a preliminary affirmative determination has been made of dumping and consequent injury to a domestic industry; and

(iii) the authorities concerned judge such measures necessary to prevent injury being caused during the investigation.

[54] The Appellate Body recognized that the *context* of a provision includes previous agreements on the same matter (report of the Appellate Body in *United States - Restrictions on Imports of Cotton and Man-made Fibre Underwear*, WT/DS24/AB/R, AB-1996-3, adopted 25 February 1997, DSR 1997:I, 11, at 25 ("the disappearance in the ATC of the earlier MFA express provision for backdating the operative effect of a restraint measure, strongly reinforces the presumption that such retroactive application is no longer permissible.")

ment procedures refer to the rights and the obligations of the Member countries, the question of whether or not there is a significant impact must be assessed in relation to the overall trade interest of the complaining Member. No other interpretation of Article 17.4 would be logical given the object and purpose of the AD Agreement and the DSU. Mexico agrees with this interpretation. In the case *United States - Anti-Dumping Duties on Grey Portland Cement and Cement Clinker from Mexico*, Mexico stressed that the General Agreement on Tariffs and Trade 1947 (GATT 1947) was designed to regulate conduct between signatory countries and that the dispute settlement process was a government-to-government process.[55] Mexico contended that the predecessor to Article 17.4 "expressly allowed *signatories* to challenge...preliminary determinations where these had a significant impact on *their* trading interests."[56]

4.88 These strict requirements, which must be met by complainants in order to challenge a provisional measure, establish an important balance between the rights of a complainant to make such challenges and the burden on the defending party in defending itself against them. In almost all cases, the underlying anti-dumping investigation is close to completion, and in no more than a few months the provisional measure will be replaced by the definitive measure.[57] In fact, the AD Agreement does not even require members to impose provisional measures as a prerequisite to the imposition of definitive measures. For example, in situations where the definitive anti-dumping measure has already been imposed, if for any reason the complainant decides to challenge the provisional measure, it is difficult to imagine how it would be possible for the complainant to show that the provisional measure has had an enduring significant impact.

(ii) Mexico does not claim that the provisional measure has had an enduring significant impact

4.89 In its request for the establishment of the panel of 15 July 1999, Mexico claims that the imposition of a provisional measure was an "action" contrary to Guatemala's obligations under the AD Agreement.[58] Although Mexico claims in its request for the establishment of a panel that the provisional measure "*had* a significant impact", it does not claim that the provisional measure "*has* a significant impact" as required by Article 17.4. Similarly, in its first written submission to this Panel, it does not argue that the provisional measure "has a significant impact". In fact, it is inconceivable that the provisional measure should have an enduring impact. That measure expired on 28 December 1996, more than three years ago.

---

55 ADP/82, Report of the Panel (unadopted), 7 July 1992, para. 3.1.11.

56 *Ibid.*, (emphasis added).

57 Article 7.4 of the AD Agreement stipulates that "the application of provisional measures shall be limited to as short a period as possible, not exceeding four months or, on decision of the authorities concerned, upon request by exporters representing a significant percentage of trade involved to a period not exceeding six months."

58 As stated above, Mexico's request for the establishment of a panel does not challenge the provisional measure *per se*, which is only mentioned as an action preceding the imposition of the definitive measure.

(iii) In the alternative, the provisional measure never had a significant impact

4.90 Mexico could claim - although Article 17.4 uses the present tense ("has a significant impact") - that proof of prior significant impact suffices. Guatemala would disagree with this idea, because it is contrary to the simple wording of Article 17.4. However, even if we were to assume, for the sake of argument, that it were enough under Article 17.4 to prove prior significant impact, Mexico does not even do that. In its first submission, Mexico neither claims not tries to prove that the provisional measure had a significant impact.

4.91 Mexico cannot prove that the provisional measure in question has a "significant impact" on its trading interests as a whole. In fact, the provisional measure was only in force for four months, and only affected an insignificant portion of Mexico's exports during those four months. According to official information on exports from Bancomex, during 1996, exports of grey Portland cement from Mexico to Guatemala represented only 0.016 per cent of Mexican exports of all products to all countries (US$15.6 million in cement exports to Guatemala/US$96 billion in total exports to all countries). Moreover, the provisional measure only affected a small fraction of Mexico's exports to Guatemala. Mexico's cement exports to Guatemala in 1996 represented only 4.3 per cent of its total exports to Guatemala (US$15.6 million in cement exports/US$360 million in overall exports).

4.92 Nor can Mexico prove that the provisional measure had a significant impact on the Mexican cement industry, even if we assume for the sake of argument that such an analysis specific to the cement sector had any relevance under Article 17.4. Guatemala is not one of Mexico's traditional cement export markets. In fact, Mexico had no interest in exporting cement to Guatemala until it suffered a severe recession resulting in an enormous excess cement production capacity in 1995. Moreover, the provisional measure applied only to Cruz Azul, one of the five producers of grey Portland cement in Mexico. The provisional measure did not apply to the leading producers and exporters in Mexico - CEMEX, S.A. de C.V., Apsaco S.A. de C.V., and Cementos de Chihuahua, S.A. de C.V.. And indeed, the provisional measure only required Guatemalan importers to provide a guarantee or a cash deposit to cover the estimated margin of dumping. If Cruz Azul or a Guatemalan importer had asked for an examination under Article 9 of the AD Agreement and had shown that there was no dumping, the guarantee provided by the importers would have been restituted and the cash deposits reimbursed. Neither Cruz Azul nor its importers requested such an examination.

4.93 Given the proliferation of disputes brought before the WTO, the competence restrictions contained in Article 17.4 should be respected in order to prevent certain Members from having recourse to the WTO dispute settlement system every time a provisional measure is imposed, when the impact of the measure is insignificant or temporary and can only affect an individual company in the territory of the Member. Article 17.4 is designed in part to preserve the WTO's resources for disputes relating to the imposition of definitive anti-dumping measures or to price commitments, unless it is proved that the imposition of a provisional measure has had an enduring "significant impact" on the trade interests of a Member.

4.94 Since Guatemala's provisional measure does not have a significant impact on Mexico's overall trading interests, Guatemala requests the Panel to issue a preliminary resolution to the effect that the Panel does not have the mandate to examine the provisional measure and all of the complaints referring to that measure.

2. *Rebuttal of Mexico*

4.95 **Mexico** makes the following rebuttal arguments to Guatemala's preliminary objection regarding the Panel's examination of the provisional measure:

4.96 Guatemala asserts that the Panel does not have the mandate to examine the provisional measure and the complaints referring thereto. To substantiate its assertion, Guatemala puts forward the following alternative arguments:

(a) Mexico did not identify the provisional measure as "the specific measure at issue".

(b) Nevertheless, if it is interpreted that Mexico did identify the provisional measure as "the specific measure at issue", Mexico failed to meet its obligation to request the holding of consultations on the provisional measure.

(c) The provisional measure does not or did not have a "significant impact", as required by Article 17.4.

4.97 Mexico responded to these assertions in its oral submission at the first substantive meeting with the parties by indicating the following:

(a) The obligations in the second sentence of Article 17.4 of the AD Agreement do not apply to cases in which the definitive anti-dumping measure is contested.

(b) The concept of "significant impact" does not refer to the "overall trading interests" of a Member.

(c) In any event, Mexico shows that it did comply with the formal and material requirements in the DSU for contesting a provisional measure.

4.98 In addition to the arguments it has already put forward, Mexico wishes to underline certain aspects that are important for its pleadings.

(a) Mexico was not obliged to hold consultations with Guatemala, nor to prove that the provisional measure imposed by Guatemala had or has a "significant impact"

(i) Holding of consultations

4.99 Mexico understands Guatemala's objection to be formulated as follows:

(a) Firstly, it sets out arguments to assert that Mexico does not contest the provisional measure as such but only as one of the actions which preceded the objection to the final measure, consequently the Panel has no mandate to examine this.[59]

[59] First submission by Guatemala, paras. 39-43.

(b) Subsequently, it argues that, if it is understood that Mexico did identify the provisional measure as the subject of its complaint, such a request violates Article 4 of the DSU because no opportunity was given for consultations with a view to reaching a mutually satisfactory solution of the matter.[60]

4.100 According to Mexico's understanding, Guatemala's reasoning provides alternatives: (i) if Mexico did not identify the provisional measure as "the specific measure at issue", then the provisional measure was outside the Panel's mandate; however, (ii) if Mexico did identify the provisional measure as "the specific measure at issue", then it failed to meet the requirement to hold consultations.

4.101 The following at least can be deduced from Guatemala's assertions:

(a) Guatemala acknowledges that Mexico did identify the provisional anti-dumping measure, at least as an action that preceded the definitive anti-dumping measure.[61]

(b) Guatemala also acknowledges that the actions do not have to be included in the request for consultations.[62]

4.102 As Mexico has already indicated, the fact of whether or not the provisional anti-dumping measure was identified as the "specific measure at issue" is irrelevant.[63]

4.103 In this rebuttal, it will be shown why, irrespective of whether or not the provisional anti-dumping measure was identified as the ("specific measure at issue"), the result is exactly the same: that is to say that the Panel is entitled to examine it.

4.104 Mexico did identify the provisional measure as an action that preceded the definitive anti-dumping measure ("specific measure at issue") and this was specifically accepted by Guatemala.[64]

4.105 In its oral submission at the first substantive meeting with the parties, Mexico showed that, when a definitive anti-dumping measure is contested as the "specific measure at issue", the complainant is at liberty to make any type of complaint regarding the provisional anti-dumping measure as the action that preceded the definitive anti-dumping measure.[65] As the Appellate Body pointed out in *Guatemala-Cement I*:

> "This requirement to identify a specific anti-dumping measure at issue in a panel request in no way limits the nature of the *claims* that may be brought concerning alleged nullification or impairment of benefits or the impeding of the achievement of any objective in a dispute under the *Anti-Dumping Agreement*."[66]

4.106 There is nothing in Article 17.4 or in any other part of the AD Agreement to prevent claims being made against any action taken during an anti-dumping investi-

---

[60] *Ibid.*, paras. 44-49.

[61] *Ibid.*, para. 43.

[62] *Ibid.*, para. 44. Guatemala claims a violation of Article 4 of the DSU "to the extent that Mexico's request for the establishment of a panel did identify the provisional measure as the subject of its complaint".

[63] Oral submission by Mexico at the first substantive meeting.

[64] First written submission by Guatemala, para. 43.

[65] Oral submission by Mexico at the first substantive meeting, paras. 34-37.

[66] Report of the Appellate Body in *Guatemala-Cement I*, *supra*, footnote 25, para. 79.

gation (even the imposition of a provisional measure), provided that the requirement to identify the definitive measure as the "specific measure at issue" is met. Article 1 of the AD Agreement itself obliges the authorities to impose anti-dumping measures only "pursuant to investigations initiated and conducted in accordance with the provisions of this Agreement". This means that the imposition of the definitive measure must be the result of an investigation conducted in accordance with the AD Agreement. In other words, all the steps taken in the investigation preceding the definitive anti-dumping measure affect the imposition of that measure. In the present case, the provisional anti-dumping measure is a step taken in the investigation (or action preceding the definitive anti-dumping measure), and therefore, Mexico can unquestionably make several claims in this regard.

4.107 Furthermore, assuming, for the sake of argument, that Article 17.4 prevents the provisional measure from being contested as an action, it should be noted that the second sentence of the Article only refers to paragraph 1 of Article 7 and not to other obligations related to the provisional measures.[67] Following Guatemala's logic, therefore, even if the Panel did not have the mandate to examine claims relating to violations of Article 7.1 of the AD Agreement, the same Panel could examine Mexico's claims regarding violations of Articles 2.2, 2.4.3 and 12.2.1. If this were the case, the absence of a mandate would be offset by the Panel's authority to examine the provisional measure under Article 1 of the AD Agreement.

4.108 Lastly, it should be noted that it is common practice for Members of this Organization to conduct dispute settlement proceedings that cover both a provisional and a definitive measure.[68]

4.109 Assuming that Mexico did identify the provisional anti-dumping measure as the "specific measure at issue", even though it is not necessary to repeat everything said in the oral submission at the first substantive meeting, it should be recalled that Mexico did request consultations on the provisional measure and that Guatemala acknowledged that it had consulted with Mexico.[69] All the background to these proceedings constitutes reliable proof that there were more than enough opportunities to try to reach a mutually satisfactory solution of this issue. Two particularly relevant aspects should be highlighted in relation to this dispute: (i) Mexico's request for consultations refers specifically to Article 7 of the DSU[70]; and (ii) Mexico and Guatemala did consult about the provisional anti-dumping measure in the context of this dispute. See the indicative list of questions at the hearing, particularly questions 27-38.[71]

---

[67] See the Report of the Panel in *Mexico-Corn Syrup, supra*, footnote 34, para. 7.54.

[68] See *inter alia*, the request for the establishment of a Panel in *European Communities - Anti-Dumping Duties on Imports of Cotton-Type Bed Linen from India* (WT/DS141/3) and *United States - Anti-Dumping Measures on Stainless Steel Plate in Coils and Stainless Steel Sheet and Strip from Korea* (WT/DS179/2). See also the GATT Report of the Panel in *Brazil - Milk Powder*, in particular, para. 368. This is proof that a Panel may note non-compliance of provisional and definitive measures in the context of the same dispute settlement proceedings.

[69] Oral submission by Mexico at the first substantive meeting with the parties.

[70] See Mexico's request for consultations WT/DS156/1, G/L/289, G/ADP/D/14/1, of 8 January 1999.

[71] In order to understand the significance of footnote 45 to Guatemala's first submission, see the Panel Report in *Canada - Civilian Aircraft, supra*, footnote 48, para. 9.12, where the Panel adopts

4.110 Consequently, to the extent that the provisional measure is interpreted as a "specific measure at issue", Mexico consulted with Guatemala and thus fully complied with Article 4 of the DSU. Moreover, the request for the establishment of a panel indicated that two series of consultations had been held: one in the context of the previous proceedings and the other relating to the present proceedings, therefore, although Guatemala does not make any claim in this regard, it is clear that Mexico complied with Article 6.2 of the DSU.

(ii) Significant impact

4.111 After reading this claim, the first remark that springs to mind is that it is an alternative. In other words, the Panel can examine the claim relating to consultations or the claim relating to significant impact, but it is not necessary to examine both claims. In any event, if the Panel decides to examine Guatemala's claim, it is important to emphasize the following:

4.112 Guatemala's reasoning has a very strange basis: according to Guatemala, Article 17.4 of the AD Agreement mainly refers to definitive anti-dumping measures because it is very difficult to contest a provisional measure (at no time does it mention price undertakings).[72] This logic seems to be an attempt to make the second sentence of Article 17.4 of the AD Agreement inoperative or, in other words, it seeks to make any objection to provisional measures inoperative.

4.113 According to Guatemala:

(a) Article 17.4 indicates that the complainant "must prove that there was a significant impact"[73];

(b) " ... the intention of the drafters of Article 17.4 must have been that the significant impact must be proven in relation to the trade interests of the complaining party and not in relation to the exporting industry under investigation."[74]

4.114 Using this interpretation, Guatemala claims that Mexico does not complain that the provisional measure has an enduring significant impact[75] or, alternatively, that the provisional measure did not have any significant impact.[76]

4.115 With regard to these claims, at the first substantive meeting with the parties Mexico asserted that.[77]

(a) There is no obligation to prove a significant impact.

an approach that "seeks to preserve due process while also recognising that the 'matter' on which consultations are requested will not necessarily be identical to the 'matter' identified in the request for establishment of a panel" Put another way, this approach supports the concept that it was not necessary for Mexico to identify the provisional anti-dumping measure as the "specific measure at issue" (concept of "matter") in its request for consultations and it was sufficient for the consultations to have covered this matter.

72 First submission by Guatemala, para. 50.

73 *Ibid.*, para. 51.

74 *Ibid.*, para. 52.

75 *Ibid.*, para. 54.

76 *Ibid.*, paras. 55-59.

77 Oral submission by Mexico at the first substantive meeting with the parties.

(b) The concept of "significant impact" does not refer to the overall trading interests of a Member because such an interpretation would give countries which impose provisional anti-dumping measures in breach of the AD Agreement almost total immunity.

4.116 Regarding this matter, Mexico wishes to put forward the following arguments in order to facilitate the Panel's work:

4.117 The logic of "significant impact" is similar to that in the case of consultations. In other words, the second sentence of Article 17.4 does not apply if the definitive measure is identified as the "specific measure at issue".

4.118 Having said this, Mexico recalls that it has already shown that, unlike Article 3.5 of the AD Agreement, Article 17.4 does not contain the word "demonstrated". It is nevertheless important to examine the wording of Article 17.4 in order to understand the obligation contained therein. According to this Article "When a provisional measure has a significant impact ...that Member may also refer such matter to the DSB". Does this mean that the significant impact must be "demonstrated" in the request for the establishment of a panel? It would appear that this is Guatemala's position, because if it is not it would not have used the word "challenged" and would not have claimed that the Panel did not have a mandate.[78]

4.119 Mexico submits that Guatemala is wrong. Guatemala's reasoning means that the second sentence of Article 17.4 of the AD Agreement makes it necessary to "demonstrate" a significant impact. If this same logic is applied to the first sentence of this Article, however, a Member requesting the establishment of a panel would have to "demonstrate" that the competent authority of the importing Member had adopted definitive anti-dumping duties or had accepted price undertakings. As can be seen, this is an illogical interpretation of the dispute settlement provisions. No Member of the WTO has had to provide such a demonstration before a panel could be established.

4.120 Neither Article 17.4 of the AD Agreement nor any other provision in the WTO dispute settlement mechanism contains an obligation to provide any demonstration in order to be able to request the establishment of a panel. Furthermore, the need to demonstrate any particular point in the request for the establishment of a panel would conflict with the virtually automatic principle in Article 6.2 of the DSU whereby panels are established automatically unless there is a consensus to the contrary. Consequently, it would be illogical to assume that a complainant Member is not obliged to provide any evidence for the establishment of a panel because when establishing a panel there is no difference according to whether or not an alleged requirement has been proved.[79] In any event, assuming for the sake of argument that

[78] First submission by Guatemala, paras. 50 and 59.

[79] The Panel which considered the complaint of the United States in the *European Communities - Regime for the Importation, Sale and Distribution of Bananas – Complaint by the United States, (WT/DS27/R/USA)*, adopted 25 September 1997, DSR 1997:II, 943, para. 7.26, recognized that it is not necessary to examine the formal requirements for the establishment of a panel prior to its actual establishment. It therefore stated the following: "Because of the application of 'reverse' consensus decision-making applicable in the case of panel establishment in the DSB, the DSB is not likely to be an effective body for resolving disputes over whether a request for the establishment of a panel meets the requirements of Article 6.2 of the DSU. Therefore, as a practical matter only the panel

there is an obligation to demonstrate a significant impact, this should be done after the establishment of a panel.

4.121 In order to clarify the different levels of demonstration when requesting the establishment of a panel and when presenting the parties' submissions to a panel, the Panel in *EC - Bananas* pointed out that:

> "... there is a significant difference between the *claims* identified in the request for the establishment of a panel, which establish the panel's terms of reference under Article 7 of the DSU, and the *arguments* supporting those claims, which are set out and progressively clarified in the first written submissions, the rebuttal submissions and the first and second panel meetings with the parties".[80]

4.122 Furthermore, it would be illogical for a Member to have to demonstrate a signficant impact in order to object to a provisional anti-dumping measure, particularly if this concept is understood according to Guatemala's unacceptable interpretation. Bearing in mind that the duration of provisional measures is four months (or, in any event, six months), by the time a Member had collected all the relevant statistics, held consultations and established a panel, the measure would already have expired or be on the point of expiring. It would not therefore make any sense to challenge this type of measure and the second sentence of Article 17.4 would be inoperative, as Guatemala would like.

4.123 Consequently, Mexico asserts that the demonstration of a current or past "significant impact" is not a requirement to be met before a Panel can examine a provisional anti-dumping measure.

3. Guatemala's Response to Rebuttal Arguments

4.124 **Guatemala** makes the following response to Mexico's rebuttal of its preliminary objection regarding Panel examination of the provisional measures:

4.125 The third preliminary objection raised by Guatemala concerns Mexico's claims directed exclusively against the provisional measure. Guatemala respectfully submits that the Panel lacks the mandate to examine the provisional measure and the complaints referring to that measure.

4.126 In *Guatemala - Cement I*, the Appellate Body considered that Article 17.4 of the AD Agreement merely specified the three types of measure which could make up the *dispute* referred to the DSB: definitive (i.e. final) anti-dumping duties, price undertakings and provisional measures.[81] In the case *Canada - Measures Affecting the Export of Civilian Aircraft* (hereinafter *Canada - Civilian Aircraft*), the Panel considered that Article 4.4 of the Agreement on Subsidies and Countervailing Measures (SCM Agreement") and Article 4.7 of the DSU read together "prevent a Member from requesting the establishment of a panel with regard to a ´dispute` on which no

---

established on the basis of the request (and thereafter the Appellate Body) can perform that function."

[80] Report of the Appellate Body in *European Communities - Regime for the Importation, Sale and Distribution of Bananas*, WT/DS/27/ABR, adopted 25 September 1997, DSR 1997:II, 591, para. 141.

[81] *Guatemala Cement I, supra*, footnote 25, para. 79.

consultations were requested".[82] In the present case, Mexico's request for consultations ***does not*** identify the provisional measure as being the subject of this dispute - it identifies only the definitive antidumping measure.[83] Thus, Article 17.4 of the AD Agreement and Article 4.7 of the DSU, read together, prevent Mexico from requesting the establishment of a panel with respect to Guatemala's provisional measure, on which consultations were not requested. The provisional measure is clearly different and separate from the definitive anti-dumping measure and the challenge of one of those measures can prevail while the challenge of the other measure fails. In other words, they are separate "disputes".

4.127 At the first meeting with the Panel, Mexico recognized that it was *not* challenging the provisional measure; but it argued that it was challenging the provisional measure "as an action preceding the definitive anti-dumping measure".[84]

> "Since Mexico had clearly challenged the definitive anti-dumping measure in its request for the establishment of a panel, it was free to assert any number of complaints regarding any aspect of the Anti-Dumping Agreement which might arise during the dispute, including the provisional measure, without having to identify them as "specific measures at issue".[85]

4.128 According to Mexico, this also means that it was under no obligation to demonstrate that the provisional measure had a "significant impact".

> "Since Mexico has the freedom to raise various complaints concerning the provisional measure as an action preceding the definitive anti-dumping measure (sic), there is no need to comply with the requirements mentioned by Guatemala".[86]

These statements at best reflect a deep misunderstanding of the report of the Appellate Body and the relevant DSU provisions.

4.129 First, the operative question is whether Mexico is seeking to obtain a recommendation by the Panel under Article 19.1 of the DSU to the effect that Guatemala's provisional measure is inconsistent with the AD Agreement. In order to obtain this recommendation, Mexico should have requested consultations on the provisional measure and should have requested the establishment of a panel in respect of the provisional measure. Mexico did neither of these two things. By identifying the final determination as the *only* measure at issue, Mexico prevented the Panel from issuing a recommendation in respect of the provisional measure.[87]

4.130 Secondly, as discussed at great length by the Appellate Body in *Guatemala - Cement I*, provisional anti-dumping measures are completely different from defini-

---

[82] Panel Report, *Canada – Civilian Aircraft*, *supra*, footnote 48, para. 9.12.

[83] Nor has it been shown that Mexico and Guatemala held consultations in respect of the provisional measure. Contrary to what Mexico suggests in its oral submission. The fact that the two Members may have held consultations in respect of the provisional measure prior to the establishment of the Panel in *Guatemala I* does not show that in the *present* dispute, similar consultations were held.

[84] Oral submission by Mexico, para. 34.

[85] *Ibid.*, para. 35.

[86] *Ibid.*, para. 39.

[87] This explains why at the first meeting Guatemala asked Mexico whether it sought to obtain a recommendation under Article 19.1 of the DSU in respect of the provisional measure.

tive anti-dumping measures. In fact, the investigating authorities could issue a definitive anti-dumping measure without having issued a provisional anti-dumping measure. Thus, even if the Panel were to rule on Mexico's complaints in respect of the provisional measure, this ruling would not include the definitive measure.[88]

4.131 Finally, the provisional measure has not had an enduring "significant impact" under Article 17.4 of the AD Agreement. Indeed, it is inconceivable that the provisional measure should have had any enduring impact since it expired on 28 December 1996, more than three years ago. Moreover, the provisional measure was only in force for four months, and affected an insignificant share of Mexico's exports during those months (i.e. only 0.016 per cent).[89]

4.132 For the above reasons, which are developed more extensively in our first written submission, Guatemala respectfully submits that the Panel lacks the authority to examine the provisional measure and all of the complaints referring thereto.

V. THIRD PARTY ARGUMENTS

A. Ecuador

5.1 Ecuador made the following arguments to the Panel:

5.2 In conformity with Article 10.2 of the Understanding on Rules and Procedures Governing the Settlement of Disputes and paragraph 17.1 of the Anti-Dumping Agreement, Ecuador would like to make the following observations:

1. Concerning the Background

5.3 Following consultations and a dispute settlement procedure between the Governments of Mexico and Guatemala, on 19 June 1998 the Panel in the case *Guatemala - Anti-Dumping Investigation Regarding Portland Cement from Mexico* issued its report (WT/DS60/R) which was appealed by Guatemala. The ruling of the Appellate Body (WT/DS60/AB/R), adopted by the Dispute Settlement Body at its meeting of 25 November 1998, concluded in paragraph 88 that: " ... the Panel erred in concluding that it could examine Mexico's claims concerning the initiation of the anti-dumping investigation." It added in paragraph 89 that: "Having found that this dispute was not properly before the Panel, we consider that the merits of Mexico's claims in this case are not properly before it. Therefore we cannot consider any of the substantive issues raised in the alternative by Guatemala in this appeal."

5.4 The Appellate Body also stated, at the end of paragraph 89, that its findings in no way precluded Mexico from seeking consultations with Guatemala regarding the latter's

---

[88] In other words, Members may attack various elements of an investigation, including the initiation, as part of their challenge of the provisional or definitive anti-dumping measures. However, they cannot challenge a provisional measure as part of their challenge of the definitive measure. As stated by the Appellate Body in *Guatemala I*, these measures are distinct from each other.

[89] Mexico's attempt to interpret Article 17.4 of the AD Agreement as not requiring "significant impact" must also be rejected. Although this provision does not use the term "prove", according to International Law and WTO practice "the burden of proof rests upon the party, whether complaining or defending, who asserts the affirmative of a particular claim or defence". Appellate Body Report *United States - Measure Affecting Imports of Woven Wool Shirts and Blouses from India*, WT/DS33/AB/R, adopted 23 May 1997, DSR 1997:I, 333 at 335.

imposition of definitive anti-dumping duties on imports of portland cement from Mexico, or from pursuing " ... another dispute settlement complaint under the provisions of Article 17 of the *Anti-Dumping Agreement* and of the DSU." In accordance with the above, Mexico held consultations with Guatemala on 23 February 1999 concerning the definitive anti-dumping measure imposed on imports of grey portland cement from the Mexican firm Cooperativa La Cruz Azul (Cruz Azul) as well as the actions that preceded it. Guatemala argues in its first submission of 10 January 2000 that Mexico did not hold consultations concerning the provisional measure which forms part of its complaint, as required under Article 6.2 of the DSU if it is to be included in the Panel's analysis.

5.5 These consultations were unable to resolve the dispute, and Mexico requested the establishment of a panel in accordance with document WT/DS156/2 of 20 July 1999, which states that the complaint covers the definitive anti-dumping measure imposed by Guatemala and the actions that preceded it, including the provisional anti-dumping measure and various matters relating to the initiation of the investigation and the anti-dumping proceeding. Among the matters to be examined are certain aspects raised during the initial dispute, such as the violation of Articles 5.3 and 5.5 of the *Anti-Dumping Agreement* on which the Appellate Body did not rule for the substantive reasons set forth in its conclusions.

2. *Concerning the Composition of the Panel*

5.6 Guatemala formally objected to the appointment of the members who served on the Panel in the previous dispute (*Guatemala I*) in the conviction that the participation of one or more of the previous panelists in the new Panel would deprive the new Panel of the independence and the objectivity it required to fulfill its purpose. Nevertheless, pursuant to Article 8.7 of the DSU, one of the previous panelists was appointed to the present Panel. Guatemala maintains that the present Panel was improperly composed, since one of its members had already issued opinions (reflected in the report of the Panel in *Guatemala I*) on matters identical to those which are now to be examined. According to the said report of the Appellate Body, that Panel did not have the jurisdiction to carry out its first examination. To this, Guatemala adds that there is a possibility that in the framework of the discussions of the new Panel, that member could refer to and/or reveal opinions or elements relating to the deliberations of the Panel in *Guatemala I*, thereby compromising the principle of confidentiality enshrined in Article 14 of the DSU and in paragraph 3 of Appendix 3 of the DSU. Given the peculiarities of this case, Ecuador considers that it is essential to ensure that the composition of the Panel is devoid of flaws from its inception and free of any objective risk of elements or circumstances which could undermine the basic principles of public international law, such as the principles of impartiality and objectivity as well as others contained in the Rules of Conduct for the DSU. From the systemic point of view, it must be recognized that Article 8.7 of the DSU grants the Director-General the authority to appoint the panelists in case of disagreement between the parties, specifying that this should be done "... after consulting with the parties to the dispute" and considering the written objections concerning the participation of the panel members. At the same time, Ecuador stresses that this authority should be applied in accordance with Article 8.2, which states that "Panel members should be selected with a view to ensuring the independence of the members ...". Otherwise, the final decisions of the Panel would be compromised. Consequently, Article 8.7 of the DSU should be implemented with due attention to the particular circumstances of each case in order to avoid problems which could lead to serious consequences if objections such as those of Guatemala reached the Appellate stage and were sustained by the competent body. At the same time, the Panel does not have the jurisdiction to rule on whether or not it has, itself, been properly composed.

3. *Concerning whether the Report in Guatemala I Constitutes a Precedent*

5.7 In view of the ruling of the Appellate Body in WT/DS60/AB/R, and taking account of the fact that the present dispute was brought by Mexico essentially to resolve the "substance of the case" that was not resolved by the Panel in *Guatemala I*, Ecuador considers that the conclusions, recommendations and suggestion of the Panel in the dispute *Guatemala - Anti-Dumping Investigation Regarding Portland Cement from Mexico* (WT/DS60/R) do not constitute a legal precedent under GATT/WTO practice, and should not be taken into consideration as such. In international law, it is acceptable for decisions of international bodies adopted in excess of their jurisdiction to be considered void and without legal effect. This is what happened in the case *Guatemala I*, and Ecuador is therefore of the opinion that Mexico's suggestion, contained in paragraph 8 of its submission OF/OMC/742/99 of 13 December 1999, that the Panel rely on various precedents of fact and law from the previous procedure is inadmissible and should not be accepted. Hence, Guatemala's request that the Panel issue a preliminary decision declaring that it will not take account of the report in *Guatemala I* is relevant.

4. *Concerning the Provisional Measure and the Consultations*

5.8 The request for the establishment of a panel by Mexico (WT/DS156/2) states that Mexico "... challenges the definitive anti-dumping measure imposed by Guatemala on imports of grey portland cement from Cruz Azul through the final resolution, 'Resolution 000113', published in the *Diario de Centroamérica* on 30 January 1997, as well as the actions that preceded it, including the provisional anti-dumping measure and various matters relating to the initiation of the investigation and of the anti-dumping proceeding, as being contrary to Guatemala's obligations under Article VI of the GATT 1994 and Articles 1, 2, 3, 5, 6, 7, 9, 10, 12 and 18 of the Anti-Dumping Agreement as well as Annexes I and II of the Anti-Dumping Agreement." In accordance with the legal reasoning and the ruling of the Appellate Body (WT/DS60/AB/R) in the case *Guatemala - Anti-Dumping Investigation Regarding Portland Cement from Mexico*, this implies that if Mexico had the intention of challenging the provisional measure, it should have identified that measure expressly and individually as a specific measure at issue pursuant to Articles 6.2 of the DSU and 17.4 of the Anti-Dumping Agreement, as it did for the definitive anti-dumping measure. Ecuador submits that the identification of the measure was at best ambiguous, casting doubt as to whether that part of the complaint was properly brought before the Panel. In any case, even supposing the Panel were to consider that Mexico had, in fact, identified the provisional measure as a specific measure at issue in its complaint, it would seem, unless it can be clearly proven otherwise, that Mexico's application does not meet the requirements of Article 4 of the DSU since Mexico has failed, in this process, to hold consultations with Guatemala concerning the provisional measure *per se* as required for the Panel to be able to examine it. Mexico's request reveals that consultations were held only in respect of the definitive measure and the "actions that preceded it" (WT/DS156/2), a generalization which does not palliate the lack of specificity concerning consultations on the provisional measure and makes it impossible to comply, pursuant to paragraph 3.7 of the DSU, with the requirements in paragraph 5 of the mentioned Article 4 of the DSU that in the course of the consultations " ... before resorting to further action under this Understanding, Members should attempt to obtain satisfactory adjustment of the matter." At the same time, the failure to hold such consultations has made it impossible for third parties to exercise their rights under Article 4.11 of the DSU, which permits them to safeguard their interests by joining in such consultations. In addition, Article 6.2 of the DSU emphasises the substantive nature of the consultation procedure as a prelude to examination by the Panel of the complainant's claims; in other words, it leads to the examination by the Panel itself of the specific measures at issue on which consultations have been requested. Finally, with reference to Article 17.4 of the Anti-Dumping Agreement, Mexico should have proved - and in Ecuador's view it did not do so convincingly - that the provisional measure "has a significant impact". In short, Ecuador submits that Mexico's complaint concerning the provisional measure was not properly brought; that the consultations concerning that measure did not take place; and that Mexico did not provide full proof of the "significant impact" of the measure.

5. *Concerning the Complaints and the Violations Alleged by Mexico: Sufficiency of the Examination of the Evidence*

5.9 In Parts III and V of its submission OF/OMC/742/99 of 13 December 1999, Mexico set out its complaints concerning the inititaion of the investigation, referring to alleged inconsistencies in the application for initiation by Cementos Progreso, as well as shortcomings in the examination of the evidence and in the initiation itself. It also refers to Guatemala's alleged failure to comply with the obligations on notification and publication of the public notice of initiation, and points out what it considers to be general violations of the Anti-Dumping Agreement. In Ecuador's view, Article 5 of the Anti-Dumping Agreement clearly indicates the type of information that an application for initiation of an investigation in this area must contain. Article 5.2 stipulates that the application must include "evidence of (a) dumping, (b) injury within the meaning of Article VI of the GATT 1994 as interpreted by this Agreement and (c) a causal link between the dumped imports and the alleged injury." It stresses that simple assertion without evidence cannot be considered sufficient to meet these requirements, and that the application "shall contain such information as is reasonably available to the applicant" on subparagraphs 5.2(i), (ii), (iii) and (iv). Mexico claims that the evidence submitted by the applicant was insufficient to initiate the investigation and that it was not properly examined by the investigating authority. In fact, Ecuador would like to observe that the investigating authority decided to gather further information during an assessment period of "three or four months" (paragraph 69 of Guatemala's submission), following which it decided that there was "sufficient evidence". In this context, the various interpretations of the sufficiency of "such information as is reasonably available to the applicant" clearly complicate the examination of the matter. In Ecuador's view and as demonstrated in paragraphs 67 and 72 to 77 of Guatemala's submission of 10 January 2000, the applicant firm - representing 100 per cent of the domestic injury - supplied such information and evidence as was reasonably available to it under subparagraphs (i) and (ii) in support of its request for the initiation of an anti-dumping investigation, in conformity with Article 5.2 of the Anti-Dumping Agreement. However, Mexico would seem to be right that in its initial application, Cementos Progreso did not properly substantiate its evidence under subparagraphs (iii) and (iv) of Article 5.2 regarding price and volume, which are significant factors in helping the applicant to support its threat of injury claim. In any case, this does not mean that the applicant did not substantiate threat of injury, but that it would have been appropriate and desirable that the information and evidence in Cementos Progreso's possession should have been more extensive. Concerning Mexico's contention that the examination of the evidence by the investigating authority was deficient in that the decision to initiate the investigation reflected shortcomings in terms of the accuracy and adequacy of the evidence, Ecuador submits that the investigating authority does in fact have a right to substantiate its findings when it considers that there is sufficient evidence. This does not indicate bias or lack of objectivity, particularly when the investigating authority is presumed to have acted in good faith. Without wishing to play down the effects of the procedural violations alleged by Mexico, it should be borne in mind that most procedural errors committed during anti-dumping investigations are generally attributable to the complexity of the actual procedure and the fact that Members who only make sporadic use of it are not familiar with it. Certain violations, for example not providing timely notification before initiating the investigation, could have been corrected long ago - perhaps through the initiation of a new investigation - if Mexico had stated its procedural objection at the time, and not several months after the initiation of the investigation. Thus, in any case, the main point to be elucidated, supposing that they turn out to be true, would be whether the possible procedural violations alleged by Mexico, many of them factual, effectively restricted Cruz Azul's right of defence, and nullified or impaired benefits accruing to Mexico under the Anti-Dumping Agreement, the DSU and the covered Agreements. Ecuador does not think so.

6. *Concerning the Definitive Measure*

5.10 Ecuador considers that the investigating authority exercised its right, under the regulations in force, in particular Article 9.1 of the Anti-Dumping Agreement, to impose the definitive measure. The extension of the period of investigation by the investigating authority was right, considering that in view of the nature and purpose of the anti-dumping investigation the authority required updated information, for example concerning Cruz Azul's sales during the extended period or its production costs, data which was requested by the Ministry but never provided by the firm. It should be added that this authority to extend the investigation is also provided for under the Mexican legal system. The same applies to the investigating authority's right to gather further evidence, since this does not conflict either with the spirit or the letter of the Anti-Dumping Agreement. The Guatemalan investigating authority provided Cruz Azul and Mexico with an opportunity to defend their interests as required under Article 6.2 of the Anti-Dumping Agreement, even granting an extension - as stipulated in the said Agreement - for Cruz Azul to submit the relevant questionnaire. Against this background, the investigating authority made its interpretation of the facts and conducted its examination and evaluation of the evidence in accordance with Article 5.3 of the Anti-Dumping Agreement, and found that there was dumping, injury and a causal relationship which led, legitimately, to the introduction of the provisional, and subsequently, the definitive measure. The fact that the investigating authority did not use the technical accounting evidence submitted by Cruz Azul in connection with the determination of the definitive measure - in Guatemala's words a "self-verification of its own information" - is not a violation because, in Ecuador's understanding, it was the Authority's exclusive right under Article 6.1 of the Anti-Dumping Agreement to establish whether the evidence was adequate or not in deciding whether to accept or reject it. Here, the objection raised by Mexico (which belatedly supplied unsubstantiated data resulting from an audit carried out by a company hired by the Mexican firm itself) is therefore unfounded, since requiring the acceptance of such information could amount to substituting for the Ministry as investigating authority.

7. *Requests by Mexico to the Panel*

5.11 Concerning Mexico's requests in Part F, subparagraphs (b), (c) and (d) of document WT/DS156/2 of 20 July 1999, it has been the general practice of the GATT and the

WTO in this area for panels and the Appellate Body to issue - in accordance with their findings and conclusions - a general recommendation along the lines of the first sentence of Article 19.1 of the DSU, which stipulates that: "Where a panel or the Appellate Body concludes that a measure is inconsistent with a covered agreement, it shall recommend that the Member concerned bring the measure into conformity with that agreement." The implementation of the second sentence of Article 19.1 is appropriate in certain cases where there is a clear and duly substantiated need which must be evaluated by the panel - for example, to ensure the prompt and effective resolution of a dispute in circumstances in which it has been demonstrated that there have been repeated breaches on the part of the Member concerned - and as a result of which the objective of Article 21.1 of the DSU cannot be achieved. In such cases it would indeed be appropriate for a panel to suggest ways in which the Member concerned could implement the recommendations of the DSB. However, this dispute does not seem to warrant any suggestion by the panel as to how the Member concerned could implement the relevant recommendations, since as a rule, it is always preferable for the parties to a dispute to be able to reach a mutually agreed solution following the adoption of a report. This leads us to the conclusion that Mexico's requests to the Panel, in particular the request contained in subparagraph (d), are excessive.

B. El Salvador

5.12 El Salvador made the following arguments to the Panel:

5.13 The Government of El Salvador would like to state clearly its interest in the dispute *Guatemala - Definitive Anti-Dumping Measure on Grey Portland Cement from Mexico.*

5.14 El Salvador and Guatemala are both members of the Treaty on Central American Economic Integration, and ever since the beginning of our history as countries, we have been linked by strong cultural and commercial ties as well as ties of friendship.

5.15 El Salvador and Guatemala are committed to building a customs union in their territories.

5.16 El Salvador is aware that dumping is an unfair trade practice which should not be tolerated because of the damage it does to the domestic industry of any country, particularly the developing countries which, as such, have more vulnerable economies.

5.17 El Salvador is an active Member of the World Trade Organization, and as such it has an interest in any case of this kind which affects any developing country, the more so when the country in question is a neighbouring country with which we are bound by strong ties.

5.18 El Salvador and Guatemala, like the other Central American countries, share the same procedural legislation in this field, and El Salvador's interest in cases of this sort is therefore to ensure strict compliance with WTO rules and regulations and to confirm the efficiency of the procedures applicable under the Central American regulations.

5.19 Through its participation, El Salvador is interested above all in ensuring the proper and correct application of the principles contained in the agreements administered by the World Trade Organization, in particular those which guarantee special and differential treatment for the developing countries.

5.20 In the light of the above considerations, we would like to submit: (i) that the mechanisms provided for in the WTO Anti-Dumping Agreement as a means of discouraging an injurious practice are valuable and legitimate as a means of defence against this reprehensible trade conduct, and in implementing them, Members should guarantee their observance, taking account of the problems facing the developing countries in applying and implementing the provisions of the WTO as well as their urgent need to defend themselves against distorting practices which have an enormous impact on their economies;

and (ii) that the dispute settlement system serves to preserve the rights and obligations of the Members under the covered agreements and to ensure that the recommendations and rulings of the dispute settlement system cannot add to or diminish the rights and obligations provided in those agreements, all of this in conformity with the principle which guarantees economies such as ours special and differential treatment.

C. European Communities

5.21 The European Communities made the following arguments to the Panel:

1. Introduction

5.22 The European Communities (hereafter "the EC") makes this third party submission because of its systemic interest in the correct interpretation of the Agreement on Implementation of Article VI of the General Agreement on Tariffs and Trade 1994 ("ADP Agreement").

5.23 Many of the issues in dispute involve questions of fact on which the EC is not in a position to comment. Accordingly, this submission will address only a number of issues of legal interpretation which are of particular interest to the EC.

5.24 Section II discusses the preliminary objections advanced by Guatemala. Section III addresses some of the claims submitted by Mexico.

2. Preliminary Objections Raised by Guatemala

(a) Is the Panel validly constituted?

5.25 Guatemala claims that the Panel was not validly constituted because one of its members served as a panelist in *Guatemala - Antidumping Investigation on Imports of Portland Cement from Mexico* ("*Portland Cement I*"). On that ground, Guatemala has requested the Panel to issue a preliminary ruling declaring that it is not "competent" to examine the matter in dispute.

5.26 The EC considers that this is not the proper venue to address Guatemala's request. It is clearly beyond a Panel's authority to decide that it has not been validly composed. The EC would suggest that if Guatemala considers that one of the members of this Panel lacks the requisite "independence", it should raise the matter with the Chair of the Dispute Settlement Body in accordance with the procedure specifically provided for in the Rules of Conduct for the Dispute Settlement Understanding[90] (the "DSU").

(b) Is the provisional anti-dumping measure properly before the Panel?

5.27 Guatemala argues that the provisional anti-dumping measure was not mentioned in the request for consultations and, therefore, is not properly before the Panel.[91]

5.28 The EC recalls that, by now, it is well established that a measure which has not been the subject of consultations cannot be examined by a Panel.[92] The fact that a meas-

---

[90] Cf. paras. 5 to 10.

[91] Guatemala's First submission, paras. 39-49.

[92] See e.g. the Panel reports in *European Communities - Regime for the Importation, Sale and Distribution of Bananas (Bananas III)*, WT/DS/27R, adopted 25 September 1997, DSR 1997:II, 803, paras. 7.18- 7.19; *Korea - Taxes on Alcoholic Beverages*, ("*Korea – Alcoholic Beverages*"), WT/DS75/R, WT/DS84/R, adopted 17 February 1999, DSR 1999:I, 44, paras. 10.17-10.20; and

ure is not mentioned in the request for consultations creates a presumption that no consultations were held with respect to such measure. Yet, a complaining party should be permitted to prove by other means that a measure not mentioned expressly in the request for consultations was, nevertheless, the subject of consultations.[93]

5.29 Mexico's request for consultations is ambiguous as to whether it extends to the provisional measure, as it refers to the definitive measure "and the actions that preceded it". The EC would note, however, that the request mentions Article 7 of the ADP Agreement, a provision which deals exclusively with the imposition of provisional measures. Moreover, significantly Guatemala does not seem to allege that the provisional measure was not discussed in the course of the consultations.

5.30 In the alternative, Guatemala argues that Mexico failed to show that the provisional measures had a "significant impact" within the meaning of Article 17.4 of the ADP Agreement[94].

5.31 The EC concurs with Guatemala's view that Mexico must demonstrate through positive evidence that the provisional measures have a "significant impact" and cannot satisfy itself simply with invoking such impact.[95]

5.32 On the other hand, the EC takes issue with Guatemala's position that the impact of the measures must be assessed with respect to Mexico's "overall trade interest".[96] The EC considers that the impact should be examined with respect to the imports covered by the measure. Indeed, Guatemala's interpretation would have the absurd consequence that Members with large economies, such as the EC, could never be in a position to challenge a provisional measure. In the absence of any indication that Article 17.4 has the purpose of affording special and differential treatment to developing countries, an interpretation which leads to such a discriminatory outcome should be rejected.

3. Claims Submitted by Mexico

(a) Initiation of the investigation

5.33 The EC notes that, unlike in *Portland Cement I*, there appears to be no substantial disagreement between the parties with respect to the interpretation of the provisions of the ADP Agreement concerning the initiation of investigations. Indeed, both Mexico and Guatemala seem to be in accord with the interpretation of Articles 5.2 and 5.3 made in *Portland Cement I* (even if, understandably, Guatemala avoids any express reference to

---

Brazil - Export Financing Programme for Aircraft, WT/DS46/R, adopted adopted 20 August 1999, DSR 1999:III, 1221, paras. 7.4-7.11.

In *Brazil - Aircraft, supra,* footnote 52, paras. 127-133, the Appellate Body clarified that Articles 4 and 6 of the DSU do not require "a precise and exact identity between the specific measures that were the subject of consultations and the specific measures identified in the request for the establishment of the panel". That case, however, concerned a measure which had been replaced by a new measure having essentially the same content (Report of the Appellate Body in.

[93] In *Korea - Definitive Safeguard Measure on Imports of Certain Dairy Products*, WT/DS98/AB/R, adopted 12 January 2000, DSR 2000:I, 3, para. 131, the Appellate Body suggested that a defective panel request does not prevent the panel from considering a claim unless it prejudices the defendant's ability to defend itself in the course of the proceeding. By the same token, a defective request for consultations should not prevent the establishment of a panel, if it can be shown that it did not cause prejudice to the defendant.

[94] Guatemala's First submission, paras. 50-59.

[95] *Ibid.*, paras. 50-51.

[96] *Ibid.*, para. 52.

that report). The disputes arise only at the stage of applying that interpretation to the facts of the case.

5.34 The EC considers that the interpretation of Articles 5.2 and 5.3 made in *Portland Cement I* was generally correct, irrespective of whether the particular application of such interpretation to the facts of the case was also correct, an issue on which the EC is not in a position to comment. Therefore, the EC would encourage this Panel to follow the same interpretation.

5.35 In particular, the EC agrees with the panel's conclusions with respect to the relationship between Articles 5.2 and 5.3, namely that

> the question whether there is 'sufficient evidence' to justify initiation is not answered by a determination that the application contains all the information 'reasonably available' to the applicant on the factors specified in Article 5.2 (i)-(iv) ... the 'reasonable available' language in Article 5.2 does not permit the initiation of an investigation based on evidence and information which, while all that is reasonably available to the applicant is not, objectively judged, sufficient to justify initiation.[97]

5.36 The EC is also in accord with the standard of interpretation of "sufficient evidence" developed by the panel[98] on the basis of the *Softwood Lumber* report.[99]

5.37 Finally, the EC agrees with the panel's view that Articles 2 and 3 of the ADP Agreement are relevant in assessing whether there is "sufficient evidence" for purposes of Article 5.3. As noted by the panel, the subject matter, or type, of evidence needed to justify initiation is the same as that needed to make a preliminary or final determination of dumping and injury, although the quality and quantity is less.[100] At the same time, however, it is obvious that, contrary to Mexico's claims, this does not mean that, by initiating an investigation on the basis of insufficient evidence of dumping and injury, a Member is in breach not only of Article 5.3, but also of Articles 2 and 3.

(b) Notification of the initiation

5.38 In the EC's view, it is beyond question that the investigation was "initiated" by Guatemala pursuant to the Notice published on 11 January 1996. Accordingly, by not notifying the initiation of the investigation to the Mexican Government until 22 January 1996, Guatemala acted inconsistently with Article 5.5 of the ADP Agreement.

5.39 Guatemala's contention that the investigation was not initiated "effectively" until 23 January 1996[101], even if true, would be devoid of relevance, as Footnote 1 to the ADP Agreement specifies that the term "initiated", as used in the ADP Agreement, means "the procedural action by which a Member *formally* commences an investigation..." [emphasis added].

5.40 Guatemala's argument to the effect that its Constitution requires to notify the interested parties before initiating an investigation is also irrelevant.[102] If anything, this argument would suggest that, by failing to notify the Mexican Government before initiat-

---

[97] *Portland Cement I, supra*, footnote 25, para. 7.53.

[98] *Portland Cement I, supra*, footnote 25, paras. 7.54-7.57.

[99] *United States - Measures affecting Softwood Lumber from Canada*, SCM/162, adopted 27 October 1993, BISD 40S/358.

[100] *Portland Cement I, supra*, footnote 25, paras. 7.64, 7.67.

[101] Guatemala's First submission, para. 79.

[102] *Ibid.*, paras. 203-204.

ing the investigation, the investigative authorities infringed not only the ADP Agreement but also Guatemala's Constitution.

5.41 As a subsidiary defence, Guatemala invokes that in any event the late notification would have to be exonerated because it is a "harmless error" (*error inocuo*).[103] The evidence adduced by Guatemala is not sufficient to show that what it calls the "harmless error" principle is in fact a general principle of international law. In any event, the examples cited by Guatemala are concerned with the consequences of the violation of a procedural rule, and not with the existence of the violation of a procedural rule. They stand for the proposition that, in certain cases, the violation of procedural rule does not entail the lack of validity of the act adopted pursuant to that procedure. At issue here, however, is not the question of whether the anti-dumping measures imposed by Guatemala are "valid", notwithstanding the violation of Article 5.5, but rather the previous question of whether Guatemala has violated Article 5.5.

5.42 As an additional subsidiary defence, Guatemala contends that Mexico is "estopped" from raising this claim, because it did not complain about the late notification until six months after the initiation of the investigation.[104] In the EC's view, Guatemala has not shown that the strict requirements for the operation of the principle of estoppel are met in the present case. In particular, it cannot be considered that Mexico's failure to complain immediately about the late notification amounts to a "clear and unequivocal representation"[105] that it acquiesced to the violation by Guatemala of Article 5.5.

5.43 Contrary to Guatemala's assertions[106], previous panel reports do not support its claim of estoppel. In *Canada/European Communities Article XXVIII rights*, the Arbitrator did not rely on the principle of estoppel, but instead on the rather vague notion that it was necessary to preserve the "stability and predictability of the GATT system".[107] More relevant is the report in *EC - Bananas I*[108], where a claim of estoppel was dismissed on the following grounds:

> "361... the Panel considered that such a modification or estoppel could only result from the express, or in exceptional cases implied, consent of [the complaining parties] or of the CONTACTRING PARTIES.
>
> 362. The Panel considered that the decision of a contracting party not to invoke a right under the General Agreement at a particular point in time could due to circumstances that change over time. The decision of a contracting party not to invoke a right vis-à-vis another contracting party at a particular point in time can therefore, by itself, not reasonably be assumed to be a decision to release that other contracting party from its obligations under the General Agreement. The Panel noted in this context that previous panels had based their findings on measures which had remained un-

---

[103] *Ibid.*, paras. 206-216.

[104] *Ibid.*, paras. 217-219.

[105] See e.g. Temple of Preah Vihear Case, where the International Court of Justice enounced the conditions for the application of the principle of estoppel as follows:

"The principle operates to prevent a State contesting before the Court a situation contrary to a clear and unequivocal representation made by it to another State, expressly or impliedly, on which representation the other state was, in the circumstances, entitled to rely, and as a result that other State has been prejudiced or the State making it has secured some benefit or advantage for itself" (ICJ reports 91962) pp. 143-144).

[106] *Ibid.*, para. 218.

[107] DS12/R, BISD 37/80, at p. 86.

[108] Panel report in *EEC - Member States' Import regimes for Bananas*, DS32/R (unadopted).

> challenged for long periods of time. The Panel therefore found that the mere fact that the complaining parties had not invoked their rights under the General Agreement in the past had not modified these rights and did not prevent them from invoking these rights now". [footnotes omitted]

5.44 As yet another subsidiary defence, Guatemala contends that the late notification did not nullify or impair any benefits.[109] For the reasons aptly explained by the panel in *Portland Cement I*[110], the EC considers that Guatemala has failed to rebut the presumption of nullification or impairment laid down in Article 3.8 of the DSU.

(c) Disclosure of essential facts

5.45 In response to Mexico's claim that Guatemala violated Article 6.9 of the ADP Agreement, Guatemala appears to be arguing that its investigating authorities complied with that provision by granting access to the public file.[111]

5.46 Guatemala's defence reflects a serious misunderstanding of the disclosure requirements imposed by Article 6.9. That Article imposes upon the investigating authorities a positive duty "to inform" the interested parties which goes beyond simply granting access to the file. The public file of an investigation consists essentially of questionnaire responses and allegations submitted by the different interested parties, which are often contradictory. Thus, the mere examination of the file may not allow the interested parties to identify the "essential facts" on the basis of which the authorities intend to impose definitive measures. For that reason, Article 6.9 requires that the investigating authorities indicate to the interested parties which, of all the facts contained in the file, are the "essential facts" that will form the basis for their decision, so that the interested parties can defend their interests adequately.

5.47 Moreover, if the obligation imposed by Article 6.9 could be fulfilled simply by granting access to the file, Article 6.9 would become totally redundant, since the obligation to provide access to the file is already prescribed by Article 6.4 of the ADP Agreement.

(d) Extension of the investigation period

5.48 Mexico claims that by extending the period of investigation Guatemala violated paragraph 1 of Annex II to the ADP Agreement, as well as Articles 6.1 and 6.2.[112].

5.49 In the EC's view, paragraph 1 of Annex II does not prevent the investigating authorities from requesting additional information in the course of the investigation, including information pertaining to a period different from that initially defined as the investigation period. The investigating authorities may not become aware that certain information is "required" for the purposes of the investigation until they have already received some information from the interested parties. In those cases, it is not "possible" for the investigating authorities to request such information at an earlier stage and, therefore, it cannot be claimed that there is a violation of paragraph 1 of Annex II.

5.50 Nevertheless, the extension of the investigation period should be justified and not impose an unreasonable extra burden on the interested parties. In addition, the investigating authorities should observe the same procedural requirements as when they made

---

[109] Guatemala's First submission, paras. 220-221.

[110] *Portland Cement I, supra*, footnote 25, para. 7.42.

[111] Guatemala's First submission, para. 339.

[112] Mexico's First submission, paras. 355-372.

the original request for information, including in particular those contained in Articles 6.1 and 6.2. Whether or not Guatemala complied with those requirements when it extended the investigation period is a question of fact on which the EC is not in a position to comment.

(e) Information on costs of production

5.51 Mexico claims that Guatemala has breached Articles 2.1 and 2.2 of the ADP Agreement because the investigating authorities requested information on costs of production from the exporter, even though the complaint did not allege that domestic sales were made below cost.[113].

5.52 This claim is clearly unfounded. The investigating authorities are entitled to request any information which is pertinent for a determination of dumping. There is nothing in the wording of Articles 2.1 and 2.2, or in any other provision of the ADP Agreement, which may be interpreted as restricting the possibility for the investigating authorities to request cost of production data to those cases where the complaining industry has alleged the existence of sales below cost.

(f) Revocation of the measures

5.53 Guatemala has submitted that, even if the Panel were to found that the definitive anti-dumping measures are inconsistent with the ADP Agreement, it should reject Mexico's request that the Panel "suggest" the revocation of those measures.[114].

5.54 It is true that, as argued by Guatemala, under the GATT 1947, panels recommended specific remedies in very few occasions. Yet, Guatemala's position that panels should never suggest "specific" remedies, including the revocation of a measure, is clearly untenable, as it would reduce to inutility the last sentence of Article 19.1 of the DSU, which provides expressly that "in addition to its recommendations, the panel or Appellate Body may suggest ways in which the Member concerned could implement the recommendations".

5.55 The EC would agree, nonetheless, that panels should be careful not to make suggestions which limit the choices available to the offending Member. Accordingly, they should not suggest the revocation of a measure, unless it can be established that there is no other possible way to "bring the measure into conformity". The panel report in *DRAMS*[115], which has been cited with approval by Guatemala, supports that view. Indeed, in *DRAMS* the panel did not rule that Panels can never suggest the revocation of a measure, but rather that

> in light of the range of possible ways in which ... the United States could appropriately implement our recommendation, we decline to make any suggestion in the present case.[116]

5.56 The report in *Portland Cement I* reflects the same principle. The Panel suggested the revocation of the definitive anti-dumping measure only after having determined that,

[113] *Ibid.*, paras. 373-379.

[114] Guatemala's First submission, paras. 399-404.

[115] Panel Report in *United States - Anti-dumping Duty on Dynamic Random Access Memory Semiconductors (DRAMS) of One Megabit Or Above from Korea*, WT/DS99/R, adopted 19 March 1999, DSR 1999:II, 521.

[116] *Ibid.*, para. 7.4.

in view of the nature of the violations of the ADP Agreement incurred by Guatemala, there was no other possible way to bring that measure into conformity:

> We have determined that an unbiased and objective investigation authority could not properly have determined, based on the evidence and information available at the time of initiation, that there was sufficient evidence to justify initiation of the anti-dumping investigation Thus, the entire investigation rested on an insufficient basis, and therefore should have never been conducted. This is, in our view, a violation which cannot be corrected effectively by any actions during the course of the ensuing investigation. Therefore, we suggest that Guatemala revoke the existing anti-dumping measure on imports of Mexican cement, because, in our view, this is the only appropriate means of implementing the recommendation.[117]

5.57 The EC agrees with the report in *Cement Portland I* that, where an investigation has been initiated on the basis of insufficient evidence, the only possible means of implementation is the revocation of the anti-dumping measure imposed pursuant to that investigation. Therefore, in those circumstances, it would be appropriate for a panel to suggest the revocation of the measure.

D. Honduras

5.58 Honduras submitted the following arguments to the Panel:

1. Interest of Honduras as a Third Party to the Dispute

5.59 The Government of Honduras welcomes the opportunity to make this written submission as a third party to the dispute brought by Mexico challenging the definitive anti-dumping measure imposed by the Guatemalan Ministry of the Economy (the Ministry) on imports of grey portland cement (cement) produced by one of its exporters, Cooperativa la Cruz Azul, S.C.L. (Cruz Azul), as well as the action that preceded it, including the provisional anti-dumping measure.

5.60 Honduras' economy is closely linked to that of Guatemala. Central America has a broad and varied programme with Mexico, and consequently we are interested in strengthening our trade links and ensuring that trade between Mexico and our countries is not affected by unfair trade practices.

5.61 Our cement industry is also highly vulnerable to the dumping practices reported to the Guatemalan investigating authority. The anti-dumping measure taken satisfactorily protects Central America's interests and, to some extent, represents an effective deterrent to dumping of other products by Mexico.

5.62 The Government of Honduras took part in the first dispute between Mexico and Guatemala in order to protect the right of any WTO Member to conduct an anti-dumping investigation and not to be cited before a panel whose terms of reference do not allow it to hear the case. Honduras is now participating in this second dispute because it considers that Guatemala correctly applied the regulations contained in the Agreement on Implementation of Article VI of the General Agreement on Tariffs and Trade 1994 (hereinafter the Anti-Dumping Agreement).

---

[117] *Cement Portland I, supra*, footnote 25, para. 8.6.

2. *Preliminary Objections*

5.63 This dispute raises considerations of competence and admissibility which affect fundamental principles and, in order to maintain the purity and integrity of the dispute settlement system, the Panel should take a preliminary decision on these.

(a) The Panel was improperly composed

5.64 Firstly, Guatemala has made an appropriate and duly reasoned complaint that the Director-General appointed to the present Panel persons who had heard the previous dispute. Honduras shares Guatemala's concern regarding the lack of independence and objectiveness of persons who had already taken positions when considering Mexico's first complaint, without having the competence to do so, in connection with claims relating to the violation of Article 5.3 and 5.5, which are again the subject of this case.

5.65 Clearly, no one is questioning the integrity or qualifications of the panellist in the first dispute who has been re-appointed to consider the present dispute, but he will undoubtedly take into account the views held by those who served with him on the first Panel and will be unable to disregard the discussions held and decisions taken during the previous dispute in which he participated.

5.66 The issue is of systemic interest and, as far as we know, this is the first time that a panel report has been rejected and the complaining Member has initiated a second dispute concerning the same complaints. The DSU and Article 17 of the Anti-Dumping Agreement do not empower the Appellate Body to refer the dispute back to the panel whose conclusions were rejected and likewise the Director-General should not act in such a way.

5.67 Article 8.2 of the DSU states that "Panel members should be selected with a view to ensuring the *independence* of the Members ...", and according to Article 11 a panel "should make an *objective* assessment of the matter before it, including an *objective* assessment of the facts of the case and the applicability of ... the relevant covered agreements ..." (emphasis added).

5.68 In order to ensure that full effect is given to the principle of public international law whereby decisions by international tribunals must be impartial and objective, the Director-General should take into account Guatemala's objections regarding a particular individual. The Preamble to the Rules of Conduct for the DSU states that the operation of the DSU "would be strengthened by rules of conduct designed to maintain the integrity, impartiality and confidentiality of proceedings conducted under the DSU".[118] The confidentiality requirement is also to be found in paragraph 3 of Appendix 3 on Working Procedures.

5.69 According to Sections II and III of the aforementioned Rules of Conduct, all members of panels "shall be independent and impartial, shall avoid direct or indirect conflicts of interest ..." and shall also "consider *only issues raised in*, and necessary to fulfil their responsibilities within, the dispute settlement proceeding ..." (emphasis added). If any member of the previous Panel were allowed to participate in the present Panel, these principles would be undermined.

5.70 Consequently, with due respect, Honduras supports Guatemala's request that a preliminary resolution be issued to the effect that the Panel was improperly composed and does not therefore have the competence to examine the matter referred by Mexico to the DSB.

[118] WT/DSB/RC/1, 11 December 1996.

(b) The report of the previous panel is without value

5.71 Mexico wishes this Panel to endorse the work and the conclusions of the Panel in the first dispute (hereinafter *Guatemala I*) and therefore repeatedly quotes the latter's report. According to Article 11 of the DSU, however, this Panel must respect its obligation to make an objective assessment of the matter and conduct its own review, completely disregarding the report published by the previous Panel.

5.72 In *Guatemala I*, the Appellate Body ruled that the Panel which examined the dispute should never have considered the claims submitted to it and rejected its report. As a result, this report has no value as a precedent, as evidence or as guidance. Honduras considers that, if this Panel is guided by the reasoning in the report in the *Guatemala I* case, this would constitute a precedent that would have a negative impact on every WTO Member.

5.73 The report published in the *Guatemala I* case cannot even be used simply for guidance, as has sometimes occurred for reports that were not adopted. There is a substantive difference between a report that was not adopted by the DSB - whose legal findings have not been rejected - and a report expressly rejected by the Appellate Body; it is clear that a report that has been rejected has no legal existence.

5.74 Honduras therefore supports Guatemala's request that a preliminary decision be taken declaring that the Panel should not take into account the report on the *Guatemala I* case.

(c) The Panel does not have the mandate to examine the provisional measure and the claims referring thereto

5.75 In anti-dumping disputes, the specificity requirement is of particular relevance. Articles 4 and 6 of the DSU and Article 17 of the Anti-Dumping Agreement define when an anti-dumping dispute can be submitted to a panel. Paragraph 4 of Article 17 of the Anti-Dumping Agreement should be interpreted in parallel with paragraph 2 of Article 6 of the DSU, which requires that the parties submit to the DSB matters regarding which consultations have been held and identify the specific measures at issue.

5.76 In the present case, Mexico's request for consultations identifies the definitive anti-dumping measure but not the provisional measure. This Panel does not therefore have any mandate to consider the provisional measure or Mexico's claims contesting it.

5.77 Mexico's request for the establishment of a panel shows that the request for consultations only identified the definitive anti-dumping measure "as well as the actions that preceded it"[119], but Mexico also challenges "the actions preceding that measure", including the provisional anti-dumping measure.[120] Mexico does not contest the provisional measure *per se*, but as one of the actions preceding the challenge of the final measure.

5.78 In any event, if it is considered that Mexico's request for the establishment of a panel did identify the provisional measure as a subject of complaint, the request violates Article 4 of the DSU. According to Article 6 of the DSU, a Member may not request the establishment of a panel to contest a measure regarding which it has not requested the consultations specified in Article 4 of the DSU. Similarly, Article 6.2 requires, that in its request for the establishment of a panel, a Member must indicate "whether consultations were held, and identify the specific measures at issue ...". As Mexico's request for con-

[119] WT/DS156/2, page 2.

[120] *Ibid.*.

sultations did not identify the provisional measure as the specific measure at issue, this measure cannot be the subject of the dispute.

5.79 The *United States - Imposition of Anti-Dumping Duties on Imports of Fresh and Chilled Atlantic Salmon from Norway,* cited by Guatemala, is indicative in this respect.

5.80 Mexico's failure to identify the provisional measure (and to present the full series of complaints relating to the provisional measure) in its request for consultations prevented the special dispute settlement rules applicable to anti-dumping cases from giving the parties an opportunity to reach a "mutually satisfactory resolution" of the dispute in accordance with Article 17.3 of the Anti-Dumping Agreement.

5.81 Consequently, Honduras considers that, as requested by Guatemala, the Panel should take a preliminary decision to the effect that it has no mandate to consider the provisional measure and all the complaints referring thereto because Mexico did not request consultations on this measure.

5.82 In the alternate, Honduras also considers that all the WTO's Members, but especially those countries which are particularly vulnerable to dumping, have an interest in ensuring full respect for Article 17.4 of the Anti-Dumping Agreement, which restricts complaints in the WTO to disputes concerning the imposition of definitive anti-dumping measures or price undertakings, unless it can be proved that the imposition of a provisional measure has an enduring "significant impact" on the trade interests of a Member.

5.83 The clear wording of Article 17.4 indicates that the complainant must prove a significant impact. The intention of those who drafted Article 17.4 was that the significant impact must relate to the trade interests of the complainant and not to the exporting industry under investigation because, in a dispute settlement procedure, the complainant is the WTO Member and not the exporter or exporters being investigated.

5.84 In the present case, Mexico does not claim that the provisional measure has had an enduring significant impact. In its first submission to this Panel, Mexico does not argue that the provisional measure had a significant impact at any time. It is in fact inconceivable that the provisional measure has had an enduring impact because it expired over three years ago.

5.85 In the alternate, Honduras endorses Guatemala's position that the provisional measure did not have any significant impact. In its first submission, Mexico neither claimed nor tried to prove that the provisional measure had had a significant impact in the past.

5.86 Consequently, Honduras requests the Panel to issue a preliminary resolution to the effect that the Panel does not have a mandate to consider the provisional measure and all the claims referring thereto.

3. Arguments

(a) Standard of review

5.87 Another aspect of particular importance is the scope of the examination to be conducted by panels in anti-dumping cases. Article 17.6(i) of the Anti-Dumping Agreement prescribes that panels may not overturn the establishment of the facts by an investigating authority, even if they do not agree with its evaluation. In other words, panels may not undertake a new examination of the facts.

5.88 Regarding legal questions, according to Article 17.6(ii) a national authority's determination should rest upon a "permissible interpretation" of the Agreement's provisions. Clearly, several interpretations may exist, but the Anti-Dumping Agreement only requires that the investigating authority use one that is permissible.

5.89 In the present case, as the Guatemalan Ministry of the Economy's determination is based on a permissible interpretation of the regulations applicable - in particular, the meaning of words that are not defined in the Agreement but are central to the action of an investigating authority, for example, "sufficient" in Article 5.3, "As soon as" in Article 6.1.3, "adequate" in Article 12.1.1, and "sufficient detail" in Article 12.1.1[*] - the Panel should respect its determination.

(b) It is up to Mexico to prove that there has been a violation

5.90 Honduras wishes to draw the Panel's attention to the fact that Mexico does not deny that Cruz Azul dumped cement in Guatemala nor does it deny material injury.
5.91 Moreover, Mexico has not assumed the burden of proving that there has been a violation of the Anti-Dumping Agreement. The WTO is no different from other legal systems which make the complainant responsible for providing prima facie proof of non-compliance and it is only when this has been done that the burden of rebutting the claim would be shifted to Guatemala.[121]

(c) Guatemala properly initiated the anti-dumping investigation

5.92 Honduras considers that, during the investigation that gave rise to the definitive anti-dumping measure challenged by Mexico, Guatemala complied with the applicable provisions in Article VI of the General Agreement on Tariffs and Trade 1994 (GATT 1994) and Articles 1-3, 5-7, 9, 12, 18, and Annexes I and II, of the Anti-Dumping Agreement.
5.93 Honduras does not share Mexico's opinion that any WTO Member requested to initiate an investigation is obliged to conduct a prior investigation. Contrary to what is claimed by Mexico, under Article 5.3 the investigating authority did not have to have evidence of injurious dumping based on a "fair comparison" of Cruz Azul's prices in Mexico and Guatemala.[122] Claiming that there must be sufficient information to establish these facts prima facie amounts to a claim that the investigating authority should conduct a prior investigation.
5.94 Mexico's claim that the Ministry did not "examine" the accuracy and adequacy of the evidence provided in Cementos Progreso's application[123] is not acceptable either. A correct reading of paragraphs 2, 3 and 1 of Article 5 of the Anti-Dumping Agreement shows that:

According to Article 5.2 of the Anti-Dumping Agreement, an applicant must substantiate its claims with relevant evidence - described in subparagraphs (i)-(iv) of

[*] *Translator's note*: These words do not appear in Article 12.1.1, but in 12.2.

[121] See, for example, the Report of the Appellate Body *United States - Measure Affecting Imports of Woven Wool Shirts and Blouses from India*, *supra*, footnote 89, at 335. See also the Report of the Appellate Body, *European Communities - Measures Concerning Meat and Meat Products (Hormones)*, WT/DS/26/AB/R, WT/DS48/AB/R, adopted 13 February 1998, DSR 1998:I, 135, para. 98.

[122] *Ibid.*, paras. 98, 103, 107 and 126.

[123] First submission by Mexico, paras. 75, 89-90 and 111.

Article 5.2 -, but this is limited to the information "reasonably available to the applicant".[124]

Article 5.3 lays down the obligation to examine the accuracy and adequacy of the evidence provided which "justify *the initiation* of an investigation".[125]

According to Article 5.1, it is during the course of the investigation and not at the time of its initiation that the authority must determine "the existence, degree and effect of any alleged dumping ...".

5.95 It is also a matter of concern that Mexico considers that the Ministry should have "ascertained" the "legitimacy or veracity" of the documentary evidence attached to Cementos Progreso's application[126], and should have proved the normal value and export price *before* initiating the investigation.[127] Honduras does not consider that it is the investigating authority's responsibility to sift the complaints before initiating an investigation.

5.96 An investigating authority cannot "prove" the normal value or the export prices and cannot "verify" the legitimacy and veracity *before* conducting an investigation in any country in the world, especially in Central America. This is why Article 6.7 and Annex I of the Anti-Dumping Agreement provide for the verification of information *during* the course of an investigation.

5.97 Even though Honduras considers that Guatemala met the provisions of Article 5.2 and 5.3 of the Anti-Dumping Agreement, others - Mexico for example - might consider that in a perfect world it would have been better if Guatemala had had more information before deciding whether an investigation was justified. But the situation in countries such as Guatemala, which is familiar to Honduras because the circumstances are the same, is that further information is not easy to obtain nor reasonably available.

5.98 The scope of the examination prior to initiating an investigation and the fact that the level of "sufficient" evidence to justify initiation is lower than the level of evidence required for a preliminary or final affirmative determination were dealt with at length in *Softwood Lumber II*, which Guatemala cites in its first written submission to the Panel.[128]

5.99 Furthermore, even though Articles 2 and 3 of the Anti-Dumping Agreement contain useful definitions of the words "dumping", "injury" and "causal relationship", there is no legal reason for claiming that these Articles apply to the initiation phase.

5.100 As already stated, Article 5 governs the initiation of an investigation, and does not mention Article 2. The sole reference to Article 3 is in subparagraph 5.2(iv), but only in relation to the factors used to demonstrate injury and as guidance for the submission of information in an application, which suggests that those drafting the text did not intend any other provision of Articles 2 or 3 to apply at the time of initiating the investigation.

5.101 To summarize, Honduras considers that the investigating authority undertook a full examination of the accuracy and adequacy of the evidence provided in Cementos Progreso's application. On the basis of this examination and of all the information before it, the Ministry reasonably determined that there was sufficient evidence to justify the initiation of an anti-dumping investigation.

---

[124] Article 5.2 does not stipulate that the complainant must attach documentary evidence. Article 5.2 and 5.3 use the words "evidence" and "information" without distinction. It is therefore clear that the "evidence" mentioned in the first sentence of Article 5.2 consists of the types of information defined in subparagraphs (i) - (iv) of the same Article.

[125] Article 5.3 (emphasis added).

[126] First submission by Mexico, paras. 75, 89-90 and 111.

[127] *Ibid.*, paras. 98, 103, 107 and 126.

[128] First submission by Guatemala, para. 134.

5.102 If the standard of review referred to in Article 17.6 of the Anti-Dumping Agreement is applied correctly, the Panel is not empowered to assess once again the evidence used when taking the decision to initiate the investigation.

(d) Guatemala correctly notified the initiation of the investigation

5.103 It is contrary to the interests of WTO's Members which could potentially conduct their own anti-dumping investigations for panels hearing complaints to impose the regulations applicable with excessive severity. On the contrary, panels should bear in mind the object and purpose of the provisions applicable.

5.104 Honduras considers that the provisions in Articles 5.5, 12.1-12.1.1 and 6.1.3 of the Anti-Dumping Agreement were not established with the object and purpose of imposing formal obstacles on investigating authorities. The goal of these provisions is to ensure that exporting Members and their exporters have the opportunity to defend their interests in a timely and appropriate manner.

5.105 As far as Article 5.5 is concerned, Honduras does not consider that the interests of Mexico and its exporters were infringed because the investigation was not actually initiated until Mexico had been notified. As Guatemala points out, in our countries the rights of the defendant have to be infringed before failure to give a proper hearing can be claimed.

5.106 In Honduras' view, Article 12.1 of the Anti-Dumping Agreement was not violated either because this provision does not lay down any time-limit for making a notification; it only requires that a notification and a public notice must be issued when the authorities are satisfied that there is sufficient evidence.

5.107 Regarding the information to be provided in the public notice, according to Article 12.1.1 the necessary details may be contained in the notice or in a separate report such as that to be found in the administrative file.[129]

5.108 Lastly, in compliance with Article 6.1.3, Guatemala gave the Government of Mexico and Cruz Azul the full text of the anti-dumping application "as soon as" the investigation was initiated.

5.109 In conclusion, Honduras considers that the Panel should take into account the fact that, if Guatemala had complied with these Articles in another way, this would not have affected the course of the investigation. For example, Article 5.5 does not provide that the Member to be investigated may undertake action or submit any evidence, or in other words, prevent the initiation of the investigation; likewise, nothing would have changed if further information had been included in the public notice or if the full text of the application had been submitted beforehand.

(e) The provisional measure was imposed in accordance with the Anti-Dumping Agreement

5.110 Although the preliminary determination of injurious dumping made by the Ministry is not the subject of this complaint and, in any event, its imposition is not subject to further requirements, in the alternative Honduras considers that it was made on the basis of duly established and reasonably assessed facts and that Guatemala respected the provisions contained in Articles 7, 2 and 3 of the Anti-Dumping Agreement. Moreover, the

[129] *Ibid.*, paras. 227 and 228.

public notice of the preliminary determination and the separate report dated 26 July 1996 comply with Article 12.2.1.

5.111 The preliminary margin of dumping (38.72 per cent) was fixed on the basis of information submitted by Cruz Azul in response to the Ministry's questionnaire. The subsequent preliminary determination of threat of injury was based on the rapid increase in dumped imports (from June 1995 - November 1995, Cruz Azul captured 25 per cent of the market) and the resulting reduction in Cementos Progreso's sales, market share, production and prices.

5.112 As pointed out with regard to the decision to initiate the investigation, as far as the preliminary determination is concerned, the Panel is not empowered to replace its own examination by the examination of the investigating authority.

(f) Conduct of the investigation

5.113 Mexico drew attention to a series of alleged violations in the course of the investigation. Although a detailed analysis of these goes beyond the purpose of this submission, after considering them Honduras is of the view that none of these alleged violations impaired the rights of Mexico or Cruz Azul.

5.114 Nevertheless, Honduras believes it necessary to emphasize that the Anti-Dumping Agreement also imposes certain obligations on the firms investigated in a Member country, and a complaint can only lawfully be made when there has been such cooperation. For example, a firm is obliged to provide the information requested in the questionnaires and must refrain from impeding the verification of information required by Article 6.7 and Annex I of the Anti-Dumping Agreement.

5.115 Unlike complaints relating to the violation of other covered agreements, the basis of an anti-dumping dispute is a complaint of an unfair trade practice by one or more exporting firms of the complaining Member. Honduras, therefore, considers that the Panel's examination should not be limited to compliance with the investigation procedures which the regulations prescribe for the respondent Member, but should also consider the attitude of the firm or firms of the complaining Member and the additional burden imposed on the investigating authority as a result of their lack of cooperation.

(g) The final affirmative determination by Guatemala

5.116 In its first submission to the Panel, Mexico did not try to prove that its firm had not been involved in dumping or had not caused injury to Cementos Progreso. Both the firm investigated and the Government confined themselves to contesting alleged procedural violations during the initiation and conduct of the investigation.

5.117 Guatemala considers that the final determination, published in the *Diario de Centro América* of 30 January 1997, contains the required information in sufficient detail relating to the conclusion reached by the Ministry that Cruz Azul had been involved in dumping, that the dumping margin was 89.54 per cent, and that the dumped imports had caused material injury to Cementos Progreso.

5.118 Mexico claims, but does not demonstrate, that Guatemala violated Articles 2, 5 and 6 of the Anti-Dumping Agreement. Regarding the normal value and the adjustments in order to make a fair comparison, the Panel should note that the lack of collaboration obliged Guatemala to base its determination on the best information available. The Panel should also take into account the fact that Mexico did not contest the export price.

5.119 Guatemala considers that, after having properly established the facts, the Ministry carried out an unbiased and objective evaluation thereof and, faced with Cruz Azul's refusal to cooperate in the investigation, the Ministry was obliged to use the facts available in order to calculate the final margin of dumping. The same applies to its subsequent conclusion that there was dumping, based on the statistical information in the file which showed a rapid increase in imports and the devastating effect on Cementos Progreso's sales, production, market share, prices and profits. The dumping margin was enormous, the increase in imports dramatic and the injury immediate and severe.

5.120 Guatemala made its analysis in a way that meets the requirements of the anti-dumping regulations and it is compelling. In this connection, reference should be made to the "supplemented report on the determination of injury caused by dumped imports of grey Portland cement from Mexico", of 15 January 1997, by the Ministry's Directorate of Economic Integration, and its final determination. Guatemala considers that it met the provisions of Article 3 because it based its determination of injury on positive evidence and an objective examination of the following:

> The volume of the dumped imports and their effect on the price of like products in the domestic market (according to Article 3.2).
>
> The resulting impact of the dumped imports on domestic producers (taking into account the factors in Article 3.4).

5.121 In conclusion, Honduras affirms that, taking into account the purpose and object sought by the drafters when laying down the formalities for an anti-dumping investigation, the point at stake is whether Guatemala gave Mexico and Cruz Azul an opportunity to defend their interests properly. There can be no question that the formalities for an anti-dumping investigation pursue this purpose, otherwise it would mean that they only existed for the purpose of hindering the investigation. An examination that takes into account this aspect would be a real contribution to anti-dumping disciplines.

E. United States

5.122 The United States made the following arguments to the Panel:

1. Introduction

5.123 The A-D Agreement recognizes a Member's right to impose anti-dumping measures, but specifies procedures that investigating authorities must follow in imposing them. Many of these procedural requirements are technical in nature, but they are not mere "technicalities". As elaborated below, the United States is of the view that Guatemala violated certain requirements codified in the A-D Agreement. For example, Article 5.5 of the A-D Agreement requires investigating authorities to notify the government of the exporting country *prior* to the initiation of an investigation, which Guatemala did not do.

5.124 At the same time, the Panel should be wary of certain arguments presented by Mexico that attempt to expand the obligations of investigating authorities under the A-D Agreement. Article 19.2 of the DSU could not be more clear that panels "cannot add to or diminish the rights and obligations provided in the covered agreements". For example, the A-D Agreement does not require investigating authorities to fix a rigid schedule for the acceptance of relevant evidence. So long as the investigating authority provides adequate time for exporters to respond to information requests, the A-D Agreement establishes no limit on *the number* of requests that may be made, or *when* they may be made.

5.125 Finally, the United States is concerned that, while Mexico has asked this Panel to issue a general recommendation that Guatemala bring its measures into conformity with its obligations under the A-D Agreement, Mexico has also asked the Panel to suggest two specific ways in which this should be accomplished - revocation of the anti-dumping duty order and refund of duties. If the Panel does determine that Guatemala has violated its obligations under the A-D Agreement, the United States urges the Panel to refrain from suggesting revocation of the measure and refund of duties. The latter, especially, is a specific, retroactive remedy of the sort panels reviewing anti-dumping and countervailing duty measures have avoided. Panels are not experts in national law, and should refrain from attempting to identify ways in which Members can best bring offending measures into conformity with their obligations.

5.126 In submitting these views, the United States notes that it has not yet received the WTO Secretariat's English translation of Guatemala's first submission and has received the translation of Mexico's first submission in draft. The United States therefore reserves the right to supplement or amend the views presented in this submission once these translations are made available.

2. *US Views Regarding the Parties' Claims and Arguments*

(a) Guatemala's conduct of the anti-dumping investigation

(i) Investigating authorities are entitled to initiate anti-dumping investigations only where an applicanbt has submitted information reasonably available regarding dumping, injury and causation, and where the evidence regarding each element is sufficient

5.127 The threshold question before this Panel - at least as far as the procedural requirements of the A.D Agreement are concerned - is whether Guatemala was authorized to accept, and subsequently act upon, the anti-dumping application filed by Cementos Progreso.

5.128 Mexico argues that Guatemala violated Article 5.2 of the A-D Agreement by initiating the investigation based upon an application that did not contain required information "reasonably available" to the applicant. According to Mexico, the application's deficiencies relate to all three fundamental elements of a dumping allegation - dumping, injury, and causation. Mexico also argues that Guatemala violated Article 5.3 of the A-D Agreement when it failed to ascertain whether there was "sufficient evidence" to justify initiation of the investigation. Mexico contends that both the "reasonably available" and "sufficient evidence" standards cannot be interpreted without reference to Articles 2 and 3 of the A-D Agreement, which set forth the basic elements of dumping and injury, respectively.

5.129 Guatemala contends that Cementos Progreso did include all pertinent information reasonably available to it in its application, and that the Guatemalan authorities properly concluded that the evidence was sufficient to warrant initiation of the investigation. Guatemala further argues that Mexico is mistaken in its position regarding the relationship between Article 5, on the one hand, and Articles 2 and 3, on the other. According to Guatemala, both the Uruguay Round negotiating history as well as panel practice confirm that the level of evidence sufficient for initiation is less than the level of evidence required for preliminary or final dumping analyses.

5.130 In the view of the United States, Article 5.2 is precise with respect to the information that must be included in an anti-dumping application. Specifically, an applicant must submit "reasonably available" information regarding each of the information categories enumerated at subarticles (i) through (iv). Article 5.2(i) dictates, among other things, that applicants shall describe "the volume and value of the domestic production of the like product by the applicant." Article 5.2(ii) requires "a complete description of the allegedly dumped product." Article 5.2(iii) sets forth requirements regarding domestic market and export prices. Finally, Article 5.2(iv) specifies that an application must contain information regarding the extent and effects of the alleged dumping.

5.131 Article 5.2 thus is intended to prevent the imposition of unreasonable information requirements that go beyond not only the normal capacity of a private entity to develop, but also beyond those of a particular applicant in a given case. Thus, for example, confidential pricing, cost of production, and profitability information pertaining to foreign producers or domestic competitors is not normally obtainable by legal means and would not normally be considered to be "reasonably available" to an applicant so as to require such information for initiation. Similarly, there may be aggregate information regarding the volume and value of imports or industry production and capacity that is available in some countries, but which may be legally or simply practically unavailable in others or to other applicants. In circumstances where a practical or legal bar exists to the acquisition of information otherwise required by the Agreement, such information in that instance also should not be considered to be "reasonably available" to an applicant.

5.132 However, Article 5.2 also specifies that "[s]imple assertion, unsubstantiated by relevant evidence, cannot be considered sufficient to meet the requirements of this paragraph." Because the "reasonably available" language in Article 5.2 was not intended to excuse any inadequacy in an application that could have been avoided or cured by reasonable efforts on the part of the domestic industry, where an applicant asserts the unavailability of critical data as a reason for not fulfilling information requirements imposed by the Agreement, some explanation of the basis for the unavailability may be required. Such explanation appears particularly appropriate when missing information pertains to the domestic entities making the application and which normally would be expected to be within their possession. Again, "simple assertions" do not suffice.

5.133 Article 5.3 sets forth the separate requirement that, once an application has been submitted, the authorities shall examine its "accuracy and adequacy" and ascertain whether "there is sufficient evidence to justify the initiation of an investigation." In the view of the United States, Articles 5.2 and 5.3 of the A-D Agreement set forth distinct obligations. First, under Article 5.2, investigating authorities must determine that an application contains such information of dumping, injury, and causation as was "reasonably available" to the applicant. If, and only if, this condition is satisfied, may authorities proceed to the second inquiry under Article 5.3 - whether the evidence presented is sufficient to warrant the initiation of an investigation.[130] Article 5 thus appears to contemplate scenarios in which an applicant provides all "reasonably available" information, but this information proves insufficient to justify initiation of an investigation.

5.134 Turning to the facts before this Panel, the United States submits that the evidentiary basis for Guatemala's initiation of the investigation appears to have been especially thin with respect to the requirements of Article 5.2(iii). Paragraph 5.2(iii) requires that applicants provide information supporting allegations of dumping. It appears that the application did not identify the type of grey portland cement upon which the Guatemalan industry based its evidence of normal value. The normal value price information consisted of two invoices reflecting two separate sales of Mexican cement in Tapachula, Mexico in

[130] As stated by the *Guatemala I* panel, "Article 5 establishes an obligation that extends beyond a determination that the requirements of Article 5.2 are satisfied." *Guatemala - Anti-Dumping Investigation Regarding Portland Cement from Mexico*, *supra*, footnote 25, para. 7.49 ("*Guatemala I*"). We do not agree with Guatemala that the findings of the *Guatemala I* panel should be rejected outright by this Panel. To the extent that they are relevant in light of the way the issues have been framed in this proceeding, we see no legal obstacle to this Panel's consideration of those findings.

August 1995. Both the invoices and the application merely identified the cement sold in Mexico as grey cement. There is no indication that either Cementos Progreso in its application, or the Guatemalan authorities in their initiation analysis, recognized the possibility that the initial product comparison may have been based on sales of different types of cement. Also, it appears that Cementos Progreso relied upon Mexican retail prices in alleging normal value, while relying upon wholesale prices in alleging export price. This component of the allegation, too, appears to have been accepted at face value.

5.135 The obvious questions for this Panel, thus, are whether this information was all that was reasonably available to Cementos Progreso, and whether the investigating authorities should have further probed its accuracy and adequacy. There is no indication in either the notice of initiation of the investigation or the memorandum recommending initiation from the Ministry of Economy that the Guatemalan authorities subjected these factual assertions to further scrutiny.[131]

5.136 With respect to information on the evolution of the volume of the allegedly dumped imports required by Article 5.2(iv), the investigating authority relied on two shipments of cement from Mexico which occurred on consecutive days and statements that other imports were being made during a three-month period. These import volumes were described as massive, but were not quantified. The applicant had explained that the dearth of import volume data was due to its lack of access to official import data, and had requested the investigating authority to develop this information. However, while Guatemala provides some explanation as to why this information was not reasonably available to the applicant, Guatemala does not explain why its investigating authority did not obtain this information on it own. Although Guatemala attempts to excuse its apparent lack of diligence by claiming that it is a small country relative to Mexico, nothing in the A-D Agreement permits such a "small country" exception. The Panel should not excuse Guatemala's actions for a reason that has no foundation in the Agreement.[132]

5.137 The views of the parties differ dramatically about the relationship between Articles 5.2 and 5.3, on the one hand, and Articles 2 and 3, on the other. Mexico argues that Guatemala's violations of Articles 5.2 and 5.3 comprised violations of Articles 2 and 3, because the evidence before the Guatemalan investigating authorities did not "establish" and "prove" the existence of dumping, injury and causal link. Guatemala argues that Articles 2 and 3 inform an authority's determination to initiate, but cannot be violated as such, because the evidence that is sufficient to justify initiation need not prove or establish dumping, injury and causal link. The United States agrees that there is a difference between allegation and proof, and that violations of Articles 5.2 and 5.3 do not comprise violations of Articles 2 and 3. Articles 2 and 3 are of course relevant in determining whether the information presented in an application justifies initiation of an investiga-

---

[131] The *Guatemala I* panel concluded that "based on an unbiased and objective evaluation of the information before it, the Ministry could not properly have determined that there was sufficient evidence of dumping to justify the initiation of the investigation." *Ibid.* at para. 7.63.

[132] The *Guatemala I* panel stated that "based on an unbiased and objective evaluation of the evidence and information before it in this case, the Ministry could not properly have determined that there was sufficient evidence of injury, that is threat of injury, to justify the initiation of the investigation." *Ibid.* at para. 7.77.

tion[133], and may reasonably be viewed as providing "context" for Articles 5.2 and 5.3 in that they set forth, respectively, detailed definitions of dumping and injury.[134]

5.138 In any event, the Panel need not define the precise relationship between Articles 5.2 and 5.3 and Articles 2 and 3. The *Guatemala I* panel did not. It simply rejected Guatemala's assertion that its authorities could compare sales of two sacks of cement at the retail level with sales of several thousand sacks of cement at the wholesale level without appearing to accord any consideration to these differences.[135] The United States respectfully submits that such an approach - that is, concluding only that the Guatemalan authorities exercised inadequate scrutiny of the applicant's pricing information - would be appropriate in this proceeding as well.

5.139 Along this same line, the United States disagrees with Mexico's characterization of the detailed price-adjustment requirements in Article 2.4 and their application in the initiation context.[136] Investigating authorities cannot be expected to analyze and ensure, for example, that all price comparisons at the initiation phase are at the same level of trade. Level-of-trade adjustments (not to mention other types of complex adjustments mandated by Article 2) must by their very nature be based on detailed (and usually confidential) information supplied by the exporting firm, and thus *cannot* be made until the investigating authority has developed an evidentiary record based on complete questionnaire responses.[137] The United States urges the Panel to exercise particular caution in this area, and not to suggest or find that investigating authorities must make level-of-trade adjustments at initiation per the requirements of Article 2.4.

5.140 Finally, the United States also urges the Panel to avoid implying in any context (initiation, preliminary or final phases) that the reference to "fair comparison" in Article 2.4 requires something more than compliance with the more specific language embodied in that Article. In the view of the United States, a price has been "fairly" adjusted where an investigating authority has complied with the detailed adjustment provisions enumerated in Article 2.4. At any rate, as explained, the legal sufficiency of Guatemala's decision to initiate the anti-dumping investigation can be assessed by the Panel without a finding regarding the extent to which Articles 2 and 3 inform Articles 5.2 and 5.3.

---

[133] The *Guatemala I* panel held that investigating authorities "may not ignore" the provisions of Article 2 of the A-D Agreement because that Article defines dumping. *See id.* at para. 7.64.

[134] The Vienna Convention on the Law of Treaties, at Article 31.1, provides that "[a] treaty shall be interpreted in good faith in accordance with the ordinary meaning to be given to the terms of the treaty in their context and in the light of its object and purpose."

[135] *Guatemala I, supra*, footnote 25, at para. 7.62.

[136] Mexico's first submission, while first recognizing that the "quantum and quality" of evidence supporting an initiation decision will by its very nature be less than the amount supporting subsequent determinations, then appears to assume that Article 2 is directly applicable to a sufficiency determination under Article 5.3. For example, para. 100 states the initial price-comparison analysis "must take due account of the differences affecting the comparability of the prices ... and to do otherwise would be a serious violation of Article 2 of the ADP Agreement."

[137] This conclusion is compelled not just by logic, but also by the structure of the AD Agreement. Articles 2 and 3 are styled, respectively, *Determination* of Dumping and *Determination* of Injury. An investigating authority cannot determine the existence of dumping or injury until it has gathered evidence. Nothing in the AD Agreement suggests that a decision to initiate an anti-dumping investigation also constitutes a "determination of dumping" or "of injury." In fact, Article 5.2 itself does not specifically refer to Article 2.

(ii) Investigating authorities must notify exporting members prior to initiation of an anti-dumping investigation

5.141 Mexico argues that Guatemala violated Article 5.5 of the A-D Agreement by failing to notify the Government of Mexico before formally initiating the investigation. Guatemala's position that its "actual investigation" did not commence until after its 11 January 1996 publication of the notice of initiation in the official government journal, the *Diario Oficial de Centro América*. Guatemala also argues in the alternative that: (1) the delay was harmless under generally accepted principles of international law; (2) the Government of Mexico acquiesced to the delay; and (3) the delay did not bring about nullification or impairment of benefits accruing to Mexico under the A-D Agreement. The United States submits that Guatemala did, for purposes of the A-D Agreement, initiate its investigation when it published notice in the *Diario Oficial de Centro América*, and that its arguments in the alternative are unpersuasive.[138]

5.142 Article 5.5 states that "after receipt of a properly documented application and before proceeding to initiate an investigation, the authorities shall notify the government of the exporting Member concerned." Footnote 1 to the A-D Agreement clarifies that "initiate" refers to "the procedural action by which a Member formally commences an investigation as provided in Article 5." Read together, these provisions allow little latitude for Guatemala to argue that the procedural action through which it formally launched its investigation was any action other than its 11 January 1996 publication of the initiation notice.

5.143 The documents before the Panel also suggest that the Guatemalan authorities themselves believed that the 11 January 1996 publication constituted the formal act of initiation. For one, the 15 December 1995 memorandum from the Director for Economic Integration to the Ministry of the Economy states, in paragraph 5, that "[t]he date of the initiation of the investigation shall be considered to be the date on which such notice is published in the Official Journal." Also, the actual published notice makes no mention of the fact that the investigation would not commence until some later date, but instead, for example, notifies interested parties that they will have thirty days from the date of publication of the notice to submit any supplementary arguments and evidence that they may consider relevant. These documents thus show that the Guatemalan authorities deemed the investigation to have commenced with the publication of notice of initiation on 11 January 1996.

5.144 Guatemala contends, citing other sources of public international law, that this Panel should apply a theory of harmless error which holds that procedural errors should not be viewed as invalidating an official determination. The Panel need not turn to other sources of law, however, as the DSU squarely resolves the issue presented. Article 3.8 of the DSU provides as follows:

> In cases where there is an infringement of the obligations assumed under a covered agreement, the action is considered prima facie to constitute a case of nullification or impairment. This means that there is normally a presumption that a breach of the rules has an adverse impact on other Member parties to that covered agreement, and in such cases, it shall be

[138] The *Guatemala I*, *supra*, footnote 25, at paras. 7.30-7.43, panel thoroughly rejected Guatemala's arguments that its notification was legally adequate or, if inadequate, excusable.

> up to the Member against whom the complaint has been brought to rebut that charge.

Thus, if a Member has violated a WTO obligation which is phrased as a categorical rule, an assertion that the violation was merely a harmless error is irrelevant. Guatemala notes that panels have not ruled out application of the harmless error doctrine in construing GATT/WTO obligations and rights.[139] However, to date, no panel has ever invoked this doctrine, and the facts of this case do not warrant its application here.

5.145 The procedural requirement in Article 5.5 of the A-D Agreement is not a mere technicality. It is obvious from Article 5.5 that Members, in negotiating the A-D Agreement, wished to safeguard the right of governments to take whatever steps they deemed necessary and appropriate in reacting to other governments' impending anti-dumping investigations. In this case, Guatemala effectively deprived Mexico of that protected right. It is impossible to show, as Guatemala would have this Panel believe, that the course of the investigation would not have been altered had Mexico received timely notification (*e.g.*, prior to publication of the initiation notice) of the decision to initiate the investigation. It is simply impossible to know what steps the Government of Mexico might have taken had it been notified pursuant to the terms of Article 5.5.[140]

5.146 Guatemala's assertion that Mexico acquiesced in the violation of its rights is without foundation. It was well-established under the GATT 1947 that the fact that a violation has taken place with the knowledge of the complaining party changes neither the violator's obligations nor the right to redress of the complaining party. In 1983, a GATT panel examined French quantitative restrictions on watches and other products from Hong Kong.[141] The EEC argued to that panel that the restrictions were of long standing and that the widespread existence of quantitative restrictions meant that "contracting parties had adopted a tolerant attitude that was tantamount to acceptance of the situation."[142] In response,

> The Panel ... recognized that restrictions had been in existence for a long time without Article XXIII ever having been invoked by Hong Kong with respect to the products concerned, but concluded that *this did not alter the obligations which contracting parties had accepted under GATT provisions*. Furthermore the Panel considered it would be erroneous to interpret the fact that a measure had not been subject to Article XXIII over a number of years, as tantamount to its tacit acceptance by contracting parties. ..."[143]

[139] The panel in *Brazil - Imposition of Provisional and Definitive Countervailing Duties on Milk Powder and Certain Types of Milk from the European Economic Community*, SCM/179, adopted 28 April 1994, at para. 271, stated: "Without wishing to exclude that the concept of 'harmless error' could be applicable in dispute settlement proceedings under the Agreement, the Panel considered that this concept was inapplicable under the circumstances of the case before it."

[140] The United States notes a recent recommendation adopted by the Committee on Anti-Dumping Practices relating to Article 5.5 which states, ". . . the Committee recommends that the notification required by the second sentence of Article 5.5 should be made as soon as possible after the receipt by the investigating authorities of a properly documented application, and as early as possible before the decision is taken regarding initiation of an investigation on the basis of that properly documented application." G/ADP/5 (3 November 1998).

[141] *EEC - Quantitative Restrictions Against Imports of Certain Products from Hong Kong*, L/5511, adopted on 12 July 1983, BISD 30S/129.

[142] *Ibid.*, 30S/135, para. 17.

[143] *Ibid.*, 30S/138, para. 28; emphasis added.

5.147 The 1993 *Bananas I* panel report [DS32/R] also rejected an EC argument that subsequent practice with respect to the banana import regimes at issue had modified GATT rights and obligations or resulted in the complaining parties being estopped from raising such rights.[144] The EC cited in particular "(a) the notoriety of the facts involved; (b) the general tolerance of these measures by the GATT contracting parties, especially by those most interested in the matter; (c) the period of time the parties tolerated restrictions associated with the EEC banana import régimes; (d) the area of law concerned; and (e) the basic aims and mechanisms of the General Agreement."[145] In examining and rejecting this argument, the Panel found that "such modification or estoppel could only result from the express, or in exceptional cases implied, consent of such parties or of the CONTRACTING PARTIES"[146] and that "[t]he decision of a contracting party not to invoke a right vis-à-vis another contracting party at a particular point in time can ... by itself, not reasonably be assumed to be a decision to release that other contracting party from its obligations under the General Agreement."[147]

5.148 Whether Mexico was aware of and complained about the violation of its rights in the course of Guatemala's investigation or not, Guatemala remained obligated to carry out Article 5.5 of the A-D Agreement, and Mexico retained the right to invoke its rights under the DSU and the WTO Agreement. Guatemala could not unilaterally alter Mexico's rights to a timely notification. In the 1992 dispute concerning United States anti-dumping duties on Atlantic salmon from Norway, the panel rejected an argument that the failure of Norway or private Norwegian respondents to raise certain issues before the investigating authorities precluded Norway from raising them before the panel. That panel considered that no such limitation existed in the Tokyo Round A-D Code, nor could it be implied.[148] In short, the consistent interpretative approach under the GATT and WTO has been to resist reliance on "subsequent practice," supposed acquiescence, or other such conduct as a source for altering the rights and obligations conferred by the positive treaty law agreed between governments.

(iii) Where separate reports replace public notices for purposes of Article 12, those reports must be adequate and accessible

5.149 Mexico argues that Guatemala's public notice of initiation in the *Diario Oficial de Centro América* does not comply with Article 12.1.1 of the A-D Agreement because the notice does not contain adequate information regarding the allegations of dumping and injury. In response, Guatemala contends that its public notice of initiation should be assessed in conjunction with the 17 November 1995 Report of the Office of Economic Inte-

---

[144] *Report of the Panel in EEC - Members States' Import Regimes for Bananas*, DS32/R, 3 June 1993 paras. 124-146 (unadopted).

[145] *Ibid.*, para. 127.

[146] *Ibid.*, para. 361.

[147] *Ibid.*, para. 362.

[148] *United States - Imposition of Anti-dumping Duties on Imports of Fresh and Chilled Atlantic Salmon from Norway*, ADP/87, 30 November 1992, paras. 347-351 (adopted); accord, *United States - Imposition of Countervailing Duties on Imports of Fresh and Chilled Atlantic Salmon from Norway*, SCM/153, 4 December 1992, paras. 216-220 (adopted).

gration, which does summarize the information presented by the applicant, Cementos Progreso.[149]

5.150 Article 12.1.1 of the A-D Agreement provides that a public notice of initiation of an anti-dumping investigation must contain "adequate information" regarding, *inter alia*, "the basis on which dumping is alleged in the application" and "a summary of the factors on which the allegation of injury is based." Importantly, the information may be made available "through a separate report," so long as that report "is readily available to the public." While Mexico entirely overlooks this alternative to publication, which is clearly spelled out in Article 12.1.1 and the accompanying footnote 23, Guatemala appears to suggest - erroneously - that the "separate report" can be *any* document, *anywhere* on the record of the investigation.

5.151 The United States is of the view that the purpose of Article 12.1.1 is to ensure transparency of decision-making. Accordingly, where an investigating authority relies upon a "separate report" to disclose information of the type outlined in subarticles (i) through (vi), that separate document should be referenced in or clear from the public initiation notice and be "available" publicly pursuant to the plain meaning of that term. Where the separate report does not clearly substitute for the public notice, or is not readily "available," the separate report should be seen as failing to satisfy the requirements of Article 12.[150]

5.152 The arguments on this point thus present the Panel with two factual questions - whether the 17 November 1995 Report of Guatemala's Department of Economic Integration was indeed "readily available to the public," and, if so, whether the information contained therein was "adequate." In this respect, the United States suggests that, in weighing the arguments of Mexico and Guatemala, the Panel be mindful of the purpose of Article 12.1, which, as mentioned, is to ensure that investigating authorities reveal the evidentiary basis for proceeding with initiation of an anti-dumping investigation. Where exporters are in no position to assess either the quality or the source of the information relied upon by the investigating authority, the purpose of Article 12.1 has presumably been subverted.

(iv) Investigating authorities enjoy considerable latitude under Article 6 of the A-D Agreement in developing the evidentiary record

5.153 Mexico contends that Guatemala violated Article 6 of the AD Agreement, as well as Annexes I and II thereto, in developing the evidentiary record of the investigation. Specifically, Mexico attempts to persuade this Panel, *inter alia*, that the Guatemalan authorities violated their obligations by: (1) failing to fix a precise time-frame for the submission of evidence; (2) attempting to gather additional evidence during an on-the-spot verification of the exporting firm; and (3) rejecting certain "technical accounting evidence" submitted late in the proceeding. The Panel should reject Mexico's arguments and refrain from supplementing the already-detailed provisions regarding the development of evidentiary records with the additional requirements proposed by Mexico.

5.154 Article 6.1 provides that "[a]ll interested parties in an anti-dumping investigation shall be given notice of the information which the authorities require and ample opportu-

[149] Guatemala makes similar arguments regarding the memoranda supporting its preliminary and final determinations of dumping. *See* Guatemala first submission, paras. 286 and 386.

[150] The same rationale applies to the use of separate reports to explain the bases for the imposition of subsequent measures.

nity to present in writing all evidence which they consider relevant in respect of the investigation in question." Articles 6.1.1, 6.1.2, and 6.1.3 further require, respectively, that exporters or foreign producers be accorded at least 30 days in which to reply to a questionnaire, that evidence submitted by one party be made available promptly to other parties, and that authorities provide the full text of an application to the known exporters and authorities of the exporting Member. Article 6.2 adds, in pertinent part, that interested parties to an investigation "shall have a full opportunity for the defence of their interests."

5.155 While Article 6 sets forth a host of procedural requirements that an investigating authority must follow in requesting information, nowhere does it specify, as Mexico appears to believe, that investigating authorities must fix a particular time-frame for the collection of evidence during an investigation. So long as the investigating authority has provided a reasonable opportunity for respondent exporters or producers to answer information requests, the A-D Agreement does not limit the timing of such requests. Indeed, depending on the complexities of a case, an investigating authority may need to solicit extensive information during the final phase of an investigation. Likewise, nothing in the A-D Agreement precludes the extension of the period of investigation, and Article 6 should not be read as prohibiting *per se* the collection of information related to this extended period.

5.156 Also contrary to Mexico's arguments, investigating authorities are free under the terms of the A-D Agreement to seek additional information - within reason - while conducting on-the-spot verification visits. According to Mexico, Guatemala was not entitled under Article 6.7 to seek new information from Cruz Azul during its planned verification. Mexico appears again to be asking this Panel to *restrict* the latitude investigating authorities possess under the A-D Agreement in developing evidentiary records.

5.157 Article 6.7 provides, in relevant part, as follows:

> In order to verify information provided *or to obtain further details*, the authorities may carry out investigations in the territory of other Members as required, provided they obtain the agreement of the firms concerned and notify the representatives of the government of the Member in question, and unless that Member objects to the investigation. The procedures described in Annex I shall apply to investigations carried out in the territory of other Members.

5.158 Paragraph 7 of Annex I elaborates on the scope of investigating authorities in conducting on-the-spot verifications:

5.159 As the main purpose of the on-the-spot investigation is to verify information provided *or to obtain further details*, it should be carried out after the response to the questionnaire has been received unless the firm agrees to the contrary and the government of the exporting Member is informed by the investigating authorities of the anticipated visit and does not object to it; further, it should be standard practice prior to the visit to advise the firms concerned of the general nature of the information to be verified and of *any further information which needs to be provided*, though *this should not preclude requests to be made on the spot for further details to be provided in the light of information obtained.*

5.160 Article 6.7 and Annex I thus expressly recognize that the examination of information already on the record at an on-the-spot verification in no way precludes the solicitation of additional information. While Mexico argues that the "further details" an investigating authority may attempt to acquire are necessarily limited to details corresponding with information already on the record, such an interpretation is neither required nor envisaged by the Agreement's text. Paragraph 7 of Annex I, after all, clearly provides that investigating authorities should, before commencing verification, inform exporting firms of "any further information which needs to be provided."

5.161 At any rate, Mexico's narrow textual argument appears to mask the real issue - Cruz Azul's unwillingness to provide information crucial to the calculation of an accurate margin of dumping. Mexico does not deny that Cruz Azul refused to provide either sales information related to the extended period of investigation, or information regarding its costs of production. The United States submits that, given the firm's intransigence in providing requested information, Guatemala acted reasonably in attempting to obtain this information while verifying the accuracy of other evidence of record. Indeed, Guatemala appears to have done more than required under the A-D Agreement by providing Cruz Azul with yet another opportunity to provide the withheld information.

5.162 Mexico makes much of the "technical accounting evidence" presented by Cruz Azul after the aborted verification, and objects strenuously to Guatemala's rejection of this evidence. Yet nothing in Article 6 requires investigating authorities, in developing an evidentiary record, to rely upon information that does not comply with the investigating authority's pre-verification information requests and is presented after verification. While Mexico contends that the Guatemalan authorities should have accepted and relied upon the "technical accounting evidence" after the failed verification attempt, nothing in the A-D Agreement required the Guatemalan authorities to base their final determination of dumping on this information.

5.163 Annex II to the A-D Agreement elaborates upon the procedures that administering authorities must follow in developing an evidentiary record. Paragraph 3, for example, states in relevant part, that:

> All information which is verifiable, which is appropriately submitted so that it can be used in the investigation without undue difficulties, which is supplied in a timely fashion, and, where applicable, which is supplied in a medium, or computer language requested by the authorities, should be taken into account when determinations are made.

In light of the fact that Cruz Azul submitted this technical accounting information *after* the scheduled verification, it is simply not tenable for Mexico to argue, as it does now, that Guatemala was required to rely upon this information in its final analysis.

5.164 Paragraph 5 of Annex II instructs that "[e]ven though the information provided may not be ideal in all respects, this should not justify the authorities from disregarding it, provided the interested party has acted to the best of its ability." Paragraph 6 further states:

> If evidence or information is not accepted, the supplying party should be informed forthwith of the reasons therefor, and should have an opportunity to provide further explanations within a reasonable period, due account being taken of the time-limits of the investigation. If the explanations are considered by authorities as not being satisfactory, the reasons for the rejection of such evidence or information should be given in any published determinations.

5.165 The Guatemalan authorities acted consistently with these provisions as well in rejecting the "technical accounting evidence." For one, this information was not just less than "ideal in all respects;" it was not even remotely compliant with Guatemala's information requests. Also, by waiting until *after* the scheduled verification to submit the information, Cruz Azul effectively ensured that the Guatemalan authorities would not be in a position to verify it at all.

5.166 Under these circumstances, the United States cannot concur with the Government of Mexico's argument that Guatemala was required to base its final determination, in whole or in part, upon the unverified "technical accounting evidence." Mexico's claims incorrectly ignore Cruz Azul's failure to provide the investigating authority with timely and complete information regarding, for example, its production costs.

(v) Investigating authorities have discretion to consider all relevant circumstances when making preliminary and final injury or threat of injury determinations and are not limited to the factors enumerated in the A-D Agreement

5.167 Mexico incorrectly argues that Guatemala erred when it relied on data on domestic inventories of clinker rather than on inventories of grey portland cement in its final injury determination. The A-D Agreement gives an investigating authority the discretion to consider all relevant circumstances when determining whether a domestic industry is injured or threatened with injury from subject imports. It does not limit an investigating authority to considering only specific factors or product comparisons. For instance, Articles 3.4 and 3.7 of the A-D Agreement specifically permit an investigating authority to consider factors which are not enumerated as injury or threat of injury factors.[151]

5.168 Therefore, Mexico is incorrect when it claims that an investigating authority may not find inventories of a dedicated input relevant when determining whether a domestic industry is injured or threatened with injury. Determining the relevance of such factors based upon the particular circumstances affecting imports and the domestic industry is central to a proper injury or threat analysis under the A-D Agreement. Considering inventories of a dedicated input can be especially relevant in cases involving a product under investigation that has a short or unstable shelf life, making it impractical for producers to maintain large inventories of the finished product. Thus, manufacturers of these types of products may find it more efficient and economical to maintain their inventories, not in the finished product, but in a semifinished, shelf stable product that can be quickly and cheaply transformed into the finished product. The Panel should not restrict the ability of investigating authorities to accord relevance to information regarding the inventories of upstream products.

5.169 The United States also disagrees with Mexico's claim that an investigating authority may not, after initiating an investigation based on allegations of threat of material injury, make a final determination of present injury without specific justification for the change. Without reaching the procedural issues that Mexico raises under Article 6, the United States submits that the AD Agreement does not limit an investigating authority's discretion to examine all relevant evidence gathered during the course of an investigation, irrespective of its determination in the preliminary phase of the investigation. At the initiation phase, Article 5.3 dictates that an authority should ascertain whether the application contains "sufficient information to justify the initiation of an investigation." Nothing in that Article suggests that the scope of an investigation is limited to the issues on which the applicant could present evidence prior to investigation. A preliminary determination serves the function of, *inter alia*, assessing whether there is sufficient evidence to justify proceeding with a full investigation, including with respect to injury. Consequently, it is

[151] The last sentence of Article 3.4 states: "This list is not exhaustive, nor can one or several of these factors necessarily give decisive guidance." The last sentence of the first para. of Article 3.7 states in part: "[i]n making a determination regarding the existence of a threat of material injury, the authorities should consider, *inter alia,* such factors as ..."

reasonably likely that a preliminary determination will not include all of the information a full investigation could obtain. Thus, a decision at the preliminary phase based on either of the two bases set out in footnote 9 of the A-D Agreement is without prejudice to a finding on full investigation that the other ground is met.

5.170 In the course of an antidumping investigation, the bulk of the evidence which forms the basis of the final determination is generally gathered after the preliminary determination. The Agreement, including Article 6, envisions that evidence at the point of a final determination may be much more expansive than the more limited evidence available at the initiation or preliminary stages. Thus, preliminary evidence may indicate that a domestic industry is threatened with material injury by reason of subject imports, but as more evidence is gathered and upon closer inspection, a final determination of present material injury may be justified.

(b) Requirements of DSU Article 19

5.171 In its first submission, Mexico argues that this Panel should (a) "recommend" that Guatemala bring the offending measures into conformity with Guatemala's obligations under the GATT 1994 and A-D Agreement, and (b) "suggest" that Guatemala revoke its anti-dumping measure concerning imports of Mexican cement and refund improperly collected duties. The United States respectfully submits that the Panel should refrain from exercising its discretion to suggest specific ways in which Guatemala might bring any offending measures into conformity with its obligations under the A-D Agreement. The Panel should particularly avoid suggesting specific remedies with a retroactive component, such as the refund of duties.

5.172 Article 19 of the DSU defines the remedial authority of panels:

> Where a panel or the Appellate Body concludes that a measure is inconsistent with a covered agreement, it shall recommend that the Member concerned bring the measure into conformity with the agreement. In addition to its recommendations, the panel or Appellate Body may suggest ways in which the Member concerned could implement the recommendations.

Article 19 thus clearly distinguishes "recommendations" from "suggestions." Where a panel finds a violation of an obligation, it *must* recommend that the offending measure be brought into conformity with the obligation at issue; however, a panel *need not* suggest specific ways in which this may be accomplished.

5.173 In addition to the express language of the DSU regarding the nature of panel and Appellate Body recommendations, it is the general practice of reviewing bodies to refrain from issuing specific recommendations. The United States urges this Panel to adhere to this practice. The requirement that panels issue general recommendations reflects the purpose and role of dispute settlement in the WTO and, before it, the GATT 1947. Article 3.4 of the DSU provides that "[r]ecommendations and rulings made by the DSB shall be aimed at achieving a satisfactory settlement of the matter," and Article 3.7 provides that "[a] solution mutually acceptable to the parties to a dispute ... is clearly to be preferred." To this end, Article 11 of the DSU directs panels to "consult regularly with the parties to the dispute and give them adequate opportunity to develop a mutually satisfactory solution." Ideally, a mutually agreed solution will be achieved before a panel issues its report. However, if this does not occur, a general panel recommendation that directs a party to bring an offending measure into conformity with its obligations still leaves parties with the necessary room to cooperate in arriving at a mutually agreed solution. A panel's suggestion of specific procedures for the correction of an offending measure could impede such cooperation because the suggested solution is likely to be perceived by the complaining Member as the panel's preferred solution to the dispute.

5.174 Retroactive remedies, such as the refund of anti-dumping duties sought by Mexico, suffer from the same defects as specific remedies. In addition, however, retroactive remedies are inconsistent with the established practice of panels of refraining from recommending - or suggesting - remedies that attempt somehow to restore the *status quo ante* or otherwise compensate the prevailing party for WTO-inconsistent actions taken by the defending party. As explained by the panel in the *Norway - Toll Collection Equipment* case, involving procurement by a Norwegian city of electronic toll collection equipment, there was no basis under GATT law for annulling the contract and recommencing procurement.[152] The panel stated that it was not appropriate to issue a recommendation that would operate retroactively because "[r]ecommendations of this nature had not been within customary practice in dispute settlement under the GATT system and the drafters of the Agreement on Government Procurement had not made specific provision that such recommendations be within the task assigned to panels under standard terms of reference."[153]

5.175 The conclusions of the *Norway - Toll Collection Equipment* panel - even though they related to government procurement rather than trade flows - are fully consistent with the general principle that GATT rules are generally considered as protecting "expectations on the competitive relationship between imported and domestic products," rather than "expectations on export volumes".[154] Thus, no GATT 1947 or WTO panel ever has awarded monetary compensation to an exporting country for lost trade. Moreover, even if GATT 1994/WTO rules were intended to restore lost trade volumes, the retroactive remedy of a duty refund requested by Mexico would not accomplish this objective, because the repayment of duties to individual importers would not reestablish the competitive conditions that a prevailing country could have expected in the absence of a WTO-inconsistent action by a party.

5.176 As Guatemala correctly notes, panels in anti-dumping and countervailing duty cases have been careful to avoid specific and retroactive remedies - even in suggesting ways in which offending measures could be brought into conformity with GATT/WTO obligations. Thus, in *United States - DRAMs*, the panel rejected Korea's request that it suggest revocation of the anti-dumping duty order at issue and amendment of a pertinent regulatory provision.[155] Instead, the panel concluded that, given "the range of possible ways in which we believe the United States could appropriately implement our recommendation, we decline to make any suggestion in the present case".[156] Similarly, the *Guatemala I* panel, citing Article 21.3 of the DSU, emphasized that "the modalities of implementation of a panel, or Appellate Body, recommendation are for the Member concerned to determine".[157]

---

[152] *Norway - Procurement of Toll Collection Equipment for the City of Trondheim*, GPR/DS2/R, adopted 13 May 1992 ("*Norway - Toll Collection Equipment*").

[153] *Ibid.*, para. 4.17.

[154] See, e.g., *United States - US Taxes on Petroleum and Certain Imported Substances*, L/6175, adopted 17 June 1987, BISD 34S/136, 158, at para. 5.1.9.

[155] Panel Report, *United States - Anti-Dumping Duty on Dynamic Random Access Memory Semiconductors (DRAMS) of One Megabit or Above from Korea*, *supra*, footnote 115.

[156] *Ibid.*, para. 7.4.

[157] *Guatemala I*, *supra*, footnote 25, para. 8.3. The *Guatemala I* panel declined to issue a suggestion on implementation with respect to its finding that Guatemala had violated Article 5.5 of the AD Agreement. *Ibid.* at para. 8.4. With respect to its finding that Guatemala had violated Article 5.3 of

5.177 Even where panels have offered suggestions in the anti-dumping and countervailing duty context, these suggestions have been general and prospective in nature. In the recent *United States - Lead and Bismuth Steel Products* decision, the panel refused to suggest, as advocated by the European Communities, that the United States amend its law to bring the offending measure into conformity with US obligations under the Subsidies and Countervailing Measures Agreement. Rather, the panel suggested "that the United States take[] all appropriate steps, including a revision of it administrative practices, to prevent the aforementioned violation of Article 10 of the SCM Agreement from arising in the future".[158]

5.178 This appropriate reluctance even to suggest specific actions a Member might take is grounded in the likelihood that a country might have at its disposal a variety of administrative or regulatory mechanisms with which to bring offending measures into conformity with its obligations. Further, panels generally lack expertise in the domestic law of a defending Member. Indeed, the DSU provides, at Article 8.3, that citizens of Members whose governments are parties to a dispute normally shall not serve on a panel concerned with that dispute, absent agreement by the parties.

5.179 For these reasons, the United States submits that, while Article 19.1 of the DSU expressly permits suggestions as to the ways in which offending measures might be brought into conformity with the obligations of a covered agreement, GATT/WTO practice reveals that - at least with respect to obligations regarding the conduct of anti-dumping and countervailing duty investigations - even the suggestion of specific and retroactive remedies is in most instances inappropriate.

VI. MAIN ARGUMENTS OF THE PARTIES CONCERNING ISSUES ARISING UNDER THE AD AGREEMENT AND GATT 1994[159]

A. *Standard of Review and Burden of Proof*

1. *Submissions of Guatemala*

6.1 **Guatemala** makes the following submissions regarding the standard of review and the burden of proof in these proceedings:

(a) Standard of review

6.2 Mexico is seeking a re-examination of the hundreds of factual matters considered by the Ministry in connection with the underlying administrative proceedings. In order to do so, the Panel would have to substitute itself for the Ministry. The Panel should not allow Mexico to interpret the standard of review unilaterally for its own purposes.

6.3 The Panel review is not a substitute for the proceedings conducted by the national investigating authorities.[160] Various panels have recognized that the role of panels is not

---

the AD Agreement, it suggested "that Guatemala revoke the existing anti-dumping measure on imports of Mexican cement, because, in our view, this is the only appropriate means of implementing our recommendation." *Ibid.* at para. 8.6. However, the panel did *not* suggest that Guatemala should also refund improperly collected duties.

[158] Panel Report, *United States - Imposition of Countervailing Duties on Certain Hot-Rolled Lead and Bismuth Carbon Steel Products Originating in the United Kingdom, supra*, footnote 34.

[159] The arguments of the parties are set out *verbatim*, as submitted to the Panel.

to carry out a *de novo* review of factual matters.[161] Describing the role of panels in reviewing factual matters, the Panel in the *Korea - Resins* case considered that:

> "the Panel should [not] substitute its own judgement for that of the KTC as to the relative weight to be accorded to the facts before the KTC. To do so would ignore that the task of the Panel *was not to make its own independent evaluation of the facts* before the KTC to determine whether there was material injury to the industry in Korea but to review the determination as made by the KTC for consistency with the Agreement, bearing in mind that *in a given case reasonable minds could differ as to the significance to be attached to certain facts*."[162]

6.4 The standard of review to be applied by this Panel is contained in Article 17.6 of the AD Agreement. In fact, the AD Agreement is unique in that it is the only covered Agreement containing its own special standard of review.[163]

6.5 Subparagraph (i) instructs panels not to substitute their own judgement for that of the national investigating authorities:

> "In its assessment of the facts of the matter, the Panel shall determine whether the authorities' *establishment of the fact was proper* and whether their *evaluation of those facts was unbiased and objective.* If the establishment of the facts was proper and the evaluation was unbiased and objective, *even though the Panel might have reached a different conclusion, the evaluation shall not be overturned.*[164]

Moreover, by applying this standard, Article 17.6(ii) instructs the Panel to limit its review to the facts that were known to the Ministry when it reached its determination (e.g. the evidence contained in the administrative file).[165]

6.6 A panel may, "in its assessment of the facts of the matter", draw conclusions on the basis of the facts contained in the file.[166] In *Canada - Civilian Aircraft*, the Appellate

---

160 Report of the Panel, *United States - Restrictions on Imports of Cotton and Man-made Fibre Underwear, WT/DS24/R,* as modified by the Appellate Body, adopted on 25 February 1997, DSR 1997:I, 31, para. 7.12.

161 See, for example, *idem*, citing the report of the Panel in *Korea - Anti-Dumping Duties on Imports of Polyacetal Resins from the United States*, ADP/92, adopted on 27 April 1993, para. 227 (hereinafter "*Korea - Resins*"); report of the Panel in *United States - Initiation of a Countervailing Duty Investigation into Softwood Lumber Products from Canada*, BISD 34S/194, adopted 3 June 1987 (hereinafter "*Softwood Lumber I*").

162 *Korea - Resins, ADP/92,* para. 227 (Emphasis added).

163 *Argentina - Safeguard Measures on Imports of Footwear,* WT/DS121/AB/R, adopted 12 January 2000, DSR 2000:I, 515, para. 118

164 Article 17.6(i) of the AD Agreement (emphasis added). In its first submission, Mexico does not recognize that the more lax standard of review set forth in Article 17.6(i) replaces the less lax standard of review established by certain panels under the GATT (see, for example, first submission by Mexico, paras. 74-76).

165 In the case *United States - Measure Affecting Imports of Woven Wool Shirts and Blouses from India* (hereinafter *United States - Wool Shirts*), the Panel refused to reinvestigate the market situation in question. Rather, it maintained that the purpose of the panel review was limited to analysing "the evidence used by the importing Member in making its determination to impose the measure" in question (Report of the Panel, *United States - Measure Affecting Imports of Woven Wool Shirts and Blouses from India* (hereinafter *United States - Wool Shirts*), WT/DS33/R, adopted 23 May 1997, , as upheld by the Appellate Body, DSR 1997:I, 343, para. 7.21). The covered Agreement in question in *United States - Wool Shirts*, the Agreement on Textiles and Clothing, does *not* contain a special standard of review like the AD Agreement.

Body recently found that "The drawing of inferences is ... an inherent and unavoidable aspect of the panel's basic task of finding and characterizing the facts making up a dispute."[167]

6.7 In examining the legal matters surrounding the true meaning of the Anti-Dumping Agreement, Article 17.6(ii) stipulates that:

> "the panel shall interpret the relevant provisions of the Agreement in accordance with customary rules of interpretation of public international law. Where the panel finds that a relevant provision of the Agreement admits of more than one permissible interpretation, the panel shall find the authorities' measure to be in conformity with the Agreement if it rests upon one of those permissible interpretations".[168]

This wording is designed to provide the authorities with a certain amount of flexibility. Article 17.6(ii) stipulates that the authorities shall establish (or maintain) their own interpretations and compliance procedures, particularly where the AD Agreement is obscure or ambiguous. The perfect example of such a situation can be found in this dispute, where the failure to define certain key terms, such as "sufficient" in Article 5.3, "as soon as" in Article 6.1.3, "adequate" in Article 12.1.1 and "sufficient detail" in Article 12.2 has led to a certain amount of obscurity.

6.8 In other words, what is important in each case is not whether the challenged determination rests on the best or "correct" interpretation of the AD Agreement, but whether it rests on a "permissible interpretation" (of which there can be many). If this is the case, then the Panel should respect the determination of the Ministry of the Economy.

(b) Burden of proof

6.9 It is a known fact that Mexico, as complainant in this dispute, bears the burden of proving that a WTO Agreement has been violated. This is explained extensively in the case *United States - Wool Shirts*, where the Appellate Body found:

> "In addressing this issue, we find it difficult, indeed, to see how any system of judicial settlement could work if it incorporated the position that the mere assertion of a claim might amount to proof. It is, thus, hardly surprising that various international tribunals, including the International Court of Justice, have generally and consistently accepted and applied the rule that the party who asserts a fact, whether the claimant or the respondent, is responsible for providing proof thereof. Also, it is a generally accepted canon of evidence in civil law, common law and, in fact, most jurisdictions, that the burden of proof rests upon the party, whether complaining or defending, who asserts the affirmative of a particular claim or defence. If that party adduces evidence sufficient to raise a presumption that what is claimed is true, the burden then shifts to the other party, who will fail unless it adduces sufficient evidence to rebut the presumption."[169]

6.10 In assuming the burden of proof, Mexico must establish a prima facie case of inconsistency with a provision of the AD Agreement or the GATT 1994 which falls

[166] Report of the Appellate Body in *Canada - Measures Affecting the Export of Civilian Aircraft* (hereinafter *Canada - Civilian Aircraft*), WT/DS70/AB/R, adopted 20 August 1999, DSR 1999:III, 1377, para. 198.

[167] *Ibid.*.

[168] AD Agreement, Article 17.6 (ii).

[169] *Supra*, footnote 89, at 335.(footnote omitted).

within the terms of reference of the Panel, and it must do so before passing on to Guatemala the burden of proving compliance with the provision in question. In *EC - Hormones*, the Appellate Body found that:

> "The initial burden lies on the complaining party, which must establish a prima facie case of inconsistency with a particular provision of the Agreement on the part of the defending party, or more precisely, of its SPS measure or measures complained about. When the prima facie case is made, the burden of proof moves to the defending party, which must in turn counter or refute the claimed inconsistency."[170]
>
> "In case of uncertainty, i.e. in case all the evidence and arguments remain in equipoise", the Panel must give Guatemala, as the respondent, "the benefit of the doubt".[171]

6.11 For example, in the case *United States - Antidumping Duty on Dynamic Random Access Memory Semiconductors (DRAMS) of One Megabit or Above from Korea (*hereinafter *United States - DRAM*), Korea challenged the rejection of an economic study in an anti-dumping investigation by the United States Department of Commerce. In rejecting the complaint, the Panel stated that Korea had erred "in failing to advance anything beyond conclusive arguments in support of its claim that the DOC should not have rejected the Flamm Study".[172]

6.12 Consequently, the Panel considered that Korea had not established prima facie that the United States had violated any provision of the AD Agreement.[173]

6.13 Similarly, it has been established that a panel cannot relieve the complainant of the burden of establishing a violation.[174] In addressing this issue in the case *Japan - Measures Affecting Agricultural Products* (hereinafter *Japan-Agricultural Products)*, the Appellate Body made the following finding:

> "... we consider that it was for the United States to establish a prima facie case that there is an alternative measure that meets all three elements under Article 5.6 in order to establish a prima facie case of inconsistency with Article 5.6. Since the United States did not even claim before the Panel that the 'determination of sorption levels' is an alternative measure which meets the three elements under Article 5.6, we are of the opinion that the United States did not establish a prima facie case that the 'determination of sorption levels' is an alternative measure within the meaning of Article 5.6".[175]

6.14 The report continues with the following finding:

> "Article 13 of the DSU and Article 11.2 of the SPS Agreement suggest that panels have a significant investigative authority. However, this authority cannot be used by a Panel to rule in favour of a complaining party which has not established a

---

170 Report of the Appellate Body in *EC - Measures Concerning Meat and Meat Products (Hormones), supra, footnote 121*, para. 98 (hereinafter *"EC-Hormones"*).

171 Report of the Panel in *United States - Sections 301-310 of the Trade Act of 1974*, WT/DS/152/R, DSR 2000:II, 815, adopted 27 January 1999, para. 7.14.

172 Report of the Panel in *United States - DRAM*, *supra*, footnote 115, para. 6.69.

173 *Ibid.*, para. 6.69. See also *Ibid.*, para. 6.80.

174 See, e.g. Report of the Panel in *EEC-Quantitative Restrictions Against Imports of Certain Products from Hong Kong*, BISD 30, page 129 (1983) (France argued that the terms of reference of the Panel stipulated that the Panel must consider all of the justifications. The Panel did not agree).

175 Report of the Appellate Body, *Japan - Measures Affecting Agricultural Products*, WT/DS76/AB/R, adopted 19 March 1999, DSR 1999:I, 277, para. 126.

prima facie case of inconsistency based on specific legal claims asserted by it. A panel is entitled to seek information and advice from experts and from any other relevant source it chooses, pursuant to Article 13 of the DSU and, in an SPS case, Article 11.2 of the SPS Agreement, to help it to understand and evaluate the evidence submitted and the arguments made by the parties, *but not to make the case for a complaining party*."[176]

6.15 In the present case, Mexico did not assume the burden of the proof, and the Panel should therefore find that the final determination (and, in the alternate, the provisional determination) is inconsistent with the Anti-Dumping Agreement and the GATT 1994.

2. *Rebuttal of Mexico*

6.16 **Mexico** makes the following rebuttal arguments to Guatemala's submissions regarding the standard of review and burden of proof in these proceedings:

(a) Standard of review

6.17 According to Guatemala, "Mexico is seeking a re-examination of the hundreds of factual matters considered by the Ministry in connection with the underlying administrative proceedings" and "In order to do so, the Panel would have to substitute itself for the Ministry."[177] It does not, however, provide one single item of evidence of this.[178] Because this is a general statement without any evidence, Mexico will not dwell on the matter. Nevertheless, the following comments are relevant:

(a) Any arguments concerning the standard of review in Article 17.6 are in vain because Mexico based its request for the establishment of a Panel on Article 17 of the AD Agreement. Furthermore, in its oral submission at the first substantive meeting, Mexico reiterated its request that the Panel reach its determinations on the basis of the standard of review in the AD Agreement.[179]

(b) The Panel which examined *Guatemala - Cement I* took its decisions on the basis of the standard of review in Article 17.6 of the AD Agreement, and, on that basis, determined that Guatemala had committed a number of violations of the Agreement, adding that the investigation should never have been initiated.[180] As is known, Mexico had included this Report in this Panel's terms of reference and so it is obvious that it is confident of a favorable outcome based on the rule in Article 17.6.

6.18 Irrespective of the foregoing, some aspects of Guatemala's arguments need to be highlighted:

---

[176] *Ibid.*, para. 129 (emphasis added). See also the Report of the Appellate Body in the case *Korea - Definitive Safeguard Measures on Imports of Certain Dairy Products, supra*, footnote 93, para. 147 (citing *Japan - Agricultural Products).*

[177] *Ibid.*, para. 116. See also paras. 196-198.

[178] See, in particular, footnote 131 to Guatemala's first submission. Guatemala omits to mention that para. 75 of Mexico's first submission deals precisely with the review criterion in Article 17.6 of the AD Agreement.

[179] Oral submission by Mexico at the first substantive meeting with the parties, 15 February 2000.

[180] See the Report of the Panel in *Guatemala - Cement I, supra*, footnote 25, in particular, paras. 7.79 and 8.6.

(a) Article 17.6(ii) of the AD Agreement has nothing to do with the facts known to the Ministry, but refers to the interpretation of the provisions of the Agreement.[181] Moreover, the consideration relating to the *Canada - Civilian Aircraft* case is unrelated to Article 17.6(ii).[182]

(b) Article 17.6(ii) does not empower the authorities to establish "their own interpretations and compliance procedures, particularly where the AD Agreement is obscure or ambiguous".[183] This Article is aimed at the Panel, not at a Member's authorities.

(c) Article 17.6(ii) is not, as Guatemala appears to suggest, a blank cheque for erroneous interpretations of the AD Agreement on the pretext that its provisions are obscure.[184] What this Article does is to instruct this Panel to apply the customary rules of interpretation of public international law and not to grant a waiver to interpret the AD Agreement as wished. In other words, if the Panel accepts the Guatemalan authority's interpretations, it must first interpret the terms of the Agreement according to the rules of interpretation of public international law and determine whether Guatemala's interpretations correspond to this interpretation. It is only if it is found that a provision has several acceptable interpretations that it should be determined whether the Guatemalan authority's interpretations are based on any of these acceptable interpretations. If this is not the case, the Panel cannot endorse the action by the Guatemalan Ministry of the Economy.

(b) Burden of proof

6.19 The way in which Guatemala deals with the concept of burden of proof is particularly strange. First of all, it states that Mexico must prove that a violation has occurred and concludes that "Mexico did not assume the burden of the proof" without furnishing any grounds for this statement other than the reports by other panels in completely unrelated cases.[185] Furthermore, Guatemala considers that it has reversed the prima facie presumption of nullification or impairment by asserting that Mexico's rights under Article 5.5 of the AD Agreement were not affected.[186] It would seem that Guatemala expects the Panel to apply different criteria to it when determining compliance with the obligation to substantiate its statements.

6.20 Mexico recognizes the procedural principle that "the burden of the proof lies with the party making the assertion". This principle has been duly incorporated in the WTO dispute settlement mechanism.[187] What Mexico categorically rejects is Guatemala's attempt to take advantage of a legitimate principle in order to cover up a ridiculous assertion which it cannot substantiate with evidence, such as "Mexico did not assume the burden of proof". In order to be able to make such a strong accusation, Guatemala should

[181] See first submission by Guatemala, para. 119.

[182] *Ibid.*, para. 120.

[183] *Ibid.*, para. 121.

[184] *Ibid.*.

[185] *Ibid.*, paras. 125-128.

[186] *Ibid.*, in particular paras. 220 and 221.

[187] See *inter alia* the reports of the Appellate Body in *United States - Measure Affecting Imports of Woven Wool Shirts and Blouses from India* , *supra*, footnote 89, at 335. See also *EC - Measures Concerning Meat and Meat Products (Hormones)*, *supra*, footnote 121, para. 98.

have identified the assertions in Mexico's first submission that were not substantiated by relevant evidence. In addition, Guatemala cannot reverse the prima facie presumption simply by asserting that Mexico was not affected by its violation of Article 5.5, inasmuch as it confines itself to speculating on what would have occurred if Guatemala had not violated the Article.

B. Initiation of the Anti-Dumping Investigation

1. Claims under Article 5 and Articles 2 and 3 - Requirements for the Initiation of an Anti-Dumping Investigation

(a) Submissions of Mexico

6.21 **Mexico** makes the following claims under Articles 5, 2 and 3 of the AD Agreement with respect to the requirements for the initiation of an anti-dumping investigation.

6.22 The application made to the Ministry of the Economy by Cementos Progreso for initiation of an anti-dumping investigation into grey Portland cement from Cruz Azul of Mexico (hereinafter the "application for initiation") did *not* include relevant evidence of dumping, threat of material injury or a causal relationship between the imports allegedly dumped and the alleged threat of material injury, as required by Article 5.2 of the AD Agreement. Moreover, the application for initiation did *not* contain the information reasonably available to the applicant on the points specified in subparagraphs (i) to (iv) of this Article.

6.23 The Ministry did *not* examine the accuracy and adequacy of the evidence provided in the application by Cementos Progreso and initiated the investigation without sufficient evidence of dumping, threat of material injury or a causal link between them to justify the initiation of an investigation, as required by Article 5.3 of the AD Agreement.

6.24 The Ministry also violated Article 5.7 and 5.8, as Article 5.7 requires that the evidence of dumping and injury shall be considered simultaneously when deciding whether or not to initiate an investigation. If the Ministry had conducted this examination when deciding upon initiation, as required by the AD Agreement, it would have been convinced that there was not sufficient evidence of dumping and injury and would have rejected the application by Cementos Progreso, as required by Article 5.8 of the AD Agreement.

6.25 An application must also contain evidence and information on the essential elements of dumping, injury and a causal link. The substantive provisions of Articles 2.1 and 2.4, 3.1, 3.2, 3.4, 3.5 and 3.7 *inter alia* on determining the existence of dumping and injury[188] respectively must be taken into account by the investigating authority in order to assess whether the evidence in an application is relevant and whether there is sufficient evidence to justify the initiation of an investigation according to Article 5.3 of the AD Agreement.

6.26 Article 5.2 states that an application for initiation must include evidence of dumping according to the definition given in Article 2 of the AD Agreement. Moreover, when assessing whether there is sufficient evidence of dumping to justify the initiation of an investigation, an investigating authority must take into account the provisions of Article 2 regarding the methodology and technical elements for calculating the dumping mar-

[188] Injury is understood as defined in footnote 9 to the AD Agreement, which defines injury, unless otherwise specified, as material injury to a domestic industry, threat of material injury to a domestic industry or material retardation of the establishment of such an industry.

gin, determining the normal value and the export price, and making the necessary adjustments to ensure a fair comparison.[189]

6.27 In order to determine the sufficiency of evidence on the existence of material injury for the purposes of initiation, it is also necessary to take into account the technical and economic factors mentioned in the various provisions of Article 3 of the AD Agreement, including those referred to in Article 3.2, 3.4 and 3.7. Article 5.2 in fact specifically refers to Article 3.2 and 3.4 and, even though it does not expressly mention Article 3.5 and 3.7, it is obvious that they also apply to the decision to initiate an investigation in cases of threat of material injury.

6.28 It cannot be argued that these substantive provisions do not apply to the decision to initiate an investigation but only to the preliminary or final determination of dumping, injury or threat of injury, because information such as that mentioned in Articles 2 and 3 must be contained in the application and must be taken into account when assessing whether there is sufficient evidence to justify initiation.

6.29 Nevertheless, when initiating the investigation, the Ministry totally disregarded the substantive provisions on the determinations of dumping and injury laid down in Articles 2 and 3 respectively of the AD Agreement, which must be duly taken into account by the investigating authority in order to comply with the requirements on initiation specified in Article 5 of the AD Agreement.

6.30 To summarize, and as can be seen throughout this section, the initiation of the anti-dumping investigation by the Guatemalan Ministry of the Economy did not comply with Article 5.2, 5.3, 5.7 and 5.8, nor the various provisions in Articles 2 and 3, of the AD Agreement.

(b) Response of Guatemala

6.31 The following are **Guatemala's** arguments in response to Mexico's claims under Articles 5, 2 and 3 of the AD Agreement:

6.32 Mexico complains that the Ministry did not "examine" the accuracy and adequacy of the evidence submitted with Cementos Progreso's application.[190] According to Mexico, the Ministry should not have initiated the investigation until it had "evidence"[191] of injurious dumping based on a "fair comparison" of Cruz Azul's prices in Mexico and Guatemala.[192] Mexico asserts that the initiation of the investigation did not comply with "Article 5.2, 5.3, 5.7 and 5.8, nor ... various provisions in Articles 2 and 3, of the AD Agreement."[193] Guatemala respectfully submits that these arguments are based on a fundamentally erroneous notion of the initiation and conduct of anti-dumping investigations under the Anti-Dumping Agreement. If the Panel were to accept such arguments, it would be undermining the spirit of the Agreement and requiring the authorities to conduct investigations before initiating the investigation. For the following reasons, Mexico's arguments must be rejected.

---

189 Even when the criteria used to determine whether there is sufficient evidence of dumping justifying the initiation of an investigation are different to those used for a preliminary or final determination of dumping, this does not mean that Article 2 should not be taken into account when determining whether an investigation should be initiated. See section 1.A "Dumping" in Mexico's first written submission.

190 First submission of Mexico, paras. 75, 89-90 and 111.

191 *Ibid.*, paras. 91, 92, 107-109.

192 *Ibid.*, paras. 98, 103, 107 and 126.

193 *Ibid.*, para. 64.

6.33 *First*, Article 5 of the AD Agreement establishes the requirements for initiating an anti-dumping investigation. Under Article 5.2, it is not enough for the complainant to assert that there is dumping and consequent injury. The complainant must support its claims with relevant evidence - that is, the information described in sub-paragraphs (i) to (iv) of Article 5.2. While the application must contain some evidence of dumping, injury and causal link, the evidence submitted must be limited to such information as is "reasonably available to the applicant".[194]

6.34 Article 5.3, for its part, stipulates that "the authorities shall *examine* the accuracy and adequacy of the evidence provided in the application to determine whether there is sufficient evidence to justify the initiation of an *investigation*".[195] If the authority determines that there is sufficient evidence, Article 5.1 authorizes the initiation of an investigation "to determine the existence, degree and effect of any *alleged* dumping ...".[196]

6.35 The AD Agreement does not define the term "investigation", but in its ordinary meaning, to investigate signifies to search or to enquire.[197] If we apply this definition in the context of the AD Agreement it follows that the "examination" that the authorities must conduct *prior* to initiation is less than the examination, search or enquiry which takes place *during* the investigation. Mexico repeatedly forgets this fact. It insists, for example, that it is up to the Ministry to "ascertain" the "legitimacy or veracity" of the documentary evidence submitted with Cementos Progreso's application[198] and to prove the normal value and export price *before* initiating the investigation.[199] This is absurd. No authority, however sophisticated and experienced, can "prove" the normal value or the export prices *before* conducting an investigation. In a way, the real purpose of an anti-dumping investigation is to "prove" the normal value and the export prices. The same applies to "verification". Verification of the information (including invoices and import certificates) is something that the authority does *during* the investigation, not *before*. Thus, Article 6.7 and Annex I of the AD Agreement provide for the verification of information *during* the course of the investigation.

6.36 A look at the history of the negotiation of the AD Agreement confirms Mexico's error.[200] During the Uruguay Round of multilateral trade negotiations, Hong Kong and the Nordic countries insisted that any application must include "information sufficient to permit the authorities concerned to establish a prima facie case of dumping, of injury and of causality".[201] According to Hong Kong, the intention of the proposed text was to clarify the circumstances under which an anti-dumping investigation shall be initiated and to introduce *a more definitive requirement* of "evidence sufficient to establish a prima facie

194 Article 5.2 of the AD Agreement.

195 *Ibid.*, Article 5.3 (emphasis added).

196 *Ibid.*, Article 5.1 (emphasis added).

197 *The Compact Edition of the Oxford English Dictionary,* Volume 1 (Oxford University Press, 1971); see also *Webster's Encyclopaedia Unabridged Dictionary of the English Language, 749* (Gramercy Books 1994) ("1. The act or process of investigating or the condition of being investigated. 2. A searching enquiry for ascertaining facts; a detailed or careful examination").

198 First submission by Mexico, paras. 75, 89-90 and 111.

199 First submission by Mexico, paras. 98, 103, 107 and 126.

200 Article 32 of the *Vienna Convention* states that recourse may be had to preparatory work to verify (or confirm) a meaning that emerges as a result of the textual approach. I. Brownlie, *Principles of Public International Law,* page 630 (Fourth Edition, 1990) (hereinafter "*Brownlie*").

201 MTN.GNG/NG8/W/83/Add.5 (23 July 1990). Sufficient evidence to establish "a prima facie case" is essentially the amount of evidence that would support a finding if proof to the contrary is not considered. The standard of "sufficient evidence" in Article 5.3 establishes a lower threshold.

case". That the investigating authorities had a particular responsibility in the vetting of complaints was emphasized.[202] This "more definitive requirement" was rejected during the negotiations, and the standard of the Tokyo Round was maintained basically intact.

6.37 The report of the Panel in *United States - Measures Affecting Imports of Softwood Lumber from Canada* (hereinafter *Softwood Lumber II*) serves as an illustration of the review which the authorities must conduct before initiating the investigation.[203]

The Panel made the following observations:

> "In analysing further what was meant by the term "sufficient evidence", the Panel noted that the quantum and quality of evidence to be required of an investigating authority prior to initiation of an investigation would necessarily have to be less than that required of that authority at the time of making a final determination. At the same time, it appeared to the Panel that "sufficient evidence" clearly had to mean more than mere allegation or conjecture, and could not be taken to mean just "any evidence". In particular, there had to be a factual basis to the decision of the national investigative authorities and this factual basis had to be susceptible to review under the Agreement".[204]

This level of "sufficient" evidence to justify initiation is lower than the level of evidence required for an affirmative preliminary or final determination, as confirmed by the Chairman of the Panel in *Softwood Lumber II*:

> "The Panel feels that a number of substantive concerns have been raised by the parties in this case. The Panel saw considerable merit in many of Canada's criticisms with respect to the United States' initiation of a countervailing duty investigation on imports of softwood lumber from Canada. In particular, the Panel recognized that the data and methodologies used by the United States contained shortcomings, in some cases of a serious nature. A number of questions arose regarding particular aspects of the evidence addressed by the US Department of Commerce. Moreover, certain facts available to the United States, for example on the impact of the recession, were, but arguably should not have been, ignored. Such information might have had an important bearing on this case, even at the initiation stage. However, the Panel had to take into account that it was not reviewing a *determination* of the existence of subsidy, injury and causality, but a finding that sufficient evidence of these elements existed to *warrant an investigation* ... The Panel was also aware, despite its rigorous application of the criteria established in paragraphs 331, 332, 333 and 335 of its report, of concerns that the threshold for initiation as applied in customary practice in several countries was relatively low. Nonetheless, the

---

[202] Document MTN.GNG/NG8/W/51, page 4 (12 September 1989) (emphasis added).

[203] Report of the Panel in *United States - Measures Affecting Imports of Softwood Lumber from Canada*, BISD-40S/358, adopted 27 October 1993. Although the *Softwood Lumber II* report analysed the sufficiency of evidence for the initiation of an investigation on countervailing measures, the aspects of the report which referred to the amount of evidence required to justify initiation are equally applicable to anti-dumping investigations. However, we must note that the standard of review set forth in Article 17.6 (i) governing this dispute settlement procedure is more lax in respect of the findings of the investigating authorities than the standard of review contained in *Softwood Lumber II*.

[204] *Ibid.*, para. 332 (emphasis added).

> Panel was of the view that the threshold required by Article 2.1 of the Agreement for initiation of a countervailing duty investigation was such that the Panel could not properly find that the United States *initiation* in this case was inconsistent with that Article, having regard to the standard of review".[205]

6.38 *Second*, contrary to what Mexico argues, an investigating authority cannot make a "fair comparison" under Article 2.4 before concluding its investigation.[206] In general, the information required to make a fair comparison is not available to the authority until it has concluded its investigation and is ready to determine whether the imports at issue are being dumped in the meaning of the AD Agreement. It is absurd to suggest, for example, that before initiating the investigation Guatemala should have adjusted the level of trade in conformity with Article 2.4. As we shall argue further on in greater detail, the adjustment of the level of trade is one of the most difficult anti-dumping adjustments for the authorities to calculate and among those that require the most data.

6.39 To summarize, Mexico is mistaken in asserting that in initiating its investigation on cement from Mexico, the Ministry "violated" Articles 2 and 3 of the Anti-Dumping Agreement. The obligation to make a "fair comparison" under Article 2 and to "prove" injury under Article 3 only applies to the final determination (and to a lesser extent, to the preliminary determinations).[207] We are not suggesting that Articles 2 and 3 are totally irrelevant during the initiation phase. Articles 2 and 3 contain definitions which give meaning to the expressions "dumping", "injury" and "causal link" used in Article 5.2. When the authorities examine the accuracy and adequacy of the evidence submitted in the application, those definitions help to establish whether there is "sufficient evidence" in the meaning of Article 5.3 to justify the initiation of the investigation.[208] However, Mexico goes too far when it states that:

> "An investigating authority must take into account the provisions of Article 2 regarding the methodology and technical elements for calculating the dumping margin, determining the normal value and the export price, and making the necessary adjustments *to ensure a fair comparison*."[209]

6.40 The Ministry carried out a full examination of the accuracy and adequacy of the evidence supplied in the application submitted by Cementos Progreso. On the basis of this examination and of all of the information before it, the Ministry reasonably determined that there was sufficient evidence to justify the initiation of an anti-dumping investigation.

---

[205] Letter from Michael Cartland, Chairman of the Panel in *Softwood Lumber II*, to G. Salembier, Chairman of the GATT Committee on Subsidies and Countervailing Measures (7 December 1992) (emphasis appears in original). (This letter transmits the observations of the Panel and the Softwood II report) (hereinafter the "Cartland Letter").

[206] First submission by Mexico, paras. 98-103, 126.

[207] Article 5.2(iv) establishes that the factors which serve to demonstrate injury listed in paras. 2 and 4 of Article 3 may be used as a guide for presenting information in an application. However, neither Article 5.2 nor Article 5.3 make any other reference to Articles 2 and 3. This suggests, the very least, that it was not the intention of the drafters that any other provision of Articles 2 or 3 should be applicable upon initiating the investigation.

[208] For example, if the applicant were to claim that imports were being dumped on the basis of the fact that the exporter's prices were higher in the importing country than in the exporting country, causing injury to the applicant's industry consuming that imported product, this allegation, however correct or well documented, would not provide *sufficient* evidence to justify the initiation of an anti-dumping investigation.

[209] First submission by Mexico, para. 60 (emphasis added).

(c) Rebuttal of Mexico

6.41 The following is **Mexico's** rebuttal of Guatemala's response to its claims under Articles 5 and Articles 2 and 3 of the AD Agreement:

6.42 First of all, Mexico wishes to reaffirm its position that Guatemala violated Article 5.2, 5.3. 5.7 and 5.8, *inter alia,* of the AD Agreement by initiating the investigation without having examined the accuracy and adequacy of the evidence and without having sufficient evidence to allow it to evaluate and establish properly the facts that have to be established in order to justify a determination to initiate an investigation, i.e. the existence of dumping, a threat of injury and a causal relationship.

6.43 The main arguments and evidence substantiating Mexico's position have been put before the Panel in Mexico's first written submission and in the evidence contained in the annexes attached thereto, which allow the Panel to examine and note that, on the basis of the evidence available to the Guatemalan Ministry of the Economy at the time of initiation, a reasonable and unbiased authority could not have determined that there was sufficient evidence of dumping, threat of material injury and a causal relationship to justify its decision to initiate an investigation against imports of grey Portland cement from Cruz Azul of Mexico. In this part of our rebuttal, therefore, we shall mainly focus on responding to and rejecting several of the assertions made by Guatemala in its first submission and at the first substantive meeting of the parties.

6.44 Mexico also reaffirms its rejection of Guatemala's distortion and manipulation in its first submission[210] in an attempt misrepresent Mexico's arguments concerning various violations committed in the course of initiation. This is why throughout this submission we shall clarify various specific aspects in this regard, but first we shall inform the Panel that in general Mexico's position in no way has the nuances or the "temporal" sense which Guatemala has tried to attribute to it on several occasions by imputing to Mexico incorrect and absurd assertions.[211]

6.45 Mexico in no way suggested that it was a question of the Ministry "taking its time" or "examining the evidence more carefully" because in certain respects the evidence was simply non-existent. Suffice it simply to read the corresponding section in Mexico's first written submission, including the paragraph to which Guatemala itself refers,[212] to see that at no time did Mexico claim what Guatemala is presenting in a distorted and tendentious way in an attempt to substantiate an initiation that is flagrantly inconsistent with the AD Agreement. What Mexico did assert is that the facts which must be established in every case in order to justify the initiation of an investigation pursuant to the AD Agreement (i.e. the existence of the alleged dumping, injury and a causal relationship) were not duly established in this case because of the insufficient evidence before the Ministry of

---

[210] See *inter alia* paras. 129, 171 and 174.

[211] Guatemala continues to distort Mexico's arguments in its oral submission at the first substantive meeting (14 and 15 February 2000), in paras. 26 and 29.

> "26. In its first submission, Mexico tries in vain to chip away at this mountain of evidence. For example, it claims Guatemala violated Articles 2, 3 and 5 of the AD Agreement because the Ministry's evidence of normal value was *somehow* deficient and because it *did not wait* for precise figures on the volume of Cruz Azul's imports ..." (emphasis added).
>
> 29. Second, Mexico errs when it asserts that Guatemala did not 'verify' the accuracy and adequacy of the information presented by Cementos Progreso, and that Guatemala should not have initiated its investigation *until* it had 'proof' of injurious dumping by Cruz Azul ..." (Emphasis added).

[212] Guatemala's first written submission, footnotes 145, 146, 205-208.

the Economy and therefore its initiation determination cannot be substantiated by any admissible interpretation of the various provisions in Article 5, which were violated by Guatemala.

6.46 Guatemala also misrepresents Mexico's arguments and is mistaken in indicating in paragraph 171 of its first submission that "Mexico never objected directly to any of the evidence mentioned". It is more than obvious in these proceedings that Mexico's complaints regarding the initiation are basically related to the lacunae in the application and, above all, to the evidence put forward by Cementos Progreso in order to comply with Article 5.2. Mexico has also objected to the lack of accuracy and adequacy of the evidence on the alleged dumping and the total absence of evidence on threat of injury and the causal relationship, all facts which prevented the Ministry of the Economy from determining the objective sufficiency of the evidence in order to justify the initiation of the investigation, as required by Article 5.3.

6.47 An examination of these matters by the Panel therefore necessitates in the first place a determination of whether the facts which lead to the acceptance of a request and, where applicable the initiation of an anti-dumping investigation (i.e. the existence of sufficient evidence of dumping, injury and the causal relationship of the evidence pursuant to Article 5.2, 5.3. 5.7 and 5.8) were duly established by the Guatemalan Ministry of the Economy; and whether the Ministry conducted an unbiased and objective assessment of these facts. It is also necessary to decide whether the various omissions and actions of the Ministry in connection with its initiation determination can be substantiated according to a permissible interpretation of the relevant provisions of the AD Agreement which lay down the conditions for the initiation of an investigation.

6.48 As we have already stated, Mexico for its part furnished the arguments and evidence of the violations committed in respect of initiation in its first written submission. The main aspects on which Mexico's claims regarding initiation of the investigation are based are the following:

6.49 FIRST: Cementos Progreso's application[213] was clearly insufficient to meet the requirements of Article 5.2. Firstly, it did not include relevant evidence of the alleged dumping. Secondly, it did not contain evidence, not to mention relevant evidence, of any sort concerning the alleged threat of material injury and the corresponding causal relationship, which is not the subject of the slightest claim in the application. Thirdly, contrary to what is argued by Guatemala[214], the information in Cementos Progreso's application cannot be considered as constituting all the information reasonably available to the complainant on the data required in accordance with subparagraphs (i) to (iv) of Article 5.2.

6.50 SECOND: The investigation was initiated by the Ministry in clear violation of Article 5.3 because the Guatemalan authority failed to examine, or in the best of cases undertook an insufficient examination of, the accuracy and adequacy of the evidence in the application, and initiated the investigation without sufficient proof to justify its initiation. If the Ministry had conducted an examination of the accuracy and adequacy as required by Article 5.3, it would have seen that not only did the evidence in the application in no way constitute accurate and adequate proof to substantiate the alleged dumping but also that evidence on the alleged threat of injury was simply non-existent in Cementos Progreso's application, which only provided a series of assertions and suspicions without

[213] Both the original application of 21 September 1995, and the supplemented application of 9 October 1995.

[214] See Guatemala's first written submission, paras. 138-151 and Guatemala's oral submission at the first substantive meeting, para. 25.

attaching any evidence to substantiate them. The same may be said of the causal relationship, which, as we have already pointed out, was not even claimed in the application. The foregoing, together with the fact that the investigating authority did not make any effort to obtain more evidence other than that in the application and confined itself to plainly and simply accepting the limited evidence and mere declarations furnished by Cementos Progreso, will necessarily lead the Panel to find that the investigation was initiated without sufficient evidence to justify initiation.

6.51 THIRD: It is also clear that the Ministry failed to comply with Article 5.7, which requires that the evidence of dumping and injury shall be considered simultaneously when deciding whether or not to initiate an investigation. If the authority had fully met this obligation, it would have perceived the lack of sufficient evidence of dumping and injury, in accordance with Articles 2 and 3, to underpin its determination on initiation.

6.52 FOUR: The Ministry violated Article 5.8 because it should have rejected the application and refrained from initiating the investigation due to insufficient evidence.

6.53 Having summarized the central elements of Mexico's position on the violations committed in respect of initiation, some important aspects substantiating Mexico's position are set out below, taking into account the relationship existing among the provisions relevant to the present case and responding to some of the arguments put forward by Guatemala in its first written submission and its oral submission at the first substantive meeting.

6.54 As regards the applicability of Articles 2 and 3 of the AD Mexico states as follows:

6.55 Guatemala contends that Article 5, and not Article 3 (or Article 2), establishes the requirements for initiation of an investigation under the AD Agreement (paragraph 180 of Guatemala's first written submission). Indeed, it is Article 5 that establishes the requirements for initiation, but this does not mean that Articles 2 and 3 are not to be taken into account in initiating an investigation. If by reading Article 5.2, 5.3, 5.7 and 5.8 together we are to understand that an investigation can only be initiated if there is sufficient evidence of dumping and injury (including evidence of a causal link), then Articles 2 and 3 indisputably apply to the initiation determination if that determination is to be consistent with the various requirements established under Article 5.

6.56 Article 5.2 and 5.7 expressly refer to evidence of *dumping and injury*, and the scope of these provisions extends to the obligations contained in Article 5.3 and 5.8 which refer to this same evidence. Meanwhile, Articles 2 and 3, which are expressly entitled "Determination of *dumping*" and "Determination of *injury*", in fact establish the substantive provisions applicable to such determinations without distinction as to the different moments at which these determinations must be made during an investigation.

6.57 Consequently, it cannot be argued that the provisions contained in Articles 2 and 3 of the Agreement do not apply to the decision to initiate an investigation, and that they apply only to the preliminary or final determination of dumping and injury or threat of injury. On the contrary, it has been recognized that in an anti-dumping investigation, dumping and injury must be established, albeit with different levels of evidence, at three different moments, i.e. in the initiation determination, in the preliminary determination and in the final determination. In this connection, the Panels in *USA - Softwood Lumber*[215] and *Guatemala - Cement I*[216] established that the subject-matter or type of evidence

[215] *United States - Measures Affecting Imports of Softwood Lumber from Canada, SCM/162*, report adopted on 27 October 1993, BISD 40S/426, para. 332.

[216] Report of the Panel in *Guatemala - Cement I, supra*, footnote 25, paras. 7.67 and 7.77.

needed to justify initiation is *the same subject-matter or type of evidence* as that needed to make a preliminary or a final determination, although the quality and quantity of the evidence needed for the initiation of an anti-dumping investigation is less than for a preliminary or final determination of dumping and injury.

6.58 Seen from this angle, we submit that for an initiation determination to be consistent with Article 5, it is *necessary* for an investigating authority to take account of the various provisions of Articles 2 and 3 in order to ensure that *the evidence of dumping and injury* on which the initiation determination is based contains *the same subject-matter* or is *of the same type* as the evidence required for a preliminary or final determination of dumping and injury, even if the level of evidence is clearly different. Only then can the investigating authority:

(i) Evaluate and establish in the first instance whether the application for initiation meets the requirements of Article 5.2, in particular whether it includes evidence of the *existence* of dumping, injury and causal link;

(ii) evaluate and establish whether the evidence of the alleged dumping and the alleged injury or threat of injury meet the standard of sufficiency contained in Article 5.3 for justifying the initiation of the investigation, or whether, on the contrary, the application should be rejected pursuant to Article 5.8. In this connection, both the examination required under Article 5.3 and that required under Article 5.7 must be conducted in the light of the substantive provisions of Articles 2 and 3, since the accuracy, adequacy and, where applicable, sufficiency of evidence to justify initiation must in fact be established in direct relation to the (determination of) dumping and injury, including as an integral part of this concept, the causal link pursuant to Article 3.5.

6.59 Moreover, we can also assert that for the purposes of an initiation determination, the investigating authority *must* take account of the various provisions of Articles 2 and 3, to ensure consideration of all areas which the provisions of Article 5 expressly or implicitly require to be considered. For example, Article 5.2 (iv) expressly refers to paragraphs 2 and 4 of Article 3; so that to evaluate the evidence of dumping implicit reference is made to the relevant provisions of Article 2 concerning the normal value and the export price, and to Article 3.5 for the establishment of a causal link between dumped imports and the alleged injury. Here, Mexico's position is perfectly consistent with the findings of the Panels in *United States - Softwood Lumber* and *Guatemala - Cement I.*

6.60 In view of the above, Mexico cannot agree with Guatemala's argument that for the purposes of an initiation determination Articles 2 and 3 are not applicable or are only applicable in a limited way with respect to the definitions of dumping and injury. If this were the case, Article 5 would refer expressly and exclusively to the definitions of dumping and injury contained in Article 2.1 and footnote 9 of the Agreement respectively.

6.61 It is up to the Panel to evaluate the need to decide whether or not there is any inconsistency *per se* with Articles 2 and 3. Mexico's position has focused more on the argument that for the initiation of an investigation to be consistent with the provisions of Article 5, the determination of dumping and injury must be consistent with the provisions of Articles 2 and 3, and not run counter to their meaning. The fact is that an initiation determination such as the one at issue, in which it is evident that the investigating authority did not take account of the nature of the evidence of dumping and injury, clearly violating a number of the relevant provisions of Articles 2 and 3, including aspects expressly provided for in Article 5, is obviously inconsistent with Article 5.2, 5.3, 5.7 and 5.8 of the Anti-Dumping Agreement.

(d) Guatemala's response to rebuttal of Mexico

6.62 **Guatemala** makes the following response to Mexico's rebuttal:

6.63 The factual record shows clearly that Cruz Azul began to export relatively large quantities of grey Portland cement to the Guatemalan market at dumped prices in the middle of 1995 in an effort to avoid the devastating effects of a severe recession in Mexico caused by the devaluation of the peso in December 1994. The record also shows that Cruz Azul's export prices were significantly lower than its prices in Mexico and the prevailing prices on the Guatemalan market. In fact, these prices were even lower than Cementos Progreso's production costs. Although Cementos Progreso responded by lowering its prices, even then it lost customers and market share to Cruz Azul. Indeed, in the six months immediately prior to the initiation of the investigation, Cruz Azul's share in the Guatemalan market went from 0 to 25 per cent.

6.64 Threatened by a flood of dumped imports in its **only** market, Cementos Progreso had no choice but to file an anti-dumping application with the Guatemalan investigating authority. In its application, dated 21 September 1995, and the supplementary application of 9 October 1995, Cementos Progreso provided the Ministry with all of the information reasonably available to it on dumping, injury and causal link in conformity with Article 5.2 of the AD Agreement. With respect to dumping, the company provided the Ministry with invoices, bills of lading and import certificates showing that Cruz Azul was selling grey Portland cement in Mexico at Q 27.62 per sack, while at the same time, just the other side of the border, it was selling grey Portland cement in Guatemala at only Q 14.77 per sack. This difference reflected a margin of dumping of 87 per cent.[217] With respect to injury, Cementos Progreso provided information concerning loss of sales, loss of customers and a trend towards penetration of imports which, in the space of *one single* day, basically went from 0 to 480 tons (representing a loss of sales of approximately US$60,000). Finally, with respect to causal link, the company provided the Ministry with evidence of price undercutting by Cruz Azul, an increase in Cruz Azul imports and the effect of Cruz Azul imports on Cementos Progreso's profits, sales and investment plans.

6.65 During the first meeting, Mexico tried desperately to cast doubt on this evidence. Firstly, it scolded Guatemala for not gathering more evidence of injurious dumping before initiating the investigation. According to Mexico, it is "incomprehensible" that Cementos Progreso should not have provided (and the Ministry collected) more evidence during the period of time between the submission of the supplementary application on 9 October 1995 and the initiation of the investigation a few months later.[218]

6.66 Furthermore, Mexico repeatedly argues that Guatemala simply "did not conduct the examination required" under Article 5.3 of the AD Agreement.[219] According to Mexico, Guatemala did not conduct the "examination required" with respect to the type of cement[220], the size of the sacks[221], "representivity" of the sales[222], level of trade[223] and exchange rates.[224]

---

[217] See, for example, first submission by Guatemala, para. 154.

[218] Oral submission of Mexico, paras. 62 and 82. Curiously, in other parts of its oral submission (paras. 107-109), Mexico accuses Guatemala of "manipulating" *similar* language contained in Mexico's first written submission. See, for example, first written submission by Mexico, paras. 128 and 134-136.

[219] See, for example, oral submission by Mexico, para. 88.

[220] *Ibid.*, paras. 86-89.

[221] *Ibid.*, paras. 92-94.

[222] *Ibid.*, paras. 96-98.

6.67 Mexico maintains that the result of this examination is not important. It does not seem to care who ended up being the "beneficiary" of any particular adjustment.[225] What is important, according to Mexico, is that Guatemala allegedly failed to carry out the examination required under Article 5.3 of the AD Agreement.[226]

6.68 Finally, Mexico continues to insist that Guatemala violated Articles 2 and 3 of the AD Agreement by initiating the challenged investigation.[227] For example, according to Mexico the investigation was initiated in spite of a "total absence of evidence of an alleged threat of injury".[228]

6.69 As we shall demonstrate below, some of these arguments make no sense and none of them have any merit.

6.70 Firstly, like the Panel, Guatemala does not really understand what Mexico means when it uses the term "representivity".[229] Mexico never explained where this "representivity" requirement comes from, nor has it explained the basis for its assertion that the alleged "lack of representivity ... without any doubt affected the comparison made between the normal value and the export price".[230] If Mexico uses this term to mean "sufficient quantity" as indicated in footnote 2 to Article 2.2 of the AD Agreement[231], then Guatemala fully respected its WTO obligations as discussed in detail in the reply to question 17 of the Panel to Mexico.[232]

6.71 Secondly, Mexico paints a false picture when it adduces that Guatemala did not conduct the "examination required" under Article 5.3 of the AD Agreement.[233] In any anti-dumping investigation, there are thousands of potential adjustments. Adjustments can be made with respect to like products, support to industry, transactions between related parties; or there could be price or cost adjustments associated with the costs of maintaining an inventory, credit expenditures, interest payments to banks, bonds, advertising costs, transport costs (pre-sale and post-sale), reimbursement of tariffs in tolling operations, tax rebates and sales commissions. The list is practically infinite. However, at the time of initiation, the factual record before the authorities is incomplete by definition. Thus, the authorities can only address the matters which appear in an affirmative form. All other adjustments, real or imaginary, must be addressed, where appropriate, during the course of the investigation.

6.72 In this dispute, for example, the Ministry had no reason whatsoever to believe at the time of initiation that the cement sold in Mexico was different from the cement that Cruz Azul sold in Guatemala. As explained in greater detail in our first written submission, the invoices for the sales in Mexico identified the cement as "grey cement" and

---

223 *Ibid.*, paras. 99-100.

224 *Ibid.*, paras. 101-103.

225 *Ibid.*, para. 90.

226 *Ibid.*.

227 See, for example, *Ibid.*, paras. 121-122.

228 See, for example, para. 111. See, also, *Ibid.*, para. 63. ("Cementos Progreso did not provide any information in support of its assertions concerning the alleged threat of material injury.")

229 See questions of the Panel to Mexico, 18 February 2000, Geneva, 17-18 (hereinafter Appendix I).

230 Oral submission by Mexico, para. 98. See, also, first submission of Mexico, paras. 122-123 and 234-236.

231 As Mexico suggests in para. 168 of its oral submission.

232 Appendix I, question 17 to Mexico.

233 See, for example, oral submission by Mexico, para. 88.

"Cruz Azul" cement.[234] The evidence of the export price - which was supported by import certificates, invoices and bills of lading - identifies the product as "grey cement", "grey Portland cement" and "type II Portland cement with pozzolana". Since the price of cement in Guatemala had been regulated for more than 50 years, this evidence indicated to the Ministry that the sales that were being compared concerned "grey cement".

6.73 It is also wrong for Mexico to state that it is not important whether a particular adjustment at the moment of initiation could have benefited Cruz Azul. This Panel was established to resolve a dispute, not to issue a consultative opinion. Mexico maintains that Guatemala initiated an anti-dumping investigation in violation of Article 5.3 of the Anti-Dumping Agreement. In particular, Mexico maintains that the evidence which the investigating authority of Guatemala had before it at the time of initiation was not "sufficient" to justify an investigation. Guatemala disagrees.

6.74 In its defence, Guatemala showed, *inter alia*, that the Ministry did have "sufficient evidence" in the meaning of Article 5.3 of the Anti-Dumping Agreement to justify the initiation of an investigation. As part of this demonstration, it was shown that even if Mexico had been right in certain of its claims, Guatemala still had sufficient evidence to justify the initiation. For example, in its first written submission, Guatemala stated that an adjustment for the size of the sacks would have left a margin of 59 per cent[235] and any adjustment for the type of cement would probably have *increased the margin*.[236] This demonstration is entirely relevant.

6.75 Mexico is the complainant in this dispute, and as such bears the burden of proving that a WTO Agreement was violated.[237] It is therefore up to Mexico to establish prima facie that there is an inconsistency with a provision of the AD Agreement or the GATT 1994 included in the Panel's terms of reference before the burden of proving the consistency of the provision in question is shifted to Guatemala. As found by the Appellate Body in the case *European Communities - Measures Concerning Meat and Meat Products (Hormones)*:

> "The initial burden lies on the complaining party, which must establish a prima facie case of inconsistency with a particular provision of the *SPS Agreement* on the part of the defending party, or more precisely, of its SPS measure or measures complained about. When that prima facie case is made, the burden of proof moves to the defending party, which must in turn counter or refute the claimed inconsistency."[238]

"In case of uncertainty, i.e. in case all the evidence and arguments remain in equipoise", the Panel must give Guatemala, as defending party, "the benefit of the doubt".[239]

6.76 Mexico did not fulfil the requirements of presenting a prima facie case of inconsistency. At least, Guatemala refuted the claimed inconsistency.[240]

---

[234] Mexico recognizes, in para. 113 of its first written submission, that the invoices documenting the sales in Mexico *did not* identify the product as a particular or special type of grey cement. If this had been the case, the invoices would probably have reflected the fact.

[235] First submission by Guatemala, para. 160, footnote 191.

[236] *Ibid.*, para. 159.

[237] *Ibid.*, paras. 123-128 (regarding the burden of proof).

[238] *Supra*, footnote 121, para. 98.

[239] Report of the Panel in *United States - Sections 301-310 of the Trade Act of 1974*, WT/DS/152/R, *supra*, footnote 171, para. 7.14.

6.77 Third, Mexico is mistaken in asserting that the initiation of the investigation was "inconsistent" with Articles 2 and 3 of the AD Agreement.[241] As we discussed in detail in our first written submission, this argument is not supported by a permissible interpretation of the AD Agreement[242] and was not supported by the United States[243] or the European Union.[244] Mexico is also mistaken in adducing that the investigation was initiated in spite of a "total absence of evidence of injury".[245] As we explained in detail in our first written submission, the Ministry had plenty of evidence of injury at the time of initiation.[246]

6.78 Finally, Mexico is right about one thing. Guatemala *could* have collected more evidence of dumping, injury and causal link before deciding whether the evidence it had before it was "sufficient" to justify the initiation of an anti-dumping investigation.[247] The Ministry could have wasted many years and millions of quetzals gathering further information; in fact, the Ministry *could still* be gathering evidence. But this is not the point. The point is, that in January 1996 Guatemala had "sufficient evidence" to launch an anti-dumping investigation. In our first written submission and during the first meeting we demonstrated that the only correct reply to this question would be "yes".

6.79 As we indicated during the first meeting with the Panel, it is possible that others, including the Panel, would have done things differently.[248] Looking back upon decisions that were taken more than four years ago, it is easy enough to identify things that might have been done differently - additional information that might have been gathered or a particular enquiry which might have been pursued before deciding on the initiation. For example, in the case *Measures Affecting Imports of Softwood Lumber from Canada* (hereinafter *Softwood Lumber II*) the Panel considered that the data and methodologies used by the United States contained "shortcomings".[249] The Panel even considered that the United States had "ignored" certain facts that were important and that "might have had an important bearing on this case, even at the initiation stage".[250] But the Panel did not reverse the decision to initiate. The Panel recognized that it was only reviewing a decision justifying the investigation and not a final determination based on a complete file.[251]

---

240 This explains why Guatemala asked Mexico during the first meeting with the Panel whether the 87 per cent *ad valorem* margin of dumping would have disappeared if all of the adjustments sought by Mexico had been made.

241 Oral submission by Mexico, paras. 121-122.

242 First submission by Guatemala, paras. 135-136.

243 Submission by the United States as third party, 27 January 2000, para. 15.

244 Submission by the European Union as third party, 27 January 2000, para. 16.

245 Oral submission by Mexico, para. 111. See also *Ibid.*, para. 63 ("Cementos Progreso did not provide any information in support of its assertions concerning the alleged threat of material injury.")

246 See first written submission by Guatemala, paras. 166-181.

247 See first oral submission by Mexico, paras. 62 and 82 (arguing that it is "incomprehensible" that neither Cementos Progreso nor Guatemala collected further evidence before deciding to initiate").

248 Oral submission by Guatemala, 14 February 2000, Geneva, paras. 31-38 (hereinafter oral submission by Guatemala).

249 Letter by Michael Cartland, Chairman of the Panel on *Softwood Lumber II*, to G. Salembier, Chairman of the GATT Committee on Subsidies and Countervailing Measures (7 December 1992) (letter transmitting the observations of the Panel and the report in *Softwood Lumber II*).

250 *Ibid.*.

251 Report of the Panel in *Measures Affecting Imports of Softwood Lumber from Canada*, BISD 40S, adopted 27 October 1993, para. 359. While the report in *Softwood Lumber II* analysed the sufficiency of evidence to initiate an investigation on countervailing measures, the elements of the report relating to the quantity of evidence needed to justify the initiation are also applicable to anti-dumping investigations. However, the standard of review contained in Article 17.6(i) governing this

6.80 The Panel in *Softwood Lumber II* also stated that the term "sufficient evidence" clearly had to mean "more than mere allegation or conjecture".[252] According to the Panel "there had to be a factual basis to the decision of the national investigative authorities".[253] In the present case, Guatemala ***had*** a factual basis for initiating the investigation. Cementos Progreso's application and the supplementary application contained more than mere "allegation or conjecture". These documents contained, among other import figures and trends, information on prices backed by invoices, bills of lading and other elements, market prices in Guatemala, and evidence of price undercutting. In fact, it was shown that the prices of the dumped imports averaged only Q 13.96 per sack, almost 15 per cent less than the average price of Q 26 charged by Cementos Progreso in Guatemala. Once again, if Mexico or the Panel had been the investigating authority, they might have done certain things differently or they might have arrived at a different conclusion. However this is not the point. It is not the Panel's job to take over from the investigating authority of Guatemala. The Panel's mandate consists in determining whether, according to Article 17.6(i) of the AD Agreement, Guatemala's decision to initiate rested on facts which were properly established and evaluated in an unbiased and objective manner. In fulfilling this task, the Panel should bear in mind that the evidence of injurious dumping available to the authority at the time of initiation will be incomplete and imperfect by definition. This is what investigations are for - to gather more complete information.

2. *Claims under Articles 5.2 and 5.3 - "Sufficient Evidence to Justify the Initiation of and Investigation"*

(a) Submissions of Mexico

6.81 **Mexico** further makes the following claims under Articles 5.2 and 5.3 of the AD Agreement:

(i) Evidence to be Included in an Application

6.82 Article 5.2 of the AD Agreement states the following:

> "An *application* under paragraph 1 *shall include evidence* of *(a) dumping*, *(b) injury* within the meaning of Article VI of GATT 1994 as interpreted by this Agreement and *(c) a causal link* between the dumped imports and the alleged injury. *Simple assertion, unsubstantiated by relevant evidence, cannot be considered sufficient* to meet the requirements of this paragraph." (emphasis added).

6.83 As the Panel may note, the *application* for initiation by the firm Cementos Progreso, in violation of Article 5.2 of the AD Agreement, *did not include relevant evidence* of dumping, threat of injury and a causal link between them, as required by Articles 2 and 3 of the Agreement. The investigation was in fact initiated on the basis of two delivery notes for cement and two import certificates, without even knowing the total amount of imports from Mexico, in the complete absence of evidence regarding the alleged threat of

---

dispute settlement procedure is more deferential to the findings of the investigating authorities than the standard of review in *Softwood Lumber II*. See oral submission by Guatemala, paras. 28-29 (where a distinction is made between the standard of review in *Softwood Lumber II* and the standard of review in Article 17.6(i) of the Anti-Dumping Agreement.

252 *Ibid.*, para. 332.

253 *Ibid.*.

injury to the Guatemalan industry and the equally complete absence of evidence or even arguments regarding a causal link or relationship between the alleged dumping and the alleged threat of injury.

6.84 Article 5.2 also states that the application must contain "such information as is reasonably available to the applicant" on:

> "(i) the identity of the applicant and a description of the volume and value of the domestic production of the like product by the applicant. Where a written application is made on behalf of the domestic industry, the application shall identify the industry on behalf of which the application is made by a list of all known domestic producers of the like product (or associations of domestic producers of the like product) and, to the extent possible, a description of the volume and value of domestic production of the like product accounted for by such producers;
>
> (ii) a complete description of the allegedly dumped product, the names of the country or countries of origin or export in question, the identify of each known exporter or foreign producer and a list of known persons importing the product in question;
>
> (iii) information on prices at which the product in question is sold when destined for consumption in the domestic markets of the country or countries of origin or export (or, where appropriate, information on the prices at which the product is sold from the country or countries of origin or export to a third country or countries, or on the constructed value of the product) and information on export prices or, where appropriate, on the prices at which the product is first resold to an independent buyer in the territory of the importing Member;
>
> (iv) information on the evolution of the volume of the allegedly dumped imports, the effect of these imports on prices of the like product in the domestic market and the consequent impact of the imports on the domestic industry, as demonstrated by relevant factors and indices having a bearing on the state of the domestic industry, such as those listed in paragraphs 2 and 4 of Article 3."

6.85 A mere glance at the application for initiation in this particular case shows clearly that the applicant, like the Ministry, failed to observe these requirements. It is not only highly doubtful whether the requirements laid down in subparagraphs (i) and (ii) were respected, for example, a description of the volume and value of the domestic production of the like product and a complete description of the product by the applicant, which in this case were obviously inadequate or incomplete, but, what is more serious, the applicant failed to provide the information required by subparagraphs (iii) and (iv), which in general was certainly reasonably available to it.

6.86 The information contained in Cementos Progreso's application (essentially two delivery notes and two import certificates, together with a number of unsubstantiated allegations) could not therefore be considered as all the information reasonably available to the applicant, nor as relevant evidence of dumping, still less a threat of material injury and a causal link between the imports allegedly dumped and the alleged threat of material injury to the domestic industry. The sections below will provide further details regarding the lack of evidence on each of these elements.

6.87 For the moment, it must be stated that, even though in principle Article 5.2 undoubtedly lays an obligation on the applicant to provide evidence of dumping, injury and a causal link between the two in its application, together with the information reasonably available to it on the points indicated in subparagraphs (i) to (iv), it is also true that, under the AD Agreement, this requirement is also incumbent upon the investigating authority because, according to Article 5.8, an investigating authority must accept an application if these requirements are met or reject it if such evidence and/or information as is reasonably available to the applicant is not provided. This should have been done by the Ministry of the Economy, as will also be explained in a subsequent section of this submission.

6.88 Mexico also argues that the Guatemalan authorities violated Article 5.3 of the AD Agreement by *not* examining the accuracy and adequacy of the evidence contained in Cementos Progreso's application and by initiating the investigation without sufficient evidence to justify this. Article 5.3 provides the following:

> "The authorities shall examine the accuracy and adequacy of the evidence provided in the application to determine whether there is sufficient evidence to justify the initiation of an investigation."

6.89 As can be seen from the text of the Agreement itself, Article 5.3 lays an obligation on the investigating authority that results from Article 5.2. In other words, once the authority has accepted an application after having determined that it contains evidence of the existence of the three elements required, namely, dumping, injury and a causal relationship, as well as the information reasonably available to the applicant on the points specified in Article 5.2, it must then examine the accuracy and adequacy of the evidence provided in the application, but in this instance to "determine whether there is sufficient evidence to justify the initiation of an investigation".

6.90 This means that Article 5.3 of the AD Agreement imposes on the investigating authority an obligation that goes beyond determining whether or not an application meets the terms of Article 5.2. This provision requires that, *once it has been determined that the requirements of Article 5.2 of the AD Agreement have been met*, the authority must also *examine* whether there is *sufficient evidence* to justify the initiation of an investigation. If it determines that the evidence and information contained in the application are not accurate nor adequate to support the conclusion that there is sufficient evidence to justify initiating an investigation, the authority must refrain from initiating the investigation or it may *ex officio* try to obtain evidence and information that will allow it to meet the sufficiency standard laid down in the AD Agreement in order to initiate an investigation. The Panel that considered this matter previously concluded that:

> "7.53 ... In particular, there is nothing in the Agreement to prevent an investigating authority from seeking evidence and information on its own, that would allow any gaps in the evidence set forth in the application to be filled. We do not suggest that such action by the investigating authority is in any case required by the AD Agreement."

6.91 The Panel that heard the case *United States -Softwood Lumber*, when referring specifically to a panel's role of examining the consistency of a decision to initiate an investigation with the provisions of the Tokyo Round Subsidies Code, stated:

> "The Panel considered that in reviewing the action of the United States authorities in respect of determining the existence of sufficient evidence to initiate, the Panel was not to conduct a *de novo* review of the evidence relied upon by the United States authorities or otherwise to substitute its judgment as to the sufficiency of the particular evidence considered by the United States authorities. Rather, in the view of the Panel, *the review to be applied in the present case required consideration of whether a reasonable, unprejudiced person could have found*, based upon the evidence re-

lied upon by the United States at the time of initiation, *that sufficient evidence existed* of subsidy, injury and causal link *to justify initiation* of the investigation."[254] (emphasis added).

6.92 In the present case as well, therefore, the Panel had to examine whether, on the basis of the evidence available to the Guatemalan Ministry of the Economy at the time of initiation, a reasonable, unprejudiced authority could have found sufficient evidence of dumping, threat of material injury and a causal link to justify its decision to initiate the investigation into imports of grey Portland cement from the Mexican firm Cruz Azul.

6.93 Although neither Article 5 nor any other provision of the AD Agreement defines what is meant by "sufficient evidence to justify the initiation of an investigation", certain Panel decisions are indicative in this regard. The report of the Panel in the *United States - Softwood Lumber* case is also important in this respect when it states the following:

> "In analysing further what was meant by the term 'sufficient evidence', the Panel noted that the quantum and quality of evidence to be required of an investigating authority prior to initiation of an investigation would necessarily have to be less than that required of that authority at the time of making a final determination. At the same time, it appeared to the Panel that 'sufficient evidence' clearly had to mean more than mere allegation or conjecture, and could not be taken to mean just 'any evidence'. In particular, there had to be a factual basis to the decision of the national investigative authorities and this factual basis had to be susceptible to review under the Agreement. Whereas the quantum and quality of evidence required at the time of initiation was less than that required to establish, pursuant to investigation, the required Agreement elements of subsidy, subsidized imports, injury and causal linkage between subsidized imports and injury, the Panel was of the view that the evidence required at the time of initiation nonetheless had to be relevant to establishing these same Agreement elements."[255] (emphasis added).

6.94 However, in the special circumstances of this investigation, it is particularly important to take into account the relationship between Article 5.2 (which lays down the requirements to be met in an application) and Article 5.3 (which establishes the requirement of sufficiency of evidence to justify the initiation of an investigation).

6.95 As we have already stated, it is obvious that the two delivery notes and the two import certificates submitted to the Ministry together with the application cannot, according to the minimum acceptable standard, be considered all the information reasonably available to the applicant because Cementos Progreso even went so far as to fail to submit information that was certainly reasonably available to it, for example, information on several of the factors mentioned in subparagraphs (iii) and (iv).

6.96 Nevertheless, even supposing - although Mexico does *not* accept this - that the evidence submitted with the application had been all the information reasonably available to the applicant, this does not imply that, in the circumstances of this particular case, the

---

[254] *United States - Measures affecting Imports of Softwood Lumber from Canada*, SCM/162, report adopted on 27 October 1993, BISD 40S, para. 335.

[255] *Ibid.*, para. 332. Although in the *United States - Softwood Lumber* case *ex officio* initiation of an investigation into countervailing duties was contested, *inter alia* because it was claimed that the evidence was insufficient to justify initiation, these aspects of the report are equally applicable to the initiation of anti-dumping investigations.

evidence was accurate or relevant to be able to conclude that there was sufficient evidence to justify initiation of the investigation within the meaning of Article 5.3.

6.97 Even if the information provided by Cementos Progreso in its application was deemed to be all the information reasonably available to it, which Mexico rejects, these two provisions (Article 5.2 and 5.3) cannot acceptably be interpreted to mean that Article 5.3 authorizes an investigating authority to initiate an anti-dumping investigation solely because an application meets the requirements of Article 5.2 of the AD Agreement (which were not even met in this case).[256]

6.98 In other words, even supposing - without agreeing - that the information needed to be able to determine that there was sufficient evidence was not reasonably available to the applicant, this does not mean that the lack of information in Cementos Progreso's application became the criterion for considering that there was sufficient evidence to justify initiation in accordance with Article 5.3 of the AD Agreement.

6.99 Moreover, as happened in this case, if an authority, prior to initiation, does not make any effort to obtain evidence other than the mere allegations and clearly insufficient evidence in the application (two delivery notes and two import certificates), it is obvious that the AD Agreement cannot authorize the initiation of an investigation on such bases. Even if it was all the information reasonably available to the applicant, an objective and unbiased examination would not allow it to be deemed sufficient to justify initiation. In fact, in its own application for initiation, Cementos Progreso requested the Ministry to collect certain information on the volume of imports that it was not in a position to obtain. The Ministry, however, only sought this information after the investigation had been initiated.

6.100 Taking into account the limited documentation submitted by Cementos Progreso in its application for initiation, as well as the fact that at no time prior to initiation did the Guatemalan authority request fuller information from Cementos Progreso or even try to obtain additional information or evidence by any other means in order to make good the deficiencies in the application, the Panel can see that the Ministry of the Economy did *not* conduct *the examination of the accuracy and adequacy of the evidence* required by Article 5.3 and therefore could not have satisfactorily established the objective *sufficiency* of *the evidence* to justify the initiation of an investigation.

6.101 Even though the recommendation of 17 November 1995 (which served as the basis for resolution 2-95 of 15 December 1995 by the Ministry's Director of Economic Integration) refers to an alleged analysis of the information submitted and appears to reach the conclusion that there was sufficient evidence of dumping and threat of injury to justify the initiation of the investigation, it is clear that neither in the determination on initiation of 9 January nor in the public notice of 11 January 1996 is there any indication whatsoever to show that the investigating authority did in fact examine the accuracy, adequacy, and above all sufficiency, of the evidence submitted by Cementos Progreso, as required by Article 5.3 of the AD Agreement.

6.102 In Mexico's opinion, the evidence submitted by Cementos Progreso in its application was far from being accurate or adequate. However, even if it were considered accurate or adequate, that would not mean that it was sufficient, and the decision to initiate an investigation must be taken in the light of the objective sufficiency of the evidence. The

[256] Compliance with the requirements of Article 5.2 does not *ipso facto* mean that there is sufficient evidence to justify initiating an investigation in accordance with Article 5.3. See *Guatemala - Cement, supra*, footnote 25, para. 7.51.

evidence cannot be accurate, adequate and, certainly not sufficient, simply because the investigating authority considers it to be so, as the Ministry did without any grounds.

6.103 An examination of the documentation prior to initiation to be found in the administrative file necessarily leads to the conclusion that an unbiased and objective investigating authority could not rightly have made the determination made by the Guatemalan Ministry of the Economy. Given the circumstances of this case, an unbiased and objective investigating authority could not rightly have determined that there was sufficient evidence of the three elements required by the AD Agreement to justify the initiation of an investigation.

6.104 Lastly, Mexico shares the view of the Panel in the case *United States - Softwood Lumber* to the effect that the quantum and quality of the evidence to be required at the time of initiation are less than the quantum and quality of the evidence required for a preliminary or final determination of dumping, injury or a causal link[257] requiring evidence of the same nature. In the present case it is obvious beyond any doubt that the information before the investigating authority was *not* in any way the *type* of evidence, nor of the quantum and quality required when initiating an investigation in order to determine the existence of dumping, threat of injury or a causal link, in accordance with the substantive provisions of the AD Agreement (i.e. Articles 2 and 3).[258]

6.105 To illustrate this, suffice it to take as an example in this particular case the two delivery notes used as the basis for calculating the alleged normal value and consequently to determine the existence of dumping. These delivery notes only mention the product as "grey cement" or "Cruz Azul cement", without specifying the type of cement, so they do not show whether this is a like product potentially the subject of the investigation (Type I PM grey Portland cement). This description only indicates that it is not white cement, but it does not specify whether it is grey Portland cement or whether or not it is pozzolanic cement.

6.106 Likewise, the Guatemalan authorities never ascertained the legitimacy or veracity of these documents which, as can be seen, are not proper invoices according to Mexican legislation but merely delivery notes issued by independent distributors that do not deal solely with Cruz Azul and may simply have falsified the entry "Cruz Azul cement" or have entered "grey cement" without it necessarily being from the firm Cruz Azul.

6.107 The fact that the Ministry did not satisfy itself as to the veracity or legitimacy of these documents nor ask Cementos Progreso for more evidence (other than the two delivery notes) nor obtain it on its own initiative shows that the Guatemalan authority did *not* examine the accuracy and adequacy of the necessarily limited evidence before it and on which it based its initiation decision. In the light of the foregoing, it is also obvious that the two delivery notes do not constitute accurate and adequate information either and are certainly not sufficient, neither in nature, quantum nor quality.

6.108 To summarize, Mexico contends that:

(i) The application by Cementos Progreso was accepted by the Ministry of the Economy in flagrant violation of Article 5.2 of the AD Agreement because the information it contained cannot be considered as the type of adequate evidence needed to prove dumping, the threat of injury and the

[257] *United States - Softwood Lumber*, para. 332.

[258] "... The subject matter, or **type**, of evidence needed to justify initiation is the same as that needed to make a preliminary or final determination of dumping, although the quality and quantity is less." *Guatemala - Anti-Dumping Investigation regarding Portland Cement from Mexico (Guatemala - Cement), supra*, footnote 25, *inter alia*, para. 7.67.

causal link, neither can the two import certificates be considered all the information reasonably available to the applicant;

(ii) in open violation of Article 5.3 of the AD Agreement, the Ministry based its initiation decision on insufficient evidence. An unbiased and objective investigating authority examining such evidence could not have properly determined that there was sufficient evidence of dumping, still less the existence of a threat of material injury, and a causal link between the imports allegedly dumped and the alleged threat of material injury to the Guatemalan domestic industry.

(ii) Evidence of Dumping

6.109 The Ministry of the Economy initiated the investigation in question only taking as adequate evidence of dumping copies of the two delivery notes to show the normal value, dated 25 and 26 August 1995, corresponding to the sale in Mexico of one load of cement each; and import certificates corresponding to two transactions for 7,035 and 4,221 sacks of cement dated 14 and 15 August 1995 as proof of the export price.[259]

6.110 These documents were submitted by Cementos Progreso in its application for the initiation of an investigation and in fact neither in the extension of the application nor in the file on the case is there any indication that the Ministry had any other information. Even the Panel which examined the case stated "There is no indication that any other information on dumping was available to or considered by the Ministry."[260]

6.111 Article 5.2 of the AD Agreement, however, provides that, for the purposes of complying with the requirements on initiation, simple assertion is *not* sufficient unless it is substantiated by relevant evidence. An application must therefore contain the information reasonably available to the applicant in relation to subparagraphs (i) to (iv) of this Article.

6.112 Although it is true that there is no minimum or maximum amount of documentation that must be submitted in order to prove dumping, this does not mean that any documentation suffices to justify the initiation of an investigation in a particular case. Article 5.2 prescribes that an application must include relevant evidence of dumping and Article 5.3 makes it necessary to determine whether there is sufficient evidence to justify the initiation of an investigation.

6.113 As we have already stated, when considering whether there is sufficient evidence of dumping to justify the initiation of an investigation, an investigating authority *cannot* disregard the provisions of Article 2 of the AD Agreement because this is the provision that expressly refers to dumping and applies both to the initiation of an investigation and to the determination of a provisional or definitive measure. The nature or type of evidence required to justify initiation are the same as the nature or type of evidence required to make a preliminary or final determination of dumping, although the quality and quantity may be less for initiation.

6.114 As we have also mentioned, Article 2 establishes the technical elements for calculating the dumping margin, determining the normal value and the export price, as well as the adjustments required for a fair comparison. In this particular case, Article 2.4 of the AD Agreement is especially relevant:

---

[259] Import certificates together with their corresponding invoices and bills of lading.

[260] *Guatemala - Cement*, *supra*, footnote 25, para. 7.61.

"A fair comparison shall be made between the export price and the normal value. This comparison shall be made at the same level of trade, normally at the ex-factory level, and in respect of sales made at as nearly as possible the same time. Due allowance shall be made in each case, on its merits, for differences which affect price comparability, including differences in conditions and terms of sale, taxation, levels of trade, quantities, physical characteristics, and any other differences which are also demonstrated to affect price comparability." (The footnote has been omitted.)

6.115 In this particular case, it can be clearly seen that the Ministry failed to make a fair comparison between the normal value and the export price for the following reasons:

(a) The transactions that were the subject of comparison were at different volumes and levels of trade, so it is obvious that the prices used to establish the normal value were retail prices to the public, whereas the export prices were the manufacturer's prices to the distributor;

(b) the conditions of sale for these transactions were under different circumstances because the information contained in the delivery notes used to prove the normal value referred to the price of 50 kg. bags of cement, whereas the import certificates used to prove the export price showed the price of 42.5 kg. bags of cement;

(c) the dollar-peso exchange rate claimed by Cementos Progreso was *not* documented and was solely based on an affirmation by the applicant without any substantiation whatsoever, i.e. there was no proof.

6.116 Regarding the above, the Panel which previously examined the *Guatemala - Cement* case,[261] when considering the differences noted in the documentation submitted to prove the normal value and the export price, particularly the volumes of the product investigated and the levels of trade, concluded:

"7.62. The two invoices reflect two separate sales at the retail level of one sack of cement of unspecified weight each. The import documents reflect two separate import transactions at the distributor (or wholesale) level of several thousand sacks of cement, each sack weighing 94 pounds (42.6 kilograms). The alleged margin of dumping is calculated in the application by comparing the average retail price for the cement bought in Mexico (converted into Guatemalan Quetzales at then current rates) with the average c.i.f. value of the cement imported into Guatemala (converted into Guatemalan Quetzales at then current rates). The Ministry recommended initiation based on this information. *In our view, this comparison ignores obvious problems with the data: (1) the transactions involve significantly different volumes; and (2) the transactions occurred at different levels of trade*." (emphasis added).

6.117 Thus, the prices shown on the delivery notes used to prove the normal value and those in the documentation used to show the export price, are *not* comparable according to Article 2.1 and 2.4. The analysis must take due account of the differences affecting the comparability of the prices shown on each and to do otherwise would be a serious violation of Article 2 of the AD Agreement.

6.118 In its letter of 26 July 1996, the Ministry acknowledged that it had *not* made adjustments to the prices shown on the alleged invoices nor on the import certificates in

---

[261] *Guatemala - Cement, supra*, footnote 25, para. 7.62.

order to place them on a comparable level, stating that it was the responsibility of the exporting firm to prove that there was no dumping:

> "With respect to the points on which you sought clarification as to the criteria used by the investigating authority to determine the existence of dumping and the threat of injury to the domestic industry, please be informed that the Department of Economic Integration of the Ministry of the Economy of Guatemala considered the evidence submitted showing differences between the prices of cement being sold on Mexican territory and that being sold in our country to be sufficient. *It was not possible to make any adjustments at the date when the initial resolution was published, as these are made on the basis of information supplied by the exporting company, which is concerned to demonstrate that the alleged dumping does not exist.*"[262] (emphasis added).

6.119 It is important to point out that this shows a total lack of understanding of and compliance with the AD Agreement as the latter does not provide that exporters are responsible for proving that there is no dumping. They obviously have the right to defend their interests in this regard. The Agreement does, however, make the applicant responsible for providing adequate evidence of dumping and the investigating authority responsible for *not* accepting an application when this evidence is lacking and not initiating an investigation when there is not sufficient evidence.

6.120 At the least, the Ministry should have recognized that such adjustments were needed in order to make a fair comparison. Concerning the failure to make the necessary adjustment to allow a fair comparison according to Article 2.4, the Panel which previously considered this matter stated:

> "...In our view, this provision" (Article 2.4 of the AD Agreement) "establishes an obligation for investigating authorities to make a fair comparison. Investigating authorities can certainly expect that exporters will provide the information necessary to make adjustments and demonstrate that particular differences for which adjustments are sought affect price comparability. However, *the authorities cannot, in our view, ignore the question of a fair comparison in determining whether there is sufficient evidence of dumping to justify initiation, particularly when the need for adjustments is apparent on the face of the application ...*".[263] (emphasis added).

6.121 The above shows that the evidence submitted together with the application was *not* sufficient to justify initiation of the investigation. It was initiated on the basis of two delivery notes/invoices for one load of cement each (to determine the normal value) and import certificates for two transactions (to determine the export price) without any relevant evidence as to the total volume of imports and the trend in imports allegedly dumped or other factors relevant to initiation.

6.122 The Ministry thus determined the normal value of the product investigated using solely the average of the retail selling price shown on the alleged invoices attached to the application, without making a fair comparison with the export price and duly taking ac-

[262] Letter of 26 July 1996 from Ms. Edith Flores de Molina, Ministry of the Economy of Guatemala, sent to Mr. Eduardo Solis, Secretary for Trade and Industrial Development of Mexico.

[263] *Guatemala - Cement*, *supra*, footnote 25, para. 7.65.

count of the different levels of trade, quantities and exchange rate, thereby violating Article 2.4 of the AD Agreement.[264]

6.123 Likewise, information on the evolution of the total volume of imports allegedly dumped was *not* supplied in the application, in violation of Article 5.2(iv) of the AD Agreement, and it *cannot* simply be claimed that this information was *not* reasonably available to the applicant for the purposes of initiating the investigation because, based on an unbiased and objective assessment of the information in its possession, the Ministry could *not* rightly have determined that there was sufficient evidence of dumping to justify the initiation of an investigation. This was acknowledged by the Ministry when, after initiating the investigation, it requested the Directorate General of Customs to supply information on the volume of imports, which could have been done by the applicant or the Ministry during the months prior to initiation of the investigation (11 January 1996) or after receiving the application for initiation (21 September 1995).

6.124 In addition, the fact that the authority simply assumed that the application contained all the information reasonably available to the applicant is *not* sufficient to obviate the fact that the applicant did *not* submit relevant evidence regarding the normal value, the export price nor the evolution in imports, thus violating Article 5.2, and that the Ministry, disregarding Article 2 of the AD Agreement, did *not* take into account the necessary adjustments in order to make a fair comparison between the normal value and the export price. In other words, lack of information in an application *cannot* become the standard for compliance with sufficiency of evidence on the premise of "information reasonably available to the applicant".

6.125 The Panel which considered the Guatemala - Cement case[265] concluded that the Ministry committed a number of violations of the AD Agreement in the following terms:

> "7.66. In this case it is apparent on the face of the application that the alleged normal value and the alleged export price are not comparable for purposes of considering whether dumping exists without adjustment. The recommendation to the Director of the Department of Economic Integration reflects this lack of comparability when it states that the normal value is the average price 'to the final consumer' and the export price is the average of 'the c.i.f. values'. However, there is no recognition of the need for any adjustments in either the recommendation or the notice of initiation. While we would not expect the authorities to have, at the initiation stage, precise information on the adjustments to be made, we find it particularly troubling that there is not even any recognition that the normal value and export price alleged in the application are not comparable, nor any indication that more information on this issue was requested from the applicant or otherwise sought by the Ministry. When, as in this case, it is evident from the information before the investigating authority that some form of adjustment will be required to make a fair comparison and establish a dumping margin, an unbiased and objective investigating authority could not, in our view, properly determine that there was sufficient evidence of dumping to justify initiation in the absence of such adjustment, or at least

---

264 All these differences necessarily increase the dumping margin artificially: indeed different volumes are compared since the normal value concerns 50 kg. of cement and the export price transactions for 4,000 to 7,000 sacks.

265 *Guatemala - Cement, supra*, footnote 25, para. 7.66.

> without acknowledging the need for such adjustment." (The footnote has been omitted.) (emphasis added).

6.126 In addition, under Article 5.3 of the AD Agreement, the documents submitted by the applicant cannot be considered as *accurate and adequate evidence* to prove the normal value nor the export price.

6.127 Firstly, with regard to the alleged invoices showing the normal value:

6.128 Neither of the two alleged invoices mentions the type of cement so the Ministry could *not* be sure whether it was a like product to that being investigated, according to the terms of Article 2.1 and 2.6 of the AD Agreement, or the content of the loads of cement (a fact that is particularly relevant in this case as 50 kg. bags are sold in Mexico and 42.5 kg. bags in Guatemala, and was curiously omitted by the applicant).

6.129 Consequently, the Ministry could *not* be certain that the product covered by the two alleged invoices was in fact the product investigated and not another more expensive product. It is *not* sufficient for the purposes of accuracy and adequacy to argue that all types of grey Portland cement, with or without pozzolana or modified pozzolana, come under tariff heading 2523.29.00 of the Central American Tariff System when, on the one hand, the product investigated is identified on the basis of declarations by the applicant and the examination of the likeness of products to be undertaken by the investigating authority according to Article 2.1 and 2.6 of the AD Agreement and, on the other, where applicable, physical and chemical differences among products result in different prices irrespective of the tariff classification.

6.130 Regarding price differences for the products, it is *not* enough to argue that this information was *not* reasonably available to the applicant because the various types of cement are *not* mentioned in the delivery notes for the cement sold in Mexico.

6.131 In fact, the Ministry did *not* in fact ask Cementos Progreso for, or collect or try in any way to obtain, further information on the type of product sold, whether it was a like product, the prices of the product sold in Mexico or the export price. This shows that the Guatemalan investigating authority did *not* undertake the examination of the accuracy and adequacy of the evidence required by Article 5.3 and incorrectly determined that there was sufficient evidence to initiate an investigation, thereby violating Article 5.2 of the AD Agreement.

6.132 In the application for initiation of an investigation submitted on 21 September 1995, the following is indicated under point X entitled "Characteristics of the product subject to unfair trade practices":

> "Cement is a product which uses clinker as a raw material (mixture of natural minerals with hydraulic properties). Five per cent gypsum (hydrated calcium sulphate, burned, milled and mixed with water) is added to the clinker, together with *10 to 15 per cent of pozzolanic material (volcanic rock)*. It is then pulverized and thoroughly mixed in special mills. The result is a powder called PORTLAND CEMENT". (emphasis added).

6.133 The documents submitted to prove the export price are two import certificates (with the corresponding invoices and two bills of lading). One of the *certificates* identifies the product as "*grey Portland cement*, tariff heading 2523.29.00". The other mentions "*Type II grey Portland cement with pozzolana*, tariff heading 2523.29.00". The two invoices from Cruz Azul define the product as "Type II grey Portland cement with pozzolana". The two bills of lading identify the product as "grey Portland cement".

6.134 In Section II entitled "GENERAL INFORMATION" of the extension of the application for initiation of an investigation of 9 October 1995, the following appears:

> "Detailed description of the domestic product

The domestic product is grey Portland cement, which is packaged in 42.5-kilogramme sacks, the equivalent of 94 pounds. The commercial name is grey Portland cement, Cementos Progreso brand, and it is intended for use in the construction industry.

Detailed description of the imported item

The imported item is grey Portland or pozzolanic cement, in 94-pound bags, under the brand name La Cruz Azul, and is intended for use in construction".

6.135 In Section IV of the extension application entitled "FEATURES OF THE DOMESTIC INDUSTRY", the following appears:

"... to produce clinker - a raw material used in the production of Portland cement - a mixture of natural ores is processed to yield an intimate mixture of artificial ores with hydraulic properties ... Once the new material is obtained, i.e. the raw material clinker, it is combined with 5 per cent gypsum (hydrated calcium sulphate, burned, milled and mixed with water) and *10 to 15 per cent pozzolanic material (volcanic rock)* and the mixture is pulverized and mixed thoroughly in special mills. The mixture of clinker, gypsum and pozzolana produces a powder called Portland cement." (emphasis added).

6.136 The above clearly highlights differences in identifying the product investigated and, for the reasons already explained, shows *the failure to examine both whether they were like products*,[266] and the price difference, which must be taken into account where applicable, as well as the failure to examine the accuracy and adequacy of the evidence prescribed by Article 5.3 of the AD Agreement.

6.137 Furthermore, on the basis of the type of evidence submitted by the applicant, it was not possible for the Ministry to satisfy itself as to the amount of the product sold because 50 kg. sacks are sold in Mexico and 42.5 kg. sacks in Guatemala, a circumstance that was curiously omitted by Cementos Progreso yet is of vital importance for a fair comparison between the normal value and the export price, thus showing once again the failure to undertake the examination of the accuracy and adequacy of the evidence required by Article 5.3.

6.138 As mentioned above, the Ministry did *not* seek from the applicant, nor collect nor in any way try to obtain more information on the volume of the product sold in Mexico for the purposes of comparison with that sold in Guatemala.

6.139 Moreover, concerning the representative nature of the transactions, the following should be noted:

(a) The operations shown on each of the alleged invoices could not be considered as representative because they only cover one load of cement each and both occurred on two days (25 and 26) of one of the months (August) of the investigation period 1 June to 30 November 1995;

[266] The failure to examine whether they were like products before initiating the investigation results in equivocal and contradictory determinations. Firstly, with respect to the initiation of the investigation, where the product being investigated is not clearly identified. Secondly, the provisional measure imposing provisional anti-dumping duties on imports of Type I (PM) grey Portland cement. Thirdly, the definitive measure imposing definitive anti-dumping duties on imports of grey Portland cement without any distinction.

(b) comparing one tenth of a tonne with the total sales of the domestic producer in the Mexican market during the period investigated (six months) *cannot* be considered a fair, unbiased, objective and reasonable comparison;

(c) the price shown on the alleged invoices for sales of cement in Mexico *cannot* be considered as representative for the purposes of determining the normal value because, even if they refer to commercial transactions that supposedly took place, the sales only reflect an insignificant share of Cruz Azul's operations on the Mexican market.

6.140 Secondly, as far as determination of the export price is concerned, the documentation submitted by Cementos Progreso cannot be considered accurate and adequate evidence either because:

(a) It cannot be assumed that two transactions for 299 and 179 tonnes each (7,035 and 4,221 bags weighing 42.5 kg.) respectively are representative of a market which, at the beginning of the investigation period, was estimated to be around 95,000 tonnes per month; and

(b) both transactions occurred over only two days (14 and 15) of one of the six months of the investigation period (August).

6.141 In addition, the documentation submitted by the applicant does *not* adequately identify the product concerned, particularly since it is variously described as grey cement, grey Portland cement or Type II grey Portland cement with pozzolana. As we have already mentioned, this information is particularly important in order to allow the Ministry to analyse properly whether they are like products.

6.142 From the foregoing, it can be seen that the Ministry of the Economy did *not* meet the standard laid down in Article 5.3 of the AD Agreement by examining the accuracy and adequacy of the evidence provided in the application and making an unbiased and objective evaluation of whether there was sufficient evidence to justify the initiation of an investigation according to Article 5.2 of the AD Agreement.

6.143 To summarize, the Ministry of the Economy violated Articles 2.1, 2.4, 5.2, 5.3 and 5.8 of the AD Agreement by initiating an investigation after accepting as accurate and adequate evidence of dumping the two delivery notes and the import certificates relating to two transactions, failing to make a proper analysis and a fair comparison and determining that the documentation submitted was sufficient to justify the initiation of an investigation.

6.144 Lastly, the Panel which previously examined this matter, when referring to the Ministry's action with regard to the information in its possession and the determination of the alleged dumping, concluded the following:

6.145 "7.67 ... while there is clearly a different standard applicable to making a preliminary or final **determination** of dumping, than to determining whether there is sufficient evidence of dumping to justify initiation of an investigation, *we cannot agree with Guatemala's position that Article 2 is irrelevant to the initiation determination.* The subject matter, or **type**, of evidence needed to justify initiation is the same as that needed to make a preliminary or final determination of dumping, although the quality and quantity is less. Thus, *in our view, based on an unbiased and objective evaluation of the evidence and information before it in this case, the Ministry could not properly have determined that* *there was sufficient evidence of dumping to justify the initiation of the investigation.*"[267] (emphasis added).

(iii) Evidence of Threat of Injury

6.146 The Ministry of the Economy initiated the anti-dumping investigation apparently taking as evidence of the threat of material injury two import certificates, although under no permissible interpretation of the AD Agreement can these be considered adequate evidence to prove a threat of material injury and still less sufficient to justify the initiation of an investigation.

6.147 In Cementos Progreso's application, the only information transmitted to the Ministry was the documentation concerning two transactions (certificates) for the import of grey Portland cement into Guatemala through the customs post at Tecún Umán, Department of San Marcos, both on 15 August 1995, through which it is apparently sought to show the volume of imports allegedly dumped.[268]

6.148 As already mentioned, on 9 October 1995, the applicant presented a new submission extending its original application ("extended application"). Despite the submission of a new application, it did not include in this extended application any more evidence to substantiate the alleged threat of injury. In fact, the extended application merely claimed that:

- Cementos Progreso was being threatened by "massive" imports of cement from Mexico and sought to substantiate the word "massive" with two photocopies of the same import certificates attached to the original application[269] and a declaration on its *suspicions* "that similar imports are also taking place through the customs posts of El Carmen, Department of San Marcos, and La Mesilla, Department of Huehuetenango".[270] (emphasis added).
- cement was entering Guatemala by land allegedly at prices lower than normal value and directly affecting investment by Cementos Progreso.

6.149 Consequently, the only additional information in the extended application regarding the threat of material injury consisted of the following claim:

> "Cementos Progreso, S.A. is being threatened by massive imports of cement from Mexico. By way of evidence, the initial complaint contained two photocopies of import certificates showing imports at prices below the normal retail price in Mexico, and which therefore threatened the company with imminent material injury, as set out below:
>
> - Cement entering Guatemala by land at prices lower than normal value is directly affecting investment planning by the company, specifically for plant improvements and expansion, which would entail:
>   - Expanding raw material milling facilities at the plant itself;
>   - maximizing the efficiency of the plant;

[267] *Guatemala - Cement, supra*, footnote 25, para. 7.67.

[268] The import certificates covered total sales of 480 metric tonnes of cement.

[269] Covering the import of 7,035 and 4,221 sacks of cement respectively.

[270] See Cemento Progreso's extended application, section entitled *Customs posts or posts via which the goods are imported into Guatemala.*

- building a third kiln at the San Miguel Sanarate plant;
- restructuring the existing electricity system by converting the plant that presently runs on bunker;
- the foregoing expansions would call for at least an additional 400 workers, who would no longer be needed if the projects were stopped;
- rather than invest in cement at below-cost prices, the company would prefer to cease production and become an importer;
- loss of market shares;
- were the company to become an importer, it would be compelled to dismiss 1,052 workers, with all the attendant social problems;
- the plant would lose its expertise or what is referred to as technology transfer."

6.150 The foregoing claims are not substantiated by any relevant evidence, as found by the Panel which previously considered this matter:

> "7.71 ... '*Sufficient evidence to justify initiation*' must, in our view, mean something whose 'accuracy and adequacy' can be objectively evaluated as required by Article 5.3 of the AD Agreement. *Mere statements do not fall into this category of information.* Moreover, *there is no indication as to what evaluation was made of the 'accuracy and adequacy' of these statements.*"[271] (emphasis added).

6.151 As may be noted, like the original, the extended application failed to provide information on the factors referred to in Article 3.2 and 3.4 of the AD Agreement, which are specifically mentioned in Article 5.2(iv). We shall refer to this omission below. Taken together with the fact that, as we have already stated, none of these claims was substantiated by relevant information or evidence in the application, there is a more serious issue, namely, in order to initiate the investigation, the Guatemalan investigating authority did *not* have more evidence or information than that simply to be found in the application.

6.152 Neither in the documentation prior to initiation to be found in the administrative file (the recommendation of 17 November, resolution 2-95 of 15 December and the initiation decision of 9 January) nor in the public notice of initiation is there evidence to indicate that, in deciding or initiating the investigation, the Ministry of the Economy had sought to obtain more information or evidence to substantiate the claims made in the original and extended applications from Cementos Progreso.

6.153 Below we explain to the Panel some of the reasons why the Guatemalan authorities failed to comply with the AD Agreement when it initiated the investigation.

6.154 Firstly, regarding the *allegedly "massive" nature of the imports*, the following remarks must be made:

(a) As we have already mentioned, the only information *both in the application and the investigating authority's administrative file* regarding the volume of imports was the two import certificates and the claims concerning the "suspicion" of possible imports through other customs posts;

---

[271] *Guatemala - Cement*, *supra*, footnote 25, para. 7.71.

(b) in this regard, it must be pointed out that, in its extended application of 9 October, Cementos Progreso stated that it denounced a "*threat of injury*, as thus far, it has not been able to prove the huge volume of the product entering the country daily";[272] it asked the Ministry of the Economy *inter alia* to request "from the customs authorities the import certificates for the last year, so as to ascertain the quantities of grey cement imports", which it claimed had caused "*material injury* to the domestic industry and to the national economy".[273]

(c) despite Cementos Progreso's request in its extended application of 9 October, the Ministry only sought information on imports from the Directorate General of Customs *after having initiated the investigation*, which highlights facts that constitute very serious violations of the AD Agreement:

- firstly: neither when accepting the application, when deciding to initiate an investigation, nor when publishing the notice of initiation, did the investigating authority possess information on the level of imports for any date other than 15 August 1995 (date of the two import transactions); nor did it have information on possible imports of grey Portland cement that might have come from other origins or sources than the firm Cruz Azul;
- secondly: neither in the Ministry's administrative file, nor in the public notice of initiation is there any indication either that, when deciding to initiate an investigation, the investigating authority knew or even tried to calculate or compare the volume of imports (represented by the two import certificates) with consumption in Guatemala, nor that it attempted, according to any criterion (e.g. production), to determine the allegedly "massive" nature of the imports. On the contrary, everything seems to indicate that the Guatemalan authorities simply accepted the claim made in the application in this respect.

6.155 This shows that the Ministry of the Economy did *not* have, nor obtain nor seek information that was essential to justify initiation according to Article 5.3 of the AD Agreement.

(d) Without the minimum relevant information on any increase in the volume of imports of grey Portland cement, *in absolute terms or relative to production or consumption in Guatemala*[274], it might be asked how the applicant could affirm that these were massive or had caused "material injury" or "threat of injury"? But above all, how could the investigating authority justify initiation on the basis of sufficient evidence regarding the threat of injury if, at the time of initiation, it only had the two import certificates and the mere suspicions or allegations on the part of Cementos Progreso referred to in the application, which do not constitute any valid grounds for qualifying the volume of imports as "massive"?

---

272 Para. 3 in the *Legal framework* section of Cementos Progreso's extended application.

273 Subparagraph (e) in the In regard to substance part of the I REQUEST section of Cementos Progreso's extended application.

274 As required by Article 3.2 of the AD Agreement.

(e) moreover, there is no evidence to show that, when taking the decision to initiate an investigation, the Ministry had conducted an analysis of the level and trend in imports for the period investigated (June-November 1995) relative to the level and trend in imports for a previous comparable period (June-November 1994). Indeed, there is no indication that the authority considered or even possessed information on the volume of imports prior to June 1995. Without such a comparative analysis, the authority could not simply assume that any increase in imports was massive.

6.156 To summarize, neither in the application nor in the investigating authority's administrative file is there any other evidence or even information to allow a determination that imports of grey Portland cement from Cruz Azul were "massive". It is obvious that the two import certificates on which the Ministry of the Economy based its decision to initiate an investigation cannot, from any standpoint, constitute "sufficient evidence" within the meaning of Article 5.3 of the AD Agreement in order to prove the allegedly "massive" nature of the imports, still less to initiate an investigation on the basis that the imports *ipso facto* threatened to cause material injury to the Guatemalan domestic industry.

6.157 Another essential factor which the Guatemalan authority failed to analyse when taking the initiation decision concerns the *effect of the imports on prices*. As we have already stated, Article 3.2 of the AD Agreement refers to Article 5.2(iv) and stipulates that the application for initiation shall include information on whether there has been significant price undercutting by the dumped imports or whether the effect of such imports has been otherwise to depress prices to a significant degree or prevent price increases which otherwise would have occurred.

6.158 The information contained in Cementos Progreso's application on the price of Mexican cement in Guatemala (c.i.f. price of Q14.77 according to the two import certificates provided) and on the price of Guatemalan cement (average retail price of Q24 in the capital and Q32 in the Department of El Petén), does not in any way make it possible to determine the effect of the dumped imports on prices because it is obvious that these prices are *not* comparable. The prices in the import certificates were c.i.f. prices applicable to independent distributors and consequently they cannot be properly compared with the retail price of Guatemalan cement because the difference in the level of trade has a significant effect on prices and their comparison.

6.159 Furthermore, an analysis of the share of imports in the Guatemalan market and their impact on prices was essential in this case, particularly in view of Cementos Progreso's monopolistic position on the Guatemalan market.

6.160 In addition, as we have stated, the claim that there was a threat of material injury was not substantiated either by relevant evidence regarding the *economic factors and indices having a bearing on the state of the industry* listed in Article 3.4 (and mentioned in Article 5.2(iv) of the AD Agreement): for example, actual and potential decline in sales, profits, output, market share, productivity, return on investments, or utilization of capacity; factors affecting domestic prices; the magnitude of the margin of dumping; actual and potential negative effects on cash flow, inventories, employment, wages, growth, ability to raise capital or investment.

6.161 Although it could be argued that the application for initiation contained allegations regarding some of these factors[275] (for example, where it is claimed that the expan-

[275] See above where the declarations in the application are cited.

sion plans would require the recruitment of 400 new workers and that, if production stopped completely, 1,052 workers would be dismissed), it is more than obvious that, contrary to the terms of the AD Agreement, the (original and extended) application submitted to the Ministry of the Economy did *not* contain relevant evidence on these factors, which involve specific and quantifiable information that is generally reasonably available to the applicant.[276]

6.162 Moreover, in the case of an industry such as cement and taking particular account of Cementos Progreso's monopoly in the Guatemalan market, it was quite reasonable for the firm to have available specific and quantifiable data and information on levels of sales, profits and employment *inter alia*, as well as on its ability to finance investment or expansion plans, and to include these in its application to the Ministry.

6.163 Likewise, Cementos Progreso's statements to the effect that, if the imported product allegedly dumped continued to be sold on the Guatemalan market, this would directly affect its investment plans (expansion and modernization of the production infrastructure) were *not* accompanied by any information regarding its ability to raise capital or finance its investment in some other way, information which should quite logically be reasonably available to the applicant.

6.164 To summarize, the statements contained in Cementos Progreso's application regarding the existence of a threat of material injury were not substantiated either by evidence on the relevant economic factors and indices having a bearing on the state of the industry listed in Article 3.4 and still less by the accurate and adequate evidence required by the AD Agreement. Moreover, *no permissible interpretation* of the AD Agreement allows these simple declarations, unaccompanied by relevant evidence to substantiate them and without the authority examining or seeking to ensure their accuracy or adequacy, to be enough to meet the standard of "sufficient evidence" of threat of material injury for the purposes of initiation. We shall go into greater detail concerning this standard below.

6.165 Before continuing, however, it is also necessary to explain that, in obvious violation of Article 5.2 of the AD Agreement, Cementos Progreso's initiation application failed to provide information and evidence on the factors listed in Article 3.7, which is particularly serious when a threat of material injury is alleged in a case.

6.166 In Mexico's opinion, no permissible interpretation of the AD Agreement can allow the argument that the factors listed in Article 3.7 do not have to be considered when deciding to initiate an investigation, for the following reasons.

6.167 Firstly, the provisions of the AD Agreement itself must be taken into account, and Article 5.2 states the following:

> An application under paragraph 1 shall include evidence of [...] *(b) injury within the meaning of Article VI of GATT 1994 as interpreted by this Agreement* [...]." (emphasis added).

6.168 The concept of "injury within the meaning of Article VI of GATT 1994" as interpreted by the AD Agreement is in turn defined in footnote 9 to Article 3 of the AD Agreement as follows:

---

[276] Even where such business information is of a confidential nature, this does not justify the fact that Cementos Progreso's application did not contain the specific information that was relevant to prove its claims regarding the threat of material injury, as not only the AD Agreement but also Central American legislation applicable in Guatemala establishes mechanisms to guarantee the confidential nature of information where this is justified.

> "Under this Agreement the term 'injury' shall, unless otherwise specified, be taken to mean *material injury* to a domestic industry, *threat of material injury* to a domestic industry or *material retardation* of the establishment of such an industry and shall be interpreted in accordance with the provisions of this Article." (emphasis added).

6.169 Thus, this footnote makes it clear that the provisions of Article 5.2 referring to the concept of "injury" should be interpreted as meaning a "threat of material injury" when it is a case of threat of injury. Article 5.2(iv) of the AD Agreement specifies that the application to initiate an investigation must also contain information on the four factors listed in Article 3.7 when a threat of material injury is claimed.

6.170 Secondly, in this regard the Panel which previously examined this matter concluded the following:

> "7.75 ... We recognize that there is no specific reference in Article 5.2 to the factors enumerated in Article 3.7 regarding threat of injury, such as there is to the factors set forth in Articles 3.2 and 3.4 regarding injury. However, we do not accept the view that the lack of a specific reference to Article 3.7 means that an applicant is not required to submit 'such information as is reasonably available to the applicant' on the question of threat of material injury, if threat of material injury is alleged in the application. Such an interpretation of the Agreement would, in our view, be entirely impermissible, as it would be inconsistent with the text, as well as the object and purpose of Article 5.2 as a whole."

6.171 The Panel confirmed the conclusion of the Panel in the *United States - Softwood Lumber* case to the effect that "the subject matter, or **type**, of evidence needed to justify initiation is the same as that needed to make a preliminary or final determination of threat of injury, although the quality and quantity is less."[277]

6.172 Consequently, in the light of the decisions by various Panels in this regard, the applicability of Article 3.7 of the AD Agreement to a decision to initiate an investigation when threat of material injury is alleged is indisputable.

6.173 In this case, therefore, when Cementos Progreso claimed threat of injury, its application for initiation should obviously have contained evidence of a threat of material injury according to the factors set out in Article 3.7 of the AD Agreement. In other words, for the Ministry to accept an application for initiation alleging threat of injury, Cementos Progreso should also have furnished evidence to demonstrate the significant rate of increase in imports, the exporter's freely disposable capacity or its imminent and substantial increase, the effect of the exports on domestic prices on the Guatemalan market and inventories of the product investigated.

6.174 The Panel in this case, however, can see that the evidence submitted in no way shows a significant rate of increase of imports, the freely disposable capacity of the exporter, an imminent, substantial increase in capacity, or the effect of Mexican imports on prices, *inter alia*. Indeed, there is no reference to surplus capacity in Mexico nor to the likelihood of increased imports in the application for initiation, nor in the recommendation by the two advisers from the Department of Economic Integration, nor in the decision to initiate an investigation.

---

[277] *Guatemala - Anti-Dumping Investigation regarding Portland Cement from Mexico (Guatemala - Cement), supra*, footnote 25, *inter alia* para. 7.77 in connection with *United States - Measures Affecting Imports of Softwood Lumber from Canada (United States - Softwood Lumber)*, Report adopted on 27 October 1993, para. 332.

6.175 It is therefore clear that Cementos Progreso failed to provide relevant evidence and that the investigating authority in turn did *not* have sufficient evidence to allow it to establish the threat of material injury alleged by the applicant. It is also obvious that, with the limited and insufficient information contained in the only two items of evidence submitted by the applicant (the two import certificates), it was impossible for the Ministry of the Economy to conduct a proper analysis of the adequacy of the evidence in accordance with Article 5.3 of the AD Agreement in relation to any of the factors enumerated in Article 3.7 in order to decide whether to initiate an investigation. Without information on these factors, an unbiased and objective investigating authority simply cannot properly determine whether there is sufficient evidence of threat of material injury to justify initiation of an investigation if a threat of material injury is alleged.[278]

6.176 The foregoing clearly leads to the conclusion that:

(a) The only information before the Ministry of the Economy when the investigation was initiated to prove the alleged threat of injury claimed by Cementos Progreso was two import certificates and a number of suspicions and allegations not substantiated by adequate evidence; these could not be considered the accurate and adequate evidence required by Article 5.2 and 5.3 of the AD Agreement in order to prove threat of injury according to Article 3. Moreover, no permissible interpretation of the AD Agreement could allow these to be considered as meeting the standard of sufficiency required by Article 5.3 in order to justify initiation.

(b) the applicant - and the investigating authority which accepted an application that was obviously not consistent with the AD Agreement - failed to respect the concepts of injury and threat of injury defined in Article 3, and the provisions of Article 5, whose purpose is "to ensure that certain conditions be met before the initiation was decided upon"[279], for example: *(i)* the application to initiate an investigation must contain evidence of the injury or threat of injury, as well as the information reasonably available to the applicant on a number of factors, in this case those enumerated in subparagraph (iv) of Article 5.2 of the AD Agreement; and *(ii)* a decision to initiate an investigation into threat of material injury must be based on facts and not on simple allegations, conjectures or remote possibilities, and these must be established on the basis of the objective sufficiency of the evidence in accordance with Article 5.3 of the AD Agreement.

6.177 On the basis of an unbiased and objective evaluation, the Guatemalan investigating authority could not properly have determined that the alleged evidence and allegations of threat of injury submitted to the Ministry by Cementos Progreso were sufficient to justify the initiation of an investigation within the meaning of Article 5.3 of the AD Agreement. This was indeed the conclusion of the Panel which previously examined this matter.[280]

---

[278] This was indeed the conclusion of the Panel which previously considered the matter. See *Guatemala - Cement, supra*, footnote 25, para. 7.77.

[279] This was the conclusion of the Panel which considered the case of *United States - Anti-Dumping Duties on Gray Portland Cement and Cement Clinker from Mexico* (*United States - Gray Portland Cement and Clinker*), ADP/82, Report of the Panel, published on 7 September 1992, not adopted, para. 5.37.

[280] See *Guatemala - Cement, supra*, footnote 25, para. 7.70.

6.178 Lastly, it is also necessary to mention another matter of particular importance which shows that, at the time of initiating the investigation, the Guatemalan investigating authority did *not* have sufficient evidence of a threat of material injury. On 22 January 1996 (11 days after publication of the notice of initiation), the Ministry of the Economy itself ordered that Cementos Progreso be sent the "Form for producers applying for the initiation of an investigation into discriminatory pricing practices", through which it requested information on the production process and technical standards, production, sales, customers, profits, cost structure, plant capacity, labour force, domestic price trends, imports, accounting statements, and matters relating to threat of injury and a causal link. This information was submitted by Cementos Progreso on 17 May 1996, in other words, eight months after the submission of its original application and four months after the initiation of the investigation.

6.179 The above must certainly lead the Panel to the conclusion that the Guatemalan Ministry of the Economy failed to act in compliance with the AD Agreement, in particular Article 5.2, 5.3, 5.7 and 5.8 (as will be seen below), or the substantive provisions in Article 3.1, 3.2, 3.4, 3.5 and 3.7.

(a) By accepting an application based on simple allegations which blatantly lacked or omitted relevant evidence to substantiate the allegations, instead of rejecting it;

(b) by failing to examine the accuracy and adequacy of the information and allegations by Cementos Progreso;

(c) by initiating an investigation, basing its decision on two import certificates and simple allegations, conjectures and remote possibilities of the alleged threat of injury, which do not constitute adequate and sufficient evidence thereof.

6.180 No permissible interpretation of the AD Agreement can in this case lead to the conclusion that the Ministry of the Economy acted properly in determining that there was sufficient evidence of threat of material injury to justify the initiation of the investigation.

(iv) Evidence of causal link

6.181 The relevant section of Article 5.2 of the AD Agreement states the following:

> "*An application* under paragraph 1 *shall include evidence of (a)* dumping, *(b)* injury within the meaning of Article VI of GATT 1994 as interpreted by this Agreement and *(c) a causal relationship between the dumped imports and the alleged injury*." (emphasis added).

6.182 In this context, it is also important to cite once again Article 5.3 of the AD Agreement:

> "The *authorities shall examine* the accuracy and adequacy of *the evidence provided in the application* to determine whether there is *sufficient evidence* to justify the initiation of an investigation." (emphasis added).

6.183 Reading these Articles shows that any application for initiation must contain, and any investigation must be initiated on the basis of, evidence not only of dumping and injury but also of a third element required by the AD Agreement, namely, *a causal link between the dumped imports and the injury*, within the meaning of Article 3.5 of the AD Agreement.

6.184 In the present case, the Ministry initiated the anti-dumping investigation without sufficient evidence regarding the causal link between the allegedly dumped imports and the alleged threat of injury to the domestic industry. The argument in this respect is quite straightforward.

6.185 In its application for initiation and in the extended application submitted by Cementos Progreso on 21 September and 9 October 1995 respectively, there was not the slightest relevant evidence of a causal relationship between the allegedly dumped imports and the alleged threat of injury to the Guatemalan domestic industry, as required by Article 5.2 of the AD Agreement. There was not even any mention of or reference to such a causal link. Likewise, in the initiation decision of 9 January 1996 and the public notice of initiation of 11 January 1996, the Ministry of the Economy did not mention any evidence or conduct any evaluation that would allow it to determine the sufficiency of the evidence of a causal relationship between the alleged dumping and the alleged threat of injury.[281]

6.186 Nevertheless, these omissions in Cementos Progreso's application and in the Ministry of the Economy's decision and notice of initiation are the result of a quite obvious and even logical situation.

6.187 As has been shown throughout this written submission, the Panel may see that *(i)* Cementos Progreso's application did *not* contain relevant evidence of dumping nor of threat of material injury to the domestic industry; *(ii)* the Guatemalan authority did *not* obtain or seek in any way additional evidence of these elements before deciding on initiation; and *(iii)* the Ministry initiated the investigation without sufficient evidence of dumping and threat of injury to justify initiation.

6.188 Consequently, it is both logical and obvious that owing to the lack of sufficient evidence of dumping and threat of material injury to justify initiation, the Ministry did not have sufficient evidence to demonstrate the existence of a causal relationship.[282] The Panel which previously considered this matter indeed concluded the following:

> "Finally, we conclude that an unbiased and objective investigating authority could not properly have determined that there was sufficient evidence of causal relationship to justify initiation if there was not sufficient evidence of dumping and threat of injury. In this case, having concluded that the evidence of dumping and threat of material injury were insufficient to justify initiation, we also conclude that the evidence of causal relationship between the dumped imports and the alleged injury was, perforce, not sufficient to justify initiation. The AD Agreement clearly requires sufficient evidence of all three elements before an investigation may be initiated."[283]

6.189 To summarize, in initiating the investigation without sufficient evidence of this third element, the Ministry of the Economy acted in a manner inconsistent with the AD Agreement, which clearly requires the investigating authority to possess sufficient evidence of three elements in order to initiate an investigation: dumping, injury and a causal relationship.

[281] The delivery notes and the import certificates submitted by Cementos Progreso as sole evidence in its application for the initiation of an investigation cannot be considered relevant evidence to substantiate a causal relationship. Still less can they be considered adequate evidence to justify the initiation of an investigation in accordance with Article 5.3 of the AD Agreement.

[282] From a technical standpoint, it can be assumed that dumping or injury may exist without there necessarily being a causal link between the dumped imports and the injury to domestic industry because the state of the industry could be the result of other distinct factors. Under no circumstances, however, is it possible simply to assume the existence of a causal link if there is not even sufficient evidence to show the existence of dumping or injury to a domestic industry, as is the case in this instance.

[283] *Guatemala - Cement*, *supra*, footnote 25, para. 7.78.

(b) Response of Guatemala

6.190 **Guatemala** makes the following arguments in response to Mexico's claims regarding the evidence required to justify the initiation of an investigation:

(i) Evidence to be included in application

6.191 The first sentence of Article 5.2 stipulates that the application shall include evidence of dumping and of injury within the meaning of Article VI of the GATT 1994 as interpreted by the AD Agreement, and a causal link. The second sentence stipulates that assertions of dumping, injury and causal link must be substantiated by "relevant evidence" that is "sufficient" to meet the requirements set forth in Article 5.2. The concept of "relevant" evidence sufficient to meet the requirements of Article 5.2 is defined in the third sentence as "such information as is reasonably available to the applicant" concerning the factors listed in sub-paragraphs (i) to (iv).

6.192 Contrary to what Mexico argues, Article 5.2 does not stipulate that the evidence required to substantiate an assertion must be documentary evidence.[284] The expression "evidence" and the expression " information" are used without distinction in Articles 5.2 and 5.3 of the AD Agreement and in the corresponding Articles (11.2 and 11.3) of the Agreement on Subsidies and Countervailing Measures (SCM Agreement). Article 11.2 (iv) of the SCM Agreement states that " ... this evidence includes information." Thus, the "evidence" referred to in the first sentence of Article 5.2 consists of the categories of "information" described in subparagraphs (i)-(iv) of the third sentence of that same article.[285]

6.193 As we shall show in greater detail further on, Cementos Progreso's application contained statements of dumping, threat of material injury and causal link. All of the information and evidence contained in the application and its annexes (and in the supplementary application) concerning the categories of information described in subparagraphs (i) and (iv) of the third sentence of Article 5.2 constitute the evidence or information in support of those statements.

6.194 Article 5.2 (i) states that the application shall contain such information as is reasonably available to the applicant on the following: (1) the identity of the applicant; (2) domestic production of the like product; (3) the industry on behalf of which the application is made. The application of 21 September 1995 identified Cementos Progreso as the applicant. The supplementary application of 9 October 1995 indicated that Cementos Progreso's production represented 100 per cent of cement production in Guatemala, that its production capacity was 1.6 million tons and that it used 100 per cent of its installed capacity.

6.195 Article 5.2(ii) states that the application shall contain such information as is reasonably available to the applicant on the following: (1) a complete description of the allegedly dumped product; (2) the names of the country or countries of origin or export in question; (3) the identity of each known exporter or foreign producer; (4) a list of known persons importing the product in question. In its application of 21 September 1995, Cementos Progreso identified the dumped product as grey Portland cement; explained how grey Portland cement was manufactured; identified Mexico as the country of export;

[284] *Ibid.*, paras. 83, 90, 93-96, 128, 136-162, 167-171.

[285] A similar position was adopted by the Panel in the case *United States - Salmon from Norway* with respect to Article 5.1 of the Tokyo Round Anti-Dumping Code which is the predecessor to Articles 5.2 and 5.3 of the AD Agreement (ADP/87, 27 April 1994, para. 362). In that case, the panel concluded that the statements in an application constituted sufficient evidence of the applicant's standing to submit an application.

identified Cruz Azul as the producer and exporter of the allegedly dumped product; and also identified Distribuidora De León and Distirbuidora Comercial Molina as the known importers of the product in question.

6.196 According to Article 5.2(iii) the application shall contain such information as is reasonably available to the applicant on the following: (1) the prices at which the product in question is sold when destined for consumption in the domestic markets of the country or countries of origin or export; (2) export prices. Cementos Progreso's application of 21 September 1995 supplied information and evidence concerning the prices at which Cruz Azul sold cement in Mexico and the prices at which it exported cement to Guatemala. In the supplementary application of 9 October 1995, Cementos Progreso stated that during the month of August 1995, the price in Mexico was Q 27.62 per sack and the export price to Guatemala was Q 14.77 per sack. Consequently, the margin of dumping was Q 12.85 per sack. In its application of 21 September 1995, Cementos Progreso furnished documentary evidence of these prices.

6.197 The price in Mexico was certified by two invoices showing the price of two different sales which took place in Tapachula, Mexico, in August 1995. One invoice was from Cruz Azul, while the other identified the brand name of the cement as "Cruz Azul". The sales price in one case was Mex$27, while in the other it was Mex$28. Consequently, the sales price information for both transactions was consistent. The Cruz Azul invoice identified the product as "grey cement", while the other invoice identified it as "Cruz Azul" cement.

6.198 The export price was certified by two sales carried out by Cruz Azul to two different importers in Tecún Umán, Guatemala, on 15 August 1995. The applicant provided an import certificate, invoices and bills of lading for both sales. The product was shipped as "grey cement", "grey Portland cement" and "Type II grey Portland cement with pozzolana" without distinction. This evidence was relevant because it showed the price of Cruz Azul cement in Mexico and its export price to Guatemala in the same month and in the same locations - Tapachula, Mexico and Tecún Umán, Guatemala - which are not very far from each other (45 kilometres).

6.199 Under Article 5.2(iv), the application shall contain such information as is reasonably available to the applicant on the following: (1) the evolution of the volume of the allegedly dumped imports; (2) the effect of these imports on prices of the like product in the domestic market; (3) the consequent impact of the imports on the domestic industry, as demonstrated by the relevant factors and indices having a bearing on the state of the domestic industry, such as those listed in paragraphs 2 and 4 of Article 3.

6.200 The application contained information and evidence of massive Cruz Azul imports which began in the middle of 1995. This information and evidence showed that imports increased rapidly from a zero base, and referred to the evolution of the volume of dumped imports.

6.201 The application also contained information and evidence of "a significant price undercutting". This information and evidence was relevant to the effect of dumped imports on the prices of the like product in the domestic market as required by Article 3.2.

6.202 Moreover, the application contained information and evidence concerning the expected adverse effects of the dumped imports. This information and evidence were relevant to the consequent impact of the imports because Cementos Progresos claimed threat of injury and not actual material injury. For the Ministry, the evidence of the risk that the dumped imports would threaten the jobs of 1,052 employees was significant. At the time, unemployment in Guatemala was approximately 42 per cent.[286]

6.203 According to Article 5.3, the investigating authorities shall "examine the accuracy and adequacy of the evidence provided in the application to determine whether there is sufficient evidence to justify the initiation of an investigation." As Guatemala will explain in the next section of this submission, the Ministry reasonably determined that the application contained "adequate" evidence because it contained such information and evidence as was reasonably available to the applicant on the categories of evidence described in subparagraphs (i) to (iv) of Article 5.2. The Ministry also determined that the application contained "accurate" evidence because it contained information and evidence that was reasonable, consistent, and plausible, and did not contain any statement contrary to the facts which were known to the Ministry at that time.

6.204 In its first submission, Mexico did not try to show that any of the information and evidence described above and contained in the application and supplementary application were false. Nor did Cruz Azul try to prove this during the course of the investigation.

(ii) Evidence of dumping

6.205 Mexico claims that Guatemala violated Articles 2.1, 2.4, 5.2 and 5.3 of the AD Agreement by initiating the investigation without sufficient evidence of dumping. In particular, Mexico argues that the evidence of normal value used by the Ministry in initiating the investigation was flawed because (i) it only covered two sacks of cement, an insignificant portion of Cruz Azul's sales on the Mexican market[287]; (ii) it only covered two days of the month of August 1995[288]; (iii) it did not identify the type of cement[289]; (iv) the invoices were not proper invoices under Mexican law.[290] In attacking the evidence that the Ministry had before it in establishing the export price and comparing it with the normal value at the time of initiation, Mexico states that: (i) Cruz Azul's sales to Guatemala were at a different level of trade than the sales in Mexico[291]; (ii) the sales to Guatemala involved smaller sacks than the sales in Mexico[292]; (iii) the Dollar-Peso exchange rate claimed by Cementos Progreso and used by the Ministry was not "documented"[293]; (iv) the sales to Guatemala represented only a small percentage of Cruz Azul's total sales to Guatemala and only covered a period of two days in August 1995.[294] Each one of these arguments is without foundation and should be rejected by the Panel.

6.206 *First*, as mentioned above, Article 5 establishes the requirements for the initiation of an investigation under the AD Agreement. An authority cannot "violate" Articles 2 and 3 simply by *initiating* an investigation into a complaint of injurious dumping.

---

[286] The subsequent investigation confirmed Cemetos Progreso's fears. In the space of only six months, the rapidly increasing imports at unfair prices captured 25 per cent of the market, causing Cementos Progreso to suffer a corresponding loss in market share, a fall in sales, loss of customers, a slump in production, an increase in the fixed costs per unit produced, a decrease in prices, a fall in profits and a negative cash flow.

[287] First submission by Mexico, para. 122.

[288] *Ibid.*, paras. 92, 122.

[289] *Ibid.*, paras. 88, 111-19 and 124.

[290] *Ibid.*, para. 89.

[291] *Ibid.*, para. 98.

[292] *Ibid.*.

[293] *Ibid.*.

[294] *Ibid.*, para. 123.

6.207 *Second*, as explained above, the level of dumping documented in the application was quite substantial. In the supplementary application of 9 October 1995, Cementos Progreso submitted evidence showing that in Mexico, Cruz Azul was selling grey Portland cement at Q 27.62 per sack and that it was selling the same cement in Guatemala for only Q 14.77 per sack Thus, the Ministry had evidence of a margin of dumping of 87 per cent - (27.62 - 14.77)/14.77 = .87. The Ministry also had documentary evidence to support the alleged margin of dumping.

6.208 The evidence of the price in Mexico was certified by two invoices showing the prices for two separate sales in Tapachula, Mexico, during August 1995. As stated above, one invoice was from Cruz Azul and identified the product as "grey cement". The other invoice identified the brand name of the cement as "Cruz Azul". The price of one of the sales was Mex$27 (i.e. the equivalent of Q 25.65). The price of the other sales was Mex$28 (i.e. the equivalent of Q 27.62). The fact that, as Mexico states, the two sales took place at a similar price and during the same period of time does not deprive them of their probative value; rather, it would tend to show that the sales were legitimate and the documentary evidence authentic. Moreover, contrary to what Mexico states, nothing in the AD Agreement required the Ministry to base its calculations of normal value (for the purposes of initiation) on a higher number of sales in Mexico. In fact, it is common at the time of initiation for the authorities of other countries, including Mexico, not to base their determinations of normal value on any sale at all (to base it, for example, on price lists).[295]

6.209 *Third*, at the time of initiation of the investigation, the Ministry did not have any reason to believe that there was any difference between the cement sold in Mexico and the cement that Cruz Azul sold in Guatemala. In fact, in its first submission to this Panel, Mexico did not ever claim, much less defend the position that the cement sold in Mexico was of better quality or value than the cement sold in Guatemala.

6.210 As explained above, the invoices for the sales in Mexico identified the cement as "grey cement" and "Cruz Azul" cement.[296] The evidence of the export price - import certificates, invoices and bills of lading - identified the product as "grey cement", "grey Portland cement" and "Type II grey Portland cement with pozzolana". In a country where the price of cement had been regulated by the Government for over 50 years, this evidence indicated to the Ministry that the sales that were being compared were of "grey cement".

6.211 Even if the Panel were to assume, at this stage, that the evidence of normal value and the export price available at the time of initiation referred to two different types of

[295] See for example *Pencils from the People's Republic of China*, 9 August 1993 (Mexico) (List of prices for normal value); *Additives for Gasoline from the United States*, 8 November 1993 (Mexico) (List of prices for normal value); *Bags and Vanity Cases from the People's Republic of China*, 29 November 1993 (Mexico) (List of prices for normal value). *Additives for Gasoline from the United States*, 25 April 1996 (Mexico) (List of prices for normal value) See also *Initiation of Anti-Dumping Duty Investigations: Certain Pasta from Italy and Turkey*, Federal Register Vol. 60, 30268, 30269 (1995) (United States) (Normal value based on price lists) Moreover, it is not rare for the anti-dumping authority of Mexico, SECOFI, to initiate an anti-dumping investigation in which the evidence of normal value is limited to one or two sales in the domestic market of the exporter. See, for example, *Rubber Belts for Use in the Automotive Industry from the Republic of Korea*, (15 May 1992) (one invoice for the calculation of normal value); *Sodium Tripolyphosphate from Spain*, 11 February 1992 (one invoice for the calculation of normal value).

[296] Mexico recognizes, in para. 113 of its submission, that the invoices backing the sales in Mexico did *not* identify the product as a rare or special type of grey cement. If this had been the case, we must assume that the invoices would have reflected this fact.

cement, the Ministry would nevertheless have been justified in initiating the investigation. It must not be forgotten that the application documented a margin of dumping of 87 per cent. There is nothing in the file of the proceedings, nor indeed is there any evidence anywhere else, to suggest that differences in types of grey Portland cement could excuse such a level of price discrimination. Cement is, after all, a fungible consumer product. In most countries, especially in developing countries, consumers are not prepared to pay a significant price difference for cement with higher industrial standards.

6.212 Moreover, if the Ministry had made an adjustment for the alleged difference in types of cement, the chances are it would have benefited Cementos Progreso rather than Cruz Azul. Some of the documents referring to exports sales suggest that the product imported into Guatemala was "Type II grey Portland cement with pozzolana", while the product sold in Mexico was simply identified as "grey cement" (i.e. standard Type I cement). Type II cement has higher industrial standards than Type I.[297] Thus, if any adjustment had been made, the margin of dumping would have *increased*, and not decreased as Mexico suggests.

6.213 *Fourth*, something similar might be said for Mexico's argument that the size of the sacks under comparison at the beginning of the investigation was different. Firstly, neither the application nor any evidence in the possession of the Ministry at the time of initiation provided any indication that the size of the sacks was in fact different. This came to light some time after the initiation of the investigation.[298] In fact, it would have been very reasonable for the Ministry, at the time of initiation, to assume that Cruz Azul would not incur additional costs by using sacks of a different size in Guatemala and Mexico. This is especially true in that the evidence of normal value and export price is based on sales transactions in two cities (Tapachula, Mexico and Tecún Umán, Guatemala) that are only 45 kilometres apart. In any case, given the substantial dumping margin shown by the invoices and other evidence in the Ministry's possession at the time of initiation, the fact is that there would still have been a significant margin of dumping even if the slight difference in the weight of the sacks had been taken into account.[299]

6.214 *Fifth*, it is absurd to suggest, as Mexico has done, that Guatemala ignored its WTO obligations when it initiated the investigation in question without adjusting for the level of trade. To begin with, the application and the evidence before the Ministry at the time of initiation provided no indication that any adjustment for level of trade would be appropriate. Even if the Panel were to assume, for the purposes of this dispute, that sales in Mexico were taking place at retail level and sales in Guatemala were taking place at another level (i.e. wholesale or distributor), this would not be sufficient to justify an adjustment in the level of trade. Article 2.4 of the AD Agreement requires an adjustment to the same level of trade only in cases where sales at a different level of trade "affect price comparability". In this case, there was no such indication, especially at the initiation stage. In fact, Cruz Azul *never* provided the Ministry with any evidence that sales in its

[297] In its communication to the Ministry of 9 May 1996 (Annex GUA-22), Cruz Azul stated that none of the invoices certifying the sales in Mexico identified the type of cement as anything other than grey cement.

[298] It eventually came to light that the two invoices certifying the sales in Tapachula, Mexico, referred to 50 kg. sacks, while the exports entering via Tecún Umán, Guatemala, concerned 42.5 kg. sacks.

[299] Allowing for the difference, the Ministry still had evidence that Cruz Azul was selling cement in Mexico at an adjusted price of Q 23.48 per sack of 42.5 kg. as compared to Q 14.77 per sack of the same weight in Guatemala, resulting in a margin of dumping of 59 per cent.

domestic market were at a different level of trade than its exports sales, *and* that those different levels affected price comparability.

6.215 Throughout the world many authorities, including SECOFI in Mexico, rely on the same methodology, which is basically the one used by the Ministry in this case. Indeed, in a *final determination* SECOFI compares levels of trade that are nominally different (i.e. retail against wholesale) unless the foreign exporter provides evidence that its sales at those different levels affect price comparability. In its main written submission to the dispute settlement panel established under Article 19 of the North American Free Trade Agreement to examine a challenge by the company Archer Daniels Midland Corp. (the claimant) against the definitive determination of dumping with respect to imports of high fructose corn syrup from the United States, SECOFI stated that:

> "This means that *the claimant must have proven* that it was involved in different sales activities in the two markets; that these activities involved differences in the costs incurred and that there is in fact a price differentiation pattern which depends on the type of customer to which the investigated products are sold."

6.216 *Sixth*, the Ministry had no reason to consider that the export price evidence was not "representative" of Cruz Azul's export activities. As Mexico was obliged to recognize in its first submission, the AD Agreement *does not* contain any minimum requirement with respect to documentation. Moreover, there was no reason whatsoever for the Ministry to conclude that the two export sales were not representative merely because they were registered on two consecutive days in the same month. The fact that the prices were basically the same on those two consecutive days would tend to confirm their probative value. The invoices, as well, were recent - from the month preceding the submission of the application. Furthermore, the dates of these export sales were contemporaneous with the dates of the sales in the exporter's domestic market.[300]

6.217 *Seventh*, Mexico argues, without evidence or confirmation of any kind, that the documents in the hands of the Ministry providing evidence of normal value were not "proper invoices according to Mexican legislation". As argued in connection with the burden of proof in this dispute, Mexico is the complainant in these proceedings, and as such, carries the burden of the proof in this case. In the case *United States - DRAM*, which we also discussed above, the Panel rejected outright certain complaints by Korea which were not substantiated by facts or arguments.[301] The same should apply to the present dispute. Moreover, it is not particularly odd (and it is certainly not inconsistent with the AD Agreement) that the authorities should base the evidence of normal value at the time of initiation on documents other than invoices. Mexico does so all the time.

6.218 Finally, Mexico claims without any grounds that the exchange rate used by Cementos Progreso in its application "was not documented and was solely based on an affirmation". The fact is that the exchange rate used by Cementos Progreso was anything but a mere affirmation. Comparing the exchange rate by Cementos Progreso with the official IMF exchange rate for December 1995, they turn out to be practically identical.[302]

---

[300] Article 2.4 of the Anti-Dumping Agreement stipulates that the authorities must make the comparison "as at nearly as possible the same time".

[301] *United States - DRAM, supra*, footnote 115, paras. 6.67-6.69.

[302] In its application of 9 September 1995, Cementos Progreso indicated the exchange rate for the new Mexican peso against the Guatemalan quetzal, relating both currencies to the US dollar (US$1 = 6 new pesos or 5.70 quetzals). From then on, all prices contained in the application, both in new pesos and in quetzals, are converted into US dollars.

(iii) Evidence of threat of injury

6.219 Article 5.2(iv) of the AD Agreement provides that the application should contain such information as is reasonably available to the applicant on the evolution of the volume of the allegedly dumped imports, the effect of these imports on prices of the like product in the domestic market and the consequent impact of the imports on the domestic industry. As shown in detail below, the application submitted by Cementos Progreso clearly met the requirements of Article 5.2(iv).

6.220 Firstly, concerning the evolution of imports, Cementos Progreso stated that for more than three months at least, a company in Mexico, Cruz Azul, had been selling cement in Guatemala. Cementos Progreso relied on the above-mentioned import documents to support its claim of massive imports. The documentary evidence showed that in one day Guatemala received substantial imports of Mexican cement from Cruz Azul through the Tecún Umán customs post. 7,035 sacks of cement were registered for one of the import transactions, while the other involved 4,221 sacks of cement. These imports were in fact fairly considerable in relation to the size of the Guatemalan market. Cementos Progreso mentioned that it suspected that other imports had entered through the customs posts of El Carmen and La Mesilla.

6.221 Cementos Progreso stated that it was claiming threat of injury, and not actual injury, because it had been impossible for it to obtain information to show the significant volume of the dumped product that was entering the country. It asked the Ministry to obtain documentation concerning the previous year to determine the volume of cement imports from Mexico that had caused injury to the Guatemalan cement industry.

6.222 Secondly, concerning the effect of imports on the prices of the like domestic product, Cementos Progreso based its assertions on a list of prices for cement in Guatemala and on the import documents identified above to show that the dumped imports were being sold at a price significantly lower than the prices of Cementos Progreso in Guatemala. It was shown that the prices of the dumped imports averaged no more than Q 13.96 per sack, which was almost 50 per cent *less* than the average price of Q 26 being charged by Cementos Progreso in Guatemala. Thus, the application contained compelling evidence of "significant price undercutting" in accordance with Article 3.2 of the AD Agreement.

6.223 Thirdly, concerning the consequent impact of imports on the domestic industry, Cementos Progreso supplied evidence that the dumped imports were threatening its investment programme for the modernization and expansion of its production capacity. In particular, the firm stated that its ongoing investment programme included the expansion of its capacity to grind clinker and produce cement, the modernization of its production equipment, the construction of a third kiln to produce clinker at its San Miguel plant, and the conversion of its kilns to coal instead of bunker. The firm mentioned that 400 employees would be dismissed if this major investment project were cancelled. Moreover, it mentioned that if it had to compete with dumped cement at prices below production costs, it would have to become a cement importer, in which case it would have to dismiss 1,052

The official IMF exchange rate for the new Mexican peso and the Guatemalan quetzal against the US dollar for September 1995 was US$1 = 6.3025 new pesos (or 5.8882 quetzals). Thus, the IMF exchange rate is very close to the exchange rate used by Cementos Progreso in its application.

production workers and the national economy would lose their know-how and expertise in cement production.[303]

6.224 Mexico never objected directly to any of the evidence mentioned. In fact, Mexico never denied that Cruz Azul was shipping cement to Guatemala at significant margins of dumping. Rather, it has argued that the Ministry was under obligation to examine *more* evidence of injury before initiating the investigation.[304] Mexico never denied that Cruz Azul flooded the Guatemalan market with cement or that in less than one year, Cruz Azul's share of the Guatemalan cement market increased from zero to 25 per cent approximately. Rather, it insisted that Guatemala should have analysed at greater length the evidence before it and should have taken more time to issue its decision to initiate the investigation.[305] For example, Mexico cites the decision of the Ministry to initiate its investigation without waiting for fuller information on the actual level of Cruz Azul's imports.[306] Mexico asserts that if the Ministry had taken its time and studied the evidence more carefully, it would have realized that there was no justification for an investigation. Guatemala contends, with due respect for its larger neighbour in the north, that these arguments are nothing short of ridiculous.

6.225 Firstly, Guatemala is a small country in comparison to Mexico. Its total cement consumption in 1994 (the year preceding the submission of the application for the anti-dumping investigation at issue) amounted to only 1,180,000 tons.[307] Mexico's total cement consumption for 1994 was approximately 29 million tons, for an installed production capacity of about 43 million tons.[308]

6.226 Moreover, when Cruz Azul suddenly began to ship great quantities of cement to Guatemala in the summer of 1995, it was not threatening an unimportant industry. Cement is not a luxury good. In Guatemala, cement is a strategically important consumer good, essential for dam and road construction and other infrastructure projects.

6.227 Mexico's suggestion that the Ministry should have delayed initiation in order to gather more information conjures up Nero playing his violin while Rome was in flames. In this submission, we have proved beyond any doubt that the Ministry had more than sufficient evidence to justify the initiation of an anti-dumping investigation under Article 5 of the AD Agreement. The Ministry knew the size of the domestic market. Cementos Progreso exported practically no cement up to 1995, and no one was interested in exporting cement to the Guatemalan market.[309] Consequently, Cementos Progreso's production reflected national consumption. The Ministry did not need complete information to know that imports were rapidly increasing. As explained above, within a period of a few months in 1995, imports increased from basically zero to 25 per cent of consumption in Guatemala. The Ministry also knew that Mexico was going through a terrible recession and that consumption and production had decreased dramatically, resulting in thousands of tons of idle capacity. Finally, the Ministry knew that Cruz Azul's prices were well below those of Cementos Progreso, because the Government regulated cement prices and

303 Article 3.4 lists the actual and potential negative effects on employment, growth, ability to raise capital and investments as the factors relevant to the impact of dumped imports on the domestic industry.

304 See, for example, first submission by Mexico, paras. 128, 134-136.

305 First submission by Mexico, 136(c) and 139.

306 *Ibid.*, para. 136 (b) and (c).

307 *The Global Cement Report.*

308 *Ibid.*, pages 176-178.

309 *Ibid.*, page 123.

because the Government itself was one of the main purchasers of cement, and because Cementos Progreso had supplied information on domestic prices.

6.228 In these circumstances, the Ministry could not wait around while its only producer of a strategic consumer good drowned in a tidal wave of imports. This might be an option for a large and developed country like the United States, where according to the latest data there are 42 different cement companies operating 105 different plants, but for Guatemala, as a small developing country with only one producer operating two plants, the collapse of Cementos Progreso would mean the collapse of the *entire* industry.

6.229 It is also unfair for Mexico to seek to impose on a developing country, like Guatemala, a level of evidence and documentation which many other small countries are not always able to achieve. Mexico appears to take it for granted that all the Ministry had to do to gather more complete information on imports of the product under investigation was to press a button and wait for it to shoot out of some computer. This may be the case in Mexico and in many developed countries, but it is definitely *not* the case in Guatemala.

6.230 Indeed, full information on imports of the product under investigation was not available to Cementos Progreso, and it took the Ministry approximately two months to obtain it.[310] As is the case in many developing countries, information on imports is not always kept in a specific register for each product corresponding to the scope of an anti-dumping claim, and even if the data were entered in a specific register for each product, the information would have to be tabulated by hand.

6.231 In short, just as Article 5.2 takes account of what is reasonably available to the applicant in judging the accuracy and adequacy of the evidence, Article 5.3 should take account of what is reasonably available to the investigating authority. The drafters of Article 5.2 were seeking to allow for the fact that access to information (such as consumption and import figures) is not universal. In other words, what is easily available in the United States may not be easily available in Guatemala or another developing country. Thus, part of the purpose of Article 5.2 would be compromised if the Panel were to ignore this reality in applying Article 5.3.[311]

6.232 In conclusion, the Ministry acted reasonably and in keeping with its WTO obligations under Article 5 of the AD Agreement. In a perfect world it would perhaps have been better for the Ministry to have had complete information on imports before deciding whether an investigation was justified, but the Panel should take account of the fact that this information was not easily and reasonably available to the Ministry. Cementos Progreso was faced with a growing flood of imports in its **only** market. In its application of 21 September and the supplementary application of 9 October 1995, the company supplied evidence concerning the injurious effects of Cruz Azul's dumping in Guatemala. In particular, Cementos Progreso furnished information relating to loss of sales, loss of customers and a trend towards the penetration of imports, which in a single day increased

[310] It is not possible for a private company in Guatemala to obtain information from Government or other sources containing figures on imports of a particular product into Guatemala. If such information is required, a private company may request that it be collected as part of an official Government investigation, and this can take some time.

[311] In the case *United States - Reformulated Gasoline*, the Appellate Body considered that the interpretation of a treaty must give meaning and effect to all the terms of the treaty: "An interpreter is not free to adopt a reading that would result in reducing whole clauses or paras. of a treaty to redundancy or inutility." Report of the Appellate Body in *United States - Standards for Reformulated and Conventional Gasoline, supra*, footnote 2, at 21.

from basically zero to 480 tons (representing a loss of sales of approximately $60,000).[312] While this sum may seem small to Mexico, projected over one year it would represent a substantial proportion of Cementos Progreso's cement sales in 1995.

6.233 Mexico also asserts that the initiation by Guatemala violated Article 3.1, 3.2, 3.4, 3.5 and 3.7 of the AD Agreement.[313] However, as we have explained in detail on several occasions throughout this submission, Article 5, and *not* Article 3 (or Article 2), establishes the requirements for initiation of an investigation under the AD Agreement. Thus, an authority cannot "violate" any of the requirements contained in Article 3 by simply initiating an investigation into allegations of injurious dumping.

6.234 Finally, Mexico claims that the fact that the Ministry sent Cementos Progreso a questionnaire after initiation shows that the application did not contain adequate evidence of threat of injury.[314] In fact, questionnaires are routinely sent to domestic producers in the vast majority of anti-dumping investigations, including those conducted by Mexico.

(iv) Evidence of Causal Link

6.235 Mexico claims that the Ministry violated Articles 5.2 and 5.3 by accepting an application that did not contain any evidence of a causal link between the alleged dumping and the alleged threat of injury.[315] Once again, Mexico's claim is without merit.

6.236 Article 5.2 provides that the application should contain evidence of a causal link between the dumped imports and the alleged injury. It does not, however, specify any particular factor that should prove the causal link, other than those contained in Article 5.2(iii) and 5.2(iv). Article 5.2 does not refer to Article 3.7, which concerns the demonstration of a causal link required in making a preliminary or final determination of threat of material injury. The clear meaning of Article 5.2 is that there is sufficient evidence of a causal link if the application provides evidence of dumping in conformity with Article 5.2(iii) and proof of consequent injury in conformity with Article 5.2(iv). Cementos Progreso met those requirements.

6.237 As shown above, the application contained accurate and adequate evidence with respect to the criteria contained in Article 5.2(iii) and 5.2(iv). Contrary to what Mexico states in its first submission, the application also referred explicitly to the causal link.[316] The application dated 21 September states that the dumped cement was entering in quantities that were causing injury to Cementos Progreso. The supplementary application states that Cementos Progreso was being threatened *by* massive imports of cement from Mexico. The supplementary application also describes how the dumped imports were directly affecting the firm's investments.

(v) Guatemala examined the accuracy and adequacy of the application

6.238 Mexico insists that the Ministry "totally disregarded" the requirements of the AD Agreement when initiating the investigation.[317] According to Mexico, the file put together

---

[312] The customs value of the imports was approximately US$30,000 and the file indicates that the export prices were at least 50 per cent lower than Cementos Progreso's prices in Guatemala.

[313] First submission by Mexico, para. 161.

[314] *Ibid.*, para. 160.

[315] *Ibid.*, paras. 163-171.

[316] *Ibid.*, para. 167.

[317] See, for example, first submission by Mexico paras. 63 and 102.

during the underlying administrative process lacks *any* evidence that the Ministry actually examined the accuracy or adequacy of the information contained in Cementos Progreso's application.[318] Mexico insists that no "unbiased and objective" investigating authority examining the information that the Ministry had before it in this case could have concluded that it constituted sufficient evidence of dumping, threat of material injury or causal link.[319] As in the case of Mexico's other arguments, this argument is flawed and must be rejected by the Panel.

6.239 It is clear from our earlier discussion of the matter that the Ministry examined the accuracy and adequacy of the evidence accompanying the application in determining whether there was sufficient evidence to justify the initiation of the investigation. As mentioned earlier on in the "Chronology of the Investigation", the initial application was submitted on 21 September 1995. The Ministry then held a number of meetings with officials from Cementos Progreso to determine whether the evidence in the application was accurate and adequate. During these meetings, the Ministry asked the Cementos Progreso officials many questions concerning the evidence and information provided in the application. The Ministry informed Cementos Progreso that the original application did not contain sufficient evidence to justify the initiation of an investigation because it did not provide sufficient information to substantiate the assertion that there was a consequent threat of material injury. In the supplementary application of 9 October 1995, Cementos Progreso furnished additional information which, read together with the application, provided evidence of dumping, injury and causal link in conformity with Article 5.2. On 6 November 1995, the Directorate of Economic Integration passed the application and the supplementary application on to the legal department for examination. In accordance with the mandate received, on 17 November 1995 two legal advisers submitted an opinion to the Directorate of Economic Integration containing their detailed analysis of the application (and the supplementary application) and accompanying evidence, and expressing their view that there was sufficient evidence to justify the initiation of an investigation. On 15 December 1995, the Directorate of Economic Integration adopted the opinion of 17 November 1995 and concluded that there was sufficient evidence to justify the initiation of an investigation. The Ministry approved this finding on 9 January 1996 and issued a public notice of its determination on 11 January 1996.

6.240 To summarize, Guatemala did not act hastily. It did not initiate its investigation until it had examined the accuracy and adequacy of the evidence and determined that there was "sufficient evidence" under Article 5.3 of the AD Agreement of dumping, injury and causal link.

(c) Rebuttal of Mexico

6.241 The following are **Mexico's** arguments in rebuttal to Guatemala's response its claims under Articles 5.2 and 5.3:

6.242 Mexico has submitted that the evidence contained in Cementos Progreso's application cannot be considered as accurate and adequate evidence, let alone sufficient to meet the standards set forth in Article 5.2 and 5.3. For its part, Guatemala has tried to defend itself by arguing that the application contained all of the information reasonably available to the applicant, and that this information was also considered by the Ministry to be sufficient to justify the initiation of the investigation.

---

[318] See, for example, first submission by Mexico paras. 63 and 102.
[319] *Ibid.*, para. 91.

6.243 However, Guatemala failed to provide an acceptable explanation of why it should have considered that the applicant, upon submitting its application for initiation, had no more information "reasonably available" to it than two notes and two import certificates. In Mexico's view, the limited information that these items provided cannot be considered as constituting all of the information reasonably available to the applicant. Similarly, Guatemala failed to demonstrate the insufficiency of the evidence, resorting to a series of *post hoc* arguments and getting involved in a series of contradictions that provide no excuse for failing to comply with its obligations under the Anti-Dumping Agreement.

6.244 As Guatemala itself recognizes in paragraph 69 of its first submission, several months elapsed between the time when it was first approached by Cementos Progreso, or between the submission of Cementos Progreso's original application, and the initiation determination and corresponding public notice. Between these two events, Cementos Progreso also had the opportunity to submit a supplement to its application. However, all that this supplementary application added to the original application was a series of simple assertions and mere suspicions concerning the alleged threat of injury and the alleged "massive" nature of the imports, unsubstantiated by any relevant evidence. It is therefore difficult to understand why, in spite of the geographical proximity[320] of Mexico and Guatemala, of the fact that several months had elapsed, and that Cementos Progreso even had the opportunity to supplement its application, it was not possible for the applicant to obtain anything more than two delivery notes and two import certificates, established on two consecutive days, as evidence of the normal value and the export price as well as the allegedly "massive" nature of the imports.

6.245 More serious and more obvious still is the fact that the application did not include the information required in Article 5.2(iv), information which to a large extent clearly had to be reasonably available to the applicant, since Cementos Progreso stated in its application that it represented 100 per cent of domestic cement production in Guatemala. In other words, the information concerning the relevant factors and indices having a bearing on the state of the domestic industry, the probable impact of the imports on the domestic industry and the relevant economic factors must have been, to a great extent, exclusively in the hands of the applicant. And yet Cementos Progreso did not supply any information in support of its assertions concerning the alleged threat of injury, information which it clearly controlled, considering in particular that this information was in fact submitted by Cementos Progreso itself during later stages of the investigation.

6.246 For example, the failure by Cementos Progreso to provide information on Cruz Azul's costs might be understandable, probably because the information in question was confidential and under the control of the exporting firm. This, then, might validly be considered as information that was not "reasonably available to the applicant", since there were factual and legal impediments barring access to the information. But since it was argued in the supplementary application that, *inter alia*, export prices "**were in fact lower than Cementos Progreso's production costs**"[321], what justification can there be for not substantiating this assertion with data in the application on *Cementos Progreso's* production costs, information which was in fact under the applicant's control.

6.247 Even if we accept, for the sake of argument only, that the information on the evolution of the volume of the imports was difficult for Cementos Progreso to obtain, how is it possible to justify the failure to submit any *information or evidence* to back its asser-

[320] First written submission by Guatemala, paras. 145 and 160, recognizing that Tapachula, Mexico and Tecún Umán, Guatemala, are separated by only 45 kilometres.
[321] *Ibid.*, para. 66.

tions on the alleged effect of the imports on prices and hence their consequent impact on the domestic industry relating to the economic factors set forth in Articles 3.2 and 3.4, such as sales, production volume, market share, profits, productivity, investment projects, inventories, employment, salaries, etc., which were also under the control of the applicant.

6.248 Thus, even though Guatemala has tried to reject Mexico's arguments concerning the insufficiency of information in the application on the grounds that Cementos Progreso's application contained such information as was reasonably available to the firm, it is an indisputable fact that there was no information or evidence at all concerning the relevant factors having a bearing on the state of the domestic industry, such as those listed in Article 3.2 and 3.4, or concerning the factors listed in Article 3.7, since the application claimed threat of material injury, as expressly and implicitly required by subparagraph (iv) of Article 5.2.

6.249 As we said earlier on, Mexico also submits that the Ministry did not comply with its obligation under Article 5.3 to examine the accuracy and adequacy of the evidence provided in the application, and that there is no way that the investigating authority could have validly determined that there was sufficient evidence to justify the initiation of the investigation. I shall therefore now turn to the lack of *accuracy and adequacy* of the evidence contained in Cementos Progreso's application, both in terms of the failure to comply with the Article 5.2 requirement that the application contain *relevant* evidence of dumping, injury and causal link, and in terms of the failure to comply with Article 5.3, which requires the authority to examine the accuracy and adequacy of the evidence provided in the application.

6.250 The relevance or adequacy of the evidence within the meaning of Articles 5.2 and 5.3 basically depends on the relationship and relevance of the information or data concerned to the facts that it is necessary to establish in order to initiate the investigation, i.e. the alleged *dumping*, the alleged *injury*, and the *causal link* between the two. Similarly, the qualification of a piece of evidence as accurate within the meaning of Article 5.3 basically depends on the quality, precision and reliability of the data and information concerned, as well as its sources.

6.251 As can be seen in paragraph 129 of its first written submission, Guatemala distorts and manipulates Mexico's position with respect to the *insufficiency of evidence of dumping* to justify the initiation of an investigation when it states that:

> "... According to Mexico, the Ministry should not have initiated the investigation *until* it had 'evidence' of injurious dumping based on a 'fair comparison' of Cruz Azul's prices in Mexico and Guatemala." (Emphasis added) (footnotes omitted).

6.252 Mexico never brought this time factor into its arguments. Mexico's position in this respect is very clear: in the investigation at issue, the evidence of dumping contained both in Cementos Progreso's original application (of 21 September 1995) and in its supplementary application (of 9 October 1995) cannot in any way be qualified as accurate and adequate, let alone *sufficient* to justify initiation within the meaning of Article 5.2 and 5.3, for the following reasons:

6.253 Firstly, because the evidence of normal value and export price differs in the identification of the product concerned by the transaction, so that it is not precise or accurate to say that it is product investigated, in this case Type I PM grey Portland cement with pozzolana; there may even have been, as a result, price comparisons involving different types of cement.

6.254 Secondly, the delivery notes that were used as evidence of normal value only referred to the sale of one load or sack of cement each; in other words they concern transactions involving insignificant volumes which cannot be considered as "representative" (in the sense of sufficient quantity) in demonstrating the normal value of the like product to that being investigated. In fact, if the Ministry had access *post hoc* to information on the size of the Mexican cement market[322], then it could have obtained that information before initiating the investigation and it would have realized that the volumes covered by the delivery notes used to document the normal value were not "representative" of the Mexican domestic market. The same is true for the two invoices and import certificates used to calculate the export price. This evidence, covering transactions involving 299 and 179 tons respectively, certainly could not be considered as representative of the volume which Cruz Azul exported to Guatemala during the period of investigation.

6.255 Thirdly, the transactions used as proof of the normal value and the export price took place at distinctly different levels of trade: retail level in the case of the normal value, and distributor level in the case of the export price. These differences preclude a proper comparison between the two prices, and thus cannot be considered as accurate and adequate as evidence of a margin of dumping.

6.256 Bearing in mind that the Ministry initiated the investigation on the basis of the same evidence that is contained in the application, some of the above considerations also apply to the insufficiency of evidence of dumping required for the initiation of the investigation. There is clear evidence that the Ministry did not examine the accuracy and adequacy of the two delivery notes which it used as evidence of normal value, or the two import certificates and their corresponding invoices which it used as evidence of the export price. If it had done so, it would certainly have noticed that there were differences between them with respect to the identification of the product involved, and in fact they do not refer to the investigated product. Moreover, they are not representative of the prices in the domestic market and the export market, they concern distinctly different volumes and the transactions took place at different levels of trade. In these circumstances, no unbiased and objective authority could possibly have determined that the evidence contained in Cementos Progreso's application warranted the conclusion that there was sufficient evidence of dumping to justify the initiation of the investigation.

6.257 At the same time it is difficult, in fact impossible to say anything about the accuracy, adequacy or insufficiency of the evidence of threat of injury required for the purposes of the Ministry's initiation determination, since such evidence was simply non-existent. In its application, Cementos Progreso merely attempts to prove the alleged massive nature of the imports with the two much-cited import certificates and the firm's "suspicions" that other imports were entering through other customs posts.[323]

6.258 We have already referred to the differences between these two certificates which preclude their being considered as accurate and adequate evidence. Apart from these suspicions, the supplementary application merely contained a series of assertions or statements by Cementos Progreso, unsubstantiated by information or evidence of any kind, which we included in our first submission to the effect that the imports of grey Portland cement from Cruz Azul were threatening to cause material injury to Guatemala's domestic industry.

6.259 Thus, it seems to us cynical and downright ridiculous for Guatemala to dare to include these suspicions and simple assertions by Cementos Progreso, on which it based

[322] *The Global Cement Report* (2nd Ed. 1996), No. 123, cited in para. 62 of Guatemala's first written submission.

[323] Concerning the explicit recognition that the Ministry took account of mere suspicions of other possible imports, see Guatemala's first written submission, paras. 75 and 167.

its initiation determination, among its arguments before this Panel to justify an initiation which was incompatible with the Anti-Dumping Agreement in every respect.

6.260 The Anti-Dumping Agreement establishes very clearly that simple assertion, unsubstantiated by relevant evidence, cannot be considered sufficient to meet the requirements of Article 5.2. Similarly, Article 3.7 could hardly be clearer when it stipulates that "a determination of a threat of material injury shall be based on fact and not merely on allegation, conjecture or remote possibility". This applies to initiation determinations as well, particularly in view of the fact that Article 5.3 and 5.8 require sufficient evidence of injury, or as in this case, of threat of injury, to initiate an investigation, failing which the investigating authority must reject the application and refrain from initiating the investigation.

6.261 Thus, it cannot be concluded that an unbiased and objective investigating authority could properly have determined that there was sufficient evidence to justify the initiation of the investigation on the basis of mere allegations or statements made by Cementos Progreso to the Ministry in its application or in the alleged meetings with officials to which Guatemala refers, and without the slightest information or evidence of the alleged threat of injury to the Guatemalan industry.

6.262 Moreover, with respect to the insufficiency of evidence, it is worth citing Guatemala's comments in paragraph 68 of its first written submission and 28 of its oral submission:

> "68. The case before it was so convincing that the Ministry was fully justified in pursuing the investigation. Firstly, the product in question was not a *luxury item* - it was a strategically important *consumer good* which was crucial to the development of the infrastructure (e.g. roads and dams) of a *small country*. Secondly, the *industry* in question was not *large and diversified* - Cementos Progreso is the *only producer* of cement in Guatemala. If Cementos Progreso collapsed, the entire industry collapsed ..." (Emphasis added).
>
> "28. Given this disparity, it is perhaps understandable that Mexico would scoff at the idea that several hundred or several thousand tons of cement could *threaten material injury within the meaning of Article 3 of the AD Agreement*. But in a small, developing country like Guatemala, this kind of threat is very real. Particularly where, as here, the product under investigation is not a *luxury item*, but a *strategically important commodity, and* the *domestic industry is not large and diverse*, but confined to only *one company that depends on its domestic market for* ***all*** *of its revenues*. As we noted in Guatemala's first submission, had Cementos Progreso failed, the entire cement industry in Guatemala would have failed. Would Mexico be making the same arguments it is today if the "shoe had been on the other foot"? I think not". (Emphasis added).

6.263 In the paragraphs cited above, Guatemala argues that the Ministry had such a convincing case before it that it was fully justified in pursuing the investigation. But far from seeking to substantiate its argument by trying to demonstrate the sufficiency of the evidence, Guatemala resorts to a series of considerations that are absurd and out of context, and which have nothing to do with the standard of sufficiency of evidence imposed by Article 5.3 to justify the initiation of an investigation. In this context, it is thoroughly inappropriate and devoid of legal value for Guatemala to try to justify the initiation of the investigation by resorting to considerations such as the fact that the product in question is a consumer good and not a luxury item, or that the industry in question is not large and diversified but consists of a single domestic producer, which merely reflects the monopolistic position enjoyed by Cementos Progreso. Guatemala also suggests that it deserves special treatment or some kind of exemption on the grounds that it is a small and developing country. However, there are no provisions or exceptions under the WTO whereby small and developing countries like Guatemala are given special treatment in the form of a lower level of evidence and standard of sufficiency than the other Members, relieving them of their obligations under the Anti-Dumping Agreement, in particular under Article 5 thereof.[324]

6.264 The fact that Guatemala should resort to such considerations simply confirms the bias and lack of objectivity with which the Guatemalan authority evaluated and improperly established the facts required for the initiation of the investigation, i.e. the sufficiency of the evidence justifying such initiation. Moreover, there is no permissible interpretation of Article 5.3 under which the "forcefulness of a case" justifying the pursuit of an investigation can be determined on the basis of considerations or criteria such as those put forward by Guatemala. On the contrary, such arguments or considerations clearly have nothing to do with the letter, the context, the object and the purpose of Article 5.3 which consists in establishing the objective sufficiency of the evidence as a requirement for an authority to be able to proceed with the initiation of an investigation. Thus, under the Anti-Dumping Agreement, the sufficiency of evidence is in any case the only standard which can serve as a measure of the "forcefulness" of a case justifying the initiation of an investigation.

6.265 Still on the subject of the insufficiency of evidence, we cite below paragraph 69 of Guatemala's first written submission:

> "Notwithstanding, the Ministry did not act hastily. In fact, as we mentioned initially, it began by rejecting Cementos Progreso's application because *it needed further information and documentation* concerning certain complaints. In the course of the *three or four* months that followed, the Ministry obtained *additional* information from Cementos Progreso and interviewed officials from that firm. It was only *after* that *extended period of evaluation* that the Ministry decided that there was "sufficient evidence" under Article 5.3 of the Anti-Dumping Agreement to initiate an anti-dumping investigation." (Emphasis added).

6.266 On the one hand, this argument by Guatemala is an express recognition of the absence of information and the insufficiency of evidence, and on the other hand, it is no more than a *post hoc* argument without foundation, since although Guatemala argues that

---

[324] We cite below para. 27 of Guatemala's oral submission at the first substantive meeting as another example of its *post hoc* arguments based on information which was reflected neither in the determination nor in the public notice of initiation, where Guatemala seeks to hide behind its status as a developing country in order to relieve itself of its obligations under Article 5:

> "First, Mexico trivializes the size and impact of Cruz Azul's imports on Guatemala. Guatemala is a small, developing country. In 1994 (the year before the challenged anti-dumping investigation was initiated), Guatemala consumed only 1.18 million metric tonnes ("tons") of cement. By comparison, Mexico consumed 28.7 million tons of cement in 1994. Guatemala also has only two cement plants (both operated by Cementos Progreso) with a total productive capacity of less than 1.4 million tons in 1994. Mexico, by comparison, had well over 25 cement plants in 1994 with a productive capacity of approximately 43 million tons. Indeed, in 1995, Mexico's *excess* capacity (18.8 million tons) was 15 times greater than Guatemala's total consumption of cement (1.2 million tons)."
>
> See also, in this connection, Guatemala's first written submission, para. 176.

the Ministry rejected the application at first because it needed further information, there is nothing in the administrative file to prove these facts. Nor is there anything to show or to clearly explain what the information originally submitted by Cementos Progreso consisted in, not to mention the alleged "additional" information which, according to Guatemala, the Ministry obtained from Cementos Progreso during the course of the following three or four months. In other words, Mexico wonders why Guatemala does not explain what information Cementos Progreso had initially, when its application was rejected, and what other information and evidence was subsequently gathered for its application to be accepted by the Ministry later on.

6.267 At the same time, how can there possibly be any validity or credibility in the simple allegation by Guatemala that the Ministry conducted alleged interviews with officials from Cementos Progreso when the file did not contain the slightest record of them, let alone of such alleged additional information as the Ministry might have obtained through the alleged interviews. Without any record in the file, such data or information that the Ministry may have obtained through these interviews, assuming that they took place, amounts to no more than simple assertion, unsubstantiated by evidence, in violation of Article 5.2 which states that the requirements contained therein cannot be met through simple assertion, unsubstantiated by relevant evidence.

6.268 Similarly, it is unacceptable and inexplicable that if several months separated this alleged rejection from the submission of the original application, and allegedly there were efforts by the authority and Cementos Progreso to obtain additional information, the *evidence* that was finally submitted and considered by the Ministry as "sufficient" to initiate the investigation should have been limited to *two* delivery notes and *two* import certificates, since there is no way that a series of unsubstantiated allegations concerning the alleged threat of injury can be considered as constituting evidence, as Guatemala seems to suggest.

6.269 In the circumstances which Guatemala has itself evoked, it is also difficult to understand why it was not possible for the investigating authority to ask its customs authorities for the information on imports of the investigated product as soon as it was first approached by Cementos Progreso or as soon as the original application was filed, but that it should have done so only after initiating the investigation. If, as Guatemala asserts, "the Ministry did not act hastily" and three or four months elapsed, providing it with an "extended period of evaluation", there was ample time for the Ministry to request and obtain the relevant information on imports of the investigated product, particularly if we consider that the information requested from the customs authorities following the initiation of the investigation took about two months for the Ministry to obtain.

6.270 Given the lack of accurate and adequate evidence of dumping, the simple acceptance of the allegations and suspicions of the applicant concerning the alleged threat of injury, and the complete absence of evidence concerning these allegations, it is clear that none of the facts could be properly established by the Guatemalan authority. Clearly, the authority did not carry out an evaluation of the alleged facts in an unbiased and objective manner, but decided to accept outright the simple allegations and suspicions of the applicant.

6.271 Similarly, there is no permissible interpretation of Article 5.3 that would warrant considering that two delivery notes, two import certificates and a series of allegations and suspicions concerning the imports and their alleged effects would permit a reasonable and unbiased investigating authority to establish that such evidence in the application complied in the least with the *objective sufficiency* standard of evidence applicable to an initiation determination.

6.272 Thus, the only possible conclusion is that the investigation was initiated in a manner contrary to Article 5.3, since although no permissible interpretation of that provision could possibly justify the insufficiency of evidence of dumping, not to mention the *total absence* of evidence of the alleged threat of injury, and hence the causal link, the investigation was nevertheless initiated.

6.273 This enables us to conclude that under Article 5.3, the Ministry of the Economy *simply should not have initiated* this investigation and that the anti-dumping measures imposed by Guatemala and challenged by Mexico in this dispute rested on an investigation initiated by the Ministry on the basis of clearly insufficient evidence of the alleged dumping, the alleged threat of injury and the corresponding causal link.

6.274 However, before continuing, we must refute a number of assertions made by Guatemala in an attempt to distort and manipulate Mexico's arguments, and respond to some of its *post hoc* arguments which not only fail to demonstrate the alleged consistency of the initiation with the Anti-Dumping Agreement, but ironically and fortunately have served to strengthen Mexico's position in this WTO proceeding.

(i) Replies to Guatemala's arguments concerning the alleged sufficiency of the evidence of dumping to justify initiation

6.275 Regarding the likeness of the investigated product, Guatemala argues that it had no reason to believe that there was any difference between the cement sold in Mexico and the cement that Cruz Azul sold in Guatemala.[325] This makes it clear that the Ministry, in making its initiation determination, did not take account of the differences that can be seen in the identification of the product both in the application for an investigation[326] filed by Cementos Progreso and in the accompanying evidence of the normal value and the export price. Similarly, the Ministry clearly did not conduct the examination stipulated in Article 5.3, in this case in particular, in checking the likeness of the product under Article 2.6.

6.276 Guatemala clearly reveals a flaw in its argument when it recognizes, in paragraph 157 of its first submission, the differences in the identification of the investigated product contained in the evidence referred to above, and reproduces the references contained in the evidence of normal value and export price, such as "grey cement" and "Cruz Azul cement" for the normal value, and "grey cement", "grey Portland cement" and "Type II grey Portland cement with Pozzolana" for the export price.

6.277 Furthermore, in the same paragraph of its first submission, Guatemala tries, through the assertion below, to maintain that in fact the price comparison carried out on the basis of the evidence provided by Cementos Progreso both for the normal value and for the export price concerned "grey cement":

> "In a country where the price of cement had been regulated by the Government for over 50 years (footnote omitted), this evidence indicated to the Ministry that the sales that were being compared were of 'grey cement'."

6.278 While this deduction by Guatemala may be valid for identifying the product exported by Cruz Azul to the Guatemalan market, it is not valid for determining the like product destined for consumption in the domestic market of Mexico, particularly when one of the delivery notes used for the calculation of normal value merely indicated "Cruz

[325] First written submission by Guatemala, para. 156.

[326] In the sections "Detailed description of the domestic product" and "Detailed description of the imported item", Cementos Progreso mentions the differences in types of cement.

Azul cement". This description merely indicates that the product in question was cement, and no more - not that it was "grey cement" as Guatemala contends. In fact, the Ministry asserted *post hoc* that: "... Mexico, which has a common border with Guatemala 963 kilometres long and whose capital (Mexico city) is the second largest city in the world, consumed 28,700,000 tons of cement in 1994".[327]

6.279 Since Guatemala recognizes that the Mexican cement market is large in comparison to its own market, even highlighting the fact that Mexico City is the second largest city in the world, and clearly has many different types of consumers with different needs, it should have been obvious that "grey" cement was not the only type of cement consumed domestically.

6.280 Further evidence that Guatemala did not conduct the examination required under Article 5.3 can be found in the fact that Cementos Progreso's application contains allegations that the investigated product was "grey Portland or pozzolanic cement in 94-pound bags" (sic) and that the evidence submitted with the application for an investigation referred to above did not clearly identify the type of cement used to prove the normal value (see MEXICO-3). Furthermore, neither Cementos Progreso's application nor the alleged analysis carried out by Guatemala recognizes the possibility that the product comparison might have been made in respect of different types of cement. Guatemala simply did not conduct the required examination.

6.281 In fact, there is no evidence that Guatemala conducted an examination of product likeness, still less that it did so in conformity with Article 2.6 of the AD Agreement, and apparently in making its determination of likeness, if indeed it made such a determination, the Ministry accepted the validity of Cementos Progreso's allegation without carrying out any check or examination under Article 5.3.

6.282 Finally, Guatemala adds that an adjustment for the alleged difference in types of cement would probably have benefited Cementos Progreso and not Cruz Azul. In Mexico's view, what counts is not who might have benefited from the adjustment, but that Guatemala violated Articles 2.6 and 5.3 by not carrying out the required examination and not making an initiation determination based, *inter alia*, on an analysis and determination of product likeness.

6.283 As regards the differences in volume in the evidence submitted in support of the alleged dumping, there is a discrepancy between the applicant's allegation that the product investigated was sold in bags, and the evidence supplied in support of the normal value which indicates that the cement was sold in loads or sacks, and not bags. Sales in sacks or loads reflect a quantity of 50 kg., while the sale in bags referred to by the applicant concerns a quantity of 42.5 kg.

6.284 Guatemala submits that neither the application, nor any evidence in the possession of the Ministry at the time of initiation, provided any indication that the size of the sacks was in fact different.[328] Here we repeat that the evidence in support of the normal value expressly states that the two transactions concerned one sack of cement and one load of cement respectively. Hence the need to examine whether the sacks or loads of cement had the same volume as the bags. Guatemala's assertion shows once again that the Ministry did not conduct the examination required under Article 5.3.

6.285 Guatemala ignored the possible differences which could result from the sale of cement in loads and sacks instead of the bags referred to by the applicant. In fact, Guatemala did not even decide on the matter, and consequently, has no evidence to show that it

[327] First written submission by Guatemala, para. 62.

[328] *Ibid.*, para. 160.

carried out the examination. Lacking the evidence, Guatemala circumvents the violation it committed in respect of Article 5.3, and in paragraph 160 of its first written submission states that:

> "In any case, given the substantial dumping margin shown by the invoices and other evidence in the Ministry's possession at the time of initiation, the fact is that *there would still have been a significant margin of dumping even if the slight difference in the weight of the sacks had been taken into account*." (Emphasis added).

6.286 On the subject of the levels of trade of the reported transactions, Mexico submits that in comparing the normal value and the export price, Guatemala failed to take account of the fact that these levels were different. Guatemala has asserted in this connection that the application and the evidence before the Ministry at the time of initiation provided no indication that any adjustment for level of trade would be appropriate.[329] By making this assertion, Guatemala shows once again that it did not examine the evidence submitted by Cementos Progreso.

6.287 As we have said, Guatemala simply did not conduct the examination required under Article 5.3. The evidence submitted by the applicant with respect to normal value referred to transactions which took place at retail price to the public, while the evidence of the export price referred to transactions at prices between the manufacturer and the distributor. In establishing price comparability, Guatemala should have recognized and evaluated the fact that the prices for normal value and the export prices were obtained on the basis of transactions which took place at different levels of trade, and in its initiation determination, in the section entitled "Estimation of the Margin of Dumping", it should have acknowledged this fact.

6.288 Another element which confirms Guatemala's violation of Article 5.2 and 5.3 is the fact that the dollar/peso exchange rate put forward by the applicant is not documented in the file. Cementos Progreso did not provide any evidence to substantiate the claimed exchange rate. Once again, Guatemala accepted the applicant's claim as valid without conducting the examination required under Article 5.3.

6.289 Now, as part of this procedure, Guatemala cites the official exchange rate of the International Monetary Fund (IMF) for September 1995, the month and year in which the application for an investigation was submitted, adding that the IMF exchange rate was very close to the exchange rate used by Cementos Progreso in its application.[330]

6.290 Thus, using *post hoc* arguments Guatemala is now seeking to show that the exchange rate used for the initiation determination was close to the official exchange rate. In doing so, however, Guatemala is disregarding two important elements. Firstly, under Article 5.2, Cementos Progreso should have provided evidence in support of its assertion concerning the exchange rate, failing which the Ministry should have requested the information from the applicant; and secondly, under Article 5.3 the examination and verification of the evidence submitted by Cementos Progreso should have been conducted and documented before the initiation determination was issued; in other words, what Guatemala is now seeking to demonstrate is, *inter alia*, what it should have demonstrated before issuing the determination of initiation of the anti-dumping investigation.

6.291 Regarding the evidence submitted by Cementos Progreso in support of the normal value, Mexico submits that the so-called invoices are in fact delivery notes. In this con-

---

[329] *Ibid.*, para. 161.

[330] *Ibid.*, para. 165 and footnote 199.

nection, Guatemala attempts[331] to shift the burden of the proof to Mexico, although as argued in the general remarks section of this second submission, this is totally unacceptable. If, instead, Guatemala had conducted the examination required under Article 5.3, it would have discovered that the evidence submitted by the applicant in support of the export price included invoices that were sent by Cruz Azul on the grounds that they complied with the relevant requirements under Mexican law in that, *inter alia*, they were identified as numbered invoices and contained a photocopy of the tax certification showing that they were registered with the corresponding Mexican tax authority (in this case, it appears at the top of the documents).

6.292 The delivery notes provided as evidence of the normal value, on the other hand, contain no clear indication that they are in fact invoices, nor do they contain the tax certification; in fact one of them refers to an order rather than a sale, suggesting there might not actually have been a sale of a sack of cement, but only an offer.

6.293 In any case, it seems fairly clear that Guatemala did not conduct the examination required under Article 5.3; *inter alia*, it did not review the accuracy and adequacy of the evidence submitted to prove the normal value and the export price. In fact, Guatemala did not recognize the differences in the evidence submitted by Cementos Progreso and in a general and arbitrary manner, the Ministry pointed out that the evidence of normal value consisted of invoices.

6.294 With respect to the alleged dumping in support of the initiation determination, it is clear to Mexico that any authority that had made an unbiased and objective evaluation of the facts in conducting the examination stipulated in Article 5.3 would have realized that in making a comparison between the normal value and the export price it could not disregard the significant and obvious differences reflected in the evidence submitted in respect of the alleged dumping, *inter alia*, differences in the products, the volumes, the levels of trade and the "representivity" of the sales, and the lack of evidence concerning the exchange rate.

6.295 It is equally serious in the light of the above considerations that Guatemala, in its initiation determination, should not have shown the slightest recognition of the fact that the normal value and export price cited by Cementos Progreso in its application for initiation were not comparable and that there was no indication that the Ministry asked the applicant for more information or tried to obtain the information by some other means.

6.296 While Mexico understands that the information contained in the application for initiation of an investigation is limited to the information reasonably available to the applicant on the factors listed in subparagraphs (i) to (iv) of Article 5.2, and that the level of evidence needed to justify the initiation of an investigation is lower than the level of evidence required for a preliminary or definitive determination, the evidence required to initiate an investigation cannot be just "any evidence".[332] How could Guatemala possibly think that two delivery notes which failed to identify the type of cement that was supposed to be a like product to that exported by Mexico to Guatemala, that failed to indicate

---

[331] *Ibid.*, para. 164.

[332] Although neither Article 5 nor any other provision of the AD Agreement defines the term "sufficient evidence to justify the initiation of an investigation", certain panel decisions shed light in this respect, as for example the report adopted on 27 October 1993, SCM/162, BISD/426, *United States - Measures Affecting Imports of Softwood Lumber from Canada*, para. 332. Although *United States - Softwood Lumber* involved the challenge of an ex officio initiation of a countervailing duty investigation, *inter alia* because it was argued that the evidence was insufficient to justify initiation, these elements apply by analogy to the initiation of anti-dumping investigations as well.

the terms and conditions of sale applicable to the prices reported in the alleged invoices for sales in the Mexican market and corresponding to two sales transactions expressed in the lowest possible unit of sale for the marketing of the investigated product, and two import certificates which showed export volumes at wholesale or distributor level, could be considered as accurate and adequate evidence, and hence, as sufficient evidence to justify the initiation of an investigation?

6.297 In short, for the purposes of its initiation determination the Ministry failed to take account of the differences between the evidence submitted by Cementos Progreso of normal value and the evidence of the export price, thereby violating Article 5.2 and 5.3, not to mention Article 2; and since it did not have accurate and adequate evidence, nor sufficient evidence to justify the initiation of the investigation, Guatemala should have promptly rejected the application for initiation of the anti-dumping investigation. By not doing so, it also violated Article 5.8 of the AD Agreement.

(ii) Reply to Guatemala's arguments concerning the alleged sufficiency of evidence of threat of injury to justify the initiation

6.298 Guatemala's arguments concerning the alleged sufficiency of evidence of threat of injury to initiate the investigation must also be rejected.

6.299 We must begin by refuting certain arguments set forth in paragraph 67 of Guatemala's first written submission:

> "Seeing itself threatened by this flood of imports on its **only** market, Cementos Progreso had no choice but to file an application for an anti-dumping investigation with the Ministry of the Economy. In its application dated 21 September 1995, and the supplementary application of 9 October 1995, Cementos Progreso presented evidence of the injurious effects of dumping by Cruz Azul in Guatemala. In particular, Cementos Progreso supplied information relating to loss of sales, loss of customers and a *trend* towards penetration of imports which *in the space of a single day increased* from basically 0 to 480 tons (representing approximately US$60,000 in loss of sales). While this amount may seem small to Mexico, projected over one year it would represent a substantial portion of the total production and income of Cementos Progreso in 1995." (Footnote omitted)

6.300 Firstly, Cementos Progreso never supplied information to show that it was threatened by a "flood" of imports; indeed, its application was supported only by the documentation concerning two import certificates and simple assertions, unsubstantiated by relevant evidence, as prohibited by Article 5.2 of the AD Agreement.

6.301 Secondly, Cementos Progreso never presented "evidence of the injurious effects of dumping by Cruz Azul", since the only documents that could have been considered as evidence in the application were, as we said, two delivery notes, two import certificates and a "flood" of simple assertions. Similarly, Guatemala is lying when it claims that Cementos Progreso supplied information relating to loss of sales, loss of customers and a "trend" towards penetration of imports. Simple assertion in respect of these factors is not enough to substantiate the argument that the application contained the information required under subparagraph (iv) of Article 5.2.

6.302 Thirdly, Guatemala cannot contend that it had information concerning an "increase" in the "trend towards penetration of imports" when the analysis of an import penetration "trend" would in any case require a study of many more indicators than the two import certificates showing an incremental difference for only one day while the original investigation period was six months; it cannot now argue, in this proceeding, that the mentioned figure (0 to 480 tons) "projected over one year ... would represent a substantial portion of the total production and income of Cementos Progreso in 1995". It should be noted that at no time prior to initiation did the applicant or the Ministry make this projection or any other projection, nor did they examine the volume of imports against production or consumption in Guatemala as the Ministry now asserts.[333] So that Guatemala cannot substantiate its allegation that the imports were massive merely by arguing that Cementos Progreso was threatened by a "flood" of imports, nor can it assert, as it did in paragraph 32 of its oral submission at the first substantive meeting, that Cementos Progreso's application contained import figures and trends.

6.303 At the same time, in its first written submission (Part III B, Section 2(b)), Guatemala maintains that the Ministry had sufficient evidence of threat of injury to initiate the investigation, and in an effort to develop its position, it also makes an unfortunate attempt to counter Mexico's arguments concerning the *insufficiency of evidence of threat of injury* to initiate the investigation.

6.304 In paragraph 174 of its first submission, in very eloquent, almost literary terms, Guatemala displays evident confusion concerning Mexico's arguments relating to the insufficiency of evidence of threat of injury:

> "174. Mexico's suggestion that *the Ministry should have delayed initiation in order to gather more information* conjures up Nero playing his violin while Rome was in flames. [...]." (Emphasis added)

6.305 Similarly, in paragraph 171 of its first submission, Guatemala tries to manipulate Mexico's position by stating that Mexico "has argued that the Ministry was under obligation to examine *more* evidence of injury before initiating the investigation". According to Guatemala, Mexico "insisted that Guatemala should have analysed *at greater length the evidence before it and should have taken more time to issue its decision* to initiate the investigation", adding that "Mexico cites the decision of the Ministry to initiate its investigation without waiting for *fuller* information on the actual level of Cruz Azul's imports." In a further attempt to counter Mexico's arguments, Guatemala states that "if the Ministry had *taken its time* and *studied the evidence more carefully*, it would have realized that there was no justification for an investigation" and contends that "with due respect for its larger neighbour in the north, [...] these arguments are nothing short of ridiculous".

6.306 It is true that Mexico's arguments, as distorted and manipulated by Guatemala, would seem ridiculous to anyone. Nowhere has Mexico suggested that Guatemala's violations in this context have anything to do with the fact that the Ministry should have "taken more time to issue its decision" or should have "delayed initiation in order to gather more information" as Guatemala absurdly suggests. Nor was it a matter of "waiting for fuller information on the actual level of Cruz Azul's imports", but rather, of the Ministry's complying with its obligation to have sufficient evidence to justify the initiation. For example, regarding the alleged "massive" nature of Cruz Azul's imports, the Ministry had ample time to obtain information on imports before initiation, but preferred to base its decision on the insufficient information contained in two import certificates, and request information on imports from the customs authorities only after the investigation had been initiated.

6.307 Still less did Mexico argue that the point at issue was that the Ministry should examine "at *greater* length the *evidence before it*" or that it was "under obligation to examine *more* evidence of injury" as Guatemala absurdly tries to suggest. We might respond to these absurd suggestions by asking what evidence the Ministry had before it of threat of

[333] First written submission by Mexico, paras. 136 and 137.

injury? When does Guatemala think that Mexico ever stated that the Ministry had any evidence before it of the alleged threat of injury when deciding to initiate? How many times do we have to repeat that the initiation was based on nothing more than simple assertions, and that the evidence in support of those assertions was non-existent?

6.308 What evidence could the Ministry have examined at "greater" length, when in fact Mexico has insisted any number of times that neither Cementos Progreso's application, nor the administrative file on initiation, contained any evidence at all, let alone relevant, accurate, or sufficient to initiate the alleged threat of injury and the corresponding causal link, and that the Ministry merely accepted and adopted outright the simple assertions and even the suspicions of the applicant with respect to the alleged massive volume of imports and this alleged effect on the Guatemalan domestic industry, in open violation of Articles 5.2 and 5.3?

6.309 But suffice it to read the relevant part of Mexico's first written submission, including the paragraphs to which Guatemala itself refers[334], to realize that Mexico never argued what Guatemala has presented in a manipulated and tendentious way in an absurd attempt to defend an initiation which was blatantly inconsistent with the Anti-Dumping Agreement owing to the indisputable fact that it took place without the slightest evidence in support of the alleged threat of injury. This complete lack of evidence of injury cannot, under any permissible interpretation of the Agreement, be considered consistent with the standard of sufficiency stipulated in Article 5.3 for the initiation of an anti-dumping investigation.

6.310 In an equally absurd attempt to support the fallacy that the Ministry had "*more than sufficient*" evidence of the alleged threat of injury to justify the initiation of the investigation, Guatemala states, in paragraph 174 of its first submission[335], that the Ministry *knew* of certain information with respect to Cementos Progreso and on aspects such as the cement market in Guatemala, prices, the increase in imports, and the fact that Mexico was going through a deep recession, from which is simply inferred that Mexico had an excess capacity.

6.311 To assert that the Ministry knew of this information is not the same as proving that these alleged facts were duly established by the Guatemalan authority for the purposes of initiating the investigation. Even assuming, for the sake of argument, that the Ministry knew of the information, there is no such indication in Cementos Progreso's

[334] First written submission by Guatemala, footnotes 205 to 208.

[335] *Ibid.*, para. 174, which reads:

"Mexico's suggestion that the Ministry should have delayed initiation in order to gather more information conjures up Nero playing his violin while Rome was in flames. In this submission, we have proved beyond any doubt that the Ministry had *more than sufficient* evidence to justify the initiation of an anti-dumping investigation under Article 5 of the AD Agreement. The Ministry *knew* the size of the domestic market. Cementos Progreso exported practically no cement up to 1995, and no-one was interested in exporting cement to the Guatemalan market. Consequently, Cementos Progreso's production reflected national consumption. The Ministry *did not need complete information to know* that imports were rapidly increasing. As explained above, within a period of a few months in 1995, imports increased from basically zero to 25 per cent of consumption in Guatemala. The Ministry *also knew* that Mexico was going through a terrible recession and that consumption and production had decreased dramatically, resulting in thousands of tons of idle capacity. Finally, the Ministry *knew* that Cruz Azul's prices were well below those of Cementos Progreso, because the Government regulated cement prices and because the Government itself was one of the main purchasers of cement, and because Cementos Progreso had supplied information on domestic prices." (Emphasis added by Mexico)

application, or in the recommendation prepared by the two advisors, or in the initiation determination, still less in the public notice of initiation. In fact, Guatemala expressly acknowledges in the cited paragraph that the Ministry "did not need complete information to know that imports were rapidly increasing" and that the Ministry merely inferred that there was excess capacity from its "knowledge" that Mexico was going through a "terrible recession", without any element of the administrative file on the initiation or the public notice of initiation making the slightest reference to any information or evidence in support of the likelihood of an increase in imports or excess capacity in Mexico. Consequently, these simple assertions cannot be taken into consideration in evaluating whether the Ministry correctly reached the conclusion that there was sufficient evidence to justify the initiation of the investigation.

(iii) Reply to Guatemala's arguments concerning the alleged sufficiency of evidence of a causal link to justify initiation.

6.312 Guatemala argues that the Ministry had sufficient evidence concerning the causal link between the alleged dumping and the alleged threat of injury, and that Mexico's claim concerning the violation of Article 5.2 and 5.3 based on lack of evidence of a causal link[336] is without merit. Guatemala's defence is based simply on the argument that:

> " ... The clear meaning of Article 5.2 is that there is sufficient evidence of a causal link if the application provides evidence of dumping in conformity with Article 5.2(iii) and proof of consequent injury in conformity with Article 5.2(iv). Cementos Progreso met those requirements".[337]

6.313 Guatemala's argument is erroneous from various points of view:

6.314 Firstly, the interpretation of Article 5.2 adduced by Guatemala is simply impermissible, since even if we assume, for the sake of argument, that there was evidence of dumping and threat of injury in the application, this does not necessarily and automatically imply, let alone prove, that there was a causal link, since the state of the domestic industry could be the result of factors other than dumping. From a strictly technical point of view it is possible to imagine that there is dumping and injury *without* there necessarily being a causal link between the dumped imports and the injury to a domestic industry, since the effects on the domestic industry could be the result of other factors. But when there is insufficient evidence of the existence of dumping or threat of injury to a domestic industry, as in this case, it cannot under any circumstances simply be assumed that there is evidence of a causal link.

6.315 Nor is it enough, secondly, to say in refutation of the argument that Article 5.2 and 5.3 were violated:

> "... the application also *referred* explicitly to the causal link. The application dated 21 September *states* that the dumped cement was entering in quantities that were causing injury to Cementos Progreso. The supplementary application *states* that Cementos Progreso was being threatened by massive imports of cement from Mexico. The supplementary application also *describes* how the dumped imports

336 From its first submission onwards, Mexico has maintained that the application did not contain, nor did the Ministry have before it, any evidence of the causal link for the purposes of its initiation determination, and that this constituted a violation of Article 5.2 and 5.3 of the AD Agreement. See paras. 165 to 171 of Mexico's first written submission.

337 First written submission by Guatemala, para. 183.

were directly affecting the firm's investments."[338] (Emphasis added by Mexico) (footnotes omitted)

6.316 A plain reading of this quotation clearly reveals that the application did not contain any evidence of the causal link between the dumping and the alleged threat of injury, but only simple assertions or statements. To "refer to", "to state" or "to describe" something cannot, under any permissible interpretation of Article 5.2, be considered as consistent with the requirement stipulated therein to *include "evidence"* of a causal link. In fact, Article 5.2 expressly prohibits what Guatemala has adduced in its defence by firmly stating that:

> "[...] Simple assertion, unsubstantiated by relevant evidence, cannot be considered sufficient to meet the requirements of this paragraph. [...]"[339]

6.317 Thirdly, Guatemala's defence is not only based on an impermissible interpretation of Article 5.2, but it also fails to answer Mexico's claim concerning the violation of Article 5.3. Simply to argue that "the application contained accurate and adequate evidence with respect to the criteria contained in Article 5.2 (iii) and 5.2 (iv) "does not answer the question of whether there was sufficient evidence of a causal link to justify the initiation by the Ministry of the Economy of an investigation.[340]

6.318 Mexico has being demonstrating throughout this proceeding that the application did not contain relevant evidence of dumping or of threat of injury, nor did the Ministry obtain ex-officio any evidence thereof, initiating the investigation without sufficient evidence of dumping and of threat of injury. Thus, the only possible conclusion is that the Ministry of the Economy could not, under any circumstances, simply assume that there was sufficient evidence to demonstrate *a causal link* either.

6.319 In short, when there is insufficient evidence of dumping and threat of injury to justify initiation as in this case, it cannot simply be argued, as Guatemala has done, that "the Ministry had sufficient evidence of a causal link", as this merely reflects a poor attempt to demonstrate what cannot be demonstrated.

3. *Claims Under Articles 5.7 and 5.8 - Simultaneous Consideration of Evidence of Both Dumping and Injury*

(a) Submissions of Mexico

6.320 **Mexico** advances the following arguments under Articles 5.7 and 5.8 of the AD Agreement:

6.321 Despite the obvious lack of sufficient evidence of the alleged dumping and the alleged threat of injury, the Ministry of the Economy did not reject Cementos Progreso's application for initiation but, on the contrary, initiated the investigation improperly basing itself on the submission of two delivery notes and two import certificates and on mere allegations and conjectures unsubstantiated by evidence.

---

338 *Ibid.*, para. 184.

339 Article 5.5 of the AD Agreement.

340 In this connection, the Panel in the case *"Guatemala - Cement I"* found:

> "7.53 We have concluded that the question whether there is 'sufficient evidence' to justify initiation is not answered by a determination that the application contains all the information 'reasonably available' to the applicant on the factors specified in Article 5.2 (i) to (iv). [...] "See also paras. 7.49 and 7.50 of the same document.

6.322 It is thus obvious that the Guatemalan authority violated Article 5.7 of the AD Agreement by failing to examine the evidence of dumping and threat of injury simultaneously, in accordance with Articles 2 and 3 of the Agreement, when deciding whether or not to initiate the investigation.

6.323 Moreover, the relevant section of Article 5.8 makes a specific reference to rejection of applications submitted in accordance with Article 5.1 *as soon as the authorities concerned are satisfied that there is not sufficient evidence* of either dumping or of injury to justify proceeding with the case:

> "5.8. An application under paragraph 1 shall be rejected and an investigation shall be terminated promptly as soon as the authorities concerned are satisfied that there is not sufficient evidence of either dumping or injury to justify proceeding with the case [...]."

6.324 This provision is clearly related to Article 5.2 and 5.3 and can only be interpreted to mean that an investigation cannot be initiated unless there is sufficient evidence of dumping and injury. Where this is not the case, the application *must* be rejected by the investigating authority and an investigation may not be initiated.

6.325 As has been established in previous decisions by panels, failure to comply with the provisions on initiation laid down in the AD Agreement cannot be remedied or replaced by measures subsequent to initiation of the investigation[341] as the very purpose of Article 5 is to ensure compliance with specific minimum criteria before deciding to initiate an investigation.[342] Not only should Cementos Progreso's application have been rejected, but the investigation should never have been initiated.

6.326 The Ministry of the Economy therefore violated Article 5.8 of the AD Agreement by not rejecting the application made by Cementos Progreso and by not refraining from initiating the investigation due to the lack of sufficient evidence of dumping and threat of injury to justify initiation in accordance with Articles 2 and 3 of the AD Agreement respectively.

(b) Response of Guatemala

6.327 The following are **Guatemala's** arguments in response to Mexico's claims under Articles 5.7 and 5.8:

6.328 Mexico asserts that Guatemala initiated the investigation at issue without sufficient evidence of dumping *and* injury.[343] Mexico argues that as a result, Guatemala violated Article 5.7 of the Anti-Dumping Agreement.[344]

6.329 Article 5.7 stipulates that "the evidence of both dumping and injury shall be considered simultaneously" when an authority makes its determination with respect to initia-

---

341 Some GATT Panels considered this issue in the context of the Tokyo Round Agreement on application of Article VI of the GATT. See, for example, *United States - Gray Portland Cement and Clinker,* above footnote 26, para. 5.37, where it is concluded that "a failure to observe the requirements in Article 5 could not be remedied by action subsequent to the initiation of the investigation ..."; and *United States - Imposition of Anti-Dumping Duties on Imports of Seamless Stainless Steel Hollow Products from Sweden*, ADP/47, Report of the Panel published on 29 August 1990 (not adopted), para. 5.20, which states that "there was no basis to consider that an infringement of this provision could be cured retroactively". See also *Guatemala - Cement, supra*, footnote 25, para. 8.6.

342 *United States - Gray Portland Cement and Clinker*, para. 5.37.

343 First submission of Mexico, para. 172.

344 *Ibid.*, para. 173.

tion.[345] Mexico's claim that Guatemala violated Article 5.7 is no more than a claim, because it is not substantiated by facts or arguments. In addressing the burden of proof above, we showed that when a complainant fails to substantiate a claim, that claim must be rejected. Mexico's claim concerning Article 5.7 must be rejected.

6.330 Even assuming, for the sake of argument, that the Panel were to allow Mexico to maintain its claim with respect to Article 5.7, that claim should not be allowed to prevail because it is without merit. Our earlier discussion of the subject (which we incorporate here by reference) shows sufficiently clearly that Guatemala fully examined the accuracy and adequacy of the evidence before it with respect to dumping *and* injury. There is no evidence, and Mexico certainly does not cite any, that could lead this Panel to conclude that the Ministry examined one category and not the other prior to the initiation of the investigation at issue.

(i) There was sufficient evidence of dumping and injury

6.331 According to Mexico, "the Ministry of the Economy ... violated Article 5.8 of the AD Agreement by not rejecting the application made by Cementos Progreso and by not refraining from initiating the investigation due to the lack of sufficient evidence of dumping and threat of injury ...".[346] This last minute argument must be rejected for the following reasons:

6.332 Like Mexico's claim with respect to Article 5.7, this claim with respect to Article 5.8 is no more than just that: a claim unsubstantiated by any facts or arguments. Thus, Mexico has failed to assume the burden of the proof as required of it, and its claims should be rejected. If, nevertheless, the Panel were to allow Mexico to maintain this claim, like all other such claims, it should not be allowed to prevail because it is without merit.

6.333 Firstly, the first sentence of Article 5.8 states that "an application under paragraph 1 shall be rejected *and* an investigation shall be terminated promptly as soon as the authorities concerned are satisfied that there is not sufficient evidence of either dumping or injury to justify proceeding with the case."[347] The next sentence identifies certain situations requiring "immediate termination" of an investigation.[348] The wording of Article 5.8 makes it clear that it is only applicable after the initiation of the investigation.

6.334 This interpretation of Article 5.8 is confirmed by negotiating history. The origins of this provision can be found in Article 5(c) of the Kennedy Round Anti-Dumping Code, the title of which was the same as that of the current Article 5: "Initiation and Subsequent Investigation". However during the Kennedy Round of multilateral trade negotiations, this text was included in Article 7 of the Draft Anti-Dumping Code under the title "Subsequent Consideration".[349] This suggests exactly what the ordinary meaning of the current text is, i.e. that Article 5.8 is applicable to the consideration and conduct of anti-dumping investigations *after* they have been initiated.

6.335 Secondly, even if we assume, for the sake of argument, that this approach to Article 5.8 were rejected, Guatemala respectfully submits that if this Panel applied the appro-

[345] AD Agreement, Article 5.7.

[346] First submission by Mexico, para. 177.

[347] AD Agreement, Article 5.8 (emphasis added).

[348] For example, when the margin of dumping is *de minimis*. See *United States - DRAM, supra*, footnote 115, para. 6.90.

[349] See TN.64/NTB/W/16,6 (3 March 1967); TN.64/NTB/W14,6 (9 December 1966).

priate standard of review, it could not conclude, as Mexico claims, that the investigation at issue was initiated without sufficient evidence of dumping and threat of injury. In earlier sections of this submission we presented our arguments and opinions on the matter, and we shall simply incorporate them here by reference.

(ii) The determination of initiation by the ministry is not subject to examination by the panel as a de novo review

6.336 Throughout its first submission, Mexico argues for a standard of review which would require this Panel, illegally, to substitute its judgement for that of the investigating authority in Guatemala. Mexico repeatedly urged the Panel to examine the evidence which the Ministry had before it and to find that the said evidence was not sufficient to justify the initiation of an anti-dumping investigation.[350] Article 17.6 of the Anti-Dumping Agreement prescribes a standard of review. Article 17.6(i) stipulates that panels should respect the factual decisions of an investigating authority when "the establishment of the facts was proper and the evaluation was unbiased and objective, even though the panel might have reached a different conclusion ... ". If these conditions are satisfied, the evaluation of the national investigating authority will not be overturned, even if the panel has reached a different conclusion.[351]

6.337 Thus, the limited scope of the Article 17.6(i) review means that: (a) panels should not reassess the evidence; and (b) panels cannot carry out a *de novo* review.[352] As long as the decision of the Ministry to initiate the investigation at issue rests on facts that were adequately established and assessed on an unbiased and objective basis, the panel should respect that decision.

6.338 Mexico asserts that the determination made by the Ministry concerning the initiation reflected a complete omission in assessing the accuracy and adequacy of the evidence and a partial analysis of the evidence. An impartial reading of the Ministry's determination and of the facts in this dispute shows that the Ministry examined the facts that it had before it completely and fairly, and made a determination that was reasonably supported by those facts. Mexico or this Panel may carry out a *de novo* review and arrive at a different conclusion, but that is not the Panel's function

---

[350] See, for example, first submission of Mexico, paras. 91, 126, 138, 159, 161-62, 170-71.

[351] As mentioned when we discussed the standard of review above, the Panel in the case *Korea - Resins* arrived at this same conclusion:

> "The Panel considered that a review of whether the KTC's determination was based on positive evidence did not mean that he Panel should substitute its own judgement for that of the KTC as to the relative weight to be accorded to the facts before the KTC. To do so would ignore that the task of the Panel was not to make its own independent evaluation of the facts before the KTC to determine whether there was material injury to the industry in Korea but to review the determination as made by the KTC for consistency with the Agreement, bearing in mind that in a given case reasonable minds could differ as to the significance to be attached to certain facts. The Panel considered that a proper review of the KTC's determination against the requirement of positive evidence under Article 3.1 meant that it should examine whether the factual basis of the findings articulated in the determination was discernible from the text of the determination and reasonably supported those findings."

ADP/92, 2 April 1993, para. 227.

[352] See the Cartland Letter, footnote 159 above.

6.339 In conclusion, Mexico did not meet the requirement to demonstrate, under the applicable standard of review, that Guatemala's factual findings were made in an inadequate and partial manner. Although Mexico argues that the factual determinations at issue were biased and partial, it has not provided any evidence in support of its arguments. Similarly, there is no indication of partiality in the way in which the evidence was interpreted by the Guatemalan authorities.[353] At best, all Mexico has done is to offer an alternative reading of the evidence, or in some cases, it has merely suggested that an alternative reading might be possible, and not that the factual record required an alternative finding. In view of this situation, there is simply no reason whatsoever why the Panel should substitute its interpretation of the facts for that of the Guatemalan authorities, and to do so would simply infringe the clear standard of review applicable to anti-dumping disputes under Article 17.6(i) of the AD Agreement.

(c) Rebuttal of Mexico

6.340 **Mexico** rebuts Guatemala's response to its claims under Articles 5.7 and 5.8 as follows:

6.341 As Mexico has argued before, it is clear from the proven circumstances in which the investigation at issue was initiated that Guatemala also violated Article 5.7 and 5.8 of the Anti-Dumping Agreement. That is, it can also be seen from the evidence that Mexico supplied to the Panel on the basis of the administrative file of Guatemala's investigation that in deciding whether or not to initiate the investigation, the Ministry failed to consider simultaneously the evidence of both dumping and injury in accordance with the provisions of Articles 2 and 3.

6.342 In Mexico's view, this is not a simple requirement under the Agreement, but a provision which in all cases reinforces the examination required under Article 5.3 and its standard of objective sufficiency of the evidence. If it had conducted this examination simultaneously as required by the Agreement, the authority would not have been able to consider two delivery notes and two import certificates as sufficient evidence of dumping within the meaning of Article 2, let alone as sufficient evidence of injury within the meaning of Article 3.

6.343 Moreover, faced with the conclusion that would inevitably have resulted from such an examination, if the authority had conduced that the evidence was insufficient, the Ministry should have rejected the application submitted by Cementos Progreso and refrained from initiating the investigation in accordance with Article 5.8. But Guatemala seems to have disregarded both the letter and the object and purpose of this provision.

6.344 Indeed, Mexico considers the interpretation of Article 5.8 proposed by Guatemala to be totally impermissible.[354] According to Guatemala, Article 5.8 is only applicable to the rejection of an application after the initiation, to terminate an investigation. Under this

---

[353] In the Panel Report *EC - Imposition of Anti-Dumping Duties on Imports of Cotton Yarn from Brazil*, ADP/137, adopted on 30 October 1995, paras. 512-513, the Panel determined that when an investigating authority had before it two sets of inconsistent data neither of which was necessarily more precise than the other, the decision of the investigating authority to base its determination on one of those sets of data and not the other did not show any bias or lack of objectivity. In Guatemala's opinion, when one of the parties tries to prove that the determination of the investigating authority is not "unbiased" in the meaning of Article 17.6(i), it must provide positive evidence that the decision was influenced by a bias or prejudgement. Mere allegation or conjecture cannot in any way discharge the burden that rests with the challenging party in this respect.

[354] First written submission by Guatemala, para. 193.

interpretation, an investigation could be initiated without sufficient evidence of dumping and injury, which would totally contradict the text of this provision which refers to the *rejection* of an application as soon as the authorities concerned are satisfied that there is not sufficient evidence of either dumping or of injury to justify proceeding with the case.[355] Likewise, Guatemala's interpretation goes against the logic of the standard of objective sufficiency established in Article 5.3. What point would there be in Article 5.3 requiring sufficient evidence to justify initiation of an investigation if Article 5.8, according to Guatemala's interpretation, permitted the initiation of the investigation in spite of insufficient evidence?

6.345 Finally, in this connection, paragraph 39 of Guatemala's oral submission at the first substantive meeting with the parties states:

> "[...] [As we explain in our written submission, this provision does **not** apply to the initiation of anti-dumping investigations. As the Panel in *Corn Syrup from the United States* recently found (paragraph 7.99), Article 5.8 only applies *after* the initiation of an investigation. ... Besides being a correct interpretation of Article 5.8, this interpretation also underscores the low evidentiary threshold for initiation under Article 5.3. In other words, if the allegations that warrant initiation are later proven not to "justify proceeding with the case", importers are protected by Article 5.8 which requires "prompt "termination of the proceeding".

6.346 We cite below paragraph 7.99 of the report of the Panel which recently examined the case *Mexico - Corn Syrup*[356] in order to refute Guatemala's erroneous reading of this conclusion:

> [...] In our view, Article 5.8 does not impose additional substantive obligation beyond those in Article 5.3 on the authority in connection with the initiation of an investigation. That is, *if there is sufficient evidence to justify initiation* under Article 5.3, there is no violation of Article 5.8 in not rejecting the application. [...] (Emphasis added)

6.347 As can be seen, the Panel in *Mexico - Corn Syrup* certainly did not establish that Article 5.8 applied only after the initiation of an investigation as Guatemala mistakenly tries to suggest. What the Panel established is that Article 5.8 does not impose any additional substantive obligations beyond those in Article 5.3 as long as there is sufficient evidence to justify the initiation of an investigation. In fact, this conclusion reaffirms Mexico's position that Article 5.8 applies before the initiation and not after, since it is a supplementary provision to Article 5.3 in that it requires the authority to reject the application and to refrain from initiating an investigation when there is not sufficient evidence to justify such initiation.

(d) Guatemala's Response to Rebuttal of Mexico

6.348 **Guatemala** responds by claiming that it did not violate Articles 5.7 and 5.8 when it notified the initiation of the investigation. The following are its arguments in this regard:

---

[355] This was the view taken by the Panel in *Guatemala - Cement I*, which added:

> "Merely that Article 5.8 continues to outline circumstances in which an investigation must be terminated, which presumes that it has been initiated, does not support the conclusion that the Article does not refer to rejection of an application prior to initiation if the authorities conclude that there is not sufficient evidence of dumping and injury". See the report of the Panel in *Guatemala - Cement I, supra*, footnote 25, para. 7.59.

[356] Report of the Panel in *Mexico - Corn Syrup, supra,* footnote 34.

6.349 Mexico also errs in asserting that Guatemala violated Article 5.7 and 5.8 of the AD Agreement when it initiated the investigation. Firstly, as we explained in our first submission, Article 5.8 does not apply to the initiation of anti-dumping investigations. As recently found by the Panel in *Corn Syrup*, Article 5.8 only applies *after* the initiation of an investigation.[357] Thus, for example, had the Ministry received import data from its customs authorities *after* the initiation of the investigation indicating that the imports were negligible, Guatemala would have been required under Article 5.8 to terminate the investigation. Besides being a correct interpretation of Article 5.8, this interpretation also underscores the low evidentiary threshold for initiation under Article 5.3. In other words, if the allegations that warrant initiation are later proven not to justify "the initiation of an investigation", importers are protected by Article 5.8, which requires "prompt" termination of the proceeding.

6.350 Secondly, even if Article 5.8 were applicable to initiations, the challenged investigation was initiated on the basis of "sufficient evidence" within the meaning of Article 5.3. As we discussed in greater detail in our first submission, the Ministry examined the "accuracy and adequacy" of the evidence accompanying the original application and the supplementary application with respect to dumping, injury and causal link.[358] Thus, Guatemala complied with Article 5.7 and 5.8 of the AD Agreement (to the extent that the latter was applicable to the initiation of the investigation).

C. Guatemala's Notification of the Initiation of the Investigation

1. Claims Under Article 5.5 - Notification on Receipt of Properly Documented Application for Investigation

(a) Submissions of Mexico

6.351 **Mexico** claims that Guatemala was in violation of its obligations under Article 5.5 of the AD Agreement. Its arguments in this regard are as follows:

6.352 Article 5.5 of the AD Agreement states the following:

> "5.5. The authorities shall avoid, unless a decision has been made to initiate an investigation, any publicizing of the application for the initiation of an investigation. However, after receipt of a properly documented application and before proceeding to initiate an investigation, the authorities shall notify the government of the exporting Member concerned."

6.353 Moreover, footnote 1 to the AD Agreement defines the concept of "initiated" relating to an investigation as follows:

> "The term 'initiated' as used in this Agreement means the procedural action by which a Member formally commences an investigation as provided in Article 5."

6.354 In the light of the foregoing, one of Guatemala's obligations was to notify the exporting Member's Government after receiving a properly documented application and before proceeding to the "procedural action" by which an investigation formally commences.

6.355 Guatemala, however, only notified the Government of Mexico of initiation of the investigation on 22 January 1996. This delay constitutes a violation of Article 5.5 of the

---

[357] *Ibid.*, para. 7.99.

[358] See first submission by Guatemala, paras. 138-87.

AD Agreement. In order to show this, the following arguments have to be taken into account.

(i) Guatemala - Cement Initiated the investigation on the same date on which it published the "Public Notice of the Initiation of the Investigation Pursuant to a Complaint of Dumping"

6.356 The initiation of an investigation is one of the structural elements of dumping disciplines. The fact that initiation is a formal act corresponds to a logical structure: an anti-dumping investigation involves several actors in addition to the authority itself and implies compliance with a timetable. The information provided by interested parties is extremely important in allowing the authorities to make their determinations. This is why it would be illogical to assume that an investigation could be initiated on just any date or as a result of an internal act by the investigating authority.

6.357 In the present case, Guatemala decided formally to initiate the investigation upon publication of the "Public notice of the initiation of the investigation pursuant to a complaint of dumping" in the *Diario Oficial de Centro América* on 11 January 1996. This has been the interpretation given by the Guatemalan authorities throughout the investigation. Several documents attest to this.

6.358 Firstly, resolution 2-95 of the Directorate of Economic Integration of the Guatemalan Ministry of the Economy, dated 15 December 1995, expressly stated that the date of initiation of the investigation was deemed to be the date of publication in the *Diario Oficial de Centro América* and ordered that the corresponding notifications be made.

6.359 Secondly, resolution 000042 of 9 January 1996, issued by the Ministry of the Economy, announcing the decision to give public notice of initiation that would take effect "on the day of publication of the notice in the *Diario Oficial*".

6.360 Furthermore, in its letter to the Government of Mexico dated 26 July 1996, Guatemala indicates the following:

> "We sincerely regret that your country was not notified before the publication of the resolution for the initiation of the investigation, and we offer our sincere apologies in that regard. This was due to a slip on the part of the persons responsible for effecting the notifications, as they were not familiar with the provisions applicable to anti-dumping investigation procedures. Once again, please accept our apologies."

6.361 It should be noted that Guatemala refers to "the publication of the resolution for the initiation of the investigation". In other words, Guatemala specifically states that the "resolution for the initiation of the investigation" *was a publication*. On 26 July 1996, the only publication concerning the investigation was the public notice of initiation of 11 January 1996.

6.362 Moreover, in Guatemala's preliminary determination it was decided "to pursue the investigation initiated on 11 January this year".

6.363 When referring to the initiation stage of the investigation, Guatemala's final determination referred solely to "Notice of the initiation of the investigation".

6.364 Thus, it is indisputable that Guatemala initiated the anti-dumping investigation on 11 January 1996, the date of publication of the "Public notice of the initiation of the investigation pursuant to a complaint of dumping". Moreover, Guatemala's interpretation that the public notice of initiation itself constituted the initiation of the investigation was consistent throughout the investigation.

(ii) The Guatemalan authorities did not notify the Government of Mexico before proceeding to initiate the investigation.

6.365 As proof of this argument, we refer to the letter sent by the Guatemalan authority to the Mexican Embassy in Guatemala City. This notification was received by the Mexican Embassy on 22 January 1996. Having noted that Guatemala initiated the investigation on 11 January 1996, it is obvious that the Guatemalan authority did *not* notify the Government of Mexico before initiating the investigation.

6.366 As mentioned above, Guatemala's letter of 26 July 1996 expressly recognizes that Mexico was not notified "before the publication of the resolution for the initiation of the investigation".

6.367 The AD Agreement obliges the investigating authority to notify the exporting Member in two instances:

(a) Initiation of an investigation (Articles 5.5 and 12.1.1);

(b) on-the-spot investigations (Article 6.7 and paragraph 6 of Annex I).

6.368 As the letter refers to publication of the resolution to open the investigation, Guatemala was certainly referring to the notification mentioned in Article 5.5 of the AD Agreement.

(iii) By not notifying the Government of Mexico before proceeding to initiate the investigation, Guatemala violated Article 5.5 of the AD Agreement

6.369 Having established the preceding facts, we shall now refer to the usual meaning of the terms in Article 5.5 of the AD Agreement, including the following: "after receipt of a properly documented application and before proceeding to initiate an investigation, the authorities shall notify the government of the exporting Member concerned". As already indicated, the facts set out in this section clearly show that Guatemala did not comply with the obligation in Article 5.5 to notify Mexico "after receipt of a properly documented application and before proceeding to initiate an investigation".

6.370 It is interesting to note that the Guatemalan authorities were aware of their obligation to notify. In resolution 2-95 of 15 December 1995, the Ministry of the Economy decided to notify the interested parties (including the Government of the exporting Member). Likewise, resolution 000042 of 9 January 1996 indicates that the interested parties (including the Government of the exporting Member) should be notified.

6.371 In addition, in its letter of 26 July 1996, the Government of Guatemala apologized to the Government of Mexico for not having notified Mexico prior to publication of the resolution to open the investigation and attributes this to "a slip on the part of the persons responsible for effecting the notifications, as they were not familiar with the provisions applicable to anti-dumping investigation procedures".[359] This letter clearly shows that the Guatemalan authorities interpreted the AD Agreement in such a way that the notification referred to in Article 5.5 was made after initiation itself and that this violated the Article.

6.372 It impossible to know the reasons which incited Guatemala to notify after having initiated the investigation. Nevertheless, it is obvious that, by failing to notify the Gov-

[359] It should be noted that there is a specific reference to the (i) personnel responsible for notification, and (ii) ignorance of the provisions applicable to anti-dumping investigation procedures.

ernment of Mexico before proceeding to initiate the investigation, Guatemala violated Article 5.5 of the AD Agreement.

(b) Response of Guatemala

6.373 The following are **Guatemala's** responses to Mexico's claims relating to notifications:

6.374 Guatemala argues, in response to Mexico's claims under Article 5.5, that its notification to Mexico did not impair the right of Mexico and Cruz Azul to mount a timely defence. Its response is as follows:

6.375 According to Article 5.5, "before proceeding to initiate an investigation, the authorities shall notify the Government of the exporting Member concerned." Article 6.1.3 stipulates that "as soon as an investigation has been initiated, the authorities shall provide the full text of the written application received... to the known exporters and to the authorities of the exporting Member", while according to Article 12.1 "when the authorities are satisfied that there is sufficient evidence to justify the initiation of an anti-dumping investigation pursuant to Article 5, the [exporting Member and other interested parties] shall be notified and a public notice shall be given."

6.376 The object and purpose of these provisions is to ensure that when an investigation is opened the exporting Member and its exporters can defend their interests in an appropriate and timely manner. Clearly, the object and purpose of these provisions is not to give an "advantage" to the exporting Member or its exporters before the investigation begins. The only Article that requires notification "before proceeding to initiate an investigation" is Article 5.5, but this Article does not specify any minimum interval between the act of notification and the act of investigation. Thus, for the purpose of complying with Article 5.5 the investigating authority could notify at 8 a.m. and initiate the investigation at 8.01 a.m.. Moreover, as distinct from Article 13.1 of the SCM Agreement, Article 5.5 does not require Members to hold consultations between the time of notification and the initiation of the investigation.

6.377 As shown below, Guatemala complied with each and all of the above-mentioned articles and did nothing to impair the right of Mexico or Cruz Azul to mount a timely and appropriate defence.

(i) Under Guatemalan legislation, the investigation was not and could not have been initiated until Mexico and Cruz Azul had received timely notice of the investigation

6.378 Guatemala complied with Article 5.5 because it did not effectively initiate the investigation until Mexico had received the official notification made on 22 January 1996. In refraining from beginning the actual investigation until Mexico had been notified, Guatemala complied with its own notification legislation. In particular, Article 12 of the Guatemalan Constitution, which takes precedence over all provisions relating to due process and the right to a hearing, establishes that notification is a *sine qua non* for the initiation of any legal proceeding.[360] The constitutional guarantee concerning the obligation

[360] See, for example, case 40-93 of the Constitutional Court of the Republic of Guatemala, 3 August 1993, Gaceta Jurisprudencial No. 29 (Article 12 of the Constitution stipulates that the defence of the person and his rights are inviolable; the guarantee of *audiator inter partes* is ensured by the notification communicating the judicial or administrative decision to the subjects of the proceedings;

to give notification is developed in Article 66 of the Code of Civil and Commercial Procedure[361] and in Article 45(e) of the Law on the Organization of Justice. In accordance with Article 26 of the Law on Administrative Appeals, these provisions are applicable to administrative acts. In strict compliance with the above-mentioned legislation, although the resolution would establish a specific date for the initiation of the investigation, the Ministry was obliged to postpone it until the working day following the day on which the Government of Mexico was notified of the decision to initiate an investigation[362] and this is what the Ministry did. If Guatemala had proceeded with the investigation without having previously notified Mexico and Cruz Azul, either of them could have brought an *amparo* action to annul the investigation, but neither Mexico nor Cruz Azul made use of that remedy.[363]

6.379 It should be noted that in its own anti-dumping investigations Mexico does not comply with the provisions of Article 5.5 as strictly as it would have Guatemala do in this proceeding. On 4 September 1997, the United States requested Mexico to hold consultations with respect to an anti-dumping investigation on corn syrup imports. These consultations were requested, *inter alia*, because Mexico had not notified the United States "before proceeding to initiate an investigation" which, in the opinion of the United States, was an infringement of Article 5.5. The file on this investigation shows that the Mexican investigating authority issued the initiation decision on 17 February 1997 and published it at 6.00 a.m. on 27 February, but the Government of Mexico did not notify the United States until 9.48 p.m. on 27 February. Mexico did not notify the Government of the United States either before issuing the initiation decision on 17 February or before publishing the notice of initiation on 27 February.

(ii) In its reply to the questionnaire Cruz Azul acknowledges that the investigation was not "initiated" until 22 January 1996

6.380 As already pointed out, Guatemalan legislation requires that notification be given before any investigation is carried out. Mexico acknowledges that Cruz Azul was notified on 20 January 1996 before any step had been taken to conduct an investigation.[364] Clearly, having received the notification on 20 January 1996, a Saturday, Cruz Azul considered that the effective initiation date was 22 January 1996, the first working day following the date of notification. In fact, Cruz Azul expressly records in its reply to the Ministry's questionnaire that the investigation was initiated on 22 January 1996 and not 11 January 1996 as the Government of Mexico now claims.

---

depriving a person of a reasonable opportunity to be heard is an infringement of the constitutional protection of due process).

361 See, for example, case 80-88 of the Constitutional Court of the Republic of Guatemala, 7 November 1988, Gaceta Jurisprudence No. 10 (notification under Article 66 in the form laid down in Article 71 gives effect to the guarantee of a hearing and preserves the right of defence; failure to notify would violate the fundamental rights fully guaranteed by the Constitution, would introduce uncertainty into the judicial system and would render the other party defenceless).

362 Article 45(e) of the Law on the Organization of Justice ("e" any time-limit must be calculated from the day following the date of the last notification).

363 The fact that neither Mexico nor Cruz Azul brought an *amparo* action shows that both considered that their right to a timely and appropriate defence was intact. Moreover, the object and purpose of the WTO provisions concerning notifications were duly respected.

364 Mexico's first written submission, para. 206.

(iii) Notifying Mexico on 11 January 1996 or before that date would not have affected the course of the investigation

6.381 The alleged delay in giving notification under Article 5.5 of the Anti-Dumping Agreement (which Guatemala does not accept) did not impair Mexico's rights in the proceeding and in accordance with generally accepted principles of international law was merely a harmless error. Article 17.6(ii) of the Anti-Dumping Agreement stipulates that "the panel shall interpret the relevant provisions of the Agreement in accordance with customary rules of interpretation of public international law". WTO panels have recognized that "the customary rules of interpretation of public international law" are those incorporated in the Vienna Convention on the Law of Treaties (the Vienna Convention).[365] Thus, the expression "customary rules of interpretation of public international law" in Article 17.6(ii) of the Anti-Dumping Agreement also refers to the rules laid down in the *Vienna Convention.*

6.382 Article 31.3 of the Vienna Convention establishes that, in addition to the text, consideration must be given to "any relevant rules of international law applicable in the relations between the parties". Accordingly, in arriving at a decision, a WTO panel should apply the relevant rules of international law.

6.383 In accordance with Article 38(1) of the Statute of the International Court of Justice, the sources of international law include, *inter alia*, the "general principles of law recognized by civilized nations".[366] The principle of harmless error, which states that a party must show injury before obtaining the right to be compensated for a procedural error, is a general principle of law recognized by civilized nations. The response to the violation of a substantive rule is very direct; the national measure is condemned and its withdrawal is requested. Violations of procedural rules may also be condemned. However, the question is whether it can be said that a decision involving such a violation is flawed. The retrospective rejection of administrative decisions can give rise to immense confusion and to avoid this most national legal systems are prepared to accept that a minor procedural error does not invalidate the decision.

6.384 The Members of the WTO make extensive use of the doctrine of harmless error in connection with infringements of procedural rules in civil and criminal proceedings. In Australia, for example, the courts agreed that a delay in lodging an application, for the purpose of examining a report and preliminary finding of the Australia Customs Service, was a harmless error since the delay was unlikely to have prejudiced the respondent.[367] Similar decisions have been taken in the United States. For example, in Intercargo Insurance company v. United States, the court applied the principle to defective notices for extension of liquidation period sent by the customs service to an importer.[368] In fact, the United States federal rules of civil procedure stipulate that "the court at every stage of the proceeding must disregard any error or defect in the proceeding which does not affect the substantial rights of the parties".[369]

---

[365] See, for example, *Japan - Taxes on Alcoholic Beverages,* WT/DS8/R, WT/DS10, WT/DS11/R, adopted 1 November 1996, DSR 1996:I, 125, para. 6.7 (11 July 1996).

[366] Statute of the International Court of Justice, 1945 ICJ, Article 381.

[367] See, for example, C.A. Ford v. Comptroller General of Customs, Fed. 854 (D.N.S.W. 24 November 1993) (Australia) (the two-week delay was judged harmless because it was unlikely to prejudice the respondents, the Australian industry or the importers).

[368] 83 F. 3d 391 (Fed. Cir. 1996) (United States).

[369] Fed. R. Civ. P. 61.

6.385 Expressions of this principle or its equivalent are also to be found in the criminal proceedings of many WTO Members. In Namibia, for example, it has been held that when a verdict has not been tainted by an irregularity committed during the trial, the verdict should stand.[370] A similar approach has been adopted by the courts of Guatemala and other Member countries of the WTO such as Spain, Canada, Australia and the United States.[371]

6.386 Harmless error is also accepted by international courts. For example, the International Court of Justice recognizes the concept.[372] It is also recognized and applied by the European Court of Justice where "an error of law made by the [court of first instance] will not suffice to quash its decision if it was harmless and the same outcome could have been properly reached in the absence of error."[373] Moreover, when a WTO Member requests the Appellate Body to "reverse a panel's ruling on matters of procedure it must demonstrate the prejudice generated by the legal ruling."[374]

6.387 For its part, Mexico incorporated the harmless error concept in articles 237-238 of its Federal Tax Code according to which an administrative decision by SECOFI in unfair trading cases will only be illegal if the procedural error harms the individual.

6.388 Within the context of the present dispute, the application of the harmless error principle means that the Panel should examine Guatemala's acts and decide whether the non-fulfilment of a procedural obligation should be overlooked on the grounds that the omission did not prejudice the rights of Mexico or Cruz Azul. A panel established under the Tokyo Round Anti-Dumping Code recognized the principle of harmless error but considered that it was inapplicable under the circumstances of the case before it. [375] The case of *Brazil - Milk Powder* was certainly decided by the panel in this way since the investigating authority had notified importers of the initiation of the investigation 22 days

---

370 See, for example, S.V. Shikunga, 1997 (9) B.C.L.R. 1321 (NmS).

371 See, for example, Constitutional Court of Guatemala, Gaceta Jurisprudencial, No. 12, Case 37-89, Cons. II (the applicant drew attention to alleged irregularities, but these did not prevent him from learning of the existence of an administrative proceeding that affected his interests and taking the necessary corrective action), 9 May 1989; Thaman, Spain Returns to Trial by Jury, Hastings Int'l. and Comp. L. Rev., 241.349 No. 478 (Winter 1998) (referring to the application of the harmless error principle in Spanish criminal proceedings); R.v. Bevan [1993] 2 S.C.R. 599 (application of the harmless error principle by the Canadian Supreme Court); Wilde v. The Queen (1988) 164 CLR.365, Slip op. (FC) (application of the principle in Australia); Fed. R. Crim. P. 52(a) (United States) ("no error, defect, irregularity or variation that does not affect substantial rights should be taken into account").

372 See, for example, Appeal relating to the jurisdiction of the ICOA Council (*India v. Pakistan*), 1972 I.C.J. 46 (18 August) (Separate Opinion of Judge Dillard) ("it would appear that even if there were error, it was harmless error").

373 See Konstantin J. Joergens, True Appellate Procedure or Only a Two-Stage Process? A comparative view of the Appellate Body under the WTO Dispute Settlement Understanding, 30 Law and Pol'y. Int'l. Bus. 193, 206 (1999).

374 See Report of the Appellate Body in *EC - Hormones*, *supra*, footnote 121, para. 152; see also Gaffney, *Due Process in the World Trade Organization: The Need for Procedural Justice in the Dispute Settlement System*, 14 Am. U. Int'l. Rev. 1173, 1219 (1999) (" it is evident that the commission of what is known in the United States as harmless error will be insufficient to warrant the reversal of a panel decision).

375 See *Brazil - Imposition of Provisional and Definitive Countervailing Duties on Milk Powder and Certain Types of Milk from the European Economic Community* (*Brazil - Milk Powder*) SCM/179, para. 271 (adopted 28 April 1994).

after the public notice of initiation and 1 day before imposing a provisional measure.[376] Meanwhile, the exporting government was notified more than two months after publication and one month after the provisional measure was imposed.[377] Accordingly, the panel did not accept the argument that these delays constituted "harmless error" because it considered that they had clearly prejudiced the defence of the interests of the interested parties.[378]

6.389 As distinct from the circumstances of *Brazil - Milk Powder*, in Guatemala's case the alleged delay in giving notification was only 11 days; between initiation and notification the investigating authority did not engage in any investigation-related activity and all the interested parties had sufficient time and opportunity to participate in the proceedings; the provisional measure was not imposed until several months after receipt of the notification. Thus, the alleged delay in notifying Mexico of the initiation of the investigation was a "harmless error", since it did not prejudice Mexico's rights under the AD Agreement.

6.390 In fact, the alleged procedural error in not having given Mexico timely notice in accordance with Article 5.5 had no effect on the development of the anti-dumping investigation. If Mexico had been notified of the initiation of the investigation on 11 January, nothing would have happened differently from then onwards, except that the initial stages of the investigation might possibly have been speeded up. Clearly, the AD Agreement does not give Mexico any right to delay or impede the initiation of an investigation or allow Mexico to make any kind of submission before the investigation is initiated. Notification given on 11 January would not have given Mexico or Cruz Azul additional time to defend their interests since under Guatemalan law grace periods are calculated from the date of notification. Similarly, under Guatemalan legislation the period allowed for replying to a questionnaire is also calculated from the date of receipt of that questionnaire. Furthermore, Cruz Azul was granted 30 additional working days to reply to the questionnaire, which is not required by the AD Agreement. The Ministry also extended to 17 May the period granted to Cruz Azul for replying to the questionnaire. Finally, instead of imposing the provisional measure within 60 days of the date of initiation, Guatemala waited until 28 August before acting, that is, until eight months after initiation. In view of all this, it is inconceivable that having notified Mexico on 11 January could have had any effect on the course of the investigation.

6.391 Consequently, in accordance with the general principles of international law recognized by civilized nations, the Panel should apply the principle of "harmless error" to Guatemala's alleged *procedural* delay under Article 5.5 of the AD Agreement and reject the Mexican argument.

6.392 In the alternate, Guatemala maintains that the Mexican Government gave rise to estoppel by not objecting to any putative delay in notification under Article 5.5. Mexico made no mention of the alleged violation of Article 5.5 until 6 June 1996, that is, almost six months after the date of publication of notice of initiation. Even then, Mexico did not send the Ministry a formal note expressly objecting to the alleged violation[379], merely

[376] *Ibid.*, para. 240.

[377] *Ibid.*, para. 228.

[378] *Ibid.*, para 271.

[379] In a communication dated 30 October 1996, Cruz Azul objected for the first time to the delay in notification under Article 5.5. In a communication dated 7 February 1996, Cruz Azul objected to the decision to initiate an investigation, but did not object to the delay in notification under Article 5.5 or under any other provision of the AD Agreement.

mentioning the alleged violation in the month of June within the context of informal consultations with Guatemala. By 6 June 1996, Guatemala and the interested parties had invested substantial resources in the investigation.

6.393 Acquiescence is an accepted principle of international law. It has been recognized and applied on numerous occasions by the International Court of Justice.[380] The principle has also been applied by GATT 1947 and WTO dispute settlement panels. For example, in the case *Canada - EEC Arbitration on the Ordinary Wheat Agreement*, the Arbitrator, Mr. Patterson, used the acquiescence principle for interpreting the GATT and the Ordinary Wheat Agreement. In the award it is expressly stated that "a properly functioning multilateral international trading system does require that after a certain period silence must be considered acceptance of a state of affairs or abandonment of a claim. The predictability and stability that are central features of the GATT system require that".[381]

6.394 If Mexico had promptly entered an objection in the administrative file with respect to the alleged violation of Article 5.5, Guatemala would have reinitiated the investigation after making the notification which, according to Mexico, was necessary under Article 5.5. Instead, Mexico waited until Guatemala had investigated for six months. By that time it was very late and from every point of view unnecessary for Guatemala to do anything about the alleged delay. Consequently, on the basis of the principle of estoppel, the Panel should reject the Mexican argument.

6.395 In the alternate, Guatemala maintains that the alleged delay did not nullify or impair benefits accruing to Mexico under the Anti-Dumping Agreement. As noted above, Guatemala did not take any step to begin the investigation until Mexico had been notified. Moreover, Guatemala granted Cruz Azul a two-month extension to reply to the questionnaire. Thus, any putative delay in notification under Article 5.5 did not prejudice Mexico's ability to defend its interests nor affect in any other way Mexico's benefits under the Agreement.

6.396 According to Article 3.8 of the DSU "There is normally a presumption that a breach of the rules has an adverse impact on other Members parties to that covered agreement, and in such cases, it shall be up to the Member against whom the complaint has been brought to rebut the charge". In the present instance, Guatemala has amply rebutted any presumption of nullification or impairment of Mexico's rights under the Anti-Dumping Agreement. It should be stressed that the obligation alleged to have been infringed in this case is a *procedural* and not a *substantive* obligation. Given that Article 3.8 of the DSU clearly states that the presumption of nullification or impairment is rebuttable and taking into account the fact that the alleged violation is procedural, Guatemala maintains that it has in fact rebutted the presumption. The Panel should therefore reject this argument.[382]

---

[380] See, for example, the case relating to the Temple of Preah Vihear, [1962] I.C.J. Rep. at 32-33.

[381] Award of the arbitrator in *Canada - European Communities Article XXVIII Rights*, BISD 37S/80 (1990).

[382] Guatemala points out that the notification under Article 5.5 of the Anti-Dumping Agreement is unique within the context of the WTO. This notification does not relate to the notification of laws under covered agreements, the subject of most WTO notification rules. The notification in question applies only to an isolated stage in an anti-dumping proceeding. Unlike Article 13.1 of the Agreement on Subsidies and Countervailing Measures (1994), the notification does not impose any obligation to hold post-notification consultations. Finally, in accordance with the Agreement, it is the only notification rule that could result in a prior notice of no consequence. For example, the investigating authority could give notice to the representative of the government of the exporting country

(c) Rebuttal of Mexico

6.397 In its rebuttal, Mexico makes the following observations concerning the concepts of 'harmless error and nullification or impairment' in the 'General Comments' section, noting that Guatemala had referred to these concepts in relation to various violations of the Anti-Dumping Agreement:

6.398 Section IV.B.3 of Guatemala's first written submission focuses on the assertion that, if Guatemala had met its obligation, this would not have affected the course of the investigation. First, it states that this was a "harmless error"[383], then it mentions that Mexico acquiesced[384] and, lastly, Guatemala asserts that it has demonstrated that there was no nullification or impairment.[385] These arguments can be found in other parts of Guatemala's submission.[386] Nevertheless, as will be shown below, in this dispute the principles of "harmless error" and "acquiescence" are not only inapplicable but are mutually exclusive and as far as nullification or impairment is concerned, Guatemala did not prove anything.

6.399 Guatemala puts forward the concepts of harmless error, acquiescence and nullification or impairment in the context of its claim relating to Article 5.5 of the ADP Agreement and repeats them in other parts of its first written submission. Consequently, the arguments set out below should be seen as supplementing those in the section concerning Article 5.5 of the ADP Agreement, but also apply when rejecting Guatemala's claims of "harmless error", "acquiescence" and "nullification or impairment" in each context where these appear.

(i) Applicability of the concept of "harmless error"

6.400 Regarding the concept of "harmless error", Guatemala asserts that its delay in notifying did not prejudice Mexico's rights and that, according to the rules governing interpretation of public international law, it is the responsibility of the Panel to "examine Guatemala's acts and decide whether the non-fulfilment of a procedural obligation should be overlooked on the grounds that the omission did not prejudice the rights of Mexico or Cruz Azul".[387]

6.401 According to Guatemala, if it had notified Mexico of the initiation of the investigation on 11 January, nothing would have changed, because the ADP Agreement does not give Mexico the right to delay or prevent the initiation of an investigation or to put forward claims.

6.402 In its oral submission to the Panel, Mexico (i) recalled that, pursuant to Article 3.8 of the DSU, failure to comply with obligations leads to a presumption of nullification or impairment so whether or not there was a harmless error has no meaning; (ii) added that it was Mexico's right to be notified before the initiation of the investigation (in this case, publication of the relevant public notice), irrespective of the action taken; (iii) emphasized that Guatemala was obliged to comply with the provisions of the ADP Agreement and non-compliance cannot be excused as a "harmless error"; and (iv) the Panel

---

under Article 5.5 and then, immediately afterwards, proceed to give that representative notice of initiation.

383 First submission by Guatemala, paras. 206-216.

384 *Ibid.*, paras. 217-219.

385 *Ibid.*, paras. 220 and 221.

386 See, for example, *Ibid.*, para. 226.

387 *Ibid.*, para. 213.

which examined *Guatemala - Cement I* found that harmless error did not apply in this case.[388]

6.403 In addition to the arguments set out above, Mexico wishes to indicate the following:

6.404 Guatemala states that harmless error does apply to this dispute because the concept can be found in a number of domestic laws and has been recognized by the International Court of Justice.[389] Subsequently, it indicates that the Panel which heard the *Brazil - Milk Powder* case did not accept this because "it considered that [these delays] had clearly prejudiced the defence of the interests of the interested parties".[390]

6.405 Mexico totally rejects the arguments outlined by Guatemala. Firstly, as the Panels have clearly indicated, Guatemala did not even prove that its theory of "harmless error" constitutes a principle of international law and, even if that were the case, the examples it mentions do not apply to the present dispute.[391] Secondly, Guatemala's interpretations are unacceptable because they are contrary to the provisions of Article 3.8 of the DSU. Thirdly, no panel has accepted such a theory.[392] In the *Brazil - Milk Powder* case, the Panel rejected Brazil's argument, not because a long time had elapsed after initiation of the investigation but, as will be seen below, because Brazil, like Guatemala, tried to reverse the burden of proof in a manner contrary to Article 3.8 of the DSU:

> "It was not incumbent upon a signatory whose procedural rights under Article 2 had been infringed by another signatory to demonstrate the harm caused by such an infringement. The Panel therefore rejected the position of Brazil that it was for the EEC to demonstrate that the results of this investigation would have been different had Brazil not committed its procedural errors."[393]

6.406 Furthermore, in another case in which the principle of harmless error was claimed, namely, *Guatemala - Cement I,* the Panel, after having considered exactly the same facts as those now being presented, rejected Guatemala's argument regarding "harmless error" stating the following:

> "7.40 Guatemala argues that, even assuming there was a violation of Article 5.5, the Panel should conclude that any delay in notification under Article 5.5 was without adverse effects on Mexico's rights and thus constitutes harmless error under customary rules of public international law. Guatemala further argues that the alleged delay did not nullify or impair Mexico's rights under the ADP Agreement.
>
> 7.41 We have concluded, as discussed above, that Guatemala failed to carry out its obligation under Article 5.5 to notify the Government of Mexico before proceeding to initiate this investigation. Article 3.8 of the DSU provides that there is a presumption that benefits are nullified or impaired when a Member fails to carry out an obligation under a WTO Agreement:

388 Oral submission by Mexico, paras. 136-141.

389 First submission by Guatemala, paras. 208-212.

390 *Ibid.*, para. 213.

391 See the first submission by the European Communities, 27 January 2000, para. 20.

392 See the first submission by the United States, 27 January 2000, para. 22.

393 Report of the Panel in *Brazil - Imposition of Provisional and Definitive Countervailing Duties on Milk Powder and Certain Types of Milk from the European Economic Community* (SCM/179), para. 271.

> 'In cases where there is an infringement of the obligations assumed under a covered agreement, the action is considered prima facie to constitute a case of nullification or impairment. This means that there is normally a presumption that a breach of the rules has an adverse impact on other Member parties to that covered agreement, and in such cases, it shall be up to the Member against whom the complaint has been brought to rebut the charge'.

In other words, there is a presumption that a violation will entitle a Member to relief, because that violation nullified or impaired a benefit accruing to the complaining Member, that is, 'harmed' the complaining Member. Article 17 of the ADP Agreement entitles a Member to relief when benefits accruing to that Member under the ADP Agreement are nullified or impaired. Moreover, while Article 3.8 of the DSU indicates that the presumption of nullification or impairment may be rebutted, GATT panels have consistently found that the presumption is not rebutted simply because the particular violation in question had no or insignificant adverse effects on trade.[394] This approach is supported by the Appellate Body's decision in *Japan Alcohol*, in which it upheld the Panel's decision not to introduce a trade effects test into the first sentence of Article III:2 of GATT 1994.[395]

7.42 In our view, having found that Guatemala failed to notify the Government of Mexico in a timely fashion, we need not determine that the failure to carry out an obligation had particular or demonstrable adverse trade effects in order to find that the benefits accruing to Mexico under the ADP Agreement were nullified or impaired. Rather, to the extent that the presumption of nullification or impairment may be rebutted in the case of the breach of a procedural obligation, it would be incumbent on the Member that has breached the obligation to demonstrate that its failure to respect the obligation could not have had any effect on the course of the in-

---

[394] In *United States - Taxes on Petroleum and Certain Imported Substances*, L/6175 (Adopted 17 June 1987), BISD 34S 136, 157-58, the Panel reviewed previous disputes in which parties had claimed that a measure inconsistent with the General Agreement had no adverse impact and therefore did not nullify or impair benefits accruing under the General Agreement to the contracting party that had brought the complaint. The Panel concluded from its review that,

> "while the CONTRACTING PARTIES had not explicitly decided whether the presumption that illegal measures cause nullification or impairment could be rebutted, the presumption had in practice operated as an irrefutable presumption".
>
> *Ibid.* at para. 5.1.7

[395] *Japan - Taxes on Alcoholic Beverages*, *supra*, footnote 365. We note also the decision of the Panel in *Brazil - Imposition of Provisional and Definitive Countervailing Duties on Milk Powder and Certain Types of Milk from the European Economic Community*, SCM/179, adopted 28 April 1994 at para. 271:

> "It was not incumbent upon a signatory whose procedural rights under Article 2 had been infringed by another signatory to demonstrate the harm caused by such an infringement. The Panel therefore rejected the position of Brazil that it was for the EEC to demonstrate that the results of this investigation would have been different had Brazil not committed its procedural errors. Without wishing to exclude that the concept of 'harmless error' could be applicable in dispute settlement proceedings under the Agreement, the Panel considered that this concept was inapplicable under the circumstances of the case before it".

vestigation in question. In this case, the procedural obligation breached was the requirement to notify the exporting Member prior to proceeding to initiate an anti-dumping investigation. A key function of the notification requirements of the ADP Agreement is to ensure that interested parties, including Members, are able to take whatever steps they deem appropriate to defend their interests. Where a required notification is not made in a timely fashion, the ability of the interested party to take such steps is vitiated. We cannot now speculate on what steps Mexico might have taken had it been timely notified, and how Guatemala might have responded to those steps.[396] Thus, while it is possible that the investigation would have proceeded in the same manner had Guatemala timely notified Mexico before proceeding to initiate the investigation, we cannot say with certainty that the course of the investigation would not have been different. Under these circumstances, we cannot conclude that Guatemala has rebutted the presumption that its failure to carry out its obligation under Article 5.5 consistent with the ADP Agreement nullified or impaired benefits accruing to Mexico under that Agreement.

7.43 With respect to Guatemala's arguments regarding harmless error, the precedents cited - assuming *arguendo* that they reflect customary rules of public international law - relate to the consequences of a violation of a procedural rule, rather than to the existence of a cause of action. Thus, we do not consider that the assertion that an error is 'harmless' should prevent us from reaching the issue whether a violation of a provision of the ADP Agreement nullifies or impairs benefits under that Agreement. However, we do not preclude that the notion of 'harmless error' could be relevant to the question of what steps a Member should take in order to implement the recommendation of a panel in a particular dispute. Since we do not view the principle of harmless error as one which would prevent us from determining that there was a violation of the ADP Agreement which nullified or impaired benefits under that Agreement, we believe it would be improper for us to fail to make a recommendation under Article 19.1. However, the effects of a particular error may, we believe, be relevant in determining what remedial actions might be appropriate - that is, what if any suggestions a panel might make as to how its recommendation may be implemented."

6.407 Lastly, Mexico simply wishes to recall that the nullification or impairment caused by non-compliance with Article 5.5 of the ADP Agreement does not vanish because Mexico could have held consultations or not. Guatemala violated one of Mexico's rights, irrespective of the action which Mexico might have decided to take.[397]

---

[396] We note Guatemala's argument that, unlike the Agreement on Subsidies and Countervailing Measures, the ADP Agreement does not require Members to afford an opportunity for consultations before initiating an investigation, and that therefore there is no action which would take place after notification but before initiation. Merely that the ADP Agreement does not **require** some action following notification of the exporting Member and before initiation does not mean that nothing useful can take place following a timely notification, or that the exporting Member therefore has no interest in timely notification.

[397] See *Brazil - Milk Powder*, para. 232, which states: "The requirement to notify other signatories and interested parties served the essential purpose of enabling these signatories and interested parties

(ii) Nullification or impairment

6.408 Guatemala asserts that as it "did not take any step to begin the investigation until Mexico had been notified ... [it] did not prejudice Mexico's ability to defend its interests."[398] In Guatemala's opinion, therefore, according to Article 3.8 of the DSU, the presumption of nullification or impairment has been amply rebutted so the Panel should reject this argument.[399] Mexico wishes to indicate the following in this regard:

(a) The only "evidence" put forward by Guatemala to rebut the presumption of nullification or impairment is two assertions: (i) that Guatemala did not take any step to begin the investigation until Mexico had been notified; and (ii) Guatemala granted Cruz Azul a two-month extension to reply to the questionnaire.[400]

(b) Nevertheless, as pointed out in this rebuttal, the investigation began on 11 January, while Mexico was notified after and not before the initiation so by then the violation had been committed.

(c) Guatemala did not respect Mexico's right to be notified by Guatemala before the investigation began and, therefore, Mexico's benefits were nullified or impaired.

(d) Guatemala cannot prove that, if there had been compliance with Article 5.5 "nothing would have happened differently"[401], particularly since in another part of its submission Guatemala itself indicates that "If Mexico had promptly entered an objection in the administrative file with respect to the alleged violation of Article 5.5, Guatemala would have reinitiated the investigation ...".[402]

(e) In fact, contrary to what Guatemala indicates[403], the Panel which examined the case of *Brazil - Milk Powder* considered that the obligation to notify the initiation of an investigation was independent of the right to hold consultations.[404] Consequently, the fact that the ADP Agreement does not provide for the holding of consultations before initiating an investigation does not constitute grounds for excusing Guatemala's non-compliance.

(f) The extension granted to Cruz Azul has nothing to do with the violation of Article 5.5. Moreover, Guatemala was obliged to grant this extension, according to Article 6.1.1 of the ADP Agreement.

---

to effectively defend their interests by participating in the investigation." See also, *Ibid.*, para. 264, which states that the "offer of consultations made to the EEC on 27 February 1992, i.e., prior to the initiation of the investigation, was immaterial to the issue of Brazil's compliance with its obligations under Article 2:5 of the Agreement" (notification). See also the first submission by the United States, para. 26.

398 First submission by Guatemala, para. 220.

399 *Ibid.*, para. 221.

400 *Ibid.*, para. 220.

401 *Ibid.*, para. 215.

402 *Ibid.*, para. 219.

403 See Guatemala's first submission, footnote 267, which asserts that Article 5.5 of the ADP Agreement is of no importance and, unlike Article 13.1 of the Agreement on Subsidies and Countervailing Measures, it does not require the holding of consultations.

404 See report of the Panel in "*Brazil - Milk Powder*", para. 264.

(g) In the GATT, there are no precedents for the successful rejection of the presumption of nullification or impairment and, in the present case, Guatemala's assertions are certainly not sufficient to rebut this presumption.[405]

6.409 In its first written submission, Guatemala mentions that Mexico gave rise to estoppel by not objecting to any putative delay in notification under Article 5.5.[406] Subsequently, it indicates that "If Mexico had promptly entered an objection in the administrative file with respect to the alleged violation of Article 5.5, Guatemala would have reinitiated the investigation."[407]

6.410 Mexico asks itself: if Guatemala did not prejudice Mexico's rights by delaying notification[408] yet, on the other hand, asserts that, if Mexico had objected to the late notification, Guatemala would have reinitiated the investigation[409], does this not imply that Mexico would at least have had the right to lodge an objection in the administrative file and that the matter is sufficiently serious for Guatemala itself to recognize that its authorities would have had to reinitiate the investigation?

6.411 In addition, the Appellate Body in *Guatemala - Cement I* determined that, pursuant to the ADP Agreement, only the definitive anti-dumping measure, the provisional anti-dumping measure and price undertakings may be contested.[410] If a Member has to wait until one of these three measures is applied, what can it do to see that the principle of estoppel is not applied?

6.412 The above examples show the absurdity of Guatemala's reasoning regarding this concept. According to its logic, Members will lose rights as time goes by and they do not object to violations committed by other Members.

6.413 As Mexico has already indicated, unlike other provisions, neither the ADP Agreement nor the DSU prescribe time-limits within which to contest a measure.[411] Moreover, as will be seen below, the legal practice in the GATT has shown the inapplicability of the concept put forward by Guatemala.

6.414 The Panel which heard the case *Quantitative Restrictions Against Imports of Certain Products from Hong Kong*[412] found the following:

> "28. ... The Panel ... recognized that restrictions had been in existence for a long time without Article XXIII ever having been invoked by Hong Kong in regard to the products concerned, but concluded that this did not alter the obligations which contracting parties had accepted under GATT provisions. Furthermore, the Panel considered it would be erroneous to interpret the fact that a measure had not been subject to Article XXIII over a number of years, as tantamount to its tacit acceptance by contracting parties."

6.415 In addition to the foregoing, in the case *United States - Imposition of Anti-Dumping Duties on Imports of Fresh and Chilled Atlantic Salmon from Norway*[413], the

---

405 See first submission by the EC, para. 23.

406 First submission by Guatemala, para. 217.

407 *Ibid.*, para. 219.

408 *Ibid.*, para. 214.

409 *Ibid.*, para. 219.

410 Report of the Appellate Body in *Guatemala - Cement I*, *supra*, footnote 25, para. 79.

411 Oral submission at the first substantive meeting with the parties, para. 132.

412 See the Report of the Panel on *EEC - Quantitative Restrictions Against Imports of Certain Products from Hong Kong* (L/5511 - 30S/129-140), adopted on 12 July 1998, para. 28.

413 See the Report of the Panel in *United States - Imposition of Anti-Dumping Duties on Imports of Fresh and Chilled Atlantic Salmon from Norway* (ADP/87), adopted on 30 November 1992, paras.

Panel rejected an argument along the same lines as that put forward by Guatemala. In that dispute, it was argued that "... the failure of Norway or private Norwegian respondents to raise these issues before the investigating authorities precluded Norway from raising them before the Panel". Later on in the same report, the Panel states the following:

> "349. ... The Panel did not find in this provision any basis for it to refuse to consider a claim by a Party in dispute settlement under the Agreement merely because the subject matter of the claim had not been raised before the investigating authorities under domestic law."

6.416 Furthermore, in *EEC - Member States' Import Regimes for Bananas*[414] an attempt was made to apply the principle of acquiescence, but the Panel decided that it was inoperative as follows:

> "362. The Panel considered that the decision of a contracting party not to invoke a right under the General Agreement at a particular point in time could be due to circumstances that change over time. For instance, a contracting party may not wish to invoke a right under the General Agreement pending the outcome of a multilateral trade negotiation, such as the Uruguay Round, or pending an assessment of the trade effects of a measure. The decision of a contracting party not to invoke a right *vis-à-vis* another contracting party at a particular point in time can therefore, by itself, not reasonably be assumed to be a decision to release that other contracting party from its obligations under the General Agreement. The Panel noted in this context that previous panels had based their findings on measures which had remained unchallenged for long periods of time. The Panel therefore found that the mere fact that the complaining parties had not invoked their rights under the General Agreement in the past had not modified these rights and did not prevent them from invoking these rights now." (Footnote omitted).

6.417 In the light of the foregoing, it is obvious that Mexico could have waited until Guatemala had imposed a definitive anti-dumping measure and then objected to the violations of Article 5.5 of the ADP Agreement, without this being construed as Mexico acquiescing in the errors made by the investigating authority. As seen above, since it is only possible to object to three measures in anti-dumping disputes[415], it is even more obvious that the concept of estoppel does not apply in these cases. Mexico could not have acquiesced in the violation of Article 5.5, as claimed by Guatemala.

6.418 In addition, in relation to Article 5.5 of the ADP Agreement, Mexico's objection was such that the Panel in *Guatemala-Cement I* decided against Guatemala. Paragraph 8.4 of the Panel's report states the following:

> "8.4 We have concluded in this case that Guatemala violated the provisions of the ADP Agreement by failing to notify the Government of Mexico before proceeding to initiate, as required by Article 5.5. We therefore

347-351. See also the Report of the Panel in *United States - Imposition of Countervailing Duties on Imports of Fresh and Chilled Atlantic Salmon from Norway* (SCM/153), adopted on 4 December 1992, paras. 216-220.

[414] See the Report of the Panel in *EEC Member States' Import Regimes for Bananas* (DS32/R), Panel Report not adopted, dated 3 June 1993, para. 362.

[415] Contrary to what Guatemala asserts in para. 218 of its first written submission, there has never been any case in the WTO nor in the GATT 1947 in which the concept of acquiescence and estoppel has been applied. In the case of *Canada - EEC Arbitration on the Ordinary Wheat Agreement* cited by Guatemala in this para., the principles in question were not applied. See also the first submission by the EC, para. 22, and the first submission by the United States, paras. 24-26.

recommend that the Dispute Settlement Body request Guatemala to bring its action into conformity with its obligations under Article 5.5 of the ADP Agreement ..."[416]

6.419 Subsequently, when referring specifically to Guatemala's violations of Article 5.5 of the AD Agreement, Mexico added the following:

6.420 As was duly shown in Mexico's first written submission[417], the Government of Guatemala violated Article 5.5 of the Anti-Dumping Agreement by notifying the Government of Mexico only 11 days after initiating the investigation (i.e. publishing the public notice of initiation in the *Diario Oficial de Centro América*). However, in its first written submission the Government of Guatemala appears not to take any notice of this violation since it does not refute the arguments or evidence submitted by Mexico against it.[418] These arguments are:

> **Resolution 2-95 of 15 December 1995** clearly stated that the date of initiation of the investigation was the same as the date of publication of the public notice, i.e. 11 January 1996. Moreover, that Resolution ordered that Mexico be notified of the initiation.
>
> In **Resolution 000042 of 9 January 1996**, the Ministry of the Economy ordered that the Government of Mexico should be expressly notified of the initiation of the investigation. Moreover, it stated that the initiation of the investigation would take effect on the day following the publication of the public notice of initiation.
>
> The **public notice of initiation of 11 January 1996** fixed a period of 30 days for the interested parties to appear and submit their evidence and arguments. It must be stressed that this time-period ran from the publication of the public notice of initiation.
>
> In its **letter of 26 July 1996** the Ministry of the Economy apologised to the Government of Mexico for not having notified it before publishing the initiation resolution, arguing that it was not familiar with the notification procedures.
>
> In the **preliminary determination published on 28 August 1996**, it was decided to continue the investigation initiated on 11 January of that year.
>
> The **final determination published on 30 January 1997** refers exclusively to the public notice of initiation of the investigation, the date on which the Mexican Government was notified having no importance for the purposes of the initiation of the investigation.

6.421 By failing to refute the arguments and evidence mentioned above, Guatemala has accepted the only logical conclusion that can be drawn from them: Guatemala initiated the investigation on 11 January 1996 and notified the Mexican Government on 22 January

[416] See the Report of the Panel in *Guatemala-Cement I*, *supra*, footnote 25, para. 8.4.

[417] See paras. 178 *et seq*.

[418] The only direct evidence submitted by Guatemala to refute Mexico's arguments was the cover page of Cruz Azul's reply to the questionnaire for exporting enterprises. The document is inoperative as far as Article 5.5 is concerned, since that Article regulates the relationship between the Government of Guatemala and the Government of Mexico without the involvement of Cruz Azul. Moreover, *assuming for the sake of argument* that this piece of evidence were applicable to Article 5.5, it would not suffice to prove that the investigation was initiated on 22 January 1996; i.e. the cover page in question cannot have a greater probative value than Guatemala's acts at the time of initiation.

1996.[419] Thus, the Government of Guatemala violated Article 5.5 of the Anti-Dumping Agreement.[420]

6.422 The arguments by which Guatemala tries to prove that it did not violate Article 5.5 of the Anti-Dumping Agreement circumvent Mexico's evidence by simply mentioning that "although the resolution would establish a specific date for the initiation of the investigation, the Ministry was obliged to postpone it until the working day follow the day on which the Government of Mexico was notified of the decision to initiate an investigation".[421]

(i) Domestic legislation

6.423 Guatemala's argument concerning its domestic legislation is very basic: since it was obliged under its constitution to provide notice before initiating any legal proceeding, Guatemala had to wait to notify Mexico until it had effectively initiated the investigation.[422]

6.424 Mexico submits in this connection that Article 5 does not provide for a distinction between "effective initiation" and "non-effective initiation". Article 5 expressly defines the concept of initiation, and does not allow for far-fetched interpretations. The fact that the Guatemalan Constitution obliges the authority to notify the interested parties before initiating a legal proceeding does not mean that the moment of initiation of the investigation is thereby implicitly changed. The only thing that this argument in fact reveals is that Guatemala also violated its constitutional requirement to notify prior to initiating a legal proceeding.

6.425 Moreover, the legal instrument that applies to Guatemala's notification to Mexico is Article 5.5 of the Anti-Dumping Agreement, not the legislation mentioned by Guatemala, and the principle of international law *pacta sunt servanda* must be applied: i.e. the Anti-Dumping Agreement is a treaty in force which is binding upon the parties to it and must be performed by them in good faith.[423]

6.426 That Guatemala should claim that compliance with its domestic legislation renders the analysis of its failure to comply with Article 5.5 of the Anti-Dumping Agreement unnecessary is contrary to international law. The Vienna Convention on the Law of Treaties, which was cited by Guatemala, stipulates that a party may not invoke the provisions of its internal law as justification for its failure to perform a treaty.[424] In other words, Guatemala cannot invoke its domestic legislation on notifications to justify its failure to comply with Article 5.5.

6.427 Finally, we would like to stress that the sophism used by Guatemala does not show that it met the requirement to notify Mexico prior to the initiation of the investigation, but is an attempt to interpret the concept of "initiation of the investigation" to fit its

[419] See, letter of notification by the Government of Guatemala to the Government of Mexico dated 22 January 1996.

[420] To supplement the interpretation of Article 5.5 of the Anti-Dumping Agreement the Panel may consult the recommendation of the Committee on Anti-Dumping Practices of 29 October 1998 (G/ADP/5).

[421] First submission by Guatemala, para. 203.

[422] *Ibid.*.

[423] The *pacta sunt servanda* principle of international law is enshrined in Article 26 of the Vienna Convention on the Law of Treaties. It should be mentioned that Guatemala has argued the application of this Treaty in the present case - see para. 206 of Guatemala's first written submission.

[424] See the Vienna Convention on the Law on the Law of Treaties, Article 27.

domestic legislation. In other words, Guatemala is attempting to justify its violation with *post hoc* arguments, an attempt which cannot work.

6.428 Similarly, Guatemala's argument that Cruz Azul expressly recorded that the investigation was initiated on 22 January 1996, apart from being deceptive, is irrelevant. The only thing this argument reveals is that Guatemala would acknowledge that the provisions of the Anti-Dumping Agreement are subject to interpretation by Cruz Azul. If Guatemala had applied this to other stages of the investigation, the result would surely have been different.

(ii) Acquiescence by the Government of Mexico

6.429 Guatemala argues that Mexico acquiesced in the violation, to its disadvantage, of Article 5.5 of the Anti-Dumping Agreement. Mexico's arguments in this respect can be found in the "General Comments" section of this written submission. We would simply add that far from acquiescing in the acts of the Guatemalan authority, Mexico has conducted two dispute settlement procedures in order to ensure that Guatemala complies with its obligations under the Anti-Dumping Agreement.

(iii) Harmless error and nullification or impairment

6.430 Guatemala invokes harmless error as a principle of public international law to justify its failure to comply with Article 5.5 of the Anti-Dumping Agreement. Guatemala assures us that the Panel must examine and decide whether to excuse the failure to comply with Article 5.5 on the basis of the fact that it did not have any adverse effects on Mexico's rights. Mexico's arguments in this respect are contained in the "General Comments" section of this rebuttal. Nevertheless, we would like to add the following:

6.431 It is surprising that Guatemala should invoke harmless error as a principle of international law[425] when it is the provisions of the WTO Agreement that form the primary source of international law applicable to this case.

6.432 The arguments of the United States are particularly relevant in that they consider that when a WTO obligation which is phrased as a categorical rule is violated, the fact that the violation was merely a harmless error is irrelevant.[426] Article 5.5 of the Anti-Dumping Agreement is a categorical rule which protects the right of Members to be notified in due time and form. Thus, it is illogical to try to justify non-compliance using the theory of harmless error.

6.433 For all of these reasons, it is clear that Guatemala did not refute the arguments submitted by Mexico in its first written submission, but simply tried to confuse the Panel with syllogisms that are devoid of any foundation, justification or applicability to the present case.

(d) Guatemala's Response to Rebuttal of Mexico

6.434 **Guatemala** responds to Mexico's rebuttal as follows:

(i) Under Guatemalan legislation, the investigation was not and could not have been initiated until

[425] See written submission by the European Communities as a third party of 27 January 2000, para. 20.

[426] See written communication by the United States as a third party, 27 January 2000, para. 22.

Mexico and Cruz Azul had received timely notice of the initiation of the investigation

6.435 In Guatemala's first written submission and during the first meeting, it was clearly established that Guatemala provided Mexico with timely notice under Article 5.5 of the AD Agreement, and that even if this were not the case, Mexico suffered no injury, and in fact acquiesced in the alleged breach (i.e. the delay).[427] We also showed that Guatemala provided Mexico and Cruz Azul with the full text of the written application "as soon as" the investigation was initiated in accordance with Article 6.1.3 of the AD Agreement.[428] Finally, the weight of evidence shows that Guatemala complied with Article 12.1 of the Anti-Dumping Agreement when it provided timely notice of the initiation and published an announcement in the *Diario de Centro América* which, together with certain reports that were readily available to the public (Cruz Azul subsequently cited them), described, *inter alia*, the basis on which dumping was alleged in the application and provided a summary of the factors on which the allegation of threat of material injury was based.[429]

6.436 Nevertheless, at the first hearing with the Panel Mexico continued to insist that Guatemala did not comply with Article 5.5, *inter alia*. In support of its position, Mexico presented various arguments which distorted the previous statements by Guatemala on the subject. As during the first meeting[430], Guatemala will once again clarify its position to ensure that in the future there is no confusion or further opportunity to distort its words.

6.437 Firstly, Article 5.5 stipulates that "before proceeding to initiate an investigation, the authorities shall notify the government of the exporting Member concerned."[431] Footnote 1 to the AD Agreement defines the term "initiated" as "the procedural action by which a Member *formally commences* an investigation as provided in Article 5."[432] According to the dictionary, the word "commence" means "begin, initiate a thing."[433] and "formally" means "according to proper form"[434], "with formality, expressly".[435]

6.438 "The procedural action" by which, in the present dispute, the challenged investigation was initiated, took place on 11 January 1996. On that date, the ministry published the notice of initiation in the *Diario de Centro América*. However, "the formal commencement" of the investigation did not occur until Mexico and Cruz Azul received the notification of initiation of the investigation, which occurred no later than 22 January 1996.

6.439 In developing its argument, Guatemala does not confuse, as Mexico persistently suggests, the *formal commencement* of the investigation with the "actual" commencement of the investigation.[436] Nor are we trying to invoke Guatemalan law as an excuse for **[not]**

---

[427] See, for example, first written submission by Guatemala, paras. 203, 221; oral submission by Guatemala, paras. 48-59.

[428] See, for example, first written submission by Guatemala, paras. 231-235; oral submission by Guatemala, para. 48.

[429] See, for example, written submission by Guatemala, paras. 222-230; oral submission by Guatemala, para. 48.

[430] See oral submission by Guatemala in English, para. 49 ("Despite our attempts to be as clear as possible regarding Guatemala's position on these issues, there appears to be some confusion that I would like to try to clarify today.")

[431] Anti-Dumping Agreement, Article 5.5.

[432] *Ibid.*, Article 1, footnote 1 (emphasis added).

[433] See *Diccionario de la Lengua Española*, page364 (Real Academia Española) (Annex GUA-61).

[434] *Ibid.*, page 696.

[435] *Ibid.*.

[436] Oral submission by Mexico, paras. 126-127.

complying with Article 5.[437] On the contrary, we are trying to show that under Guatemalan law, in fact according to our Constitution, the investigation did not begin until *after* Mexico and Cruz Azul had received notice in accordance with Article 5.5 of the AD Agreement. As we explained in our first written submission (paragraph 203), Article 12 of the Guatemalan Constitution states that notification is a *sine qua non* requirement for the initiation of any legal procedure.[438] This requirement is reaffirmed in Article 66 of the Code of Civil and Commercial Procedure[439] and Article 45(e) of the Law on the Organization of Justice. Moreover, under Article 26 of the Law on Administrative Appeals, those provisions apply to administrative acts.

6.440 This evidence is fatal to Mexico's claim because it is an accepted principle of international law that municipal law (and practice) is a *fact* which must be proven before an international dispute settlement body such as this Panel.[440] Guatemala has supplied evidence to show when an anti-dumping investigation "formally commences" according to its law. Mexico has not refuted this evidence. Under these circumstances and for all of the reasons set forth in Guatemala's first written submission plus those presented during the first meeting, Mexico's complaint with respect to Article 5.5 should be rejected.

(ii) Any alleged delay in notification under Article 5.5 was harmless under the generally accepted principles of international law

6.441 In its first submission, Guatemala showed that any alleged delay in notification under Article 5.5 of the AD Agreement (and Guatemala does not accept that there was a delay) did not prejudice Mexico's rights in the procedure and constituted a harmless error under the generally accepted principles of international law.[441] In response, Mexico argued during the first meeting that: (1) violations of the AD Agreement give rise to the

---

[437] *Ibid.*, para. 129.

[438] See, for example, Case 40-93 of the Constitutional Court of Guatemala, 3 August 1993 - *Gaceta Jurisprudencial* No. 29 (The Constitution of the Republic states, in Article 12, that the defence of the person and his rights are inviolable; the *audiator inter partes* guarantee is fulfilled with the notification which is the procedural act whereby the judicial or administrative decision is authentically communicated to the persons concerned in accordance with all of the formalities required by law; i.e. the notification must be fulfilled in fact and in law for its procedural function to be fulfilled. The deprivation of a reasonable opportunity to be heard violates the constitutional protection of the process)

[439] See, for example, Case 80-88 of the Constitutional Court of Guatemala, 7 November 1988, *Gaceta Jurisprudencial* No. 10 (With the notification stipulated in Article 66 of the Code of Civil and Commercial Procedure in the form prescribed in Article 71 thereof, the guarantee of the right to be heard is fulfilled, and ultimately, the right of defence is preserved; on the other hand, any other way of proceeding would surely result in a violation of fundamental rights fully guaranteed under the Constitution of the Republic, causing uncertainty in the legal and juridical system and, even worse, leaving the opposing party defenceless).

[440] See the Report of the Appellate Body in *India - Patent Production for Pharmaceutical and Agricultural Chemical Products*, WT/DS50/AB/R, adopted 16 January 1998, DSR 1998:I, 9, para. 65, citing the case *Certain German Interests in Polish Upper Silesia*, [1926], PCIJ, Series A, No. 7, page 19. See also I. Brownlie, Principles of Public International Law, 4th edition, (Clarendon Press, 1990, pages 40-42).

[441] First submission by Guatemala, paras. 206-216.

presumption of nullification or impairment under Article 3.8 of the DSU[442]; and (2) Mexico "had the right to be notified".[443]

6.442 None of these replies satisfies Guatemala's argument. As we explained clearly in the first meeting, the entire Guatemalan discussion proceeds from the assumptions (which we state solely for the purposes of this analysis) that Mexico's right to be notified *was* violated and that this violation gave rise to the presumption of nullification or impairment under Article 3.8.[444] What we are trying to say is that any alleged violation of Article 5.5 was harmless given the indisputable facts of this case. Thus, the presumption contained in Article 3.8 has been refuted unless Mexico proves otherwise.

(iii) The Government of Mexico acquiesced in the alleged delay according to the generally accepted principles of international law

6.443 Apart from the fact that any alleged delay in notification under Article 5.5 of the AD Agreement (and once again, Guatemala does not accept that there was a delay) was harmless, in its first submission Guatemala also showed that any alleged delay was acquiesced in by Mexico.[445] In response, Mexico has presented three arguments which make little sense; (1) no provision of the AD Agreement or the DSU imposes a time-limit for submitting complaints[446]; (2) the concept of estoppel has no place in the AD Agreement[447]; (3) Mexico challenged Guatemala's compliance with Article 5.5 before the previous Panel which examined the *Guatemala - Cement I* case.[448]

6.444 Firstly, estoppel and acquiescence are legal *concepts*. The fact that they do not have direct counterparts in the AD Agreement or the DSU is of no importance. What is really important is that their application is *not* prohibited by any provision of the AD Agreement or the DSU. Secondly, Guatemala cannot even begin to guess why Mexico thinks that the issuing of a provisional or definitive measure would prevent a Member from challenging the initiation of an investigation. In fact, as we said above, in certain circumstances such challenges are clearly permitted by the DSU and the AD Agreement. Finally, the issue before this Panel is whether Mexico acquiesced in any alleged delay in the notification under Article 5.5 by not stating any objection until 6 June 1996, almost six months after the date of publication of the notice of initiation.[449] The fact that a few months later Mexico sought the establishment of a Panel on this subject is irrelevant.

6.445 In its oral submission at the second substantive meeting with the parties, Mexico made the following comments:

6.446 As for the concept of the "harmless error" which Guatemala has repeatedly invoked and described as a "generally accepted principle of international law", Mexico does not agree with the Guatemalan statement that its violation did not prejudice Mexico's rights. If Mexico had the right to be notified at a given moment and Guatemala did not do so, it is undeniable that Mexico's rights were prejudiced. On the other hand, if the Gua-

---

[442] Oral submission by Mexico, paras. 136-137.

[443] *Ibid.*, para. 138. See also *Ibid.*, para. 139 ("the obligation exists or does not exist").

[444] Oral statement by Guatemala, para. 55-56.

[445] First submission by Guatemala, paras. 217-219.

[446] Oral submission by Mexico, para. 132. Mexico also states, without any explanation, that "there are various precedents in this organization which point in a diametrically opposite direction". *Ibid.*.

[447] *Ibid.*, para. 133.

[448] *Ibid.*, para. 134.

[449] See first [written] submission by Guatemala, paras. 217-219.

temalan interpretation were to have any validity, how can Members know which obligations of the Anti-Dumping Agreement give rise to harmless errors and which ones do not? In fact, the sole effect of the Guatemalan interpretation would be that Members would be able to violate provisions of the Anti-Dumping Agreement or any other agreement and then argue that the violations constituted harmless errors.

6.447 As for the concepts of estoppel and acquiescence, Mexico does not understand the logical consequence of the fact that these concepts are not prohibited by the Anti-Dumping Agreement or the Understanding. In the first place, the rules for interpreting the WTO Agreements are contained in the Vienna Convention on the Law of Treaties, not the principles of civil law. Secondly, Mexico wonders precisely what is implied by the fact that the concepts are not expressly prohibited. Does this mean that Mexico, without knowing it, has waived its right to challenge the actions of Guatemala? No permissible interpretation of the Anti-Dumping Agreement can sustain this position.

6.448 Guatemala underestimates the violation it committed at the initiation of the investigation. In fact, it disdained the fulfilment of the obligation imposed upon it by Article 5.5, stating that the lack of notification was of no consequence[450] and was simply a harmless error. Mexico categorically rejects this position.

6.449 Guatemala is trying to justify its non-fulfilment by impermissible interpretations of the Anti-Dumping Agreement. On the one hand, it argues that the initiation of the investigation occurred on 11 January 1996, and on the other, that the formal commencement occurred on 22 January when Mexico was notified. According to Guatemala, the initiation takes place in two acts, namely, "the procedural action" on the one hand and the "formal commencement" on the other. However, footnote 1 of the Anti-Dumping Agreement is very clear: "the procedural action" by which an investigation is initiated is a single action and the term "initiated" means "the procedural action by which a Member formally commences an investigation." In this connection, Mexico has three comments to make:

(a) Guatemala has accepted that the publication in the *Diario de Centro América* was the procedural action that initiated the investigation, and Mexico does not deny this.

(b) According to Guatemala, "formally" means *inter alia*, "expressly". Nobody in this room can deny that a publication in an official journal is something express.

(c) Now, if the publication in the *Diario de Centro América* was a "formal procedural action", and complied with the requisites of footnote 1, how is it possible to fail to recognize that the investigation was initiated on 11 January 1996, through the publication of the notice of initiation in the *Diario de Centro América*?

6.450 The facts and evidence submitted[451] in these proceedings, *inter alia*, Resolutions 2-95 of 15 December 1995, and 000042 of 9 January 1996 and the public notice of initiation, demonstrate that Guatemala *formally* initiated the investigation on 11 January

---

[450] Guatemala maintains that the notification under Article 5.5 " ... is the only notification rule that could result in a prior notice *of no consequence*". See the first written submission by Guatemala, footnote 267.

[451] See Resolution 2-95 of 15 December 1995, Resolution 000042 of 9 January 1996 (MEXICO-6), public notice of initiation, letter of 26 July 1996, public notice of the imposition of the provisional anti-dumping measure, public notice of the conclusion of the investigation and Annex to the Commitment on the Protection of Confidential Information.

1996[452]; at the same time, it was recognized in the letter of 26 July 1996 and in the public notices of imposition of the provisional and definitive measures that Guatemala had notified Mexico at a later date, namely, 22 January 1996.[453] Consequently, it is indisputable that Guatemala has violated Article 5.5 of the Anti-Dumping Agreement.

6.451 The above was clearly confirmed in the report of the Panel in *Guatemala - Cement I* which, after analysing the facts of the case, concluded that " ... the act by which Guatemala 'formally commenced the investigation' in this case was the publication of the notice of initiation of the investigation".[454] and that " ... Guatemala violated the provision of the ADP Agreement by failing to notify the Government of Mexico before proceeding to initiate, as required by Article 5.5".[455]

2. *Claims Under Article 12 - Sufficiency of Evidence to Justify Initiation of Investigation and Notification of Initiation*

(a) Submissions of Mexico

6.452 **Mexico** claims that Guatemala breached various obligations contained in Article 12 of the AD Agreement. Its arguments are as follows:

6.453 Article 12.1 of the AD Agreement provides the following:

> "12.1. When the authorities are satisfied that there is sufficient evidence to justify the initiation of an anti-dumping investigation pursuant to Article 5, the Member or Members the products of which are subject to such investigation and other interested parties known to the investigating authorities to have an interest therein shall be notified and a public notice shall be given."

6.454 This Article obliges the investigating authority to notify the government of the exporting Member and the other interested parties known *when it is satisfied* that there is sufficient evidence to justify initiation of an investigation.

6.455 In this case, Guatemala violated the AD Agreement in two ways:

(a) By publishing the public notice of initiation of the investigation without having first satisfied itself that there was sufficient evidence to justify initiating an investigation;

(b) by not notifying the Government of the exporting member or Cruz Azul when the Ministry of the Economy had allegedly satisfied itself that there was sufficient evidence to justify initiating an investigation.

6.456 The complaints regarding the former violation are set out in Section V.A.1(b) of this written submission. Nevertheless, it is useful to add one further element, namely, in order to make the relevant public notice, Guatemala should have ascertained that there was sufficient evidence to justify initiating an anti-dumping investigation, but it did not do so. Although not legally entitled to do so, the Ministry issued the public notice of initiation and initiated the investigation. In addition to failing to comply with Article 5.3,

---

452 For the Mexican analysis of the acts by Guatemala, see the first written submission by Mexico, para. 182 et seq. and the second written submission by Mexico para. 183 et seq..

453 See the first written submission by Guatemala, para. 203 and second written submission by Guatemala, para. 52.

454 See *Guatemala - Cement I*, *supra*, footnote 25, para. 7.39.

455 *Ibid.*, para. 8.4.

Guatemala also violated Article 12.1 of the AD Agreement by publishing the notice of initiation of the investigation.

6.457 With regard to the second obligation, according to the usual meaning of the terms in Article 12.1, the Ministry of the Economy should have notified the Government of Mexico and Cruz Azul *when* it had satisfied itself that there was sufficient evidence to justify initiating an anti-dumping investigation. The violation of this Article is described below.

(i) On 15 December 1995, the Guatemalan authorities already considered that there was sufficient evidence to justify initiation of an anti-dumping investigation.

6.458 In this particular case, there are at least two documents which indicate that the Ministry of the Economy considered that there was sufficient evidence to justify initiating an investigation:

(a) Resolution 2-95 of 15 December 1995 of the Directorate of Economic Integration of the Guatemalan Ministry of the Economy, which states that "as there is sufficient evidence to justify initiating an investigation into dumping and threat of injury, the notifications to the persons concerned should be made, as provided in Articles 6.11 and 12.1 of (the AD Agreement)".

(b) resolution 000042 of 9 January 1996 issued by the Ministry, containing the decision to issue a public notice of initiation. In the preambular part of this resolution it is stated that "there is sufficient evidence to justify the initiation of an investigation into dumping and threats (*sic*) of injury to domestic industry, therefore, the notifications to the persons concerned should be made, as provided in Articles 6.11 and 12.1 of (the AD Agreement)".

(ii) The Guatemalan authorities did not notify the Government of Mexico or Cruz Azul when they had satisfied themselves that there was sufficient evidence to justify the initiation of an anti-dumping investigation, as provided in Article 5.

6.459 As already mentioned[456], the Government of Mexico was only notified of the initiation of the investigation on 22 January 1996.

6.460 As far as Cruz Azul is concerned, the Guatemalan authorities only notified it on 20 January 1996.

6.461 The Guatemalan authorities had already considered that there was sufficient evidence to justify the initiation of an anti-dumping investigation on 15 December 1995 (or 9 January 1996). As the Government of Mexico and Cruz Azul were only notified on 22 and 20 January respectively, it is obvious that these notifications were *not* made when the authorities had allegedly satisfied themselves that there was sufficient evidence to justify initiating an investigation.

---

[456] Section V.A.1(e) of this submission.

(iii) Guatemala violated Article 12.2 of the AD Agreement.

6.462 The obligation to notify the exporting Member and the other interested parties must be met "*When* the authorities are satisfied that there is sufficient evidence to justify the initiation of an anti-dumping investigation". Guatemala did not do this and thus violated Article 12.2 of the AD Agreement.

6.463 Guatemala was aware of its obligation to notify, as can be seen from the aforementioned resolutions (2-95 and 000042). Both of these recognize the need to notify the interested parties.

6.464 Even more serious is the fact that the public notice was issued on 11 January 1996. It would seem that the Ministry of the Economy exercised its right to initiate the investigation, but took the "political" decision not to notify either the Government of Mexico or Cruz Azul until later.

6.465 Thus, Guatemala violated Article 12.1 of the AD Agreement:

(a) By publishing the public notice of initiation without having sufficient evidence to justify the initiation of an investigation;

(b) by not notifying Cruz Azul nor the Government of Mexico when the authorities considered that there was sufficient evidence to justify the initiation of an anti-dumping investigation.

(iv) The public notice of initiation is inconsistent with Article 12.1.1 of the AD Agreement

6.466 The public notice of the initiation of an investigation into allegedly dumped imports of grey Portland cement from the Mexican firm Cruz Azul published in the *Diario Oficial de Centro América* of 11 January 1996 ("notice of initiation")[457] did *not* comply with the provisions of Article 12.1.1 of the AD Agreement because it did *not* provide the necessary information on the basis for the allegation of dumping in the application, nor the requisite information summarizing the factors on which the allegation of threat of material injury was based.

6.467 Article 12.1.1 provides the following:

"12.1.1. A public notice of the initiation of an investigation shall contain, or otherwise make available through a separate report, adequate information on the following:

(i) the name of the exporting country or countries and the product involved;

(ii) the date of initiation of the investigation;

(iii) the basis on which dumping is alleged in the application;

(iv) a summary of the factors on which the allegation of injury is based;

(v) the address to which representations by interested parties should be directed;

(vi) the time-limits allowed to interested parties for making their views known." (The footnote has been omitted.)

[457] "Public notice of the initiation of the investigation pursuant to a complaint of dumping" (hereinafter called the "notice of initiation").

6.468 Consequently, Article 12.1.1. requires that the public notice of initiation contain "adequate information" on the basis on which dumping is alleged in the application *inter alia* (subparagraph (iii)).

6.469 However, irrespective of the violations in the application with regard to information and evidence proving dumping to which we have referred, it should be noted that the notice of initiation published by the Ministry did *not* contain "*adequate information*" on the basis on which dumping was alleged by Cementos Progreso in its application. On the contrary, in part 3 entitled "Legal basis of the allegations of dumping stated in the application", there is simply a reference to Articles 7.2, 10.2 and 10.6 of the AD Agreement concerning the form and criteria for the application of anti-dumping duties. As proof of this, we offer section 3 of the aforementioned notice of initiation:

> "3. *Legal basis of the allegations of dumping stated in the application*:
>
> Agreement on Implementation of Article VI of the General Agreement on Tariffs and Trade 1994; and the Central American Regulations on Unfair Business Practices and Safeguard Clause (Government Agreement No. 221-93).
>
> Article 7.2 of the first above-mentioned legal basis provides that measures may take the form of a *provisional duty* equal to the amount of the anti-dumping duty provisionally estimated, being not greater than the provisional estimated margin of dumping. Similarly, Articles 10.2 and 10.6 of the same document stipulate that a duty may be levied equivalent to the *amount of a definitive anti-dumping duty* levied on products imported not more than 90 days prior to the date of application of provisional measures, if allegations of discriminatory prices are substantiated."

6.470 As will be noted, none of this section of the notice of initiation can be deemed to contain "adequate information" on the allegation of dumping in the application. Indeed, this text *completely omits* any allegation of dumping that might have emerged from the application for initiation of an investigation by Cementos Progreso. The text has no relevance whatsoever and is in no way related to the requirements of Article 12.1.1. On the contrary, it simply refers to the bases laid down in various provisions of the Agreement for the application of provisional and definitive anti-dumping measures, thereby highlighting a clear violation of the AD Agreement because the notice of initiation did *not* contain the adequate information called for by Article 12.1.1, subparagraph (iii).

6.471 In addition, as can be seen, Article 12.1.1 of the AD Agreement provides that the public notice of initiation of an investigation shall contain "*adequate information*" *inter alia* on *a summary of the factors on which the allegation of injury is based* (subparagraph iv).

6.472 It should be borne in mind that footnote 9 to the Agreement states the following:

> "Under this Agreement the term 'injury' shall, unless otherwise specified, be taken to mean material injury to a domestic industry, threat of material injury to a domestic industry or material retardation of the establishment of such an industry and shall be interpreted in accordance with the provisions of this Article."

6.473 The Ministry of the Economy decided to initiate an investigation into an alleged threat of material injury, so the initiation notice published in the *Diario Oficial de Centro América* should have contained "*adequate information*" summarizing the factors on which the allegation of *threat of material injury* was based. Likewise, according to Article 3 and footnote 9 to the AD Agreement, the summary referred to in Article 12.1.1(iv) should contain factors such as those indicated in paragraphs 1, 2, 4, 5 and 7 of Article 3 of the AD Agreement.

6.474 Nevertheless, and subject to the violations indicated concerning the information and allegation of threat of injury in the application, the notice of initiation published by the Ministry did not contain "*adequate information*" summarizing these factors either. As proof of this, we cite section 4 entitled "Summary of the factors on which the allegation of threat of injury is based":

> "4. Summary of the factors on which the allegation of threat of injury is based
>
> Cementos Progreso S.A. appeared before this Ministry to lodge a complaint that massive quantities of grey Portland cement produced by the Mexican company La Cruz Azul, S.C.L. are being imported into Guatemala by land at a price less than the normal value and are threatening injury to the domestic industry, the margin of dumping being calculated at 77 per cent. These imports are adversely affecting investment in improvements and expansions of the Guatemalan cement production plant and, should they continue, would lead to the dismissal of a large number of workers with all the resulting economic and social problems."

6.475 As can be seen from this excerpt, the notice of initiation published by the Ministry did *not* contain "*adequate information*" summarizing the factors on which the allegation of injury was based according to the applicable provisions of Article 3. In fact, in the notice, the Guatemalan authority simply took over, in a very limited way, some of the allegations made by the applicant which once again, as mentioned, were not substantiated by adequate evidence, although this is required by Article 5.2 of the AD Agreement. Section 4 of the notice of initiation *cannot* therefore, according to any permissible interpretation of the AD Agreement, be considered a sufficiently adequate summary in order to meet the standard of "*adequate information*" required by Article 12.1.1. for the content of initiation notices in conformity with its subparagraph (iv).

6.476 To summarize, the notice of initiation did *not* meet the standard of "*adequate information*" required by Article 12.1.1. for the content requirements laid down in subparagraphs (iii) and (iv) of the Article because it did *not* contain adequate information on the basis on which dumping was alleged in the application nor adequate information summarizing the factors on which the allegation of injury, in this case threat of material injury, was based.

(b) Response of Guatemala

6.477 **Guatemala** makes the following response to Mexico's claims that it breached its obligations prescribed by Article 12 of the AD Agreement:

6.478 Article 12.1 of the Anti-Dumping Agreement states that "when the authorities are satisfied that there is sufficient evidence to satisfy the initiation of an anti-dumping investigation pursuant to Article 5" the exporting Member and its known exporters "shall be notified and a public notice shall be given". Mexico claims that Guatemala infringed Article 12.1 because it waited until 20 January 1996 to notify Cruz Azul of the investigation and because it waited until 22 January 1996 to notify Mexico of the investigation, although Guatemala had already decided that there was sufficient evidence to justify initiation on 15 December or 9 January. The Mexican arguments are mistaken.

(i) Article 12.1

6.479 *Firstly*, the "authorities" in charge of the investigation were the Ministry, not the Directorate of Economic Integration which issued the ruling dated 15 December 1995. This is a subordinate directorate and therefore the Ministry could have rejected its report of 15 December. Thus, the competent "authorities", to which Article 12.1 refers, were not satisfied that there was sufficient evidence until 9 January. After taking its decision, the Ministry promptly issued a public notice within the next two days and quickly notified Mexico and Cruz Azul, within the next two weeks.

6.480 *Secondly*, the Mexican argument is based on a faulty interpretation of Article 12.1. Contrary to what Mexico says, Article 12.1 does not oblige Guatemala to notify Mexico and Cruz Azul *immediately* after Guatemala was satisfied that there was sufficient evidence to justify initiation. This is not what Article 12.1 requires. Article 12.1 does not establish any time-limit for notification. Guatemala certainly notified Mexico and Cruz Azul "when" it was satisfied that there was sufficient evidence. Just as Article 5.5 does not specify any interval between notification and initiation, Article 12.1 does not specify any interval between the determination that there is sufficient evidence and the notification of the parties and the giving of a public notice. By contrast, other provisions of the Anti-Dumping Agreement establish definite time limits for taking certain steps.[458]

6.481 Finally, as noted above in connection with the discussion of Mexico's argument that Guatemala violated Article 5.5, the notifying of Mexico or Cruz Azul would not have affected the course of the investigation. The alleged delay was harmless, Mexico demonstrated its acquiescence in the alleged delay and the alleged delay did not nullify or impair Mexico's benefits under the Anti-Dumping Agreement.

6.482 Guatemala's notification under Article 12.1 gave Mexico and Cruz Azul a timely and appropriate opportunity to defend their interests when the investigation began to unfold on 23 January. Cruz Azul never complained that its notification under Article 12.1 was not given in good time.[459] For three and a half years Mexico acquiesced in the notification under Article 12.1 having been made in good time, until it submitted its request for the establishment of a panel on 20 July 1999.[460] Prior to that Mexico does not even mention Article 12 of the Anti-Dumping Agreement.

(ii) Article 12.1.1

6.483 Mexico next alleges that Guatemala's notice of initiation violated Article 12.1.1, because it did not provide sufficient information on the factors on which the allegation of dumping and consequent injury was based. However, the Mexican argument fails to acknowledge that according to Article 12.1.1 this information is to be contained in a public notice or in a separate report available to the public.

6.484 In Guatemala, all administrative investigation files are available to the public, because the Constitution requires that administrative acts be published.[461] Thus, the report

---

458 See, for example, Articles 9.3.1 and 9.3.2.

459 The first time that Cruz Azul alleged that notification was not made in good time under Article 5.5 was in its communication dated 30 October 1996. However, the communication made no mention of notification not being made in good time under the terms of Article 12.1.

460 WT/DS60/2.

461 See Article 30 of the Constitution (interested parties have the right to obtain the reports, copies and certificates they may request and the disclosure of files, except ... for information provided by individuals under a guarantee of confidentiality) and Article 171 of the Guatemalan Law on the

of the Directorate of Economic Integration of 17 November 1995 was available to the public and that report contains relevant information concerning the basis on which dumping was alleged in the application, as well as a summary of the factors on which the allegation of threat of material injury was based. In fact, in its submission dated 9 May 1996, Cruz Azul referred to the report of 17 November 1995.

6.485 Moreover, as mentioned above in discussing Mexico's arguments concerning Guatemala's alleged violation of Article 5.5, including more details in the public notice of initiation would not have affected the course of the investigation. As already noted, Cruz Azul had ample access to the report by the Directorate of Economic Integration of 17 November 1995. The alleged irrelevance of the public notice (which Guatemala does not accept) was harmless; Mexico and Cruz Azul acknowledge the relevance of the public notice during the course of the investigation; and the alleged lack of relevance of the public notice does not constitute nullification or impairment of Mexico's rights under the Anti-Dumping Agreement.

6.486 The report by the Directorate of Economic Integration, dated 17 November 1995, gave Mexico and Cruz Azul a timely and adequate opportunity to defend their interests when the investigation began to unfold on 23 January 1996. In its submissions dated 7 February 1996 and 9 May 1996, in which it objected to the initiation of an anti-dumping investigation, Cruz Azul did *not* object that the public notice of initiation required under the terms of Article 12.1.1 was not relevant. Similarly, Cruz Azul did not raise this objection in its submission dated 30 October 1996. For three and a half years Mexico acquiesced with regard to the relevance of the public notice under the terms of Article 12.1.1, until it submitted its request for the establishment of a panel on 20 July 1999. In its request for the establishment of a panel (*Guatemala - Cement I)* dated 4 February 1997, Mexico did not even mention Article 12 of the Anti-Dumping Agreement.

(c) Rebuttal of Mexico

6.487 **Mexico** rebuts Guatemala's claims as follows:

6.488 Guatemala did not refute the arguments submitted by Mexico proving violation of Article 12.1 of the Anti-Dumping Agreement. It only responded partially, evasively and without presenting any solid counter-arguments.

6.489 Mexico bases its arguments on the provisions of Article 12.1, under which there was an obligation to notify Mexico and Cruz Azul and to give public notice of the initiation as soon as the authorities were satisfied that there was sufficient evidence:[462]

(i) Guatemala issued the public notice of initiation without first satisfying itself that there was sufficient evidence to justify the initiation of an investigation.[463]

(ii) Guatemala effected the notifications and issued the public notice of initiation 38, 36 and 27 days after allegedly satisfying itself that there was sufficient evidence.[464]

Organization of Justice which sets out the requirements for requesting copies and certificates, including payment of the corresponding fees.

[462] See first written submission by Mexico, para. 201.

[463] See the section on sufficiency of evidence in this second written submission by Mexico.

[464] Guatemala allegedly satisfied itself that there was sufficient evidence to initiate the investigation on 15 December 1995 and 9 January 1996 and issued the public notice of initiation on 11 January 1996; and disregarding these circumstances, Guatemala notified the Government of Mexico and

6.490 Guatemala's reply is essentially based on three elements: (i) the competence of the authority to determine the alleged sufficiency of the evidence[465]; (ii) an alleged misinterpretation by Mexico[466]; and (iii) justification of its violation on the grounds of harmless error and acquiescence.[467]

(i) Competent authority for the determination of the alleged sufficiency of the evidence

6.491 Guatemala asserts that the competent authority is the Ministry of the Economy, not the Directorate of Economic Integration.[468]

6.492 As Mexico stated earlier, according to footnote 3 of the Anti-Dumping Agreement, the word "authorities" should be interpreted as meaning authorities at an appropriate senior level. Merely stating that the Directorate of Economic Integration was not competent to determine the alleged sufficiency of evidence is not enough to prove that the said Directorate does not have "an appropriate senior level". Guatemala merely mentioned that the Ministry of the Economy was hierarchically superior to the Directorate of Economic Integration, just as it could have said that the Ministry was not competent to determine the sufficiency of evidence because the President of Guatemala was hierarchically superior. Moreover, it should be pointed out that the footnote in question does not specify the appropriate level for an authority to issue determinations.[469]

6.493 As stated earlier, the term "authorities" can vary depending to the specific context. In this particular case, "the authorities" that must be satisfied that "there is sufficient evidence to justify the initiation of an anti-dumping investigation" are the Directorate of Economic Integration and not the Ministry of the Economy, since the former is a technical body responsible for reviewing the arguments and evidence submitted.[470]

6.494 Moreover, the actual wording of the resolution of the Directorate of Economic Integration (which, incidentally, is under the authority of the Ministry of Economy) does not suggest that there would be any ratification. Unlike the opinion referred to in paragraph 1 of the resolution, paragraph 4 orders that notification should be made to the parties concerned, paragraph 5 requires that a public notice of initiation be given and paragraph 6 states that the investigation procedure should be pursued.[471]

6.495 In fact, Guatemala argues that "the competent 'authorities' to which Article 12.1 refers, were not satisfied that there was sufficient evidence until 9 January".[472] It would be useful to have evidence in support of Guatemala's argument; in particular, it would be useful to know what evidence was submitted between 15 December and 9 January which satisfied the authorities.

6.496 However, supposing for the sake of argument that this Panel should determine that the resolution of 15 December 1995 is not the document by which Guatemala deter-

---

Cruz Azul on the 22 and 20 January 1996 respectively. Finally, we stress the fact that Guatemala already knew of its obligation to notify on 15 December 1995 and 9 January 1996.

465 First written submission by Guatemala, para. 223.

466 *Ibid.*, para. 224.

467 *Ibid.*, paras. 225 and 226.

468 *Ibid.*, para. 223.

469 Oral submission by Mexico at the first substantive meeting with the parties, paras. 145 and 146.

470 *Ibid.*, para. 147.

471 *Ibid.*, para. 149.

472 First written submission by Guatemala, para. 223.

mined the alleged sufficiency of evidence, then it would be the resolution of 9 January 1996. Either of the two dates considered would imply a violation of Article 12.1.[473]

(ii) Alleged faulty interpretation by Mexico of Article 12.1

6.497 Guatemala contends that the Article at issue did not oblige it to notify Mexico and Cruz Azul immediately after it was satisfied that there was sufficient evidence to justify initiation. Similarly, it argues that the Article does not specify any interval between the determination of the alleged sufficiency of evidence, the notification of the parties and the public notice of initiation.[474]

6.498 Since the Anti-Dumping Agreement does not establish a precise interval or define the term "when", under Article 31 of the Vienna Convention, the term must be interpreted in accordance with its ordinary meaning, in its context and in the light of its object and purpose. The ordinary meaning of the term "*cuando*" ("when") is "*entiempo que*" ("at which time").[475] Now, we must consider that "when" refers to the time at which the authorities satisfied themselves that there was sufficient evidence to justify the initiation of the anti-dumping investigation, the notification and the public notice. In other words, at the time at which there is sufficient evidence, the notification and public notice must be effected. While it will be argued that there are various permissible interpretations of the term "when", in this context and in the light of its object and purpose, it is impossible to accept that in notifying Mexico and Cruz Azul 38 and 36 days late respectively and publishing the public notice of initiation 27 days after the sufficiency of the evidence had been established, Guatemala had fulfilled its obligations under Article 12.1 of the Anti-Dumping Agreement. Consequently, Guatemala has not proven that it complied with that provision of the Anti-Dumping Agreement.

(iii) Harmless error and acquiescence

6.499 Please refer to the arguments set forth in the section on Article 5.5 of the Anti-Dumping Agreement.

6.500 On the basis of those arguments, Mexico states categorically that Guatemala has not refuted the evidence of its violation of Article 12.1 of the Anti-Dumping Agreement which Mexico has established ever since its first written submission. It has simply tried to evade the conclusive arguments against it.

(iv) Violations of Article 12.1.1 of the Anti-Dumping Agreement

6.501 Guatemala argues that it fulfilled its obligation under Article 12.1.1 through the report of the Directorate of Economic Integration of 17 November 1995, and that that report contained relevant information concerning the basis on which dumping was alleged as well as a summary of the factors on which the allegation of threat of material injury was based.[476]

6.502 Firstly, Guatemala recognizes that the public notice of initiation did not comply with the requirements of Article 12.1.1, and now, using a post hoc argument, it contends

[473] Oral submission by Mexico at the first substantive meeting with the parties, para. 149.
[474] First written submission by Guatemala, para. 224.
[475] Diccionario Larousse, 1987 Edition.
[476] First written submission by Guatemala, para. 228.

that it complied with its obligation under that Article by submitting a separate report prepared by the Directorate of Economic Integration. Guatemala is trying to suggest, erroneously, that any document in the file can constitute the separate report, an argument that cannot in any circumstances be accepted as validly complying with the transparency requirements for determinations by the investigating authority.

6.503 The public notice of initiation does not even make any reference to the existence of a separate report nor does it suggest that the notice was replaced or supplemented by a separate report which, moreover, must be available to the interested parties in accordance with footnote 23 of the Anti-Dumping Agreement.[477] Guatemala's argument is entirely inconsistent with the purpose of Article 12.1.1 of ensuring the transparency of the Ministry's initiation determination.

6.504 Secondly, not only is there no indication that the Ministry sought to comply with its obligation under Article 12.1.1 through a separate report, but the report to which Guatemala refers also fails to provide adequate information on the elements listed in Article 12.1.1(i) to (vi).[478]

6.505 Mexico submits that the separate report does not contain, *inter alia*, "adequate information" concerning the allegation of dumping in the application or "adequate information" summarizing the factors on which the allegation of material injury is based. Hence, the separate report does not contain the sufficient grounds on which the Ministry initiated the investigation, and as a result of this omission Cruz Azul was in no position to assess either the quality or the sources of information relied upon by the investigating authority for its initiation determination.[479]

6.506 Thus, for example, in referring to Cementos Progreso's standing in its "Analysis" section, the report refers to the firm as a producer of cement that is identical or similar to the imported cement without anywhere referring to the product likeness analysis which, if it was actually conducted, was simply omitted. At the same time, in referring to the evidence submitted in the application, it refers to evidence concerning the export price and does not speak of the existence of evidence of the normal value. In spite of this omission, the section "Estimation of the Margin of Dumping" presents a table in four columns showing how the Ministry obtained the margin of dumping without adequate evidence. Consequently, it is impossible to consider that this complies with the purpose and requirements of Article 12.1.1 - in other words, the separate report does not contain the "adequate information" on which the allegation of dumping is based in the application.

[477] In para. 228 of its first written submission, Guatemala tries to suggest that it complied with the requirement to make the separate report available to the public because, in its submission dated 9 May 1996, Cruz Azul referred to the report of 17 November 1995; however, this does not mean that we should accept that it is a separate report which contains the required information and complies with the requirements of Article 12.1.1.

[478] Unlike the public notice of initiation, the separate report fails to indicate, *inter alia*, the address to which representations by interested parties should be directed or the time limits allowed to interested parties for making their views known.

[479] In para. 30 of its third-party submission, the United States agrees that what is at issue is whether the separate report mentioned by Guatemala contains adequate information and whether it is was available to the public. It adds that the Panel should also be mindful of whether Article 12.1 has been complied with, i.e. whether the investigating authority reveals the evidentiary basis for proceeding with the initiation of the investigation. Where exporters are in no position to assess either the quality or the source of the information relied upon by the investigating authority, the purpose of Article 12.1 has been subverted.

6.507 Nor does the report provide a summary of the factors referred to in paragraphs 1, 2, 4 and 7 of Article 3 on which the allegation of injury, or in this case threat of injury, is based. The report merely refers to simple allegations by the applicant and makes no reference to any relevant evidence. For example, according to the report:

> "The complainant states that the massive imports of grey Portland cement from Mexico at less than their normal value constitutes a threat of injury to the domestic industry in that it would prejudice investment in improvements and expansion of the Guatemalan cement industry. Furthermore, due to the extremely low prices at which this product is imported from Mexico, the Guatemalan company would become an importer and would be obliged to lay off 1,052 workers, with the consequent negative impact on the level of employment in Guatemala and concomitant economic and social problems".

6.508 Under no circumstances can the simple allegations by the applicant be considered as "adequate information" constituting a summary of the factors on which the allegation of threat of injury was based in accordance with the relevant provisions of Article 3. The lack of evidence relating to the allegation of threat of injury prevented the investigating authority from providing, in the separate report, adequate information concerning the summary of factors on which the allegation of threat of injury was based, while at the same time preventing Cruz Azul from assessing the quality and sources of information taken into account by the Ministry in reaching its initiation determination - indeed, the evidence relating to the allegation of threat of injury was non-existent.

6.509 Consequently, Mexico submits that Guatemala failed to comply with Article 12.1.1 in that neither the public notice of initiation, nor the separate report, contained adequate information concerning the basis on which dumping was alleged in the application, nor did they contain a summary of the factors on which the allegation of threat of material injury was based. Nor can Guatemala's argument that the Ministry met its obligation under Article 12.1.1 by submitting a separate report be accepted, since neither the public notice of initiation nor the file of the investigation makes any such reference, besides which, not just any document from the file can be accepted as a separate report.

6.510 In the alternative, Guatemala points out that the irrelevance of the public notice was harmless and does not constitute nullification or impairment of the rights accruing to Mexico under the AD Agreement, adding that in any case Mexico acquiesced in respect of the relevance of the public notice under the terms of Article 12.1.1.[480]

6.511 To avoid repetition, as the subjects of harmless error, nullification or impairment and acquiescence have already been addressed in the "General Comments" section of Mexico's second written submission, we shall not revert to them here.

(d) Guatemala's Response to Rebuttal of Mexico

6.512 **Guatemala** responds to Mexico's rebuttal by arguing that the public notice of initiation complied with Article 12.1.1. It makes the following arguments:

6.513 In its first written submission, Guatemala showed that the public notice of initiation, including the Report of the Directorate of Economic Integration of 17 November 1995, complied with Article 12.1.1 of the AD Agreement.[481] Guatemala also stated that the report of 17 November was available to Cruz Azul, and Cruz Azul cited it several

---

[480] First written submission by Guatemala, paras. 229 and 230.

[481] *Ibid.*, paras. 227-230.

times.[482] Finally, Guatemala explained why any alleged flaws in the notification (assuming there were any) were either harmless or acquiesced in by Mexico, or both.[483]

6.514 During the first meeting, Mexico adduced that neither the notice nor the report contained the type of information or the level of detail required by Article 12.1.1. For example, Mexico asserted that Guatemala was under the obligation to discuss its "analysis" of the like product and to show how it calculated its margin of dumping.[484]

6.515 It is surprising indeed that Mexico should resort to this argument, because it conflicts with a case which Mexico knows fairly well, *Corn Syrup*. In that case, the Panel refused to find that Article 12.1.1 required notices of initiation to contain the level of detail which Mexico asks of Guatemala. In particular, it submitted that the simple terms of Article 12.1.1 merely required, *inter alia, a summary* of the factors on which the *allegation* of injury is based".[485] The Panel expressly rejected the argument presented by the United States in *Corn Syrup* and by Mexico in this case that the authorities must summarize their "conclusions" and the factors underlying those conclusions.[486]

6.516 Thus, it is enough that Guatemala's notice and the separate report should contain "adequate information" under the categories described in subparagraphs (i) to (vi). Guatemala was not required to supply, *inter alia*, its "analysis" of the like product or its conclusions concerning the margin of dumping.

3. *Claim Under Article 6.1.3 - Provision of Full Text of Written Application by Guatemala*

(a) Submissions of Mexico

6.517 **Mexico** claims that Guatemala breached its obligation to provide the full text of the written application "as soon as the investigation was initiated" as required by Article 6.1.3 of the AD Agreement. It makes the following arguments in this regard:

6.518 As already seen[487], the Ministry of the Economy initiated the investigation on 11 January 1996. It only notified Cruz Azul and the Government of Mexico, however, on 20 and 22 January respectively. These letters were the first official contact between the investigating authority and the Government of Mexico, on the one hand, and Cruz Azul on the other. Consequently, the fact that the full text of the written application was not provided as soon as the investigation was initiated is sufficient proof that Guatemala violated Article 6.1.3 of the AD Agreement.

6.519 Article 6.1.3 provides the following:

> "As soon as an investigation has been initiated, the authorities shall provide the full text of the written application received under paragraph 1 of Article 5 to the known exporters and to the authorities of the exporting Member and shall make it available, upon request, to other interested parties involved. Due regard shall be paid to the requirement for the protection of confidential information, as provided for in paragraph 5."

---

482 *Ibid.*. See also (submission by Cruz Azul of 9 May 1996).

483 First submission by Guatemala, paras. 229-230.

484 Oral submission by Mexico, paras. 155-159.

485 Panel Report, *Corn Syrup, supra*, footnote 34, para. 7.87 citing Article 12.1.1 (iv) of the AD Agreement (emphasis added by the Panel).

486 *Ibid.*.

487 See Sections V.A.1(e) and V.A.1(f) of this submission.

6.520 The authority's violation is not, however, limited to the above. When Guatemala notified the Government of Mexico and Cruz Azul of the initiation of the investigation, it did not provide the text of the application. In other words, Mexico did not receive the text of the application for initiation, even when it received the tardy notification from the Guatemalan Ministry of Foreign Relations on 22 January 1996.

6.521 In addition, the Ministry of the Economy's notification to Cruz Azul of 20 January 1996 did not contain the full text of the application for initiation. As it did not have the full text of the application for initiation of an investigation, Cruz Azul had to turn to the administrative file on the case to find the application and be able to defend its interests. In other words, Cruz Azul only saw the full text of the application for initiation of an investigation for the first time when it examined the administrative file, since Guatemala had not provided it previously.

6.522 The foregoing is a serious procedural violation that mainly affected Cruz Azul and clearly infringes Article 6.1.3 of the AD Agreement. In this particular case, the violation was to be of the utmost importance. By not allowing Cruz Azul nor the Government of Mexico to know precisely what was in the full text of the application, Guatemala did not give ample opportunity to the exporter to defend its interests, and this alone impairs the rights of Mexico and Cruz Azul under Article 6.1 of the AD Agreement.

(b) Response of Guatemala

6.523 **Guatemala** makes the following response to Mexico's claims under Article 6.1.3:

6.524 Mexico alleges that Guatemala violated Article 6.1.3 of the Anti-Dumping Agreement by omitting to provide Cruz Azul and the Mexican Government with the full text of the written application as soon as the investigation was initiated. While Mexico is correct in saying that the purpose of Article 6.1.3 is to provide the exporter and its government with "ample opportunity to defend their interests, "[488] the rest of its argument is fallacious.

6.525 *Firstly*, Mexico is simply confusing the facts. On 22 January 1996, the Ministry sent Mexico the full text of the application together with the notice of initiation. On 29 January 1996, the Ministry provided Cruz Azul with the full text of the written application together with the notice of initiation and the questionnaire. In fact, Guatemala's procedural rules require that upon notification a copy of the application be provided together with the corresponding transcription.[489]

6.526 *Secondly*, it is clear from the administrative file that Cruz Azul had the application and had ample opportunity to defend its interests. For example, in its submissions of 7 February 1996 and 9 May 1996, Cruz Azul argued vigorously - before the preliminary determination was issued - that the Ministry should not have initiated the investigation.

6.527 Finally, as mentioned above in discussing Mexico's argument concerning the alleged violation of Article 5.5 by Guatemala, providing Mexico or Cruz Azul with the full text of the written application would not have affected the course of the investigation. The alleged delay was harmless, Mexico and Cruz Azul clearly acquiesced in the alleged delay and the alleged delay did not constitute nullification or impairment of Mexico's rights under the Anti-Dumping Agreement.

6.528 The fact that Guatemala supplied the full text of the application to Mexico and Cruz Azul meant that they had ample and adequate opportunity to defend their interests

[488] See Mexico's first written submission, para. 227.

[489] See Article 70 of the Code of Civil and Commercial Procedure (these provisions are applicable to the proceedings of the executive branch, Article 26 of the Law on Administrative Appeals).

when the investigation began to unfold on 23 January 1996. In its submissions of 7 February 1996 and 9 May 1996, in which it objected to the initiation of the anti-dumping investigation, Cruz Azul did not object to the alleged delay in receiving the full text of the application under the terms of Article 6.1.3. Instead, Cruz Azul waited until 30 October 1996, ten months after the beginning of the investigation, to complain about not having received a full copy of the application as soon as the investigation began. By then Cruz Azul had already had many opportunities to defend its interests in a timely fashion.

(c) Rebuttal of Mexico

6.529 **Mexico** rebuts Guatemala's arguments on the basis that Guatemala has not shown that it acted in accordance with Article 6.1.3 of the AD Agreement when it failed to provide the full text of the application to Cruz Azul and to the Government of Mexico as soon as the investigation was initiated. Mexico makes the following submissions in this regard:

6.530 There are two disputed points concerning Article 6.1.3: (i) the provision of the full text of the application to the Government of Mexico; (ii) the provision of the text to Cruz Azul. In neither of the two cases did Guatemala manage to refute the argument that it had violated the said article.

6.531 Nevertheless, before turning to the specific arguments of the case, it is important once again to highlight the contradiction in the arguments put forward by Guatemala. On the one hand Guatemala acknowledges that "the purpose of Article 6.1.3 is to provide the exporter and its government with 'ample opportunity to defend their interests,'"[490],[491] while on the other hand, it invokes once again its arguments concerning harmless error, acquiescence and absence of nullification or impairment.[492] Once again, Mexico poses the question: if Guatemala recognizes the right of defence while at the same time denying that there is any right of defence, which of its arguments is the correct one?

(i) Provision of the full text of the application to the Government of Mexico

6.532 Firstly, Guatemala has not refuted Mexico's argument that it waited until at least 11 days after the initiation of the investigation to allegedly supply the full text of the application. The only arguments put forward by Guatemala with respect to this obligation are those concerning harmless error, acquiescence and nullification or impairment, on the one hand, and the assertion that it provided Mexico and Cruz Azul with "ample and adequate opportunity to defend their interests when the investigation began to unfold on 23 January 1996".

6.533 Since it has been demonstrated that the concepts invoked by Guatemala are not applicable, and that in addition, an assertion that it had provided ample opportunity does not constitute evidence, Mexico notes that this argument has not been refuted by Guatemala at all.

6.534 Secondly, Guatemala tries to prove that it supplied the full text of the application with a document attached by Mexico to its first written submission (the letter presented as Annex MEXICO-12). As mentioned earlier, the letter in question does not prove that the full text of the application was provided to the Government of Mexico. Guatemala did not

490 *Ibid.*, para. 231.
491 *Ibid.*, para. 231.
492 *Ibid.*, para. 234.

provide the full text of the application when it notified Mexico on 22 January 1996, and this letter does not prove the contrary. Thus, Guatemala has been unable to refute Mexico's assertion that it violated Article 6.1.3.

(ii) Provision of the full text of the application to Cruz Azul

6.535 Firstly, Guatemala assures us that it supplied the full text of the application to Cruz Azul on 29 January 1996.[493] This points to the conclusion that if the application was indeed supplied on that date and not at a later date, Guatemala supplied the full text of the application 18 days after the initiation of the investigation. Since it initiated the investigation on 11 January 1996 and supplied the text of the application to Cruz Azul on 29 January 1996, it clearly took Guatemala 18 days to supply the application for initiation of the investigation, and it did not do so "as soon as the investigation was initiated". In other words, Guatemala is acknowledging that it did not comply with Article 6.1.3 of the Anti-Dumping Agreement.

6.536 Worse still, Guatemala submitted a copy of the air consignment note allegedly certifying that it sent the text of the application for initiation to Cruz Azul, although the document does not provide proper evidence that the full text was sent to Cruz Azul. Under the heading "date", the note contains the inscription "04-02-96". At best for Guatemala, the note is dated 4 February 1996 although the inscription could actually be understood to refer to the second day of the fourth month of 1996, that is 2 April 1996. Thus, if we follow Guatemala's logic, the complete text of the initiation application was presumably supplied to Cruz Azul on 4 February 1996, i.e. 24 days after the initiation of the investigation. Consequently, Guatemala is acknowledging that it waited at least 24 days before supplying the initiation application to Cruz Azul, thereby clearly violating Article 6.1.3.

6.537 As a second argument, Guatemala mentions Cruz Azul's communications of 7 February and 9 May 1996. These documents do not provide evidence that Guatemala supplied the full text of the application. The fact that on those dates Cruz Azul stated that the Ministry of the Economy should not have initiated the investigation does not in any way constitute evidence that Guatemala provided the full text of the application to Cruz Azul. In other words, it is not necessary to have the full text of the application in order to argue that Guatemala should not have initiated the investigation. Moreover, as already stated earlier, Cruz Azul had to consult the file in order to obtain the application for initiation and thus be in a position to defend its interests.

6.538 Thirdly, Guatemala argues that its procedural rules require that upon notification, a copy of the full text of the application be provided.[494] As was the case with the violation of Article 5.5 of the Anti-Dumping Agreement, the only thing Guatemala shows through this argument is that it also violated its domestic legislation. Thus, even if this is not a matter at issue, Guatemala also violated its domestic legislation by not supplying the full text of the application.

6.539 Finally, Guatemala once again invokes acquiescence, estoppel, harmless error and nullification or impairment.[495] And once again, Mexico refers to the corresponding sec-

[493] *Ibid.*.

[494] First written submission by Guatemala, para. 232.

[495] *Ibid.*, para. 234.

tions in the "General Comments" section and to its arguments concerning Article 5.5 of the Anti-Dumping Agreement.

6.540 Thus, Guatemala has not been able to refute Mexico's arguments that it violated Article 6.1.3 of the Anti-Dumping Agreement by not supplying the full text of the application to the Government of Mexico until 11 days after the initiation of the investigation. Moreover, and worse still, Guatemala has not been able to prove that it supplied the full text to Mexico, even at the time of notification on 22 January 1996. At the same time, it has failed to prove that it provided Cruz Azul with the full text of the application, even on 4 February 1996. In other words, there can no longer be any doubt that Guatemala violated Article 6.1.3 of the Anti-Dumping Agreement.

D. Guatemala's Application of the Provisional Measure

1. Claims Under Articles 2.4 and 7.1 - Information Received and Used by Guatemala's Investigating Authority

(a) Submissions of Mexico

6.541 **Mexico** claims that by applying the provisional anti-dumping measure without properly meeting the requirements for its imposition, Guatemala violated Articles 2 and 7 of the AD Agreement. Further, the application of the provisional measure under these circumstances violates the provisions of Article VI of the GATT 1994.

6.542 Notwithstanding Guatemala's preliminary objections, Mexico claims that the Ministry did not comply with the obligation set forth in subparagraph (i) of Article 7.1 of the AD Agreement as it applied a provisional measure without having given Cruz Azul an adequate opportunity to comment on the information provided to the Ministry in the reply to the questionnaire it had received. In this regard Mexico makes the following arguments:

6.543 Article 7.1 of the AD Agreement provides the following:

> "Provisional measures may be applied only if:
>
> (i) an investigation has been initiated in accordance with the provisions of Article 5, a public notice has been given to that effect and interested parties have been given adequate opportunities to submit information and make comments; ..."

6.544 The Ministry calculated a dumping margin using information provided by Cruz Azul that was unclear to it in certain respects and simply relied on assumptions concerning the way in which the dumping margin should be calculated, without giving Cruz Azul a clear prior indication of the deficiencies or inaccuracies in its reply to the questionnaire and requesting the relevant clarifications.

6.545 Moreover, the Ministry also violated the final part of Article 2.4 of the AD Agreement, which provides the following:

> "...The authorities shall indicate to the parties in question what information is necessary to ensure a fair comparison ...".

6.546 After receiving the reply to the questionnaire for exporting firms, even though the Ministry acknowledged that it had doubts about the information provided by Cruz Azul, it did *not* request the exporter to supply additional information in order to clarify the inaccuracies and thus ensure that it could make a fair comparison between the normal value and the export price indicated by Cruz Azul, thus violating Article 2.4 of the AD Agreement.

(b) Response of Guatemala

6.547 **Guatemala** responds to Mexico's claims under Articles 7.1 and 2.4 as follows:

6.548 Article 7 of the Anti-Dumping Agreement does not lay down any particularly onerous requirements for the application of provisional measures. According to Article 7.1, provisional measures may be applied if:

(i) An investigation has been initiated in accordance with the provisions of Article 5, a public notice has been given to that effect and interested parties have been given adequate opportunities to submit information and make comments;

(ii) a preliminary affirmative determination has been made of dumping and consequent injury to a domestic industry; and

(iii) the authorities concerned judge such measures necessary to prevent injury being caused during the investigation.

6.549 Thus, Article 7 clearly envisages a very limited preliminary investigation in which before they can impose a provisional measure the investigating authorities are only required to provide timely notification of the initiation of an investigation and to give interested parties adequate opportunities to submit information and make comments so that they can be considered by the authorities.

6.550 The limited nature of the preliminary investigation is further confirmed by the fact that, despite Article 5.10 requiring the investigation to be concluded within one year after initiation (or 18 months in special circumstances), Article 7.3 states that "provisional measures shall not be applied sooner than 60 days from the date of initiation of the investigation". Thus, it is clearly permissible to apply provisional measures as early as 60 days after the investigation was initiated. Since provisional measures can be imposed so early in a 12 or 18 month investigation, it is clear that under the Agreement the investigating authorities can impose such measures on the basis of a much less exhaustive investigation (and with much less detailed documentary evidence) than would be required to justify the imposition of a definitive measure.[496]

6.551 Another indication that the provisional measure is not subject to any particular requirements is the fact that the Agreement does not impose definitive standards for the formulation of a preliminary determination by the investigating authority. Article 7.1(ii) only requires that an preliminary affirmative determination has been made of dumping and consequent injury and Article 7.1(iii) only requires that "the authorities concerned judge such measures necessary to prevent injury being caused during the investigation." At the same time, the Article does not provide any further guidance as to the nature of the decision which must be taken or as regards the adequacy or quality of the evidence. The lack of definitive standards for making a preliminary determination in an anti-dumping case contrasts sharply with the standard provided in Article 6 of the Agreement on Safeguards: "... a Member may take a provisional safeguard measure pursuant to a preliminary determination that there is *clear evidence* that increased imports have caused or are threatening to cause serious injury ...".[497]

---

[496] Article 7.4, which limits the application of provisional measures "to as short a period as possible", normally not exceeding four months, also supports the conclusion that the Agreement requires a less exhaustive investigation for the preliminary than for the final phase of the process. This Article ensures that any provisional measure based on documentary evidence less complete than that required for a definitive anti-dumping duty will only have a limited duration.

[497] Agreement on Safeguards, Article 6 (emphasis added).

6.552 The Panel in the dispute *Brazil - Milk Powder*[498], which dealt with the similar rules in Article 5.1 of the Tokyo Round Subsidies Code, clarified the necessary requirements for the imposition of provisional measures. The Panel found that, in accordance with the Subsidies Code, a preliminary affirmative determination should be preceded by an investigation, that is, "a preliminary affirmative finding could be made only at some point in time after the initiation of an investigation, when interested signatories and interested parties have been afforded an opportunity to submit their views to the investigating authorities and to have access to the information used by the investigating authorities".[499] Brazil failed to comply with these requirements by not giving interested parties relevant and timely notice of the initiation of the investigation and not sending out the questionnaire before making a preliminary determination. Thus, the parties had no way of making their views known or providing information before Brazil applied provisional duties.[500]

6.553 Guatemala's anti-dumping investigation clearly exceeded the requirements laid down in Article 7 for applying a provisional measure and far exceeded the action taken in the case *Brazil - Milk Powder*. As the chronology of the investigation makes clear, the Ministry published its decision to initiate an investigation on 11 January 1996. It then notified the Mexican Government, as required, and provided it with a full copy of the application on 22 January 1996. Notification of the initiation of an investigation, the full text of Cementos Progreso's application and a questionnaire was sent by the Ministry to Cruz Azul via DHL on 26 January 1996. Subsequently, Cruz Azul requested and was granted an extension until 17 May 1996 to reply to the questionnaire. Cruz Azul gave a partial reply to the questionnaire dated 9 May 1996, which accompanied a long submission bearing the same date; both documents were lodged on 13 May 1996. The Ministry's preliminary determination was issued on 16 August 1996 and the application of the provisional measure entered into effect with the publication of the preliminary determination on 28 August 1996, long after the expiration of the period of 60 days required by Article 7.3 for the application of provisional measures. The determination establishing dumping and consequent injury was based on a careful and complete examination of the evidence gathered during the preliminary investigation, including the information submitted by Cruz Azul.

6.554 Mexico challenges the preliminary affirmative determination of dumping and consequent injury on the grounds that the Ministry did not properly evaluate various pieces of evidence and thus did not establish the facts correctly. However, the role of the panel is not to make an independent evaluation of the evidence. On the contrary, Article 17.6(i) requires the panel to respect Guatemala's sovereignty and the authority of the Ministry as the investigating agency responsible for evaluating the relevant facts and drawing the appropriate conclusions. Under Article 17.6(i) the panel may only "determine whether the authorities' establishment of the facts was proper and whether their evaluation of those facts was unbiased and objective." The text of this Article leaves no doubt that the panel can only reject the factual findings made by the national authorities in special cases in which the conclusions drawn by the authorities are simply not supported by the evidence or when there is clear evidence of bias in their evaluation of the facts.

6.555 Quite inappropriately, Mexico suggests that the panel should carry out a new investigation and make a new evaluation of the evidence instead of confining itself to determining "whether the authorities' establishment of the facts was proper and whether

---

[498] SCM/179, adopted 28 April 1994.

[499] *Ibid.*, para. 223.

[500] *Ibid.*, paras. 251-53.

their evaluation of those facts was unbiased and objective".[501] The fact is that the Ministry carried out a careful and complete examination of the evidence in accordance with the relevant criteria established in the Anti-Dumping Agreement. Clearly, Mexico has not shown that the Ministry's establishment of the facts was not proper or that its evaluation of those facts was biased.

6.556 Mexico argues that Guatemala violated Article 7.1 by not giving Cruz Azul an adequate opportunity to comment on the information provided in the replies to the anti-dumping questionnaire and therefore based its provisional calculation of the dumping margin on information from *Cruz Azul* that was unclear in certain respects. The essence of the Mexican argument is that after the Ministry received the replies to the questionnaire from Cruz Azul it should have asked Cruz Azul for explanations and additional information before making a preliminary determination of dumping. There is no support for Mexico's arguments in the Anti-Dumping Agreement.

6.557 According to Article 7.1, provisional measures may only be applied if, *inter alia*, "interested parties have been given adequate opportunities to submit information and make comments". Article 2.4 states, *inter alia*, that "the authorities shall indicate to the parties in question what information is necessary to ensure a fair comparison ...".

6.558 Guatemala complied with Article 7.1 by giving Cruz Azul the opportunity to submit information and make comments before issuing a provisional determination. Guatemala complied with Article 2.4 by providing Cruz Azul with a written anti-dumping questionnaire specifying the information necessary to calculate the dumping margin. In fact, the Ministry used the same anti-dumping questionnaire as the Mexican investigating authority, SECOFI, in its anti-dumping investigations.

6.559 On 11 January 1996, a notice was published inviting all importers, exporters, representatives of the Mexican Government and anyone who considered himself to have a legitimate interest in the outcome of the investigation to appear and present their views and any evidence they considered relevant. As indicated in Section I.C. of the preliminary determination, entitled "Notification", a number of interested parties, including Cruz Azul, responded to the notice of initiation. Cruz Azul appeared on 7 February 1996 and requested a 30-day extension to reply to the anti-dumping questionnaire. Subsequently, the Ministry extended the time-limit to 17 May 1996 for all the interested parties in order that they might submit evidence and reply to the questionnaires. Cruz Azul presented its written arguments on 9 May 1996 and on 13 May 1996 lodged a submission that contained a partial reply to the anti-dumping questionnaire.

6.560 For calculating the preliminary dumping margin the Ministry used the information that Cruz Azul had supplied in its reply to the questionnaire. The Ministry made adjustments for tariff differences and freight costs requested by Cruz Azul. Cruz Azul's to the questionnaire was internally inconsistent and confused, *inter alia*, with respect to the adjustments to the normal value which it asked to have made for discounts for wholesalers and discounts for prompt payment.[502] However, the Ministry also accepted these adjustments as valid on the basis of the discount procedure described by Cruz Azul.

6.561 In short, it is absurd for Mexico to argue that Guatemala did not comply with Articles 2.4 and 7.1, since the Ministry used the information submitted by Cruz Azul to determine the preliminary dumping margin.

[501] AD Agreement, Article 17.6(i).

[502] For example, in some cases the total alleged discount exceeded the total for the corresponding sale.

(c) Rebuttal of Mexico

6.562 **Mexico**, in rebuttal, argues that the imposition of the provisional anti-dumping measure violated Articles 2 and 7 of the AD Agreement. It submits as follows:

6.563 Here, Guatemala contends that it complied with Article 7.1 by giving Cruz Azul the opportunity to submit information and make comments before issuing a provisional determination. It adds that the Ministry made adjustments for tariff differences and freight costs, and in spite of the fact that according Guatemala Cruz Azul's reply to the questionnaire was inconsistent and confused, it accepted the validity of adjustments for wholesalers and discounts for prompt payment. In short, the Ministry used the information submitted by Cruz Azul to determine the preliminary margin of dumping.[503]

6.564 Following the replies by Guatemala in its first written submission, Mexico will not pursue the issue of the adjustments claimed by Cruz Azul. Nevertheless, Mexico repeats that Guatemala did not properly interpret Article 7.1, and in fact violated that Article by not giving Cruz Azul a proper opportunity to make comments after its reply to the investigation questionnaire and before Guatemala issued its preliminary determination.

(d) Guatemala's Response to Rebuttal of Mexico

6.565 **Guatemala** responds by arguing that the preliminary determination of dumping complied with Articles 2 and 7.1. It makes the following arguments in this regard:

6.566 As already mentioned, Guatemala is of the view that the provisional measure and the complaints against that measure are not properly before the Panel. But even if Guatemala's preliminary objection were to be rejected, it is clear that Mexico's arguments are without merit.

6.567 The gist of Mexico's argument is that after Guatemala had received Cruz Azul's reply to the questionnaire, it was under an obligation to seek clarifications and additional information from Cruz Azul before making a preliminary determination of injurious dumping. As we explained during the first meeting, this argument is absurd.

6.568 Firstly, a preliminary determination, by its very nature, cannot be based on a complete factual record. Thus, if Cruz Azul was concerned about the accuracy and completeness of the preliminary determination, it should have provided complete and accurate answers to the questionnaire. Instead, it provided a partial and confusing reply which in many respects was self-contradictory. For example, Cruz Azul only provided pricing data on its sales of Type II and Type II Pz cement sold in Mexico. Yet, in an annex to its reply (Annex 1), Cruz Azul indicated that all home market and export sales were of Type I (PM) cement.

6.569 In short, if anyone is to blame for the preliminary determination, it is Cruz Azul. Guatemala based its preliminary determination primarily from Cruz Azul's data. It gave Cruz Azul ample opportunity, in accordance with Article 7.1 of the AD Agreement, to "submit information and make comments". Indeed, it extended the deadline for submission of Cruz Azul's response by more than 60 days. Guatemala even used the same anti-dumping questionnaires as Mexico uses.

6.570 If anything, the preliminary determination *understated* Cruz Azul's dumping margin. As we explained in our first written submission, the Ministry made adjustments for taxation differences and freight costs that lowered Cruz Azul's margin.[504] It also made adjustments favourable to Cruz Azul for wholesaler and prompt payment discounts in

---

[503] First written submission by Guatemala, paras. 246, 248 and 249.

[504] First submission by Guatemala, para. 248.

spite of the fact that its reply to the questionnaire was self contradictory and confusing on both these subjects. Most investigating authorities would not have given Cruz Azul the benefit of the doubt on these issues.

6.571 These facts, which we developed in greater detail in our first written submission, support the conclusion that Guatemala carried out a careful and complete examination of the evidence in accordance with the relevant criteria provided in the AD Agreement. Mexico clearly has not demonstrated either that Guatemala's establishment of the evidence in the file was improper or that Guatemala's evaluation of the evidence was biased.

2. *Claims Under Article 2.2 - Determination of Normal Value*

(a) Submissions of Mexico

6.572 **Mexico** claims that Guatemala violated Article 2.2 for the following reasons:

6.573 The Ministry never examined whether the product for consumption in Mexico like to that exported to Guatemala was representative, thus violating Article 2.2 of the AD Agreement, notably footnote 2, which reads as follows:

> "Sales of the like product destined for consumption in the domestic market of the exporting country shall normally be considered a sufficient quantity for the determination of the normal value if such sales constitute 5 per cent or more of the sales of the product under consideration to the importing Member, provided that a lower ratio should be acceptable where the evidence demonstrates that domestic sales at such lower ratio are nonetheless of sufficient magnitude to provide for a proper comparison."

6.574 The Ministry in fact inferred that the sales of Type I (PM) cement for domestic consumption in Mexico were representative because the sales of Type I (PM) cement to Guatemala accounted for 4 per cent of sales destined for domestic consumption. It should be noted, however, that when determining the normal value the Ministry used sales of Type II Pz cement, arguing that this was the like product to that exported to Guatemala by Cruz Azul. This is why the file on the case does *not* include any examination of the representativeness of the sales of Type II Pz cement for consumption in Mexico.

6.575 The Ministry, therefore, never satisfied itself that the volume of sales on the Mexican domestic market of the like product to that exported to Guatemala was of a sufficient magnitude to provide for a proper comparison, thereby violating the provision in Article 2.2 of the AD Agreement.

(b) Response of Guatemala

6.576 **Guatemala's** arguments in response to Mexico's claims under Article 2.2 are as follows:

6.577 Mexico alleges that the Ministry did not make a valid determination of the normal value because it used sales of Type II Pz cement made by Cruz Azul in Mexico instead of certain sales of Type I (PM) cement. Again, Mexico's arguments are beside the point since the Ministry based its calculation of the normal value on the sales of cement in Mexico which Cruz Azul reported in its reply to the anti-dumping questionnaire.

6.578 The anti-dumping questionnaire instructed Cruz Azul to draw up a list itemizing all its sales of the commodity in question on the domestic market during the investigation period. It also instructed Cruz Azul to provide information on each type of cement sold. As described in the preliminary determination, Cruz Azul only provided selling price information relating to its sales of Type II and Type II Pz cement in Mexico. The Ministry did not find any difference in the prices reported for Type II and Type II Pz cement.

Moreover, Cruz Azul did not provide any information on domestic market prices for sales of Type I (PM) cement. However, in Annex 1 to its reply to the questionnaire, Cruz Azul indicated that all the sales on the domestic market and export sales involved of Type I (PM) cement. The volume of export sales reported was 61,279 tons while the volume sold on the domestic market was reported as 1,538,962 tons. As explained in section VI.C of the provisional determination, entitled "Procedure used to calculate the normal value", the Ministry used only the selling prices of Type II cement with pozzolana sold to distributors in Mexico. Since the Type I (PM) cement exported to Guatemala contained pozzolana, the Ministry considered that the Type II cement with pozzolana sold in Mexico was the product most like to the product exported to Guatemala.

6.579 In view of these facts, Mexico has no reason to complain that Guatemala used selling prices for Type II cement with pozzolana for calculating the normal value. There was nothing in Cruz Azul's questionnaire to suggest that the Ministry ought not to have used this information for calculating the normal value. In fact, it was the company that provided the information.

(c) Rebuttal of Mexico

6.580 **Mexico** makes the following arguments in response to Guatemala's submissions:

(i) Product likeness

6.581 Regarding product likeness, Guatemala states in its first submission[505] that Cruz Azul only provided price information concerning its sales of Type II and Type II Pz cement sold in Mexico, and that it could find no difference between the prices reported for the two types. It adds that Cruz Azul did not provide any information on domestic market prices for sales of Type I (PM) cement, which corresponds to the product exported to Guatemala.

6.582 In spite of the differences between the products reported (Type II, Type II Pz and Type I PM), the Ministry decided that since the Type I (PM) cement exported to Guatemala contained pozzolana, the Type II cement with pozzolana sold in Mexico was the product most like to the product exported to Guatemala. Mexico submits that the Ministry did not conduct a likeness analysis of the product to support its preliminary affirmative determination.

(ii) "Representativeness" of the domestic market prices

6.583 In connection with the preliminary determination of the normal value, the Ministry used the sales of Type II Pz cement, arguing that it was the "product most like to" the product exported by Cruz Azul to Guatemala. However, there is *no* examination of the "representativeness" of the sales of Type II Pz cement for consumption in Mexico in the file of the case.

6.584 Mexico repeats its argument that the Ministry never satisfied itself that the volume of sales in the Mexican domestic market of the like product to that exported to Guatemala could be considered a sufficient quantity (within the meaning of footnote 2 of the Anti-Dumping Agreement) to permit a proper comparison, so that Guatemala violated Article 2.2 of the Anti-Dumping Agreement.

505 *Ibid.*, para. 251.

3. *Claims Under Article 3.7 and Related Provisions - Preliminary Determination of Threat of Material Injury*

(a) Submissions of Mexico

6.585 **Mexico** argues that the Ministry of the Economy's preliminary affirmative determination of threat of material injury is contrary to the provisions in Article 3.1, 3.2, 3.4, 3.5 and 3.7, *inter alia*, of the AD Agreement. Its various arguments in respect of its Article 3.7 claim are as follows:

6.586 Firstly, it should be noted that, in arriving at this determination, the Ministry did *not* evaluate whether there had been a significant increase in imports in absolute terms or relative to domestic production or consumption. It did not consider either whether the imports entered the Guatemalan market at significantly undercut prices that had an impact on domestic prices by depressing them to a significant degree or preventing their increase. The Ministry violated Article 3.2, in particular by *not* considering whether there had been significant price undercutting by the dumped imports as compared with the domestic price on the Guatemalan market. Instead of this, the Ministry simply confined itself to mentioning in its preliminary affirmative determination of threat of material injury that the domestic prices had fallen, without making the necessary comparison with the price of imports of grey Portland cement.

6.587 In addition, according to Article 3.7[506] of the AD Agreement, a determination of threat of material injury must be based on facts and not merely on allegation, conjecture or remote possibility, and it requires that, in reaching such a determination, a number of factors must be considered, *inter alia* the following: a significant rate of increase of imports, the freely disposable capacity of the exporter (taking into account the availability of other export markets to absorb any additional exports), the effect of the exports on domestic prices, and the inventories of the product.

6.588 Nevertheless, an examination of the Ministry of the Economy's preliminary determination shows that the Ministry apparently limited itself to considering the factors enumerated in Article 3.7 of the AD Agreement, and we say apparently because there can be no doubt that the consideration of these factors was inadequate and insufficient, as will be seen throughout this section. We must submit, however, that the Ministry did not

---

[506] Article 3.7 of the AD Agreement provides the following:

"A determination of a threat of material injury shall be based *on facts and not merely on allegation, conjecture or remote possibility*. The change in circumstances which would create a situation in which the dumping would cause *injury must be clearly foreseen and imminent*. In making a determination regarding the existence of a threat of material injury, the authorities should consider, *inter alia*, such factors as:

(i) a significant rate of increase of dumped imports into the domestic market indicating the likelihood of substantially increased importation;

(ii) sufficient freely disposable, or an imminent, substantial increase in, capacity of the exporter indicating the likelihood of substantially increased dumped exports to the importing Member's market, taking into account the availability of other export markets to absorb any additional exports;

(iii) whether imports are entering at prices that will have a significant depressing or suppressing effect on domestic prices, *and would likely increase demand for further imports*; and

(iv) inventories of the product being investigated.

No one of these factors by itself can necessarily give decisive guidance but the totality of the factors considered must lead to the conclusion that further dumped exports are imminent and that, unless protective action is taken, material injury would occur." (emphasis added).

properly evaluate the factors enumerated in Article 3.7 in order to arrive at a valid conclusion that, over the investigation period, there was a change in circumstances which would create a situation in which the dumped imports of grey Portland cement would cause material injury to the domestic industry.

6.589 In addition, it must be borne in mind that, even though the factors listed in Article 3.7 are elements which the investigating authority must necessarily consider in cases of threat of material injury, for such cases the AD Agreement requires an examination that goes beyond the consideration of these factors. The last paragraph of Article 3.7 of the Agreement states that:

> "No one of these factors by itself can necessarily give decisive guidance but the totality of the factors considered must lead to the conclusion that further dumped exports are imminent and that, unless protective action is taken, material injury would occur."

6.590 This text, and particularly the words "material injury would occur", indicates that the authority must evaluate all relevant factors having a bearing on the state of the domestic industry and listed in Article 3.4 of the AD Agreement when making a preliminary determination of threat of material injury. This is also clear from Article 3.1 of the AD Agreement. The Ministry of the Economy should, therefore, have considered all the relevant factors listed in Article 3.4 of the AD Agreement[507] and not have based its determination on the trend in only one of them (volume of sales) and on an incomplete and inadequate examination of the factors in Article 3.7, when examining the possible impact of dumped imports on this industry.

6.591 One important conclusion which an investigating authority must reach when determining threat of material injury is whether there has been any change in the circumstances of the domestic industry that would lead to a situation in which dumping caused material injury. In order to be able to reach such a conclusion, the Ministry of the Economy should not only have examined the trend in the volume of imports and prices, but should also have obtained sufficient information on the state of the domestic industry to be able to evaluate whether it was likely that the entry of new imports of the product investigated would cause a change in this state and whether this change would cause material injury to the domestic industry.

6.592 In this particular case, however, the investigating authority did *not* analyse the relevant factors enumerated in Article 3.4 of the AD Agreement, for example, the profits of the domestic industry, output, market share, productivity, return on investments or the utilization of the domestic producer's plant capacity, cash flow, inventories, employment, wages, growth, the ability to raise capital or investments, consequently the Ministry's preliminary determination does not contain any findings on the possible impact of future dumped imports on the domestic industry.

6.593 An examination of the administrative file on the investigation and the public notice of imposition of the provisional anti-dumping measure clearly shows that, with one

[507] Article 3.4 of the AD Agreement provides that, in order to determine the impact of the dumped imports on the domestic industry, the investigating authority must evaluate "...all relevant economic factors and indices having a bearing on the state of the industry, including actual and potential decline in sales, profits, output, market share, productivity, return on investments, or utilization of capacity; factors affecting domestic prices; the magnitude of the margin of dumping; actual and potential negative effects on cash flow, inventories, employment, wages, growth, ability to raise capital or investments. This list is not exhaustive, nor can one or several of these factors necessarily give decisive guidance."

exception, the Ministry of the Economy did *not* evaluate the relevant factors enumerated in Article 3.4 of the AD Agreement and did not give proper consideration to the factors listed in Article 3.7 of the Agreement. The Ministry's evaluation could *not* therefore lead to a valid conclusion regarding the existence of a threat of material injury to the industry manufacturing grey Portland cement.

6.594 In turn, these facts mean that the Ministry could not have established a causal relationship between the dumped imports and the threat of injury claimed by the domestic producer. Furthermore, the Ministry of the Economy's determination was not based on positive evidence to substantiate adequately a preliminary affirmative determination of threat of injury to the domestic industry.

6.595 The Ministry of the Economy thus made a preliminary affirmative determination of threat of injury after inadequate and insufficient consideration of the following:

(a) An alleged increase in imports from Cruz Azul, without taking into account relevant factors to prove this;

(b) the likelihood of an increase in Mexican exports to Guatemala as a result of plant capacity at Cruz Azul, based on alleged surplus plant capacity at the exporting firm and the demand situation on the Mexican market, without having undertaken a proper analysis and without having relevant and sufficient evidence of the actual likelihood that these exports would increase in the immediate future;[508]

(c) a decrease in the price of the domestic product in certain Guatemalan cities, without proper comparison of prices;

(d) an accumulation of inventories based on a subjective and biased analysis that referred to a product not under investigation;

(e) under-utilization of plant capacity;

(f) a decrease in sales by Cementos caused by other factors;

(g) loss of the applicant's customers, without verifying their existence nor the substitution effect.

6.596 The above clearly shows what has already been stated, namely, when adopting its preliminary affirmative determination of a threat of material injury the Ministry of the Economy limited itself to carrying out an inadequate and insufficient analysis of the factors enumerated in Article 3.7 of the AD Agreement without taking into account the fact that the Agreement requires positive evidence and an objective examination of the impact of the dumped imports when determining threat of material injury, evaluating not only the factors listed in Article 3.7 but also those set out in Article 3.2 and 3.4 of the AD Agreement, and certain other factors which simultaneously have an adverse effect on the domestic industry, as provided in Article 3.5.

6.597 Mexico's arguments are set out below and show in more detail that the alleged examination carried out by the Ministry of the Economy (essentially of the factors in Article 3.7) was insufficient and inadequate to substantiate its preliminary affirmative determination of threat of material injury.

(i) Increase in imports

6.598 In its preliminary determination, the Ministry of the Economy indicated that during the investigation period (June to November 1995) exports from the Mexican firm

[508] Section F, part 2, points 2.1, 2.2 and 2.4-2.7 of the preliminary determination.

increased significantly and allegedly reached 23.54 per cent of domestic apparent consumption.[509] In this connection, certain facts necessarily lead to the conclusion that the preliminary determination of threat of injury was contrary to the AD Agreement and this must be considered:

6.599 The figures used by the Ministry of the Economy to determine the performance of imports from Mexico are *not* accurate as they do not take account of the existence of types of cement other than that investigated. There is an indication in the administrative file that products other than that investigated were imported under the tariff heading 2523.29.00 of the Central American Tariff System[510], for example, white cement and grey cement. Consequently, the import figures for grey Portland cement obtained by the Ministry of the Economy and attributed to the firm Cruz Azul are *not* correct and cannot therefore substantiate the Ministry's analysis and determination.

6.600 The conclusions concerning the volume of dumped imports on which the Ministry of the Economy based its preliminary affirmative determination of material injury are inconsistent with the criteria set out in Article 3.7(i) of the AD Agreement. The Ministry of the Economy violated this Article by *not* taking into account whether or not there was a significant increase in imports and confining itself to obtaining monthly import figures for the investigation period, without noting that a determination of threat of injury requires the investigating authority to analyse the trend in imports in relation to previous comparable periods in order to see whether the trend towards an increase in the imports investigated persists and thus be able to estimate their future trend.

6.601 In addition, the figures included in the preliminary determination by the Ministry of the Economy on the alleged increase in the volume of imports of the product investigated are inaccurate because the Ministry did *not* take into account the trend in imports over the investigation period (June to November 1995) in comparison with the previous comparable period, which in this case would be June to November 1994.

6.602 In its application for initiation of an investigation, the domestic producer Cementos Progreso claimed that the exports from the Mexican firm Cruz Azul were threatening to cause it material injury. Nevertheless, in the corresponding paragraph of the public notice of imposition of the provisional anti-dumping measure, the Ministry of the Economy does *not* in any way refer to a rate of increase in exports by the firm under investigation which would indicate the likelihood, based on facts rather than simply on allegations, of a substantial increase in exports, as required by Article 3.7(i) of the AD Agreement.

6.603 Thus, it can be seen that the analysis of imports by the Ministry of the Economy in the preliminary determination of threat of material injury is not consistent with the provision in the AD Agreement so it was *not* possible for the Ministry of the Economy to obtain a rate of increase in dumped imports in the domestic market and therefore it could *not* have determined a causal link between the alleged increase in dumped imports and the alleged threat of material injury to the domestic industry in accordance with the provisions of Article 3.5 of the AD Agreement.

---

[509] Point 2.1, Section F, of the preliminary determination.

[510] Imports of grey Portland cement, heading 25232900 for 1995.

(ii) Surplus plant capacity and demand in Mexican Market

6.604 In order to make a preliminary affirmative determination of threat of injury[511], the Ministry incorrectly assumed that the fact that Cruz Azul had alleged freely disposable capacity for cement production of 360,000 tonnes, combined with negative growth in the Mexican economy and an alleged decrease in demand on the Mexican market, according to its evaluation, indicated the likelihood that the dumped exports would increase. It is important in this respect to stress the following:

6.605 As far as Cruz Azul's disposable capacity is concerned, the Ministry of the Economy ignored the fact that the Mexican producer manufactured several types of cement, not only grey Portland cement - a like product to that investigated. The alleged amount of freely disposable capacity taken by the Ministry as a basis, therefore, *cannot* be considered accurate information or adequate for the purposes of reaching an affirmative determination of threat of material injury.

6.606 Regarding the likelihood of increased exports by Cruz Azul in the future, it should be emphasized that the preliminary determination shows that the Ministry of the Economy reached this conclusion on the basis of mere conjecture because there is no indication that the investigating authority carried out an analysis on the basis of evidence substantiating the actual likelihood that exports from Cruz Azul would increase in the immediate future. It will be remembered that Article 3.7 of the AD Agreement states that "The change in circumstances which would create a situation in which the dumping would cause injury must be clearly foreseen and imminent" and not be based on "allegation, conjecture or remote possibility".

6.607 It can thus be concluded that the Ministry of the Economy's determination regarding the likelihood of a significant increase in exports from Cruz Azul to the Guatemalan market is a violation of Article 3.7 of the AD Agreement.

(iii) Reduction in prices of domestic producer

6.608 In the preliminary determination, the investigating authority found that:

> "As a result of dumped imports, there was a fall in the price of cement in those cities where the product under investigation is sold, despite an increase in the cost of fuel, which is the major cost element in cement production. This is demonstrated both by the outcome of the investigation conducted by the Department for Consumer Welfare (DIACO) and by information furnished by the complainant concerning prices obtained in this segment of the Guatemalan market and the relationship between these prices and those that might have been established in keeping with the Government formula for setting a maximum sale price."

6.609 Pursuant to Article 3.7(iii) of the AD Agreement, in order to make an affirmative determination of threat of injury, the investigating authority should have considered, *inter alia*, whether imports were at prices that would depress or significantly suppress domestic prices and whether this would perhaps lead to increased demand for further imports. Instead, the Ministry of the Economy quite simply asserted that "as a consequence of dumped imports, there was a fall in the price of cement in those cities where it is sold". In order to reach this conclusion, the Ministry took as a basis the DIACO investigation, the information supplied by the applicant and the relationship between these prices and those

511 Point 2.7, Section F, of the preliminary determination.

that might have been established in keeping with the Government formula for setting a maximum selling price.

6.610 The conclusion of the Ministry of the Economy suffers from the following inconsistencies:

6.611 The preliminary determination does *not* explain the procedure (i.e. the methodological steps and the circumstances) followed in establishing that the fall in prices was due to the allegedly dumped imports, but simply asserts that this was so.

6.612 The conclusion and the study by DIACO refer only to some Guatemalan cities, as though the anti-dumping investigation had been conducted on the basis of a regional investigation under Article 4.2 of the AD Agreement, when in fact it involved the whole of the domestic industry.

6.613 The preliminary determination does *not* indicate how the comparison was made between the price of imported cement and the selling price of the domestic product, nor does it state whether the prices were compared at the same level of trade, whether the transactions were on the same terms of trade, whether the products were comparable, the dates of the comparisons, and whether the prices were the result of simple or weighted, moving or progressive averages.

6.614 The comparison with the prices that might have been established in keeping with the formula introduced by the Guatemalan Government in 1990 for setting the selling price ceiling could distort the entire exercise in that the formula does not correspond to the market prices that would result in a situation of free competition. In any case, it is a theoretical price ceiling and not a price that must necessarily be reached.

6.615 The conclusions concerning the trend in domestic prices used by the Ministry of the Economy to reach a preliminary determination of threat of material injury are inconsistent with the criteria laid down in Article 3.7(iii) of the AD Agreement. The Ministry of the Economy therefore violated the Article by *not* taking account of whether the price of imports of the product investigated had had the effect of depressing domestic prices or suppressing them significantly, because in its preliminary determination the Ministry confined itself to giving simplistic indications of the price trend with no mention that the investigating authority had made the relevant calculations to show the trend in prices of the imported product and domestic prices for comparable previous periods in order to determine whether the trend in such prices might increase demand for further imports of the product investigated.

6.616 In the administrative file on this case, there is *no* indication to show that, as required by Article 3.2 of the AD Agreement, the Ministry of the Economy considered whether there was significant undercutting of the price of the imports investigated during the investigation period in comparison with the price of the domestically manufactured product. The Ministry of the Economy thus violated Article 3.2 by not making the corresponding evaluation. It could not therefore determine that the situation envisaged in Article 3.7(iii) existed inasmuch as if there is no analysis of the trend in import prices and domestic prices, it is impossible to make the estimates and forecasts needed to be certain that this effect would occur in the future.

(iv) Accumulation of inventories and under-utilization of plant capacity

6.617 In its preliminary determination[512], the Ministry of the Economy indicates the following:

> "As a result of the increase in cement imports, there was a build-up of clinker in the complainant's warehouses, and three kilns at its production plant therefore had to be closed (two in the Pedrera Plant and one in the San Miguel Plant).
>
> The shutdown of the kilns at the complainant's production plant came at the time of peak demand for the product, which is also the period of highest production, as emerges from the analysis of sales and milling curves for the years 1993, 1994 and 1995, included in the file.
>
> As regards the facts indicated, the Notary Jorge Edwin Rosales Pichardo certified the existence of 76,252 tonnes (one day after the kilns were ordered closed) and the Director of Economic Integration ascertained that the kilns had been stopped and that there were 51,875 tonnes of material accumulated at the San Miguel plant. This final figure indicated was derived from records kept by the production department of the complainant and amounts to 65,665 tonnes of cement."

6.618 In this regard, the following facts should be highlighted:

6.619 The alleged increase in stocks of clinker[513] and the consequent shutdown of the kilns in which this raw material is produced were recorded after the investigation period and, indeed, almost two months after the initiation of the investigation. The investigation period fixed by the investigating authority spanned June to November 1995, yet, the facts noted by the Ministry itself[514] and by a notary[515] concern events that took place subsequently.

6.620 In this connection, it must be pointed out that the analysis needed to determine threat of injury was limited to the period fixed by the investigating authority for the determination, namely June-November 1995. In other words, the events that occurred in 1996 *cannot* explain nor affect what happened in the past. The evidence of alleged threat of injury claimed by the domestic producer during the investigation period could *not* in any way be proved by events that would occur in the future. The causal link between dumped imports and the alleged threat of injury must be verified over the same period of time because the causal link is contemporaneous and not sequential.

6.621 Pursuant to Article 3.6 of the AD Agreement, the effect of imports is to be evaluated in relation to domestic production of the like product when available data permit separate identification on the basis of such criteria as the production process, producer's sales and profits. Yet the Ministry of the Economy attributed to the alleged imports investigated an impact on the inventory of a product other than the one investigated. Indeed,

---

[512] Point 2.2, Section F, of the preliminary determination.

[513] Produced by incipient fusion of limestone, bauxite, hematite and silica at 1380ºC, and used in the manufacture both of the product under investigation and of any other type of cement (grey, white or any other hydraulic cement).

[514] Document of the Ministry of the Economy to prove the accumulation of inventories of clinker and the stoppage of the kilns producing clinker, dated 29 March 1996. Point 2.2 of section F of the preliminary determination.

[515] Notary's Act (verification of stocks of clinker within Cementos Progreso's plant, dated 29 February 1996).

a reading of the preliminary determination reveals that the Ministry of the Economy determined that there was an accumulation of inventories of one of the raw materials (clinker) used in the manufacture of the product under investigation (grey Portland cement). The Ministry did *not*, however, mention in its determination that this input *cannot only be used to manufacture grey Portland cement but also any other type of cement*, including those that not under investigation. The investigating authority therefore erred in determining an increase in the inventory of an input while forgetting that the inventory that should have been evaluated was that of the product under investigation.

6.622 Moreover, there is *no* certainty that the material accumulated at the industrial plant of Cementos Progreso actually was clinker as neither the Notary who certified the existence of the material nor the Director of Economic Integration of the Ministry of the Economy who conducted the on-the-spot investigation have the technical and scientific capacity to vouch that the material that they observed was in fact clinker, and whether the product in question would be used for the manufacture of the product being investigated and not for some other type of cement.

6.623 As of the publication of the public notice of initiation (11 January 1996), imports from Cruz Azul remained constant, a fact that was *not* analysed at any stage by the Ministry of the Economy and in Mexico's opinion this calls into question the causal link between the imports and the closure of the kilns for a product other than that investigated, particularly when the Ministry of the Economy itself during the consultations agreed that, even after the closure of the kilns supplying clinker, Cementos Progreso continued to manufacture grey Portland cement.

6.624 In its preliminary determination, the Ministry of the Economy admitted as proof several statements and documents that are *not* relevant for the purposes of demonstrating the existence of stocks of grey Portland cement and the consequent shutdown of the kilns[516], for example, the administrative inspection carried out by two officials of the Ministry of the Economy and the notarial deed by Mr. Edwin Rosales, the eight colour pictures and graph showing the alleged inventories of clinker and cement. These documents *cannot* be considered relevant since, in order to ascertain the existence of stocks and the shutdown of kilns, technical inspections need to be made and, as emerges from the text of the resolution itself, these were *not* carried out.[517]

6.625 It is clear that the mere observation of heaps of material is *not* enough to prove either the existence of stocks of clinker, their volume or the use to which they will be put, neither is it therefore possible to deduce that the supposed accumulation of materials was the result of the allegedly dumped imports from Cruz Azul.

6.626 To illustrate the flaws in the analysis made by the Ministry of the Economy, it must be pointed out that in the cement industry the accumulation of clinker is not such an important fact in itself since it may be attributable to a variety of reasons, as Cruz Azul told the Ministry of the Economy in due course.[518] These reasons may include the following:

(a) Buffer stocks consisting of 14 days output from the principal kiln. Operation manual II Cement. In Cement Review. Philippe A. Alsop;

(b) seasonal demand;

---

[516] Flow of the production process for the manufacture of cement contained in Cemontos Progreso's reply of 17 May 1996 to the form.

[517] The Ministry of the Economy does *not* explain how the shutdown of the kilns came to result from alleged imports and how this effect came to be a case of threat of injury.

[518] See Cruz Azul's hearing of 30 October 1996.

(c) imbalances within the production plant. Clinker vs. final milling;

(d) strikes, power cuts and lack of fuel;

(e) rain (climatic factors).

6.627 The Ministry of the Economy should have ascertained whether the alleged inventories were related to any of the foregoing factors, or whether they were caused wholly or partly by imports of cement from Cruz Azul.

6.628 Finally, it is noteworthy that the preliminary determination does *not* mention the under-utilization of plant capacity, even though this is expressly included in the title of the corresponding section.

6.629 The foregoing shows that the Ministry of the Economy violated Article 3.7(iv)of the AD Agreement by conducting an incorrect, subjective and biased analysis of the inventories of the product being investigated, which referred to a product that was *not* the product under investigation and was based on evidence that could *not* be considered relevant. The Ministry also omitted important elements that negate the causal relationship between the inventories of the product investigated and the increase in imports investigated. The Ministry of the Economy thus violated Article 3.5 of the AD Agreement.

(v) Reduced sales

6.630 In its preliminary determination[519], the Ministry of the Economy states that, due to an increase in the imports investigated, there was a reduction in sales by Cementos Progreso during the month of September 1995 in comparison with sales during the preceding year, a situation that persisted throughout the first three months of the following year. Nevertheless, it should be pointed out that:

6.631 According to the preliminary determination, *sales by Cementos Progreso fell during the month of September 1995*. Nevertheless, as the determination itself recognizes, this fall could not be attributed to the imports investigated[520] as *there was a fall in imports of 40.14 per cent during that month* and in September 1995 demand in the Guatemalan market fell in comparison with the preceding month. It is obvious that the trend in sales of the domestic product on the domestic market shadows the trend in the imports investigated in September 1995.

6.632 As regards the pattern of sales for the first quarter of 1996, the said sales do not fall within the period of investigation and should therefore not be considered. What is more, the Ministry of the Economy did *not* collect at this stage of the investigation information on the increase in imports, which means that such information cannot justifiably be included in an examination of the relationship between Cementos Progreso's sales and the imports investigated.

6.633 It may be concluded from the foregoing that the determination of the alleged effect on Cementos Progreso's sales caused by the imports investigated was due to factors other than the import of grey Portland cement from Mexico and this was even expressly recognized by the Ministry of the Economy in its own preliminary determination. Therefore, the determination does *not* reflect an objective and unbiased analysis of the factual elements available to the Guatemalan investigating authority when issuing the preliminary determination, thus violating Guatemala's obligations under Article 3.5 and 3.7 of the AD Agreement.

---

519 Point 2.4, section F, of the preliminary determination.

520 Line 7 *et seq* of the third para. of point 2.1, section F, of the preliminary determination.

(vi) Loss of customers

6.634 In its preliminary determination, the Ministry of the Economy considered that Cementos Progreso had lost some of its customers, without having ascertained the truthfulness of the claim and of the list of alleged customers submitted by the applicant.

6.635 Thus, the investigating authority in its preliminary determination accepted that the alleged customers switched from domestically manufactured cement to imported grey Portland cement, though it did not ascertain the existence of these clients and the effect of substitution of one product by the other. The list in question shows only the names of alleged customers and no further data bearing out the applicant's affirmations.

6.636 The investigating authority should also have considered that the list which was presented as "proof" might also have contained "customers" who had been driven out of the applicant's market as a result of its own intimidatory, exclusive and monopolistic policy, as was found by the Ministry itself through the DIACO studies of the market for the cement being investigated, which, by their very nature, constitute irrefutable proof.

(b) Response of Guatemala

6.637 **Guatemala's** response to Mexico's Article 3.7 arguments are as follows:

6.638 Contrary to Mexico's claims, the Ministry carefully and properly considered the factors which, according to Article 3.7, can be used to determine the existence of a threat of material injury. The Ministry made an evaluation of the evidence as reflected in the report of the Directorate of Economic Integration of 26 July 1996, in the Ministry's preliminary determination dated 16 August 1996, and in the public notice of the determination dated 28 August 1996. The report of 16 August and the public notice of 28 August 1996 are identical. The report of 26 July contains some additional information which is summarised in the documents mentioned below.

(i) Increased imports

6.639 The Ministry found that during the investigation period (June-November 1995) Cruz Azul imports had increased in absolute and relative terms with respect to domestic production and apparent consumption. During the period investigated Cruz Azul imports increased from 140 tons in June 1995 to 25,740 tons in November 1995. Imports from Cruz Azul increased sharply from 0.15 per cent of domestic production in June to 32.65 per cent of domestic production in November. Cruz Azul's market share increased from 0.15 in June to 23.54 per cent in November. This led to Cementos Progreso's market share falling from 99.85 per cent in June to 75.42 per cent in November. This significant rate of increase in dumped imports clearly indicated the likelihood that imports would continue to increase and that Cementos Progreso's market share would be reduced.

6.640 Contrary to Mexico's unfounded allegations, the Ministry was not unaware of the existence of other types of cement imported under tariff heading 2523.99.00. In its analysis the Ministry only considered Cruz Azul imports.[521] The Ministry noted that imports from Cruz Azul represented 91 per cent of total Guatemalan grey cement imports during the period investigated. However, the Ministry did not assume that all the imports under this tariff heading were from Cruz Azul.

6.641 Mexico has criticized the Ministry for not taking into account the level of imports during June-November 1994. However, Mexico is well aware that Cruz Azul did not be-

[521] Report of the Directorate of Economic Integration, dated 26 July 1996.

gin exporting cement to Guatemala until 1995[522], after the devaluation of the peso in December 1994, which led to a sharp downturn in the construction industry and in the demand for cement in Mexico during the following year. Comparing imports for June-November 1995 with those for June-November 1994 would only have served to strengthen support for an preliminary affirmative determination.

(ii) Surplus plant capacity and demand in Mexico

6.642 The Ministry found that because of the high fixed costs involved in cement production the cement producer's profitability depends on maintaining a high degree of utilization of capacity. If there is a weakening of demand, new outlets must be found for the product. The Ministry found that, following the devaluation of the peso in December 1994, the Mexican economy was experiencing negative growth of at least 3 per cent and that spending in the construction sector had fallen by 22 per cent. According to the consultancy firm Arthur D. Little Mexicana, Cruz Azul had 360,000 tons per year of excess production capacity. The Ministry found that the evidence of excess production capacity and depressed demand supported the conclusion that "dumped exports are likely to increase".

6.643 Mexico argues that the finding with respect to excess production capacity does not take into account the fact that Cruz Azul is said to manufacture several types of cement different from grey Portland cement. However, Mexico does not allege that the same plant cannot be used for producing all types of cement. Thus, Mexico's unsupported argument to the effect that Cruz Azul can produce different types of cement does not mean that Cruz Azul did not have 360,000 tons of excess production capacity available for producing grey Portland cement. On the contrary, the company could have used all this excess capacity for producing grey Portland cement for export to Guatemala.

(iii) Reduction in the prices of the domestic producer

6.644 The Ministry found that as a result of the dumped imports the price of domestic cement fell in those cities in which Cruz Azul cement was being sold, despite the fact that Cementos Progreso's production costs had increased. The Ministry referred to the findings of a study prepared by the Directorate of Consumer Affairs (BIACO) which showed that the imported product consistently undercut domestic prices.[523] The Ministry also referred to the evidence submitted by Cementos Progreso concerning the widening of the gap between the maximum price fixed by the Government and Cementos Progreso's actual prices. Once again, Mexico requests the Panel to conduct a *de novo* review of this finding.

6.645 *Firstly*, Mexico maintains that the preliminary determination fails to explain the methodology used to determine that prices were being depressed by dumped imports. Article 12.2.1 of the Agreement, which describes the information that a public notice of the imposition of a provisional measure must contain, does not require the investigating authority to describe the methodology used to arrive at a factual conclusion. This Article only requires the notice to set forth findings and conclusions and "sufficiently detailed

---

522 In its communication of 30 October 1996, Cruz Azul stated that it began to export to Guatemala during the investigation period which began in June 1995.

523 As described in Section IV.B.3 of the determination dated 16 August 1996, BIACO investigated the prices, inventories and characteristics of the cement being sold in nine different Guatemalan departments.

explanations for the preliminary determinations...". In any case, the methodology used is obvious from the determination itself. The Ministry found that Cruz Azul imports were giving rise to undercutting of Cementos Progreso's cement prices and thus were obliging Cementos Progreso to reduce its prices in those cities in which Cruz Azul cement was being sold.[524] The price undercutting and consequent fall in prices resulted in the widening of the gap between the maximum prices authorized by the Government and Cementos Progreso's actual prices.

6.646 *Secondly*, Mexico argues that the DIACO reports cover only some Guatemalan cities, as if it were a question of an investigation of a regional industry. Because of the low price/weight ratio and high freight costs for cement, Cruz Azul concentrated its sales effort in the western part of Guatemala, which lies closer to its plant in Lagunas, Oaxaca. Accordingly, DIACO directed its attention to the cities closer to the Mexican frontier, where Cruz Azul sales were concentrated. The existence of underpriced sales in the area of Guatemala most affected clearly pointed to a threat of injury to Cementos Progreso. According to Cruz Azul's submission dated 9 May 1996, Cruz Azul imports caused prices in Guatemala to fall by between Q 6.00 and Q 8.00 per sack. Despite the fact that initially Cruz Azul concentrated its sales effort in western Guatemala, the lower prices enabled it to capture almost one-quarter of the total Guatemalan market in only six months.

6.647 *Thirdly*, Mexico claims that the preliminary determination does not show how price comparisons were made between the imported and domestic products. The price comparison is explained in detail in the DIACO reports. DIACO officials visited cement sales establishments in many cities distinguishing those which were selling Cruz Azul cement from those which were selling Cementos Progreso cement. This made possible a direct comparison of selling prices at the same level of trade, under the same conditions, at the same time and with the same buyers. In almost all cases Cruz Azul cement was being sold at prices that undercut those of Cementos Progreso cement. Moreover, many of these establishments confirmed that Cruz Azul cement had caused a fall in the price of cement in Guatemala.

6.648 *Finally*, Mexico argues that it was not appropriate to compare the prices made by Cementos Progreso with the maximum prices it was entitled to charge under the formula imposed by the Government. The evidence showed that before the influx of imports from Cruz Azul the prices made by Cementos Progreso were generally as high as permitted by the Government formula. During the period investigated, Cementos Progreso was not able to charge the maximum permissible price in those cities where Cruz Azul cement was being sold, but was able to charge that price in cities further from the Mexican frontier where Cruz Azul cement was not available. This is conclusive evidence that Cruz Azul imports were entering at prices that were depressing the prices of the like domestic product.

(iv) Accumulation of small inventories and under utilization of plant capacity

6.649 The Ministry found that increased Cruz Azul imports had led to an accumulation of the domestic producer's clinker inventories, which had forced it to suspend the operation of three clinker kilns (two at the La Pedrera plant and one at the San Miguel plant). On the basis of an analysis of the sales and production figures for 1993-1995, the Minis-

[524] The determination also referred to a newspaper Article published in La República on 22 August 1998 indicating that cement imports were causing prices to fall in Guatemala.

try also found that the kilns were shut down during a period of high demand for cement when production is also higher. A notary recorded clinker stocks amounting to 76,252 tons on the day after the kilns were shut down. The Directorate of Economic Integration verified the shutdown of the kilns and accumulated stocks of 51,875 tons of clinker at the San Miguel plant. As the clinker is mixed with hydrated calcium sulphate and other additives and then ground up to make the finished cement, the Ministry found that clinker stocks of 51,875 tons were equivalent to 65,665 tons of cement.

6.650 *Firstly*, Mexico claims that the evidence of excessive inventories and kiln shutdown during the months of February to March 1996 is irrelevant since it post-dates the investigation period which ran from June 1995 to November 1995. Mexico does not cite any provision of the Agreement preventing an investigating authority from considering recent information. Article 3.7 does not contain any such restriction. Guatemala respectfully maintains that it is particularly desirable for the investigating authority to use as much of the recent information available as possible.

6.651 *Secondly*, Mexico argues that the Ministry should not have considered the accumulation of clinker inventories since the product being investigated was cement. Moreover, Mexico alleges that clinker can be used for making products other than grey cement. This is not true. As noted above, clinker is a semi-finished product which is ground to produce cement in the last phase of the production process. It can be stored outdoors in large quantities, whereas finished cement must be stored in concrete silos. Thus, clinker inventories provide better evidence of inventory trends than the cement inventories themselves. Likewise, the file shows that Cementos Progreso was only producing grey Portland cement. Thus, the Ministry correctly established that 51,875 tons of clinker stocks were equivalent to 65,665 tons of finished cement.

6.652 *Thirdly*, Mexico challenges the Ministry's factual finding to the effect that the material stocked was clinker. However, it does not suggest what alternative clinker-like material could have been stocked in a plant devoted to producing cement. The preliminary determination notes that the file contained eight colour photographs of clinker and a notarial deed certifying the clinker stored, together with a graph showing Cementos Progreso's monthly inventories from June 1995 to February 1996.

6.653 *Fourthly*, contrary to what Mexico says, Cruz Azul imports did not remain constant after January 1996. The imports continued to increase, reaching 45,859 tons in March 1996.

6.654 *Fifthly*, Mexico denies that the inspection carried out by two officials from the Ministry, the notarial deed and the colour photographs are valid evidence of clinker inventories. Guatemala would respectfully maintain that it is not the function of the panel to evaluate the admissibility and value of the evidence considered by the Ministry. Moreover, the Ministry confirmed that the increased clinker inventories were the result of increased Cruz Azul imports and not the result of other factors such as seasonal demand, strikes or rain.

6.655 *Sixthly*, curiously, Mexico points out that this part of the preliminary determination did not refer to underutilization of installed capacity, even though this factor was included in the section title. In Guatemala's view the underutilization of capacity is clearly demonstrated by the shutdown of three kilns.

(v) Reduced sales

6.656 The Ministry found that in September 1995 and thereafter as a result of increased imports sales of the like domestic product fell as compared with those recorded during the previous year. Sales continued to decline during the first quarter of 1996. Mexico's objections to these findings are unfounded.

6.657 *Firstly*, Mexico claims that the reduced sales were the result of a fall in demand in the month of September rather than increased imports. Although there was in fact a fall in demand in September 1995, the Ministry found that there had been a continuous decline in sales from September 1995 to March 1996 as compared with the previous year. Moreover, in challenging the preliminary determination of reduced sales due to dumped imports, Mexico disregards the fact that in Guatemala cement demand is seasonal. Demand is stronger during the dry season (October-May) than in the rainy season (June-September). Thus, the Ministry properly evaluated Cruz Azul's sales by comparing them with the volume of sales in the same months of the previous year. This comparison showed that Cementos Progreso's sales fell during the latter part of 1995 and the first quarter of 1996 as compared with the same months of the previous year.

6.658 *Secondly*, Mexico claims that the Ministry should not have considered sales during the first quarter of 1996 since those sales fell outside the initial investigation period. The Agreement does not prohibit the investigating authority from considering the most recent information available. In fact, this is a better practice, especially where it is a question of analysing a threat of material injury.

(vi) Loss of customers

6.659 The Ministry found that despite the fact that Cementos Progreso reduced its prices to compete with Cruz Azul it lost certain customers who were identified in the file. Mexico challenges this finding on the grounds that the Ministry did not ascertain the truthfulness of the evidence submitted by Cementos Progreso in support of its claim to have lost customers to Cruz Azul. It is an indisputable fact that in only six months Cruz Azul increased its market share from 0.15 per cent to 23.54 per cent and that Cementos Progreso's market share fell from 99.85 per cent to 75.42 per cent during the same period. DIACO based itself on the fact that cement from Cruz Azul was cheaper than that from Cementos Progreso. Thus, it is logical to conclude that Cementos Progreso lost customers to Cruz Azul. The evidence of loss of customers submitted by Cementos Progreso is corroborated by the shift of market share to Cruz Azul.

(vii) The Ministry also considered important factors contained in paragraphs 1, 2 and 4 of Article 3

6.660 Mexico also argues that in making its preliminary determination Guatemala did not consider the factors contained in paragraphs 1, 2 and 4 of Article 5. Guatemala has stressed the factors listed in paragraph 7 of Article 3, because those factors are relevant to the consideration of threat of injury and not present injury. However, Mexico is wrong in suggesting that the Ministry did not *consider* other factors.

6.661 Contrary to Mexico's assertion, the Ministry explicitly took into account the possibility of a significant increase in imports, in accordance with Article 3.2. As the preliminary determination states, imports increased dramatically in absolute and relative terms, in relation to both domestic production and apparent consumption during the investigation period. It is ridiculous that Mexico should suggest the contrary.

6.662 Contrary to what Mexico alleges, the Ministry explicitly considered whether significant price undercutting was responsible for the fall in prices, under the terms of Article 3.2. It also referred to the DIACO report and other evidence of price depression. In its submission of 9 May 1996, Cruz Azul itself acknowledged that Cruz Azul imports had caused cement prices in Guatemala to fall by Q 6.00 to Q 8.00 per sack.

6.663 Contrary to what Mexico says, the Ministry explicitly evaluated the impact of dumped imports on the domestic industry, in accordance with Article 3.4. Among other things, the Ministry explicitly considered the decline in sales, productivity, market share and utilization of capacity suffered by Cementos Progreso and whether imports from Cruz Azul had had an adverse impact on domestic prices and Cementos Progreso's inventories.

6.664 Moreover, the Anti-Dumping Agreement does not oblige the investigating authorities to provide details in writing of all the factors considered or make an explicit report on each of the factors taken into account. The Ministry listed all the evidence considered in its preliminary determination, provided detailed explanations of the preliminary determination of dumping and injury and carefully spelled out "the main reasons leading to the determination".[525] No more is required.

(c) Rebuttal of Mexico

6.665 **Mexico** rebuts Guatemala's submissions by maintaining that Guatemala's preliminary determination of threat of injury is inconsistent with Article 3 of the Anti-Dumping Agreement. It argues the following:

6.666 Mexico categorically rejects Guatemala's argument that the preliminary determination of threat of material injury complied with Article 3 of the AD Agreement, and repeats that the preliminary determination of the Ministry of the Economy of threat of material injury to the Guatemalan domestic industry was inconsistent with the provisions of Article 3.1, 3.2, 3.4, 3.5 and 3.7 of the Anti-Dumping Agreement.

6.667 Specifically, Mexico begins by rejecting the argument by Guatemala that "[...] the Ministry carefully and properly considered the factors which, according to Article 3.7, can be used to determine the existence of a threat of material injury [...]¡", [526] and reiterates its position that in the case at issue, the Ministry did not properly analyse the factors listed in Article 3.7 in reaching its preliminary determination of threat of injury.

6.668 However, to avoid unnecessary repetition, we refer the Panel to the specific arguments made by Mexico in this respect in its first written submission.[527] In this section of our rebuttal, we shall refer to the violations of Article 3.7[528] only in relation to other elements which demonstrate the inconsistency of the Ministry's preliminary determination with Article 3 of the Anti-Dumping Agreement, and to the extent necessary to respond to Guatemala's arguments.

6.669 We begin by referring to paragraph 275 of Guatemala's first written submission which states that:

---

525 Anti-Dumping Agreement, Article 12.2.1.

526 *Ibid.*, para. 253.

527 See parts B2a, B2b, B2c and B2d of Mexico's first written submission.

528 It is worth adding one small comment concerning an opinion expressed by the United States in para. 15 of its oral submission as third party to these proceedings according to which the evaluation of inventories of a semi-finished product can help an investigating authority to obtain a clearer picture of the state of the domestic industry. Mexico agrees with this opinion, *provided* the evaluation is indeed used to provide supplementary assistance in determining more precisely the state of the industry. However, in this case, the Ministry, in its preliminary determination, considered *that the analysis of the inventories of one input exclusively sufficed to infer the behaviour of the inventories of the investigated product*. This is inconsistent with Article 3.7(iv) of the AD Agreement, which expressly states that the authorities should consider, *inter alia*, such factors as "inventories *of the product being investigated*". Thus, it is unacceptable for an investigating authority not to conduct an analysis of the inventories of the product under investigation, but rather, merely to look at the behaviour of the inventories of one of the inputs used in manufacturing grey Portland cement and simply to infer or deduce that the inventories of the investigated product would have behaved similarly to the clinker inventory during the investigation period.

> "275. [...] Guatemala has stressed the factors listed in paragraph 7 of Article 3, because *those factors are relevant to the consideration of threat of injury* and not present injury. However, Mexico is wrong in suggesting that the Ministry did not *consider* other factors."

6.670 Thus, according to Guatemala the Ministry also considered important factors contained in Article 3.1, 3.2 and 3.4.

6.671 However, the evidence in the administrative file of the investigation which Mexico supplied to the Panel in various annexes clearly contradicts Guatemala's post hoc argument in paragraphs 275 to 279 of its first submission. Thus, contrary to what Guatemala has said, Mexico repeats that the Ministry of the Economy did not properly and sufficiently examine the factors listed in Article 3.2 and 3.4 of the AD Agreement which should have been taken into account in examining the increase in imports, their effect on domestic prices and their consequent impact on the domestic industry.

6.672 According to footnote 9 of the Anti-Dumping Agreement, the term "injury" also covers threat of material injury:

> "Under this Agreement *the term 'injury'* shall, unless otherwise specified, be taken to mean *material injury* to a domestic industry, *threat of material injury* to a domestic industry or *material retardation* of the establishment of such an industry and shall be interpreted in accordance with the provisions of this Article". (Emphasis added)

6.673 Thus, while it is true that Article, 3.7 lists the specific factors to be considered in determining a threat of injury, it is also true that Article 3.1 is a general provision which establishes that *the determination* of 'injury' for purposes of Article VI of GATT 1994, i.e. in the sense *of material injury and threat of material injury* in accordance with the scope of footnote 9:

> "shall be based on *positive evidence* and involve an *objective examination* of (a) the *volume of the dumped imports* and the *effect* of the dumped imports *on prices* in the domestic market for like products, and (b) the *consequent impact* of these products on domestic producers of such products."

6.674 In accordance with the requirements of Article 3.1, Article 3.2 establishes the factors which need to be taken into consideration with regard to the *volume of imports* and their *effect on the prices* which need to be examined, while Article 3.4 lists the factors to be taken into account in examining the *consequent impact* of the dumped imports on the domestic industry.

6.675 Thus, Article 3.1 of the Anti-Dumping Agreement establishes in a general way the elements to be examined for a threat of injury determination in accordance with an evaluation of the specific factors indicated in Article 3.2 and 3.4.

6.676 This means that while it is true that Article 3.7 requires a prospective analysis of certain specific factors to determine threat of injury, it is also true that threat of injury determinations made by an investigating authority through insistent and exclusive analysis of the factors listed in Article 3.7 would be based on an insufficient and illogical analysis if the investigating authority failed, as it did in this case, to take proper account of the factors listed in Articles 3.2 and 3.4 as stipulated in Article 3.1.

6.677 However, Guatemala seems to disregard these provisions and argues that on the basis of a partial and inadequate analysis of some of the factors listed in Article 3.7 and 3.4 it was possible for the Ministry to determine threat of material injury without taking account of the fact that the analysis of the behaviour or the factors on which the preliminary determination was based is insufficient and is closely related to the behaviour of other relevant factors which it failed to analyse in its determination. In fact, as the Panel will be able to see, the Ministry's preliminary determination and the public notice of imposition of the provisional anti-dumping measure clearly show that the threat of injury analysis was not based on positive evidence or on an objective and sufficient examination of the various relevant factors listed in Article 3.2 and 3.4 such as:

> *A significant increase* in imports relative to domestic production or consumption in the importing Member;
>
> *the effect of dumped imports on domestic prices* and a significant undercutting of those prices by the dumped imports, or whether the effect of such imports is otherwise to depress prices or prevent their increase to a significant degree;
>
> *actual or potential* decline in profits, output or return on investments;
>
> *potential* decline in sales, market share, productivity and utilization of installed capacity;
>
> actual and potential negative effects on cash flow, inventories, employment, wages, growth, ability to raise capital or investment.

(i) Violation of Article 3.2

6.678 In paragraph 276 of its first written submission, Guatemala states that:

> "276. [...] the Ministry explicitly took into account the possibility of a significant increase in imports, in accordance with Article 3.2. As the preliminary determination *states*, imports increased dramatically in absolute and relative terms, in relation to both domestic production and apparent consumption during the investigation period."

6.679 Firstly, the fact that the preliminary determination "states" that imports increased in absolute and relative terms is not sufficient to demonstrate that the Ministry actually evaluated whether there had been a significant increase in imports in absolute terms or relative to domestic production or consumption. On the contrary, the evidence would tend to indicate that in order to obtain figures which favoured a positive determination of threat of injury, the Ministry blatantly made an improper calculation, considering exclusively the share in domestic consumption of *imports registered in the month of June 1995* in relation to their share *in the month of November 1995*.

6.680 This indicates that the Ministry's calculation was tendentiously manipulated, in that it did not consider the variations in the share of imports during the entire period of investigation, and only considered the extremes which were more convenient. For example, if the investigating authority had considered in an unbiased and objective manner the sum of the allegedly dumped imports during the period of investigation against the sum of domestic *consumption* in Guatemala during the same period, it would have obtained a share of 10 per cent, which is considerably less than the 23 per cent it in fact obtained. By failing to analyse the increase in imports during the entire investigation period (June-November 1995) relative to production or domestic consumption during the same period, the Guatemalan authority violated Article 3.2.

6.681 Even if we assume for the sake of argument that the Ministry was merely trying to reach the conclusion required under Article 3.7(i) concerning the likelihood of substantially increased importation of cement based on the increase in imports during the period investigated and Cruz Azul's disposable capacity, the Ministry's preliminary determination contains no analysis based on facts of the likely impact of further dumped imports on the domestic industry according to the examination of the relevant factors listed in Article 3.4 In other words, there is no analysis to substantiate the conclusion that the likelihood of a substantial increase in imports would cause an increase in the share of imports in the

Guatemalan market affecting, for example, Cementos Progreso's production, sales or profits so as to cause material injury. However, we shall revert to this matter further on.

(ii) Effects of the imports on domestic prices

6.682 In paragraph 277 of its first written submission, Guatemala argues that:

> "277. [...] the Ministry explicitly considered whether significant price undercutting was responsible for the fall in prices, under the terms of Article 3.2. It also referred to the DIACO report and other evidence of price depression. [...]"

6.683 Mexico categorically rejects Guatemala's assertion that it explicitly considered whether there was a significant price undercutting by the dumped imports as compared with the domestic prices of the investigated product. Clearly, the Ministry did not even bother to obtain a figure indicating the alleged price decrease of the investigated product manufactured by Cementos Progreso, let alone compare the domestic prices with the price of imports under alleged conditions of price discrimination.

6.684 In its preliminary determination, the Ministry simply states that:

> "As a result of dumped imports, there was a fall in the price of cement in those cities where the product under investigation is sold, despite an increase in the cost of fuel, which is the major cost element in cement production. This is demonstrated both by the outcome of the investigation conducted by the Department for Consumer Welfare (DIACO) and by information furnished by the complainant concerning prices obtained in this segment of the Guatemalan market and the relationship between these prices and those that might have been established in keeping with the Government formula for setting a maximum sale price."

6.685 As can be seen, the Ministry merely made a series of unsubstantiated statements which in no way prove that the authority actually demonstrated or documented the behaviour of import prices and domestic prices, let alone conduct an objective examination based on positive evidence of the effect of such imports on domestic prices. The following points confirm this:

(a) There is no analysis or calculation suggesting a decrease in the price of the domestic product; the Ministry simply considered that the mere mention of a price decrease was sufficient to show that an objective examination had been conducted of the behaviour of prices and the alleged effect of imports on domestic prices.

(b) Similarly, the Ministry limited itself to mentioning the decrease in the price of the like product without even explaining the basis on which this alleged decrease was determined. In particular, the Ministry makes no reference in any document to the periods used in the comparison to determine the price behaviour of either the imported product or the domestic product.

(c) Nor did the Ministry provide any explanation of the effect of the increase in the cost of energy - according to Guatemala, the most significant factor in the cost of cement production - on the behaviour of prices during the investigation period. In fact, the file of the investigation does not contain any information on such increases which presumably were also taken into account by the investigating authority in conducting an objective examination of the effect of imports on the price of the domestic product.

(d) Guatemala asserts that "As a result of dumped imports, there was a fall in the price of cement *in those cities in which the product under investigation is sold*". This assertion contains elements which reflect an incorrect price analysis by the Ministry. The alleged examination of the effects of imports on domestic prices by the Ministry of the Economy during the preliminary stage of the investigation was based on:

(i) The report prepared by the Department for Consumer Welfare (DIACO), which refers to the prices recorded exclusively in four "departments" of Guatemala, whereas if it had considered the price of cement at the national level, it would have analysed the prices in the 22 "departments" making up the territory of Guatemala, and not only in a part of the country;

(ii) "information furnished by the complainant concerning prices *obtained in this segment of the Guatemalan market*".

6.686 This shows that the Ministry conducted a regional price analysis, considering only the prices reported in certain "departments" of Guatemala and equating the alleged behaviour of prices in part of the Guatemalan market with the behaviour of prices at the national level. Moreover, it should be borne in mind that the investigation conducted by DIACO was different from every point of view from the kind of analysis of the effect of imports on domestic prices required under Article 3.2 of the AD Agreement, particularly where the DIACO report makes a price comparison using the price of the investigated product at the regional level and not the national level. Consequently, because the Ministry's determination was based on this DIACO report, it could not reflect the effect that dumped imports during the investigation period may have had on *national prices* of grey Portland cement.

6.687 In short, there is nothing to show that the Ministry's preliminary determination of threat of injury was based on an objective examination of the effect of the imports on the prices in the domestic market for like products as required by Article 3.1 and 3.2 of the AD Agreement. In fact, the evidence shows the Ministry of the Economy reached the conclusion that the dumped imports had depressed the prices of cement in a certain region of Guatemala without properly analysing the behaviour of imported and domestic grey Portland cement prices during the investigation period, i.e. without examining the price fluctuations of the cement or of the dumped imports showing that the prices of the imported product actually had "caused prices" of cement to fall during the investigation period.

6.688 Without this analysis, any conclusion which simply assumes that the dumped imports would cause prices to fall in the future is purely speculative. One cannot, merely on the basis of the likelihood that imports are at lower prices than the like domestic product, assume threat of injury to the domestic industry. On the contrary, injury or threat of injury may be unlikely if the price level of the like domestic product generated sufficient income and profits for the domestic industry. But no such analysis (i.e. of fluctuations, behaviour and level of prices) was made by the Ministry, which simply took as the relevant reference price the maximum price established by the Government itself.

6.689 Nor does the public notice or the alleged separate report provide sufficiently detailed explanations concerning the examination of the effect of imports on domestic prices under Article 3.2 as a basis for the Ministry's preliminary determination of threat of injury. Besides which, under no permissible interpretation of the Anti-Dumping Agreement may the DIACO report be considered to constitute a separate report within the meaning of

Article 12.2.1 as Guatemala claims. It is the Ministry of the Economy, as the Guatemalan anti-dumping authority, and not DIACO, as a consumer authority, that is responsible for ensuring compliance with the obligations arising from Article 12.2.1 of the AD Agreement. Nor can the letter or purpose of Article 12.2.1 be interpreted as permitting the authority to issue a "separate report" as an alternative to the public notice, or as allowing Members to present, as a "separate report" any document contained in the administrative file. This would be contrary to the actual text of Article 12 and to its purpose of ensuring transparency and publicity therein.[529]

6.690 For all of the above reasons, Mexico submits that the Ministry did not conduct an objective examination based on positive evidence of the volume of imports or increase in imports and their effect on the prices in the domestic market for the like product to support its preliminary determination of threat of injury as stipulated in Article 3.1 and 3.2 of the Anti-Dumping Agreement.

6.691 At the same time, even assuming, for the sake of argument, that the Ministry had acted in conformity with Article 3.2, and had properly concluded that the dumped imports were increasing and would have adverse effects on domestic prices, it cannot be concluded *ipso facto* that there was a threat of injury, i.e. that further imports would cause injury to the domestic industry. If the situation of the domestic industry is favourable or if it is affected by factors other than the dumped imports, the dumped imports may not represent a threat of injury. Consequently, in making a threat of injury determination, the investigating authority must also analyse the likely impact of further dumped imports on the domestic industry, evaluating all of the relevant economic factors and indices listed in Article 3.4. The Ministry of the Economy simply did not conduct this analysis. We shall revert below this added aspect of the inconsistency of Guatemala's preliminary determination with the Anti-Dumping Agreement.

(iii) Violation of Article 3.4 and 3.7

6.692 It is indeed surprising that in an attempt to argue, now, before the Panel, that its preliminary determination of threat of material injury was consistent with Article 3.4, Guatemala should dare to state, in paragraph 278 of its first written submission, that:

> "278 [...] the Ministry explicitly evaluated the impact of dumped imports on the domestic industry, in accordance with Article 3.4, Among other things, the Ministry explicitly considered the decline in sales, productivity, market share and utilization of capacity suffered by Cementos Progreso and whether imports from Cruz Azul had had an adverse impact on domestic prices and Cementos Progreso's inventories."

6.693 Contrary to what Guatemala contends, Mexico submits that the Ministry of the Economy did not properly and sufficiently evaluate the factors listed in Article 3.4 which should have been taken into account in examining the impact of dumped imports on the domestic industry.

6.694 We have established that threat of injury determinations cannot be based solely on an examination of the factors listed in Article 3.7 of the Anti-Dumping Agreement[530], as Guatemala has more or less done in this case, but also requires an evaluation of the impact

[529] Here, Mexico agrees with the opinion expressed by the United States in its third-party submission in these proceedings.

[530] Report of the Panel in *Mexico - Corn Syrup*, *supra*, footnote 34, paras. 7.111 et seq.

of imports on the domestic industry, which involves considering the relevant economic factors listed in Article 3.4.

6.695 The requirement for a threat of injury determination to include a specific analysis of the impact of dumped imports on the domestic industry flows from the text of Article 3.1 and 3.4 in conjunction with footnote 9 of the Anti-Dumping Agreement, as well as from Article 3.7 itself. Article 3.1 stipulates that a determination of "injury" shall involve an examination of the impact of imports, and Article 3.4 expressly indicates the factors which must be considered relevant in examining the impact of imports on the domestic industry. Both articles are applicable both to material injury determinations and threat of material injury determinations in view of the scope of footnote 9 of the AD Agreement. Article 3.7, for its part, requires that the investigating authority determine whether, unless protective action is taken, material injury would occur.

6.696 At the same time, to make a threat of material injury determination in accordance with Article 3.7, it is essential that the investigating authority evaluate whether there is a clearly foreseen and imminent change in circumstances which would create a situation in which the dumping would cause injury, and conclude that further dumped exports are imminent and that, unless protective action is taken, material injury would occur. The Ministry could not validly have reached either of these conclusions given that it failed to examine the relevant economic factors listed in Article 3.4.

6.697 Thus, for the authority to be in a position to conduct this evaluation, not only does it have to assess the information concerning the likelihood of an increase in exports owing to the freely disposable capacity of the exporter at prices that will have a significant depressing or suppressing effect on domestic prices, and owing to the level of inventories of the product investigated, but it would also have to have information on the state of the domestic industry during the period under investigation. Only then would the investigating authority be in a position to evaluate whether further imports would be likely to produce a change in the state of a domestic industry and whether that change would cause material injury to the domestic industry.

6.698 In other words, for the Ministry to have been in a position to decide on the effect of the likelihood of a substantial increase in dumped imports on the domestic industry, it would have had to analyse the relevant factors listed in Article 3.4.[531] Its determination

---

[531] Concerning the nature of this type of analysis, see the report of the Panel in *Korea - Definitive Safeguard Measure on Imports of Certain Dairy Products ("Korea - Dairy")*, WT/DS98/R, adopted 12 January 2000, DSR :2000:I, 49, paras. 7.55 and 7.58.

"7.55 In conducting our review of Korea's serious injury determination we are mindful of the obligations contained in Article 4.2 of the Agreement on Safeguards. This provision mandates that competent authorities when performing a serious injury investigation:

> ... shall evaluate all relevant factors of an objective and quantifiable nature having a bearing on the situation of that industry, in particular, the rate and amount of the increase in imports of the product concerned in absolute and relative terms, the share of the domestic market taken by increased imports, changes in the level of sales, production, productivity, capacity utilization, profits and losses, and employment.

This provision sets out the general principle regarding the economic factors which need to be considered in a serious injury investigation, *and provides a list of factors that are a priori considered to be especially relevant and informative of the situation of the domestic industry. The use of the wording 'in particular' makes it clear to us that, among 'all relevant factors' that the investigating authorities 'shall evaluate', the consideration of the factors listed is always relevant and therefore required, even though the authority may later dismiss some of them as not having a bearing on the situation of that industry.* Under the applicable standard of review, our function is to

was therefore based on an improper and insufficient analysis: because it did not even familiarize itself with the situation prevailing in the industry, it was impossible for the authority to project the effect of the increase in dumped imports on the market under analysis, and still less to determine the effect of those imports on domestic production indicators.

6.699 Thus, in the present case, having focused its analysis (also improper) almost exclusively on the factors contained in Article 3.7, the Ministry did not show that the further imports could cause injury within the meaning of the Anti-Dumping Agreement, since it never established the current condition of the industry which could have served as a basis for determining the likelihood of an increase in further dumped imports and hence, the effect they could have on the domestic industry for grey Portland cement.[532]

---

assess whether Korea (i) examined all relevant facts in its possession or which it should have obtained in accordance with Article 4.2 of the Agreement on Safeguards at the time of the investigation; and (ii) provided an adequate explanation of how those facts as a whole supported the determination made. Thus, we shall examine whether at the time of the determination all factors listed in Article 4.2 were appropriately considered; *whether the Korean authorities explained how each factor considered supports (or detracts from) a finding of serious injury; and whether valid reasons have been put forward for dismissing a considered factor as not being relevant to the serious injury determination in this case*." (Emphasis added)

"7.58 In our evaluation of Korea's serious injury determination there are three issues that we find particularly troublesome. First, we find that there *is a lack of consideration* in the OAI Report *of some of the factors listed in Article 4.2*. This is the case for instance for capacity utilization and productivity. In both cases Korea offers explanations in its submissions to the Panel of why it considered these factors not to bear on the situation of the domestic industry. *While these explanations seem plausible, there is nothing in the OAI Report which would indicate to the Panel that these factors were taken into consideration in the serious injury finding of the Korean authorities.* Second, as we noted above, the definition of the domestic industry in this case as comprising two different segments of the dairy products market has consequences for the evaluation of the situation of the industry. In assessing the serious injury to the whole domestic industry, we find that it is acceptable to analyse distinct market segments but, as stated above, *all factors listed in Article 4.2 must be addressed. In considering each of the factors listed in Article 4.2, and any others found to be relevant by the authority*, the investigating authority has two options: for each factor, the investigating authority can consider it either for all segments, or if it decides to examine it for only one or some segment(s), it must provide an explanation of how the segment(s) chosen is (are) objectively representative of the whole industry. A lack of consideration of all segments, without any explanation, is a flaw that we find present in Korea's analysis of the domestic industries' profits and losses, prices, debt to equity ratio, capital depletion and production cost. How Korea relates developments in one segment to its determination regarding the industry as a whole is for Korea to decide in the first instance. Our point here is that an analysis of only a segment of the domestic industry, without any explanation of its significance for the whole industry, will not satisfy the requirements of the Agreement on Safeguards. Third, we find that for certain factors considered by Korea *it has failed to provide sufficient reasoning on some of the choices made in the analysis of such factors which may have affected the result of the consideration. Also, there is a lack of reasoning in some cases on how the factor considered supports (or detracts from) a finding of serious injury*. This lack of explanation or reasoning is perceived in Korea's consideration of market share, production, profits and losses, employment and inventory." (Emphasis added)

[532] In this connection, the Panel in *Mexico - Corn Syrup* stated, in para. 7.126 of its report:

> "While an examination of the Article 3.7 factors is required in a threat of injury case, that analysis alone is not a sufficient basis for a determination of threat of injury, because the Article 3.7 factors do not relate to the consideration of the impact of the dumped imports on the domestic industry. The Article 3.7 factors relate specifically to the questions of the likelihood of increased imports (based on

6.700 Even if we were to accept that the Ministry actually did evaluate the real decline in sales, productivity, market share and utilization of installed capacity, it was not enough for the Ministry to examine only those factors in Article 3.4 which supported a threat of material injury finding: it was required to examine other relevant factors listed in Article 3.4 which were also necessary in order to assess the situation of the industry, and which it failed to analyse, such as:

> The *actual and potential* decline in profits, output, and return on investment;
>
> the *potential* decline in sales, market share, productivity, and utilisation of installed capacity;
>
> the *actual and potential negative effects* on cash flow, inventories, employment, wages, growth, ability to raise capital or investment.

6.701 In short, the preliminary determination of threat of material injury by the Ministry of the Economy did not involve a proper and sufficient examination of the factors listed in Article 3.4 concerning the impact of dumped imports on the Guatemala industry. Without that analysis, the Ministry's determination could not validly establish how the future imports of grey Portland cement could affect the state of the domestic industry in a way that would imply material injury thereto. Bearing in mind that for a threat of injury determination to be consistent with the provisions of Article 3.1 and 3.7, the factors mentioned in Article 3.4 must be evaluated in examining the consequent impact of the imports, we can only conclude that the preliminary determination of threat of injury made by the Ministry of the Economy is inconsistent with Article 3.1, 3.4 and 3.7 owing to the Ministry's failure to carry out an objective examination of the impact of dumped imports on the Guatemalan industry based on an analysis of the factors having a bearing on the state of the industry during the period of investigation or on its state in the near future according to projections.

6.702 At the same time, Guatemala naively argues in paragraph 279 of its first submission that:

> "Moreover, the Anti-Dumping Agreement does not oblige the investigating authorities to provide details in writing of all the factors considered or make an explicit report on each of the factors taken into account. The Ministry listed all the evidence considered in its preliminary determination, provided detailed explanations of the preliminary determination of dumping and injury and carefully spelled out 'the main reasons leading to the determination'.[533] No more is required."

6.703 Guatemala is mistaken in stating that the Anti-Dumping Agreement does not oblige the authorities to provide details in writing of the all the factors considered or make an explicit report on each of the factors taken into account. Contrary to what it contends, it is not enough to list the evidence and to explain the reasons taken into account in the

---

the rate of increase of imports, the capacity of exporters to increase exports, and the availability of other export markets), the effects of imports on future prices and likely future demand for imports, and inventories. They are not, in themselves, relevant to a decision concerning what the 'consequent impact' of continued dumped imports on the domestic industry is likely to be. However, it is precisely this latter question - whether the 'consequent impact' of continued dumped imports is likely to be material injury to the domestic industry - which must be answered in a threat of material injury analysis. Thus, we conclude that an analysis of the 'consequent impact' of imports is required in a threat of material injury determination".

[533] Anti-Dumping Agreement, Article 12.2.1.

determination, and it is essential that the investigating authority should make it clear in the determination that it has considered each one of the factors listed in Article 3.4 in making a preliminary affirmative determination of material injury.[534]

(d) Guatemala's Response to Rebuttal of Mexico

6.704 **Guatemala** responds by alleging that the preliminary determination of threat of material injury complied with Article 3. It argues as follows:

6.705 During the first meeting, Mexico attacked the Ministry's preliminary determination of injury. According to Mexico, the determination was flawed because it was based exclusively on the criteria listed in Article 3.7 of the AD Agreement. Mexico adduces that it should have included an examination of the factors contained in paragraphs 1, 2 and 4 of Article 3.[535] This argument is without merit for the following reasons.

6.706 Firstly, Guatemala emphasized the factors contained in Article 3.7 because those were the most relevant factors in evaluating threat of injury, as opposed to actual injury. But this does mean that the Ministry did not *consider* other factors. As we discussed at length in our first written submission, the Ministry did in fact examine whether there had been a significant increase in imports within the meaning of Article 3.2. As explained in the determination, imports increased dramatically both in absolute terms and relative to domestic production and apparent consumption during the period of investigation. It is ridiculous for Mexico to suggest otherwise.

6.707 The Ministry also explicitly examined whether there had been any price undercutting causing prices to be depressed within the meaning of Article 3.2. Reference was made to the DIACO report and other evidence of price depression. In its submission of 9 May 1996, Cruz Azul stated that imports of Cruz Azul cement had caused cement prices in Guatemala to fall by Q 6 to Q 8 per sack.

6.708 Contrary to what Mexico has said, the Ministry also explicitly evaluated the impact of dumped imports on the domestic industry within the meaning of Article 3.4. Among other things, the Ministry expressly considered the drop in sales, production, market share and utilization of installed capacity suffered by Cementos Progreso and the adverse impact of Cruz Azul imports on domestic prices and Cementos Progreso's inventories.

6.709 Moreover, as we stated in our first submission, the AD Agreement does not oblige the investigating authorities to provide details in writing of each factor considered or to make an explicit report on each of the factors taken into account.[536] In this case, the Ministry listed all of the evidence taken into account in its preliminary determination, provided detailed explanations for the preliminary determinations on dumping and injury,

---

[534] In this connection, it is also necessary to consider Article 12.2.1 of the Anti-Dumping Agreement. The mere recitation of data does not constitute explanation, or findings and conclusions, sufficient to satisfy the requirements of Article 12.2 of the AD Agreement. Although Guatemala also referred to certain documents in the administrative file, such as an alleged separate report, unless the Ministry's determination or public notice reflects the consideration of a particular factor, not just any document in the file can be taken into consideration. See the report of the Panel *Korea-Resins*, paras. 210 and 212, and the report of the Panel in *Argentina - Safeguard Measures on Imports of Footwear*, WT/DS121/R, adopted 12 January 2000, DSR 2000:II, 575, para. 8.126.

[535] Oral submission by Mexico, paras. 169-186.

[536] See first submission by Guatemala, para. 279.

and carefully listed the "main reasons leading to the determination".[537] Nothing more was required.

4. *Claims Under Article 3.5 - Preliminary Determination of Causal Relationship*

(a) Submissions of Mexico

6.710 **Mexico** claims that the Ministry of the Economy violated Article 3.5 of the AD Agreement by imposing a provisional anti-dumping measure without demonstrating the *causal relationship* between the imports allegedly dumped and the alleged threat of injury to the Guatemalan domestic industry. The following are Mexico's arguments in support of its claim under Article 3.5:

6.711 Article 3.5 of the AD Agreement provides the following:

> "It must be demonstrated that the dumped imports are, through the effects of dumping, as set forth in paragraphs 2 and 4, causing injury within the meaning of this Agreement. The demonstration of a *causal relationship* between the dumped imports and the injury to the domestic industry shall be based on an examination of all relevant evidence before the authorities. The authorities shall also examine any known factors other than the dumped imports which at the same are injuring the domestic industry, *and the injuries caused by these other factors must not be attributed to the dumped imports*. Factors which may be relevant in this respect include, *inter alia*, the volume and prices of imports not sold at dumping prices, *contraction in demand* or changes in the patterns of consumption, *trade restrictive practices of* and competition between the foreign and *domestic producers*, developments in technology and the export performance and productivity of the domestic industry." (emphasis added).

6.712 In its preliminary determination, the Ministry of the Economy indicated that during the investigation period the imports from Mexico under investigation threatened to cause injury to the domestic industry. The threat of injury to the domestic industry was determined on the basis of the following effects: (i) an increase in imports of grey Portland cement from Mexico; (ii) the likelihood of an increase in Mexican exports to Guatemala as a result of surplus plant capacity at the exporting firm; (iii) depressed price of the domestic product in certain Guatemalan cities; (iv) accumulation of inventories of the raw material used to manufacture the product investigated; (v) decline in domestic sales of cement; (vi) under-utilization of the domestic producer's plant capacity; and (vii) loss of customers.

6.713 Reading Article 3.5 of the AD Agreement and the preliminary determination of threat of injury made by the Ministry of the Economy shows that the investigating authority could *not* have proved the existence of a causal relationship between the dumped imports and the alleged threat of injury to the domestic industry producing grey Portland cement for the following reasons:

6.714 Firstly, the investigating authority did *not* evaluate whether the price of the allegedly dumped imports was significantly undercutting the price of the like domestic product nor did the Ministry of the Economy evaluate the trend in economic factors and indices having a bearing on the state of the domestic industry, as required by Article 3.2, 3.4 and

[537] AD Agreement, Article 12.2.1.

3.7 of the AD Agreement. The investigating authority was therefore not in a position to determine the change in circumstances which would create a situation in which the dumping would cause injury to the domestic industry. Consequently, in its preliminary determination the Ministry could *not* have concluded that during the investigation period the imports investigated threatened to cause material injury to the domestic industry.

6.715 Secondly, in the preliminary determination, the Ministry of the Economy did *not* establish the causal relationship between the alleged dumping and threat of injury, simply indicating that: "On the basis of the facts indicated in the section on threat of injury, there is a causal relationship between the imports dumped and the injury caused to the domestic industry ..."[538] This statement highlights the bias and lack of objectiveness with which the Ministry of the Economy made the preliminary determination of threat of material injury because it did *not* make any specific reference to the form or procedure followed by the investigating authority in order to show that the imports investigated were the cause of the alleged threat of injury.

6.716 The investigating authority could *not* have established a causal relationship between the imports of grey Portland cement and the alleged threat of injury to the domestic industry as required by Article 3.5 of the AD Agreement because it did *not* determine the existence of a threat of material injury. The Ministry of the Economy therefore violated Article 3.5 of the AD Agreement by imposing a provisional anti-dumping measure without proving the existence of a causal relationship between the alleged dumping and the alleged threat of material injury.

6.717 To summarize, as the Panel will be able to see, the Ministry of the Economy's preliminary affirmative determination of a threat of material injury is contrary to Article 3.1, 3.2, 3.4, 3.5, 3.6. 3.7 and 3.8 of the AD Agreement, for the following reasons *inter alia*:

(a) The Ministry of the Economy did *not* base its determination of threat of injury on positive evidence nor on an objective examination of the volume of imports dumped, their effect on prices of the like product on the Guatemalan market, and their subsequent impact on the domestic industry, evaluating the factors enumerated in paragraphs 2, 4, 5, and 7 of Article 3 of the AD Agreement;

(b) the Ministry did *not* comply with the obligation that the determination must be based on facts and not simply on allegation, conjecture or remote possibility, as required by Article 3.7 of the AD Agreement;

(c) the causal relationship between the imports dumped and the threat of injury to the domestic industry was *not* demonstrated, as required by Article 3.5 of the AD Agreement; and

(d) although it was a case of threat of injury, the Guatemalan authority *failed* to examine with *special care* its decision to apply provisional anti-dumping measures, as required by Article 3.8 of the AD Agreement.

6.718 Consequently, the Guatemalan authority could *not* have justifiably considered that the provisional measures were *necessary*, in accordance with Article 7.1(iii) of the AD Agreement, to prevent injury being caused to the Guatemalan domestic industry during the investigation

[538] Point 3, section G, of the preliminary determination.

(b) Response of Guatemala

6.719 In response to Mexico's arguments regarding the demonstration of a causal relationship between imports allegedly dumped and the alleged threat of injury, **Guatemala** makes the following arguments:

6.720 Mexico maintains that the Ministry violated Article 3.5 of the Anti-Dumping Agreement by imposing a provisional measure without demonstrating a causal relationship between the dumped imports and the threat of injury. Article 3.5 actually refers to causal relationships within the context of the determination of present material injury. The Article establishes the factors which investigating authorities must examine in assessing whether the dumped imports are currently causing injury to the domestic industry. As the preliminary determination showed that there was threat of injury, the Ministry referred to causal relationship under Article 3.7.

6.721 Article 3.7 makes express reference to the question of causality in the event of injury. It refers to the change in circumstances which would create a situation in which "the dumping *would cause* injury...".[539] A provisional measure may be applied if the totality of the factors considered leads to the conclusion that further dumped exports are imminent and that, unless protective action is taken, material injury would occur. In any event, in its final determination the Ministry considered the causal relationship in accordance with Article 3.5, having established the existence of present material injury. More specifically, in its final determination the Ministry found that the dumped imports were causing material injury.

6.722 In any case, the Ministry clearly referred to the question of causality in Section VI.F of the preliminary determination, entitled "Threat of injury to the domestic industry and the causal relationship between dumping and the threat of injury". The Ministry found that Cruz Azul imports had led to the domestic producer's losing a significant share of the market, to a decline in its sales, to the loss of customers, to the accumulation of excessive inventories and the shutdown of its kilns, and to a fall in prices. On the basis of these findings the Ministry concluded that the application of a provisional measure was necessary to prevent greater injury being caused to the domestic industry. Thus, there can be no doubt that the Ministry demonstrated a causal relationship between the dumped imports and the threat of injury.

6.723 Contrary to Mexico's allegations, the Ministry determined significant price undercutting in accordance with Article 3.2. This was confirmed by DIACO's investigation and other evidence in the file.

(c) Rebuttal of Mexico

6.724 **Mexico** rebuts Guatemala's Article 3.5 arguments on the following grounds:

6.725 To help refute Guatemala's arguments with respect to the inconsistency of its preliminary determination with Article 3.5, we cite below the relevant parts of paragraphs 280-282 in part E of section V of its first written submission:

> "E. THE PRELIMINARY DETERMINATION OF CAUSAL RELATIONSHIP COMPLIED WITH ARTICLE 3.5[540]
>
> "[...] Article 3.5 actually refers to causal relationships within the context of the determination of present material injury. The Article establishes the factors which investigating authorities must examine in assessing whether

[539] *Ibid.*, Article 3.7 (emphasis added).

[540] Heading of part E of section V of Guatemala's first written submission.

> the dumped imports are currently causing injury to the domestic industry. As the preliminary determination showed that there was threat of injury, the Ministry referred to causal relationship under Article 3.7."[541]
>
> "[...] In any event, in its final determination the Ministry considered the causal relationship in accordance with Article 3.5, having established the existence of present material injury. [...]"[542]
>
> "In any case, the Ministry clearly referred to the question of causality in Section VI.F of the preliminary determination, entitled 'Threat of injury to the domestic industry and the causal relationship between dumping and the threat of injury'. (...)"[543]

6.726 Firstly, from the outset Guatemala's position clearly contains a contradiction which brings to light the inconsistency of its preliminary determination of threat of injury with Article 3.5. On the one hand, in its heading, it states that "the preliminary determination of causal relationship complied with Article 3.5", while on the other hand, it denies the applicability of Article 3.5 when the determination is of threat of material injury, suggesting erroneously that in threat of injury cases, the applicable provision for the purposes of establishing a causal relationship is Article 3.7.

6.727 Secondly, Mexico rejects the impermissible interpretation that Guatemala tries to make of Article 3.5 and 3.7 when it states that "Article 3.5 actually refers to causal relationships within the context of the determination of present material injury" and that "as the preliminary determination showed that there was threat of injury the Ministry referred to causal relationship under Article 3.7." Guatemala's interpretation is impermissible in the light of both the text of Article 3.5 and its context, which is Article 3, including footnote 9 and Article 3.7.

6.728 Article 3.5 expressly states that:

> "It must be demonstrated that the dumped imports are, through the effects of dumping, as set forth in paragraphs 2 and 4, causing *injury within the meaning of this Agreement*. The demonstration of a causal relationship between the dumped imports and the injury to the domestic industry shall be based on an examination of all relevant evidence before the authorities. [...]." (Emphasis added)

6.729 Footnote 9, in its turn, states that:

> "*Under this Agreement the term 'injury'* shall, unless otherwise specified, be taken to mean material injury to a domestic industry, *threat of material injury* to a domestic industry or material retardation of the establishment of such an industry and shall be interpreted in accordance with the provisions of this Article." (Emphasis added)

6.730 Article 3.7, for its part, lays down the specific factors to be considered in a threat of injury analysis. But even if we were to suppose, for the sake of argument, that under Article 3.7 the Ministry had reached a proper conclusion that there was "a clearly foreseen and imminent" "change in circumstances which would create a situation in which the dumping would cause injury", that "further dumped exports are imminent and that, unless protective action is taken, material injury would occur", this is no reason for assuming that the Ministry conducted an analysis and properly concluded that there was a causal

---

[541] First written submission by Guatemala, para. 280.

[542] *Ibid.*, para. 281.

[543] *Ibid.*, para. 282.

relationship under Article 3.5 enabling it to support its preliminary determination of threat of injury. While it is true that these are the specific factors that the Ministry had to demonstrate under Article 3.7 (and did not demonstrate) in order to make a threat of injury determination, it cannot be accepted that by virtue of an analysis under Article 3.7, a preliminary determination also complies with Article 3.5. Given the scope of footnote 9 of the Anti-Dumping Agreement, Article 3.5 requires an analysis and a separate conclusion, distinct from the analysis and conclusions concerning the factors listed in Article 3.7, in order to establish the causal relationship on which a determination of the threat of material injury rests. This shows how flawed and mistaken Guatemala's arguments with respect to causal relationship are.

6.731 Nor is it possible to accept from any point of view Guatemala's attempt to argue now that because it conducted its (improper) analysis of the factors listed in Article 3.7, the Ministry established a causal relationship between the dumped imports and the threat of injury, when as we have shown, the Guatemalan authority did not make a proper and sufficient analysis covering the evaluation of the factors listed in Article 3.2 and 3.4. Suffice it to look at the actual text of Article 3.5. In particular, the investigating authority must examine in an unbiased and objective manner the impact of dumped imports on the domestic industry, evaluating the factors listed in Article 3.4, in order to be in a position, as we have said, to reach a conclusion concerning the Article 3.7 factors and to determine, as well, the existence of a causal relationship under Article 3.5. Consequently, in this case, even though Guatemala argues that the Ministry, in making its determination of threat of material injury, established the causal relationship in accordance with Article 3.7, there is no way of showing that the Ministry actually did establish a causal relationship if in the analysis in connection with the preliminary determination of threat of injury the Ministry failed to examine the relevant factors having a bearing on the state of the domestic industry.

6.732 Finally, it should also be stressed that in order properly to establish all of the facts that an authority must consider to determine the cause and effect relationship between the dumped imports and the injury or, as in this case, threat of injury, Article 3.5 clearly stipulates that the investigating authorities:

> "[...] shall also examine any known factors other than the dumped imports which at the same time are injuring the domestic industry, and the injuries caused by these other factors must not be attributed to the dumped imports. [...]"

6.733 Nevertheless, in the case at issue, as stated in paragraph 294 of Mexico's first submission, in its analysis in connection with its preliminary determination of threat of injury, the Ministry never addressed *factors other* than the dumped imports, such as the volume and prices of the imports that were not dumped, the effect on the state of the domestic industry of the increase in energy costs, and the existence of a maximum price fixed by the Government of Guatemala for grey Portland cement as well as restrictive trade practices on the part of the domestic producer.

6.734 With respect to this last point, it should be stressed that the Ministry disregarded one of the substantial parts of the DIACO report of 17 May 1996 which states that the domestic producer Cementos Progreso engaged in a series of *restrictive practices* in order to avoid fair competition from the product imported under the brand name Cruz Azul:

> "As an example, we were informed (sic) that the company Cementos Progreso S.A. set up (sic) in the departmental capitals companies known as CEPESA which sell cement and other building materials, and that this was considered unfair competition for local retailers; that they were constantly subject to pressure and threats by Cementos Progreso to prevent them from buying or selling Cruz Azul cement, failing which they would not be supplied with the lime and other products they

ordered, a situation which was creating a feeling of insecurity among traders. [...] Some of the persons surveyed were suspicious when asked for information, hinting that among other things they had been visited by representatives of Cementos Progreso who, after asking them a number of questions, informed them that they should not buy Cruz Azul cement because if the import of that product were to be prohibited, they would not sell them Cementos Progreso cement afterwards. [...] Considering the result of the visits, the statements made by certain persons involved in the marketing of cement, the opinion of consumers and the views we were able to gather, it would seem that the arrival of Cruz Azul cement had revolutionized the obsolete market which for a long time had been a monopoly that in no way benefited the Guatemalan population, which now had a better quality, higher-yielding product."

6.735 The Ministry completely ignored these conclusions of the DIACO report, and made its determination of threat of material injury without even bothering to examine the possible effect of these restrictive practices by the domestic producer which DIACO brought to its attention. This shows that the investigating authority did not make an unbiased and subjective evaluation of all of the facts (factors other than dumped imports) that had to be established in order to make a preliminary determination of the causal relationship between the likelihood of an increase in dumped imports and the injury they could cause to the domestic industry.

6.736 On the contrary, it reveals more clearly than ever the bias and lack of objectivity with which the Ministry made its preliminary determination of threat of injury to the domestic industry, disregarding the fact that Article 3.5 requires the authority to examine *any known factors* other than dumped imports. Thus, once again, Guatemala's argument that its Ministry of Economy made a preliminary determination of causal relationship in conformity with Article 3.5 of the Anti-Dumping Agreement is unacceptable.

6.737 In short, although Article 3.5 sets forth the requirements for the analysis of causal relationship both for cases of material injury and for cases of threat of material injury, the Ministry simply disregarded Article 3.5 and failed to conduct any analysis of factors other than dumped imports which could have accounted for the threat of injury.

6.738 For all of these reasons, Mexico submits that the Panel should find that the preliminary determination of threat of material injury by the Ministry of the Economy was inconsistent with Guatemala's obligations under Article 3.1, 3.2, 3.4, 3.5 and 3.7 of the Anti-Dumping Agreement. Moreover, Mexico repeats that by failing to take account of the likely impact of dumped imports on the domestic industry affected in determining the existence of a threat of material injury, Guatemala also violated paragraph 6(a) of Article VI of the GATT 1994.

5. *Claims Under Article 12.2.1 - Public Notice of Imposition of Provisional Measure*

(a) Submissions of Mexico

6.739 **Mexico** makes the following arguments in support of its claim that Guatemala breached its obligations regarding the public notice of the imposition of the provisional measure under Article 12.1.1:

6.740 The public notice of imposition of the provisional anti-dumping measure on allegedly dumped imports of grey Portland cement from the Mexican firm Cruz Azul, published in the *Diario Oficial de Centro América* on 28 August 1996 ("provisional notice")[544], did *not* comply with Article 12.2.1 of the AD Agreement because it failed to include sufficiently detailed explanations of the preliminary determination on dumping. In particular, it did not provide a full explanation of the determination of likeness of the product sold in Mexico and that exported to Guatemala, thus affecting the comparison of the normal value and the export price required under Article 2. The sufficiently detailed explanations on the alleged threat of material injury required by Article 3 were not provided either. Sufficiently detailed explanations of the causal relationship between the imports allegedly dumped and the alleged threat of injury were not provided, although required by Article 3.5 of the AD Agreement.

6.741 Article 12.2 provides that public notice shall be given of any preliminary or final determination, whether affirmative or negative, and that each such notice shall set forth, or otherwise make available through a separate report, in sufficient detail the findings and conclusions reached on all issues of fact and law considered material by the investigating authorities.

6.742 Article 12.2.1 provides the following with regard to the requirements to be met in public notices of preliminary determinations:

> "12.2.1. A public notice of the imposition of provisional measures shall set forth, or otherwise make available through a separate report, sufficiently detailed explanations for the preliminary determinations on dumping and injury and shall refer to the matters of fact and law which have led to arguments being accepted or rejected. Such a notice or report shall, due regard being paid to the requirement for the protection of confidential information, contain in particular:
>
> (i) The names of the suppliers, or when this is impracticable, the supplying countries involved;
>
> (ii) a description of the product which is sufficient for customs purposes;
>
> (iii) the margins of dumping established and a full explanation of the reasons for the methodology used in the establishment and comparison of the export price and the normal value under Article 2;
>
> (iv) considerations relevant to the injury determination as set out in Article 3;
>
> (v) the main reasons leading to the determination."

6.743 The provisional notice published by the Ministry did *not* contain explanations, still less sufficiently detailed explanations, on a number of aspects that must be clarified and examined during the course of an investigation and must appear in the provisional notice of the preliminary affirmative determination leading to the imposition of a provisional anti-dumping duty.

6.744 Firstly, the provisional notice did *not* contain sufficiently detailed explanations on the authority's examination of whether the products sold in Mexico by Cruz Azul were like products to those exported by Cruz Azul to Guatemala during the investigation period, which means that the price comparison between the normal value and the export price was *not* valid.

6.745 Without examining whether they were like products, the Ministry simply indicated that the Type II Pz cement sold in Mexico and the Type I PM cement were like products within the meaning of Article 2.6 of the AD Agreement. This was set out in the

[544] "Public notice of imposition of the provisional measure" (hereinafter "provisional notice").

provisional notice in section "VI. LEGAL CONSIDERATIONS", part "B. Price comparison" as follows:

> "2.1.1. When submitting the information requested, the exporter only provided data on its selling prices on the domestic market for type II cement and type II Pz cement and not for type I (PM) cement which is under investigation. Annex I to the questionnaire, which it requested should be considered a summary of information on its sales in the domestic market, however, refers to type I (PM) cement, so it can be assumed that the product investigated and that sold in Mexico (type II Pz) are like products within the meaning of Article 2.6 of the WTO Agreement."

6.746 The Ministry did *not* examine the physical characteristics and chemical composition of Cruz Azul products sold in Mexico and exported to Guatemala, limiting itself to indicating that:

> "2.1.2. The exporter indicated the same international technical standard for producing type I (PM) cement and type II Pz cement (ASTM-C-595 standard). This standard contains the specifications for producing mixed hydraulic cements, including type I (PM) cement but not type II Pz cement."

6.747 The above shows that the Ministry based itself on inferences or the straightforward exclusion of one of the products and considered that both products - that sold in Mexico and that exported to Guatemala by Cruz Azul - were like products.

6.748 The Ministry recognized that Type II Pz cement (mixed cement) has a higher clinker content than Type II cement, and that its production accounts for the major part of the cost of producing cement, thus making even more confusing the explanation on the assumption that Type I (PM) cement and Type II (Pz) cement are like products. The following excerpt attests to this:

> "2.1.4. In addition, based on the information supplied by the exporter, the Directorate of Economic Integration considered that there was no price variation between type II (unmixed cement) and type II Pz (mixed cement) products, even though type II cement has a higher clinker content, whose production is the major cost element in cement production."

6.749 The above excerpts from the provisional notice *cannot* in any way be considered sufficiently detailed explanations within the meaning of Article 12.2.1 to show that the Cruz Azul products sold in Mexico (Type II Pz) and those exported to Guatemala (Type I PM) are like products.

6.750 Secondly, when referring to the determination of threat of injury, the provisional notice does *not* contain sufficiently detailed explanations of the examination and comparison made by the Ministry, if applicable. The notice does *not* state what previous comparable periods were used as a basis for the calculations nor the conclusions reached.

6.751 The lack of sufficiently detailed explanations on previous comparable periods can also be seen in the provisional notice where it refers *inter alia* to the indices and factors on increase in imports, accumulation of inventories, decline in sales, depressed prices of the domestic product and loss of customers.

6.752 The provisional notice also fails to refer to Article 3.1, 3.2 and 3.4 of the AD Agreement, although, in the same way as Article 3.7, they are among the legal grounds and requirements that must be met when examining and determining threat of material injury. In other words, there is *no* reference to the questions of fact and law on which acceptance or rejection of the arguments mentioned in Article 12.2.1 of the AD Agreement were based.

6.753 The explanations in the provisional notice do *not* refer to various factors and indices defined in Article 3.4 concerning the state of the domestic industry. Not only are these *not* to be found in the provisional notice but they were not examined by the Ministry either. These factors include profits, productivity, actual and potential effects on cash flow, employment, wages, growth, the ability to raise capital or investments, and the magnitude of the dumping margin.

6.754 The above shows that the provisional notice does *not* contain sufficiently detailed explanations on the evaluation of all the relevant economic factors and indices that had a bearing on the state of the domestic industry, as provided in Article 3.4, and does not refer either to the acceptance or rejection of all the factors considered relevant by the Ministry and which affected the state of the domestic industry.

6.755 In the case of inventories, the notice does *not* contain sufficiently detailed explanations on the trend in inventories in previous comparable periods and, if applicable, the accumulation of grey Portland cement in the applicant's warehouses. Indicating the volume of clinker stocks does not constitute a sufficiently detailed explanation on the inventories of the product investigated, as required by Article 12.2.1. of the AD Agreement.

6.756 The provisional notice does not contain explanations either, still less sufficiently detailed explanations, on the causal relationship between the dumped imports and the alleged threat of injury. Section "VI. LEGAL CONSIDERATIONS", part "F - Threat of injury to the domestic industry and the causal relationship between the dumping and the threat of injury" is inadequate because nowhere does it refer to a causal relationship, as required by Article 3.5 of the AD Agreement.

6.757 In addition, where the provisional notice does refer to a causal relationship, it does so confusedly. In other words, the preliminary determination concerns threat of material injury and, in the final section, the notice only refers to a causal relationship equivocally as "injury caused to the domestic industry". As proof of this, the following is an excerpt from part "G. Provisional measures":

> "3. On the basis of the facts set out in the section on the threat of injury, which show a causal link between the dumped imports and the injury caused to domestic industry, as well as the opinion issued to this effect by the Directorate of Economic Integration, the Ministry considers it appropriate to impose provisional measures in order to prevent more serious damage to domestic industry while the investigation is concluded."

6.758 The above clearly shows that the provisional notice does *not* contain explanations, still less sufficiently detailed explanations, on the causal relationship that must exist between the allegedly dumped imports and, in this case, the threat of material injury, in order to reach a preliminary affirmative determination leading to the imposition of provisional anti-dumping duties. The notice is therefore inconsistent with Article 12.2.1.

6.759 In the light of the foregoing arguments, it can justifiably be considered that the public notice imposing a provisional measure on allegedly dumped imports of grey Portland cement from the Mexican firm Cruz Azul does *not* contain sufficiently detailed explanations on the determinations of dumping and threat of material injury or on the causal relationship between the two. It does not refer either to the issues of fact and law on which the acceptance or rejection of the arguments was based, thus the notice is inconsistent with Article 12.2.1 of the AD Agreement.

(b) Response of Guatemala

6.760 **Guatemala** states that Mexico is wrong in arguing that the public notice of the preliminary determination did not comply with the requirements of Article 12.2.1. Its arguments in support of this response are as follows:

6.761 Article 12.2.1 requires the notice to contain the names of the suppliers, a description of the product which is sufficient for customs purposes, the margins of dumping established and a full explanation of the reasons for the methodology used in the establishment and comparison of the export price and the normal value under Article 2, considerations relevant to the injury determination as set out in Article 3, and the main reasons leading to the determination. No reasonable person reading the public notice could consider it deficient in any of these respects.

6.762 As Article 12.2.1 allows, the file also includes a separate report dated 26 July 1996 containing further evidence which the Ministry also considered. This report was also used by Cruz Azul. The file likewise includes the DIACO report and all the other evidence carefully identified in the public notice. Cruz Azul had timely access to all this evidence.

6.763 The points made by Mexico in paragraphs 301 to 317 were previously mentioned in Section E. Likewise, Guatemala noted that the object and purpose of Article 12.2.1 did not oblige investigating authorities to list every aspect of their deliberations in the conclusions. It would be unduly burdensome and unreasonable to require an investigating authority to give a detailed explanation of all the factors considered and quickly verify each of those factors.[545] In fact, the Article only requires the investigating authorities to provide "the main reasons leading to the determination". Guatemala certainly complied with this requirement in the public notice of preliminary determination.

(c) Rebuttal of Mexico

6.764 **Mexico** rebuts Guatemala's arguments on the following grounds:

6.765 Guatemala argues that its public notice of imposition of the provisional measure complied with the requirements set forth in subparagraphs (i) to (v) of Article 12.2.1 in that it included, *inter alia*, the names of the suppliers, a description of the product which is sufficient for customs purposes, the margin of dumping, the methodology used, and the main reasons leading to the determination. It adds that the file includes a separate report dated 26 July 1996 containing further evidence which the Ministry also considered in its preliminary determination, and that the file likewise includes the DIACO report and all the other evidence carefully identified in the public notice.[546]

6.766 Once again, Guatemala has used *post hoc* arguments to try to cure the flaws that have occurred, in this case in respect of the public notice and the fulfilment of its obligations under Article 12.2.1. Guatemala erroneously suggests that any document contained in the file can constitute the separate report, a claim which cannot be accepted as valid since it runs counter to the transparency requirements for the determinations of the investigating authority.

6.767 The separate report argument is a *post hoc* argument, as shown by the simple fact that the public notice does not refer to the existence of any separate report or suggest that the notice was replaced or supplemented by a separate report, and if so that that report was intended to fulfil the transparency requirements for the preliminary determination and the obligations laid down in Article 12.2.1.

---

[545] See Negev Phosphates, Ltd. v. United States Department of Commerce, 699 F. Sup. 938, 947 (Ct. Int'l Trade 1988) ("The fact that the Commission did not explicitly declare that the volume of imports was significant is not fatal, for the Court may uphold a decision of less than ideal clarity if the agency's path may reasonably be discerned").

[546] *Ibid.*, paras. 285 and 286.

6.768 Mexico submits that Guatemala not only failed to refer in its first submission to the provisions of the first paragraph of Article 12.2.1, but that in fact it did not comply with the obligation laid down in that paragraph, as we shall now show.

6.769 With the exception of certain changes in the wording and in the tables in certain sections relating, *inter alia*, to adjustments to the normal value, determination of the export price, behaviour of cement imports, share of imports in domestic production and apparent consumption, Opinion 002/96 of 26 July 1996, which Guatemala now claims to be the separate report, could reasonably be described as identical to the public notice; it provides no explanations, let alone sufficiently detailed explanations, concerning the aspects discussed below.[547]

6.770 Mexico submits that Guatemala did not include either in its public notice or in its alleged separate report explanations, let alone sufficiently detailed explanations, concerning a variety of elements on which its preliminary determination was based. Thus, for example, neither the notice nor the report contains sufficiently detailed explanations of the product likeness analysis which the Ministry may or may not have made between the product sold in the domestic market and the exported product, and which affected the price comparison between the normal value and the export price pursuant to Article 2.

6.771 Nor did either the public notice or the separate report include any explanations concerning the Ministry's threat of injury determination containing the elements referred in Article 3.1, 3.2 and 3.4 of the AD Agreement, in particular the factors mentioned in Article 3.2 and 3.4. The fact is, no reference is made at all to the factors considered by the Ministry as relevant and which affected the state of the domestic industry.[548]

6.772 Nor do either the public notice or the alleged separate report contain sufficiently detailed explanations concerning the causal relationship between the dumped imports and the alleged threat of injury referred to in Article 3.5.

6.773 At the same time, Guatemala's claim in paragraph 286 of its first written submission that a report such as that prepared by DIACO, which does not form part of the anti-dumping investigating authority and has separate functions and purposes[549], can be considered as fulfilling the Article 12.2.1 obligation simply because it is included in the file of the investigation, cannot be accepted under any circumstances.

6.774 Nor can it be accepted that Guatemala fulfilled its Article 12.2.1 obligations by stating that the file likewise includes "all the other evidence carefully identified in the public notice"[550], simply because all this evidence was accessible to Cruz Azul.

6.775 For the above reasons, Mexico submits that neither in the public notice of imposition of the provisional anti-dumping measure, nor in Opinion 002/96 of 26 July 1996 (alleged separate report), did Guatemala provide sufficiently detailed explanations concerning matters of fact and law relating to its preliminary determination, and that Guatemala therefore violated its obligations under Article 12.2.1 of the AD Agreement.

---

[547] Mexico also maintains that Resolution 001215 of 16 August 1996 and the public notice of imposition of the provisional measure are identical, so that neither the alleged separate report, nor the mentioned resolution, nor the public notice enable Guatemala to comply with its obligations under Article 12.2.1 of the AD Agreement, particularly in the areas mentioned by Mexico.

[548] See report of the Panel in *Korea - Dairy*, *supra*, footnote 531, para. 7.55 and 7.58.

[549] Department for Consumer Welfare.

[550] See the first written submission by Guatemala, para. 286.

E. *Conduct of the Anti-Dumping Investigation by Guatemala*

6.776 **Mexico** also claims that Guatemala committed several procedural violations under the AD Agreement which had a direct impact on the outcome of the investigation and consequently on the imposition of the definitive anti-dumping measure. Mexico's specific claims regarding procedural violations and Guatemala's responses are set out below.

1. *Claims Under Articles 6.1 and 6.2 - Establishment of Period for Acceptance and Receipt of Evidence During Final Phase of Investigation*

(a) Submissions of Mexico

6.777 **Mexico** makes the following arguments in support of its claim that Guatemala violated Articles 6.1 and 6.2 of the AD Agreement:

6.778 The Ministry violated Article 6.1 and 6.2 of the AD Agreement by *not* fixing a period for the acceptance and receipt of evidence during the final phase of the investigation and accepting new evidence from Cementos Progreso during the public hearing of the parties.

6.779 Article 6.1 and 6.2 provide the following concerning the opportunities to be given to the parties during the investigation procedure:

> "6.1 All interested parties in an anti-dumping investigation shall be given notice of the information which the authorities require and ample opportunity to present in writing all evidence which they consider relevant in respect of the investigation in question.
>
> ...
>
> 6.2 Throughout the anti-dumping investigation all interested parties shall have a full opportunity for the defence of their interests..."

6.780 On the one hand, the Ministry fixed the time limit for Cruz Azul to reply to the questionnaire for exporters and to respond to the request made on 14 October 1996. On the other, however, during the final stage of the investigation the Ministry did *not* set a period for the parties interested in the investigation to submit information, documents and evidence in defence of their interests.

6.781 The public notice of imposition of the provisional anti-dumping measure did *not* set a time limit for the presentation of arguments and evidence by the parties in defence of their interests, which was not the case at the initiation of the investigation when the public notice of initiation fixed a period of 30 days for the interested parties to appear to defend their rights.

6.782 Section 5 of the notice of initiation entitled "Invitation to appear" states the following:

> "... *importers, exporters, representatives of the Government of Mexico and any person* claiming to have a legitimate interest in the outcome of this investigation, to appear before the Ministry of the Economy (8a Avenida, 10-43 zona 1, Guatemala City) to state their legal interest in the matter and to document same within *30 days* as from the publication of this notice. *The same period is given to the interested parties to submit any supplementary arguments and evidence that they may consider relevant.*" (emphasis added).

6.783 In the notice imposing the provisional measure, the Ministry did *not* give Cruz Azul an opportunity to present further evidence and subsequently, in October 1996, it requested information from Cruz Azul, only allowing it to put forward its final pleadings at the public hearing, without being able to submit further evidence.

6.784 The denial of Cruz Azul's right of defence can be seen in the Ministry's rejection of the technical accounting evidence submitted by Cruz Azul on 18 December 1996 and the acceptance of new evidence from Cementos Progreso during the public hearing between the Ministry and the parties. According to the following rules of the hearing, this was also prohibited:

> "Attach the above submission to the background information. In view of the request from Cooperativa La Cruz Azul, S.C.L., the parties are informed that the hearing set for 19 December 1996 will be subject to the following rules:
>
> ...
>
> 2. The hearing is not intended to be a debate among the parties and *additional evidence will not be taken into account or accepted*; therefore, it will be restricted to giving each of the parties an opportunity to present its conclusions on the facts investigated and the investigating authority may not seek additional information." (emphasis added).

6.785 This shows that the Ministry did *not* give Cruz Azul a further opportunity, although it accepted arguments and new evidence from Cementos Progreso, thus violating Article 6.1 and 6.2 of the AD Agreement.

(b) Response of Guatemala

6.786 **Guatemala's** response to Mexico's Article 6.1 and 6.2 arguments are set out below:

6.787 During the course of the investigation, the Ministry established specific periods for the presentation of information, with a view to receiving information from all the interested parties in time for it to be taken into consideration. For example, the Ministry fixed 17 May 1996 as the last date for replying to the original questionnaire, 30 October 1996 for responding to the supplementary questionnaire and 19 December 1996 for the final arguments. In some cases, the periods were extended to give the parties more time to prepare their replies and defend their interests.[551] Thus, in accordance with the provisions of Article 6.1 and 6.2, Cruz Azul was given notice of the information which the authorities required and a full opportunity to present relevant evidence in defence of its interests in each of the critical phases of the investigation.

6.788 Contrary to Mexico's allegation, the Ministry did set time limits for the interested parties to submit information, documents and evidence in defence of their interests. On 14 October 1996, the Ministry sent Cruz Azul and Cementos Progreso supplementary questionnaires and set a time-limit of 30 October 1996 for submitting the new information. Cruz Azul did not request an extension of that time-limit. In fact, on 30 October 1996, Cruz Azul submitted an incomplete reply to the supplementary questionnaire and presented new information, evidence and arguments. Mexico asked the Ministry to "consider presented and accepted all of the arguments, evidence, reports and data contained in this document and its annexes...". The Ministry agreed to this request. In short, Cruz Azul was aware of the time-limit for presenting information and took advantage of the opportunity to do so.

[551] Cruz Azul was allowed a two month extension to reply to the original questionnaire.

6.789 Contrary to what is alleged by Mexico, the Ministry did not deny Cruz Azul its right of defence by rejecting the technical accounting evidence submitted by Cruz Azul on 18 December 1996 and accepting new evidence from Cementos Progreso during the public hearing. As explained below under Section G, the Ministry had the right to reject the technical accounting evidence submitted by Cruz Azul. Cruz Azul prevented the Ministry from making a verification visit and tried to substitute its own verification. No investigating authority would permit the respondent to prevent verification. Moreover, it is not true that the Ministry received new evidence from Cementos Progreso during the public hearing. The Ministry received final arguments from both Cementos Progreso[552] and Cruz Azul. This approach was consistent with the rules laid down for the public hearing.
6.790 It is significant that Mexico does not identify the evidence which Cruz Azul was not allowed to present as not being the technical accounting evidence which the Ministry had the right to reject. Similarly, Mexico does not identify any evidence presented by Cementos Progreso that the Ministry should have rejected. In short, Mexico's claim that Cruz Azul was denied its right of defence is totally unfounded.

(c) Rebuttal of Mexico

6.791 **Mexico** rebuts Guatemala's claim by arguing that Guatemala violated Article 6.1 and 6.2 of the AD Agreement by admitting and receiving evidence during the final stage of the investigation. It asserts as follows:
6.792 Guatemala argues that it established specific periods for the presentation of information with a view to receiving information from all of the interested parties in time for it to be taken into consideration. It adds that in the supplementary questionnaire to Cementos Progreso and Cruz Azul, it set a time-limit for replying.
6.793 Mexico contends that Guatemala did not set a time-period for admitting and receiving evidence during the final stage of the investigation, i.e., it did not enable the parties to present information and evidence once it had published the preliminary determination as it had done with the public notice of initiation, in which it provided the interested parties with a period of 30 days.
6.794 In Mexico's view, the supplementary request sent by the Ministry to Cruz Azul was certainly not a substitute for the opportunity that should have been granted to the exporter to defend its interests, i.e., for the parties to be able to submit information and evidence in defense of their interests without such information and evidence at any point being requested by the investigating authority.
6.795 For evidence of the lack of opportunity for the parties to submit information and evidence that was not requested by the authority, we need only refer to the fact that the Ministry rejected the technical accounting evidence even though it was submitted in a proper and timely manner by Cruz Azul in defence of its interests. The decision by the Ministry to reject the technical accounting evidence was not consistent with the acceptance by the Ministry during the public hearing of further evidence from Cementos Progreso[553], thereby treating Cruz Azul unequally and unfairly.

[552] Cementos Progreso's submission for the public hearing of 19 December 1996 summarises and comments on evidence that already existed in the file.
[553] During the public hearing held on 19 December 1996 the Ministry received from Cementos Progreso further evidence which, *inter alia*, was referenced in its final pleadings in paras. 36, 46 and 54, as Annexes 1, 2 and 3 respectively.

2. *Claims Under Articles 6.1, 6.2, and 6.4 - Access to Administrative File*

(a) Submissions of Mexico

6.796 **Mexico** argues that the Guatemalan Ministry of the Economy violated several provisions of Article 6 of the AD Agreement. Its arguments are set out below:

(i) The Ministry did not promptly make evidence submitted by Cementos Progreso available to Cruz Azul

6.797 Article 6.1.2 of the AD Agreement provides the following:

> "6.1.2. Subject to the requirement to protect confidential information, evidence presented in writing by one interested party shall be made available promptly to other parties participating in the investigation."

6.798 This Article shows that Guatemala was obliged to make available to Cruz Azul promptly *any* evidence submitted by Cementos Progreso, subject to the provisions on confidential information.[554]

6.799 The provisions governing confidential information require that it be (i) confidential by nature; or (ii) supplied on a confidential basis, provided that the authorities consider that it should be treated as such. Such information can, however, be disclosed with the specific permission of the party submitting it. A party submitting confidential information must furnish a non-confidential summary thereof, in sufficient detail to permit a reasonable understanding of its content.

6.800 In this case, the Ministry of the Economy failed to comply with the obligation to make the evidence submitted by Cementos Progreso available promptly to Cruz Azul by (i) denying Cruz Azul access to the administrative file on the investigation; and (ii) not providing Cruz Azul with a copy of Cementos Progreso's final pleadings made at the final hearing.

6.801 Regarding the first point, on a number of occasions, orally and in writing, Cruz Azul sought access to the information and evidence put forward by Cementos Progreso, but on none of these occasions did the Ministry make them available promptly. Cruz Azul encountered such problems that it had to use the services of a notary to record the negative attitude of the Guatemalan authority. The following documents are evidence of some of the attempts made by Cruz Azul to obtain the evidence submitted by Cementos Progreso from the Ministry:

(a) Attestation of 4 November 1996, issued by the notary Luis Ernesto Rodriguez, recording that the staff at the Ministry of the Economy refused access to the file on the investigation, claiming that the only person authorized to allow this was not in Guatemala and that, before providing the information, "the Ministry has to evaluate and review the documents in it".

[554] Article 6.5 of the AD Agreement defines confidential information as "Any information which is by nature confidential (for example, because its disclosure would be of significant competitive advantage to a competitor or because its disclosure would have a significantly adverse effect upon a person supplying the information or upon a person from whom that person acquired the information), or which is provided on a confidential basis by parties to an investigation ...".

(b) document dated 13 November 1996 in which Cruz Azul requested "all the information submitted by CEMENTOS PROGRESO S.A. and other interested parties ..".

6.802 The foregoing reflects the difficult situation faced by Cruz Azul because the Ministry of the Economy did *not* promptly make available the evidence submitted by Cementos Progreso, in violation of Article 6.1.2 of the AD Agreement.

6.803 Concerning the second point, as evidenced by the record of the public hearing of 19 December 1996, at that time Cruz Azul requested access to the document supplied by Cementos Progreso, but received the reply that "the copy would be transmitted when the necessary notifications were made". On 20 December 1996, Cruz Azul vigorously protested at the Ministry of the Economy's refusal to allow it access to the document containing Cementos Progreso's final pleadings during the hearing. Cruz Azul did *not* in fact have access to this document until 8 January 1997 (less than two weeks before the final determination).

(ii) The Guatemalan authorities did not provide Cruz Azul with a timely opportunity to examine the information relevant to the presentation of its case

6.804 Article 6.4 of the AD Agreement states the following:

> "6.4. The authorities shall whenever practicable provide timely opportunities for all interested parties to see all information that is relevant to the presentation of their cases, that is not confidential as defined in paragraph 5, and that is used by the authorities in an anti-dumping investigation, and to prepare presentations on the basis of this information."

6.805 The facts set out in the preceding section show that Article 6.4 was violated for the following reasons:

(a) On several occasions Cruz Azul contacted the Guatemalan Ministry of the Economy in order to see the file, but it was repeatedly denied access;

(b) as confirmed in the record of the public hearing, despite a specific request for Cementos Progreso's letter, the Ministry refused to furnish it until 8 January of the following year;

(c) furthermore, on 17 January 1997, Cruz Azul sent a further letter requesting two certified copies of all the records in the file. In May 1997 (when the proceedings before the WTO Panel were well under way[555]), Cruz Azul had still not received the whole file;

(d) lastly, Mexico wishes to mention the copy of the record of the public hearing held on 19 December 1996 furnished by the Ministry of the Economy. This copy bears the numbers 02736 to 02739, but it is only part of the record of the public hearing. In other words, the Ministry did *not* give Cruz Azul a full copy of the record of the public hearing. This shows the lack of order in the Ministry of the Economy's file and the ease with which it could be modified to the prejudice of Cruz Azul.

[555] See *Guatemala - Cement*, *supra*, footnote 25, para. 4.384.

(iii) Guatemala did not give Cruz Azul a full opportunity to defend its interests

6.806 Article 6.2 of the AD Agreement provides the following:

> "6.2. Throughout the anti-dumping investigation all interested parties shall have a full opportunity for the defence of their interests. To this end, the authorities shall, on request, provide opportunities for all interested parties to meet those parties with adverse interests, so that opposing views may be presented and rebuttal arguments offered. Provision of such opportunities must take account of the need to preserve confidentiality and of the convenience to the parties. There shall be no obligation on any party to attend a meeting, and failure to do so shall not be prejudicial to that party's case. Interested parties shall also have the right, on justification, to present other information orally."

6.807 Article 6.2 of the AD Agreement gives the parties the right to defend their interests, but the Ministry of the Economy violated this Article in the following manner:

(a) By not allowing access to the full administrative file throughout the course of the investigation;

(b) by delaying communication of the evidence submitted by Cementos Progreso and the other documents in the file;

(c) by not supplying Cruz Azul with the documentation requested, claiming that it might contain confidential information;

(d) by delaying notification to Cruz Azul and the Government of Mexico;

(e) by failing to furnish the full text of the application for initiation of an investigation submitted by Cementos Progreso.

6.808 These arguments show that the Guatemalan investigating authority violated Article 6.1.2, 6.2 and 6.4 of the AD Agreement, without prejudice to other violations due to these acts or omissions.

(b) Response of Guatemala

6.809 **Guatemala** responds to Mexico's claims under 6.1.2, 6.2 and 6.4 as follows:

6.810 Guatemala complied with the provisions of Article 6.1.2, 6.2 and 6.4 by affording Cruz Azul and all the interested parties the opportunity to examine the information, arguments and evidence presented during the course of the investigation. Mexico's complaints in this respect are groundless.

6.811 *Firstly*, during the investigation Cruz Azul was allowed timely access to the public documents. It should be noted that in Guatemala neither the law nor administrative practice requires a reason or justification to be given every time that the parties consult a specific document. Accordingly, the Ministry did not monitor the consultations of the file by the parties. However, Cruz Azul's numerous submissions in which it alludes to evidence in the file shows that it had full access to the file and that it was given ample opportunity to examine the information, arguments and relevant evidence during the various phases of the proceeding. In a resolution dated 6 December 1996 the Director of Economic Integration informed the interested parties that he was preparing a technical study on the result of the investigation and that any of the parties could obtain, at their own expense, copies of the documents and the file. In Guatemala, the acts of the administration are public and interested parties have access to the administrative files.[556] Cruz Azul did not request a copy of any document. Moreover, in its submission for the hearing on December 1996, Cruz Azul did not argue that it had been denied access to any document in the file. On the contrary, Cruz Azul based its arguments on the evidence that had been produced, which shows that Cruz Azul had access to all the information it needed to defend its position. Finally, Mexico does not identify any specific evidence that was allegedly denied to Cruz Azul, still less show that such evidence had any effect on the result of the investigation.

6.812 *Secondly*, Mexico claims that on 4 November 1996 Cruz Azul was denied access to the file. It bases this claim on a notarial deed that was never submitted to the Ministry during the investigation. Even if it were true, as Mexico would have it, that the Ministry was unable to make the file available on the date indicated (which Guatemala does not accept), Cruz Azul had full access to the file on many other occasions. As pointed out above, in accordance with the constitutional guarantee concerning the publication of administrative acts, which is confirmed in the resolution of the Directorate of Economic Integration of 6 December, Cruz Azul had the right to request copies of any document in the file not yet in its possession. However, Cruz Azul did not request that a copy of any document be supplied at its expense. At this stage of the proceeding, Cruz Azul did not request copies of any document because it had already examined the file on many occasions and had been supplied with copies in the course of the investigation.

6.813 *Thirdly*, Mexico complains that at the public hearing held on 19 December 1996, the Ministry unfairly denied Cruz Azul the opportunity to examine the written pleadings submitted by Cementos Progreso at that time. Contrary to what Mexico says, the Ministry had a valid reason for not giving Cruz Azul immediate access to this document. In fact, in the rules which the Ministry laid down for the hearing in its Resolution of 6 December, it specified that "the hearing is not intended as a debate between the parties nor will additional evidence be recognized or admitted; accordingly, each of the parties will merely be given an opportunity to submit its arguments in relation to the facts investigated, without the investigating authority requesting additional information". The instructions also authorized the parties to make written submissions, but did not specify whether these submissions should be part of the public record or whether they could include confidential information. However, a written submission was the only means at the parties' disposal for presenting their final pleadings on the basis of confidential information.

6.814 Consequently, it was reasonable for the Ministry to conclude that the lengthy written submission of 19 December prepared by Cementos Progreso would contain confidential information that ought not to be revealed to Cruz Azul. However, the fact that Cruz Azul did not have immediate access to Cementos Progreso's written submission of 19 December did not deprive Cruz Azul of the opportunity to give its view on the factual information in the file. As stated in the resolution of 6 December, which contains the rules for the hearing, the purpose of any written pleadings submitted by the parties for the hearing was to sum up the arguments and not to provide new evidence. Consequently, during the hearing the Ministry informed Cruz Azul that it would provide a copy of the Cementos Progreso submission once it had been determined whether it contained confidential information. Moreover, Cruz Azul did not have the right to refer to Cementos Progreso's final pleadings in the public hearing. The hearing was not intended as a "de-

[556] (Article 30 of the Constitution: ... Interested parties have the right to obtain, at any time, any reports, copies, or certificates they may request and disclosure of files they may wish to consult, except for ... data supplied by individuals who have been guaranteed confidentiality).

bate between the parties". Thus, in accordance with the Anti-Dumping Agreement, Cruz Azul received a copy of Cementos Progreso's final pleadings a week before the final determination was issued. Any rejoinder to the pleadings that the parties submitted on 19 December would not have been taken into account in presenting the corresponding technical study and, thus, in accordance with the provisions of Article 6.4, no submission prepared in order to refute pleadings made at the hearing would have been "practicable" in the context of the investigation. Moreover, as stated in Article 6.14, the procedures set out in the previous paragraphs of Article 6 "are not intended to prevent the authorities of a Member from proceeding expeditiously". The Ministry was not obliged to delay the conclusion of the investigation in order to allow either of the parties to prepare rejoinders to the final submissions of 19 December 1996.

6.815 *Fourthly*, Mexico maintains that Cruz Azul was refused a complete copy of the file. During the investigation the Ministry provided the interested parties with a copy of the documents in the file. Prior to the date at which the parties had to submit their final pleadings and before the Directorate of Economic Integration presented its final technical study, the parties were reminded that they had the right to obtain, at their own expense, a copy of any document in the file. By 19 December 1996 Cruz Azul had not requested a copy of any document. The document in question, the pleadings which Cementos Progreso submitted to the hearing on 19 December, was made available to Cruz Azul as soon as the Ministry had verified that it did not contain confidential information. The Ministry did not refuse Cruz Azul the certified copy of the whole file which it requested on 17 January 1997. A copy was not issued on that occasion because, according to Guatemalan law, copies are issued at the expense of the interested party and Cruz Azul had not paid the corresponding fee.

6.816 Finally, Mexico does not argue, still less prove that Cruz Azul was denied the right to submit the evidence it wished to submit. The fact is that Cruz Azul refused to reply to the Ministry's requests for information and refused to permit verification of the partial and incomplete information it had submitted. Its unwillingness to cooperate obliged the Ministry to issue its final determination on the basis of the information available.

(c) Rebuttal of Mexico

6.817 **Mexico** rebuts Guatemala's arguments by asserting that it has not shown that it gave Cruz Azul the opportunity to examine the information used by the Ministry, and it has violated Article 6.1.2, 6.2 and 6.4 of the AD Agreement. Mexico expands on these arguments as follows:

6.818 Under Article 6.1.2 Guatemala was under an obligation to make any evidence submitted by Cementos Progreso available promptly to Cruz Azul. Similarly, under Article 6.4 Cruz Azul had the right to see any information relevant to the presentation of its case. Finally, under Article 6.2 Cruz Azul was entitled to an opportunity for the defense of its interests. However, Guatemala acted in violation of these obligations on several occasions. Among the violations argued by Mexico in its first written submission, Guatemala has not refuted, and has thus accepted, the following:

> On 13 November 1996, Cruz Azul requested a copy of all of the information submitted by Cementos Progreso, a request which was never complied with.
>
> On 17 January 1997 Cruz Azul requested at its own expense two copies of the entire file; six months later Cruz Azul had not received the requested copies.

> The copy furnished to Cruz Azul of the record of the public hearing held on 19 December 1996 is incomplete. Even though the page numbers follow on, the document was not supplied in full, i.e. the copy supplied by Guatemala to Cruz Azul is incomplete.
>
> The Ministry of the Economy did not provide Cruz Azul with the text of the application filed by Cementos Progreso.[557]
>
> Guatemala was late in notifying the Government of Mexico and Cruz Azul.[558]

6.819 The fact that Guatemala did not refute the above-mentioned facts is enough to consider them as having been accepted. Thus, Guatemala violated Article 6.1.2, 6.2 and 6.4 of the Anti-Dumping Agreement. Nevertheless, we shall reply below to the weak arguments submitted by Guatemala.

(i) Arguments by Guatemala concerning access to the file[559]

6.820 Firstly, Guatemala argues that it does not keep a record of access to the file. In this case, it is up to Guatemala to prove a positive fact, since Mexico is at a disadvantage in having to prove a negative fact; in other words, it is easier for Guatemala to prove that it granted Cruz Azul access to the file than for Mexico to prove that it did not grant Cruz Azul such access. However, even if Guatemala cannot prove that it provided access to the file because it does not keep a register, Mexico does have evidence of the authority's refusal to grant access to the file (at least one case among many). The notarial deed, which we shall discuss further on, provides public certification that the Ministry of Economy denied Cruz Azul access to the file.

6.821 Secondly, Guatemala argues that there are various Cruz Azul documents which refer to evidence in the files. This argument does not prove that Cruz Azul was given full access to the file. Guatemala does not mention specific cases in which access was granted, let alone full access; because it may have given such an opportunity on limited occasions does not mean that it complied with its obligations under the cited Articles.

6.822 Guatemala then goes on to mention that the Director of Economic Integration decided, in a resolution dated 6 December 1996, to prepare a technical study, announcing that it was possible to request copies. To this, Mexico replies that it is not up to the Director of Economic Integration to announce the opportunity of access to specific documents; access is a right of the parties which should not be granted for certain documents, but should be granted for the entire file. Worse still, *the example cited by Guatemala shows that access to the documents was denied during the procedure*; this resolution of 6 December 1996 refers to the technical study which reportedly contained the essential facts that would allegedly be furnished to Cruz Azul. However, Guatemala did not hand over the technical study until 31 January 1997, i.e. the document mentioned by Guatemala as an example of access to the information in the file was not transmitted to Cruz Azul until 1 day after the publication of the public notice of conclusion of the investigation and of imposition of the definitive anti-dumping duties.

---

557 See the section on Article 6.1.3 of this second written submission by Mexico.

558 See the arguments concerning Articles 5.5 and 12.1 in this second written submission by Mexico as well as the relevant arguments in the "General Comments" section.

559 First written submission by Guatemala, para. 293.

6.823 Finally, Guatemala cites its domestic legislation, an argument that only serves to confirm that Guatemala not only violated the Anti-Dumping Agreement, but also violated its domestic legislation.

(ii) Arguments by Guatemala concerning the notarial deed showing denial of access to the file[560]

6.824 On 4 November 1996, a notary public provided certification that the staff of the Ministry of the Economy had denied Cruz Azul access to the file.

6.825 Guatemala's first argument against this evidence is that it was never submitted to the Ministry of the Economy. We would like to stress that Guatemala is once again trying to justify its failure to comply with the Anti-Dumping Agreement by invoking the theories of estoppel and acquiescence. We have already sufficiently proven that these theories are inoperative in the present case.[561]

6.826 Guatemala then goes on to state that "even if it were true, as Mexico would have it, that the Ministry was unable to make the file available on the date indicated (which Guatemala does not accept) ..." Here, we would like to stress that Guatemala is once again trying to justify its violation through the alleged nullity of its acts, since it is not Mexico that is arguing, but Guatemala through its notary public. Guatemala cannot argue that its own acts are invalid, and then use them at its convenience in the present case.

6.827 Finally, Guatemala assures us that "at this stage of the proceeding [about 4 November 1996], Cruz Azul did not request copies of any document ... ". Once again, Guatemala is using sophisms and lies as a means of bending the facts to suit itself. Mexico did request copies of the documents submitted by Cementos Progreso, since it did not have them at that time; for example, on 13 November 1996 Cruz Azul requested all of the information submitted by Cementos Progreso. The request was not met.

(iii) Guatemala's arguments concerning the refusal to provide Cruz Azul with the document submitted by Cementos Progreso during the public hearing[562]

6.828 During the public hearing of 19 December 1996, Cruz Azul requested access to the document submitted on the same day by Cementos Progreso. The Ministry of the Economy refused this access, on the grounds that there were confidential elements. A copy of the document was provided to Cruz Azul on 8 January 1997.

6.829 Firstly, Guatemala adduces that the public hearing was not intended to be a discussion; the parties were only meant to present their conclusions (final pleadings). Mexico replies that the fact that the public hearing was not a discussion does not authorize Guatemala to deny Cruz Azul access to a document submitted by Cementos Progreso. Guatemala had an obligation to make every document submitted by Cementos Progreso available to Cruz Azul. Thus, the justification put forward by Guatemala does not constitute sufficient reason for violating the Anti-Dumping Agreement.

---

560 First submission by Guatemala, para. 294.

561 See the relevant arguments in the "General Comments" section as well as the arguments concerning Article 5.5 in this second written submission by Mexico.

562 First written submission by Guatemala, para. 295.

6.830 Secondly, Guatemala cannot conclude that a document contains confidential information simply because it was lengthily written, as it states in paragraph 296 of its first submission. In that case, Guatemala should have proceeded according to the confidential information provisions of the Anti-Dumping Agreement. In this connection we refer to the arguments on confidential information in this second written submission by Mexico.

6.831 Finally, Guatemala argues that Cruz Azul received the document submitted by Cementos Progreso one week before issuing the final determination.[563] This argument merely reveals yet another contradiction in Guatemala's reasoning. It cannot be argued that Cruz Azul was given the opportunity to review the document in question when Guatemala submitted it one week before the public notice of conclusion of the investigation and imposition of the definitive anti-dumping duties was issued. This is one more example of Guatemala's denial of access to information submitted by Cementos Progreso.

(iv) Arguments by Guatemala concerning the alleged accessibility to the file during the final stage of the investigation[564]

6.832 Guatemala argues that prior to the date at which the parties had to submit their final pleadings and before the final technical study was presented, the parties were reminded that they had the right to obtain any document in the file.

6.833 In this case, we would like to revert to Cruz Azul's request for copies of 13 November 1996. Guatemala cannot support its claim that it offered certified copies when it did not provide Cruz Azul with the copies requested on 13 November 1996. Moreover, Guatemala has not substantiated its statement since it did not provide any document confirming this offer of copies. Finally, assuming for the sake of argument that Guatemala did make this offer, this would not constitute sufficient evidence that it respected the principle of accessibility for Cruz Azul to the copies during the course of the investigation, since the alleged offer was only made at the end of the investigation. Thus, Mexico wonders why Guatemala does not substantiate its claim and explain what took place during the rest of the investigation.

6.834 For all of these reasons, we conclude that Guatemala violated Article 6.1.2, 6.2 and 6.4 of the Anti-Dumping Agreement. On the one hand, Guatemala did not refute the evidence and the arguments presented in the first part of this section, which in itself is sufficient confirmation that it violated the said Articles. On the other hand, Guatemala's arguments, in addition to being weak, are inoperative, as shown above.

3. *Claims Under Article 6.6 and Paragraph 7 of Annex II - Accuracy of Information Supplied by Cementos Progreso*

(a) Submissions of Mexico

6.835 The following are **Mexico's** arguments under Article 6.6 and paragraph 7 of Annex II regarding the accuracy of information supplied by Cementos Progreso:

6.836 The Ministry violated Article 6.6 of the AD Agreement by *not* satisfying itself as to the accuracy of the information supplied by Cementos Progreso and used by the Ministry for the purposes of its final determination.

---

[563] *Ibid.*, para. 296.

[564] *Ibid.*, para. 297.

6.837 Article 6.6. obliges the authorities to satisfy themselves as to the accuracy of the information received during the investigation, especially the information upon which their findings are based. The Article states the following:

> "6.6. Except in circumstances provided for in paragraph 8, the authorities *shall* during the course of an investigation *satisfy themselves as to the accuracy of the information* supplied by interested parties upon which their findings are based." (emphasis added).

6.838 The Ministry did *not* satisfy itself as to the information supplied by Cementos Progreso and used as a basis for its final affirmative determination. On the one hand, the information it used to determine the normal value is similar to that submitted upon initiation of the investigation, i.e. four alleged invoices, two of which served to initiate the investigation, which did *not* clearly specify or identify the product sold.

6.839 The Ministry did *not* undertake any action that was clearly needed to satisfy itself as to the accuracy of the information supplied by Cementos Progress to determine the normal value. Indeed, bearing in mind that in its final determination the Ministry took a decision according to the best available information[565] within the meaning of Article 6.8 and Annex II to the AD Agreement, the Ministry violated paragraph 7 of Annex II, which provides the following, by not acting with special circumspection when determining the normal value:

> "*If the authorities have to base their findings, including those with respect to normal value*, on information from a secondary source, including the information supplied in the application for the initiation of the investigation, *they should do so with special circumspection*. In such cases, the authorities should, where practicable, check the information from other independent sources at their disposal, such as published price lists, import statistics and customs returns, and from the information obtained from other interested parties during the investigation. It is clear, however, that if an interested party does not cooperate and thus relevant information is being withheld from the authorities, this situation could lead to a result which is less favourable to the party than if the party did cooperate." (emphasis added).

6.840 As can be seen from the public notice of conclusion of the investigation, the Ministry did *not* comply with its obligations, it simply did *not* check or ascertain the accuracy of the information supplied by Cementos Progreso (two of the alleged invoices) and

[565] The following appears in the Considerations section, part B. Determination of dumping, of the notice of conclusion of the investigation, which determined the imposition of definitive anti-dumping duties:

"6. ... this Ministry considers that the information submitted by the exporter cannot be taken into account when calculating the normal value of the product investigated because it could not be verified and the technical evidence submitted by the exporter on 18 December 1996 (confidential information) could not replace verification of the information by the Guatemalan investigating authority, as required by Article 6.6 of the Anti-Dumping Code (sic)." (The footnote has been omitted.)

"7. Consequently, on the basis of Articles 6.6, 6.8 and Annex 2 of the Anti-Dumping Code (sic), this Ministry considers that the normal value should be calculated on the basis of the invoices for purchases on the Mexican market contained within the file, which are proof of transactions carried out in that market and are the best available information contained in the file." (emphasis added).

the other two alleged invoices, whose source was neither justified nor explained, and did not consider them in the light of other information from other independent sources.

6.841 The Ministry did *not* act with special circumspection either in its final determination, fully aware that the type and amount of information (two alleged invoices) supplied by Cementos Progress were neither sufficient nor precise enough to permit initiation of the investigation, and in the final stage it considered accurate and adequate four alleged invoices, including the two original ones, when such documentation was *neither* accurate nor representative of Cruz Azul's sales on the domestic market nor a sufficient basis for its findings in the final determination of the normal value.

6.842 In addition, the Panel should turn to section E.1 of this first written submission by Mexico, which sets out the arguments on the inaccuracy of the documentation used by the Ministry for its final determination of the normal value.

6.843 For the foregoing reasons, the Ministry of the Economy, by *not* checking the information supplied during the investigation and by *not* acting with special circumspection in determining the normal value, violated Article 6.6 and paragraph 7 of Annex II to the AD Agreement.

6.844 With regard to the volume of allegedly dumped imports used as a basis for the affirmative determination of injury, the Ministry did *not* satisfy itself as to the accuracy of the information supplied during the investigation, so it violated Article 3.2 of the AD Agreement by not considering whether there had been a significant increase in imports in absolute terms as there is a marked difference between growth in absolute terms and a rate of growth, as indicated in Article 3.7(i) of the Agreement.

6.845 The calculations made in order to obtain the increase in the volume of imports of grey Portland cement from Mexico for the purposes of the final determination are *not* accurate, however, and are even wrong because the Ministry confined itself to obtaining the maximum and minimum amounts imported during the investigation period instead of the import trend in absolute terms or relative to the previous comparable period, which in this case would be 1 June 1994 to 31 May 1995.

6.846 Moreover, the figures for imports obtained by the Ministry are *not* accurate and are indeed wrong because tariff heading 2523.29.00 of the Central American Tariff System, which includes grey Portland cement, also covers products other than that investigated. Nevertheless, the Ministry improperly considered that all imports under this tariff heading corresponded to the product investigated.

6.847 Even more serious is the fact that the Ministry considered that the total volume of imports under the tariff heading over the period January-June 1996 corresponded to the product of Mexican origin without taking account of the fact that imports of grey Portland cement from other sources entered Guatemala during this period.

6.848 Consequently, the Ministry made its final determination without giving due consideration to the information received during the investigation and without checking its accuracy in the light of the claims made by Cementos Progreso, which led to an incorrect determination of the volume of imports of grey Portland cement from Mexico inasmuch as it did *not* exclude imports from other sources nor other types of cement, for example, grey cement or slow-setting cement imported under the same tariff heading.

6.849 The Ministry did not satisfy itself either as to the accuracy of the information on clinker inventories supplied by Cementos Progreso and accepted during the investigation, thus violating Article 6.6.

6.850 In order to demonstrate the Ministry of the Economy's non-compliance, it should be noted that the Ministry did *not* examine the trend in inventories of grey Portland cement and instead limited itself to indicating that clinker, an input used in cement production, accumulated from August 1995 onwards. The Ministry was therefore *not* in a position to determine that inventories of the like domestic product might have been affected as a result of the imports from Mexico.

6.851 As a result of these arguments, it may justifiably be concluded that, by not satisfying itself as to the accuracy of the information received during the investigation, the Ministry acted in a manner inconsistent with Article 6.6 and paragraph 7 of Annex II to the AD Agreement.

(b) Response of Guatemala

6.852 **Guatemala** responds to Mexico's arguments under Article 6.6 and paragraph 7 of Annex II to the AD Agreement as follows:

6.853 Mexico alleges that the Ministry violated Article 6.6 by not satisfying itself as to the accuracy of the four invoices submitted by Cementos Progreso which were used for calculating the normal value in the final determination of dumping. There is no support for Mexico's allegation in the Anti-Dumping Agreement.

6.854 Under Article 6.6, the Ministry was required to satisfy itself as to the accuracy of the information supplied by Cementos Progreso upon which its findings were based "except in circumstances provided for in paragraph 8". Paragraph 8 was in fact applicable to the calculation of the normal value because Cruz Azul had refused to provide necessary information and had significantly impeded the investigation by refusing to permit verification of the information which would have been used to establish the normal value. Thus, under Article 6.8, the Ministry was authorized to calculate the normal value on the basis of the facts available. What is more, under paragraph 7 of Annex II, since Cruz Azul did not cooperate and withheld relevant information from the authorities, the Ministry was authorized to use the facts available, even if that could have led to a result less favourable to Cruz Azul than if that party had cooperated.

6.855 As stated in the case *United States - DRAM:*

> "Article 6.6 simply requires Members to 'satisfy themselves as to the accuracy of the information'. In our view, Members could 'satisfy themselves as to the accuracy of the information' in a number of ways without proceeding to some type of formal verification, including, for example, reliance on the reputation of the original source of the information. Indeed, we consider that anti-dumping investigations would become totally unmanageable if investigating authorities were required to actually verify the accuracy of all information relied on."[566]

In the investigation in question, the Ministry did not use unfounded allegations of the applicant as available facts for calculating the normal value. On the contrary, it used documentary evidence - four invoices. During the course of the investigation, Mexico did not suggest that the documents used by the Ministry were fraudulent. The Ministry used these documents instead of relying on the information of Cruz Azul itself, as it did in the preliminary determination, because Cruz Azul refused to supply the information requested and refused to permit a verification visit in the final phase of the investigation. Accordingly, Mexico cannot complain that the Ministry used documentary evidence as available information for computing the normal value.

6.856 Next, Mexico alleges that the Ministry did not satisfy itself as to the accuracy of the information supplied during the investigation with regard to the volume of allegedly dumped imports. In fact, as explained above, the Ministry used the information supplied by Cruz Azul itself for calculating the volume of dumped imports. The Ministry did not

---

[566] *DRAMS, supra*, footnote 115, para. 6.78.

take into account imports from other countries or imports of other types of cement not subject to investigation. On the basis of Cruz Azul's own information, the Directorate found that imports had increased from 140 tons in June 1995 to 25,079 tons in May 1996. The maximum volume of imports was recorded in May 1996 when it rose to 45,859 tons. In the light of this irrefutable evidence Guatemala cannot understand why Mexico has chosen to argue this point before the panel. As such, Guatemala complied with Article 6.6 in establishing the volume of imports.

6.857 Mexico also claims that the Ministry did not confirm the authenticity of the information supplied by Cementos Progreso with regard to its inventories. Specifically, Mexico again complains that the Ministry relied on clinker inventories instead of cement inventories. As explained above, clinker inventories are highly relevant for evaluating the performance of a cement producer. Clinker is used only for making cement and can be stored in greater quantities than the finished cement. As such, Guatemala complied with Article 6.6 in establishing Cementos Progreso's clinker inventories.

(c) Rebuttal of Mexico

6.858 **Mexico** makes the following rebuttals with respect to the accuracy of the information on which the authority based its findings throughout the various stages of the investigation:

6.859 Guatemala argues that it was not required to satisfy itself as to the accuracy of the information submitted by Cementos Progreso on which its findings were based[567] since Cruz Azul refused to provide the information it required and refused to allow the verification visit to take place, so that the investigating authority proceeded in accordance with Article 6.8.

6.860 Mexico submits that Cruz Azul did not obstruct the verification for the reasons given in Mexico's first written submission[568], in the Section concerning the on-the-spot investigation. Similarly, Mexico submits that the Ministry was required to satisfy itself at the various stages of the investigation (initiation, preliminary and final) as to the accuracy of the information, above all in view of the differences and discrepancies in the information as indicated in the sections on dumping.

6.861 Regarding the final determination, if we assume that Guatemala acted in accordance with Article 6.8, Mexico submits that Guatemala should have proceeded in conformity with Annex II, paragraph 7 in determining the normal value, i.e. with special circumspection, since the information on normal value, four alleged invoices, only certified the sale of one sack or load of cement each. Moreover, the Ministry never justified or explained the origin of the two alleged invoices used in its final determination, nor did it consider them in the light of other information from other independent sources, as also provided for in paragraph 7 of Annex II.

6.862 With respect to the volume of the allegedly dumped imports, Guatemala asserts that the Ministry did not take account of imports from other countries or imports of other types of cement not subject to investigation.[569] However, the Ministry improperly considered that all imports under tariff heading 2523.29.00 corresponded to the product investigated, when in fact, products other than grey Portland cement were being imported under the same tariff heading.[570] Nor did Guatemala satisfy itself that the imports under that

[567] *Ibid.*, paras. 300 and 301.

[568] First written submission by Mexico, paras. 383 *et seq.*

[569] First written submission by Guatemala, para. 302.

[570] First written submission by Mexico, para. 349.

tariff heading during the period January-June 1996 did not also correspond to grey Portland cement of other origins, not only Mexican.

6.863 At the same time, with respect to the clinker inventories considered by the Ministry, Guatemala asserts that they were highly relevant for evaluating the performance of a cement producer, since clinker is used only for making cement and can be stored in greater quantities than finished cement.[571]

6.864 Mexico submits that the analysis of the inventories of clinker, an input used in manufacturing cement, shows that the Ministry neither analysed nor ascertained the behaviour of grey Portland cement inventories, nor was it in a position to determine whether these inventories might have been affected as a result of the Mexican imports.[572]

6.865 Finally, Mexico submits that by failing to satisfy itself as to the accuracy of the information which served as a basis for the findings of its final determination or, if applicable, by not acting with special circumspection and checking the information from other independent sources, Guatemala acted in violation of Article 6.6 and paragraph 7 of Annex II.

4. *Claims Under Articles 6.1 and Paragraph 1 of Annex II - Guatemala's Extension of the Investigation Period*

(a) Submissions of Mexico

6.866 **Mexico** argues that the Guatemalan Ministry extended the investigation period without any legal justification and without consulting or properly notifying Cruz Azul. Its arguments are as follows:

(i) Facts

6.867 On 17 November 1995, the Ministry of the Economy's advisers recommended opening the investigation procedure, considering that the investigation and examination of evidence should cover the period 1 June to 30 November 1995. The questionnaire submitted by Cruz Azul also mentioned this period. Subsequently, the preliminary determination of 28 August 1996 fixed the period mentioned as the investigation period. The provisional duties were in fact imposed on the basis of the evidence submitted for this period.

6.868 Nevertheless, on 4 October 1996, i.e. nine months after the public notice of initiation had been published and three months prior to publication of the final determination, Guatemala issued an official letter containing its decision to extend the original investigation period from 1 December 1995 to 31 May 1996, i.e. the period investigated was now to be 1 June 1995 to 31 May 1996. As a result, on 14 October 1996, the Ministry requested Cruz Azul to supply information for the new investigation period.

6.869 The Ministry of the Economy's letter of 4 October 1996 itself shows that a request for extension of the investigation period had been submitted by Cementos Progreso on 1 October that year. The Ministry's letter stated the following:

> "... Regarding the extension of the investigation period, this cannot be accepted in the form requested because the period must be continuous. This Department will therefore extend the period from 1 December 1995 to 31 May 1996 in the request for additional information."

[571] First written submission by Guatemala, para. 303.

[572] First written submission by Mexico, para. 353.

6.870 The Ministry decided to extend the period without justification or any legal grounds, and without consulting Cruz Azul. In its letters of 30 October and 13 November 1996, Cruz Azul stated that Cementos Progreso had *not* provided any technical or legal grounds for extending the investigation period, for which it should have presented evidence of dumping, injury and a causal relationship, it also specifically requested that the extension of the investigation period be declared without effect and that the period originally fixed be confirmed, but the Ministry disregarded this request.

6.871 Finally, in a communication dated 2 December 1996, the Government of Mexico expressed its disagreement with the extension of the investigation period.

(ii) Guatemala did not specify the information actually required from Cruz Azul as soon as possible after having initiated the investigation, in violation of paragraph 1 of Annex II to the AD Agreement

6.872 Paragraph 1 of Annex II to the AD Agreement provides the following:

> "1. As soon as possible after the initiation of the investigation, the investigating authorities should specify in detail the information required from any interested party, and the manner in which that information should be structured by the interested party in its response. The authorities should also ensure that the party is aware that if information is not supplied within a reasonable time, the authorities will be free to make determinations on the basis of the facts available, including those contained in the application for the initiation of the investigation by the domestic industry."

6.873 As can be seen, Guatemala first sought information from Cruz Azul on the extended period in its letter dated 14 October 1996, i.e. nine months after publication of the initiation decision and three months prior to publishing the final determination.

6.874 This clearly shows that Guatemala did not specify in detail the information actually required from Cruz Azul as soon as possible after the initiation of the investigation. It did so when the investigation was already fairly advanced, when provisional anti-dumping duties had been applied for over a month and a short time before the investigation ended. The extension of the investigation period in itself is a violation of paragraph 1 of Annex II. Cruz Azul had already had several meetings with the investigating authority and had transmitted information concerning the investigation.

6.875 This new requirement not only violates the letter of paragraph 1 of Annex II but is also contrary to the logic of the structure of investigations. Changing the investigation period between the preliminary and final decisions can completely distort the procedure because the bases used to determine dumping, injury or threat of injury and the causal relationship between the dumping and the injury or threat of injury will not be the same. Nevertheless, this is not the substantive problem in this case.

6.876 The problem here goes beyond a straightforward modification of the investigation period because the Guatemalan authority made a preliminary determination on the bases of biased data that exceeded the investigation period it had itself established and went against the interests of the exporter, without any substance or reason. As the determination shows, the only party that supplied information concerning the extended period was the applicant, a fact that once again shows the partiality with which the Ministry of the Economy conducted this investigation. [573]

(iii) Guatemala did not notify Cruz Azul of the information required by the authorities or give it ample opportunity to present in writing all the evidence it considered relevant, in violation of Article 6.1 of the AD Agreement. Nor did it give Cruz Azul full opportunity for the defence of its interests, in violation of Article 6.2 of the AD Agreement

6.877 Article 6.1 and 6.2 of the AD agreement provide the following:

> "6.1. All interested parties in an anti-dumping investigation shall be given notice of the information which the authorities require and ample opportunity to present in writing all evidence which they consider relevant in respect of the investigation in question.
>
> ...
>
> 6.2. Throughout the anti-dumping investigation, all interested parties shall have a full opportunity for the defence of their interests. To this end, the authorities shall, on request, provide opportunities for all interested parties to meet those parties with adverse interests, so that opposing views may be presented and rebuttal arguments offered. Provision of such opportunities must take account of the need to preserve confidentiality and of the convenience to the parties. There shall be no obligation on any party to attend a meeting, and failure to do so shall not be prejudicial to that party's case. Interested parties shall also have the right, on justification, to present other information orally."

6.878 Whereas Article 6.1 gives interested parties the right to be notified of the information required by the authorities and ample opportunity to be heard in connection with the investigation, Article 6.2 also gives the parties an opportunity to defend their interests during the proceedings. In other words, the AD Agreement guarantees Cruz Azul's right to be informed of the other party's arguments and to be heard by the authority in defence of its interests.

6.879 The Ministry's decision extending the investigation period is so inadequate that Cruz Azul could not have known the legal grounds nor the justification for which Cementos Progreso sought extension of the investigation period, on the one hand, and why the Ministry decided in favour of Cementos Progreso, on the other. Even more serious is the fact that the Ministry did not reply to the requests from Cruz Azul for information on extension of the period or for confirmation of the period fixed when the investigation was initiated. In fact, at no time was Cruz Azul given the opportunity to make comments or provide evidence that would allow proper defence of its interests.

---

573 Despite not having reached a preliminary affirmative determination of dumping for the period subsequent to the investigation, the attempt to attribute the alleged adverse effects on the domestic industry violates Article 3.5 of the AD Agreement.

6.880 Cruz Azul, being precluded from meeting the requirements relating to the new period, responded fully concerning the period fixed at the initiation of the investigation, thus showing that it was ready to cooperate provided that its rights were respected.

6.881 The fact that the investigating authority took such an important decision during the investigation, modifying the investigation period without giving the exporting firm a proper opportunity to present what, in its opinion, had been agreed before the decision to extend the investigation period had been taken, is clearly a denial of the opportunity that Cruz Azul should have been given to present the evidence it considered relevant and consequently to defend its interests.

6.882 Guatemala not only failed to give the exporter an opportunity to put forward arguments against its decision but also sought full information concerning the extended period, imposing an excessive and unreasonable burden on the exporter. As it had prepared information in response to the original questionnaire, it is obvious that Cruz Azul's involvement in the proceedings was solely based on that information.

6.883 The fact that the Ministry of the Economy extended the investigation period in the form and at the stage it did leads to the assumption that, when making its preliminary determination, it did *not* have relevant and adequate evidence to determine threat of material injury, and in fact it did not have such evidence. This is borne out by an examination of the inadequate preliminary determination of threat of injury and the corresponding change in the final determination in which the Ministry determines material injury without having adequate information and evidence to show that the domestic industry was affected, even at the cost of violating the principles and precepts in Article 6.1 and 6.2, as well as paragraph 1 of Annex II to the AD Agreement.

6.884 If the foregoing does not suffice, the fact that the authority did *not* mention the justification or the legal grounds on which it extended the investigation period is a clear demonstration of the partiality of the Guatemalan investigating authority and the lack of objectiveness with which it accepted the applicant's request, possibly with the intention of defending the latter's interests.

(b) Response of Guatemala

6.885 **Guatemala** responds to Mexico's arguments regarding the alleged violations of Article 6.1 and 6.2 and paragraph 1 of Annex II as follows:

6.886 Mexico claims that Guatemala violated Article 6.1 and 6.2 and paragraph 1 of Annex II to the Agreement by extending the investigation period by six months. There is no support for this argument in the Anti-Dumping Agreement.

6.887 Neither Article 6.1 nor Article 6.2 nor paragraph 1 of Annex II nor any other provision of the Agreement imposes any requirement on the investigating authority with respect to the period to be investigated. The investigation period will vary from case to case and its length is left to the discretion of the investigating authority. Nor does the Agreement prohibit the investigating authority from using different investigation periods for the preliminary and final determinations. Guatemala understands that it is common practice for the investigating authorities in other countries to gather more information in the final phase of the investigation in order that the final determination may be based on more up-to-date information. In fact, Article 76 of the Regulations implementing the Mexican Foreign Trade Act states that "the period of investigation to which the foregoing paragraph refers may be modified at the discretion of the Ministry to cover a period which includes imports made subsequent to the commencement of the investigation".[574] Subsequently, Mexico confirmed that "Article 76 of the Regulations empowers the investigating authority to extend the investigation period, where necessary".[575]

6.888 In the present case, the Ministry initially established the investigation period as the period from 1 June to 30 November 1995. In a submission dated 18 September 1996, Cementos Progreso asked the Ministry to extend the investigation period for the final determination so as to include the period from 1 January to 30 June 1996 in order that the final determination might be based on more recent evidence of the existence of dumping and consequent injury. With respect to dumping, Cementos Progreso submitted evidence showing that the margin of dumping had increased since November 1995, the period considered in the preliminary investigation. Specifically, during 1996, prices in Mexico had increased substantially, whereas the prices of exports to Guatemala had remained unchanged. With respect to consequent injury, Cementos Progreso indicated that massive imports during 1996 - subsequent to the preliminary investigation period (June-November 1995) - were causing it material injury. In other words, the threat of material injury identified in the application had turned into actual material injury during 1996. Accordingly, the Ministry asked for additional information for the period from 1 December 1995 to 31 May 1996, but not for the period from January 1995 to June 1996, as Cementos Progreso had requested.

6.889 Mexico claims that the supplementary questionnaire requesting information for the extended investigation period imposed an excessive and unreasonable burden on Cruz Azul. However, Cruz Azul made no such claim at the time and did not request an extension of the period for replying to the questionnaire. The panel will recall that the Ministry granted Cruz Azul, in accordance with its own request, an extension of several months to reply to the original questionnaire. Far from seeking an extension to complete the questionnaire, Cruz Azul simply objected to having to submit the information requested.

6.890 Mexico alleges that the extension of the investigation period was in itself a violation of paragraph 1 of Annex II, since the Ministry did not specify all the information required from Cruz Azul as soon as possible after the initiation of the investigation. This is an absurd proposition. According to Mexico, an investigating authority could never ask for information additional to that required at the time of initiation of the investigation. Mexico would prevent the investigating authority from gathering additional information during the final phase of the investigation.

6.891 If paragraph 1 of Annex II were understood to prevent the investigating authority from gathering additional information, including information from the most recent period, other provisions of the Anti-Dumping Agreement would be compromised, such as Articles 7.4 and 9.1 (information necessary to determine whether a duty lower than the margin of dumping would be sufficient to remove injury) and Article 10.2 (post-provisional information necessary to determine the effect of the imports).[576] Certainly, the implementation of these provisions would be more difficult, if not impossible, if the investigating authorities were unable to seek additional information for making these determinations.

[574] G/ADP/N/1MEX/1 (18 May 1995).

[575] G/ADP/W/66 (25 October 1995).

[576] As already noted on various occasions in the course of Guatemala's submission, in international law it has been established that "an interpreter is not free to adopt a reading that would result in reducing whole clauses or paras. of a treaty to redundancy or inutility". Report of the Appellate Body, *United States - Standards for Reformulated and Conventional Gasoline*, *supra*, footnote 2, at 21.

Moreover, the Anti-Dumping Agreement, particularly with respect to the threat of injury, recognizes the importance of using as much up-to-date information as possible. An interpretation of paragraph 1 of Annex II that made it impossible for the investigating authorities to gather up-to-date information would certainly be incompatible with the spirit of the Agreement. In the alternate, if the Agreement were interpreted as permitting the authorities to make only one request for information, the investigating authorities would make their requests for information excessively long. Such an outcome would be of benefit to no one.

6.892 Finally, contrary to what Mexico alleges, Guatemala notified Cruz Azul of the information requested and granted Cruz Azul ample opportunity to submit in writing all the evidence it considered appropriate. The Ministry issued a supplementary questionnaire and supplied it to Cruz Azul, which obviously alerted it to the information that was being requested. The Ministry set 30 October 1996 as the deadline for replying to the questionnaire and Cruz Azul did not ask for an extension of that deadline. Moreover, on 30 October Cruz Azul lodged a voluminous submission containing pleadings and evidence, together with its replies to the questionnaire. Thus, Cruz Azul had ample opportunity to incorporate any information it chose in the investigation file. Instead, as described below, Cruz Azul took the decision not to supply the information requested by the Ministry and not to cooperate with the verification. Thus, the Ministry was obliged to use the facts available for its final determination.

(c) Rebuttal of Mexico

6.893 **Mexico** maintains that Guatemala has not refuted the argument that it violated Article 6.1 and 6.2, and paragraph 1 of Annex II of the AD Agreement by extending the period of investigation without justification. It makes the following arguments in this regard:

6.894 Mexico's position, which has not been refuted by Guatemala, is based on two arguments:[577]

> Guatemala did not justify, either in fact or in law, its extension of the investigation period; moreover, Guatemala failed to comply with paragraph 1 of Annex II. In this case, the first request to Cruz Azul concerning the extended period was made on 14 October 1996.
>
> As regards the decision to extend the investigation period, contrary to Article 6.1, Guatemala did not grant Cruz Azul the right to receive notice of the information which the authorities required or ample opportunity to present its evidence. Contrary to Article 6.2 it also failed to give Cruz Azul a full opportunity for the defence of its interests. In other words, Guatemala did not grant Cruz Azul the right to familiarize itself with the arguments of the opposing party or to be heard by the authority in defence of its interests in connection with the decision to extend the investigation period. Thus Guatemala violated Article 61. and 6.2 of the Anti-Dumping Agreement.

6.895 We shall provide evidence below of the weakness of Guatemala's arguments in justifying its violations it committed in extending the investigation period.

---

[577] *Ibid.*, para. 355 *et seq.*

(i) Extension of the period of investigation

6.896 Guatemala argues that there is nothing in the Anti-Dumping Agreement which imposes any requirements with respect to the period to be investigated. The Anti-Dumping Agreement does not prohibit the use of different investigation periods for the preliminary and final determination. Furthermore, Mexico permits changes in the investigation period.[578] Mexico replies that the fact that the Anti-Dumping Agreement does not prohibit the kind of change in the investigation period made by Guatemala does not necessarily mean that it permits such a change. The Ministry of the Economy, as the investigating authority, has the obligation to justify its acts in fact and in law, on the basis of the applicable legislation, in this case, the Anti-Dumping Agreement. Mexican legislation has nothing to do with this case.

(ii) Guatemala violated Articles 6.1 and 6.2 by extending the period of investigation

6.897 Cruz Azul was never acquainted with the legal basis on which Cementos Progreso requested an extension of the investigation period. Cementos Progreso's written request for an extension of the period of investigation does not show cause, in fact or in law, for making the request. Worse still, the Ministry of the Economy did not justify to Cruz Azul, either in fact or in law, its decision to extend the investigation period. Accordingly, Cruz Azul was not afforded an opportunity to make observations or submit evidence on the extension, since Cruz Azul could not defend itself against something that was unknown to it. Hence, the procedural principles of equity and transparency were violated. What is more, not only was Cruz Azul given no opportunity to present arguments against the decision to extend the period but the Ministry of the Economy also placed an excessive and unreasonable burden on it. Lastly, Guatemala cannot show cause for any act whereby it violated transparency and equity to the detriment of Cruz Azul, and still less by merely submitting Annex MEXICO-39 as evidence.[579]

6.898 Actually, it may be inferred a posteriori that Guatemala extended the investigation period because it did not have sufficient relevant evidence to determine the existence of a threat of material injury. This is reflected in the faulty determination of threat of injury in the preliminary determination, and in the change from a threat of injury to injury in the final determination. Guatemala tried, though unsuccessfully, to find elements of injury at any cost and did not mind violating Article 6.1 and 6.2 to the detriment of Cruz Azul.

6.899 Finally, Guatemala is again endeavouring to justify its violations by contending that Cruz Azul did not challenge them when Guatemala committed them. Our repeated answer to Guatemala is that the principles of acquiescence and estoppel do not apply in the present case.[580]

6.900 Consequently, Guatemala violated Article 6.1, 6.2 and paragraph 1 of Annex II of the Anti-Dumping Agreement. On the one hand, Guatemala was not entitled to extend the investigation period, since it did not justify such a course either in fact or in law; on the other, in the determination to extend the investigation period Guatemala did not afford Cruz Azul an opportunity to be heard or to defend its interests, because Cruz Azul was unable even to find out the basis for extending the investigation period.

---

[578] First written submission by Guatemala, para. 305.

[579] See Mexico's replies to Panel questions 4 and 14 of 18 February 2000.

[580] See the arguments set out in the "General Comments" section as well as those concerning Article 5.5 in this second written submission by Mexico.

5. *Claims Under Article 2.1 and 2.2 - Guatemala's Request for Information on Production Costs From Cruz Azul*

(a) Submissions of Mexico

6.901 **Mexico** argues that Guatemala's request for information on production costs from Cruz Azul violated Articles 2.1 and 2.2 of the AD Agreement. The following are Mexico's arguments in support of its claims:

6.902 During the final phase of the investigation, after having imposed a provisional anti-dumping measure, the Ministry requested from Cruz Azul information, *inter alia*, on production costs for the investigation period fixed upon initiation of the investigation and for the extended period, even though the Ministry gave no justification or grounds for doing so.

6.903 On 14 October 1996, the Ministry made a request to the applicant and Cruz Azul for the purpose of updating the information supplied to the Ministry and asking for information for the period 1 December 1995 to 31 May 1996, covering the original period and the extended period. In its request, the Ministry asked Cruz Azul to supply information on production costs:

> "In order to pursue the investigation initiated on 11 January of this year:
>
> Requires the firm Cooperativa La Cruz Azul, S.C.L., and the domestic producer to update the information supplied to the Ministry of the Economy to include information for the period 1 December 1995 to 31 May 1996.
>
> In addition, requires the firm Cooperativa La Cruz Azul, S.C.L. to provide the following information and documentation:
>
> ...
>
> Production costs, per metric tonne, for Type II Pz and Type I PM cements, indicating separately the cost of the raw materials and labour (variable costs). The report should contain information for both plants: Hidalgo and Lagunas Oaxaca and show the weighted average of the variable cost for both plants."

6.904 As can be seen from the above, there is *no* justification nor any grounds for the request to Cruz Azul for information on production costs. However, even assuming that the extension of the investigation period was acceptable, this argument in itself would *not* be sufficient to require information on costs.

6.905 The request made to Cruz Azul is unjustified for the following reasons.

(i) The application for an investigation made by Cementos Progreso did *not* include a claim of selling below cost. Implicitly, the applicant acknowledged the prices to be valid because they were in the course of normal commercial transactions and it only argued that the price at which the product investigated was exported to Guatemala was lower than the price at which it was sold on the Mexican domestic market.

Article 2.1 and 2.2 of the AD Agreement set out the methodology to be used to determine the alleged dumping and the information that has to be required:

> 2.1 For the purpose of this Agreement, a product is to be considered as being dumped, i.e. introduced into the commerce of another country at less than its normal value, if the export price of the product exported from one country to another is less than the

> comparable price, in the ordinary course of trade, for the like product when destined for consumption in the exporting country.
>
> 2.2 When there are no sales of the like product in the ordinary course of trade in the domestic market of the exporting country or when, because of the particular market situation or the low volume of the sales in the domestic market of the exporting country, such sales do not permit a proper comparison, the margin of dumping shall be determined by comparison with a comparable price of the like product when exported to an appropriate third country, provided that this price is representative, or with the cost of production in the country of origin plus a reasonable amount for administrative, selling and general costs and for profits." (The footnote has been omitted.)

(ii) Based on this, the Ministry only received information on prices from Cruz Azul so in the administrative file on the case there is *no* information nor arguments justifying the Ministry's request to Cruz Azul for information on costs referred to in Article 2.2.1 of the AD Agreement.

(iii) In the preliminary determination imposing a provisional anti-dumping duty, a dumping margin has been calculated for Cruz Azul using *price information* specific to the firm.

6.906 It is obvious that the Ministry decided to ask Cruz Azul for information on production costs even though Cementos Progreso had not claimed that Cruz Azul's sales on the Mexican domestic market were below production costs. The Ministry had no grounds nor any basis to justify the request to Cruz Azul for additional information.

6.907 The absence of claims by the applicant and justification or grounds by the Ministry can be seen in the notice of conclusion of the investigation because in its final determination the Ministry again utilizes information on prices to determine the dumping margin imposed on Cruz Azul in the absence of any claim that sales were below cost or any information in this respect.

6.908 In the light of the above arguments, it may justifiably be considered that the Ministry of the Economy's action in requiring Cruz Azul to provide information on production costs for the original and extended investigation periods was inconsistent with Article 2.1 and 2.2. of the AD Agreement.

(b) Response of Guatemala

6.909 **Guatemala** responds to Mexico's arguments under Articles 2.1 and 2.2 as follows:

6.910 Mexico alleges that the Ministry violated Articles 2.1 and 2.2 in requesting information on production costs from Cruz Azul. According to Mexico, the Ministry did not have the right to request information on costs, because it was calculating the normal value on the basis of prices in Mexico, because Cementos Progreso had not alleged that Cruz Azul selling prices were below production costs and because the preliminary determination of normal value was based on price information. However, Articles 2.1 and 2.2 clearly do not prevent an investigating authority from gathering cost information.

6.911 In fact, under the criteria established in Article 2, Cruz Azul's production costs were extremely relevant. Firstly, Article 2.2.1 provides that sales of the like product in the domestic market of the exporting country at prices below per unit (fixed and variable) costs of production plus administrative, selling and general costs may be disregarded in determining normal value if they meet certain requirements. Secondly, Article 2.4 states that in comparing the export price and the normal value, due allowance shall be made for differences in physical characteristics that affect price comparability. In the present investigation, Cruz Azul replied to the initial anti-dumping questionnaire by providing a list of sales of Type II and Type II Pz cement on the domestic market and export sales of Type 1 (PM) cement. It claimed that the cement sold in Mexico had a higher production cost.[581] Consequently, as it was necessary, it was entirely appropriate for the Ministry to seek to know the variable cost of producing the cement sold in Mexico and the cement sold in Guatemala in order to make an adjustment for physical differences.

6.912 The Ministry requested information on production costs from Cruz Azul in Section C2, Part 3.5 of the original questionnaire submitted on 26 January and in Section 2(f) of the supplementary questionnaire submitted on 14 October. Cruz Azul failed to supply its production costs in replying to the original questionnaire. It gave only a partial reply (for one of two plants) to the supplementary questionnaire.

6.913 Cruz Azul's reluctance to provide information on production costs for both plants prevented the Ministry from determining whether Cruz Azul's sales were below cost and from calculating any adjustment for the alleged difference in physical characteristics between the product sold in Mexico and the product exported to Guatemala.

(c) Rebuttal of Mexico

6.914 **Mexico** rebuts Guatemala's arguments dealing with its claims under Articles 2.1 and 2.2 as follows:

6.915 Guatemala states that Articles 2.1 and 2.2 do not prevent an authority from gathering information on production costs and, as part of the same argument, asserts that pursuant to Article 2.4 allowance shall be made for differences in characteristics that have a bearing on the comparability of export prices and the normal value. Guatemala says that Cruz Azul answered the questionnaire by providing a list of sales of Type II and Type II Pz cement on the domestic market and export sales of Type I (PM) cement, that Cruz Azul claimed the cement sold in Mexico had a higher production cost and, accordingly, it was appropriate for the Ministry to find out the variable cost of producing cement sold in Mexico and the cement sold in Guatemala in order to make an adjustment for physical differences.[582]

6.916 In this connection, Mexico reiterates that Cementos Progreso made no argument to the effect that Cruz Azul's selling prices were below its production costs and that the preliminary determination of normal value was based on price information; for these reasons, it is unjustified and inappropriate for Guatemala to require Cruz Azul, in the final stage of the investigation, to provide information on production costs, particularly when no arguments were advanced that the sales were not made in the ordinary course of trade.

6.917 The argument whereby Guatemala seeks to justify requiring further cost information in order to make an adjustment for physical differences is false, mistaken and flimsy if we bear in mind what the Ministry decided in its preliminary determination and reproduced in the relevant public notice.

6.918 First, in that notice[583] the Ministry determined that there was no price variation between Type II and Type II Pz cement products, even though Type II has a higher clinker content, wherein lies the higher production costs of the cement, and second, the Ministry decided on the basis of the information supplied to it by the interested parties

---

581 However, in its reply to the supplementary questionnaire, Cruz Azul indicated that any differences between the cement sold in Mexico and that exported to Guatemala were insignificant.

582 First written submission by Guatemala, paras. 311 and 312.

583 Public notice, section VI.B, "Price comparison".

that the product under investigation, Type I (PM) cement, and the cement sold in Mexico (Type II Pz) are like products.[584]

6.919 Consequently, Mexico maintains that there was no justification whatsoever for Guatemala subsequently to submit a request for supplementary information (14 October 1996) from Cruz Azul, information on costs whereby it rejected any differences between the product exported to Guatemala and the product sold in Mexico, and furthermore, that it had no new arguments from Cementos Progreso to warrant the request for information on production costs.[585]

6.920 Despite the fact that Guatemala had no grounds to justify the supplementary request for information on production costs, in its reply to that request Cruz Azul provided the cost information from its plant at Lagunas, Oaxaca, because that was the only plant supplying the Guatemalan market, something it made clear in its reply.[586] However, Guatemala wrongly interprets this by saying that Cruz Azul provided a partial reply.[587]

6.921 Again, it is inconsistent for Guatemala to have tried in the verification visit (on-the-spot investigation) to obtain production cost information at the plant that was not producing the product under investigation and when it had no below-cost sales arguments and did not recognize in its preliminary determination that there were physical differences between the products exported to Guatemala and the one sold in Mexico.

6.922 In short, in the absence of below-cost sales arguments Guatemala did not have grounds to require production cost information from Cruz Azul; Guatemala therefore acted in violation of Article 2.1 and 2.2.

6. *Claims Under Article 6.7 and Paragraphs 2, 3, 7, and 8 of Annex I The Verification Visit to Cruz Azul*

(a) Submissions of Mexico

6.923 **Mexico** argues that the Guatemalan Ministry intended to carry out a verification visit to Cruz Azul in violation of various provisions contained in Annex I to the AD Agreement, for example, by not notifying the Government of Mexico of the participation of non-governmental experts, by verifying information that had *not* been supplied by Cruz Azul, and by the fact that the Ministry intended to conduct the verification visit with the participation of non-governmental experts with an obvious conflict of interest. Mexico claims that the Ministry's actions violate Article 6.7 and paragraphs 2, 3, 7 and 8 of Annex I to the AD Agreement. Its arguments in this regard are as follows:

6.924 It should be noted that, on 14 October 1996, the Ministry requested from Cruz Azul certain information on the original and extended investigation periods covering 1 December 1995 to 31 May 1996. For the reasons and arguments put forward by Cruz Azul in its reply of 30 October 1996 on the impropriety of the Ministry requesting information on a period other than that originally fixed, Cruz Azul did *not* provide the Ministry with information on the extended period.

---

[584] Even though the Ministry did not conduct an examination to determine the likeness of the product exported to Guatemala and the product sold in Mexico.

[585] In any case, to make an adjustment for physical differences, the only thing needed was information on variable production costs and not on production costs as a whole.

[586] See, Submission by Cruz Azul of 30 October 1996, pp.36-37.

[587] First written submission by Guatemala, para. 313.

6.925 Subsequently, on 6 November 1996[588], the Ministry of the Economy notified Cruz Azul of its intention to carry out an on-the-spot verification visit, indicating that it would verify information both for the original investigation period and the extended period.

6.926 On 7 November 1996, Cruz Azul informed the Ministry of its agreement to the verification visit. Following a review and examination of the Ministry's notification, however, on 25 November 1996, Cruz Azul sent an official letter stating the following *inter alia*:

(i) The Ministry could not and should not verify information that had not been supplied by Cruz Azul for the extended period, in accordance with Article 6.7 and paragraph 7 of Annex I to the AD Agreement;

(ii) during the verification visit, the Ministry could not and should not be accompanied by non-governmental experts with an obvious conflict of interest, for which Cruz Azul submitted relevant proof.

6.927 Cruz Azul requested that, prior to the verification visit, the points mentioned above should be clarified so as to permit the smooth conduct of the visit. The Ministry did not respond, however, and did not clarify the essential points raised by Cruz Azul, which is an obvious violation of paragraph 8 of Annex I to the AD Agreement, which provides the following:

> "Enquiries or questions put by the authorities or firms of the exporting Members and essential to a successful on-the-spot investigation should, whenever possible, be answered before the visit is made."

6.928 Even though it had not responded to Cruz Azul, the Ministry wished to carry out the visit to verify information that had *not* been supplied by the exporter, with the participation of non-governmental experts with an obvious conflict of interest and without having obtained the express agreement of Cruz Azul to these terms, in violation of paragraphs 3 and 7 of Annex I to the AD Agreement.

6.929 It should be pointed out that the purpose of the verification visit or on-the-spot investigation is to confirm or verify that the information supplied to the investigating authority by the firm is reliable and accurate, as is clearly stated in Article 6.7 of the AD Agreement, which provides the following:

> "6.7. *In order to verify information provided or to obtain further details*, the authorities may carry out investigations in the territory of other Members as required, provided they obtain the agreement of the firms concerned and notify the representatives of the government of the Member in question, and unless that Member objects to the investigation. *The procedures described in Annex I shall apply to investigations carried out in the territory of other Members*. Subject to the requirement to protect confidential information, the authorities shall make the results of any such investigations available, or shall provide disclosure thereof pursuant to paragraph 9, to the firms to which they pertain and may make such results available to the applicant."

6.930 Paragraph 7 of Annex I confirms the purpose of the visit as set out above by providing that:

> "7. ... the main purpose of the on-the-spot investigation is *to verify information provided or to obtain further details*..." (emphasis added).

[588] Official letter from the Ministry of the Economy of 31 October 1996, which was notified to Cruz Azul on 6 November the same year.

6.931 The intention was to conduct the verification visit on the terms indicated by the Ministry in violation of Article 6.7 and paragraph 7 of Annex I because it would have included a review of information *not* provided by Cruz Azul.

6.932 According to paragraph 7 of Annex I, what the Ministry should have verified in this case was the information provided by Cruz Azul and it should have obtained further details concerning this information, but under no circumstances was the Ministry entitled to require or review other or even different information, as was intended in this case.

6.933 As we have already indicated, the purpose of the visit is solely to verify "information provided" or to "obtain further details" thereon. The AD Agreement does *not* allow the investigation to be extended to matters as fundamental as information *not* provided by the firm. This goes beyond the obtaining of further details, which by definition concern information already provided and *not* new information. A detail cannot go beyond the matter to which it relates.

6.934 On 26 November 1996, the Ministry notified the Government of Mexico of the verification visit to Cruz Azul. This notification did *not*, however, inform Mexico that non-governmental experts would participate in the visit, nor did it explain the exceptional circumstances that justified their participation. This fact was not brought to the attention of Cruz Azul either, so that the Ministry failed to comply with the obligations imposed by paragraph 2 of Annex I to the AD Agreement.

6.935 The above arguments and reasoning show that the Ministry of the Economy failed to comply with a number of obligations laid down in the AD Agreement, and more precisely the Ministry's action violated Article 6.7 and paragraphs 2, 3, 7 and 8 of Annex I to the AD Agreement.

(b) Response of Guatemala

6.936 **Guatemala** makes the following arguments in response to Mexico's claims regarding alleged violations of the AD Agreement arising from the verification visit:

6.937 According to Mexico, Guatemala violated Article 6.7 and paragraphs 2, 3, 7 and 8 of Annex I by not notifying the Government of Mexico of the participation of non-governmental experts, by verifying information relating to Cruz Azul's production costs, which the latter had not supplied, and by trying to conduct the verification visit with non-governmental experts subject to conflicts of interest. These allegations are entirely without foundation.

6.938 *Firstly*, Mexico argues that Guatemala violated Article 6.7 and paragraphs 7 and 8 of Annex I by trying to verify information that did not form part of Cruz Azul's reply to the questionnaire. However, Article 6.7 is silent on the permissible scope of the verification and paragraphs 7 and 8 of Annex I do not support the Mexican argument.

6.939 The basis of the Mexican argument is that the Ministry sought to verify information which Cruz Azul had not supplied. Mexico omits to tell the panel that the Ministry had requested the information in question and Cruz Azul had failed to supply it. Specifically, the Ministry requested information from Cruz Azul on its production costs in Section C2, Part 3.5 of the original questionnaire dated 26 January 1996 and in Section 2(f) of the supplementary questionnaire dated 14 October. In its reply to the original questionnaire, Cruz Azul failed to supply information on its production costs. In its reply to the supplementary questionnaire, Cruz Azul failed to supply cost information for its two plants. Cruz Azul also refused to provide any information on sales during the period from 1 December 1995 to 30 May 1996, as requested in Section 2(g) of the supplementary questionnaire.

6.940 Cruz Azul's reluctance to supply complete information on its production costs at both plants prevented the Ministry from determining whether Cruz Azul's sales in Mexico were being made at below cost and from calculating adjustments for differences in physical characteristics between the product sold in Mexico (Type II PZ) and the product exported to Guatemala (Type I PM). Cruz Azul's reluctance to supply information on its sales during the period from 1 December 1995 to 30 May 1996 prevented the Ministry from calculating a final margin of dumping based on the latest information.

6.941 Cruz Azul's failure to provide the information requested would have justified the Ministry in cancelling the verification visit and proceeding on the basis of the "facts available", in accordance with Article 6.8. Instead, acting in good faith and allowing Cruz Azul a last chance, the Ministry decided to obtain the missing information during the verification visit. Paragraph 7 of Annex I expressly stipulates that prior to the visit the investigation authority should "advise the firms concerned of the general nature of the information to be verified and *of any further information which needs to be provided*".[589]

6.942 Mexico also claims that the Ministry never responded to the letter from Cruz Azul dated 25 November 1996 in which Cruz Azul set out its conditions for accepting the verification visit. However, in accordance with paragraph 8 of Annex I, the Ministry replied on 26 November 1996 and, as Cruz Azul requested, clarified its conditions for the verification visit.

6.943 Despite the fact that the Ministry acted in good faith and went as far as it could to accommodate Cruz Azul, Cruz Azul refused to give the Ministry an opportunity to verify the information it had in its possession. The result was that since that it was not possible to verify the information in accordance with paragraph 3 of Annex II and since Cruz Azul did not supply other necessary information in accordance with Article 6.8, the Ministry used the facts available for calculating the margin of dumping.

6.944 *Secondly*, the Ministry notified the Government of Mexico of its intention to be accompanied by non-governmental experts. In a letter dated 26 November 1996, the Ministry advised Cruz Azul and SECOFI who the non-governmental experts participating in the verification would be. The letter was addressed to Cruz Azul and indicated that a copy had been forwarded to SECOFI. In a document attached to the letter, the Ministry informed Cruz Azul that the verification would take place from 3-6 December and stated that the purpose of the visit would be to verify the information already provided and to obtain further information, that the period to be verified was from 1 June 1995 to 31 May 1996, that it was for the Ministry, as the investigating authority, to decide whether non-governmental experts should be included and that if Cruz Azul refused to cooperate the Ministry would be obliged to use the facts available. In the first paragraph of its letter to the Ministry dated 2 December 1996, Mexico acknowledged having received this notification from the Ministry on 26 November.

6.945 In addition, under the Anti-Dumping Agreement, Guatemala was not obliged to explain the exceptional circumstances which had made necessary the participation of non-governmental experts. Article 6.2 does not refer to non-governmental experts. Paragraph 2 of Annex I simply requires that the exporting firm and its government should be informed of the intention to include non-governmental experts in the investigating team. This provision does not oblige the investigating authority to inform the exporting country of the exceptional circumstances that justify the use of non-governmental experts nor does it require the exporting member to have agreed to the use of such experts. In any case, Mexico knew that this was Guatemala's first anti-dumping investigation. The exceptional circumstance that made it necessary for Guatemala to resort to the assistance of anti-dumping experts was the fact that the Ministry had never previously carried out a verifi-

[589] Anti-Dumping Agreement, Annex I, para. 7 (emphasis added).

cation visit. The experts were engaged to assist the Ministry to carry out the verification visit at Cruz Azul and to coach the Ministry on how to conduct future verifications.

6.946 With regard to Mexico's contention that the non-governmental experts had a conflict of interest, in its letter dated 26 November 1996 the Ministry specifically pointed out that the persons who would act as non-governmental experts had signed an agreement to protect the confidentiality of any information to which they had access. Moreover, the experts had signed confidentiality agreements applicable to administrative reviews connected with the United States anti-dumping order concerning cement from Mexico, in which they undertook not to divulge any information obtained in those proceedings. Consequently, in carrying out the verification at Cruz Azul, the non-governmental experts would not have been able to use any outside information obtained in the United States anti-dumping case.

6.947 Furthermore, Cruz Azul was not an interested party in any of the administrative reviews in which the non-governmental experts participated on behalf of the United States cement producers. Guatemala notes that Cruz Azul has made no claim to the effect that the United States clients of the non-governmental experts had any interest in the results of the anti-dumping proceeding in Guatemala. The Mexican claims regarding the existence of a conflict of interest are therefore without foundation, and in any event the alleged conflict was irrelevant since Cruz Azul declined to allow the Ministry to verify certain categories of information, with or without non-governmental experts.

6.948 Thus, in endeavouring to carry out the verification visit, Guatemala complied with Article 6.7 and paragraphs 2, 3, 7 and 8 of Annex I.

(c) Rebuttal of Mexico

6.949 **Mexico** makes the argument that Guatemala has not disproved its violation of Article 6.7 and paragraphs 2, 3, 7 and 8 of Annex I to the AD Agreement in respect of the verification visit. It makes the following rebuttal arguments:

6.950 Guatemala claims that Cruz Azul's reluctance to supply full information on production costs at both plants prevented the Ministry from determining whether Cruz Azul's sales in Mexico were being made at below cost and from calculating adjustments for differences in physical characteristics between the product sold in Mexico (Type II Pz) and the product exported to Guatemala (Type I PM).[590]

6.951 In this connection, Mexico reiterates that Cementos Progreso has not advanced any argument that Cruz Azul's sales on Mexico's domestic market were being made at below production cost and that, although the Ministry did not conduct an examination to determine the likeness of the product exported to Guatemala and the product sold in Mexico, the Ministry, in both its preliminary and final determinations, decided that they were like products. Hence, Guatemala's argument is completely false and inconsistent, because the Ministry determined the likeness of the products and rejected Cruz Azul's argument.[591]

6.952 Guatemala says that, although Cruz Azul's reply to the additional request was inadequate, which would have justified cancelling the verification and proceeding on the

[590] *Ibid.*, para. 318.

[591] The public notice of conclusion of the investigation, in the section on "Considerations" Subsection B ("Determination of dumping"), states that according to the exporting firm, the difference between the cement sold on the Mexican market and that exported to Guatemala was not significant. Conversely, Cruz Azul, in its submission of 30 October 1996, p.19, accompanied by an Annex II, indicated the differences between the two products.

basis of the facts available, the Ministry, acting in good faith, allowed Cruz Azul a last chance and, on the basis of paragraph 7 of Annex I, indicated to the exporting firm the further information which needed to be provided.[592]

6.953 As already stated, the Ministry had the production cost information for the Cruz Azul plant at Lagunas, Oaxaca, where the product exported to Guatemala was manufactured and the verification should have been made in connection with this information, pursuant to Annex I, particularly, paragraph 7 of the Annex.

6.954 In Mexico's opinion, which may be confirmed by the anti-dumping practices of other Members, the information which can be verified is that supplied by the interested parties, and before the verification takes place. In fact, no Member agrees that an interested party should supply it with further information which was not provided within the established time-limits; in other words, the authority would in no way receive further information at the verification. The simple and logical reason is that this would be information submitted outside the prescribed time-period.[593]

6.955 Furthermore, when paragraph 7 of Annex I says that it should be standard practice to advise the firms concerned of the further information which needs to be provided, in Mexico's view it is unquestionably referring to the accounting information and documentation that the party concerned used in order to back up the veracity of the information it has supplied to the investigating authority before the verification is carried out.

6.956 As part of its argument, Mexico reiterates that the first part of the paragraph in question, like Article 6.7, specifies that the main purpose of the on-the-spot investigation is to verify the information received by the authority, and when paragraph 7 of Annex I speaks of further information which needs to be provided it is understood that it will be provided to the authority in order to demonstrate the veracity of the information already supplied and even with further details on it, regardless of the fact that, during the verification and in light of the information obtained, more details will be requested.

6.957 It is apparent from the foregoing that Guatemala's interpretation of paragraph 7 of Annex I is wrong and impermissible and that the Ministry's action regarding the so-called verification was carried out in breach of the terms of Article 6.7 and paragraph 7 of Annex I of the AD Agreement.

(i) Essential questions

6.958 With reference to the essential questions raised by Cruz Azul regarding the verification, which had to be resolved in order for the exporting firm to give its express consent and for the verification to be conducted, Guatemala states that on 26 November 1996, it replied to the letter by Cruz Azul, a document submitted as Annex GUA-57.[594]

6.959 In this connection, it should be noted that, while the document was indeed prepared by a Ministry official and addressed to Cruz Azul, this is not apparent from the document nor does any attached document demonstrate that it was sent and delivered to Cruz Azul. Secondly, a perusal of the document does not show that its purpose was to reply to Cruz Azul's letter of 25 November 1996. In fact, it simply indicates which persons would be at the verification; in other words, its aim was not to reply to the essential questions raised by Cruz Azul, under the terms of paragraph 8 of Annex I.

---

592 First written submission by Guatemala, para. 319.

593 In fact, if the authority accepted further information that was not reported within the specified time-limits, it would be an incentive for the parties not to reply to the questionnaires or to do so inadequately.

594 First written submission by Guatemala, para. 320.

6.960 In addition, document GUA-57 does not make it clear to Cruz Azul what it wanted, let alone request it to give its express consent for a verification to be conducted in accordance with Article 6.7 and paragraph 3 of Annex I. This is obvious and is corroborated by the facts, because at no time did the Ministry seek to obtain Cruz Azul's express consent; what it did do was to turn up at the exporting firm's plant in an attempt to conduct the verification.

6.961 From the foregoing it is plain to see that, by not replying to Cruz Azul on the essential questions raised and not obtaining the exporting firm's express consent before finally arranging the verification, Guatemala acted in violation of Article 6.7 and paragraphs 3 and 8 of Annex I.

(ii) Notification to the Government of Mexico

6.962 As to notifying the Government of Mexico, Guatemala says that, in a letter dated 26 November 1996, it notified Mexico of its intention for the Ministry to be accompanied by non-governmental experts. It added that the letter was addressed to Cruz Azul and the letter said that a copy had been sent to SECOFI.[595] To demonstrate this, Guatemala submitted the letter in question as Annex GUA-57.

6.963 It should be pointed out that it *cannot* be inferred from the letter that it was sent by Guatemala and received by the Government of Mexico; in other words, it is not enough for the letter to state that a copy has been forwarded to the Secretary for Trade and Industrial Development to prove that Guatemala did actually send it and that the Government of Mexico did receive it. In this regard, Mexico maintains that it did *not* receive a copy of the letter by the Ministry identified as GUA-57, dated 26 November 1996.

6.964 Guatemala also states that in a document attached to the letter (GUA-57), the Ministry advised Cruz Azul of a number of matters pertaining to the verification.[596] It should be noted that *no* document was attached to the letter submitted as GUA-57.

6.965 In addition, there is nothing in the letter or in any attached document to show that it was delivered to Cruz Azul and still less that the Government of Mexico received a copy of it. On the other hand, the Government of Mexico did receive the letter submitted as Annex MEXICO-27, also dated 26 November 1996 and there is a record that it was actually sent by Guatemala and received by the Government of Mexico; this is demonstrated both by the heading of the attached fax and the fact that it records the date and time of receipt at the SECOFI offices.[597]

6.966 Accordingly, when Mexico affirms in its submission of 2 December 1996 (MEXICO-29) that it received the letter dated 26 November 1996, it is referring to Mexico's exhibit, MEXICO-27, and not as Guatemala falsely implies by exhibiting Annex GUA-57.

6.967 Again, the letter that was indeed received by the Government of Mexico, identified as MEXICO-27, fails to mention that the verification would be attended by non-governmental experts; in other words, by not reporting the participation of those experts, Guatemala violated paragraph 2 of Annex I.

---

[595] *Ibid.*, para. 322.

[596] *Ibid.*, para. 332.

[597] The documents demonstrating that they were received by Cruz Azul include Annex MEXICO-24 and the note of 6 February 1997 stating that the representative of Cruz Azul received a copy of the record of the public hearing.

(iii) Participation of non-governmental experts

6.968 Guatemala asserts that it is for the investigating authority to decide whether non-governmental experts should be included and that paragraph 2 of Annex I does not require the authorities to inform the exporting country of exceptional circumstances that justify the use of non-governmental experts, nor does it require any consent from the exporting Member to use such experts.[598]

6.969 Mexico does not argue whether or not it was for Guatemala to decide on the participation of non-governmental experts or to obtain the consent of the exporting Member to use such experts. What is does claim is that, in its notification to the Government of Mexico, Guatemala did *not* indicate the participation of non-governmental experts in the verification. In this regard, paragraph 2 of Annex I specifies that the authorities of the exporting Member should be informed of the participation of non-governmental experts, but this did not happen. Therefore, Guatemala violated paragraph 2 of Annex I.

6.970 Furthermore, in the matter of the conflict of interest of the non-governmental experts, Guatemala contends that the persons who would act as such experts had signed an agreement to protect the confidentiality of any information to which they had access, that the same had been done in the proceedings in which they had participated in the United States and that, in any event, Cruz Azul had not been an interested party in them.[599]

6.971 Mexico's argument concerning the obvious conflict of interest of the non-governmental experts lies in the fact that two of them, Daniel Joseph Cannistra and Joanna Schlesinger, were advisors to United States cement firms that called for investigations against Mexican cement exporters, and that those persons were still advisors to the firms in question when the Ministry sought to conduct the verification. So, with the participation of those non-governmental experts, the evaluation of the Cruz Azul information could prove flawed or biased.[600]

6.972 In a letter dated 25 November 1996, Cruz Azul informed the Ministry of the conflict of interest of the non-governmental experts the Ministry had appointed. To Cruz Azul's arguments the Ministry simply replied that the non-governmental experts had signed confidentiality undertakings[601]; in other words, the Ministry did not resolve the essential issue raised by Cruz Azul that the experts' work could prove biased towards Mexican cement exporting firms, including Cruz Azul. Nor did the Ministry seek or try to obtain the express consent of Cruz Azul to conduct the verification, as required under paragraph 3 of Annex I.

6.973 Moreover, the confidentiality agreements in question were not shown either to Cruz Azul or to the Government of Mexico, as can be seen from documents such as MEXICO-24, or in the communication sent to the Mexican Government, Annex

---

598 First written submission by Guatemala, para. 323.

599 *Ibid.*, paras. 324-325.

600 In addition, the document whereby the Ministry sought to conduct the verification evidenced the attitude of the non-governmental experts when Mr. Daniel Joseph Cannistra said that opposition to him participating in the verification would be penalized by "using the adverse information available".

601 It should be noted that Guatemala has not submitted anything to demonstrate that the communication identified as GUA-57 was notified to Cruz Azul and still less to the Government of Mexico. Nor can it be inferred from the content of the communication that the purpose was to resolve the issue of the possible bias of the non-governmental experts in the verification, nor that it was intended as a reply to Cruz Azul's letter of 25 November 1996.

MEXICO-27, nor were they attached to the letter Guatemala submitted as GUA-57 nor produced when the Ministry sought to conduct the verification at the Cruz Azul plant.

6.974 Consequently, in the view of Cruz Azul's arguments about the participation of non-governmental experts, an unbiased and objective authority should, pursuant to the terms of paragraphs 3 and 8 of Annex I, have resolved the essential issue raised by Cruz Azul and have obtained the exporter's express consent before making final arrangements for the verification. However, Guatemala did not resolve the essential issues raised by Cruz Azul, nor did it obtain the firm's express consent, for which reason the Ministry, in endeavouring to conduct the verification in the way it did, acted in violation of paragraphs 2 and 3 of Annex I.

6.975 Lastly, in view of the facts and the arguments adduced in connection with the failure to notify the Government of Mexico about the participation of non-governmental experts, about additional information not reported to the authority that the authority was seeking to verify, by not resolving the essential questions raised by Cruz Azul and not obtaining Cruz Azul's express consent to conduct the verification and, as a result of the way and the terms in which Guatemala tried to conduct it, Guatemala acted in violation of Article 6.7 and paragraphs 2, 3, 7 and 8 of Annex I of the Anti-Dumping Agreement.

7. *Claims Under Articles 6.1, 6.2, 6.8 and Paragraphs 5 and 6 of Annex II - Rejection of Technical Accounting Evidence on Normal Value and Export Price*

(a) Submissions of Mexico

6.976 **Mexico** claims that the Guatemalan Ministry rejected the technical accounting evidence submitted by Cruz Azul on the normal value and the export price during the investigation period fixed at the initiation of the investigation, by so doing the Guatemalan Ministry resultingly violated Article 6.1, 6.2 and 6.8 and paragraphs 5 and 6 of Annex II to the AD Agreement. Mexico's arguments in this regard are as follows:

6.977 Article 6.1, 6.2 and 6.8 provide the following in this respect:

> "6.1. All interested parties in an anti-dumping investigation shall be given ... ample opportunity to present in writing all evidence which they consider relevant in respect of the investigation in question.
>
> 6.2 Throughout the anti-dumping investigation all interested parties shall have a full opportunity for the defence of their interests. ...
>
> 6.8 In cases in which any interested party refuses access to, or otherwise does not provide, necessary information within a reasonable period or significantly impedes the investigation, preliminary and final determinations, affirmative or negative, may be made on the basis of the facts available. The provisions of Annex II shall be observed in the application of this paragraph."

6.978 On 18 November 1996, Cruz Azul provided the Ministry with technical accounting evidence so that the investigating authority would have objective and reasonable information on the normal value and the export price in order to calculate the alleged dumping margin for transactions during the investigation period fixed at the initiation of the investigation, namely 1 June to 30 November 1995.

6.979 In its letter, Cruz Azul explained the nature of the technical accounting evidence and its importance for the investigation, as well as the objectiveness and impartiality with which it had been prepared because its formulation had been entrusted to an external firm of accountants specialized in the field and independent of Cruz Azul. Nevertheless, on 15

January 1997, in its technical report on the final outcome of the anti-dumping investigation[602], the Ministry decided:

> "... that the technical evidence submitted by the exporter on 18 December 1996 (confidential information) could not replace verification of the information by the Guatemalan investigating authority, as required by Article 6.6 of the Anti-Dumping Code (*sic*)."

6.980 As can be seen, the Ministry rejected the evidence without reviewing its content or its relevance, thus violating Article 6.1 and 6.2 because the evidence was provided during the procedure and Cruz Azul supplied it for the purpose of defending its interests. It is clear that the Ministry did *not* give Cruz Azul ample and full opportunity to defend its interests, in violation of Article 6.1 and 6.2 of the AD Agreement.

6.981 It should be pointed out that, in view of the cancellation of the verification visit and in pursuance of its right of defence, Cruz Azul submitted the technical accounting evidence in conformity with Article 6.8 and paragraphs 5 and 6 of Annex II to the AD Agreement, which provide the following:

> "5. Even though the information provided may not be ideal in all respects, this should not justify the authorities from disregarding it, provided the interested party has acted to the best of its ability.
>
> 6. If evidence or information is not accepted, the supplying party should be informed forthwith of the reasons therefor, and should have an opportunity to provide further explanations within a reasonable period, due account being taken of the time-limits of the investigation. If the explanations are considered by the authorities as not being satisfactory, the reasons for the rejection of such evidence or information should be given in any published determinations."

6.982 Indeed, even supposing that the information in the technical accounting evidence was not ideal in all respects, this fact should not be sufficient to allow the Ministry to reject it, so that in doing so it violated paragraph 5 of Annex II.

6.983 If there had been justification for rejecting the evidence, the Minister should have informed Cruz Azul in due time during the procedure of the reasons why it did not accept the evidence. This would have enabled Cruz Azul to put forward explanations and arguments to defend its interests within a reasonable period, as called for by paragraph 6 of Annex II. The Ministry, however, denied Cruz Azul an opportunity to exercise its right of defence, thereby violating paragraph 6 of Annex II of the AD Agreement.

6.984 From the above arguments it is quite obvious that the Ministry's action in rejecting the technical accounting evidence submitted by Cruz Azul was inconsistent with Article 6.1, 6.2 and 6.8 and paragraphs 5 and 6 of Annex II to the AD Agreement.

(b) Response of Guatemala

6.985 **Guatemala** makes the following response to Mexico's claims under Articles 6.1, 6.2, 6.8 and paragraphs 5 and 6 of Annex II to the AD Agreement:

6.986 There is no basis for Mexico's contention that Guatemala acted in violation of Articles 6.1, 6.2 and 6.8 and paragraphs 5 and 6 of Annex II by rejecting the "self-verification" report that Cruz Azul submitted after preventing the Ministry from carrying out a verification visit.

---

[602] "Technical report on the outcome of the anti-dumping investigation into imports of cement from Mexico", preambular section, part "B. Determination of dumping", para. 6, page 16.

6.987 Article 6.8 of the Anti-Dumping Agreement reads as follows:

> "In cases in which any interested party refuses access to, or otherwise does not provide, necessary information within a reasonable period or significantly impedes the investigation, preliminary and final determinations, affirmative or negative, may be made on the basis of the facts available. The provisions of Annex II shall be observed in the application of this paragraph."

6.988 According to paragraph 3 of Annex II:

> "All information which is *verifiable, which is appropriately submitted* so that it can be used in the investigation without undue difficulties, which is *supplied in a timely fashion* ... should be taken into account when determinations are made." (Emphasis added)

6.989 Cruz Azul's "technical accounting evidence" was not verifiable, was not appropriately introduced into the investigation and was not supplied in a timely fashion, as required by paragraph 3 of Annex II. According to the Mexican submission, Cruz Azul supplied the Ministry with the "technical accounting evidence" on 18 November 1996.[603] However, the report was not prepared until 6 December 1996 and was not received by the Ministry until 18 December 1996, after the planned verification visit and the day before the public hearing.

6.990 Nor was the technical accounting evidence "appropriately submitted". It was neither requested by the Ministry nor supplied in a timely fashion. It was submitted one day before the date on which the parties were to present their final arguments at the public hearing. In its notice of 6 December, the Ministry's Directorate of Economic Integration had already informed Cruz Azul that the final determination would be made on the basis of the facts available in the file on that date. The submission by Cruz Azul on the eve of the cut-off date of 19 December for the presentation of final arguments effectively denied other interested parties the opportunity to express their views on the new factual information. Under the Anti-Dumping Agreement, the appropriate and timely juncture for the presentation of evidence in support of the information submitted by Cruz Azul would have been during the verification visit which the Ministry was prevented from carrying out. Consequently, pursuant to Article 6.8 and paragraph 3 of Annex II, the Ministry's decision not to accept the "technical accounting evidence" of Cruz Azul was perfectly appropriate.

6.991 Paragraph 6 of Annex II stipulates that:

> "If evidence or information is not accepted, the supplying party should be informed forthwith of the reasons therefor, and should have an opportunity to provide further explanations within a reasonable period, *due account being taken of the time-limits of the investigation*. If the explanations are considered by the authorities as not being satisfactory, the reasons for rejection of such evidence or information should be given in any published determinations."[604]

6.992 Because the submission by Cruz Azul was presented the day before the public hearing and in view of the "time-limits of the investigation", the Ministry was unable to give the reasons for its rejection, as required by paragraph 6 of Annex II. In its first written submission Mexico notes that during the hearing on 19 December Cruz Azul "... explained the nature of the technical accounting evidence and its importance for the investi-

---

603 Mexico's first written submission, para. 395.

604 Anti-Dumping Agreement, Annex II, para. 6 (emphasis added).

gation, ...".[605] The explanations provided by Cruz Azul were not considered satisfactory by the Ministry. Consequently, pursuant to paragraph 6 of Annex II, the Ministry set out the grounds for its rejection of the explanations by Cruz Azul in the final determination of 17 January 1997.

6.993 In the words of the duly published notice:

> "... this Ministry considers that the information supplied by the exporting firm cannot be taken into account for the calculation of the normal value of the product under investigation, in view of the fact that the information could not be verified and that the technical evidence submitted by the exporting firm on 18 December 1996 (confidential information) cannot be a substitute for such verification of the information by the Guatemalan investigating authority, as indicated in Article 6.6 of the Anti-Dumping Agreement".

6.994 These were the grounds on which the Ministry rejected this evidence. The Ministry did not allow Cruz Azul to take on the role of investigating authority and did not allow Cruz Azul to dictate to it how the verification was to be carried out. When the Ministry was prevented from carrying out the verification, it did not accept the self-verification report by Cruz Azul. All these actions were perfectly appropriate. It is absurd for Mexico to suggest that Cruz Azul had the right to tell the Ministry how to conduct the investigation.

6.995 The disregarding of the "technical accounting evidence" is in keeping with Articles 6.1 and 6.2 of the Anti-Dumping Agreement. In accordance with the terms of Article 6.1, Cruz Azul was given "ample opportunity" throughout the investigation, to present evidence which it considered relevant to the investigation. As provided by Article 6.2, Cruz Azul was given "a full opportunity for the defence of its interests".[606] Consequently, the Panel should reject this claim.

(c) Rebuttal of Mexico

6.996 **Mexico** maintains that Guatemala has not disproved its violation of Article 6.1, 6.2 and 6.8 and paragraphs 5 and 6 of Annex I of the AD Agreement. It makes the following rebuttal of Guatemala's arguments:

6.997 Guatemala claims that the Cruz Azul's technical accounting evidence was not verifiable, was not appropriately introduced into the investigation and was not supplied in a timely fashion, as required by paragraph 3 of Annex II.[607] On this point Mexico reiterates that the technical accounting evidence was appropriately submitted by Cruz Azul to the Ministry on 18 December 1996[608], one day before the hearing, within the time-limits established for the investigation, for which reason the evidence was submitted on time, in the course of the proceedings and in order for the Ministry to have true, accurate and relevant information on Cruz Azul's domestic sales and export sales during the investigation period and for it to be considered by the Ministry in its final determination.

6.998 The technical accounting evidence was submitted appropriately and on time, because the Ministry, in the decision of 6 December 1996, said that the hearing would be held on 19 December 1996 and that any request made after that date would not be taken

---

[605] Mexico's first written submission, para. 89.

[606] Guatemala invites the panel to take note that, according to Article 6.6 of the Anti-Dumping Agreement, "the authorities shall during the course of an investigation satisfy themselves as to the accuracy of the information supplied by interested parties upon which their findings are based".

[607] First written submission by Guatemala, para. 329.

[608] First written submission by Mexico, para. 52.

into account by the Ministry in its technical study on the result of the investigation. Accordingly, before the hearing the interested parties could submit requests or documents, as did Cruz Azul in this case with the technical accounting evidence. Guatemala's decision to reject the technical accounting evidence was unwarranted.

6.999 Moreover, Guatemala affirms that, since the technical accounting evidence was submitted on the day before the hearing and because of the time-limits established for the investigation, the Ministry was unable to give the reasons for its rejection, as required by paragraph 6 of Annex II.[609] The Ministry could have reported on the rejection of the technical evidence during the hearing that was held the day after the technical accounting evidence was submitted, or before the final determination was issued, in other words, before 17 January 1997.

6.1000 Since the technical accounting evidence was presented on time and in the course of the investigation, in no way is it possible to accept Guatemala's contention that it was unable to provide the reasons for its rejection. Clearly, because of the Ministry's omissions in not informing Cruz Azul of the reasons for not accepting the technical accounting evidence and in not granting the exporter an opportunity to provide further explanations within a reasonable period, Guatemala violated paragraph 6 of Annex II.

8. *Claims Under Articles 6.1, 6.2, 6.3, and 6.5 - Acceptance by the Guatemalan Authority of Confidential Information*

(a) Submissions of Mexico

6.1001 **Mexico** argues that several times during the investigation Guatemala failed to comply with its obligations on confidential information as mandated by Articles 6.1, 6.2, 6.3 and 6.5 of the AD Agreement. Mexico highlights the following facts and makes the following submissions in support of its claims:

6.1002 Firstly, the on-the-spot investigation at Cementos Progreso. As can be seen from the relevant "Report on the Verification Visit", Cementos Progreso requested that the following information be considered confidential:

(a) Technical information on the firm's principal equipment;

(b) plans for a new mill;

(c) work sheets used to prepare information submitted to the Ministry of the Economy;

(d) list of customers with addresses and volume of sales made;

(e) expansion plans for the plant, *Proyect 9636*;

(f) contract between Cementos Progreso and F.L. Smith & Co.;

(g) tables used to prepare questionnaires and reconcile the cost structure calculated for production of grey Portland cement with the accounting statements.

6.1003 Cementos Progreso requested that this information be considered confidential, but at no time did it justify its request nor furnish non-confidential summaries thereof.

6.1004 In its letter of 13 November 1996, Cruz Azul asked for the public version of all the information supplied by Cementos Progreso, but the Ministry never furnished the non-confidential summaries of the confidential information provided.

[609] First written submission by Guatemala, para. 332.

6.1005 In addition, Cruz Azul brought this to the attention of the Ministry in its letter dated 27 December 1996[610], but the authority did not require Cementos Progreso to comply with this provision and refused to agree not to take account of this information.[611]
6.1006 Secondly, as already indicated[612], at the public hearing of 19 December 1996, the Government of Guatemala refused to give Cruz Azul the document containing Cementos Progreso's final pleadings. Cruz Azul asked for access to the document at that time and the Ministry of the Economy refused, arguing that "the copy would be transmitted when the necessary notifications were made".
6.1007 Thirdly, see the facts mentioned in sections V.A.1(e) and (f), V.A.2, V.B, V.C.3, V.D.1, 2, 4, 9 and 10, E.2 and 4.
6.1008 Lastly, it will be recalled that Cruz Azul requested two certified copies of all the documents, but these were not transmitted at any time during the investigation.
6.1009 Mexico further argues that Guatemala violated the provisions of the AD Agreement regarding confidential information
6.1010 Article 6.1, 6.2 and 6.5 of the AD Agreement provide the following:

> "6.1. All interested parties in an anti-dumping investigation shall be given notice of the information which the authorities require and ample opportunity to present in writing all evidence which they consider relevant in respect of the investigation in question.
>
> 6.2. Throughout the anti-dumping investigation all interested parties shall have a full opportunity for the defence of their interests. To this end, the authorities shall, on request, provide opportunities for all interested parties to meet those parties with adverse interests, so that opposing views may be presented and rebuttal arguments offered. Provision of such opportunities must take account of the need to preserve confidentiality and of the convenience to the parties. There shall be no obligation on any party to attend a meeting, and failure to do so shall not be prejudicial to that party's case. Interested parties shall also have the right, on justification, to present other information orally.
>
> 6.3 Oral information provided under paragraph 2 shall be taken into account by the authorities only in so far as it is subsequently reproduced in writing and made available to other interested parties, as provided for in subparagraph 1.2.
>
> 6.5 Any information which is by nature confidential (for example, because its disclosure would be of significant competitive advantage to a competitor or because its disclosure would have a significantly adverse effect upon a person supplying the information or upon a person from whom that person acquired the information), or which is provided on a confidential basis by parties to an investigation shall, upon good cause shown, be treated as such by the authorities. Such information shall not be disclosed without specific permission of the party submitting it.

---

610 It should be noted *inter alia* that Cruz Azul specifically requested the investigating authority not to take this information into account, as provided in Article 6.5.2 of the AD Agreement.

611 It should be noted that, when responding to the first questionnaire from the investigating authority, Cruz Azul supplied some confidential information and indicated that Annex I to these replies was the relevant non-confidential summary. As can be seen from the preliminary determination, however, the Ministry did not accept this and requested the "non-confidential" version.

612 See Section V.D.2 of this written submission.

6.5.1 The authorities shall require interested parties providing confidential information to furnish non-confidential summaries thereof. These summaries shall be in sufficient detail to permit a reasonable understanding of the substance of the information submitted in confidence. In exceptional circumstances, such parties may indicate that such information is not susceptible of summary. In such exceptional circumstances, a statement of the reasons why summarization is not possible must be provided.

6.5.2. If the authorities find that a request for confidentiality is not warranted and if the supplier of the information is either unwilling to make the information public or to authorize its disclosure in generalized or summary form, the authorities may disregard such information unless it can be demonstrated to their satisfaction from appropriate sources that the information is correct."

6.1011 The facts set out in the first paragraph of this section show the following violations of the AD Agreement:

6.1012 Firstly (on-the-spot investigation at Cementos Progreso):

(a) By accepting Cementos Progreso's request that the information mentioned should be considered confidential, without justification for such a request, Guatemala violated Article 6.5.2 of the AD Agreement;

(b) irrespective of the above, by not requiring Cementos Progreso to furnish non-confidential summaries of the information or the reasons why it could not be made public, Guatemala violated in particular Article 6.4, 6.5, subparagraphs 6.5.1. and 6.5.2;

(c) by not accepting Cruz Azul's request that a non-confidential summary be required or that the information not be taken into account, Guatemala violated Article 6.1, 6.2 and 6.4 of the AD Agreement;

(d) alternatively, by accepting a verbal justification that the information in the letter be considered confidential, Guatemala acted in violation of Article 6.1, 6.2, 6.3 and 6.4.

6.1013 Secondly (public hearing of 19 December 1996):

(a) By not allowing proper access to the information submitted by Cementos Progreso at this hearing, Guatemala violated Article 6.1, 6.2 and 6.4;

(b) by denying access to this information, Guatemala on its own initiative granted the documentation confidential status, in violation of Article 6.5 and its subparagraphs 6.5.1 and 6.5.2;

(c) alternatively, by accepting a verbal justification that the information contained in the pleadings at the hearing should be considered confidential, Guatemala acted in violation of Article 6.1, 6.2, 6.3 and 6.4.

6.1014 Thirdly (the facts mentioned in section V.A.1(c) and (f), V.A.2, V.B, V.C.3, V.D.1, 2, 4, 9 and 10, E.2 and 4)

6.1015 All these instances concern misleading information by Cementos Progreso, impairing the rights of Cruz Azul. Each fact and each violation of specific Articles is mentioned in the corresponding section. Nevertheless, all these violations imply the following breaches in relation to confidentiality.

6.1016 By failing to fulfil these provisions, Guatemala:

(a) On its own initiative gave these documents confidential status, thereby violating Article 6.5 and its subparagraphs 6.5.1 and 6.5.2;

(b) alternatively, by accepting a verbal justification that the information contained in the application or any evidence submitted by Cementos Progreso and to be found in the file should be considered confidential, Guatemala acted in violation of Article 6.1, 6.2, 6.3 and 6.4.

6.1017 Guatemala was obliged to provide Cruz Azul promptly with all the investigation documents, with the exception of the provisions on confidentiality. It decided not to do this, however, and also decided not to respect the disciplines concerning confidential business information. If it had done so, Cruz Azul would have had ample opportunity to present all relevant evidence in writing and would have had full opportunity to defend its interests, therefore, these acts or omissions by Guatemala nullify or impair the benefits accruing to Mexico under the AD Agreement.

(b) Response of Guatemala

6.1018 **Guatemala** responds to Mexico's arguments regarding confidential information as follows:

6.1019 Contrary to Mexico's allegations, in its handling of the information supplied by Cementos Progreso Guatemala complied with Articles 6.5.1 and 6.5.2. Specifically, Mexico claims that the Ministry did not require Cementos Progreso to provide public versions of certain documents which the Ministry had obtained from Cementos Progreso during the verification visit on 27-29 November 1996. An examination of the information set out in Mexico's first written submission reveals that the documents obtained during the verification visit were clearly of a confidential nature and could not be summarized in accordance with Article 6.5.1. In fact, Guatemala understands that in other countries it is common practice for the investigating authorities not to require public versions of confidential documents obtained during verification visits.

6.1020 Furthermore, contrary to Mexico's allegation in paragraph 405 of its first written submission, Cruz Azul did not ask for the public version of this information in its letter of 13 November 1996. In that letter, Cruz Azul requested the public versions of the documents provided on 30 October. Mexico does not claim that Cruz Azul did not receive these public versions. Clearly, on 13 November Cruz Azul could not have requested public versions of documents which the Ministry was not to obtain until 27 November.

6.1021 In reply to Mexico's allegations to the effect that the Ministry failed to provide Cruz Azul with the public version of Cementos Progreso's submission to the public hearing on 19 December 1996 and failed to supply Cruz Azul with certified copies of all the documents in the administrative file, Guatemala refers to its replies to these same allegations in paragraphs 292-298 above and respectfully requests that they be incorporated by reference.

(c) Rebuttal of Mexico

6.1022 **Mexico** proved Guatemala's violation of Article 6.1, 6.2, 6.3, 6.5, 6.5.1 and 6.5.2 of the AD Agreement[613] and Guatemala did not rebut various arguments, including the following:

1. On 27 December 1996 Cruz Azul asked the Ministry of the Economy not to take account of the Cementos Progreso information classified as confidential, since that information was not justified as such, nor were non-confidential summaries provided. By ignoring Cruz Azul's request, Guatemala violated Article 6.1, 6.2, 6.3, 6.5, 6.5.1 and 6.5.2.

[613] First written submission by Mexico, paras. 402 et seq.

2. Similarly, various acts by Guatemala also violated the Anti-Dumping Agreement in connection with confidentiality. First, the Ministry of the Economy's action at the time of notification and the failure to provide both Mexico and Cruz Azul with the full text of the request is a violation of those provisions. Moreover, Guatemala did not give Cruz Azul an opportunity to examine the information used by the Ministry in the investigation, as well as that used to extend the investigation period and the period for submitting evidence, thereby violating those provisions. It also violated the provisions of the Anti-Dumping Agreement by acting as it did with regard to essential facts and the change from threat of injury to injury. Lastly, Guatemala again committed those violations in issuing the public notices.[614]

6.1023 As for Guatemala's arguments concerning confidentiality, they were presented in a poor and, in many cases, inconsistent fashion.

6.1024 Guatemala's arguments in this section are very limited, since Guatemala merely argues that it did not violate Articles 6.5.1 and 6.5.2 of the Anti-Dumping Agreement. Hence it accepts that it has violated the other Articles. Furthermore, Guatemala simply develops four points: verification (on-the-spot investigation) at Cementos Progreso, public hearing, communication of 13 November 1996 and the alleged issue of certified copies at the proper time.

6.1025 First, Mexico's arguments concerning the verification at Cementos Progreso are based on the following violations:[615]

(a) By accepting Cementos Progreso's request for confidentiality, without justification, Guatemala breached Article 6.5.2.

(b) By not requiring Cementos Progreso to furnish non-confidential summaries, or the reasons why it could not make such information public, Guatemala violated Article 6.4, 6.5, 6.5.1 and 6.5.2.

(c) By not agreeing to Cruz Azul's request to require non-confidential summaries or to disregard the information, Guatemala violated Article 6.1, 6.2 and 6.4.

(d) By accepting any oral justification for confidentiality, Guatemala violated Article 6.1, 6.2, 6.3 and 6.4.

6.1026 As to the verification, for its part Guatemala says Mexico's first written submission reveals that the verification documents could not be summarized. In addition, other countries do not require public versions of confidential documents obtained in verifications.[616] Consequently from its own words it is clear that Guatemala does not in the slightest way rebut Mexico's arguments concerning the verification at Cementos Progreso.

6.1027 In this connection, to Guatemala's flimsy argument Mexico replies that the first written submission by Mexico is not the best means to reveal whether the verification documents are or are not confidential. The Anti-Dumping Agreement stipulates specific treatment for them and Guatemala should have followed it at the time. In failing to do so,

[614] In this case, see in this second written submission by Mexico the arguments concerning Articles 5.5, 12.1, 6.1.3, the public notices, the period of evidence, the information used by the Ministry, the investigation period, the confidential information, the essential facts and change from threat of injury to injury.

[615] See the facts mentioned in paras. 403 and 404 of Mexico's first written submission.

[616] First written submission by Guatemala, para. 336.

Guatemala violated the Anti-Dumping Agreement. Furthermore, the fact of mentioning that other countries violate the Anti-Dumping Agreement is no justification for Guatemala doing so at Mexico's expense.

6.1028 Secondly, with regard to the hearing on 19 December 1996, Guatemala committed the following violations.

(a) By not permitting timely access to the information supplied by Cementos Progreso, Guatemala violated Article 6.1, 6.2 and 6.4.

(b) By granting the information confidential status of its own accord, Guatemala violated Article 6.5, 6.5.1 and 6.5.2.

(c) By accepting any oral justification for deeming the information confidential, Guatemala violated Article 6.1, 6.2, 6.3 and 6.4.

6.1029 For its part Guatemala again sidesteps Mexico's arguments, in this case by referring to another section of its first written submission. Guatemala mentions that "... it was reasonable for the Ministry to conclude that the lengthy written submission of 19 December prepared by Cementos Progreso would contain confidential information that ought not to be revealed to Cruz Azul ... Consequently, during the hearing the Ministry informed Cruz Azul that it would provide a copy of the Cementos Progreso submission once it had determined whether it contained confidential information."[617] Accordingly, it is plain that Guatemala expressly accepts that it did not follow the confidentiality procedures stipulated in the Anti-Dumping Agreement; hence, it violated the confidentiality rules.

6.1030 Thirdly, Mexico argued that, on 13 November, Cruz Azul asked the Ministry of Economy for the public version of all information supplied by Cementos Progreso, and the non-confidential summaries were not supplied. Guatemala thereby violated Article 6.2, 6.3, 6.5, 6.5.1 and 6.5.2.

6.1031 For its part, very feebly Guatemala refers to paragraph 405 of Mexico's first written submission and says that in the letter of 13 November 1996 "... Cruz Azul did not request the public version of this information ... " and moreover " ... Mexico does not claim that Cruz Azul did not receive these public versions ...".[618] In paragraph 405 Mexico does expressly claim that Cruz Azul did not receive the non-confidential summaries following the request on 13 November 1996. Hence, Mexico did claim that Cruz Azul did not receive such versions. What is more, the fact that Cruz Azul expressly requested the public versions of the documents is yet further evidence that Guatemala did not comply with its confidentiality obligations.

6.1032 Lastly, Guatemala argues that the Ministry of the Economy provided Cruz Azul with certified copies of all the documents in the administrative file. For this reason Mexico asks Guatemala whether it has any acknowledgement of receipt of the alleged certified copies - since it has Annex MEXICO-57[619] it should have some acknowledgement of receipt of the copies. We then refer to the argument about access to the information used by the Ministry of the Economy in the investigation that is developed in this second written submission by Mexico. The section in question deals in greater detail with the repeated refusals by Guatemala to provide Cruz Azul with copies of the file. Finally, it is not possible, as Guatemala claims, that Cruz Azul did not want to pay the fees for certi-

617 *Ibid.*, para. 296.

618 *Ibid.*, para. 337.

619 Annex MEXICO-57 contains the acknowledgement of receipt, one day after the publication of the final notice, of the document containing the essential facts in the investigation.

fied copies when what was at stake was access to the Guatemalan market. Furthermore, Cruz Azul asked for certified copies at its expense.

6.1033 Consequently, Guatemala violated Article 6.1, 6.2, 6.3, 6.5, 6.5.1 and 6.5.2 of the Anti-Dumping Agreement. On the one hand, the arguments not rebutted by Guatemala are enough proof of the violation of the Anti-Dumping Agreement. On the other, it has been demonstrated that Guatemala's counter arguments have not disproved what was proved by Mexico, in other words, the violation of the confidentiality requirements.

9. *Claims Under Articles 6.1, 6.2, and 6.9 of the AD Agreement - Essential Facts Taken Into Account for Imposition of Definitive Anti-Dumping Measure*

(a) Submissions of Mexico

6.1034 **Mexico** argues that Guatemala violated Articles 6.1, 6.2 and 6.4 of the AD Agreement because it did not inform Cruz Azul promptly of the essential facts that would form the basis for imposition of the definitive anti-dumping measure and only informed Cruz Azul after making the final determination. Mexico makes the following submissions with respect to this issue:

6.1035 On at least three occasions, Cruz Azul asked to be informed of the essential facts. First of all, in its letter of 30 October 1996, Cruz Azul asked the Ministry to inform it of the essential facts considered that would form the basis for the final determination and to set a sufficient period of time to allow the firm to defend its interests. Subsequently, on 4 December the same year, it reiterated its request to the Guatemalan Ministry of the Economy. Finally, Cruz Azul once again asked the Ministry to inform it of the essential facts of the procedure at the public hearing held on 19 December 1996.

6.1036 On 6 December 1996, the Ministry responded to the repeated requests from Cruz Azul stating that the essential facts would be set out in the technical report[620] on the case to be prepared, without specifying when this would be made available to Cruz Azul.

6.1037 The technical report was made available to Cruz Azul on 31 January 1997, i.e. after the final determination had been made.

6.1038 Mexico claims that by making such an omission, Guatemala prevented Cruz Azul from defending its interests and violated Article 6.1, 6.2 and 6.9 of the AD Agreement

6.1039 Article 6.9 of the AD Agreement provides the following:

> "6.9. The authorities shall, before a final determination is made, inform all interested parties of the essential facts under consideration which form the basis for the decision whether to apply definitive measures. Such disclosure should take place in sufficient time for the parties to defend their interests."

6.1040 The final determination was made on 17 January 1997 and the Ministry sent the technical report on the outcome of the anti-dumping investigation (essential facts which form the basis for the decision to apply definitive measures) on 31 January that year. Consequently, the essential facts cannot be deemed to have been given to Cruz Azul "in sufficient time for [it] to defend [its] interests". Guatemala therefore acted in a manner inconsistent with Article 6.9 of the AD Agreement.

[620] Technical report on the outcome of the anti-dumping investigation into imports of cement from Mexico.

6.1041 In addition, by presenting the essential facts of the procedure *after* having made the final determination, the Ministry denied Cruz Azul the opportunity to defend its interests by submitting the evidence it considered relevant because it is not possible to defend oneself against something one does not know. This again means that the Ministry acted in violation of Article 6.1 and 6.2 of the AD Agreement.

(b) Response of Guatemala

6.1042 **Guatemala** makes the following arguments in response to Mexico's claims under Articles 6.1, 6.2 and 6.9:

6.1043 Guatemala complied with Article 6.9 of the Anti-Dumping Agreement by "informing all interested parties of the essential facts under consideration" which would form the basis for the imposition of definitive anti-dumping duties by Guatemala. In a notice dated 6 December 1996, the Ministry informed all the parties that its Directorate of Economic Integration would carry out a technical study of the evidence in the file and that the file to be studied was itself available to the parties for making copies. In other words, the essential facts on which the final determination was to be based were those contained in the file as of 6 December, and the file was available for the parties to examine and request copies. Moreover, the Ministry had already issued a detailed report setting out its preliminary findings concerning the essential facts. The parties had the opportunity to present their final arguments regarding these essential facts at the hearing on 19 December. Thus, Guatemala complied with Articles 6.1, 6.2 and 6.9 of the Anti-Dumping Agreement by informing the interested parties of the essential facts under consideration in sufficient time for them to defend their interests.

6.1044 Moreover, under Article 6.14, Guatemala was authorized to proceed expeditiously with the issuing of a final determination, rather than delay the investigation in order to comply with Cruz Azul's request to issue another description of the essential facts.

(c) Rebuttal of Mexico

6.1045 **Mexico** rebuts these arguments by asserting that Guatemala did not prove that it had duly reported the essential facts that would be taken into account in imposing the definitive anti-dumping measure, and that it thereby violated Articles 6.1, 6.2 and 6.9 of the AD Agreement. Its argument in this regard are as follows:

6.1046 On the one hand, Cruz Azul asked Guatemala on three occasions to inform it of the essential facts to be taken into account in imposing the definitive anti-dumping measure. The first two requests were made in letters dated 30 October and 4 December 1996 and the third at the public hearing on 19 December 1996.[621] On the other hand, Guatemala issued a decision on 6 December 1996 stating that it would prepare a technical study setting out the essential facts. It is important to emphasize that the technical study also specified the imposition of definitive anti-dumping duties and, consequently, Guatemala did not afford Cruz Azul opportunities to defend its interests.

6.1047 First, Guatemala provided Cruz Azul with the technical study in question only on 31 January 1997. In other words, the document was made available to Cruz Azul one day after publication of the public notice of the conclusion of the investigation. Accordingly, there can be no doubt about Guatemala's violation of Article 6.9. Second, Guatemala decided to inform Cruz Azul of the essential facts at the same time as it reported the imposition of the definitive measure. Article 6.9 stipulates that "the authorities shall, *before a*

[621] First written submission by Mexico, para. 419.

final determination is made [*or declared*], inform all the interested parties of the essential facts ... which form the basis of the decision whether to apply definitive measures ...". Hence Guatemala cannot be deemed to have complied with Article 6.9 because it informed about the essential facts in the same document as the one in which it decided to impose a definitive anti-dumping measure. The violation of Article 6.9 is therefore confirmed.

6.1048 For its part, Guatemala argues that the essential facts forming the basis for the final determination were those contained in the file as at 6 December 1996, and they were available for the parties to examine them and to request copies. Guatemala adds that, in conformity with Article 6.14, the Ministry was authorized to proceed to issue a final determination, instead of delaying the investigation to meet Cruz Azul's request concerning the description of the essential facts.

6.1049 Mexico's reply is that under the decision of 6 December, the essential facts were to be set out in the technical study; and that because the file contains various facts it does not mean they are the essential facts forming the basis for the authority to issue its final determination. In other words, the facts contained in the file are not the same as the essential facts mentioned in Article 6.9. If there were no difference between them, Article 6.9 would be pointless and it would not use the term "essential facts".

6.1050 Again, Article 6.14 provides that the procedures set out in Article 6 cannot be used to prevent the investigation from proceeding. At no time does this provision allow the investigating authority to violate the rights of the parties, such as the right to notification of the essential facts, in a desire to speed up the investigation. In other words, Guatemala cannot comply with the Anti-Dumping Agreement by violating Cruz Azul' s right to know the essential facts and claiming a need to proceed with the investigation or to meet the investigation's time-limits to the detriment of Cruz Azul's right to due process.

6.1051 What is more, not only did Guatemala not inform Cruz Azul of the essential facts that would be taken into account by the Ministry in its final determination, but it also prevented Cruz Azul from being able to defend its interests. Consequently, Guatemala also acted in violation of Article 6.1 and 6.2 of the AD Agreement.

6.1052 As a result, Guatemala violated Article 6.9 by not duly informing Cruz Azul of the essential facts so as to enable it to defend its interests; in addition, it violated this provision by notifying the final determination in the same document as the one in which it informed Cruz Azul of the essential facts. In doing so it also violated Article 6.1 and 6.2 to the detriment of Cruz Azul.

10. Claims Under Articles 6.1, 6.2, and 6.9 - Mexico's Allegation that Guatemala Prevented Cruz Azul From Defending its Interests

(a) Submissions of Mexico

6.1053 **Mexico** claims that the Guatemalan Ministry acted in a manner inconsistent with Article 6.1, 6.2 and 6.9 of the AD Agreement by changing its determination of threat of material injury to material injury during the final stage of the investigation[622] without giving Cruz Azul full and ample opportunity to defend itself. The following are Mexico's arguments in this regard:

[622] This change was also dealt with in connection with Articles 3 and 12 of the AD Agreement in section E of this first written submission.

6.1054 The extended application by Cementos Progreso indicated that the anti-dumping investigation was being conducted into threat of injury and the Ministry decided to initiate the investigation on this basis. For example, in subparagraph 4 of the notice of initiation of the investigation entitled "Summary of the factors on which the allegation of threat of injury is based", it is stated that:

> "Cementos Progreso S.A. appeared before this Ministry to lodge a complaint that massive quantities of grey Portland cement produced by the Mexican company La Cruz Azul, S.C.L. are being imported into Guatemala by land at a price less than the normal value and are threatening injury to the domestic industry ..."

6.1055 Subsequently, the Ministry made its *preliminary affirmative determination of a threat of material injury*. See Section E of the public notice of imposition of the provisional anti-dumping measure entitled "Threat of injury to the domestic industry and the causal relationship between the dumping and the threat of injury".

6.1056 During the course of the investigation and up until the public hearing which the Ministry held with the parties, i.e. 11 months after the initiation of the investigation, Cruz Azul did *not* know that the Ministry had changed the examination and determination of threat of material injury.

6.1057 It should be pointed out that during the final stage of the investigation, in letters dated 30 October and 4 December 1996, Cruz Azul asked the Ministry to inform it of the essential facts that would serve as a basis for the final determination so that it could defend its interests adequately, on the basis of Article 6.9 of the ADP, which provides the following:

> "6.9. The authorities *shall, before a final determination* is made, *inform* all interested parties of *the essential facts* under consideration which form the basis for *the decision whether to apply definitive measures*. Such disclosure should take place in sufficient time for the parties to defend their interests." (emphasis added).

6.1058 On 6 December 1996, the Ministry replied as follows to Cruz Azul stating that the Directorate of Economic Integration would prepare a technical report on the outcome of the investigation and this would set out the facts investigated and the evidence available:

> "The technical report to be published by this Directorate will set out the facts investigated and the evidence available, as well as the results of the verifications conducted. These documents will be included in the file and the parties may obtain copies at their own expense."

6.1059 The technical report was published on 15 January 1997 but was only made available to Cruz Azul on 31 January, one day after publication of the notice of conclusion of the investigation. At no time during the investigation was Cruz Azul informed that the authority had made a change in the original examination and determination of threat of material injury with a view to a final affirmative determination of material injury, so Cruz Azul was denied an opportunity to exercise the right of defence given under Article 6.1, 6.2 and 6.9, including the opportunity to provide relevant information and evidence that might have counteracted the determination of injury by the authority.

6.1060 It can thus justifiably be concluded that the Ministry failed to meet the obligations imposed by Article 6.1, 6.2 and 6.9 of the AD Agreement by *not* giving Cruz Azul ample and full opportunity to defend its interests and by *not* furnishing the exporter with information in due time so that it could defend its interests, particularly when the final determination changed the determination of threat of material injury into one of material injury.

(b) Response of Guatemala

6.1061 **Guatemala** makes the following arguments in response to Mexico's claims under Articles 6.1, 6.2 and 6.4:

6.1062 Mexico alleges that in changing the grounds for its affirmative determination of threat of material injury in the preliminary determination to material injury in the final determination the Ministry somehow violated Articles 6.1, 6.2 and 6.9 of the Anti-Dumping Agreement. Essentially, Mexico is suggesting that an investigating authority must inform the exporter of its intention to base its final determination on threat of injury or material injury in order that the exporter may have an adequate opportunity to defend its interests. There is no support for this argument in the Anti-Dumping Agreement.

6.1063 Article 6.1, 6.2 and 6.9 contain nothing to suggest that an investigating authority must inform an exporter of the legal basis for the final determination. Article 5 of the Anti-Dumping Agreement itself provides the legal basis for a final determination. This determination may be based either on threat of injury or material injury. Thus, an exporter defending an anti-dumping case knows, through Article 5, that to escape unscathed he must show no threat of injury *and* no material injury. Cruz Azul can only blame itself for having failed to mount a defence for material injury. However, the fact is that Cruz Azul never tried to show either that it was not involved in dumping cement in Guatemala or that the dumped imports had not caused a threat of injury or material injury to the domestic industry. On the contrary, in its submissions dated 7 February 1996, 9 May 1996 and 30 October 1996, Cruz Azul chose only to challenge the sufficiency of the evidence provided by the applicant and the investigation proceedings. Cruz Azul never supplied evidence to show that it had not been engaged in dumping and never supplied evidence that Cementos Progreso had not been exposed to threat of material injury or had not been materially injured as a result of the dumped imports.

6.1064 Finally, it is significant that Mexico does not identify any particular evidence that Cruz Azul would have supplied if it had known that the Ministry was going to consider material injury and not threat of injury. As noted above, Cruz Azul never provided any evidence that it had not been engaged in dumping or that Cementos Progreso had not been adversely affected by the dumped imports. Cruz Azul merely objected to the procedures followed by the investigating authority. So far, Mexico has not told the panel that Cruz Azul was not engaged in dumping or that Cementos Progreso was not materially injured. All Mexico's arguments before the panel, like Cruz Azul's complaints to the investigating authority, relate to procedural, not substantive issues.

6.1065 However, facts are facts. In August 1996, when the preliminary determination was issued it was clear that Cementos Progreso was being threatened with material injury. By January 1997, when the final determination was issued, the files showed that Cementos Progreso had already been injured. The rapid increase in imports during the period initially investigated (June-November 1995) continued during the rest of the final investigation period (June 1995-May 1996). During the first part of 1996, the domestic industry's sales fell as compared with the first part of 1995, despite the fact that the demand for cement was higher in the first part of 1996 than in the first part of 1995. During the first part of 1996, domestic production fell by 14 per cent as compared with the same period in 1995. Similarly, the utilization of clinker capacity, the utilization of cement capacity and profitability all declined during the first part of 1996 as compared with the previous year. Thus, at the time the final determination was made, what had clearly been a threat of injury on the basis of the information for June-November 1995 had become material injury on the basis of the information for June 1995-May 1996. Cruz Azul does not dispute these facts.

(c) Rebuttal of Mexico

6.1066 **Mexico** maintains that Guatemala violated Article 6.1, 6.2 and 6.9 by not affording opportunities for a defence in connection with its change from a determination of threat of material injury to one of material injury. Its rebuttals to Guatemala's submissions on this point are as follows:

6.1067 Guatemala claims that Article 5 of the AD Agreement provides the legal basis for a final determination, which may be based either on a threat of injury or material injury and that, under Article 5, the exporter must show no threat of material injury and no material injury. Guatemala adds that Cruz Azul has only itself to blame for failing to mount a defence for material injury.[623]

6.1068 Mexico maintains that the analysis required of an authority in order to determine the existence of a threat of material injury is different from the analysis needed to determine the existence of material injury. In this respect, it should be reiterated that in its preliminary determination, the Ministry concluded that threat of injury did exist but its analysis did not include, *inter alia*, the factors and indices set out in Article 3.4, which it is essential to analyse in order to reach a valid determination of material injury.

6.1069 In this respect, there is *no* record after the preliminary determination of Cementos Progreso having supplied further information and evidence to warrant changing the analysis from a threat of material injury to material injury. Actually, at no time did the Ministry communicate to Cruz Azul or advise it of this change and, in failing to do so, it affected Cruz Azul's rights and prevented the exporter from preparing arguments in its own defence to demonstrate that the Guatemalan domestic industry was not suffering material injury as a result of Mexican exports of the product under investigation.

6.1070 Guatemala did not afford Cruz Azul ample and full opportunity to defend its interests despite Cruz Azul's request for the Ministry to inform it of the essential facts that would form the basis of the final determination.[624] In this connection, if the Ministry had information and evidence to support an analysis of the existence of material injury, it should have advised Cruz Azul during the investigation in order for the latter to prepare its defence.[625]

6.1071 It must be reiterated that Cementos Progreso's arguments in the investigation were of a threat of material injury and the preliminary determination was made accordingly. Cruz Azul was unaware that the Ministry had changed its analysis from a threat of material injury to one of material injury and, as we have already pointed out, the two analyses are different. Mexico therefore maintains that Cruz Azul should have been advised of the change in the analysis and the determination in order for it to defend its interests. Consequently, the Ministry's omission prevented Cruz Azul from being able to exercise its right to a defence. In other words, the absence of a defence by the exporter can be ascribed to Guatemala because it did not inform Cruz Azul of the change of analysis. Guatemala's omission constituted a violation of Article 6.1, 6.2 and 6.9 of the AD Agreement.

---

[623] First written submission by Guatemala, para. 342.

[624] *Ibid.*, para. 425.

[625] In referring to the essential facts the Ministry said that they would be set out in a technical study to be prepared by the Directorate of Economic Integration. It was made available to Cruz Azul a day after the public notice of conclusion of the investigation was published, for which reason the Ministry did not afford Cruz Azul the opportunity to prepare its defence with respect to an evaluation and determination of material injury.

F. *Guatemala's Final Affirmative Determination*

6.1072 **Mexico** argues that by applying the definitive anti-dumping measure without duly fulfilling the requirements for its imposition, Guatemala violated Articles, 1, 2, 3, 5, 6, 9, 12 and 18 of the AD Agreement and Article VI of the GATT 1994. Mexico's arguments and Guatemala's responses on the final affirmative determination are set out below:

1. Claims Under Articles 2, 5 and 6

(a) Submissions of Mexico

6.1073 **Mexico** makes the following arguments in support of its claim that Guatemala violated Articles 2, 5 and 6 of the AD Agreement in making its final determination of dumping:

6.1074 In its final determination of dumping, the Ministry determined the normal value on the basis of four alleged invoices dated 25 and 27 August 1995[626], 24 January and 17 February 1996, covering the sale of one load of cement in Mexico. The invoices dated 25 August 1996 and 24 January 1996 were issued by the distributor Cruz Azul en Tapachula S.A. de C.V. The cement specified in both invoices corresponds to one load of grey cement. The invoices dated 27 August 1995 and 17 February 1996 were issued by the distributors Proveedora de Láminas y Materiales Bonampak S.A. de C.V. The cement indicated on both invoices allegedly corresponds to one sack or load of Cruz Azul cement, without specifying the type of cement. It should be noted that during the investigation period the three firms were distributors independent of Cruz Azul.

6.1075 In the final determination, the export price was calculated on the basis of the invoices covered by import certificates for cement in August 1995 and January and February 1996. The export prices were weighted by the volume of exports at the f.o.b. level It is important to underline that the variation in volume of these exports for the months mentioned ranges from 60,000 to 2,640,000 kg.[627] (60 and 2,640 metric tonnes).

(i) Description of the cement considered for the normal value (Article 2.1 of the AD Agreement)

6.1076 With regard to the description or precise identification of the cement considered when determining the normal value, the Ministry naively, non-objectively and even equivocally confirmed the prices shown on the four alleged invoices for sales in the domestic market, without ascertaining whether the type of cement covered by the documents actually corresponded to the *like product exported to the Guatemalan market.* In fact, two of the four alleged invoices only described the product as "grey cement", whereas the other two only mentioned "Cruz Azul cement", facts which should have been investigated by the Ministry, particularly as the product investigated has several characteristics that must be taken into account when comparing products, for example, its durability, resistance, efficiency and adhesion.

6.1077 According to the aforementioned characteristics, Portland cement can be classified into different types such as Type I, Type II and Type III. Other types of cement such as I A, II A and III A contain an air-entraining agent. Portland cement can in turn be

[626] According to the information in the file on the case, the dates of these invoices were 26 and 25 August 1995, respectively.

[627] Annex I to the "Full report for the determination of dumping of imports of grey Portland cement from Mexico".

mixed with other components giving it another classification, including blast-furnace slag Portland cement (Type I S), pozzolanic Portland cement (Type I P and Type P), blast-furnace slag Portland cement (Type S), Portland cement modified with pozzolana (Type I PM) and Portland cement modified with blast-furnace slag (Type I SM). The product exported to Guatemala was Type I PM grey Portland cement.[628]

6.1078 It should be noted that, with the information it had for the purposes of calculating the normal value, the Ministry could not have identified the like product to that exported to Guatemala destined for consumption in Mexico, and so use the right methodology to compare the normal value and the export price in accordance with Article 2 of the AD Agreement.

6.1079 Consequently, the Ministry did *not* compare the export price with the comparable price of a like product sold on the Mexican market, thus violating Article 2.1 of the AD Agreement.

(ii) Unrepresentative invoices (Article 2.2 of the AD Agreement)

6.1080 Concerning the representative nature of the sales, the Ministry violated Article 2.2 of the AD Agreement by *not* considering whether the sales covered by the alleged invoices were representative of the Mexican domestic market. In particular, the Ministry did *not* examine whether the prices shown on the documents reflected the prices actually noted on the domestic market and were not simply isolated examples of prices, especially as the volumes of the sales transactions indicated on the alleged invoices corresponded to the lowest volume in which the product investigated could be marketed, i.e. a load, bag or sack. The Ministry did *not* therefore ascertain whether the price references used to determine the normal value allowed a proper comparison, as required by Article 2.2 of the AD Agreement.

(iii) Unfair comparison (Article 2.4 of the AD Agreement)

6.1081 The above information shows that the Ministry violated Article 2.4 of the AD Agreement by *not* making a fair comparison between the normal value and the export price and by *not* considering the differences affecting price comparability.

6.1082 The four invoices used to determine the *normal value* show four *retail* sales of a sack, bag or load of cement of unspecified weight, whereas the information used to determine the *export price* refers to import transactions at the wholesale level. It is obvious that these transactions involve different volumes and levels of trade.

6.1083 By not taking into account such differences, the Ministry determined a low export price because high volumes of sales at the wholesale level were involved, but a high normal value, because low levels of retail sales were involved. Consequently, the dumping margin obtained was over-estimated as a result of the effect on prices of the differences in the volumes sold and the levels of trade.

6.1084 In addition, the Ministry did *not* satisfy itself as to the terms of sale for the prices on the domestic market indicated on the alleged invoices and consequently did *not* take

[628] "Public notice of conclusion of the investigation which reached an affirmative determination on the imposition of definitive anti-dumping measures" ("hereinafter notice of conclusion") published in the *Diario Oficial de Centro América* of 30 January 1997, section on "Information regarding the product under investigation", para. 3.

due account of the differences that might have affected the comparability of the domestic prices and export prices used to calculate the dumping margin. In particular, as the alleged invoices corresponded to sales made by distributors independent of Cruz Azul, it is obvious that the selling prices shown on these documents include as a minimum freight and insurance from Cruz Azul's plant to the independent distributor's warehouse. The export prices used in the calculation were shown ex-factory, so they did not include the same selling costs as the domestic prices.

6.1085 The Ministry did not apply the necessary adjustments to the domestic price either in order to ensure a fair comparison with the export price, which again led to an over-estimation of the dumping margin calculated.

6.1086 This over-estimation of the dumping margin was recognized by the Guatemalan authority itself in its "Full report for the determination of dumping of imports of grey Portland cement from Mexico".

> "The percentage difference calculated on the basis of the best available information in the file was over-estimated as the evidence available did not allow adjustments to be made for the level of trade, transport, commission or discounts. The evidence available for the establishment of the normal value of the like product is not statistically representative of the sales of the Mexican cement industry in this market during the investigation period."

6.1087 According to the indications in the paragraph above, the Ministry violated Article 2.4 of the AD Agreement by *not* taking into account the differences in the volumes of sales, the levels of trade and the terms of sale in order to make a fair comparison of the prices.

(iv) Extension of the investigation period (Article 5.2 of the AD Agreement)

6.1088 The Ministry decided to extend the investigation period without substantiating or justifying its decision. When the Ministry decided to extend the investigation period (from 1 December 1995 to 31 May 1996), there was already a preliminary affirmative determination on the basis of the information supplied by Cruz Azul for the investigation period (1 June to 30 November 1995), which the Ministry had fixed when the investigation was initiated. Extending the investigation period by six months in the course of the final stage of investigation in practice amounted to initiating a new investigation, thus imposing an extra and unjustified burden on the exporter.

6.1089 The extension of the investigation period was decided following a specific request[629] from the applicant, although Cementos Progreso did *not* provide any information to justify or support its request. By accepting this extension, the Ministry violated Article 5.2 of the ADP, which provides the following:

> "5.2 ... Simple assertion, unsubstantiated by relevant evidence, cannot be considered sufficient to meet the requirements of this paragraph..."

6.1090 Cementos Progreso's request did not only *contain no information to support it*, but also referred to a split period compared with the original investigation period (1 January to 30 June 1996), thus claiming isolated dumping practices and not *discriminatory prices* during an investigation period. Although the Ministry did not specifically accede to

[629] Letter from Cementos Progreso dated 18 September 1996, received by the Ministry of the Economy on 1 October 1996.

the request, it agreed to extend the investigation period[630] by six months, thus violating Article 5.2 of the AD Agreement.

(v) The final determination of the Ministry of the Economy (Article 6.8 of the AD Agreement)

6.1091 As the notice of conclusion shows, the Ministry declined to use the information furnished by Cruz Azul on the basis of Article 6.6 and 6.8 of the AD Agreement.

6.1092 In this connection, Article 6.8 provides that:

> "In cases in which any interested party refuses acccss to, or otherwise does not provide, necessary information within a reasonable period or significantly impedes the investigation, preliminary and final determinations, affirmative or negative, may be made on the basis of the facts available. The provisions of Annex II shall be observed in the application of this paragraph."

6.1093 The Ministry erred in basing its final determination on Article 6.8 as Cruz Azul never denied access to the necessary information and did not significantly impede the investigation. According to Cruz Azul's letter to the Ministry after the verification visit, Cruz Azul simply declined to provide the information for the extended investigation period unjustifiably requested by the Ministry and refused the participation of non-governmental experts with a conflict of interest. It agreed, however, to verification of all the other information, which had already been provided to the Ministry, and that non-governmental experts who had *no* conflict of interest could take part in the verification.

6.1094 Supposing, without agreeing, that Cruz Azul should have been evaluated on the basis of the facts available to the Ministry, as laid down in Article 6.8, the Ministry also violated Article 6.8 and Annex II to the AD Agreement for the following reasons.

6.1095 Firstly, the Ministry did not comply with paragraph 3 of Annex II to the AD Agreement because, when making its final determination, it should have taken account of all the verifiable information properly presented. Cruz Azul properly presented the information requested by the Ministry covering the original investigation period and agreed that the Ministry could verify this information. However, the Ministry declined to verify the information or utilize it when calculating the final dumping margin applicable to Cruz Azul.

6.1096 Secondly, the Ministry also violated paragraph 5 of Annex II, which states the following:

> "5. Even though the information provided may not be ideal in all respects, this should not justify the authorities from disregarding it, provided the interested party has acted to the best of its ability."

6.1097 Cruz Azul supplied the information on the normal value and the export price for the original investigation period to the best of its ability, but the Ministry declined to use this information when making the final affirmative determination imposing a definitive measure on Cruz Azul.

6.1098 Thirdly, the Ministry did not comply with paragraph 7 of Annex II, which reads as follows:

> "7. If the authorities have to base their findings, including those with respect to normal value, on information from a secondary source, including

[630] The Ministry's agreement *inter alia* to extending the investigation period from 1 December 1995 to 31 May 1996.

> the information supplied in the application for the initiation of the investigation, they should do so with special circumspection. In such cases, the authorities should, where practicable, check the information from other independent sources at their disposal, such as published price lists, import statistics and customs returns, and from the information obtained from other interested parties during the investigation. It is clear, however, that if an interested party does not cooperate and thus relevant information is being withheld from the authorities, this situation could lead to a result which is less favourable to the party than if the party did cooperate."

6.1099 The Ministry did *not* act with the special circumspection prescribed by this provision. In particular, it did not verify the information used to determine the normal value in the light of information from other independent sources, but automatically considered as reliable the information on the four alleged invoices for the domestic market. In the administrative file on this case, there is *no* verification of the information used in the final determination to calculate the normal value and then to estimate the dumping margin.

6.1100 As already stated, Cruz Azul cooperated and transmitted to the Ministry the relevant information requested in the questionnaire for exporters, but even so the Ministry's final determination concerning this firm was *not* more favourable to it than to those firms that did not cooperate during the anti-dumping investigation.

(vi) Quality and quantity of information

6.1101 In determining the definitive measure, the Ministry repeated the same mistakes and violations committed at the initiation of the investigation.

6.1102 In the initial determination, the Ministry used two alleged invoices for sales on the domestic market covering an investigation period comprising six months (1 June 1995 to 30 November 1995), whereas for the final determination the period was extended by another six months (1 June 1995 to 30 May 1996), without any justification, and only two further invoices were added when determining the normal value on the basis of the extended period.

6.1103 The Ministry *failed* to comply with the requirements of its own legislation by not seeking "a legal permit"[631], by taking into account the two latest invoices used to determine the normal value, which was not done during the initiation of the investigation phase, and by not satisfying itself that the cement sold by the independent distributors corresponded to the cement manufactured by the firm Cruz Azul, so the nature of the evidence used to prove the normal value in the final determination is questionable.

6.1104 As already stated, the quantity and quality of the evidence used to calculate the normal value in the final determination are similar to those used to calculate the normal value at the beginning of the investigation. If this evidence was insufficient for the purposes of initiating the investigation, it was also clearly insufficient for determining a definitive measure. The conclusion reached by the Panel which heard the case *Guatemala - Cement* is set out below.[632]

---

[631] On 12 February 1996, in decision no. 20/96, the Directorate of Economic Integration informed Cooperativa La Cruz Azul S.C.L. that "Documents from abroad must be duly certified by the Ministry of Foreign Relations in order to have effect in Guatemala ...". In order to maintain a procedural balance between the parties during the proceedings, the same requirement should apply to Cementos Progreso in respect of documents from abroad.

[632] *Guatemala - Cement*, *supra*, footnote 25, para. 7.76.

> "7.79. In sum, in our view, based on an unbiased and objective evaluation of the evidence and information that was before it at the time of initiation in this case, the Ministry could not properly have determined that there was sufficient evidence of dumping, threat of injury, and causal relationship to justify the initiation of the investigation." Likewise, the Panel that heard the *United States - Softwood Lumber* case noted that "the quantum and quality of evidence to be required of an investigating authority prior to initiation of an investigation would necessarily have to be less than that required of that authority at the time of making a final determination."[633]

6.1105 In other words, for a final determination, the quality and volume of evidence required must be greater than that required by an authority in order to initiate an investigation. It is obvious that the Ministry did *not* comply with this standard of evidence and established definitive anti-dumping measures on the basis of the same level of information used to initiate the investigation.

6.1106 Moreover, the Ministry violated Article 6.9 of the AD Agreement, which provides the following:

> "The authorities shall, before a final determination is made, inform all interested parties of the essential facts under consideration which form the basis for the decision whether to apply definitive measures. Such disclosure should take place in sufficient time for the parties to defend their interests."

6.1107 In this connection, the Ministry did *not* inform Cruz Azul of the essential facts to be considered for its final determination. Furthermore, the Ministry neither justified nor explained the origin of the two additional invoices issued by Cruz Azul in Tapachula, S.A. de C.V. and Materiales Bonampak, S.A. de C.V., dated 24 January and 17 February 1996, and used to calculate the dumping margin, nor did it indicate the stage of the investigation at which they were furnished.

(vii) Unjustified request for information on costs

6.1108 Concerning the methodology used to compare the normal value and the export price, it should be pointed that Cementos Progreso's application for an investigation did *not* contain any allegation of sales below cost. Implicitly, the applicant accepted the prices and only claimed that the price at the which the investigated product was exported to Guatemala was lower than the price at which it was sold on the Mexican domestic market. For this reason, as from initiation of the investigation, Cruz Azul only furnished the Ministry with information on prices, so in the administrative file on the case there is *no* information or claims to justify the Ministry's request to Cruz Azul for information on costs.

6.1109 In the preliminary determination imposing a provisional anti-dumping duty, notice of which was published in the *Diario Oficial de Centro América* on 28 August 1996, a dumping margin was calculated for Cruz Azul using *price information* specific to this firm. Following publication of the notice, the Ministry decided to request Cruz Azul for information on production costs, even though Cementos Progreso had not alleged that Cruz Azul's sales on the Mexican domestic market were below its production costs and the Ministry did not explain the grounds for its request to Cruz Azul for new information.

6.1110 The notice of conclusion of the investigation determining the imposition of definitive anti-dumping duties does *not* contain any complaint about selling below cost or

[633] *United States - Softwood Lumber*, para. 332.

information of such nature and in its final determination the Ministry again used price information in order to determine the dumping margin attributed to Cruz Azul.

6.1111 For the above reasons, it can be concluded that the Ministry of the Economy did *not* make a proper determination of the normal value or the export price and, consequently, the dumping margin, so its action was inconsistent with Articles 2, 5 and 6 of the AD Agreement.

(b) Response of Guatemala

6.1112 **Guatemala** makes the following arguments in response to the Mexican claims regarding Articles 2, 5 and 6 of the AD Agreement:

6.1113 Mexico alleges that the Ministry's dumping calculations contained in the final determination violated Articles 2, 5 and 6 of the Anti-Dumping Agreement. In particular, Mexico maintains that (a) Guatemala failed to verify the accuracy and representativeness of the information it used as a basis for calculating the normal value; (b) it failed to make certain adjustments, such as for alleged differences in levels of trade in order to ensure "a fair comparison"; and (c) it improperly based its determination on the facts available in accordance with Article 6.8.[634] Mexico also repeats various assertions made in other parts of its submission. For example, it reiterates its claim that the Ministry: (i) unjustifiably extended the investigation period; (ii) unjustifiably requested information on production costs; and (iii) failed to inform Cruz Azul of the essential facts that would form the basis for its final determination.[635] Mexico does *not* challenge the calculation of the export price in the final determination.

6.1114 Guatemala has already shown that it complied with the relevant provisions of the Anti-Dumping Agreement when it extended the investigation period.[636] Guatemala has also established that it communicated to Cruz Azul the essential facts that were taken into consideration in formulating the final determination[637], and that in requesting information about Cruz Azul's production costs it acted reasonably and in keeping with Articles 2.1 and 2.2 of the Anti-Dumping Agreement.[638] There would be no point in repeating our arguments here. Rather, in this section of Guatemala's first written submission we will show that Mexico's remaining arguments are spurious and should be rejected by the panel.

---

634 Mexico's first written submission, paras. 433-48, 452-66.

635 *Ibid.*, paras. 449-51, 467-72.

636 See paras. 304-310 above. To add to Guatemala's previous comments on this question, it is worth mentioning that Mexico is wrong in maintaining that the extension of the investigation period violated Article 5.2 of the Anti-Dumping Agreement. Firstly, Article 5.2 establishes the requirements which must be met by an "application". If what Mexico is suggesting is that Cementos Progreso's views on the investigation period were fixed at the time of the application, that would be absurd. This approach finds no support in the Anti-Dumping Agreement or in the ordinary practice of Members of the WTO. See, for example, *Preliminary Affirmative Countervailing Duty Determination: Circular Welded Non-Alloy Steel Pipe from Brazil*, 57 Fed. Reg. 24466 (1962). Secondly, if what Mexico is suggesting is that Cementos Progreso's application should have been ignored because it was not supported by documentary evidence, it is again wrong. As Guatemala has already noted, Article 5.2 does not distinguish between "evidence" and "information" and Cementos Progreso's application certainly contained supporting information. Section VI.D above sets out the information concerning price increases in Mexico during 1996 which Cementos Progreso submitted as part of its application.

637 See paras. 339-340 above.

638 See paras. 311-314 above.

6.1115 Firstly, Mexico questions the accuracy of the Ministry's final calculation of the normal value. According to Mexico, the Ministry should have "ascertained" that it was not comparing different types of cement and, as regards prices, that they "were not simply isolated examples of prices".[639] This argument totally ignores the fact that Cruz Azul refused to provide the Ministry with precise and complete information relating to its costs and sales. As Guatemala has made clear in the course of this submission, Cruz Azul refused to supply the requested information on its production costs, refused to supply the requested information concerning its sales between 1 December 1995 and 31 May 1996 and refused to cooperate with the Ministry during the on-the-spot verification.[640] In these circumstances, the Ministry had no alternative but to base its final determination on the "facts available". The Ministry could not yield control of the investigation to Cruz Azul. Without a complete file, including relevant cost information, the Ministry could not be certain, among other things, that the prices on Cruz Azul's domestic market provided an appropriate basis for determining the normal value.[641]

6.1116 According to Article 6.6 of the Anti-Dumping Agreement, the authorities must "satisfy themselves as to the *accuracy* of the information supplied by interested parties ..."[642] However, an exception to this requirement is made when one of the interested parties "refuses access to, or otherwise does not provide, necessary information within a reasonable period or significantly impedes the investigation".[643] In these circumstances, the authority does not have to satisfy itself as to the accuracy of the information supplied. Instead, at its discretion, it may base its final determination on the "facts available"[644], which may include those contained in the original application.[645] Furthermore, it is expressly understood that when an interested party has not cooperated "to the best of its ability"[646] the authority may use adverse inferences as facts available.[647]

6.1117 In the present dispute, Cruz Azul "significantly impeded" the Ministry's investigation. It is also clear that Cruz Azul did not cooperate to the best of its ability. Accordingly, in its final determination the Ministry concluded:

> "... this Ministry considers that the information provided by the exporting firm cannot be taken into account in calculating the normal value of the product investigated in view of the fact that it could not be verified and the technical evidence submitted by the exporting firm on 18 December 1996 (confidential information) cannot replace such verification of the information by the Guatemalan investigating authority, in accordance with Article 6.6 of the Anti-Dumping Agreement".

---

[639] Mexico's first written submission, paras. 437-441.

[640] In its first written submission, Mexico has wrongly stated that Cruz Azul only withheld the information corresponding to the extended investigation period. (see *Ibid.*, para. 454). Guatemala has already shown that this is untrue and that during the initiation of the investigation Cruz Azul withheld information concerning its production prices. See, for example, paras. 311 to 314 above.

[641] According to the Ministry's "Technical Report", with regard to dumping: "The lack of information on the costs of Mexican manufacturers prevents us from confirming that the sales made on their market were at prices above per unit (fixed and variable) costs of production ...".

[642] Anti-Dumping Agreement, Article 6.6 (emphasis added).

[643] *Ibid.*, Article 6.8 (referred to in Article 6.6).

[644] See, *United States - Salmon from Norway*, ADP/87, adopted 27 April 1994, para. 449 (discussing the "discretion" enjoyed by authorities in choosing the "facts available").

[645] Anti-Dumping Agreement, Article 6.8 and para. 1 of Annex II.

[646] Ibid., para. 5 of Annex II. Mexico's first written submission, paras. 456-58.

[647] Anti-Dumping Agreement, para. 7 of Annex II.

6.1118 If it had so wished, the Ministry would have been fully justified, given the facts, in basing its calculation of the normal value on adverse inferences, including the highest normal value claimed in the application.[648] Instead, Guatemala was prudent and used a weighted average price derived from Cruz Azul's four sales in Mexico.

6.1119 Even assuming, for argument's sake, that the Ministry was obliged to "verify" the accuracy of its normal value calculations, Mexico has in no way fulfilled its obligation to demonstrate a violation of the WTO Agreement. The Ministry based its determination of the normal value on the facts available in four sales transactions, all supported by invoices, which in their turn reflected the sale of Cruz Azul grey Portland cement during the investigation period. There is nothing in the underlying administrative file to suggest that the invoices were fraudulent or that the selling prices were not accurate.

6.1120 In its first written submission, Mexico speculates that the "alleged invoices" might not have been "representative".[649] However, at no point does Mexico explain why invoices which are otherwise accurate and lawful should be disregarded when an investigating authority calculates the normal value - especially when the normal value is based on the facts available. Moreover, Mexico never asserts that the calculation is wrong.

6.1121 Next, Mexico complains about the Ministry's reluctance to make certain adjustments under Article 2.4 in order to make "a fair comparison".[650] Again, Mexico's argument totally disregards the fact that the Ministry was prevented from making adjustments under Article 2.4 because Cruz Azul refused to cooperate with the investigation. Accordingly, in its final determination the Ministry considered that:

> "No evidence of these adjustments was provided that would prove the veracity of the exporter's arguments, except for the packagings of the product distributed on the Mexican market and a copy of the Law on Value Added Tax in force in the Republic of Mexico during the investigation period (footnote omitted). *Neither was it possible to verify the veracity of the information provided by the exporter because it objected to the procedure, as noted in the report on the verification visit ...*"

6.1122 Mexico also fails to show *prima facie* that any adjustment, apart from the two actually made (that is, for the weight of the sacks and value-added tax), was justified. For example, Mexico says, without offering any evidence in support, that the normal value was calculated at a different level of trade from the export price.[651] However, it does not provide any facts or evidence to support its claim, since none exist. If Mexico were to

---

[648] In fact, Guatemala respectfully maintains that many investigating authorities, including some much more experienced that Guatemala in the administration of anti-dumping legislation, might have responded to this situation by assigning Cruz Azul a *margin* of dumping based on the adverse information available. See, for example, *Notice of Final Determination of Sales at Less than Fair Value: Certain Pasta from Italy*, 61 Fed. Reg. 30327-28 (1996); *Final Determination on Exports of Polybutadylene Styrene (SBR Synthetic Rubber) from the Federative Republic of Brazil, Diario Oficial de la Federación* (Official Journal), 27 May 1996, para. 104; *Definitive Resolution on the Importation of Dinner Services and Loose Table and Kitchen Ware Articles from the People's Republic of China, Diario Oficial de la Federación* (Official Journal), 25 May 1992; *Decision amending the Final Decision of the Anti-Dumping and Anti-Subsidy Investigations of Coiled Sheet Imports from the Federative Republic of Brazil, Canada, Republic of Korea, United States of America, Republic of South Africa and Republic of Venezuela. Diario Oficial de la Federación* (Official Journal), 29 February 1998, para. 39.

[649] Mexico's first written submission, para. 441.

[650] *Ibid.*, paras. 442-48.

[651] Mexico's first written submission, para. 443.

submit this same argument to its own investigating authority, SECOFI, it would be summarily dismissed. As noted above, SECOFI imposes the burden of proving both a difference in the level of trade *and* an effect on price comparability.[652] Mexico did neither the one nor the other. Instead, it supported its claim with nothing but conclusory arguments. According to the findings of the Panel in *United States - DRAMS*, conclusory arguments are not enough to satisfy the burden of proof on the respondent.[653]

(c) Rebuttal of Mexico

6.1123 **Mexico** rebuts Guatemala's submissions as follows:

6.1124 Guatemala argues that at no point does Mexico explain why invoices which are otherwise accurate and lawful should be disregarded when an investigating authority calculates the normal value and that there is no evidence whatever in the file to suggest that the invoices were fraudulent or that the selling prices were not accurate.[654]

6.1125 First, it should be pointed out that Mexico's argument is not that an authority should disregard evidence but indeed that the Ministry had to verify its accuracy and so comply with Article 6.2. Second, we must bear in mind that the Ministry, in a final determination based on the argument of the best information available[655], used as evidence of the normal value four delivery notes (alleged invoices[656] for the reasons we have already stated in this submission), two of which were used for the initial determination and the other two for transactions in January and February 1996 for a load of cement in each case; in none of them is the type of cement specified or detailed.

6.1126 Guatemala argues that the four transactions are supported by invoices which reflect the sale of Cruz Azul grey Portland cement. Guatemala's argument is false, on the one hand because not all the evidence relates to grey cement, for the product is not identified and, even if it were, it is not the product under investigation, and on the other hand, the firms from which the cement was brought were distributors independent of Cruz Azul.[657]

6.1127 Mexico maintains that in its final determination Guatemala did not verify the accuracy of the information and, as at the initiation of the investigation, did not examine the type of cement on the four alleged invoices to satisfy itself whether they effectively corresponded to the like product exported to Guatemala. Accordingly, yet again Guatemala failed to comply with its multilateral obligations by not verifying the accuracy of the evidence which was submitted to it by the parties and which formed the basis for its conclusions; it thereby violated Article 6.6 of the AD Agreement.

6.1128 Guatemala also argues that in cases where an interested party denies access to the requisite information or does not provide it within a reasonable period or significantly impedes the investigation, the authority need not verify the accuracy of the information furnished and, at its discretion, may base its determination on the facts available to it.

---

[652] See para. 162 above.

[653] *DRAMS*, *supra*, footnote 115, paras. 6.69 and 6.73.

[654] First written submission by Guatemala, paras. 351-352.

[655] *Ibid.*, para. 347.

[656] Only the evidence of the transaction concerning a load of cement on 17 February 1996 actually constitutes an invoice. The document clearly indicates that it is invoice 15439 and on the lower left it bears the fiscal stamp, just one of the requirements under Mexican law for it to be considered an invoice. In addition, Annex MEXICO-62 gives a description of invoice requirements.

[657] Independent distributors "Cruz Azul en Tapachula, S.A. de C.V." and "Proveedora de Láminas, y Materiales Bonampak, S. A. de C.V." See Mexico's first written submission, para. 435.

Even from this standpoint, paragraph 7 of Annex II specifies that, if the authority has to base its findings on information from a secondary source, it should do so with special circumspection and, where practicable, check the information from other independent sources. Paragraph 7 of Annex II establishes a standard that Guatemala did not comply with either.

6.1129 Because the Ministry had not identified the like product to the exported product, the information available to it to calculate the normal value did not meet the accuracy standard required by Article 6.6, a situation which affected the comparison of the export price with the comparable price of a like product destined for consumption on the Mexican market, for which reason Guatemala also violated Article 2.1.

6.1130 As to the lack of "representativeness" of the transactions that formed the basis for calculating the normal value, Guatemala argues that Mexico speculates that the alleged invoices could not have been representative and that Mexico never asserts that the calculation is wrong.[658] In this connection, Mexico maintains that Guatemala violated Article 2.2 by not evaluating, or if it did do so, incorrectly evaluating whether sales under the alleged invoices were representative of the Mexican market. The four alleged invoices pertained to the sale of a load or sack of cement in each case, in other words, the lowest volume at which the product under investigation can be marketed. Clearly, the Ministry did not make sure that the price references used for the normal value determination allowed for an appropriate comparison.

6.1131 In addition, Guatemala pursues an absurd and simplistic argument when its states that Mexico speculates that the alleged invoices might not be representative and that the calculation of the normal value is wrong. It is more than plain that, if Guatemala did not review the accuracy of the evidence furnished to show the normal value and did not examine the "representativeness" of the transactions, and given the differences in volume, levels of trade and lack of identification of the product, it now seeks to reverse the pattern of speculation that Guatemala itself followed in its determination of normal value.

6.1132 As to the adjustments to be made for a fair comparison between the normal value and the export price, Guatemala argues that Mexico does not provide either facts or evidence in support of its claim and adds that the reason is that they do not exist. In principle, Mexico reiterates that the evidence used for the normal value and the export price are clear proof that the transactions were made for different amounts and at different levels of trade.

6.1133 Clearly, Guatemala did not make a fair comparison between the normal value and the export price because it did not consider that the four alleged invoices used reflected retail sales and the evidence used for the export price related to wholesale transactions.

6.1134 In addition, by not bearing in mind that the transactions were made for different amounts and at different levels of trade, the Ministry determined a low export price because high volumes of sales at the wholesale level were involved, and a high normal value because low volumes of sales at the retail level were involved. Consequently, the margin of dumping obtained was overestimated because of the effect of these differences, and for this reason Guatemala did not make a fair comparison, thereby violating Article 2.4.

6.1135 Mexico also maintains that Guatemala made an unfair comparison because the Ministry did not satisfy itself as to the terms and conditions of sale for the prices on the alleged invoices of sales on the domestic market and did not take account of the differences that affect the comparability of domestic prices and export prices. It is all too obvious that, in regard to domestic prices, the alleged invoices included at least freight and

[658] First written submission by Guatemala, para. 352.

insurance from the Cruz Azul plant to the warehouse of the independent distributors and the export prices used in the calculation were at the ex-factory level and, therefore, did not include the selling costs incurred in the case of domestic prices.

6.1136 Thus, by not considering the differences in the volumes of sales, the various levels of trade and the terms and conditions of sale for calculating the normal value and the export price, Guatemala did not make a fair price comparison and acted in violation of Article 2.4.

6.1137 Guatemala also argues that the Ministry was unable to make adjustments under Article 2.4 because Cruz Azul refused to cooperate in the investigation. However, no arguments were needed from the exporting firm to recognize the inaccuracy of the evidence submitted for the normal value and the very obvious differences between the items of evidence for a fair comparison between the normal value and the export price.

6.1138 With regard to cost information, Guatemala argues that, without a complete file, the Ministry could not be certain, among other things, that the prices on Cruz Azul's domestic market provided an appropriate basis for determining the normal value.[659] Mexico maintains that, in its reply to the questionnaire, Cruz Azul did not furnish information on production costs because there was no argument by the applicant that Cruz Azul's sales were below cost. Cementos Progreso's assertion was that the price of the product under investigation exported to Guatemala was below the price at which the product was sold on Mexico's domestic market. Nevertheless, in its reply to the request, Cruz Azul supplied information on costs at one of its plants, the one producing the product actually exported to Guatemala, for the original period of investigation.

6.1139 With reference to the use of the best information available, Guatemala argues that it based its final determination on the facts available to it because Cruz Azul refused to supply the requested information on its production costs, the information on its sales between 1 December 1995 and 31 May 1996, and refused to cooperate with the Ministry during the verification.[660] Mexico reiterates that Cruz Azul did not receive a reply from the Ministry regarding essential questions which it had raised before the verification visit (on-the-spot investigation) and which the Ministry should have resolved beforehand so that Cruz Azul would agree to the verification under the terms of paragraphs 3 and 8 of Annex I. Similarly, the verification should have been confined to the information Cruz Azul had supplied or to obtaining further details thereon, in accordance with paragraph 7 of Annex I.

6.1140 In spite of this, Guatemala proceeded with its final determination on the basis of the best information available. In this connection, Mexico maintains that, in its normal value determination, the Ministry violated paragraph 7 of Annex II of the Anti-Dumping Agreement, for two reasons.

6.1141 The first is that the Ministry did not act with special circumspection in issuing its conclusions on the calculation of the normal value, *inter alia*, by not satisfying itself as to the accuracy of the evidence submitted to show the normal value, particularly with regard to the identification of the like product, the lack of "representativeness" of the sales, by not taking account of the obvious differences in volume, in the levels of trade at which the transactions took place and in the terms and conditions of sale, which together reflected that the Ministry made an unfair comparison between the normal value and the export price.

---

[659] *Ibid.*, para. 347.

[660] *Ibid.*.

6.1142 The second reason is that Guatemala did not comply with paragraph 7 of Annex II. In other words, the Ministry never checked the information used to calculate the normal value in the light of information from other independent sources, among others, price lists, official import statistics and customs returns, and there is no record in the file to show that such a check was made. If such a check was not possible, the Ministry did not explain or justify, still less document, in any part of the file, in its final report or in its notice of conclusion of the investigation, that it had not been possible to make the check referred to in paragraph 7 of Annex II.

6.1143 In short, in its normal value determination Guatemala ignored the obvious anomalies and differences mentioned above and, in its findings on normal value, the Ministry did not comply with the minimum standard required for the use of the best information available established in Article 6.8 and in paragraph 7 of Annex II of the AD Agreement.

6.1144 Indeed, Guatemala's incorrect interpretation of the relevant provisions on an authority issuing its determinations on the basis of the best information available goes so far as to make Guatemala argue that, when an interested party has not cooperated to the best of its ability, an authority may use "adverse inferences" as facts available.[661] This is what Guatemala actually did by grounding its final determination on conclusions drawn from adverse inferences concerning Cruz Azul, on the basis of what Guatemala calls the best information available. Mexico submits it is clear that neither Article 6.8 nor Annex II confirms the interpretation Guatemala used to support its final determination. For example, paragraph 7 of Annex II establishes that, if an interested party does not cooperate and thus relevant information is being withheld from the authorities, *this situation could lead to a result which is less favourable* to the party than if the party did cooperate.

6.1145 Guatemala ignored the quality and amount of the information that an authority should consider in making a final determination. As we pointed out earlier, Guatemala's final determination of the normal value was made from an analysis of four alleged invoices, two of which were taken into account to initiate the investigation despite the fact that they were inaccurate and irrelevant and were not enough for the initiation. Similar failings were repeated in the two other items of evidence submitted to show the normal value in the extended period of investigation, and we have already discussed them.

6.1146 In fact, on the basis of the conclusions of the Panels in the *Guatemala - Cement* and *United States - Softwood Lumber* cases, Mexico maintains that for, the purposes of a final determination, the evidence Guatemala should have taken into consideration should have been of a higher quality and amount than those required to initiate the investigation. However, Guatemala did not do this. It did not meet a higher standard of evidence, and the evidence used to determine the normal value is proof of this.

6.1147 Mexico contends that, for a final determination, it is not enough, as Guatemala says, to have made its determination by using a weighted average price from four Cruz Azul sales in Mexico[662], when there are a large number of anomalies, imprecisions and differences which were not heeded and resolved by Guatemala, nor did the Ministry's final determination comply with a standard of evidence higher than that of the initiation.

6.1148 As to the extension of the period of investigation in the final stage, Mexico maintains that in practice the extension constituted a new investigation and unjustifiably imposed an extra burden on the exporter. In this connection, Mexico reiterates that the extension of the investigation period was made at the request of Cementos Progreso but that

---

661 *Ibid.*, para. 348.

662 *Ibid.*, para. 350.

the firm did not submit information or in any way justify its request. Despite the lack of information and justification to extend the period, the Ministry decided in favour of Cementos Progreso's request and extended the investigation period from six months to one year, thereby failing to comply with the provisions of Article 5.2.

(d) Guatemala's Response to Rebuttal of Mexico

6.1149 **Guatemala** makes the following response to Mexico's allegations that it: (a) failed to verify the accuracy and representativeness of the information relied upon to calculate normal value; and, (b) failed to make certain adjustments, such as for alleged differences in levels of trade, to ensure a "fair comparison."

6.1150 Guatemala's position on these issues boils down to two basic points. Firstly, Mexico's arguments do not take account of the fact that Cruz Azul refused to provide Guatemala with accurate and complete information on its costs and sales. Specifically, it refused to provide essential information that was requested in the original questionnaire and in the supplementary questionnaire. It refused to cooperate with Guatemala's attempts to verify its information as provided for in Article 6.7 and Annex I of the AD Agreement. In fact, with the backing of the Mexican Government, Cruz Azul tried to usurp the role of the Ministry by deciding for itself what type of evidence was relevant to the investigation. For example, after refusing to allow the verification to take place, Cruz Azul provided Guatemala with a report containing its own on-the-spot verification conducted by a firm hired and paid for by Cruz Azul. In these circumstances, the Ministry had no choice but to base its final determination of dumping on the "facts available". It could not let Cruz Azul control the investigation and determine what information it would (or would not) provide.

6.1151 In fact, given the statistical data in the record, Guatemala had no choice but to conclude dumping and consequent injury in its final determination. Among other things, the record established the following undisputed facts: first, that the volume of imports increased significantly, from 140 tons in June 1995 to 25,079 tons in May 1996, with 45,859 tons imported during March 1996. Second, that the dumped imports forced Cementos Progreso to reduce its prices significantly in order to compete with Cruz Azul cement. Third, that Cementos Progreso's sales declined beginning with the commencement of Cruz Azul's imports in mid-1995. Fourth, that Cementos Progreso's sales dropped by 14 per cent from the first quarter of 1995 to the first quarter of 1996, notwithstanding a 15 per cent increase in demand. Fifth, that domestic production began to decline in October 1995. Sixth, that domestic production dropped by 14 per cent from the first quarter of 1995 to the first quarter of 1996. Seventh, that Cementos Progreso's market share dropped by between 20 and 30 per cent. Eighth, that Cementos Progreso under-utilized its installed capacity for both clinker and finished cement between June 1995 and May 1996. Ninth, that from June 1994-May 1995 to June 1995-May 1996, domestic capacity utilization declined by 12 per cent for cement grinding and by 16 per cent for clinker. Tenth, that Cementos Progreso suffered negative cash flows during the first months of 1996. Eleventh, that starting in August 1995 Cementos Progreso began to accumulate excess inventories. Finally, that deteriorating conditions of demand in Mexico and investments made to increase capacity in Mexico forced the Mexican cement industry to increase its exports.

6.1152 The second point concerns the argument that in order to ensure a "fair comparison", Guatemala should have made certain adjustments, such as for alleged differences in levels of trade. During the substantive meeting with the Panel, Mexico said that the need for these adjustments was "obvious" and did not depend on cooperation by Cruz Azul during the investigation.[663] However, as we explained in our reply to question 19 of the Panel to Mexico, the only persons who normally have information which would enable the authorities to make adjustments to prices and costs in an anti-dumping investigation are the exporters.[664] Thus, the authorities, such as the Guatemalan Ministry, must be able to require the parties to justify their adjustments as long as the "burden of proof" is not unreasonable.[665]

6.1153 In this case, Cruz Azul did not justify most of the adjustments it requested. In fact, as we have explained throughout this dispute, Cruz Azul refused to cooperate in the Ministry's investigation. Under these circumstances, the Ministry could not, however much it may have wanted to do so, make the adjustments requested by Cruz Azul. For example, the Ministry had no way of knowing whether Cruz Azul's sales in its domestic market and its export sales had been made at two different levels of trade, and if so, it did know the magnitude of the adjustment to be made. There is no evidence of this kind in the record because Cruz Azul refused to provide it and refused to cooperate in the investigation.

6.1154 In short, this was not even a close case. The margin of dumping was enormous, the increase in imports was dramatic and the injurious effect was swift and severe.

2. *Claims Regarding the Guatemalan Ministry's Change of Determination of Threat of Material Injury to Final Determination of Material Injury*

(a) Submissions of Mexico

6.1155 **Mexico** claims that the Guatemalan Ministry of the Economy, without any justification, changed its determination of threat of injury on which it based the initiation of the investigation and imposed a provisional anti-dumping measure into a final affirmative determination of material injury, which improperly served as a basis for imposing definitive anti-dumping duties. It advances the following arguments in respect of this issue:

6.1156 As already explained, the absence of justification for this change constituted a serious violation of Mexico's right of defence under Article 6 of the AD Agreement. Likewise, the lack of sufficiently detailed explanations in the public notice of imposition of the definitive anti-dumping measure regarding the considerations of fact and law and the reasons used as a basis for this change are also contrary to the requirements laid down in Article 12 of the AD Agreement. We shall refer to these below. Nevertheless, we must point out that, in addition to these violations, the change was made even though the Ministry had not carried out an objective examination based on positive and sufficient evidence of either the threat of material injury or the material injury apparently attributed to imports of grey Portland cement, as required by Article 3.1, 3.2, 3.4, 3.5 and 3.7 of the AD Agreement.

6.1157 As already stated, neither in the determination on initiation nor the preliminary determination of the investigation did the Ministry of the Economy undertake an examination that included an evaluation to show the existence of significant price undercutting by the imports investigated in comparison with domestic prices for the like product, nor

[663] Oral submission by Mexico, para. 231.

[664] Appendix I, question 19 to Mexico.

[665] AD Agreement, Article 2.4.

an evaluation of all the relevant factors and indices affecting the state of the domestic industry.

6.1158 Furthermore, as the Ministry did not evaluate the factors indicated in Article 3.2 and 3.4 of the AD Agreement in its determination on initiation and its preliminary determination, on the basis of positive evidence and an objective examination, it could not have concluded that the entry of new dumped imports would have an impact on the state of the domestic industry. In addition, bearing in mind that, as shown above, these determinations were inconsistent with the examination required by Article 3.7, when initiating and imposing the provisional measure, the Ministry could not have made a proper determination of the existence of a threat of material injury to the domestic industry manufacturing grey Portland cement.

6.1159 During the final stage of the investigation, moreover, the Ministry decided without any justification to extend the investigation period by a further six months at the request of Cementos Progreso[666], in other words the original investigation period fixed as June-November 1995 was extended until May 1996 following a request by the domestic producer. An examination of the information in the administrative file of the investigation clearly shows that the Ministry decided arbitrarily and unjustifiably to extend the investigation period with the sole objective of utilizing the new information to allow it to determine material injury in the absence of threat of material injury.

6.1160 In particular, consideration of the new information improperly added during the final stage of the investigation as a result of the arbitrary and unjustifiable extension of the investigation period allowed the investigating authority to manipulate the figures corresponding to the factors indicated in Article 3.2 and 3.4 of the AD Agreement so that an evaluation of these factors would indicate the existence of an alleged impact on the domestic industry apparently due to the entry of dumped imports. Nevertheless, the results of this alleged analysis were statistically invalid[667], and moreover the comparison of the factors by the Guatemalan authority did *not* correspond to the same extended investigation period in relation to previous comparable periods. Consequently, the Ministry illogically and inconsistently took a decision regarding the alleged impact of the economic factors and indices on the domestic industry during the investigation period as a result of imports of grey Portland cement from Mexico.

6.1161 As the Panel can see, this unjustified decision by the Ministry of the Economy to extend the investigation period was made with the objective of seeking to manipulate the information available for both periods so as to allow the investigating authority improperly to reach an affirmative determination of material injury. It is also shown that the decision to extend the period was closely related to the unjustified change in the determination of threat of injury (at the time of initiation and imposition of the provisional measure) to determination of material injury (at the time of imposing the definitive measure).

6.1162 In other words, according to no permissible interpretation of the AD Agreement can it be considered that the Ministry made a substantiated and justified change from the initial and preliminary determination of threat of material injury to a final determination of material injury because it was not possible for the Ministry to determine threat of injury at the initiation of the investigation and in the preliminary determination and then in the final determination to try to substantiate an alleged impact of the imports on the economic factors having a bearing on the state of the domestic industry on the basis of *unjustified extension* of the investigation period. The above shows that the Ministry did *not* have

[666] See the Ministry of the Economy's agreement of 4 October 1996.

[667] See part E.2 of this first submission by Mexico.

positive evidence, either in sufficient quantum nor quality, in accordance with the standard required at the various stages of the investigation, in order to substantiate its determinations, still less to be able to determine a deterioration in the factors of the domestic industry producing grey Portland cement as a result of dumped imports.

6.1163 As Mexico has already explained, the Ministry of the Economy violated Article 12.2 and 12.2.2 of the AD Agreement as neither the public notice of conclusion nor the full report on injury contain or refer to sufficiently detailed explanations of the considerations and reasons for which the Ministry decided: (i) to extend the investigation period; and (ii) to change its determination of the threat of injury according to which it initiated the investigation and imposed provisional duties to a final affirmative determination of material injury under which it imposed definitive anti-dumping duties, bearing in mind also that the Guatemalan authority initiated the investigation on the assumption of the existence of a threat of injury without being in possession of sufficient evidence to substantiate this.

(b) Response of Guatemala

6.1164 **Guatemala** makes the following arguments in response to Mexico's claims regarding the change of determination of threat of material injury to final determination of material injury:

6.1165 Guatemala states that the change from threat of injury to injury was fully justified by the facts.[668] According to Mexico, the Ministry's final affirmative determination of injury was made possible by the unjustified extension of the investigation period.[669] Both these arguments have been dealt with by Guatemala in the course of this submission.[670] Accordingly, they are incorporated here only by reference.

3. *Claims under Articles 3.1, 3.2, 3.4 and 3.5 of the AD Agreement*

(a) Submissions of Mexico

6.1166 **Mexico** makes the following arguments that the final determination of material injury to the domestic industry violated Articles 3.1, 3.2, 3.4 and 3.5 of the AD Agreement:

6.1167 The final affirmative determination of material injury to the Guatemalan domestic industry made by the Ministry of the Economy was *not* based on positive evidence nor did it include an objective examination of the volume of dumped imports, their effect on prices of the like product on the Guatemalan market and the consequent impact of the imports of grey Portland cement on the domestic industry because it failed to evaluate the relevant economic factors and indices having a bearing on the state of the industry. Moreover, the Guatemalan authority did *not* establish a causal relationship between the imports of grey Portland cement and the alleged material injury to the domestic industry, as required by Article 3.5 of the AD Agreement.

6.1168 The Ministry of the Economy's final determination of material injury to the domestic industry therefore violated Article 3.1, 3.2, 3.4 and 3.5 of the AD Agreement. The

668 Mexico's first written submission, paras. 473-80.

669 *Ibid.*, paras. 477-80.

670 See paras. 304-310, 341 and 344 above.

imposition of definitive anti-dumping duties by the Ministry of the Economy under such circumstances also violated paragraphs 1 and 6 of Article VI of the GATT 1994.

(i) The final determination of injury was not based on an objective examination of the volume of dumped imports

6.1169 According to Article 3.2 of the AD Agreement, when determining injury, the investigating authority must consider whether there has been a significant increase in the volume of dumped imports, in absolute terms or relative to production or consumption in the importing Member.

6.1170 Notwithstanding this, in its final affirmative determination of injury, the Ministry of the Economy did not take into account Article 3.2 of the AD Agreement but reached the conclusion that the imports of grey Portland cement from Mexico had shown a significant rate of increase during the investigation period on the basis of the following considerations:

(i) The tariff heading for the imports of cement from Mexico is 2523.29.00 of the Central American Tariff System;

(ii) in June 1995, there was a minimum volume of imports of grey Portland cement from Mexico;

(iii) the Ministry of the Economy determined that in May 1996 the volume was significantly larger than during first month of the extended investigation period[671];

(iv) in an intermediate month during the alleged investigation period, namely, March 1996, the volume of imports was larger than that recorded for the other months in its examination;

(v) the Ministry found that the trend in imports during the investigation period (June 1995 to May 1996) showed a significant rate of increase in the volume of imports.

6.1171 Finally, Mexico does not deem it necessary to repeat its specific requests, since they have been exhaustively set out. Nevertheless, it reiterates the importance of its request that the Panel suggest that Guatemala should revoke the anti-dumping measure adopted against imports of grey portland cement from Mexico and should refund the anti-dumping duties collected. As is known, Guatemala has been collecting anti-dumping duties unduly since 28 August 1996 and Mexico has had to suffer the problems of access to the Guatemalan market simply because the Appellate Body interpreted the Mexican request in a specific way.

6.1172 Mexico hopes that all the time and resources invested in this procedure will be duly considered and that the Panel will exercise its power to suggest the way in which Guatemala should implement the recommendations contained in its report.

6.1173 We are aware of the fact that this power can be exercised only with great prudence, but we consider that, in this particular case, given the background and considering the manifold violations committed in the initiation, the Panel will recognize that Guatemala should never have initiated the investigation and will be able to formulate its sug-

[671] It will be recalled that, on 4 October 1996, without any grounds and on the basis of a request from Cementos Progreso, the Ministry of the Economy decided to extend the investigation period by a further six months, i.e. the original period of June-November 1995 was extended until May 1996.

gestions with the strictest regard for the powers entrusted to it by Article 19.1 of the Dispute Settlement Understanding.

6.1174 As can be seen, the Ministry's reasoning concerning the volume of dumped imports used to reach an affirmative determination of injury is not compatible with the criteria laid down in Article 3.2. The Ministry of the Economy therefore violated Article 3.2 of the AD Agreement by *not* considering whether there had been a significant increase in imports *in absolute terms*. There is a difference between growth in absolute terms, as specified in Article 3.2 of the AD Agreement, and the rate of increase referred to in Article 3.7(i), and the purpose of considering a rate of increase is to examine the trends in the imports investigated.

6.1175 In addition, throughout the final determination there is *no* evaluation of the significant increase in imports *relative to* production or consumption in the importing Member. This led the Ministry of the Economy arbitrarily and unjustifiably to change its determination of threat of material injury into a determination of material injury, without making the examination that might have substantiated this change. Such an examination was necessary because what has to be determined in a case of threat of injury is the likelihood of a substantial increase in imports, whereas in a case of material injury the investigating authority must consider whether the increase has already occurred. Consequently, it is obvious that in this case the Ministry did not consider that *the change* from a threat of material injury to *material injury would in any case require* an evaluation of the imports in accordance with Article 3.2 of the AD Agreement, which is quite different to that required under Article 3.7(i) for cases of determination of threat of injury.

6.1176 Moreover, the calculations made to estimate the increase in the volume of imports of grey Portland cement from Mexico are inaccurate because the Ministry of the Economy confined itself to maximum and minimum volumes imported during the investigation period instead of the trend of imports in absolute terms or relative to the previous comparable period, which in this case would be June 1994 to May 1995, and relative to previous periods, in order to analyse long-term trends in imports. Furthermore, the import figures obtained by the Ministry are also incorrect because the tariff heading under which grey Portland cement is classified also covers products other than the one investigated. Nevertheless, the Ministry improperly considered that all the imports under this tariff heading corresponded to the product investigated and also considered that the total volume of imports under this tariff heading during the months of January to June 1996 corresponded to the Mexican product, without taking into account that Guatemala imported grey Portland cement from other sources during this period. Consequently, the Ministry of the Economy made an erroneous determination of the volume of imports of grey Portland cement from Mexico by *not* excluding imports from other sources and other types of cement, for example, grey cement or slow-setting cement, which are imported under the same tariff heading.

6.1177 There is also information in the administrative file of the investigation that the firm Cementos Progreso imported grey Portland cement from Mexico during the investigation period through a firm called Materiales Industriales S.A. (hereinafter "MATINSA"). In this connection, when responding to the request by the Ministry of the Economy, MATINSA stated that it had no direct commercial relations with Cementos Progreso and that the volume imported during the investigation period was 79,426 tonnes of cement.

6.1178 Contrary to the above, in a full report on the determination of injury, the Ministry of the Economy acknowledged the relationship between Cementos Progreso and MATINSA, but considered that it did not impair the domestic producer's right to complain of the injury caused by the grey Portland cement because (i) the product imported by MATINSA was non-pozzolanic Portland cement and was thus not within *the definition of like product*; (ii) imports of this cement only represented a small proportion of the domestic production of Portland cement; and (iii) the cement imported by MATINSA was sold on the Guatemalan market under the domestic producer's label.

6.1179 Mexico expressly objected to the findings of the Ministry of the Economy regarding the effect of the relationship between the importer MATINSA and the domestic cement producer on the anti-dumping investigation. Firstly, because in the investigation's final determination the Ministry of the Economy determined that the product investigated was grey Portland cement, without making any distinction giving the impression that the pozzolana content of the product investigated differed. In fact, the Ministry of the Economy classified grey Portland cement into 14 sub-categories of cement[672], including those that do not contain pozzolana such as the cement imported by MATINSA.

6.1180 Secondly, Mexico rejected the Ministry's determination for the following reasons: (i) even though the amount of the product imported by MATINSA was irrelevant in comparison with domestic production of the product investigated, the volume of these imports was of particular importance in comparison with the total volume of imports of grey Portland cement into Guatemala during the investigation period, because they accounted for at least *one third* of total imports; (ii) by disregarding the imports by MATINSA corresponding to the like product, the effect of imports of Cruz Azul grey Portland cement on the domestic industry was magnified; (iii) by failing to consider the volume and price of these imports not sold at dumping prices, the Ministry clearly failed to take account of factors other than the dumped imports which also injured the domestic industry, as required by Article 3.5 of the AD Agreement.

6.1181 Based on the foregoing, Mexico argues that the evaluation of imports by the Ministry of the Economy in the final determination of injury is inconsistent with the provisions of the AD Agreement because it is impossible to estimate the penetration of imports of grey Portland cement from Mexico into the Guatemalan market on the basis of incorrect findings, inconsistent data and in the absence of information. By making an inaccurate analysis of the penetration of imports, the Ministry of the Economy compromised the rest of the investigation and could *not* have determined a causal relationship between the allegedly dumped imports and the alleged injury to the domestic industry in accordance with Article 3.5 of the AD Agreement.

6.1182 Furthermore, the Ministry of the Economy's evaluation of imports was also inconsistent with the AD Agreement because in none of the Ministry's determinations is there any indication that the investigating authority considered the total imports of grey Portland cement into Guatemala, neither for the investigation period nor for previous comparable periods. In other words, without knowing and evaluating *the trend in total imports* irrespective of their country of origin, it is *not* possible for any investigating authority to determine *the significance* of the volume of the alleged dumped imports being investigated.

(ii) The final determination of injury did not include an objective examination of the effect

[672] The Ministry of the Economy indicated that there were 14 types of grey Portland cement, namely: Type I, Type I A, Type II, Type II A, Type III, Type III A, Type IV and Type V; if Portland cement is mixed with other components, it is classified into Type I S, Type I P, Type P, Type S, Type I PM and Type I S.

of the imports on prices of the like product on the Guatemalan market

6.1183 According to Article 3.2 of the AD Agreement, the investigating authority shall consider whether there has been significant price undercutting by the dumped imports as compared with the price of a like product of the importing Member, or whether the effect of such imports is otherwise to depress prices to a significant degree or prevent price increases, which otherwise would have occurred to a significant degree.

6.1184 In its final affirmative determination of injury, the Ministry of the Economy indicated that imports of grey Portland cement from Mexico had exercised pressure on the prices of the domestic industry. According to the Ministry, its conclusion was substantiated by the following:

(i) When Cruz Azul cement was first imported, the domestic producer significantly lowered prices in order to be able to compete in each region;

(ii) the increases in the indices considered in the official formula for fixing the maximum selling price did not lead to adjustments in the price of the domestic product;

(iii) during the investigation period (1 June 1995 to 31 May 1996), the domestic industry undertook a significant number of transactions below the maximum authorized selling price;

(iv) the domestic industry's selling price in the border area suffered a greater impact as a result of the dumped imports because prices had to be adjusted to add the relevant transport costs.

6.1185 The Ministry of the Economy did *not* comply with Article 3.2 of the AD Agreement because in its final affirmative determination of injury it included a series of affirmations concerning the price trend without having any elements to uphold the conclusion that the price of the grey Portland cement imported from Mexico undercut the price of domestic grey Portland cement manufactured by Cementos Progreso, or that the effect of the imports on the latter had led to a significant reduction or prevented an increase or, if applicable, to substantiate the finding that the dumping, allegedly by the imports, was the cause of any negative effect on domestic prices and not other elements, for example, the loss of Cementos Progreso's monopoly on the domestic market.

6.1186 In addition, in its examination of prices in the final affirmative determination of injury, the Ministry of the Economy did *not* indicate what methodology was used to analyse prices nor how the comparison between the price of imported cement and the selling price of cement by the domestic industry was made. If this was done, it did not mention either at what level of trade the prices were compared, if they were on the same terms of trade, what were the comparable periods in which the prices were recorded, and whether the prices were the result of simple, weighted, moving or progressive averages.

6.1187 In its final determination, the Ministry of the Economy mentioned that the domestic producer of grey Portland cement lowered its prices during the investigation period without indicating in any way the amount of the alleged reduction, thus showing that the investigating authority did *not* have the necessary elements to determine the trend in domestic prices. Consequently, the Ministry of the Economy could *not* have reached the conclusion that the price of the imports had a negative effect on the domestic price of the like product. The final determination or the full report do not contain either any examination of the price trend in imports for the investigation period, which obviously makes the Ministry of the Economy's findings on alleged price undercutting by the imported product as compared to the price of the domestic product inconsistent with the AD Agreement because, as shown, the investigating authority did not undertake the examination that would allow it to perceive any undercutting.

6.1188 The Ministry of the Economy did not determine either the amount by which the price of the domestic like product fell as compared to the price of the imports allegedly dumped. Because of this, the Ministry did *not* have the elements to allow it to establish a causal relationship between the effect on domestic cement prices and the level of prices at which Mexican imports were entering Guatemala. This means that during the investigation period, the Ministry of the Economy sought to establish a fall in domestic prices in certain regions of Guatemala without considering that these reductions, if they occurred, were due to factors other than the entry of imports.

6.1189 In this connection, in its final determination, the Ministry of the Economy recognizes that in 1990 the Government of Guatemala developed a formula for fixing the ceiling price for cement so that the profits of the domestic producer would not be affected by increases in the various inputs used to manufacture cement. In fact, in the final determination, the Ministry of the Economy stated that the fixing of a maximum selling prices is a disadvantage for the domestic industry confronted by cement imports from any source. The Ministry also declared that the price of imports of the product investigated was based on a policy of shadowing the price in the Guatemalan domestic cement industry, setting the price at a *level slightly below* that of the like domestic product.

6.1190 In the final affirmative determination, the Ministry of the Economy also stated the following:

> " ... that, although other factors may have contributed indirectly to the deterioration in the domestic industry's financial situation, for example, the emergence of a new competitor in a market where there was only one rival, which necessarily has an impact on prices, and the fact that energy and fuel costs constitute a disadvantage for the domestic industry in comparison with the Mexican competition ..."

6.1191 The above shows that the Ministry recognized that factors other than imports might have had a negative impact on the Guatemalan industry manufacturing the product investigated.

6.1192 To summarize, Mexico argues that the price evaluation made by the Ministry of the Economy was inconsistent with the AD Agreement. The final determination clearly shows that the investigating authority did *not* have sufficient elements to determine undercutting, a significant depression of domestic prices or an obstacle to their increase, as a result of imports of grey Portland cement from Mexico. Consequently, the final determination is also contrary to the provisions of Article 3.2 of the AD Agreement on the consideration to be given by the investigating authority to the effect on prices.

(iii) The final determination of injury was not based on positive evidence and did not include an objective examination of the impact of the dumped imports on the domestic industry

6.1193 According to Article 3.4 of the AD Agreement, in order to determine the impact of the dumped imports on the domestic industry, the investigating authority must evaluate:

> " ... economic factors and indices having a bearing on the state of the industry, including actual and potential decline in sales, profits, output, market share, productivity, return on investments, or utilization of capacity; factors affecting domestic prices; the magnitude of the margin of dumping; actual and potential negative effects on cash flow, inventories,

employment, wages, growth, ability to raise capital or investments. This list is not exhaustive, nor can one or several of these factors necessarily give decisive guidance."

6.1194 Notwithstanding the above, the Ministry of the Economy's final determination of injury was not based on positive evidence and did not include an objective evaluation of the impact of the dumped imports on the domestic industry. On the contrary, in its final determination of injury the Ministry confined itself to the following conclusions regarding the alleged impact of imports of grey Portland cement from Cruz Azul on the domestic industry:

(i) Sales of the product investigated fell during the first half of 1996 in comparison with the first half of 1995;

(ii) profits were lower in the second half of 1995 and the first half of 1996;

(iii) output fell by 17 per cent in October and November 1995 and by 14 per cent in the first half of 1996 in comparison with the previous period;

(iv) Cementos Progreso's market share decreased by 20 to 30 per cent;

(v) "the capacity used to grind cement fell by 12 per cent in comparison with the period June to May the previous year" and regarding capacity utilization for clinker, the Ministry of the Economy indicated that "During the period June 1995 to May 1996, utilized capacity fell by 16 per cent in comparison with the same period the previous year";

(vi) during the first months of 1996, the domestic product had a negative operating cash flow, which corresponded to the period during which imports of Mexican cement into the Guatemalan market increased;

(vii) from August 1995 onwards there was an increase in clinker stocks;

(viii) the decrease in sales in 1996 did not have any impact on the number of employees. The number of employees involved in production had remained relatively constant since 1993, wages and salaries had remained steady in comparison with selling prices;

(ix) concerning growth and investment, from 1993 to 1995 fixed assets increased, as a result of expansion liabilities decreased and capital increased, thereby increasing the risk for Cementos Progreso's shareholders;

(x) magnitude of the margin of dumping. There may be other factors which may have indirectly contributed to the deterioration in the financial situation. Nevertheless, the magnitude of the dumping that existed - 89.54 per cent - leads to the conclusion that the injury caused to the domestic industry is the result of the dumped imports.

6.1195 As the Panel can see, the alleged evaluation of injury by the Ministry of the Economy was *not* based on statistically valid comparisons and did *not* properly evaluate the relevant economic factors and indices having a bearing on the state of the domestic industry. By *not* basing its determination on positive evidence and by failing to carry out an objective evaluation of the impact of the imports on the Guatemalan domestic industry producing grey Portland cement, the Guatemalan authority violated Article 3.1 and 3.4 of the AD Agreement.

6.1196 In particular, the investigating authority did *not* undertake a proper evaluation of the impact of the dumped imports on the sales of the domestic industry because it tried to relate the trend in sales in monetary terms to the trend in terms of volume (metric tonnes), indicating in the final determination that:

"... Sales by the domestic industry varied in parallel with variations in demand, except for the year 1995 when the growth in real sales compared with 1994 was 6.97 per cent, although demand rose by 31.89 per cent ..."

6.1197 As can be seen, the Ministry of the Economy on the one hand used the words "real sales" to show the growth in sales in monetary terms and, on the other, referred to the increase in demand (apparent domestic consumption - ADC) expressed in terms of volume, thereby minimizing the growing sales trend in value terms and showing higher growth in apparent domestic consumption in terms of volume, which in any light is inconsistent and not comparable.

6.1198 In the part relating to profits in its final determination, the Ministry of the Economy indicated that Cementos Progreso's financial situation deteriorated in the second half of 1995, a fact that is inconsistent and cannot be substantiated, by stating that in 1995 domestic sales of grey Portland cement showed growth in real terms of 7 per cent, while in the first half of 1996 they fell by 14 per cent as compared to the same period in 1995. This shows that the Ministry of the Economy decided to compare periods that are not comparable and have nothing to do with the period investigated. Contrary to this statement, in the full report on determination of injury, the Ministry of the Economy mentions that Cementos Progreso's operating profits in 1995 were relatively high compared with the comparable period the preceding year, which again is inconsistent with the statement that there was a deterioration in finances that year and cannot be the case if the operating profits are higher as compared to the previous period.

6.1199 In response to the request made by the investigating authority, Cementos Progreso furnished a list of customers who allegedly stopped purchasing Guatemalan cement and bought the imported product under investigation. In the full report on the determination of injury, the Ministry of the Economy stated in this connection that: "During the period investigated, a representative number of customers of the domestic industry ceased to sell the domestic product and replaced their stocks with the imported product". However, from the information in the administrative file, it is *not* possible for the Ministry to substantiate its statement because in order to reach such a determination it would have had to relate the volume purchased by Cementos Progreso's customers to the volume of the imported product purchased by the same customers during the investigation period, an exercise that was not effected by the Ministry of the Economy, so it is *not* able to demonstrate that the domestic product was replaced by the imported product of Mexican origin.

6.1200 To summarize, the Ministry of the Economy made an incorrect determination of the alleged impact of the dumped imports on sales of grey Portland cement by the domestic industry because it made inappropriate comparisons and lacked consistency with regard to the investigation period, the list of customers and the increase in sales.

6.1201 The Ministry of the Economy also violated Article 3.6 of the AD Agreement by assessing all the *profits* earned by Cementos Progreso instead of assessing separately the profits earned from sales of grey Portland cement and the extent to which they affected the total profits earned by the domestic producer as a whole, as the Ministry had information on sales, costs and profits for the like product to allow it to evaluate the profits in accordance with Article 3.6 of the AD Agreement.

6.1202 Mexico also considers that Cementos Progreso's profits do *not* reflect profits for transactions in the product investigated because there are other production lines that could affect the overall profits of the domestic producer, a fact that was clearly *not* taken into account by the Ministry of the Economy in its final determination. It should also be pointed out that at no time did the Ministry of the Economy mention in its final affirmative determination of injury the trend in the domestic producer's profits for the investigation period (June 1995 to May 1996) and for the previous comparable period (June 1994 to May 1995), so it could *not* have determined that the trend in profits earned by the domestic industry had been affected by the declining sales.

6.1203 Moreover, in the final determination, the Ministry of the Economy indicated that domestic *production* of grey Portland cement rose from 1993 to 1995 due to an increase in demand. On this basis, the investigating authority arbitrarily decided to evaluate the trend in domestic production by month and determined a series of decreases in production in October, November and December 1995, as well as during the first half of 1996. The comparison made by the Ministry of the Economy is improper, however, because in reflecting the trend in production the investigating authority left out the months of June, July, August and September 1995 and added one month to the investigation period, June 1996. The cumulative data therefore vary considerably and do not correspond to the trend in production for the investigation period as compared to the previous comparable period.

6.1204 The Ministry of the Economy's evaluation of the trend in production clearly violated Article 3.1 and 3.4 of the AD Agreement because when it perceived increases in production in annual terms, it decided to change its evaluation so as to show decreases using monthly comparisons, and did not take into account the investigation period. Consequently, the Ministry of the Economy could *not* have been in a position to determine objectively that the imports might have had an impact on the volume manufactured by the domestic producer.

6.1205 With regard to Cementos Progreso's *share* of the domestic market, the Ministry of the Economy incorrectly determined that it fell by between 20 to 30 per cent. In its final determination, the Ministry mentioned a range for the share, clearly showing that the investigating authority did not even take the trouble to evaluate and define a precise figure for the share, neither did it indicate what periods the range covers. Furthermore, the Ministry did *not* evaluate the trend in the share in relation to imports from Mexico, from other sources, and the like domestic product, so it could *not* have based its determination on objective and consistent elements that could allow it to determine the impact of the dumped imports on this factor.

6.1206 With regard to *return on investments*, the Ministry of the Economy once again violated Article 3.4 of the AD Agreement by *not* making an adequate examination of the domestic producer's return on investments in its final determination and trying to reflect profitability using only one indicator, because the final determination states that the operating margin in 1995 was 3.4 per cent. This clearly shows that the Ministry of the Economy did *not* have sufficient elements to determine a trend in this factor during the investigation period

6.1207 In its final determination, the Ministry of the Economy attributes the reduction in the *utilization of production capacity* for grey Portland cement to the alleged accumulation of inventories of clinker - which is the basic input used in cement production - without considering that the trend in the utilization of plant capacity for manufacturing grey Portland cement cannot be determined by wrongly looking at the accumulation of inventories of inputs because such a determination can lead to equivocal findings, as happened to the Ministry of the Economy. For example, if we consider that a manufacturer has no stocks of an input, according to the Ministry of the Economy's logic, the conclusion would certainly be that the producer was under-utilizing its production capacity for manufacturing the final product because of the presence of imports on its market.

6.1208 Moreover, in the administrative file there are indications that the volume of clinker inventories at the end of the period, in May 1996, was substantially less than in May 1995, and this amount of stocks can barely be considered the minimum buffer stock needed when producing grey Portland cement, so Cementos Progreso's argument that the accumulation of clinker meant a reduction in the utilization of plant capacity for producing cement is quite wrong and its acceptance by the Ministry of the Economy is incorrect, tendentious and biased.

6.1209 The Ministry of the Economy also indicated that, in evaluating the utilization of plant capacity for grey Portland cement, the months of June 1994 to May 1995 were compared with June 1995 to May 1996 in order to obtain a better indicator of the seasonal nature of production and sales, without justifying such a "methodology". Mexico considers in this connection that the latter indication shows that, in its final determination, the Ministry of the Economy acted inconsistently and in a biased and tendentious manner when determining the impact of the dumped imports because, as Mexico shows in this submission, as far as the production and sales factors are concerned, the Ministry of the Economy did *not* make a comparison with the same periods used to evaluate the utilization of plant capacity. In other words, in a very simplistic way, it decided that the seasonal effects of the market were not relevant for the statistical comparison of these variables, although they were relevant when determining the utilization of plant capacity.

6.1210 Concerning *cash flow*, the Ministry of the Economy did *not* objectively determine the causes of the negative trend in the domestic producer's cash flow. It first stated that Cementos Progreso had an outflow of cash to pay off liabilities and, secondly, as it did not determine the extent of the impact of the like product on Cementos Progreso's profits, the Ministry did *not* have elements that would allow it to determine that the alleged deterioration in the domestic sales of the like product necessarily had an effect on the operational cash flow.

6.1211 In the final determination, the Ministry of the Economy indicated that the decrease in sales of the product investigated had *not* had an impact on the number of *workers directly employed* by the firm Cementos Progreso. The investigating authority could *not* therefore have determined an effect as a result of the dumped imports for this factor.

6.1212 The information in the administrative file does *not* contain any indication that the Ministry of the Economy evaluated the *ability of the domestic industry to raise capital*, as required by Article 3.4 of the AD Agreement, because in order to make such an evaluation at the very least the investigating authority would have to obtain the trend in Cementos Progreso's state of solvency and leverage so the Ministry did *not* reach a determination of the impact on this indicator, without having justified either why it considered this factor not relevant for its determination.

6.1213 The Ministry of the Economy violated Article 3.1 and 3.4 of the AD because in its final determination it did *not* evaluate the trend in *inventories* of grey Portland cement, but simply noted that inventories of clinker, i.e. the input used in cement production, had accumulated from August 1995 onwards. Mexico considers that, as the Ministry of the Economy did not evaluate the trend in inventories of grey Portland cement and did not justify either why it considered this factor irrelevant to its determination, it was *not* in a position to determine that inventories of the like domestic product could have been affected by the imports from Mexico.

6.1214 The Ministry of the Economy did *not* have information on the alleged *investment plans* of the Guatemalan industry, in order to conclude that such projects in fact existed, that they were viable even without the presence of imports, and that they had been affected by the imports of Mexican origin.

6.1215 It may thus justifiably be concluded that the Ministry of the Economy did *not* adequately evaluate the possible impact of the imports on the Guatemalan industry, nor the relevant economic factors and indices having a bearing on the state of the domestic industry so its action was inconsistent with Article 3.1, 3.2, 3.4 and 3.5 of the AD Agreement.

(b) Response of Guatemala

6.1216 **Guatemala** makes the following responding arguments to Mexico's various claims under Articles 3.1, 3.2, 3.4 and 3.5 of the AD Agreement:

6.1217 In accordance with Article 3.1 of the Anti-Dumping Agreement, the Ministry's final determination of injury was based on "positive evidence" and on "an objective examination of: (a) the volume of dumped imports and the effect of the dumped imports on prices in the domestic market for like products, and (b) the consequent impact of these imports on domestic producers of such products". The Ministry's examination of the relevant evidence in the file is contained in the document entitled Supplemented Report for the Determination of Injury Caused by Dumped Imports of Grey Portland Cement from Mexico of 15 January 1997, prepared by the Ministry's Directorate of Economic Integration and in the final determination of 17 January 1997, which was published in the Diario de Centro América on 30 January 1997.[673]

(i) Guatemala objectively examined the volume of dumped imports

6.1218 Article 3.2 allows the import volumes to be analysed in absolute *or* relative terms. If the volumes are examined in relative terms, the comparison must be relative to "production *or* consumption in the importing Member".[674]

6.1219 In the present dispute, the Guatemalan investigating authority examined positive evidence of import volumes on many bases. Firstly, it established that Cruz Azul's dumped imports totalled 236,149.21 tons during the investigation period (June 1995 - May 1996). Secondly, the Ministry determined, again based on positive evidence, that in absolute terms the increase in imports was significant. Specifically, in accordance with Article 3.2, the Ministry determined that during the investigation period imports from Cruz Azul increased from 140 tons in June 1995 to 25,079 tons in May 1996, with a maximum in March 1996 (45,859.31 tons).

6.1220 Next, the Ministry examined the import volumes in relative terms. Firstly, it compared imports of the product under investigation with domestic production. The Ministry found that cement from Cruz Azul jumped from 0.15 per cent of domestic production in June 1995 to 25.84 per cent in May 1996. It then compared import volumes with domestic consumption. In just one year, after having had less than one per cent of the Guatemalan market (in June 1995) Cruz Azul managed to capture an absolute 21 per cent of the market (May 1996). In fact, in March 1996, Cruz Azul controlled about 32 per cent of the Guatemalan cement market.

6.1221 Mexico tries in vain to lessen the impact of these figures. Firstly, it alleges that Guatemala should not have considered the "rate" at which imports from Cruz Azul were increasing.[675] Apart from its obvious absurdity, this argument contradicts the express wording of Article 3.2 which requires the investigating authority to consider whether the "increase" in imports is significant. "Increase" means the "growth or extension of a thing".[676] Thus, contrary to Mexico's assertion, in the final determination of its anti-

673 Final determination, DCA 77 2098.

674 Anti-Dumping Agreement, Article 3.2 (emphasis added).

675 Mexico's first written submission, para. 486.

676 Diccionario de la Lengua Española, Real Academia Española, twenty-first edition 1992, page 162. Webster's Unabridged Dictionary, page 722 (Gramercy Books 1994); See also The Compact

dumping investigation Guatemala properly examined the *rate* at which import volumes were increasing.

6.1222 Secondly, Mexico tries to capitalize on the fact that the Ministry's final determination does not appear to compare import volumes during the investigation period with import volumes during previous periods.[677] In fact, there were no imports during the immediately preceding periods. Mexico is aware that Cruz Azul did not begin to export cement to Guatemala until about June 1995. Mexico is also aware that traditionally its producers have not exported cement to Guatemala. This changed dramatically in 1995 when Mexico suffered a severe economic crisis largely due to the devaluation of the Mexican peso. In short, a comparison of imports during periods prior to the investigation period would only have served to strengthen support for the final affirmative determination of injury.

6.1223 Contrary to Mexico's claims, Cementos Progreso did not import cement from Mexico. Cementos Progreso did buy some cement from MATINSA which that firm was importing from a company other than Cruz Azul. As described in the final determination, the Ministry decided not to apply the anti-dumping measure to cement imported by MATINSA from other Mexican companies because it had not been shown that MATINSA's imports had caused injury to the domestic industry during the investigation period. For example, the cement which Cementos Progreso brought from MATINSA did not cause injury because it was marketed under the Cementos Progreso label and because it was a type of cement which Cementos Progreso was not manufacturing. Mexico can hardly complain that the Ministry had excluded other Mexican cement producers from the scope of its anti-dumping measure.

6.1224 Contrary to Mexico's unfounded allegations, MATINSA's imports did not represent a third of all imports. The Ministry found that the volume imported by MATINSA was insignificant as compared with the total volume of cement imported during June 1995 - May 1996. The Ministry also found that during the investigation period MATINSA's imports decreased substantially relative to the previous period.

6.1225 Contrary to Mexico's allegations, the Ministry did consider the MATINSA imports in evaluating whether dumped imports from Cruz Azul had injured Cementos Progreso. The Ministry concluded that taking MATINSA's imports into account did not weaken its determination of injury caused by cement imports from Cruz Azul.

6.1226 Finally, contrary to Mexico's unfounded claim, the Ministry did not disregard the existence of other types of cement, if any, imported under tariff heading 2523.29.00 In its analysis, the Ministry only considered imports from Cruz Azul. The Ministry noted that imports from Cruz Azul represented 91 per cent of total imports of grey cement into Guatemala during the investigation period. The Ministry did not assume that all the imports under this tariff heading were from Cruz Azul.

(ii) Guatemala objectively examined the effect of the dumped imports on prices in the domestic market for like products.

6.1227 As pointed out above, Article 3.1 requires that the determination of injury be based, among other things, on "an objective examination of ... the effect of the dumped

Edition of the Oxford English Dictionary, Vol. 1, page 1409. ("To grow in size, quantity, duration or degree").

[677] Mexico's first written submission, para. 488.

imports on prices in the domestic market for like products ...". Article 3.2 develops this requirement by specifying that the investigating authorities must consider whether: (a) there has been "a significant price undercutting by the dumped imports as compared with the price of a like product of the importing Member" or (b) "the effect of such imports is otherwise to depress prices to a significant degree or prevent price increases, which otherwise would have occurred, to a significant degree". Contrary to Mexico's allegation, Guatemala conducted both types of analysis and based its final determination of injury on an objective examination of positive evidence.

6.1228 Firstly, the Ministry examined information on prices at both wholesale and retail level in Guatemala during the investigation period. This examination revealed significant price undercutting by Cruz Azul at both levels. Next, the Ministry examined Cruz Azul's pricing policies in Guatemala. Again, it found significant evidence of price undercutting by the dumped imports as compared with the price of the like product in Guatemala. In particular, the supplemented report for the determination of injury prepared by the Ministry's Directorate of Economic Integration dealt with the "policy of following the price set by the competition, situating prices at a level slightly *below* the selling price of the domestic industry, thereby forcing the latter [(that is, Cementos Progreso)] to lower its selling price".

6.1229 Secondly, the Ministry examined whether imports from Cruz Azul were depressing prices or preventing price increases in Guatemala to a significant degree. Among other things, the Ministry found that "(a) imports from Cruz Azul had an immediate and adverse effect on Cementos Progreso's prices; (b) the dumped imports made a greater impact in the area adjacent to the Mexican frontier (especially in the Departments of San Marcos, Quetzaltenango and Retalhuleu) where Cruz Azul concentrated its sales; (c) despite increases in the maximum price for cement established by the government during the investigation period, Cementos Progreso "undertook a significant number of transactions at below the maximum selling price ..."; and (d) if there had been no imports from Cruz Azul, Cementos Progreso "would have been able to sell at the maximum prices established [by the government]".

6.1230 Mexico is desperately trying to find some flaw in these conclusions. For example, it alleges that the Ministry should have explained whether it was examining price undercutting or a reduction in prices.[678] It also mentions Guatemala's alleged failure to explain whether its price comparisons were the result of "simple, weighted, moving or progressive averages".[679] None of these arguments deserves to be taken seriously.

6.1231 If Mexico had conducted this investigation, it might have proceeded differently or have reached a different conclusion.[680] The only question is whether Guatemala established the facts "properly" and if its evaluation of those facts was "unbiased and objective".[681]

6.1232 Mexico has not shown, as required by the standard of review applicable, that Guatemala's factual findings were not properly established or were biased. In short, Mexico has only offered an alternative interpretation of the evidence or, in some cases, has merely suggested that an alternative interpretation might be possible and not that the factual record should contain an alternative finding. Accordingly, there is absolutely no basis for the panel to substitute its interpretation of the facts for that of the Guatemalan authori-

678 Mexico's first written submission, para. 498.

679 *Ibid.*.

680 Anti-Dumping Agreement, Article 17.6(i).

681 *Ibid.*.

ties and to proceed in this way would be to contravene the clearly established standard of review applicable to anti-dumping disputes under Article 17.6(i).

(iii) Guatemala objectively examined the impact of the dumped imports on the domestic industry

6.1233 In addition to examining import volumes and the effect on prices, Guatemala also examined, in accordance with Articles 3.1 and 3.4 of the Anti-Dumping Agreement, the impact which dumped imports from Cruz Azul were having on the Guatemalan cement industry. As already mentioned, Article 3.1 stipulates that the investigating authorities must examine, among other things, the impact the dumped imports were having on the domestic producers concerned. Article 3.4 develops this requirement by specifying that:

> "The examination of the impact of the dumped imports on the domestic industry concerned shall include an evaluation of all relevant economic factors and indices having a bearing on the state of the industry, including actual and potential decline in sales, profits, output, market share, productivity, return on investments, or utilization of capacity; factors affecting domestic prices; the magnitude of the margin of dumping; actual and potential negative effects on cashflow, inventories, employment, wages, growth, ability to raise capital or investments. *This list is not exhaustive, nor can one or several of these factors necessarily give decisive guidance.*"[682]

6.1234 In the present dispute, Guatemala based its final determination on positive evidence and an objective examination of, *inter alia*, the consequent impact of Cruz Azul imports on the domestic industry, in accordance with Article 3.1 and 3.4 of the Anti-Dumping Agreement. The Ministry's examination revealed that, among other things, Cruz Azul imports had:

- Caused Cementos Progreso's sales to decline by 14 per cent between the first quarter of 1995 and the first quarter of 1996. This decline coincided with Cruz Azul's entry into the market;
- caused Cementos Progreso to lose customers;
- caused domestic cement production to record a reduction of 14 per cent between the first quarter of 1995 and the first quarter of 1996. This reduction began when Cruz Azul started importing cement into Guatemala;
- caused a reduction of between 20 and 30 per cent in Cementos Progreso's share of the domestic market;
- caused a decline in Cementos Progreso's capacity to utilize both clinker and finished cement;
- caused a 12 per cent fall in domestic utilization of cement grinding capacity and a 16 per cent fall in domestic utilization of clinker production capacity;
- caused Cementos Progreso to experience negative cash flow during the first months of 1996;
- caused Cementos Progreso to postpone investment plans which would have modernized its plant and increased its production capacity; and

682 *Ibid.*, Article 3.4 (emphasis added).

- caused Cementos Progreso to accumulate excessive inventories as from August 1995.

6.1235 Once again, Mexico is trying to find a possible flaw in the Ministry's analysis and conclusions. Instead of referring to the correct standard of review, Mexico explains how it would have conducted the investigation differently. For example, Mexico says that it would not have compared sales trends (measured in monetary terms) with levels of consumption (measured in volume terms).[683] It also alleges that the Ministry could have used annual rather than monthly domestic production figures.[684] As will be shown below, none of these claims is relevant to the settlement of this dispute.

6.1236 First of all, there is no flaw in the Ministry's analysis of injury. For example, it is not wrong for the authority to compare domestic sales during the investigation period with domestic sales during the previous period. It is also consistent with Article 3 of the Anti-Dumping Agreement that an authority should make the same type of analysis for apparent domestic consumption and the relation between consumption and sales. In fact, as part of a broader examination of the impact which the dumped imports had on Guatemala's domestic industry, such an analysis is unquestionably logical and reasonable.

6.1237 Secondly, in the course of its first written submission Mexico asserts that it would have acted differently. It also expresses its displeasure with the facts revealed by the information examined by Guatemala.[685] Unfortunately for Mexico, the facts do not lie. Moreover, although Mexico might have proceeded differently if it had been the investigating authority, the fact is that this has no relevance to the settlement of this dispute. As observed by the panel in the case *EC - Cotton Yarn*, the mere fact that an authority has not selected a set of information rather than another different set of information does not indicate, in the absence of other information, bias or lack of objectivity.[686]

6.1238 As we have been obliged to point out on several occasions, the issue before this panel is whether the establishment of the facts by Guatemala was "proper" and whether its evaluation of those facts was "unbiased and objective".[687] Mexico has not shown Guatemala to have violated any of these standards; therefore, Mexico being the complainant in this dispute, its arguments should fail.

(c) Rebuttal of Mexico

6.1239 **Mexico** makes the following rebuttals to Guatemala's assertions under Articles 3.1, 3.2, 3.4 and 3.5 of the AD Agreement:

6.1240 Mexico reiterates and maintains what it said in its first submission about the final determination of the existence of material injury reached by the Ministry, namely, the determination was not based on positive evidence, nor did it involve an objective examination of the volume of the dumped imports and the effect of the dumped imports on prices of the like product, and the consequent impact of imports of grey Portland cement on the domestic industry, because it failed to evaluate the relevant economic factors and indices having a bearing on the state of the industry, required under Article 3.1, 3.2 and 3.4 of the AD Agreement. Similarly, the investigating authority did not establish a causal

683 Mexico's first written submission, paras. 508-09.
684 *Ibid.*, paras. 515-516.
685 *Ibid.*, paras. 508-09.
686 ADP/137, adopted 30 October 1995, paras. 512-13.
687 Anti-Dumping Agreement, Article 17.6(i).

relationship between the imports of cement and the alleged material injury to the domestic industry, in accordance with Article 3.5 of the Anti-Dumping Agreement.

6.1241 In particular, the Ministry's examination in arriving at an affirmative final determination of material injury did not comply with the provisions of Article 3.1, 3.2 and 3.4 of the Anti-Dumping Agreement. In its first submission, Guatemala mentions that, in accordance with Article 3.2, it examined the increase in the volume of dumped imports.[688] However, for Mexico such an assertion is unacceptable because, neither in the supplemented report on injury, nor in the final determination can it be seen that the Ministry obtained the variations in the dumped imports factor. Article 3.2 states that:

> "With regard to the volume of the dumped imports, the investigating authority shall consider whether there has been *a significant increase in dumped imports either in absolute terms* or relative to production or consumption in the importing Member ..." (Emphasis added)

6.1242 The fact is that the Ministry confined itself to specifying an alleged import volume in the *month of June 1995* and another in the *month of May 1996*, without at any time indicating the factor's behaviour in absolute terms. In other words, the Ministry considered that simply by indicating the import figures at both ends of the investigation period it was possible to infer the factor's behaviour, without thereby demonstrating the absolute increase in dumped imports.

6.1243 Moreover, it is important to mention that, in keeping with Article 3.5 of the AD Agreement, the investigating authority should evaluate, in addition to the dumped imports, imports which are not dumped, such as imports of the investigated product from other sources. In this way, an impartial and objective investigating authority is in a position to determine, on the one hand, total imports of the investigated product entering its market and, on the other, it obtains a reliable figure for imports to be included in apparent domestic consumption. However, the Ministry did not obtain either the volume or the price of imports from other sources so as to establish the real penetration of the allegedly dumped imports. This meant that the Ministry had a partial and unobjective view of the behaviour of total imports and was ignorant of the real effect they might have on relevant domestic production.

6.1244 The Ministry's analysis of imports is incorrect because it did not identify the proportion of imports of the investigated product (grey Portland cement) entering under tariff item 2523.29.00 in total imports under that tariff heading.[689] Again, the Ministry should have identified total imports of the investigated product, which of them were from Mexico, which from Honduras, which from El Salvador, and so on. By not doing this, the Ministry could hardly have reached valid conclusions on the behaviour of grey Portland cement imports on its market, as required under Article 3.2 and 3.5 of the Anti-Dumping Agreement.

6.1245 Mexico also submits that, during the investigation period, Cementos Progreso imported cement *through* a firm known as MATINSA and that the imports accounted for at least *one third* of total imports of Mexican origin. Guatemala mentions in its first submission that Mexico makes unfounded allegations that MATINSA imports represented a third of all imports and that the volume of those imports is insignificant.[690] In this con-

---

[688] *Ibid.*, para. 358.

[689] Mexico's understanding is that products other than the one under investigation (grey Portland cement) fall under tariff heading 2523.29.00 of the 1993 Central American Tariff System.

[690] First written submission by Guatemala, para. 363.

nection, Mexico wishes to make it clear that in the final determination the Ministry of the Economy said:

> "The Directorate of Economic Integration also requested the Guatemalan company, Guatemalteca Materiales Internacionales, S.A. (MATINSA), to provide information on the value and volume of its cement imports during the period 1 June 1995 to 31 May 1996 ... *During the period investigated, imports amounted to 79,426 tonnes.*" (Emphasis added)
>
> "... During the period indicated, *imports of grey Portland cement* rose to 236,149.21 metric tonnes ..." (Emphasis added)

6.1246 From these assertions it is not possible to agree with what the Ministry says. Obviously the quotient of these two figures represents at least a third of all imports, for which reason Guatemala's argument that MATINSA imports were insignificant is, in Mexico's opinion, impermissible.

6.1247 Accordingly, Mexico maintains that the Ministry's analysis of imports is inconsistent with the Anti-Dumping Agreement because it seeks to determine the penetration of dumped imports on the Guatemalan market from incorrect data about the volume of total imports originating in Mexico, and because this volume of imports by the MATINSA firm is not taken into account. What is said by the Ministry in its final determination reveals how incorrect the analysis of imports is and also the lack of information. Hence the Ministry did not validly establish its affirmative determination of injury.

6.1248 In addition, the Ministry is contradictory in regard to total cement imports by the domestic industry when it says in its supplemented report[691] that the product imported by Cementos Progreso is different from the one under investigation because it is a *PSI 5000 cement not containing pozzolana*, and also, the Ministry's import statistics show various operations in which the description of the cement imported by MATINSA is of *TI cement with pozzolana*. This indicates that the product MATINSA imported during the investigation period is the same as the one Cruz Azul exported in that period. Accordingly, the Ministry's imports analysis is wholly incorrect and biased and the import figures can in no sense be regarded as reliable.

6.1249 Furthermore, in the final determination the Ministry says that MATINSA imported cement *at a price below* that of the export firm, Cruz Azul, and that MATINSA's imports did not cause injury to the domestic industry. Regarding this assertion, there is no evidence in the investigation file to show that the Ministry made any comparison between the price of Cruz Azul exports and MATINSA imports. This demonstrates that the Ministry made a number of assertions without corroborating the facts and that the Ministry merely confined itself to copying out the arguments of the domestic industry instead of examining the behaviour of imports in order to arrive at an objective and impartial final determination of the existence of injury to the domestic industry producing grey Portland cement.

---

[691] See MEXICO-43 (Section A, Annex II, p.2), which states:

> "The second segment of domestic industry consists of the manufacture of other types of cement. The most important is the one known as 5,000 PSI, a cement without pozzolana which up to 1995 had been imported for marketing under its own brand. There have been imports of this product from Mexico. This product has characteristics different from those of Type I PM cement, which is a pozzolana cement. At the present time, domestic production of non-pozzolana cement has increased. The domestic industry's import strategy for this product was an evaluation of its market potential".

6.1250 Another example of the inconsistency in Guatemala's analysis and of its erroneous, biased and non-objective assessments is the assertion about imports undercutting domestic prices. There is in fact a serious contradiction on Guatemala's part when it states:

> "... This examination revealed *significant* price undercutting by Cruz Azul at both levels ... In particular, the supplemented report for the determination of injury prepared by the Ministry's Directorate of Economic Integration dealt with the "policy of following the price set by the competition, situating prices at a level slightly *below* the selling price of the domestic industry ...".[692] (Emphasis added)

6.1251 This confirms Mexico's contention in its first submission, namely that the Ministry's price analysis was inconsistent with Article 3.2[693], for in order to determine the imported product's undercutting of the prices of the domestic product the Ministry based itself on a series of statements about price trends without anything to support the conclusion that undercutting existed during the investigation period.

6.1252 Again, there is no analysis in the investigation file to support the Ministry's assertion that, in the absence of imports under dumping conditions, the domestic industry would have been in a position to sell at the *maximum* prices (theoretical price) established by the Government of Guatemala. In other words, there is no evidence of the trend in cement prices in periods before the imports were made, for which reason the Ministry mistakenly assumes that domestic cement prices behaved in accordance with the maximum established price and that, when the allegedly dumped imports came in, cement prices took a downturn. This shows that the Ministry, without any grounds, established a causal relationship between import prices and the trend in domestic prices.

6.1253 What is more, in the final determination the Ministry said that the transactions which showed the most marked differences between the real prices and the formula prices (formula used to establish the maximum price) were found on the market in the west of the country. This demonstrates that the Ministry confined itself to an analysis of regional prices, something which shows price trends in one region of the country, and it cannot be inferred what the price trend was in the rest of the country. Consequently, Mexico submits that the price analysis by the Ministry was not made in accordance with Article 3.2 of the Anti-Dumping Agreement because no reference was made in the final determination to the impact that the entry of dumped imports during the investigation period would have on the *domestic prices* of grey Portland cement.

6.1254 In addition, as stated by the Ministry in the course of the investigation, the price of cement in Guatemala is subject to a formula that allows for increases in various inputs used in manufacturing the product (Ministerial Decision 1-90 of the Ministry of Communications, Transport and Public Works). In this connection, the investigation file does not contain any document reflecting increases in transport, energy, fuel, etc. or the way in which these increases were absorbed by domestic grey Portland cement prices. Hence the Ministry could not find out the real trend in the price of the product under investigation and compare it with the price of the allegedly dumped imports. Therefore, the Ministry's price analysis is completely wrong and is inconsistent with Article 3.2 of the Anti-Dumping Agreement because it does not make valid comparisons between domestic prices and the prices of the imported product from which an impartial and objective investigating authority could conclude that there was significant undercutting by import prices relative to the prices of the domestic product.

---

[692] See first written submission by Guatemala, para. 367.

[693] See first written submission by Mexico, paras. 496-497.

6.1255 Mexico wholly rejects Guatemala's argument in its first submission that the analysis of the impact of the dumped imports on the domestic industry was impartial and objective.[694] In fact, in examining the impact of the imports the investigating authority should have taken account of the terms of Article 3.4 of the AD Agreement:

> " ... economic factors and indices having a bearing on the state of the industry, including actual and potential decline in sales, profits, output, market share, productivity, return on investments, or utilization of capacity; factors affecting domestic prices; the magnitude of the margin of dumping; actual and potential negative effects on cash flow, inventories, employment, wages, growth, ability to raise capital or investments. This list is not exhaustive, nor can one or several of these factors necessarily give decisive guidance".

6.1256 To begin with, in its first submission Mexico said that the Ministry's examination did not consider statistically valid information to enable it to reach proper conclusions on the degree of injury allegedly suffered by the domestic industry.[695] In Mexico's view, the purpose of an evaluation of the factors listed in Article 3.4 is not to reflect what those factors were at a particular point in time but to find out the industry's situation by evaluating the behaviour of those various factors *throughout the period*, so as to be in a position to determine the fluctuations, both real and potential.

6.1257 As a result, and because it did not find out the behaviour of the factors indicated in Article 3.4, the Ministry was unable to arrive at an analysis encompassing the interrelationships between the trends in those factors. For example, from a decline in sales and an increase in production of a good over a particular period it can be expected that inventories will rise. Therefore, the Ministry could not make a positive final determination of the existence of material injury to the domestic industry.

6.1258 Secondly, the investigation file does not *contain an examination of the potential effect on the domestic industry* of dumped imports. In other words, the Ministry never sought to find out the potential behaviour of the factors described in Article 3.4 of the AD Agreement so as to determine that the alleged dumped imports would have an adverse effect on domestic production of grey Portland cement in the investigation period. In accordance with the last sentence of Article 3.4, the investigating authority must bear in mind that the list of factors is not exhaustive, nor can one or several of those factors necessarily give decisive guidance.

6.1259 Thirdly, the Ministry failed to evaluate the potential factors in the domestic industry, in keeping with the requirements of Article 3.4, as well as evaluate the trend in such factors as cash flow, wages, growth, ability to raise capital or investments, since neither in the final examination nor in the public notice nor in the supplemented report is there any document to conclude otherwise. Consequently, it is not possible to determine the general state of the domestic industry with regard to the factors listed in Article 3.4. Actually, without an evaluation of the state of the industry, it is impossible for the Ministry to have reached a reasoned conclusion, based on an objective evaluation of the facts, about the probable impact of the dumped imports in the investigation period.

6.1260 It should be noted that, under the Agreement on Safeguards, the Panel in *Korea - Definitive Safeguard Measure on Imports of Certain Dairy Products*[696], said that the in-

---

[694] First written submission by Guatemala, paras. 372-373.

[695] First written submission by Mexico, paras. 507-508.

[696] See report of the Panel in *Korea - Dairy, supra*, footnote 531, Section G, which says:

> "7.55. In conducting our review of Korea's serious injury determination we are mindful of the obligations contained in Article 4.2 of the Agreement on Safe-

guards. This provisions mandates that competent authorities when performing a serious injury investigation:

"... shall evaluate all relevant factors of an objective and quantifiable nature having a bearing on the situation that industry, in particular, the rate and amount of the increase in imports of the product concerned in absolute and relative terms, the share of the domestic market taken by increased imports, changes in the level of sales, production, productivity, capacity utilization, profits and losses and employment.

These provisions sets out the general principle regarding the economic factors which need to be considered in a serious injury investigation, *and provides a list of factors that are a priori considered to be especially relevant and informative of the situation of the domestic industry. The use of the word "in particular" makes it clear to us that, "among all the relevant factors" that the investigating authorities shall "evaluate", the consideration of the factors listed is always relevant and therefore required, even though the authority may later dismiss some of them as not having a bearing on the situation of that industry.* Under the applicable standard of review, our function is to assess whether Korea (i) examined all relevant facts in its possession or which it should have obtained in accordance with Article 4.2 of the Agreement on Safeguards at the time of the investigation; and (ii) provided an adequate explanation of how those facts as a whole supported the determination made. Thus, we shall examine whether at the time of the determination all factors listed in Article 4.2 were appropriately considered; *whether the Korean authorities explained how each factor considered supports (or detracts from) a finding of serious injury; and whether valid reasons have been put forward for dismissing a considered factor as not being relevant to the serious injury determination in this case.*" (Emphasis added)

"7.58. In our evaluation of Korea's serious injury determination there are three issues that we find particularly troublesome. First, we find that *there is a lack of consideration in the OAI report of some of the factors listed in Article 4.2.* This is the case for instance for capacity utilization and productivity. In both cases Korea offers explanations in its submissions to the Panel of why it considered these factors not to bear on the situation of the domestic industry. *While these explanations seem plausible, there is nothing in the OAI report which would indicate to the Panel that these factors were taken into consideration in the serious injury finding of the Korean authorities.* Second, as we noted above, the definition of the domestic industry in this case as comprising two different segments of the dairy products market has consequences for the evaluation of the situation of the industry. In assessing the serious injury to the whole domestic industry, we find that it is acceptable to analyse distinct market segments but, as stated above, *all factors listed in Article 4.2 must be addressed. In considering each of the factors listed in Article 4.2, and any others found to be relevant by the authority,* the investigating authority has two options: for each factor the investigating authority can consider it either for all segments, or if it decides to examine it for only one or some segment(s), it must provide an explanation of how the segment(s) chosen is (are) objectively representative of the whole industry. A lack of consideration of all segments, without any explanation, is a flaw that we find present in Korea's analysis of the domestic industry's profits and losses, prices, debts to equity ratio, capital depletion, and production cost. How Korea relates developments in one segment to its determination regarding the industry as a whole is for Korea to decide in the first instance. Our point here is that an analysis of only a segment of the domestic industry, without any explanation of its significance for the whole industry, will not satisfy the requirements of the Agreement on Safeguards. Third, we find that for certain factors considered by Korea it has failed to provide sufficient reasoning on some of the choices made in the analysis of such factors which may have affected the result

vestigating authorities are required to consider all factors relative to the determination of injury that are included in the relevant provisions of the corresponding WTO Agreements, and that their determination should reflect consideration of all those factors. In addition, the Panel reached the conclusion that, although the investigating authorities may determine that some factors are not relevant to their decision or have no crucial bearing on it, they cannot simply dismiss those factors and must explain in their conclusions why they are not relevant or significant. It is important to emphasise that, in the present instance, the Ministry's determination was made in the context of an anti-dumping investigation and not in a safeguard context. Nevertheless, both Agreements provide for the same type of evaluation for the determination of injury. In fact, Article 3.4 of the Anti-Dumping Agreement establishes the following:

> "The examination of the impact of the dumped imports on the domestic industry concerned shall include an evaluation of all relevant economic factors and indices having a bearing on the state of the industry ...".

6.1261 Similarly, Article 4.2 of the Agreement on Safeguards states the following:

> "In the investigation to determine whether increased imports have caused or are threatening to cause serious injury to a domestic industry under the terms of this Agreement, the competent authorities shall evaluate all relevant factors of an objective and quantifiable nature having had a bearing on the situation of that industry, in particular, the rate and amount of the increase in imports of the product concerned in absolute and relative terms, the share of the domestic market taken by increased imports, changes in the level of sales, production, productivity, capacity utilization, profits and losses and employment."

6.1262 It is worth noting that both Agreements say that the investigating authorities shall evaluate all relevant factors, even some which the authority may subsequently dismiss because they have no bearing on the situation of the domestic industry.[697]

6.1263 Furthermore, the United States, as a third party in this proceeding, says that the evaluation of inventories of a semi-finished product may help an investigating authority to obtain a clearer picture of the situation of the domestic industry.[698] Mexico agrees with what the United States says, provided the evaluation *is an aid* in determining more precisely the situation of the industry. However, in its final determination the Ministry considered that *exclusively analysing an input was enough to point to the trend in inventories of the product under investigation*. This is inconsistent with the terms of Article 3.4 of the AD Agreement, which states that the investigating authority shall consider among other factors, inventories *of the product under investigation*. Accordingly, it is inadmissible for an investigating authority to fail to analyse inventories of the product under investigation and merely find out the trend in inventories of one of the inputs used in the manufacture of grey Portland cement and infer therefrom that the trend in the inventory of the product under investigation was similar to that of the clinker inventory in the investigation period.

> of the consideration. *Also, there is a lack of reasoning in some cases on how the factor considered supports (or detracts from) a finding of serious injury*. This lack of explanation or reasoning is perceived in Korea's consideration of market share, production, profits and losses, employment and inventory." (Emphasis added)

697 See report of the Panel in *"Argentina - Safeguard Measures on Imports of Footwear"* WT/DS121/R, adopted 12 January 2000, DSR 2000:II, 575.

698 See oral statement by the United States of America at the first substantive meeting, held on 16 February 2000, para. 15.

4. *Claims Under Article 3.5 - Causal Relationship Between Dumped Imports and Injury*

(a) Submissions of Mexico

6.1264 **Mexico** makes the following arguments in support of its claim that Guatemala did not adequately demonstrate the existence of a causal relationship between allegedly dumped imports and alleged injury:

6.1265 Article 3.5 of the AD Agreement provides the following:

> "3.5. It must be demonstrated that the dumped imports are, through the effects of dumping, as set forth in paragraphs 2 and 4, causing injury within the meaning of this Agreement. The demonstration of a causal relationship between the dumped imports and the injury to the domestic industry shall be based on an examination of all relevant evidence before the authorities. The authorities shall also examine any known factors other than the dumped imports which at the same are injuring the domestic industry, and the injuries caused by these other factors must not be attributed to the dumped imports. Factors which may be relevant in this respect *include, inter alia, the volume and prices of imports not sold at dumping prices*, contraction in demand or changes in the patterns of consumption, trade restrictive practices of and competition between the foreign and domestic producers, developments in technology and the export performance and productivity of the domestic industry." (emphasis added).

6.1266 In its final determination, the Ministry of the Economy indicated that during the investigation period imports of pozzolanic Portland cement from Mexico caused injury to the domestic industry. It determined the injury to the domestic industry on the basis of the following effects: (i) reduced volume and value of sales: (ii) pressure on selling prices; and (iii) resulting deterioration in the domestic industry's financial situation, which led to a loss of in market share and postponement of investment decisions and the creation of new jobs.

6.1267 A reading of Article 3.5 of the AD Agreement and the final affirmative determination reached by the Ministry of the Economy shows that the investigating authority could *not* have demonstrated the existence of a causal relationship between the dumped imports and the alleged injury to the domestic industry producing grey Portland cement for the following reasons:

6.1268 Firstly, the investigating authority did *not* evaluate the alleged impact of the imports investigated on the value and volume of sales, pressure on selling prices, deterioration in the financial situation, market share and employment, as required by Article 3.4 of the AD Agreement. *Neither* did it make statistically valid comparisons to allow it to undertake an objective examination of the effect of the imports allegedly dumped, as required by Article 3.1 of the AD Agreement.

6.1269 Secondly, in the final determination, the Ministry of the Economy recognized that the fixing of a maximum selling price was a disadvantage for the domestic industry in comparison with products imported from any country. In the full report on determination of injury, the Ministry gives more precise indications, however, stating:

> " ... that, *although other factors may have contributed indirectly to the deterioration in the domestic industry's financial situation*, for example, the emergence of a new competitor in an industry where there was only one rival, which necessarily has *an impact on prices*, if demand remains steady larger supplies lower prices. Regarding production and distribution costs, it should be noted that the relative importance of energy and fuel

> costs places the domestic industry at a disadvantage in comparison with Mexican competition ..." (emphasis added).

6.1270 The above shows that the Ministry of the Economy did *not* evaluate the injury caused by *factors other* than dumped imports because in its final determination the Ministry merely gave simplistic indications of other factors of injury, without showing how these affected the state of the domestic industry. As it had not undertaken such an examination, it was *not* possible for the Ministry of the Economy to satisfy itself of the extent to which the deterioration was attributable to the imports allegedly dumped or to other factors.

6.1271 Thirdly, in its final determination the Ministry of the Economy could *not* have established a causal relationship between the imports allegedly dumped and the alleged injury to the domestic industry producing grey Portland cement as it indicated in the full report on determination of injury:

> "The supply of grey Portland cement on the Guatemalan market has been met by the domestic industry, subject to a price ceiling and *a commitment to supply the State's requirements at a price lower than the selling price to the public.*" (emphasis added).

6.1272 The above statement highlights the Ministry of the Economy's partiality and lack of objectiveness when making the final determination of injury as it did *not* evaluate the impact of the imports on the state of the domestic industry in the light of a commitment by the domestic producer to the Guatemalan State according to which Cementos Progreso agreed to sell the product investigated to the Guatemalan State at a price lower than the selling price to the public. Consequently, by omitting this in its evaluation, the Ministry of the Economy violated Article 3.1, 3.2 and 3.4 of the AD Agreement. Contrary to Article 3.5 of the AD Agreement, the Ministry was *not* able either to establish a causal relationship between the imports of grey Portland cement and the alleged injury to the domestic industry because it had not determined the existence of material injury.

(b) Response of Guatemala

6.1273 **Guatemala** responds to Mexico's arguments regarding the final determination of injury under Article 3.5 as follows:

6.1274 In accordance with Article 3.5 of the Anti-Dumping Agreement, the investigating authorities must demonstrate that the dumped imports are causing injury to the domestic industry. The second sentence of Article 3.5 requires the demonstration of a causal relationship to be "based on an examination of all relevant evidence before the authorities". In particular, the authorities must examine:

> "Any known factors other than the dumped imports which at the same time are injuring the domestic industry, and the injuries caused by these other factors must not be attributed to the dumped imports. Factors which may be relevant in this respect include, *inter alia*, the volume and prices of imports not sold at dumping prices, contraction in demand or changes in the patterns of consumption, trade-restrictive practices of and competition between the foreign and domestic producers, developments in technology and the export performance and productivity of the domestic industry."[699]

6.1275 Guatemala complied with Article 3.5 of the Anti-Dumping Agreement in its determination of the causal relationship between Cruz Azul's dumping and the material in-

---

[699] Article 3.5.

jury suffered by the domestic industry. The Guatemalan investigating authority examined all the relevant evidence, including all the factors listed in Article 3.4, in an unbiased and objective manner. Among other things, this examination showed that:

- Cruz Azul's prices were significantly lower than the price of the like domestic product, which obliged Cementos Progreso to sell at prices much lower than the maximum price authorized by the government.
- The magnitude of the dumping by Cruz Azul was significant (that is, 89.54 per cent) and was a source of injury for Cementos Progreso.
- The influx of dumped imports obliged Cementos Progreso to implement a new price structure, in September 1995.
- The imported product and the like domestic product were marketed through the same distribution channels and in the same geographical markets.
- Representative customers switched to Cruz Azul cement during the investigation period.
- The impact of the loss of customers was greater in the border area to which Cruz Azul had easier access.
- The imported product and the like domestic product were interchangeable and, from the customer's point of view, there were no differences in the way they were used.
- As a result of declining sales, depressed prices and falling profits, Cementos Progreso was obliged to postpone the investment decisions that would have enabled it to modernize and extend its production plants.

6.1276 Mexico asserts that Guatemala did not evaluate the potential injury due to factors other than dumped imports.[700] Mexico maintains that, as it did not make this evaluation, "in its final determination the Ministry of the Economy could *not* have established a causal relationship between the imports allegedly dumped and the alleged injury to the domestic industry".[701] Mexico is wrong.

6.1277 The Ministry simply examined all the relevant evidence it had before it, including all the known factors that suggested that the injury which the domestic producer was suffering might be attributable to factors other than dumped imports. For example, the file clearly shows that the Ministry examined whether the injury suffered by the domestic producer was attributable to a contraction in demand. On finding that this was not the case, the Ministry stated:

> "... according to official statistics, the construction sector has experienced growing demand since 1985 .... Subsequently, growing demand in the construction sector remained constant, even though in comparison with other countries per capita consumption appears low (footnote omitted). This constant growth in the market prompted the domestic producer to carry out feasibility studies with a view to expanding its production capacity ... *Consequently, this Ministry considers that there has been no contraction in demand that could have affected the domestic industry.*

6.1278 In developing its point concerning the alleged failure to assess these "other factors", Mexico alleges that in its final determination Guatemala attributed the injury caused

[700] Mexico's first written submission, para. 533.
[701] *Ibid.*, para. 534 (original emphasis).

by these factors to imports from Cruz Azul.[702] The corresponding passage of the Ministry's final determination reads as follows:

> "... although other factors may have contributed indirectly to the deterioration in the domestic industry's financial situation, for example, the emergence of a new competitor in the market where there was only one rival, which necessarily has an impact on prices, and the fact that energy and fuel costs constitute a disadvantage for the domestic industry ..."

6.1279 What Mexico does not mention is that the Ministry took great care not to attribute the effect of these other factors to Cruz Azul imports. The supplemented report on determination of injury which, according to Mexico itself, is very accurate, reads as follows:

> "Although the above-mentioned factors are affecting the deterioration of the situation of the domestic industry, they do not affect the determination of injury caused by dumped imports, nor are they the subject of analysis or quantification in the present report".

6.1280 In short, the Mexican arguments against the Ministry's final determination concerning causal relationship lack merit. They are nothing other than conclusory arguments lacking any factual or legal basis. Thus, Mexico has not satisfied the complainant's burden of proof. For the reasons explained above, the Mexican arguments should be rejected and the final determination of injury should be respected.

(c) Rebuttal of Mexico

6.1281 **Mexico** rebuts Guatemala's submissions by asserting that the final determination of material injury to the domestic industry infringed Article 3.5 of the AD Agreement by not establishing the causal relationship between the dumped imports and the injury to the domestic industry. It makes the following rebuttal arguments:

6.1282 Guatemala's final determination on the causal relationship between the allegedly dumped imports and the alleged injury suffered by the domestic grey Portland cement industry did not comply with the provisions of Article 3.5. Guatemala did not make appropriate comparisons of the trend in the factors mentioned in Article 3.2 and 3.4 and, as a result its analysis did not have reliable figures to reach proper conclusions about the existence of material injury to the domestic industry.

6.1283 Again, in no part of the final determination of material injury is there any element to imply that in the course of the investigation Guatemala took up such aspects as an analysis of injury to the domestic industry attributable to factors other than the dumped imports. In fact, there is in the file no analysis of the trend in those factors which indicates the adverse effect that may have caused on the performance of the domestic industry, as well as the alleged effect caused by the dumped imports.

6.1284 Neither in the final determination, nor in the supplemented report on the determination of injury, does one find an analysis of investment programmes (economic feasibility studies) to enable the Ministry to conduct any financial simulations in the course of the investigation and conclude that, in the absence of dumped imports, the investment projects mentioned by Cementos Progreso were viable and feasible. Since such analyses were not made, there is no way the Ministry, acting as an impartial and objective authority, could satisfy itself as to the viability of the investment projects, in the absence and in the presence of the dumped imports.

---

[702] Mexico's first written submission, paras. 532 - 33.

6.1285 What is more, the Ministry never saw fit to emphasize that Cementos Progreso is obliged to sell cement to the Government of Guatemala at a price below the price at which it is sold to the public (in accordance with Government Decision 517-90). In what way did the Ministry consider the injury caused to the domestic cement industry as a result of the sales to the Government below the selling price to the consumer? Did the Ministry not consider it relevant to attribute this injury to the someone who really caused it and not to a cement exporter? The Ministry alone has answers to these questions and it is therefore clear that the Ministry did not act as an impartial and objective authority and that it acted in flagrant violation of Article 3.5 of the AD Agreement by not considering in its analysis the existence of this type of "pact" between the domestic cement industry and the Guatemalan Government.

6.1286 Similarly, the Ministry did not analyse the effects during the investigation period of increases in energy and fuel costs on the operating profits of the domestic producer of grey Portland cement:

> "... although *other factors* may have contributed indirectly to the *deterioration in the domestic industry's financial situation*, for example, the emergence of a new competitor in the market where there was only one rival, which necessarily brings pressure to bear on prices, for with constant demand greater supply brings down prices. As for the costs relating to production and energy costs, *attention should be paid to the relative importance of energy and fuel, which placed the domestic industry at a disadvantage in regard to Mexican competition* ..." (Emphasis added)
>
> "Although the above-mentioned factors are effecting the deterioration of the situation of the domestic industry, they do not effect the determination of injury caused by dumped imports, nor are they the subject of analysis or quantification in the present report." (Emphasis added)

6.1287 Under the terms of Article 3.5 it is not enough, as did the Ministry, simply to mention in the final determination the matters which might cause injury to the domestic industry and which are not attributable to the dumped imports. In fact, Article 3.5 states the following:

> "... The authorities shall also examine any known factors other than the dumped imports which at the same time are injuring the domestic industry, and the injuries caused by these other factors must not be attributed to the dumped imports ...".

6.1288 In other words, an impartial and objective investigating authority will make an analysis to support its decision to set aside or even deny the potential impact on the domestic industry of factors other than the dumped imports.

6.1289 Accordingly, Mexico confirms its argument regarding the bias and lack of objectivity in the Ministry's final determination of injury because it did not evaluate the impact of the dumped imports on the state of the domestic industry and because it was unable to establish the causal relationship between the imports and the alleged injury to the domestic industry. The Ministry therefore acted in violation of Article 3.1, 3.2, 3.4 and 3.5 of the Anti-Dumping Agreement.

5. *Claims Under Article 12.2 - Public Notice of Final Determination*

(a) Submissions of Mexico

6.1290 **Mexico** argues that the public notice of conclusion of the investigation, which contained the final affirmative determination on the imposition of definitive anti-dumping duties, published in the *Diario Oficial de Centro América* of 30 January 1997 ("notice of conclusion")[703] did *not* comply with the requirements in Article 12.2 and 12.2.2. of the AD Agreement. Its arguments on this issue are as follows:

6.1291 The final determination did *not* contain all the relevant information on the issues of fact and law nor did it include sufficiently detailed explanations of the reasons that led the Ministry to impose the definitive anti-dumping measure nor several of its determinations, for example, the unjustified extension of the investigation period from six months to one year and the equally unjustified change from threat of material injury to material injury, which was made when imposing the definitive anti-dumping measure.

6.1292 Article 12.2 provides the following with regard to the content of the public notice of the preliminary and final determinations:

> "12.2. Public notice shall be given of any preliminary or final determination, whether affirmative or negative, ... Each such notice shall set forth, or otherwise make available through a separate report, in sufficient detail the findings and conclusions reached on all issues of fact and law considered material by the investigating authorities...".

6.1293 In the case of public notice of conclusion of an investigation in particular, Article 12.2.2 lays down the requirements to be met in the notice:

> "12.2.2 *A public notice of conclusion* or suspension of an investigation in the case of an affirmative determination providing for the imposition of a definitive duty or the acceptance of a price undertaking *shall contain*, or otherwise make available through a separate report, *all relevant information on the matters of fact and law and reasons which have led to the imposition of final measures* or the acceptance of a price undertaking, due regard being paid to the requirement for the protection of confidential information. *In particular, the notice or report shall contain the information described in subparagraph 2.1, as well as the reasons for the acceptance or rejection of relevant arguments or claims made by the exporters and importers*, and the basis for any decision made under subparagraph 10.2 of Article 6." (emphasis added).

6.1294 The following are among the requirements in Article 12.2.1 referred to in the above paragraphs:

> "12.2.1 A public notice of the imposition of provisional measures *shall set forth*, or otherwise make available through a separate report, *sufficiently detailed explanations* for the preliminary determinations *on dumping and injury and shall refer to the matters of fact and law which have led to arguments being accepted or rejected*. Such a notice or report *shall*, due regard being paid to the requirement for the protection of confidential information, *contain in particular*:
>
> ...
>
> (iii) the margins of dumping established *and a full explanation of the reasons for the methodology* used in the establishment and comparison of the export price and the normal value under Article 2;
>
> (iv) considerations relevant to the injury determination as set out in Article 3;

[703] Public notice of conclusion of the investigation which reached an affirmative determination on the imposition of definitive anti-dumping duties (hereinafter also "notice of termination").

(v) *the main reasons* leading to the determination." (emphasis added).

6.1295 In this particular case, the notice of conclusion published by the Ministry of the Economy did *not* meet some of the requirements in the AD Agreement. In particular, it failed to provide a full explanation of the reasons which at a particular time had justified the methodology used by the Ministry to determine and compare the export price and the normal value and, as we have already explained above, these comparisons and determinations were *not* consistent with Article 2.

6.1296 The notice also failed to provide explanations, still less sufficiently detailed explanations, on some of the considerations *related to the determination of injury in accordance with Article 3*. One very important element in this respect is the extension of the investigation period after imposition of the provisional measure, without due justification, and without taking into account the opinion of the exporter nor the impact on its right of defence.

6.1297 As we have already mentioned above, there were no grounds whatsoever for the extension of the period, except that the Ministry sought to reach a determination of material injury instead of threat of material injury, which had been the case at the initiation of the investigation and in the preliminary determination. This change was not even mentioned in the notice of conclusion and still less were the reasons explained.

6.1298 The importance of including in the notice of conclusion sufficiently detailed explanations of the Ministry's agreement to extension of the investigation period and the reasons therefor, as well as the change from threat of material injury to material injury, is particularly significant if we consider that the extension was made after the publication of the public notice of imposition of the provisional anti-dumping measure (nine months after the initiation of the anti-dumping investigation and three months prior to its conclusion).

6.1299 Thus, *without any explanation* in the notice of conclusion, not to mention sufficient explanation, in other words in complete contravention of Article 12.2.2 of the AD Agreement, the Ministry decided: (i) to extend the investigation period without explaining the reasons for doing so; and (ii) to change the determination of threat of material injury to one of material injury.

6.1300 Another matter that was omitted from the notice of conclusion was any explanation of the considerations or physical, chemical and qualitative aspects taken into account by the Ministry in determining that the cement sold in Mexico (Type II Pz grey Portland cement) and the cement exported to Guatemala by Cruz Azul (Type I PM grey Portland cement) were like products.

6.1301 In this connection, in the section of the notice of conclusion entitled "*ARGUMENTS OF THE PARTIES*", point 1.4, it can be noted that Cementos Progreso only put forward in its final pleadings of 19 December 1996 (hearing of the parties) arguments that the products Type I PM Portland cement and Type II Pz Portland cement were like products in the following terms:

> "1.4 At the hearing for submission of the final pleadings (19 December 1996), Cementos Progreso S.A. ... also stated that chemical and physical tests carried out in the complainant's laboratory showed that there were no significant differences among type II Pz, I PM and I P cements produced by Cooperativa La Cruz Azul S.C.L. and that the three products were the same type of cement so the definitive measure should apply to all grey Portland cement imported from the United Mexican States regardless of its source and type specification ..."

6.1302 Regarding these arguments put forward by the applicant, the "CONSIDERATIONS" section of the notice of conclusion does *not contain any evaluation or explanation for acceptance or rejection* of this argument.

6.1303 In addition, with regard to the change from a determination of threat of material injury to a definitive determination of material injury, the "*ARGUMENTS OF THE PARTIES*" section in the notice of conclusion indicates that the applicant first put forward a claim that the dumped imports of cement had caused injury to the domestic industry during the course of the investigation (at the public hearing of 19 December 1996).

6.1304 The letter drawn up by the applicant and submitted at the hearing of 19 December 1996 was also confusing regarding the statement in the notice of conclusion on the change in evaluation from threat of material injury to material injury, and to show this the following is an extract from the relevant sections:

> "THREAT OF INJURY AND INJURY
>
> 48. The injury or threat of injury expressed (*sic*) in paragraph 1 of Article 3 of the WTO Agreement includes the premise of the existence of dumping. This assumption has been proved during the investigation: there is dumping, so it is necessary to consider the imports, their volume, their effects and their impact.
>
> 56. The purpose of the foregoing was to reiterate what has already been demonstrated: the injury to the domestic industry caused by dumped imports of the like product, and to warn of the possibility that it may recur...
>
> COMPLAINTS
>
> 11. That due note be taken of the arguments, evidence, statistical and all documentary information which, in the course of this investigation, has been provided to substantiate the terms of its complaint of dumping, threat of injury and the establishment of a causal link between the first two elements."

6.1305 Even assuming that there had in fact been a change in the applicant's complaint from threat of material injury to material injury, it should be made clear that this complaint was made by Cementos Progreso *eleven months after the initiation* of the investigation and less than one before the publication of the definitive determination. Even more serious is the fact that this claim was made at a phase or procedural stage at which no new evidence could be allowed. The rules[704] governing the hearing state the following:

> "Attach to this background information the above submission. In view of the request from Cooperativa La Cruz Azul, S.C.L., the parties are informed that the hearing set for 19 December 1996 will be subject to the following rules:
>
> ...
>
> 2. The hearing is not intended to be a debate among the parties and *additional evidence will not be taken into account or accepted*, therefore, it will be restricted to giving each of the parties an opportunity to present

[704] The rules governing the hearing were issued in a document of 6 December 1996 by the Directorate of Economic Integration.

its conclusions on the facts investigated and the investigating authority may not seek additional information." [705]

6.1306 Having clarified the above, we must point out that the notice of conclusion *does not contain any explanation* of the acceptance or rejection of the pleadings presented by the applicant nor any explanation of the determination reached by the Ministry in concluding the investigation and imposing the definitive anti-dumping duties, i.e. for material injury instead of threat of material injury.

6.1307 In addition, the final determination of material injury by the Ministry is *not* and cannot be recognized as a determination based on positive evidence and an objective examination in accordance with Article 3.1 of the AD Agreement, for the reasons explained in part E.2 of this first written submission by Mexico. This lack of evidence is no doubt the reason why the notice of conclusion does *not* explain in sufficient detail the considerations relating to the determination. As proof of this, we refer the Panel to the notice of conclusion, particularly the "CONSIDERATIONS" section, part C "Injury caused to the domestic industry".

6.1308 As one example of the lack of sufficiently detailed and clear explanations in the notice of conclusion, among other items we refer to subparagraph 4.5 of the aforementioned section C referring to productivity. This subparagraph does *not* explain, and certainly not in sufficient detail, what was the effect on the productivity of the domestic industry. The explanation is not only insufficient but is also confused, referring to the plant capacity factor without clearly defining the effect on productivity.

6.1309 The above clearly shows that the notice of conclusion did *not* comply with the requirements in Article 12.2 and 12.2.2 because it did *not* contain detailed explanations concerning the determinations of dumping and material injury nor explanation of certain determinations regarding the investigation made by the Ministry. There were no explanations *inter alia* on the extension of the investigation period nor the change in the determination of threat of material injury into one of material injury. In addition, the notice did not include sufficiently detailed explanations on the issues of fact and law which formed the basis for accepting or rejecting various arguments put forward by the parties during the investigation.

6.1310 To summarize, the public notice of conclusion of the anti-dumping investigation which reached an affirmative determination on the imposition of definitive anti-dumping duties on allegedly dumped imports of grey Portland cement from the Mexican firm Cruz Azul is inconsistent with Article 12.2 and 12.2.2 of the AD Agreement.

(b) Response of Guatemala

6.1311 The following are **Guatemala's** responding arguments to Mexico's claims regarding the public notice of final determination under Article 12.2 of the AD Agreement:

6.1312 In accordance with the provisions of Article 12.2.2, the public notice of 30 January 1997 provided the names of the suppliers; a description of the product sufficient for customs purposes; the margin of dumping and a full explanation of the methodology used in the establishment and comparison of the export price and the normal value under Article 2; the considerations relevant to the injury determination as set out in Article 3; and

[705] This was reiterated by Licenciada Ileana Polanco Cordón, Director of Economic Integration at the Guatemalan Ministry of the Economy, at the public hearing of the parties on 19 December 1996 in the following terms: "Beforehand, Licenciada Polanco Cordón indicated that *during the hearing evidence would not be accepted* and that explanations would solely be taken as such and not as evidence ..." (emphasis added).

the main reasons leading to the determination. The notice filled 38 single-spaced pages and was more than 15,000 words long. No reasonable person could read the public notice and conclude that it was lacking in any respect.

6.1313 As Article 12.2.2 allows, the Ministry also issued a separate report (supplemented report on dumping and injury prepared by the Ministry's Directorate of Economic Integration, dated 15 January 1997) which provided additional information on the Ministry's findings and conclusions on all the issues of fact and law. The report was issued in two parts, one for dumping and the other for injury. The report runs to approximately 40 pages and more than 14,000 words. All this information was made available to Cruz Azul in good time.

6.1314 Mexico objects to the notice on grounds that are irrelevant under Article 12. Instead of focusing on the adequacy of the analysis and the transparency of the process, Mexico uses Article 12 as an opportunity to formulate new arguments relating to substantive provisions of the Anti-Dumping Agreement. For example, it devotes several pages to its arguments concerning the extension of the investigation period and the change in the Ministry's injury analysis.

6.1315 However, Article 12 does not deal with the content of the laws, regulations, decisions or determinations of a Member. Instead, Article 12 is exclusively concerned with the interest shared by all Members in the transparent application of anti-dumping measures. Thus, Article 12.2 requires the publication of a notice that contains "sufficient detail" concerning "the findings and conclusions reached on all issues of fact and law considered material by the investigating authorities". The Article does not mention the substantive correction of the authorities' findings and conclusions, since Article 12 is not concerned with these questions.

6.1316 Secondly, Mexico seems to believe that an authority's every thought and every finding that it makes during the course of an investigation should be incorporated in writing in the final determination. Mexico disregards the Ministry's lengthy discussion of the important issues raised in the underlying administrative file and, instead, concentrates on a few topics not mentioned in the notice.[706] According to Mexico, these omissions are somehow fatal.

6.1317 Clearly, this interpretation of Article 12 is absurd. If the investigating authorities had to put down every thought and every decision on paper, they would never have the time nor the resources to conduct an investigation and, even if they had, the notice would be a worthy rival for Tolstoy's *War and Peace*. Judged by any reasonable standard, the public notice of Guatemala's final determination complied with the requirements of Articles 12.2 and 12.2.2.

(c) Rebuttal of Mexico

6.1318 **Mexico** makes the following rebuttal arguments on the subject of the public notice of final determination:

6.1319 Guatemala wrongly asserts that a large number of pages and words is sufficient for a reasonable person to read the public notice and to conclude that it was not lacking in any respect under the terms of Article 12.2.2.[707] Guatemala also says that it issued a separate report (supplemented report on dumping and injury prepared by the Ministry's Directorate of Economic Integration) which provided additional information on the Minis-

[706] See Mexico's first written submission, paras. 540-54.

[707] First written submission by Guatemala, para. 385.

try's findings and conclusions on all matters of fact and law.[708] And misinterpreting the Anti-Dumping Agreement and Mexico's arguments, Guatemala even manages to suggest, absurdly and rhetorically, that a public notice of conclusion would then have to be as long as a book like Tolstoy's *War and Peace*.[709]

6.1320 Mexico submits that the volume or extent of a public notice of conclusion of an investigation is not and cannot be enough to consider that the notice meets the requirements of Article 12.2 and 12.2.2. On the one hand, Article 12.2 specifies that "... the notice or separate report" shall set forth "in sufficient detail the findings and conclusions reached on all issues of fact and law considered material by the investigating authorities", and in addition Article 12.2.2 establishes that the public notice or the separate report shall contain or make available "... all relevant information on the matters of fact and law and reasons that have led to the imposition of final measures ... as well as the reasons for the acceptance or rejection of relevant arguments or claims made by the exporters and importers ...".

6.1321 In this connection, Mexico maintains that neither the public notice of conclusion of the investigation nor the supplemented report[710], which Guatemala now claims to have prepared as a separate report, sets out in detail the findings and conclusions reached by the authority, nor all the relevant information and reasons which have led the authority to impose final anti-dumping measures, nor the reasons for the acceptance or rejection of the exporter's arguments. For example, neither the public notice nor the supplemented report sets forth in detail the relevant information, conclusions and findings concerning the extension of the investigation period and the causes therefor, nor is any reference made to the grounds on which the extension was accepted. Neither is any mention made of the basis for the change in the final determination from threat of material injury to material injury, particularly when, at the time the investigation was initiated, there was no evidence of a threat of material injury and the Ministry's preliminary determination did not analyse the factors in Article 3.2 and 3.4 of the AD Agreement.

6.1322 In Mexico's view, the above-mentioned matters, because of their relationship with the relevant facts or circumstances of the investigation and their impact on the final determination are matters which, because of their "relevance", the Ministry should have included in the public notice or in the separate report. Even under the terms of Article 12.2.2, regardless of the validity of the final determination challenged by Mexico, the public notice or separate report should have contained matters pertaining to information, matters of fact and law, and the reasons for extending the period of investigation, as well as the change in the determination from threat of material injury to injury, for they led the Ministry to impose definitive anti-dumping measures. It should be added that:

6.1323 The investigation period was extended from six months to one year without Cementos Progreso supplying in its request any further evidence to justify an extension[711], in its determination on extending the investigation period the Ministry did not explain the

---

[708] *Ibid.*, para. 386.

[709] *Ibid.*, para. 390.

[710] In fact, these documents are annexes to the "Technical study of the result of the anti-dumping investigation into imports of cement from Mexico", and neither they nor the technical study indicate that they are designed to act as a separate report under the terms of Articles 12.2 and 12.2.2 of the AD Agreement.

[711] See Mexico's reply to Panel question 14 of 18 February 2000 and the communication by Cementos Progreso of 18 September 1996, submitted to the Ministry on 1 October.

bases or legal reason for the extension, nor did it do so in the notice or in the supplemented report.

6.1324 As already pointed out, the public notice makes no reference to the change from threat of material injury to material injury. It is relevant that the Ministry in its "Technical study of the result of the anti-dumping investigation into cement imports from Mexico" stated:

> "... in the present case, the domestic producer requested the initiation of the investigation, indicating that massive imports of Portland cement under dumping conditions were threatening to cause injury to the domestic industry. Later, in its final claim [19 December 1996] it said that it had suffered injury to its production ..."

6.1325 It may be inferred from the Ministry's assertion that, as from this statement made at the public hearing, the Ministry proceeded to conduct a different analysis. In other words, instead of analysing the existence of a threat of material injury, it conducted an analysis of material injury itself. However, neither the public notice nor the supplemented report gives any explanations in this regard.

6.1326 In addition, how can Guatemala's argument that it complied with Article 12.2 and 12.2.2 by means of a supplemented report be valid when the public notice gives no such indication, nor is the purpose of the supplemented report in question intended to comply with the obligations set out in those Articles? Quite simply, Guatemala does not meet the criterion of transparency[712] in the determinations the authority adopts. Hence we emphasize that, with post hoc arguments Guatemala is trying to make good its violations of Article 12.2 and 12.2.2. The result that it is not possible to accept the validity of Guatemala's argument that it fulfilled its obligations by pointing out that it has a report, when in fact that report does not meet the requirements of the articles mentioned.

6.1327 Again, it is inadmissible and unacceptable for Guatemala to suggest that any document contained in the file can constitute the separate report referred to in Articles 12.2 and 12.2.2. To accept this would be to violate the transparency essential to the authority's determinations. It should be reiterated that, in the case at issue, no part of the public notice or the file or the supplemented report establishes that the report constitutes the separate report referred to in the articles mentioned.

6.1328 For the reasons expressed above, Mexico maintains that, in connection with Guatemala's final determination and despite Guatemala's extensive public notice or alleged separate report, Guatemala did not comply with its obligations under Article 12.2 and 12.2.2 of the AD Agreement.

6. *Claims Under Articles 1, 9, and 18 of the AD Agreement and Article VI of GATT 1994 - Application of Anti-Dumping Measure*

(a) Submissions of Mexico

6.1329 The following are **Mexico's** submissions regarding Guatemala's alleged violations of Articles 1, 9 and 18 of the AD Agreement and Article VI of GATT 1994:

6.1330 Having demonstrated that neither on initiation of the investigation nor when imposing the provisional and definitive measures did the Guatemalan authority make a valid

[712] Guatemala recognizes the transparency required in applying anti-dumping measures; see Guatemala's first written submission, para. 388.

determination of dumping nor the alleged threat of injury nor the alleged injury, and also failed to demonstrate a causal relationship between them, as required by Articles 2 and 3 of the AD Agreement, and in view of the violations of Article 5, 6, 7 and 12 of the Agreement committed when initiating the investigation and during its course, the Panel can see that:

(i) Guatemala decided to establish definitive anti-dumping duties on grey Portland cement from the Mexican firm Cruz Azul without having duly complied with all the requirements for their establishment prescribed by Article 9.1 of the AD Agreement;

(ii) the application of the definitive anti-dumping measure under such circumstances is contrary to the provisions of Article VI of the GATT 1994 and in turn constitutes a violation of Article 1 and 18 of the AD Agreement.

(b) Response of Guatemala

6.1331 **Guatemala** responds to Mexico's arguments advanced under Articles 1, 9 and 18 of the AD Agreement and Article VI of GATT as follows:

6.1332 Article 9.1 of the Anti-Dumping Agreement deals with two questions: the imposition of anti-dumping duties and whether the amount of those duties should be equal to the full margin of dumping. In both cases, Article 9.1 leaves the decision to the investigating authority where "all requirements for the imposition [of duties] *have been* fulfilled".[713] Note that this provision does not leave the decision to the authorities "if" all requirements for the imposition are fulfilled, but in cases where all requirements "have been" fulfilled. In other words, Article 9.1 does not relate to and in no way incorporates the substantive requirements for the imposition of definitive anti-dumping duties contained in other provisions of the Anti-Dumping Agreement. Thus, Mexico's arguments under Article 9.1 lack merit and should be rejected by the Panel.

6.1333 Finally, Mexico's arguments under Articles 1 and 18 of the Anti-Dumping Agreement lack merit in that they are based on the premise that there have been violations of other provisions of the Agreement (for example, Articles 2, 3, 5, 6, 7 and 12), which is not the case. As has been shown in the course of this first written submission, the investigation at issue complied fully with Article VI of the GATT 1994 and the rules of the Anti-Dumping Agreement.

G. Are Any Errors Guatemala Might Be Found to Have Committed Insufficient to Justify the Formulation of a Recommendation by the Panel?

1. Submissions of Guatemala

6.1334 **Guatemala** advances the arguments that any error(s) it might be found to have committed is/are insufficient to justify the formulation of a recommendation by the Panel. It advances the following arguments in this regard:

6.1335 In its first written submission, Mexico asks the Panel to recommend that Guatemala "bring its measure into conformity with the GATT 1994 and the AD Agreement".[714] For the reasons set out below, Guatemala maintains that this request should be rejected.

[713] Anti-Dumping Agreement, Article 9.1 (emphasis added).

[714] Mexico's first written submission, para. 556, Section VI(f)(b).

6.1336 Firstly, Guatemala has shown, without resorting to legal ruses, that its definitive anti-dumping measure as well as the actions that preceded it were totally consistent with the GATT 1994 and all the provisions of the Anti-Dumping Agreement. Secondly, even assuming, for the sake of argument, that Guatemala has violated its obligations under the WTO, the panel should conclude that any error of a technical nature which Guatemala may have committed during the course of the investigation does not merit recommendations being made in accordance with Article 19.1 of the DSU.

6.1337 In the course of this submission, Guatemala has replied to a barrage of allegations intended to challenge procedural or (technical) aspects of the Ministry's investigation. The actions challenged include (a) Guatemala's timely notification under Article 5.5; (b) whether Guatemala complied in good time with the provisions of Article 6.1.3; (c) whether its public notices were sufficiently detailed in accordance with Article 12; (d) whether Guatemala established in a timely and reasonable fashion the time-limits for the submission of information laid down in Article 6; (e) whether Cruz Azul had timely and full access to the administrative file as required by Article 6; and (f) the handling of confidential information in accordance with Article 6.

6.1338 As far as these arguments are concerned, Guatemala has shown that it duly complied with its obligations under the GATT 1994 and the Anti-Dumping Agreement. Moreover, Guatemala has shown that neither Cruz Azul nor Mexico suffered any injury as a result of the actions to which these complaints relate. We have shown, for example, that even if assuming that Guatemala's notification under Article 5.5 had not been made in good time, the error was harmless.[715] Consequently, if the panel were to conclude with respect to these complaints that Guatemala did in fact violate its obligations under the WTO, it should *not* make any recommendation since Guatemala has rebutted any assumption of nullification or impairment under Article 3.8 of the DSU.

6.1339 Guatemala has rebutted any presumption of nullification or impairment. Moreover, Guatemala has shown that during the investigation both Cruz Azul and Mexico acquiesced in many of these actions. For example, we have shown that even though the notification under Article 5.5 may not have been made in good time, Mexico did not raise the question until 6 June 1996, almost six months *after* the publication of the notice of initiation.[716] Therefore, in accordance with the principles of international law, any injury that might have been caused is not legally worthy of consideration. Consequently, any presumption of nullification or impairment derivable from Guatemala's actions has been rebutted and there is no justification for issuing any recommendation.

6.1340 On the above grounds, Guatemala respectfully maintains that the panel should reject the Mexican application and should not make any recommendation under Article 19.1 of the DSU.

6.1341 The alleged delay in giving notification under Article 5.5 of the Anti-Dumping Agreement (which Guatemala does not accept) did not impair Mexico's rights in the proceeding and in accordance with generally accepted principles of international law was merely a harmless error. Article 17.6(ii) of the Anti-Dumping Agreement stipulates that "the panel shall interpret the relevant provisions of the Agreement in accordance with customary rules of interpretation of public international law". WTO panels have recognized that "the customary rules of interpretation of public international law" are those incorporated in the Vienna Convention on the Law of Treaties (the Vienna Conven-

---

[715] See paras. 206-216 above.

[716] See paras. 217-219 above.

tion).[717] Thus, the expression "customary rules of interpretation of public international law" in Article 17.6(ii) of the Anti-Dumping Agreement also refers to the rules laid down in the *Vienna Convention.*

6.1342 Article 31.3 of the Vienna Convention establishes that, in addition to the text, consideration must be given to "any relevant rules of international law applicable in the relations between the parties". Accordingly, in arriving at a decision, a WTO panel should apply the relevant rules of international law.

6.1343 In accordance with Article 38(1) of the Statute of the International Court of Justice, the sources of international law include, *inter alia*, the "general principles of law recognized by civilized nations".[718] The principle of harmless error, which states that a party must show injury before obtaining the right to be compensated for a procedural error, is a general principle of law recognized by civilized nations. The response to the violation of a substantive rule is very direct; the national measure is condemned and its withdrawal is requested. Violations of procedural rules may also be condemned. However, the question is whether it can be said that a decision involving such a violation is flawed. The retrospective rejection of administrative decisions can give rise to immense confusion and to avoid this most national legal systems are prepared to accept that a minor procedural error does not invalidate the decision.

6.1344 The Members of the WTO make extensive use of the doctrine of harmless error in connection with infringements of procedural rules in civil and criminal proceedings. In Australia, for example, the courts agreed that a delay in lodging an application, for the purpose of examining a report and preliminary finding of the Australia Customs Service, was a harmless error since the delay was unlikely to have prejudiced the respondent.[719] Similar decisions have been taken in the United States. For example, in Intercargo Insurance company v. United States, the court applied the principle to defective notices for extension of liquidation period sent by the customs service to an importer.[720] In fact, the United States federal rules of civil procedure stipulate that "the court at every stage of the proceeding must disregard any error or defect in the proceeding which does not affect the substantial rights of the parties".[721]

6.1345 Expressions of this principle or its equivalent are also to be found in the criminal proceedings of many WTO Members. In Namibia, for example, it has been held that when a verdict has not been tainted by an irregularity committed during the trial, the verdict should stand.[722] A similar approach has been adopted by the courts of Guatemala and other Member countries of the WTO such as Spain, Canada, Australia and the United States.[723]

---

[717] See, for example, Panel Report, *Japan - Taxes on Alcoholic Beverages, supra*, footnote 365.

[718] Statute of the International Court of Justice, 1945 ICJ, Article 381.

[719] See, for example, C.A. Ford v. Comptroller General of Customs, Fed. 854 (D.N.S.W. 24 November 1993) (Australia) (the two-week delay was judged harmless because it was unlikely to prejudice the respondents, the Australian industry or the importers).

[720] 83 F. 3d 391 (Fed. Cir. 1996) (United States).

[721] Fed. R. Civ. P. 61.

[722] See, for example, S.V. Shikunga, 1997 (9) B.C.L.R. 1321 (NmS).

[723] See, for example, Constitutional Court of Guatemala, Gaceta Jurisprudencial, No. 12, Case 37-89, Cons. II (the applicant drew attention to alleged irregularities, but these did not prevent him from learning of the existence of an administrative proceeding that affected his interests and taking the necessary corrective action), 9 May 1989; Thaman, Spain Returns to Trial by Jury, Hastings Int'l. and Comp. L. Rev., 241.349 No. 478 (Winter 1998) (referring to the application of the harmless error principle in Spanish criminal proceedings); R.v. Bevan [1993] 2 S.C.R. 599 (application of the

6.1346 Harmless error is also accepted by international courts. For example, the International Court of Justice recognizes the concept.[724] It is also recognized and applied by the European Court of Justice where "an error of law made by the [court of first instance] will not suffice to quash its decision if it was harmless and the same outcome could have been properly reached in the absence of error."[725] Moreover, when a WTO Member requests the Appellate Body to "reverse a panel's ruling on matters of procedure it must demonstrate the prejudice generated by the legal ruling."[726]

6.1347 For its part, Mexico incorporated the harmless error concept in articles 237-238 of its Federal Tax Code according to which an administrative decision by SECOFI in unfair trading cases will only be illegal if the procedural error harms the individual.

6.1348 Within the context of the present dispute, the application of the harmless error principle means that the Panel should examine Guatemala's acts and decide whether the non-fulfilment of a procedural obligation should be overlooked on the grounds that the omission did not prejudice the rights of Mexico or Cruz Azul. A panel established under the Tokyo Round Anti-Dumping Code recognized the principle of harmless error but considered that it was inapplicable under the circumstances of the case before it. [727] The case of *Brazil - Milk Powder* was certainly decided by the panel in this way since the investigating authority had notified importers of the initiation of the investigation 22 days after the public notice of initiation and 1 day before imposing a provisional measure.[728] Meanwhile, the exporting government was notified more than two months after publication and one month after the provisional measure was imposed.[729] Accordingly, the panel did not accept the argument that these delays constituted "harmless error" because it considered that they had clearly prejudiced the defence of the interests of the interested parties.[730]

6.1349 As distinct from the circumstances of *Brazil - Milk Powder*, in Guatemala's case the alleged delay in giving notification was only 11 days; between initiation and notification the investigating authority did not engage in any investigation-related activity and all the interested parties had sufficient time and opportunity to participate in the proceedings; the provisional measure was not imposed until several months after receipt of the notifi-

---

harmless error principle by the Canadian Supreme Court); Wilde v. The Queen (1988) 164 CLR.365, Slip op. (FC) (application of the principle in Australia); Fed. R. Crim. P. 52(a) (United States) ("no error, defect, irregularity or variation that does not affect substantial rights should be taken into account").

[724] See, for example, Appeal relating to the jurisdiction of the ICOA Council (*India v. Pakistan*), 1972 I.C.J. 46 (18 August) (Separate Opinion of Judge Dillard) ("it would appear that even if there were error, it was harmless error").

[725] See Konstantin J. Joergens, True Appellate Procedure or Only a Two-Stage Process? A comparative view of the Appellate Body under the WTO Dispute Settlement Understanding, 30 Law and Pol'y. Int'l. Bus. 193, 206 (1999).

[726] See Report of the Appellate Body in *EC - Hormones*, supra, footnote 121, para. 152; see also Gaffney, *Due Process in the World Trade Organization: The Need for Procedural Justice in the Dispute Settlement System*, 14 Am. U. Int'l. Rev. 1173, 1219 (1999) (" it is evident that the commission of what is known in the United States as harmless error will be insufficient to warrant the reversal of a panel decision).

[727] See *Brazil - Imposition of Provisional and Definitive Countervailing Duties on Milk Powder and Certain Types of Milk from the European Economic Community* (*Brazil - Milk Powder*) SCM/179, para. 271 (adopted 28 April 1994).

[728] *Ibid.*, para. 240.

[729] *Ibid.*, para. 228.

[730] *Ibid.*, para 271.

cation. Thus, the alleged delay in notifying Mexico of the initiation of the investigation was a "harmless error", since it did not prejudice Mexico's rights under the ADP Agreement.

6.1350 In fact, the alleged procedural error in not having given Mexico timely notice in accordance with Article 5.5 had no effect on the development of the anti-dumping investigation. If Mexico had been notified of the initiation of the investigation on 11 January, nothing would have happened differently from then onwards, except that the initial stages of the investigation might possibly have been speeded up. Clearly, the ADP Agreement does not give Mexico any right to delay or impede the initiation of an investigation or allow Mexico to make any kind of submission before the investigation is initiated. Notification given on 11 January would not have given Mexico or Cruz Azul additional time to defend their interests since under Guatemalan law grace periods are calculated from the date of notification. Similarly, under Guatemalan legislation the period allowed for replying to a questionnaire is also calculated from the date of receipt of that questionnaire. Furthermore, Cruz Azul was granted 30 additional working days to reply to the questionnaire, which is not required by the ADP Agreement. The Ministry also extended to 17 May the period granted to Cruz Azul for replying to the questionnaire. Finally, instead of imposing the provisional measure within 60 days of the date of initiation, Guatemala waited until 28 August before acting, that is, until eight months after initiation. In view of all this, it is inconceivable that having notified Mexico on 11 January could have had any effect on the course of the investigation.

6.1351 Consequently, in accordance with the general principles of international law recognized by civilized nations, the Panel should apply the principle of "harmless error" to Guatemala's alleged *procedural* delay under Article 5.5 of the ADP Agreement and reject the Mexican argument.

6.1352 In the alternate, Guatemala maintains that the alleged delay did not nullify or impair benefits accruing to Mexico under the Anti-Dumping Agreement. As noted above, Guatemala did not take any step to begin the investigation until Mexico had been notified. Moreover, Guatemala granted Cruz Azul a two-month extension to reply to the questionnaire. Thus, any putative delay in notification under Article 5.5 did not prejudice Mexico's ability to defend its interests nor affect in any other way Mexico's benefits under the Agreement.

6.1353 According to Article 3.8 of the DSU "There is normally a presumption that a breach of the rules has an adverse impact on other Members parties to that covered agreement, and in such cases, it shall be up to the Member against whom the complaint has been brought to rebut the charge". In the present instance, Guatemala has amply rebutted any presumption of nullification or impairment of Mexico's rights under the Anti-Dumping Agreement. It should be stressed that the obligation alleged to have been infringed in this case is a *procedural* and not a *substantive* obligation. Given that Article 3.8 of the DSU clearly states that the presumption of nullification or impairment is rebuttable and taking into account the fact that the alleged violation is procedural, Guatemala maintains that it has in fact rebutted the presumption. The Panel should therefore reject this argument.[731]

[731] Guatemala points out that the notification under Article 5.5 of the Anti-Dumping Agreement is unique within the context of the WTO. This notification does not relate to the notification of laws under covered agreements, the subject of most WTO notification rules. The notification in question applies only to an isolated stage in an anti-dumping proceeding. Unlike Article 13.1 of the Agreement on Subsidies and Countervailing Measures (1994), the notification does not impose any obli-

2. *Rebuttal of Mexico*

6.1354 **Mexico** rebuts Guatemalas arguments on "harmless error" and "nullification and impairment" and "acquiescence" as follows:

6.1355 Guatemala's first written submission focuses on the assertion that, if Guatemala had met its obligation, this would not have affected the course of the investigation. First, it states that this was a "harmless error"[732], then it mentions that Mexico acquiesced[733] and, lastly, Guatemala asserts that it has demonstrated that there was no nullification or impairment.[734] These arguments can be found in other parts of Guatemala's submission.[735] Nevertheless, as will be shown below, in this dispute the principles of "harmless error" and "acquiescence" are not only inapplicable but are mutually exclusive and as far as nullification or impairment is concerned, Guatemala did not prove anything.

6.1356 Guatemala puts forward the concepts of harmless error, acquiescence and nullification or impairment in the context of its claim relating to Article 5.5 of the AD Agreement and repeats them in other parts of its first written submission. Consequently, the arguments set out below should be seen as supplementing those in the section concerning Article 5.5 of the AD Agreement, but also apply when rejecting Guatemala's claims of "harmless error", "acquiescence" and "nullification or impairment" in each context where these appear.

(a) Applicability of the concept of "harmless error"

6.1357 Regarding the concept of "harmless error", Guatemala asserts that its delay in notifying did not prejudice Mexico's rights and that, according to the rules governing interpretation of public international law, it is the responsibility of the Panel to "examine Guatemala's acts and decide whether the non-fulfilment of a procedural obligation should be overlooked on the grounds that the omission did not prejudice the rights of Mexico or Cruz Azul".[736]

6.1358 According to Guatemala, if it had notified Mexico of the initiation of the investigation on 11 January, nothing would have changed, because the AD Agreement does not give Mexico the right to delay or prevent the initiation of an investigation or to put forward claims.

6.1359 In its oral submission to the Panel, Mexico (i) recalled that, pursuant to Article 3.8 of the DSU, failure to comply with obligations leads to a presumption of nullification or impairment so whether or not there was a harmless error has no meaning; (ii) added that it was Mexico's right to be notified before the initiation of the investigation (in this case, publication of the relevant public notice), irrespective of the action taken; (iii) emphasized that Guatemala was obliged to comply with the provisions of the AD Agreement

---

gation to hold post-notification consultations. Finally, in accordance with the Agreement, it is the only notification rule that could result in a prior notice of no consequence. For example, the investigating authority could give notice to the representative of the government of the exporting country under Article 5.5 and then, immediately afterwards, proceed to give that representative notice of initiation.

[732] First submission by Guatemala, paras. 206-216.

[733] *Ibid.*, paras. 217-219.

[734] *Ibid.*, paras. 220 and 221.

[735] See, for example, *Ibid.*, para. 226.

[736] *Ibid.*, para. 213.

and non-compliance cannot be excused as a "harmless error"; and (iv) the Panel which examined *Guatemala - Cement I* found that harmless error did not apply in this case.[737]

6.1360 In addition to the arguments set out above, Mexico wishes to indicate the following:

6.1361 Guatemala states that harmless error does apply to this dispute because the concept can be found in a number of domestic laws and has been recognized by the International Court of Justice.[738] Subsequently, it indicates that the Panel which heard the *Brazil - Milk Powder* case did not accept this because "it considered that [these delays] had clearly prejudiced the defence of the interests of the interested parties".[739]

6.1362 Mexico totally rejects the arguments outlined by Guatemala. Firstly, as the Panels have clearly indicated, Guatemala did not even prove that its theory of "harmless error" constitutes a principle of international law and, even if that were the case, the examples it mentions do not apply to the present dispute.[740] Secondly, Guatemala's interpretations are unacceptable because they are contrary to the provisions of Article 3.8 of the DSU. Thirdly, no panel has accepted such a theory.[741] In the *Brazil - Milk Powder* case, the Panel rejected Brazil's argument, not because a long time had elapsed after initiation of the investigation but, as will be seen below, because Brazil, like Guatemala, tried to reverse the burden of proof in a manner contrary to Article 3.8 of the DSU:

> "It was not incumbent upon a signatory whose procedural rights under Article 2 had been infringed by another signatory to demonstrate the harm caused by such an infringement. The Panel therefore rejected the position of Brazil that it was for the EEC to demonstrate that the results of this investigation would have been different had Brazil not committed its procedural errors."[742]

6.1363 Furthermore, in another case in which the principle of harmless error was claimed, namely, *Guatemala - Cement I,* the Panel, after having considered exactly the same facts as those now being presented, rejected Guatemala's argument regarding "harmless error" stating the following:

> "7.40 Guatemala argues that, even assuming there was a violation of Article 5.5, the Panel should conclude that any delay in notification under Article 5.5 was without adverse effects on Mexico's rights and thus constitutes harmless error under customary rules of public international law. Guatemala further argues that the alleged delay did not nullify or impair Mexico's rights under the AD Agreement.
>
> 7.41 We have concluded, as discussed above, that Guatemala failed to carry out its obligation under Article 5.5 to notify the Government of Mexico before proceeding to initiate this investigation. Article 3.8 of the DSU provides that there is a presumption that benefits are nullified or impaired when a Member fails to carry out an obligation under a WTO Agreement:

---

737 Oral submission by Mexico, paras. 136-141.

738 First submission by Guatemala, paras. 208-212.

739 *Ibid.*, para. 213.

740 See the first submission by the European Communities, 27 January 2000, para. 20.

741 See the first submission by the United States, 27 January 2000, para. 22.

742 Report of the Panel in *Brazil - Imposition of Provisional and Definitive Countervailing Duties on Milk Powder and Certain Types of Milk from the European Economic Community* (SCM/179), para. 271.

> 'In cases where there is an infringement of the obligations assumed under a covered agreement, the action is considered prima facie to constitute a case of nullification or impairment. This means that there is normally a presumption that a breach of the rules has an adverse impact on other Member parties to that covered agreement, and in such cases, it shall be up to the Member against whom the complaint has been brought to rebut the charge'.

In other words, there is a presumption that a violation will entitle a Member to relief, because that violation nullified or impaired a benefit accruing to the complaining Member, that is, 'harmed' the complaining Member. Article 17 of the AD Agreement entitles a Member to relief when benefits accruing to that Member under the AD Agreement are nullified or impaired. Moreover, while Article 3.8 of the DSU indicates that the presumption of nullification or impairment may be rebutted, GATT panels have consistently found that the presumption is not rebutted simply because the particular violation in question had no or insignificant adverse effects on trade.[743] This approach is supported by the Appellate Body's decision in *Japan Alcohol*, in which it upheld the Panel's decision not to introduce a trade effects test into the first sentence of Article III:2 of GATT 1994.[744]

7.42 In our view, having found that Guatemala failed to notify the Government of Mexico in a timely fashion, we need not determine that the failure to carry out an obligation had particular or demonstrable adverse trade effects in order to find that the benefits accruing to Mexico under the AD Agreement were nullified or impaired. Rather, to the extent that the presumption of nullification or impairment may be rebutted in the case of the breach of a procedural obligation, it would be incumbent on the Member that has breached the obligation to demonstrate that its failure to respect the obligation could not have had any effect on the course of the in-

[743] In *United States - Taxes on Petroleum and Certain Imported Substances*, L/6175 (Adopted 17 June 1987), BISD 34S 136, 157-58, the Panel reviewed previous disputes in which parties had claimed that a measure inconsistent with the General Agreement had no adverse impact and therefore did not nullify or impair benefits accruing under the General Agreement to the contracting party that had brought the complaint. The Panel concluded from its review that,

> "while the CONTRACTING PARTIES had not explicitly decided whether the presumption that illegal measures cause nullification or impairment could be rebutted, the presumption had in practice operated as an irrefutable presumption".
>
> *Ibid.* at para. 5.1.7

[744] *Japan - Taxes on Alcoholic Beverages, supra*, footnote 19. We note also the decision of the Panel in *Brazil - Imposition of Provisional and Definitive Countervailing Duties on Milk Powder and Certain Types of Milk from the European Economic Community*, SCM/179, adopted 28 April 1994 at para. 271:

> "It was not incumbent upon a signatory whose procedural rights under Article 2 had been infringed by another signatory to demonstrate the harm caused by such an infringement. The Panel therefore rejected the position of Brazil that it was for the EEC to demonstrate that the results of this investigation would have been different had Brazil not committed its procedural errors. Without wishing to exclude that the concept of 'harmless error' could be applicable in dispute settlement proceedings under the Agreement, the Panel considered that this concept was inapplicable under the circumstances of the case before it".

vestigation in question. In this case, the procedural obligation breached was the requirement to notify the exporting Member prior to proceeding to initiate an anti-dumping investigation. A key function of the notification requirements of the AD Agreement is to ensure that interested parties, including Members, are able to take whatever steps they deem appropriate to defend their interests. Where a required notification is not made in a timely fashion, the ability of the interested party to take such steps is vitiated. We cannot now speculate on what steps Mexico might have taken had it been timely notified, and how Guatemala might have responded to those steps.[745] Thus, while it is possible that the investigation would have proceeded in the same manner had Guatemala timely notified Mexico before proceeding to initiate the investigation, we cannot say with certainty that the course of the investigation would not have been different. Under these circumstances, we cannot conclude that Guatemala has rebutted the presumption that its failure to carry out its obligation under Article 5.5 consistent with the AD Agreement nullified or impaired benefits accruing to Mexico under that Agreement.

7.43 With respect to Guatemala's arguments regarding harmless error, the precedents cited - assuming *arguendo* that they reflect customary rules of public international law - relate to the consequences of a violation of a procedural rule, rather than to the existence of a cause of action. Thus, we do not consider that the assertion that an error is 'harmless' should prevent us from reaching the issue whether a violation of a provision of the AD Agreement nullifies or impairs benefits under that Agreement. However, we do not preclude that the notion of 'harmless error' could be relevant to the question of what steps a Member should take in order to implement the recommendation of a panel in a particular dispute. Since we do not view the principle of harmless error as one which would prevent us from determining that there was a violation of the AD Agreement which nullified or impaired benefits under that Agreement, we believe it would be improper for us to fail to make a recommendation under Article 19.1. However, the effects of a particular error may, we believe, be relevant in determining what remedial actions might be appropriate - that is, what if any suggestions a panel might make as to how its recommendation may be implemented."

6.1364 Lastly, Mexico simply wishes to recall that the nullification or impairment caused by non-compliance with Article 5.5 of the AD Agreement does not vanish because Mexico could have held consultations or not. Guatemala violated one of Mexico's rights, irrespective of the action which Mexico might have decided to take.[746]

---

[745] We note Guatemala's argument that, unlike the Agreement on Subsidies and Countervailing Measures, the AD Agreement does not require Members to afford an opportunity for consultations before initiating an investigation, and that therefore there is no action which would take place after notification but before initiation. Merely that the AD Agreement does not **require** some action following notification of the exporting Member and before initiation does not mean that nothing useful can take place following a timely notification, or that the exporting Member therefore has no interest in timely notification.

[746] See *Brazil - Milk Powder*, para. 232, which states: "The requirement to notify other signatories and interested parties served the essential purpose of enabling these signatories and interested parties

(b) Nullification or impairment

6.1365 Guatemala asserts that as it "did not take any step to begin the investigation until Mexico had been notified ... [it] did not prejudice Mexico's ability to defend its interests."[747] In Guatemala's opinion, therefore, according to Article 3.8 of the DSU, the presumption of nullification or impairment has been amply rebutted so the Panel should reject this argument.[748] Mexico wishes to indicate the following in this regard:

(a) The only "evidence" put forward by Guatemala to rebut the presumption of nullification or impairment is two assertions: (i) that Guatemala did not take any step to begin the investigation until Mexico had been notified; and (ii) Guatemala granted Cruz Azul a two-month extension to reply to the questionnaire.[749]

(b) Nevertheless, as pointed out in this rebuttal, the investigation began on 11 January, while Mexico was notified after and not before the initiation so by then the violation had been committed.

(c) Guatemala did not respect Mexico's right to be notified by Guatemala before the investigation began and, therefore, Mexico's benefits were nullified or impaired.

(d) Guatemala cannot prove that, if there had been compliance with Article 5.5 "nothing would have happened differently"[750], particularly since in another part of its submission Guatemala itself indicates that "If Mexico had promptly entered an objection in the administrative file with respect to the alleged violation of Article 5.5, Guatemala would have reinitiated the investigation ...".[751]

(e) In fact, contrary to what Guatemala indicates[752], the Panel which examined the case of *Brazil - Milk Powder* considered that the obligation to notify the initiation of an investigation was independent of the right to hold consultations.[753] Consequently, the fact that the AD Agreement does not provide for the holding of consultations before initiating an investigation does not constitute grounds for excusing Guatemala's non-compliance.

(f) The extension granted to Cruz Azul has nothing to do with the violation of Article 5.5. Moreover, Guatemala was obliged to grant this extension, according to Article 6.1.1 of the AD Agreement.

---

to effectively defend their interests by participating in the investigation." See also, *Ibid.*, para. 264, which states that the "offer of consultations made to the EEC on 27 February 1992, i.e., prior to the initiation of the investigation, was immaterial to the issue of Brazil's compliance with its obligations under Article 2:5 of the Agreement" (notification). See also the first submission by the United States, para. 26.

747 First submission by Guatemala, para. 220.

748 *Ibid.*, para. 221.

749 *Ibid.*, para. 220.

750 *Ibid.*, para. 215.

751 *Ibid.*, para. 219.

752 See Guatemala's first submission, footnote 267, which asserts that Article 5.5 of the AD Agreement is of no importance and, unlike Article 13.1 of the Agreement on Subsidies and Countervailing Measures, it does not require the holding of consultations.

753 See report of the Panel in "*Brazil - Milk Powder*", para. 264.

(g) In the GATT, there are no precedents for the successful rejection of the presumption of nullification or impairment and, in the present case, Guatemala's assertions are certainly not sufficient to rebut this presumption.[754]

(c) Acquiescence

6.1366 In its first written submission, Guatemala mentions that Mexico gave rise to estoppel by not objecting to any putative delay in notification under Article 5.5.[755] Subsequently, it indicates that "If Mexico had promptly entered an objection in the administrative file with respect to the alleged violation of Article 5.5, Guatemala would have reinitiated the investigation."[756]

6.1367 Mexico asks itself: if Guatemala did not prejudice Mexico's rights by delaying notification[757] yet, on the other hand, asserts that, if Mexico had objected to the late notification, Guatemala would have reinitiated the investigation[758], does this not imply that Mexico would at least have had the right to lodge an objection in the administrative file and that the matter is sufficiently serious for Guatemala itself to recognize that its authorities would have had to reinitiate the investigation?

6.1368 In addition, the Appellate Body in *Guatemala - Cement I* determined that, pursuant to the AD Agreement, only the definitive anti-dumping measure, the provisional anti-dumping measure and price undertakings may be contested.[759] If a Member has to wait until one of these three measures is applied, what can it do to see that the principle of estoppel is not applied?

6.1369 The above examples show the absurdity of Guatemala's reasoning regarding this concept. According to its logic, Members will lose rights as time goes by and they do not object to violations committed by other Members.

6.1370 As Mexico has already indicated, unlike other provisions, neither the AD Agreement nor the DSU prescribe time-limits within which to contest a measure.[760] Moreover, as will be seen below, the legal practice in the GATT has shown the inapplicability of the concept put forward by Guatemala. The Panel which heard the case *Quantitative Restrictions Against Imports of Certain Products from Hong Kong*[761] found the following:

> "28. ... The Panel ... recognized that restrictions had been in existence for a long time without Article XXIII ever having been invoked by Hong Kong in regard to the products concerned, but concluded that this did not alter the obligations which contracting parties had accepted under GATT provisions. Furthermore, the Panel considered it would be erroneous to interpret the fact that a measure had not been subject to Article XXIII over a number of years, as tantamount to its tacit acceptance by contracting parties."

---

[754] See first submission by the EC, para. 23.
[755] First submission by Guatemala, para. 217.
[756] *Ibid.*, para. 219.
[757] *Ibid.*, para. 214.
[758] *Ibid.*, para. 219.
[759] Report of the Appellate Body in *Guatemala - Cement I, supra*, footnote 25, para. 79.
[760] Oral submission at the first substantive meeting with the parties, para. 132.
[761] See the Report of the Panel on *EEC - Quantitative Restrictions Against Imports of Certain Products from Hong Kong* (L/5511 - 30S/129-140), adopted on 12 July 1998, para. 28.

6.1371 In addition to the foregoing, in the case *United States - Imposition of Anti-Dumping Duties on Imports of Fresh and Chilled Atlantic Salmon from Norway*[762], the Panel rejected an argument along the same lines as that put forward by Guatemala. In that dispute, it was argued that "... the failure of Norway or private Norwegian respondents to raise these issues before the investigating authorities precluded Norway from raising them before the Panel". Later on in the same report, the Panel states the following:

> "349. ... The Panel did not find in this provision any basis for it to refuse to consider a claim by a Party in dispute settlement under the Agreement merely because the subject matter of the claim had not been raised before the investigating authorities under domestic law."

6.1372 Furthermore, in *EEC - Member States' Import Regimes for Bananas*[763] an attempt was made to apply the principle of acquiescence, but the Panel decided that it was inoperative as follows:

> "362. The Panel considered that the decision of a contracting party not to invoke a right under the General Agreement at a particular point in time could be due to circumstances that change over time. For instance, a contracting party may not wish to invoke a right under the General Agreement pending the outcome of a multilateral trade negotiation, such as the Uruguay Round, or pending an assessment of the trade effects of a measure. The decision of a contracting party not to invoke a right *vis-à-vis* another contracting party at a particular point in time can therefore, by itself, not reasonably be assumed to be a decision to release that other contracting party from its obligations under the General Agreement. The Panel noted in this context that previous panels had based their findings on measures which had remained unchallenged for long periods of time. The Panel therefore found that the mere fact that the complaining parties had not invoked their rights under the General Agreement in the past had not modified these rights and did not prevent them from invoking these rights now." (Footnote omitted).

6.1373 In the light of the foregoing, it is obvious that Mexico could have waited until Guatemala had imposed a definitive anti-dumping measure and then objected to the violations of Article 5.5 of the AD Agreement, without this being construed as Mexico acquiescing in the errors made by the investigating authority. As seen above, since it is only possible to object to three measures in anti-dumping disputes[764], it is even more obvious that the concept of estoppel does not apply in these cases. Mexico could not have acquiesced in the violation of Article 5.5, as claimed by Guatemala.

---

[762] See the Report of the Panel in *United States - Imposition of Anti-Dumping Duties on Imports of Fresh and Chilled Atlantic Salmon from Norway* (ADP/87), adopted on 30 November 1992, paras. 347-351. See also the Report of the Panel in *United States - Imposition of Countervailing Duties on Imports of Fresh and Chilled Atlantic Salmon from Norway* (SCM/153), adopted on 4 December 1992, paras. 216-220.

[763] See the Report of the Panel in *EEC Member States' Import Regimes for Bananas* (DS32/R), Panel Report not adopted, dated 3 June 1993, para. 362.

[764] Contrary to what Guatemala asserts in para. 218 of its first written submission, there has never been any case in the WTO nor in the GATT 1947 in which the concept of acquiescence and estoppel has been applied. In the case of *Canada - EEC Arbitration on the Ordinary Wheat Agreement* cited by Guatemala in this para., the principles in question were not applied. See also the first submission by the EC, para. 22, and the first submission by the United States, paras. 24-26.

6.1374 In addition, in relation to Article 5.5 of the AD Agreement, Mexico's objection was such that the Panel in *Guatemala-Cement I* decided against Guatemala. Paragraph 8.4 of the Panel's report states the following:

> "8.4 We have concluded in this case that Guatemala violated the provisions of the AD Agreement by failing to notify the Government of Mexico before proceeding to initiate, as required by Article 5.5. We therefore recommend that the Dispute Settlement Body request Guatemala to bring its action into conformity with its obligations under Article 5.5 of the AD Agreement ..."[765]

3. Guatemala's Response to Rebuttal of Mexico

6.1375 In its second submissions, **Guatemala** expanded on its request for a finding that any technical error which Guatemala may have committed is insufficient to justify the formulation of a recommendation by the Panel. Its submissions in this regard are as follows:

6.1376 Even if the Panel were to find that Guatemala had violated some procedural requirement during the course of the investigation, it does not follow, as a matter of law, that the challenged measure (i.e., the definitive anti-dumping measure) is "inconsistent" (as that term is used in Article 19.1 of the DSU) with the AD Agreement. As we explained at length during the first hearing, claims directed at an anti-dumping investigation generally are not like claims directed at a quota, a licensing scheme, a technical barrier, or a host of other *measures* that may be the subject of WTO Dispute Settlement proceedings. When the Members challenge a quota or one of these other types of measures, they will typically attack the measure itself. But when Members challenge an anti-dumping duty measure, they often do so on the basis of claims directed at specific procedural requirements which may number in the thousands over the course of an investigation that could take as long as eighteen months.

6.1377 Nothing in the AD Agreement or the DSU mandates that every little procedural error that may be committed during the course of an anti-dumping investigation renders the *entire* measure illegal. For example, it would be absurd to suggest that an entire investigation resulting in the introduction of a definitive anti-dumping measure should be declared "inconsistent" under Article 19.1 of the DSU if the only error committed by the investigating authority were to fail to provide the exporter and the exporting Member with a page of the application as provided for under Article 6.1.3 of the AD Agreement.

6.1378 If the Member that has conducted the investigation can show that a particular error was harmless, or otherwise did not nullify or impair the benefits accruing to the complainant, no recommendation should follow from Article 19.1 of the DSU. Otherwise, a Member whose exporters have engaged in egregious, injurious dumping could be totally exonerated by an inconsequential procedural violation that had no impact whatsoever on the course of the investigation. Such an interpretation of the DSU and the AD Agreement would place form over substance and to make a mockery of the importing Member's right to remedy injurious dumping.

---

[765] See the Report of the Panel in *Guatemala-Cement I*, *supra*, footnote 25, para. 8.4.

H. *Should the Panel Decline to Suggest that Guatemala Revoke the Definitive Anti-Dumping Measure or Refund the Anti-Dumping Duties Collected?*

1. Submissions of Guatemala

6.1379 **Guatemala** makes an alternative argument that the Panel should decline to suggest that Guatemala revoke the definitive anti-dumping measure or refund the anti-dumping duties collected. Its supporting arguments are as follows:

6.1380 In its first written submission, Mexico requested that the panel *suggest* that Guatemala "revoke the anti-dumping measure adopted against imports of Mexican cement and refund the anti-dumping duties collected."[766] In so doing, Mexico requested a specific remedy which is inconsistent with established GATT/WTO practice. Thus, even should the panel agree with Mexico on the merits of its argument, it should reject the remedy requested.

6.1381 The specific remedy[767] requested by Mexico, namely that Guatemala revoke its measure, goes far beyond the type of remedies recommended by the overwhelming preponderance of prior GATT 1947 and WTO panels. In virtually every case in which a panel has found a measure to be inconsistent with a GATT obligation, panels have confined themselves to issuing the *general* recommendation that the country "bring its measures ... into conformity with the General Agreement"[768], and have refrained from making a *suggestion* which would prejudice the respondent Member's ability to apply the general recommendation.[769] In addition to being true of GATT disputes in general, this is especially applicable to the case of disputes relating to anti-dumping measures (and countervailing duties).[770]

6.1382 In fact, in the second dispute examined under the WTO dispute settlement system, these principles are carefully adhered to in the recommendation *and* suggestion formulated by the panel. In *United States - DRAMS*, Korea requested the panel to suggest that the United States revoke its order relating to DRAMS from Korea and eliminate a specific provision in its anti-dumping legislation.[771] In rejecting Korea's request, the panel made clear the general nature of its recommendation (that is, "recommends that ... request the United States to bring ... [the measure] into conformity with its obligations under ... the Anti-Dumping Agreement") and added that "in light of the range of possible ways in which we believe the United States could appropriately implement our recommendation, we decline to make any suggestion in the present case".[772]

---

[766] Mexico's first written submission, Section VI, para. (f)(b).

[767] By "specific" remedy Guatemala means a remedy that requires a party to take a particular, specific action in order to cure a WTO inconsistency found by a panel.

[768] See, for example, the Panel report on *Canada - Measures Affecting Exports of Unprocessed Herring and Salmon*, L/6268, adopted 22 March 1988, BISD 35S/98, 115, para. 5.1. Guatemala will not weary the panel by invoking at length all the other reports in which panels have made recommendations in similar terms. There are more than 100 such reports.

[769] See, for example, the Panel Report on *United States - Standards for Reformulated and Conventional Gasoline*, WT/DS2/R, adopted 20 May 1996, DSR 1996:I, 29, para. 8.2.

[770] See, for example, the Panel report on *Korea - Resins*, ADP/92, para. 302. See also the Panel report on *United States - Imposition of Countervailing Duties on Certain Hot-Rolled Lead and Bismuth Carbon Steel Products Originating in the United Kingdom*, WP/DS138/R, circulated on 23 December 1999, para. 8.2.

[771] *DRAMS*, *supra*, footnote 115, para. 7.3.

[772] *Ibid.*, para. 7.4.

6.1383 In fact, in general, a Member has many options for bringing a measure into conformity with its obligations under the WTO. The panel cannot and should not prejudge the matter by making a specific suggestion with regard to the solution which the parties to the dispute should reach once the DSB has adopted the panel report.

6.1384 Moreover, the position that panels should refrain from making specific suggestions is consistent with the nature of the function of the panel members, which is to interpret the agreements covered. In general, panels are not well versed in the domestic legislation of the respondent Member.[773] Thus, although it is appropriate in a particular case for a panel to determine that a Member's legislation was applied in a manner inconsistent with its obligations under a covered WTO agreement, in general it is not appropriate for the panel to prejudge, even by way of a suggestion, which of the available options the party should adopt in order to bring its actions into conformity with its international obligations.

6.1385 In short, it is contrary to established GATT/WTO practice for a panel to suggest specific remedies. Therefore, regardless of what is decided in the present case, the Panel should reject Mexico's request to the effect that the Panel suggest that Guatemala revoke its anti-dumping measure.

6.1386 Guatemala added simply in its second submission that like most Members of the WTO, Guatemala has a variety of administrative or regulatory mechanisms at its disposal which could be used to bring an offending anti-dumping measure into conformity with its obligations. Thus, if the Panel were to find that the challenged measure was inconsistent with the AD Agreement, the suggestion of a specific way of complying with that finding would be inappropriate.

VII. INTERIM REVIEW

7.1 On 11 September 2000 both parties submitted written requests for the Panel to review precise aspects of the interim report. Neither party requested a further meeting with the Panel.

7.2 Guatemala notes that in paragraph 8.13 of the interim report the Panel misrepresents Guatemala's position. Guatemala argues that it does not equate the value of the panel report in *Guatemala - Cement I* to that of an unadopted panel report. In consequence, the Panel has decided to strike out the third sentence of paragraph 8.13 of the interim report.

7.3 Guatemala also submits that in paragraph 8.17 of the interim report, the Panel misrepresents Guatemala's position and that the second sentence of this paragraph contains a generalization which does not properly reflect Guatemala's position. We consider that paragraph 8.17 contains an accurate, although not exhaustive, summarization of the arguments presented by Guatemala with respect to Article 17.6(i) of the AD Agreement. We are of the view that the summary in paragraph 8.17 is sufficient for purposes of the findings. Should the reader require a more thorough description of the arguments presented by Guatemala on this matter the reader may refer to the section of the descriptive part where these arguments have been reflected in full.

[773] Indeed, Article 8.3 of the DSU stipulates that citizens of Members whose governments are parties to the dispute should not normally serve on the panel concerned with that dispute, unless the parties agree otherwise.

7.4 Guatemala requests that the findings of the Panel contain a separate section "setting forth Guatemala's position according to which Mexico bears the burden of proof of violation of a WTO Agreement, and to that end, must establish a *prima facie* case of inconsistency with a provision of the AD Agreement or the GATT 1994, and that it must do so before passing on to Guatemala the burden of proving compliance with the provision in question." We are of the view that the question of the burden of proof as presented by Guatemala does not warrant a separate set of findings. Since, Mexico has asserted that it does not deny that as a complainant in this dispute it bears the burden of proof to show that there has been a violation of the AD Agreement by Guatemala[774].

7.5 Guatemala also requests that section VIII.B.5 titled "Guatemala's defence based on the principle of harmless error, acquiescence or estoppel, and rebuttal of the presumption in Article 3.8", should be relocated so as to follow the Panel's findings (in sections VIII.C.4, VIII.C.5 and VIII.C.6) concerning Articles 5.5, 12.1.1 and 6.1.3. This Guatemala argues that such relocation would make it clear that Guatemala's central argument is that it did not violate the mentioned provisions (Articles 5.5, 12.1.1 and 6.1.3), and that Guatemala's defence based on the principles of harmless error, acquiescence or estoppel, and the rebuttal of the presumption in Article 3.8, is not their only defence. In drafting our report we noticed that Guatemala's defence based on the principle of harmless error, acquiescence or estoppel, and rebuttal of the presumption in Article 3.8 was made as a subsidiary argument under several of the claims of violation made by Mexico. Thus, we decided to deal with such a defence up front as a preliminary issue. This decision regarding the structure of the interim report was made in order to avoid repetition and improve its readability. We see no reason to change the structure of the report at this stage.

7.6 Guatemala also requests that in addressing the subject of harmless error, the review of the Panel should draw a distinction between cases involving measures and cases involving administrative acts in the course of an investigation. We consider that this distinction is akin to the distinction between substantive and procedural violations, this issue is dealt with in paragraph 8.111 of the report.

7.7 Guatemala submits that paragraph 8.27 of the interim report should reflect the arguments made in paragraphs 138 and 139 of its first written submission. Our findings merely contain a summary of the parties' arguments. Our findings do not repeat fully the arguments of the parties, as this is the function of the descriptive part. In this regard, the reader may refer to the descriptive part for a full description of Guatemala's arguments on this matter. Moreover, the arguments presented by Guatemala in the above-mentioned paragraphs pertain to the question of whether the application contained such information as was reasonably available to the applicant (Article 5.2). We note that in light of our findings under Article 5.3 we decided not to rule on claims regarding Article 5.2.[775]

7.8 Guatemala also claims that the summary set forth in paragraph 8.30 concerning Guatemala's position on the obligation to examine the accuracy and adequacy of the evidence places Guatemala's assertions out of context. To correct this situation

---

774 Mexico second written submission, para. 13.

775 See, *infra* para. 8.59.

Guatemala requests certain changes and additions to paragraph 8.30. In order to accommodate Guatemala's concerns we have decided to make some changes to that paragraph. In the first sentence of the paragraph the phrase "prior to initiation of the investigation" will be added after the words "in the application". With regard to the other changes suggested by Guatemala, we consider that the summarization of the arguments is sufficient to present an overview of Guatemala's position. Should the reader require more detail on the arguments they can refer to the appropriate sections in the descriptive part.

7.9 Guatemala also claims that the summarization of its arguments presented in paragraph 8.34 of the interim report is inaccurate in that the Panel's statement that Guatemala asserted that there was no requirement to provide evidence on possible adjustments of an application is a generalization. Guatemala never made such an assertion. Similarly, Guatemala claims the Panel's summary in that paragraph of Guatemala's position with respect to the relationship of Articles 2 and 3 of the AD Agreement with Article 5 is inaccurate[776], and in that Guatemala never argued that during the initiation stage, Cruz Azul was required to prove that the difference in levels of trade in any way affected price comparability. We disagree with Guatemala on this point. In our view the summarization presented in the findings is sufficiently accurate, especially since the full extent of Guatemala's arguments are reflected in the descriptive part of the report.

7.10 Guatemala claims that in the last sentence of paragraph 8.44, the Panel distorts Guatemala's position as set forth in its various submissions by giving the impression that Guatemala refused to collect the information from its Customs concerning the volume of imports. We disagree with Guatemala on this point. In our view the summarization presented in the findings is sufficiently accurate, especially since the full extent of Guatemala's arguments are reflected in the descriptive part of the report.

7.11 Guatemala claims that in paragraph 8.49, the Panel makes its own evaluation of the facts and assumes the Ministry's role by establishing what the imports from Mexico amounted to. With respect to Guatemala's comments regarding paragraph 8.49 of the interim report, we wish to clarify that in our findings the Panel does not attempt to substitute itself for the investigating authority. In paragraph 8.49 of the interim report we have examined to what extent the investigating authorities considered the volume of imports relative to domestic production and consumption in Guatemala. In that analysis we conclude that there is no evidence that at the time of investigation the Ministry possessed the necessary information to appropriately consider the increase in the volume of imports relative to domestic production and consumption in Guatemala. In an attempt to ascertain whether there was any factual support for Guatemala's assertion that there was a "massive" increase in the volume of imports relative to domestic production of Guatemalan Cement, taking evidence on the record before the Panel, we put together the information available to the Ministry at the time of inititaion and performed the calculation refered to in paragraph 8.49. We found that assertions that imports of Mexican cement were "massive" did not find support in the data available to the Ministry at the time of initiation. The calcu-

[776] Guatemala did, however, maintain that Article 5.8 was not applicable to the initiation stage.

lation performed by us to verify support for Guatemala's claims of massive imports, does not affect our findings that there is no evidence to suggest that, at the time of initiation, the Ministry considered the volume of imports relative to domestic production.

7.12 Guatemala also complains that in paragraph 8.79 of the interim report, the Panel failed to mention that Guatemala maintains that it complied with Article 5.5 of the Anti-Dumping Agreement for the reasons set forth in that paragraph and because if it had proceeded with the investigation without having previously notified Mexico and Cruz Azul, either of them could have brought an *"amparo"* action to annul the investigation, but neither Mexico nor Cruz Azul made use of that remedy. We are of the view that the summary in paragraph 8.79 is sufficient for purposes of the findings. Should the reader require a more thorough description of the arguments presented by Guatemala on this matter the reader may refer to the section of the descriptive part where these arguments have been reflected in full. Moreover, we have addressed this issue and draw Guatemala's attention to our finding in paragraph 8.83 that "whether Mexico choose not to pursue its rights under Guatemalan law is of no concern to us, as this would not affect its rights under the WTO Agreements". With regard to Guatemala's comments on the Panel's treatment of its defence based on the principle of harmless error, acquiescence or estoppel, and rebuttal of the presumption in Article 3.8, we have already addressed this issue in paragraph 7.4 *supra.*

7.13 With regard to Guatemala's claim that the Panel misrepresents its position in paragraph 8.91 of the interim report by stating that Guatemala claimed that the public notice itself provided adequate information, we have decided to change the first sentence of this paragraph. The first sentence of paragraph 8.91 shall now read: "Guatemala responds that the public notice as supplemented by the report of the Directorate of Economic Integration of 17 November 1995 is adequate to fulfill the requirements of Article 12.1.1". Regarding Guatemala's comments on the Panel's treatment of its defence based on the principle of harmless error, acquiescence or estoppel, and rebuttal of the presumption in Article 3.8, we have already addressed this issue in paragraph 7.4 *supra.*

7.14 Guatemala requests changes to the summarization of the arguments in paragraph 8.123, as it considers that the summarization does not record Guatemala's position in full. We are of the view that the summary in paragraph 8.123 is sufficient for purposes of the findings. Should the reader require a more thorough description of the arguments presented by Guatemala on this matter the reader may refer to the section of the descriptive part where these arguments have been reflected in full. Guatemala also points out a slight difference in the punctuation of the second sentence of paragraph 8.123, between the Spanish and the English versions of the interim report. We have changed the English version so it would read exactly as the Spanish.

7.15 Guatemala requests changes to paragraph 8.128 of the interim report consisting of a summary of the arguments presented by Guatemala. We consider that the changes requested are not necessary as the summary of Guatemala's arguments in paragraph 8.128 is sufficient for purposes of the findings. Should the reader require a more thorough description of the arguments presented by the parties it may refer to the section of the descriptive part where these arguments have been reflected in full.

7.16 Guatemala has asked the Panel to include Guatemala's reply to Question 39 from Mexico after paragraph 8.131 of the interim report. According to Guatemala, "[t]his reply provides evidence concerning the probative value of the notarial deed of 4 November". We note that Question 39 from Mexico concerns the status of notarial deeds in Guatemalan law. This is also the context for Guatemala's reply to that question. Since the status, or "probative value", of a notarial deed under Guatemalan law is not relevant to our findings, we decline to make the change requested by Guatemala.

7.17 Guatemala maintains that our summarization of their arguments with respect to the alleged violation of Article 6.1.2. is incomplete and inaccurate. Therefore, it requests the inclusion of a reference to the rules laid down by the investigating authority for the public hearing. We are of the view that the summary in paragraph 8.143 is sufficient for purposes of the findings. Should the reader require a more thorough description of the arguments presented by Guatemala on this matter the reader may refer to the section of the descriptive part where these arguments have been reflected in full. Guatemala also requests that reference should be made to the fact that Article 6.5 distinguishes between two types of confidential information. We would like to point out that the issue of the types of confidential information provided for in Article 6.5 is explored in depth in paragraph 8.219 of the report.

7.18 Guatemala's requests an expansion of the quotation that appears in the last sentence of paragraph 8.147 of the interim report, in order to make it a complete quotation of the sentence. We wish to highlight that the quotation is made from the second to last sentence of paragraph 294 of Guatemala's first submission and not to the last sentence of that paragraph, as Guatemala seems to believe. The sentence quoted by us in the findings does not contain the words that Guatemala requests us to include, thus, we decline to make the change suggested by Guatemala. Guatemala also requests the Panel to clarify, in paragraph 8.150, that on 17 January 1997 Cruz Azul requested two copies. We would like to point out that the preceeding paragraph makes it clear that "On 17 January 1997, Cruz Azul requested that ...". We believe that no further clarification is necessary.

7.19 With respect to the third sentence of paragraph 8.153 of the interim report, Guatemala has asked the Panel to "also indicate that the text of the provision establishing the fee was attached". We are uncertain whether Guatemala asserts that the relevant text was attached to Guatemala's submissions to the Panel, or to the 6 December 1996 Resolution of the Directorate of Economic Integration sent to Cruz Azul. If the former, we fail to see how the provision of the relevant text *to the Panel* is relevant to our findings in the present dispute. If the latter, we note that Guatemala has failed to adduce any proof that the relevant text was attached to its 6 December 1996 Resolution. In particular, no such text was attached to the copy of the Resolution made available to the Panel during the course of these proceedings (Annex Mexico-36). Nor, indeed, did the 6 December 1996 Resolution contain any reference to that text. Nor has Guatemala adduced any evidence that Cruz Azul was otherwise provided with a copy of the relevant provision. For these reasons, we decline to make the change requested by Guatemala.

7.20 Guatemala points to a typographical error in the second to last sentence of paragraph 8.211. We have accepted the correction suggested by Guatemala and the word "not" has been added in "information was not 'susceptible of summary'".

7.21 Mexico requests us to suggest, in the final report, that Guatemala should refund the anti-dumping duties collected on imports of grey Portland cement from Mexico as a result of an anti-dumping measure which was found to be in violation of the AD Agreement. We see no reason to change our decision not to suggest repayment of the duties.

7.22 Mexico also requests certain changes due to typographical errors and inconsistencies between the Spanish and English versions of the report. We have made the necessary corrections in paragraphs 4.21, 4.97, 6.140, 6.445, 6.1071, 6.1111, 8.49, 8.94, 8.84 and 8.122.

VIII. FINDINGS

A. *Introduction*

8.1 This dispute involves the imposition of a definitive anti-dumping measure by the Guatemalan Ministry of Economy ("the Ministry") on imports of portland cement from Mexico. Mexico raises claims concerning the initiation of the investigation, the conduct of the anti-dumping investigation, the imposition of a provisional measure and the imposition of the definitive measure.

8.2 On 21 September 1995, Cementos Progreso S.A. ("Cementos Progreso"), the sole Guatemalan producer of cement, filed a request for initiation of an anti-dumping investigation. A supplementary request was filed on 9 October 1995. On 11 January 1996, the Ministry published a notice of initiation of an anti-dumping investigation regarding allegedly dumped imports of grey portland cement from Cooperativa la Cruz Azul, S.C.L. of Mexico ("Cruz Azul"). The Ministry notified the Government of Mexico of the initiation of the investigation on 22 January 1996. The Ministry requested certain import data from Guatemala's Directorate-General of Customs by letter dated 23 January 1996.

8.3 Guatemala established as the period of investigation the period from 1 June 1995 to 30 November 1995. On 16 August 1996, Guatemala imposed a provisional anti-dumping duty of 38.72% on imports of type I (PM) grey portland cement from Cruz Azul of Mexico. The provisional duty was imposed on the basis of a preliminary affirmative determination. On 14 October 1996 Guatemala extended the period of investigation, after the extension the period of investigation covered the period 1 June 1995 to 31 May 1996. On that same date Guatemala provided an additional questionnaire to the parties in the investigation to be responded by 30 October 1996.

8.4 After an exchange of letters between Guatemala, Mexico and Cruz Azul the date for the verification at Cruz Azul was fixed for the week of 3-6 December 1996. The scheduled verification did not take place due to Cruz Azul's objections to the Ministry's intent to: a) verify information concerning the period of 1 December 1996 to 31 May 1996; b) verify information concerning Cruz Azul's cost of production; and c) use certain non-governmental experts.

8.5 On 17 January 1997, Guatemala imposed a definitive anti-dumping duty of 89.54% on imports of grey portland cement from Cruz Azul of Mexico.

8.6 On 15 October 1996, after the imposition of the provisional anti-dumping duty but before the imposition of the definitive anti-dumping duty, Mexico requested consultations with Guatemala under Article 4 of the DSU and Article 17.3 of the AD Agreement. Consultations were concluded on 9 January 1997, before the imposition of the definitive anti-dumping duty, but the parties failed to reach a mutually satisfactory solution.

8.7 On 13 February 1997, after the imposition of the definitive anti-dumping duty, Mexico requested the establishment of a panel to examine the consistency of Guatemala's anti-dumping investigation with its obligations under the AD Agreement. A first panel concerning this matter was established by the DSB on 20 March 1997. The report of the panel was issued on 19 June 1998.

8.8 On 4 August 1998, Guatemala notified the DSB of its intention to appeal certain issues of law covered in the panel report and legal interpretations developed by the panel, and filed a Notice of Appeal with the Appellate Body. The Appellate Body issued its report on 2 November 1998. In its report, the Appellate Body reversed: a) the panel's finding that Article 17 of the *Anti-Dumping Agreement* "provides for a coherent set of rules for dispute settlement specific to anti-dumping cases ... that replaces the more general approach of the DSU"; b) the panel's alternative finding in paragraph 7.26 of the panel report relating to the term "measure"; and c) the panel's conclusion in paragraph 7.27 of the panel report that "the matters referred to in Mexico's request for establishment of a panel" were properly before it. The DSB adopted the report of the Appellate Body on 25 November 1998.

8.9 The Appellate Body's ruling did not concern the substantive question of whether Guatemala's investigation was consistent with the provisions of the AD Agreement. Consequently, on 5 January 1999, Mexico requested consultations with Guatemala under the DSU and the AD Agreement regarding Guatemala's definitive anti-dumping measure on imports of grey portland cement from Cruz Azul as well as the actions that preceded it. Mexico and Guatemala held consultations on 23 February 1999, but failed to reach a mutually satisfactory solution. On 26 July 1999, Mexico requested the establishment of a panel to examine the consistency of the definitive anti-dumping measure, and the actions preceding that measure, with the provisions of the AD Agreement. At its meeting on 22 September 1999, the DSB established a panel in accordance with Article 6 of the DSU with standard terms of reference.

B. Preliminary Issues Raised by Guatemala

1. The Panel Was Improperly Composed and is not Competent to Review the Matter

8.10 Guatemala requests us to rule that the composition of this Panel is inconsistent with WTO and international law principles, and that we therefore lack competence to review the matter before us. Specifically, Guatemala considers that the presence on this Panel of a member who served on a previous panel relating to the same matter ("*Guatemala - Cement I*"[777]) detracts from the objectivity and independence that a panel should have when reviewing a matter brought before it. Mexico requested us to reject Guatemala's preliminary objection, arguing that the Panel was composed in conformity with the DSU, and that we have competence to examine the matter before us.

[777] Panel Report, *Guatemala – Cement I, supra*, footnote 25, adopted as reversed on 25 November 1998.

8.11 Prior to the first meeting of the Panel with the parties, we issued the following preliminary ruling on this issue through a communication addressed to the parties and third parties, dated 24 February 2000:

> "1.4 In order to determine whether the substance of Guatemala's preliminary objection is an issue that is susceptible of a ruling by the Panel, we have carefully analysed the provisions of the DSU governing panel composition. It is clear that Article 8.6 of the DSU imposes primary responsibility for panel composition on the parties to the dispute. In cases where the parties are unable to agree on the composition of a panel, such as this one, Article 8.7 of the DSU imposes responsibility for panel composition on the Director General. According to Article 8 of the DSU, therefore, the composition of a panel is determined by the parties to the dispute and, in certain circumstances, by the Director General. Neither Article 8 nor any other provision of the DSU prescribes any role for the panel in the panel composition process. For this reason, we find that we are unable to rule on the substance of the issue raised by Guatemala.
>
> 1.5 Should Guatemala persist with its substantive concerns regarding the composition of the Panel, Guatemala may avail itself of the procedure provided for in the Rules of Conduct for the Understanding on Rules and Procedures Governing the Settlement of Disputes."

8.12 We are not aware whether Guatemala has decided to avail itself of its right under Article VIII:1 of the Rules of Conduct for the Understanding on Rules and Procedures Governing the Settlement of Disputes[778] to submit evidence of a violation of the obligations of independence or impartiality by a panel member to the Chairman of the DSB. As we indicated in our preliminary ruling, we conclude that this would have been the only proper way for Guatemala to raise the issue. In light of this ruling, we also requested the parties not to submit any further arguments on this issue in subsequent stages of the procedure.

---

[778] Article VIII:1 of the Rules of Conduct provides:

> "1. Any party to a dispute, conducted pursuant to the WTO Agreement, who possesses or comes into possession of evidence of a material violation of the obligations of independence, impartiality or confidentiality or the avoidance of direct or indirect conflicts of interest by covered persons which may impair the integrity, impartiality or confidentiality of the dispute settlement mechanism, shall at the earliest possible time and on a confidential basis, submit such evidence to the Chair of the DSB, the Director-General or the Standing Appellate Body, as appropriate according to the respective procedures detailed in paras. VIII:5 to VIII:17 below, in a written statement specifying the relevant facts and circumstances. Other Members who possess or come into possession of such evidence, may provide such evidence to the parties to the dispute in the interest of maintaining the integrity and impartiality of the dispute settlement mechanism. (WT/DSB/RC/1)"

2. *The Panel Report from the Previous Case Should not be Used as Precedent or in Any Way Constitute Guidance for the Present Panel*

8.13 Guatemala requests us not to take into account in our decision the report of the panel in *Guatemala - Cement I*. Guatemala argues that the report of the panel in *Guatemala - Cement I* has no legal status and cannot constitute a valid precedent because the Appellate Body concluded that the panel did not have the mandate to examine the complaints before it. Thus, Guatemala is of the view that recourse to the report issued in *Guatemala - Cement I* as useful guidance in respect of any matter being examined in the present dispute would be a violation of the decision of the Appellate Body. Guatemala equates the value of the previous panel report to that of an unadopted panel report. Guatemala requests that we not take into account in our decision the report of the panel in *Guatemala - Cement I*. Guatemala argues that the previous panel lacked the mandate to review the case. Thus, its opinion on this matter has no legal value as precedent or guidance.

8.14 Mexico considers that: (a) the arguments presented by it in the present dispute are put before the Panel independently of their having been supported, or not, by a previous panel; (b) the panel report in *Guatemala-Cement I* is an adopted panel report; (c) the panel report in *Guatemala - Cement I* was an integral part of the request for establishment of this Panel and as such is part of its mandate; and (d) assuming *arguendo* that the panel report in *Guatemala-Cement I* was not adopted, it nevertheless contains useful guidance pertinent to the issues before us.

8.15 We note that the Appellate Body ruled in *Guatemala - Cement I* that "the dispute was not properly before the Panel", and that it therefore could not consider any of the substantive issues raised in the alternative by Guatemala.[779] In other words, the Appellate Body found that the panel in *Guatemala - Cement I* should never have reached the substance of the dispute. We therefore consider that the substantive findings of the panel in *Guatemala - Cement I* are in this respect similar to those of unadopted panel reports, i.e., while they have no legal status, they may nevertheless provide useful guidance to the extent that we consider them relevant and persuasive.[780] We recall in any event Mexico's assertion that its arguments in this dispute are put before us independently of their having been supported, or not, by a previous panel.

3. *The Panel Lacks an Appropriate Mandate to Review the Provisional Measure*

8.16 Guatemala requests us to rule that the provisional measure and any claims related to it fall outside our terms of reference. In light of our decision to make no substantive rulings regarding the claims relating to the provisional measure for rea-

---

[779] Appellate Body report , *Guatemala - Cement I, supra*, footnote 25, para. 89.

[780] Panel Report, *Japan - Taxes on Alcoholic Beverages, Supra*, footnote 365. This conclusion is consistent with that reached by the panel in *Mexico - Anti-dumping Investigation on High Fructose Corn Syrup from the United States (Mexico - HFCS), supra*, footnote 34, footnote 556.

sons of judicial economy,[781] we consider that we need not decide whether the provisional measure is properly before the Panel.

4. *Standard of Review Under Article 17.6(i) of the AD Agreement*

8.17 Guatemala argues that Article 17.6(i) of the AD Agreement requires the panel to "determine whether the authorities' establishment of the facts was proper and whether their evaluation of those facts was unbiased and objective." Guatemala contends that this provision precludes an independent evaluation of the various pieces of evidence that the Ministry considered. In consequence, the Panel may only reject the factual findings made by the national authorities in special cases, such as where the conclusions drawn by the authorities were not supported by the evidence or where there was clear evidence of bias in their evaluation of the facts.

8.18 Article 17.6(i) of the AD Agreement sets forth the standard of review to be applied by a panel under the AD Agreement when considering issues of fact. That Article provides:

> "(i) in its assessment of the facts of the matter, the panel shall determine whether the authorities' establishment of the facts was proper and whether their evaluation of those facts was unbiased and objective. If the establishment of the facts was proper and the evaluation was unbiased and objective, even though the panel might have reached a different conclusion, the evaluation shall not be overturned;"

8.19 We consider that it is not our role to perform a *de novo* review of the evidence which was before the investigating authority in this case. Rather, Article 17 makes it clear that our task is to review the determination of the investigating authorities. Specifically, we must determine whether its establishment of the facts was proper and the evaluation of those facts was unbiased and objective.[782] In other

---

[781] See, section VIII.F *infra*.

[782] We note that, in the context of safeguard measures, the panel in *Korea - Dairy Safeguard*, *Supra*, footnote 531, said the following of the need for a panel to perform an objective assessment pursuant to Article 11 of the DSU:

> "7.30 We consider that for the Panel to adopt a policy of total deference to the findings of the national authorities could not ensure an "objective assessment" as foreseen by Article 11 of the DSU. This conclusion is supported, in our view, by previous panel reports that have dealt with this issue. However, we do not see our review as a substitute for the proceedings conducted by national investigating authorities. Rather, we consider that the Panel's function is to assess objectively the review conducted by the national investigating authority, in this case the KTC. For us, an objective assessment entails an examination of whether the KTC had examined all facts in its possession or which it should have obtained in accordance with Article 4.2 of the Agreement on Safeguards (including facts which might detract from an affirmative determination in accordance with the last sentence of Article 4.2 of the Agreement on Safeguards), whether adequate explanation had been provided of how the facts as a whole supported the determination made, and, consequently, whether the determination made was consistent with the international obligations of Korea. Finally, we consider that the Panel should examine the analysis

words, we must determine whether an unbiased and objective investigating authority evaluating the evidence before it at the time of the investigation could properly have made the determinations made by Guatemala in this case. In our review of the investigating authorities' evaluation of the facts, we will first need to examine evidence considered by the investigating authority, and second, this examination is limited by Article 17.5(ii) to the facts before the investigating authority. That is, we are not to examine any new evidence that was not part of the record of the investigation.[783]

5. *Guatemala's Defence Based on the Principle of Harmless Error, Acquiescence or Estoppel, and Rebuttal of the Presumption in Article 3.8 of the DSU*

8.20 As a defence common to Mexico's claims regarding the notification under Article 5.5, public notice of initiation under Article 12.1.1 and the provision of the full text of the application under Article 6.1.3, Guatemala submitted the following arguments.[784] Guatemala argues that, should we find a violation of Articles 5.5, 12.1.1 and 6.1.3, such violations, that is, delay in notification under Article 5.5, insufficient public notice of initiation or delay in the provision of the full text of the application, did not affect the course of the investigation. Guatemala posits that (a) the alleged violations of Article 5.5, 12.1.1 and 6.1.3 were not harmful to Mexico according to the principle of harmless error, (b) Mexico "convalidated" the alleged violations by not objecting immediately after their occurrence, and (c) the alleged violations did not cause nullification or impairment of benefits accruing to Mexico under the AD Agreement.

8.21 Guatemala first argues that these alleged violations constituted harmless error. Guatemala states that it is a general principle of law that in case of a violation of a procedural rule, prejudice must be shown before a party obtains the right to be compensated for this procedural error. Guatemala refers to certain Members' practice in civil and criminal proceedings in this regard. Guatemala asserts that the International Court of Justice has recognized the concept of harmless error as well. On the basis of this principle, Guatemala argues that the alleged violations of Articles 5.5, 6.1.3, 12.1.1 were of a procedural nature, did not affect Mexico's rights in any way, and thus constituted harmless errors.

8.22 In our view, the GATT panel referred to by Guatemala in support of its position merely stated that it did not wish "to exclude that the concept of harmless error

---

> performed by the national authorities at the time of the investigation on the basis of the various national authorities' determinations and the evidence it had collected. [Footnote deleted]"

[783] We note that this standard is consistent with the approach followed by the panel in *Guatemala - Cement I* in para. 7.57 of its report. In that instance the panel was of the opinion that its role was:

> "... to examine whether the evidence relied on by the Ministry was sufficient, that is, whether an unbiased and objective investigating authority evaluating that evidence could properly have determined that sufficient evidence of dumping, injury, and causal link existed to justify initiating the investigation." (footnote deleted)

[784] For a full description of the parties' arguments and the substantive findings of the Panel regarding these claims please refer to sections VIII.C.4, VIII.C.5(b) and VIII.C.6 *infra*.

could be applicable in dispute settlement proceedings under the Agreement. "[785] It therefore cannot be concluded that the GATT panel referred to "recognized the principle of harmless error "as alleged by Guatemala.[786] We do not consider that the concept of "harmless error" as presented by Guatemala has attained the status of a general principle of public international law. In any event, we consider that our first task in this dispute is to determine whether Guatemala has acted consistently with its obligations under the relevant provisions of the AD Agreement. To the extent that Mexico can demonstrate that Guatemala has not respected its obligations under the relevant provisions of that Agreement, we must next consider arguments raised by Guatemala in respect of the nullification or impairment of benefits accruing to Mexico thereunder.[787] Thus, while arguments regarding the existence and extent of the possible harm suffered by Mexico may be relevant to the issue of nullification or impairment,[788] we do not consider that an argument of harmless error represents a defence in itself to an alleged infringement of a provision of the WTO Agreement.

8.23 A second argument raised by Guatemala is based on the lack of reaction from Mexico to the alleged late notification, the alleged insufficient public notice and the alleged delay in providing the full text of the application to Mexico and Cruz Azul. Guatemala asserts that, by not reacting at the earliest possible moment, Mexico waived its rights to object to the above-mentioned alleged violations. Guatemala uses both the concepts of "acquiescence" and "estoppel" in support of this argument. We note that "acquiescence" amounts to "qualified silence", whereby silence in the face of events that call for a reaction of some sort may be interpreted as a presumed consent.[789] The concept of estoppel, also relied on by Guatemala in support of its argument, is akin to that of acquiescence. Estoppel is premised on the view that where one party has been induced to act in reliance on the assurances of another party, in such a way that it would be prejudiced were the other party later to change its position, such a change in position is "estopped", that is precluded.[790]

8.24 Regarding both arguments of acquiescence and estoppel we note that Mexico was under no obligation to object immediately to the violations it now alleges before the Panel.[791] Mexico raised claims concerning Articles 5.5, 12.1.1 and 6.1.3 at an appropriate moment under the dispute settlement procedure envisaged by the AD Agreement and the DSU. Thus, Mexico cannot therefore be considered as having acquiesced to belated notification by Guatemala, to insufficiency in the public notice or to delay in providing the full text of the application, much less to have given "assurances" to Guatemala that it would not later challenge these actions in WTO dispute settlement. Since Mexico raised its claims at an appropriate moment under the

---

785 *Brazil - Imposition of Provisional and Definitive Countervailing Duties on Milk Powder and Certain types of Milk from the European Economic Community*, SCM/179, adopted 28 April 1994, para. 271.

786 Guatemala first submission, para.213.

787 *See* paras. 8.105- 8.112, *infra*.

788 Or in the event Article 22 is invoked, to the issues of compensation and/or suspension of equivalent concessions.

789 V.D. Degan, *Sources of International Law*, Martinus Nijhoff Publishers, p. 348-349.

790 Brownlie, *Principles of International Law*, Clarendon Press, p. 640-642.

791 Regarding acquiescence we note that the precise scope and applicability of this concept is still a matter of debate, and it is clear that not any silence can be considered to constitute consent.

WTO dispute settlement procedures, Guatemala could not have reasonably relied upon Mexico's alleged lack of protest to conclude that Mexico would not bring a WTO complaint. In any event, Guatemala has not satisfied us that, had Mexico complained after the fact, but during the course of the investigation, Guatemala could or would have taken action to remedy the situation. Specifically, with respect to the delay in the Article 5.5 notification, Guatemala asserts that had Mexico objected to the notification delay in a timely manner, the Guatemalan authorities would have reinitiated the investigation after presenting Mexico with the notification under Article 5.5. We are of the view that this argument presented by Guatemala is highly speculative and notes that the Panel has been established to rule on the WTO conformity of the actions by Guatemala and not on the WTO conformity of the actions Guatemala alleges it could have taken. In any event, Guatemala states at para. 217 of its first written submission that Mexico first raised the Article 5.5 issue on 6 June 1996, that is at a relatively early stage of the Ministry's investigation, and precedes the Ministry's preliminary affirmative determination. Nevertheless, Guatemala failed to take any steps to address the delayed Article 5.5 notification at that time. Based on these considerations the Panel rejects Guatemala's defence that Mexico "convalidated" the alleged violations of Articles 5.5, 6.1.3 and 12.1.1 of the AD Agreement.

8.25 Finally, Guatemala argues that the presumption of nullification or impairment of Article 3.8 DSU, if a violation is found, is rebuttable, and that none of the alleged violations nullified or impaired benefits accruing to Mexico under the AD Agreement. As noted above, we will address the issue of nullification or impairment after we have considered whether Guatemala has acted consistently with its obligations under the AD Agreement. See paras. 8.105 - 8.112, *infra.*

C. Claims by Mexico Concerning the Initiation of the Investigation

8.26 Mexico asserts that Guatemala's initiation of the anti-dumping investigation at issue in this dispute was inconsistent with Articles 5.2 and 5.3 of the AD Agreement. Mexico considers that the anti-dumping investigation should never have been initiated, and that its initiation and subsequent conduct resulted in the nullification or impairment of benefits accruing to Mexico under the WTO and in particular the AD Agreement. Mexico asserts that the Ministry's decision to initiate the investigation is also inconsistent with Articles 2, 3 and 12 of the AD Agreement.[792]

8.27 Guatemala considers that the initiation of the investigation was fully in accordance with the requirements of Articles 5.2 and 5.3 of the AD Agreement, with respect to both the procedures and the substance of the initiation determination. Guatemala also argues that, as a result of the scope of application of Articles 2 and 3 of the AD Agreement, an investigating authority's decision to initiate an investigation cannot be found to be inconsistent with those provisions.

8.28 We note that Article 5.2 refers to the contents of the application by the domestic industry requesting the initiation of an investigation, and establishes that the

[792] In its conclusions presented in Mexico's first submission (see, p. 96), Mexico also requests the Panel to find that the initiation is inconsistent with Article 1 of the AD Agreement. However, since there is nothing in Mexico's submissions to the Panel to substantiate this purported Article 1 claim, we do not consider it necessary to consider this issue further.

application must include *inter alia* information on certain specific areas to the extent that it is "reasonably available" to the applicant. In this regard, Article 5.2 states that "[s]imple assertion, unsubstantiated by relevant evidence, cannot be considered sufficient to meet the requirements of this paragraph". Article 5.3 requires the investigating authorities to examine the accuracy and adequacy of the evidence in the application to determine whether there is sufficient evidence to justify the initiation of an investigation. Thus, we are confronted with two issues: whether the application contained such information as was reasonably available to the applicant (Article 5.2), and whether the investigating authority examined the accuracy and adequacy of the evidence to arrive at a justified determination that there was sufficient evidence to justify the initiation of the investigation (Article 5.3). We proceed by examining Mexico's claims under Article 5.3 first.

1. Sufficiency of Evidence to Justify Initiation of the Investigation - Article 5.3

8.29 Mexico argues that the Ministry based its initiation decision on insufficient evidence, in violation of Article 5.3 of the AD Agreement. Mexico considers that an unbiased and objective investigating authority examining the evidence that was before the Ministry could not have properly determined that there was sufficient evidence of dumping, still less of the existence of a threat of material injury, and of a causal link between the imports allegedly dumped and the alleged threat of material injury to the Guatemalan domestic industry, to justify initiation of an anti-dumping investigation. Mexico considers that, even if the information provided by Cementos Progreso in its application constituted all the information reasonably available to it, Articles 5.2 and 5.3 cannot acceptably be interpreted to mean that Article 5.3 authorizes an investigating authority to initiate an anti-dumping investigation solely because an application meets the requirements of Article 5.2. Thus, even if one were to suppose that the information needed to be able to determine that there was sufficient evidence to justify the initiation of an investigation was not reasonably available to the applicant, this did not mean that there was sufficient evidence to justify initiation in accordance with Article 5.3 of the AD Agreement. Mexico also argues that Guatemala failed to examine the adequacy and accuracy of the evidence included in the application.

8.30 Guatemala argues that the authorities of the importing country must examine the accuracy and adequacy of the evidence provided in the application to determine whether there is sufficient evidence to justify the initiation, as set forth in Article 5.3 of the AD Agreement, but they are not required to carry out any investigation or confirm or verify the claims contained in the application. Referring to the decision in *Softwood Lumber*, Guatemala asserts the we should consider whether "a reasonable, unprejudiced person could have found ... that sufficient evidence existed" to justify initiation, and that the level of "sufficient" evidence to justify initiation is significantly lower than the level of evidence required for a preliminary or final determination. Guatemala argues that the Ministry properly examined the accuracy and adequacy of the evidence submitted with the application, and that we must accept the Ministry's establishment of the fact that there was sufficient evidence, reasonably available to the applicant, to justify the initiation of the investigation. Otherwise,

Guatemala asserts, the Panel would be assuming the role of the investigating authority.

8.31 We recall that, in accordance with our standard of review, we must determine whether an objective and unbiased investigating authority, looking at the facts before it, could properly have determined that there was sufficient evidence to justify the initiation of an anti-dumping investigation. Article 5.3 requires the authority to examine, in making this determination, the accuracy and adequacy of the evidence in the application. Clearly, the accuracy and adequacy of the evidence is relevant to the investigating authorities' determination whether there is sufficient evidence to justify the initiation of an investigation. It is however the sufficiency of the evidence, and not its adequacy and accuracy *per se*, which represents the legal standard to be applied in the case of a determination whether to initiate an investigation.

8.32 With these considerations in mind, we now turn to consider whether Guatemala acted consistently with Article 5.3 in initiating the investigation. We will examine the determination with respect to each of the elements of a dumping investigation, that is, dumping, injury and causation, separately.

(a) Dumping

8.33 Mexico argues that the evidence before the Guatemalan authorities on the question of dumping was insufficient for an initiation of an investigation. Mexico asserts that the only evidence submitted with the application on the question of normal value consisted of two invoices, dated 25 and 26 August 1995, for one bag each of cement, and that the only evidence of export price was two import certificates, dated 15 August 1995,[793] for 7,035 and 4,221 sacks of cement. In Mexico's view, this evidence "cannot qualify as adequate and accurate evidence" of normal value and export price. With respect to normal value, Mexico argues that the invoices do not sufficiently specify the product in question, or the amounts or the source, the sales are not representative of sales over the period of investigation, and the sales represent only an insignificant share of Cruz Azul's operations. With respect to export price, Mexico argues that the import certificates are not representative of Mexico's exports to the Guatemalan market, and that the imports occurred on only two days of the period of investigation. Moreover, Mexico argues that the prices reflected in the documents were not comparable within the meaning of Articles 2.1 and 2.4 of the Agreement, and that the Guatemalan authorities did not make any allowances for differences affecting price comparability. Mexico notes that: a) there were differences in the description of product referred to in the invoices; b) the evidence was not representative of the prices in the domestic and export markets; c) there were differences between the volumes presented in the invoices and the export certificates; and d) the transactions taken as evidence of the export price and the normal value were at different levels of trade. In these circumstances, Mexico asserts that, no ob-

[793] Although the import certificates were both stamped on 15 August 1995, the certificate for 7,035 sacks of cement is also dated 14 August 1995. The Panel understands that it is for this reason that Mexico subsequently referred to the Ministry considering the volume of imports on two days during the period of investigation.

jective and unbiased authority could properly have determined that the evidence before it was sufficient to justify initiation of an investigation.

8.34 Guatemala argues that the evidence of normal value and export price before its investigating authority was sufficient to justify the initiation of an investigation. Guatemala asserts that the AD Agreement does not require that an application contain information on prices for a particular number of transactions or a particular minimum value or volume of sales, and that there is no requirement to provide evidence on possible adjustments, since the relevant information is not available to applicants. In Guatemala's view, Articles 2.1 (defining dumping), 2.4 (requirement of a fair comparison), and 5.8 (rejection of application and termination of investigation for lack of sufficient evidence) are not applicable to the decision to initiate. Guatemala asserts that it complied with Articles 5.1, (written application), 5.2 (requirement of evidence in application), and 5.3 (examination of accuracy and adequacy of evidence in application to determine sufficiency to initiate), which in its view are the only provisions of the AD Agreement which apply at the initiation stage.

8.35 In light of Guatemala's arguments, we need to examine the relationship between the requirements of Article 5.3 regarding sufficiency of evidence to justify the initiation of an investigation and the substantive provisions in Article 2 regarding dumping. In this respect, we first observe that, although there is no express reference to evidence of dumping in Article 5.3, evidence on the three elements necessary for the imposition of an anti-dumping measure may be inferred into Article 5.3 by way of Article 5.2. In other words, Article 5.2 requires that the application contain sufficient evidence on dumping, injury and causation, while Article 5.3 requires the investigating authority to satisfy itself as to the accuracy and adequacy of the evidence to determine that it is sufficient to justify initiation. Thus, reading Article 5.3 in the context of Article 5.2, the evidence mentioned in Article 5.3 must be evidence of dumping, injury and causation. We further observe that the only clarification of the term "dumping" in the AD Agreement is that contained in Article 2. In consequence, in order to determine that there is sufficient evidence of dumping, the investigating authority cannot entirely disregard the elements that configure the existence of this practice as outlined in Article 2. This analysis is done not with a view to making a determination that Article 2 has been violated through the initiation of an investigation, but rather to provide guidance in our review of the Ministry's determination that there was sufficient evidence of dumping to warrant an investigation. We do not of course mean to suggest that an investigating authority must have before it at the time it initiates an investigation evidence of dumping within the meaning of Article 2 of the quantity and quality that would be necessary to support a preliminary or final determination. An anti-dumping investigation is a process where certainty on the existence of all the elements necessary in order to adopt a measure is reached gradually as the investigation moves forward. However, the evidence must be such that an unbiased and objective investigating authority could determine that there was sufficient evidence of dumping within the meaning of Article 2 to justify initiation of an investigation.[794]

[794] On this question we concur fully with the reasoning of the panel in *Guatemala - Cement I* , when they state that:

8.36 We note that Article 2.1 states that a product is to be considered as dumped "if the export price ... is less than the *comparable* price, in the ordinary course of trade, for the like product when destined for consumption in the exporting country." (emphasis added). Other provisions of Article 2 that further elaborate on this basic definition include Article 2.4, which sets forth certain principles regarding the comparability of export prices and normal value. In particular, Article 2.4 specifies that comparisons between the export price and the normal value shall be made at the same level of trade, and that due allowance shall be made in each case, on its merits, for differences which affect price comparability, including differences in level of trade and quantity. Consistent with our discussion above, we consider that, although these provisions of Article 2 do not "apply" as such to initiation determinations, they are certainly relevant to an investigating authorities' consideration as to whether sufficient evidence of dumping exists to justify the initiation of an investigation.[795]

8.37 Turning to the case at hand, the evidence on normal value relied on by the Ministry for initiation consisted of two invoices from Mexican retailers for one sack of cement each, while the evidence of the export price consisted of two import certificates for 7,035 and 4,221 bags of cement. In our opinion, the evidence on normal value and export prices presents obvious differences with regards to the quantities for the involved transactions and the level of trade of the sales. It is clear on the face of these documents that the invoices reflecting prices in Mexico are for sales occurring at the very end of the commercialisation chain and the import certificates reflect prices at the point of importation which is the beginning of the commercialisation chain for Mexican cement in Guatemala. The existence of these stark differences in quantity and in level of trade, differences of the kind that Article 2.4 of the AD Agreement recognizes may affect price comparability, should have triggered at a minimum some reflection on the part of the investigating authorities as to the possible non-comparability of the sales in question.

8.38 Guatemala argues that there was no indication that the sales were at different levels of trade, nor that any difference in the level of trade affected price comparability. Additionally, Guatemala argues that Cruz Azul never presented any evidence to support its argument that the sales in the domestic market and export market had

---

> "In our view, the reference in Article 5.2 to "dumping" must be read as a reference to dumping as it is defined in Article 2. This does not, of course, mean that the evidence provided in the application must be of the quantity and quality that would be necessary to make a preliminary or final determination of dumping. However, evidence of the relevant **type** is, in our view, required in a case such as this one where it is obvious on the face of the application that the normal value and export price alleged in the application will require adjustments in order to effectuate a fair comparison. At a minimum, there should be some recognition that a fair comparison will require such adjustments." *Guatemala - Cement I, supra*, footnote 25, para. 7.64

[795] We understand Guatemala to agree to our approach concerning the relationship between Article 2 and Article 5.3. At para. 136 of its first written submission, Guatemala asserted that it is "not suggesting that Articles 2 and 3 are totally irrelevant during the initiation phase. Articles 2 and 3 contain definitions which give meaning to the expressions 'dumping', 'injury' and 'causal link' used in Article 5.2. When the authorities examine the accuracy and adequacy of the evidence submitted in the application, those definitions help to establish whether there is 'sufficient evidence' in the meaning of Article 5.3 to justify the initiation of the investigation."

been conducted at different levels of trade and affected price comparability. In our view, however, the fact that the sales in the Mexican and Guatemalan markets were at different levels of trade was apparent from the application itself, and an unbiased and objective investigating authority should have recognized this fact without the need for it to be pointed out. Nor do we consider that an investigating authority can completely ignore obvious differences that could affect the comparability of the prices cited in an application on the ground that the foreign exporter has not demonstrated that they have affected price comparability. Moreover, at the point where the investigating authority is considering whether there is sufficient evidence to initiate an investigation, potentially affected exporters have not even been notified of the existence of an application, much less been provided a copy thereof. Thus, the logical implication of Guatemala's argument is that an investigating authority need never take into account issues of price comparability when considering whether there is sufficient evidence of dumping to initiate an investigation. We cannot agree with such an interpretation of the AD Agreement, particularly in light of the criteria set out in para. 8.36 above.

8.39 After a thorough review of all the actions by the Ministry leading up to the initiation of the investigation, we find that no attempt was made to take into account glaring differences in the levels of trade and sales quantities and their possible effects on price comparability. Under these circumstances, an unbiased and objective investigating authority could not in our view have concluded that there was sufficient evidence of dumping to justify the initiation of an anti-dumping investigation.

8.40 We would like to emphasize that we do not expect investigating authorities at the initiation phase to ferret out all possible differences that might affect the comparability of prices in an application and perform or request complex adjustments to them. We do however expect that, when from the face of an application it is obvious that there are substantial questions of comparability between the export and home market prices being compared, the investigating authority will at least acknowledge that differences in the prices generate questions with regards to their comparability, and either give some consideration as to the impact of those differences on the sufficiency of the evidence of dumping or seek such further information as might be necessary to do so.

(b) Threat of Material Injury

8.41 We recall that the Ministry initiated its investigation into imports of cement from Mexico on the basis of an alleged threat of material injury to the domestic industry.

8.42 Mexico argues that the Ministry did not have sufficient evidence of threat of material injury to justify the initiation of an investigation. Mexico asserts that, in order to initiate an anti-dumping investigation on the basis of a threat of injury, the existence of threat of injury must be demonstrated on the basis of adequate evidence, and not merely on the basis of allegation, conjecture, or remote possibility. In Mexico's view, this requires an applicant alleging threat of injury to provide, at a minimum, evidence with respect to the factors concerning threat of injury set forth in Article 3.7. Mexico asserts that neither Cementos Progreso's original application, nor its supplementary application, contained evidence on any of these factors. Mexico argues that the only evidence on threat of injury was the two import certificates supplied by the domestic producer, which in its view is entirely insufficient to justify the initiation of an investigation.

8.43 Mexico asserts that Guatemala admits that the Ministry "did not need complete information to know that imports were rapidly increasing",[796] and argues that the Ministry just inferred that Mexican cement producers had excess capacity on the basis of its "knowledge" that Mexico was undergoing a "horrendous recession". Mexico adds that incomplete information and mere knowledge do not constitute evidence, and may not be taken into consideration to arrive at a finding of sufficient evidence of threat of injury to justify the initiation of an investigation.

8.44 Guatemala argues that the allegation of threat of injury was substantiated by adequate evidence. In Guatemala's view, Article 3.7 of the AD Agreement does not apply to an investigating authority's determination as to whether there is sufficient evidence to justify the initiation of an investigation. Guatemala argues that Article 5.2(iv) of the Agreement requires that an application contain such information as is reasonably available to the applicant on the evolution of the volume of imports, their effect on prices of the like product in the domestic market, and the consequent impact on the domestic industry, and refers to Articles 3.2 and 3.4 (which address the factors concerning the evaluation of the volume of imports, their effects on prices, and their impact on the domestic industry), but does not refer to the threat of injury factors set forth in Article 3.7. Guatemala also argues that information on the volume of imports is not available to private parties in Guatemala, and that its authorities were not obliged to obtain information on the volume of imports from the Directorate of Customs prior to initiation.

8.45 In order to review the Ministry's determination that there was sufficient evidence of threat of injury to justify the initiation of an investigation, we must first consider the relationship between Article 5.3 and Article 3. We recall our earlier analysis of the relationship between Article 5.3 and Article 2, and consider that an identical approach should be taken to the relationship between Article 5.3 and Article 3.[797] Thus, when considering whether there is sufficient evidence of threat of injury to justify the initiation of an investigation, an investigating authority cannot totally disregard the elements that configure the existence of threat of injury outlined in Article 3.[798] We do not mean to suggest that an investigating authority must have before it at the time it initiates an investigation evidence of threat of material injury within the meaning of Article 3 of the quantity and quality that would be necessary to support a preliminary or final determination of threat of injury. However, the investigating authority must have before it evidence of threat of material injury, as defined in Article 3, sufficient to justify the initiation of an investigation.

---

[796] Guatemala first submission para. 174.

[797] See para. 8.35 above.

[798] We recall that, at para. 136 of its first written submission, Guatemala asserted that it is "not suggesting that Articles 2 and 3 are totally irrelevant during the initiation phase. Articles 2 and 3 contain definitions which give meaning to the expressions 'dumping', 'injury' and 'causal link' used in Article 5.2. When the authorities examine the accuracy and adequacy of the evidence submitted in the application, those definitions help to establish whether there is 'sufficient evidence' in the meaning of Article 5.3 to justify the initiation of the investigation."

8.46 Article 3.1 of the AD Agreement provides that a determination of injury, which is defined in footnote 9 of the AD Agreement to include threat of material injury, "shall be based on positive evidence and involve an objective examination of both *(a)* the volume of the dumped imports and the effect of the dumped imports on prices in the domestic market for like products, and *(b)* the consequent impact of these imports on domestic producers of such products." In addition, Article 3.7 contains a number of factors specifically concerning threat of injury. We shall examine to what extent, if any, the Ministry examined these Article 3 factors when determining that there was sufficient evidence of threat of injury to justify the initiation of an investigation.

8.47 Regarding the volume of the allegedly dumped imports, Article 3.2 of the AD Agreement provides that an investigating authority shall consider whether there has been a significant increase in dumped imports, either in absolute terms "or relative to production or consumption in the importing Member". Guatemala asserts in its submissions before us that there was a "massive" increase in the volume of imports of cement prior to initiation. However, Guatemala has failed to demonstrate that there was any evidence on the volume of imports in the Ministry's file at the time of initiation other than two import certificates for 7,035 and 4,221 bags of cement respectively. Both these importations appear to have taken place on the same day, 15 August 1995, at the same (Tecún Umán) customs post.[799] Other than these two import certificates, Cementos Progreso's application referred only to unsubstantiated "suspicions" that Mexican cement imports may be entering Guatemalan territory through other customs posts.[800] We fail to see how the data contained in the two aforementioned import certificates, combined with Cementos Progreso's unsubstantiated "suspicions", could properly support a finding by an objective and impartial investigating authority that there was sufficient evidence of threat of injury to justify the initiation of an investigation.

8.48 In support of its argument that the imports referred to in the above-mentioned import certificates represented a "massive" increase in the volume of imports, Guatemala argues that since there were no imports into Guatemala of Mexican cement prior to 1995, any increase in imports from a level of zero would be qualified as "massive". However, there is nothing in Cementos Progreso's application, or in the report to the Director of Economic Integration recommending initiation,[801] or in the Ministry's resolution initiating the investigation, to suggest that at the time of initiation the Ministry had any information regarding the volume of imports of cement from Mexico prior to or after 15 August 1995. Thus, we fail to see how the Ministry could have compared the volume of imports on 15 August 1995 with the allegedly zero volume of imports prior to 1995. In these circumstances, we consider Guatemala's argument that any increase in imports from a level of zero would be "massive" to constitute *ex post* rationalization. Such *ex post* rationalization is irrelevant for the

[799] Both import certificates were stamped on 15 August 1995. However, the certificate concerning 7,035 sacks of cement also contained a reference to 14 August 1995. We are proceeding on the basis of the date on which the import certificates were stamped by the Guatemalan authorities.

[800] Cementos Progreso's application, Annex Mexico-2, pg.4.

[801] Annex Mexico-4.

purpose of determining whether, at the time of initiation, the Ministry acted consistent with Article 5.3 of the AD Agreement.

8.49 Given our findings concerning the Ministry's consideration of the volume of imports in absolute terms, we shall now consider to what extent, if any, the Ministry considered the volume of imports relative to production or consumption in Guatemala. There is no evidence before us to suggest that, at the time of initiation, the Ministry had any evidence that imports had increased relative to domestic consumption. Indeed, there is no evidence before us to suggest that, at the time of initiation, the Ministry had any information concerning domestic consumption *per se*. Nor is there any evidence before us to suggest that, at the time of initiation, the Ministry considered the volume of imports relative to domestic production of cement. Even if the Ministry had considered this at the time of initiation, the only weighing of imports against domestic production that could have been inferred from the evidence before the Ministry at the time of initiation derives from the statement in Cementos Progreso's application that the industry was working at full capacity, and that capacity was 1.6 million metric tonnes. Based on this statement, and assuming that capacity utilization was the same for the whole of 1995 and that production equalled capacity, the Ministry could at most have concluded that the evidenced Mexican imports represented only 11 per cent of domestic production for one day, or 0,03 per cent of domestic production for one year.[802] Thus, even if the Ministry had considered this matter, the available evidence was hardly indicative of a "massive" increase in the volume imports relative to domestic production of Guatemalan cement.

8.50 Article 3.2 of the AD Agreement provides that, with regard to the effect of dumped imports on prices, the investigating authority shall consider whether there has been a significant price undercutting by the relevant imports, or whether the relevant imports have depressed domestic prices to a significant degree, or prevented price increases that would otherwise have occurred. There is no evidence before us to suggest that, at the time of initiation, the Ministry considered any of these elements concerning the effect of the relevant imports on Guatemalan cement prices. Even if the Ministry had considered possible price undercutting, for example, the only prices available to the Ministry were not comparable since they concerned transactions taking place at different levels of trade. In this regard, the Ministry could have determined the price of imports of cement from Mexico on the basis of the *wholesale* price reported in the two import certificates. The Ministry could have determined the price of cement produced in Guatemala on the basis of the price cited in the report recommending initiation[803] (*i.e.*, Quetzals ("Q") 26.00). This price is presumably a *retail* price, given its similarity to the retail prices reported in the application for the Guatemalan product (*i.e.*, Q 24 in Guatemala City and Q 32 in the Department of El Petén). Thus, even if the Ministry had considered whether there was significant price undercutting, it only had access to prices reported for different levels of trade.

---

[802] These calculations were also performed by the *Guatemala - Cement I* panel, which also found: "There is simply no discernible basis that was before the Ministry at the time of its initiation determination on which the volume of imports could properly have been characterized as 'massive'". *Guatemala - Cement I, supra*, footnote 25, para. 7.72.

[803] Recommendation presented to the Director of Economic Integration on 17 November 1995, Annex Mexico-4.

8.51 Similarly, there is no evidence before us to suggest that, at the time of initiation, the Ministry considered all of the factors concerning the effect of dumped imports on the domestic industry enumerated in Article 3.4 of the AD Agreement.[804] It would appear that, once again, the Ministry relied solely on the limited information provided in the application. While the application contains statements which may be relevant to some of the factors enumerated in Article 3.4 (such as "employment" and "investments" for example), it contains no quantifiable information except for some data on the expansion plan and the number of workers to be laid off in case of a shut down of the Guatemalan cement industry.[805] We consider that statements and assertions unsubstantiated by any evidence do not constitute sufficient evidence of threat of injury to justify the initiation of an investigation.

8.52 We also note that in this case the Guatemalan domestic industry claimed that there was a threat of material injury caused by the allegedly dumped imports. Article 3.7 provides specific guidance on the factors to be considered by an investigating authority when making a determination of threat of injury. Although we do not necessarily believe that an investigating authority must have before it information on all Article 3.7 factors in a case where initiation of an investigation is requested on the basis of an alleged threat of injury, a consideration of those factors is certainly pertinent to an evaluation of whether there was sufficient evidence of threat of material injury to justify the initiation of an investigation. There is no evidence before us to suggest that, at the time of initiation, the Ministry had information concerning any of the four factors listed in Article 3.7. In particular, no such information was contained in the application, or in the aforementioned report to the Director of Economic Integration recommending initiation, or in the Ministry's resolution initiating the investigation. The Panel fails to see how an unbiased and objective investigating authority could properly have found that there was sufficient evidence of threat of injury to justify the initiation of an investigation when no information concerning any of the factors listed in 3.7 was examined.

8.53 Additionally, Guatemala makes some general arguments concerning the evidence required in an application that the Panel wishes to address. In its submissions, Guatemala seeks to characterize Mexico's arguments with respect to the evidence in the application as being that Article 5.2 requires that such evidence be supported by "documentary proof". In our view, however, Mexico is in fact arguing that statements of conclusion unsubstantiated by facts cannot satisfy the requirement of Article 5.3. We agree with Mexico that statements of conclusion unsubstantiated by facts do not constitute evidence of the type required by Article 5.2, and which allows an objective examination of its adequacy and accuracy by an investigating authority as provided in Article 5.3.[806]

---

[804] Article 3.4 identifies the following factors: actual and potential decline in sales, profits, output, market share, productivity, return on investments, or utilization of capacity; factors affecting domestic prices; the magnitude of the margin of dumping; actual and potential negative effects on cash flow, inventories, employment, wages, growth, ability to raise capital or investments.

[805] This was also noted by the *Guatemala - Cement I* panel in Para. 7.74.

[806] Another argument by Guatemala was that there were certain facts that, even when there was no evidence on them in the application, were "known" to the investigating authority. This same argument was also made before the panel in *Guatemala-Cement I,* the Panel finds that in their comments

8.54 Based on all the considerations detailed above, the Panel is of the view that an objective and unbiased investigating authority could not have properly determined that there was sufficient evidence of threat of injury to justify the initiation of an investigation.

(c) Causation

8.55 Finally, Mexico argues that the Ministry did not have sufficient evidence of a causal link between the alleged dumping and the alleged threat of injury to justify the initiation of the investigation. In Mexico's view, since the application did not contain adequate evidence of dumping or threat of injury, it follows that it did not demonstrate a causal link. Moreover, Mexico asserts that the application and supplement did not contain any argument regarding the existence of a causal link. Thus, Mexico maintains that the Guatemalan authorities did not have any evidence or arguments on this aspect when the investigation was initiated.

8.56 Guatemala asserts that there was adequate evidence to support the claim of the existence of a causal link. In Guatemala's view, Article 5.2 requires only evidence of the factors listed in subparagraphs (iii) and (iv), that is, such information as is reasonably available to the applicant on prices for the calculation of normal value and export price, and on the evolution of the volume of imports, their effect on prices of the like product in the domestic market, and the consequent impact on the domestic industry. It does not refer to Article 3.5, which Guatemala argues related to the evidence of a causal link required for a preliminary or final determination.

8.57 We are of the view that, having determined that the Ministry did not have sufficient evidence of dumping and injury to justify the initiation of an investigation,

---

contained footnote 242 of the report the *Guatemala - Cement I* panel provides useful guidance on this issue:

> "We note that Guatemala asserted that the Ministry "knew" certain information, such as transport costs in Guatemala, information concerning Cementos Progreso and the market for cement in Guatemala, that Mexico was going through a severe recession, particularly in the construction sector, etc., and that such knowledge was brought to bear on its evaluation of the information in the application and together with that information constituted sufficient evidence to justify initiation. Thus, for instance, Guatemala asserted before the Panel that there was sufficient information to establish a presumption that there was excess capacity in Mexico, and a decline in demand for cement in Mexico, which caused Cruz Azul to start exporting to Guatemala in 1995, and indicated that exports would increase. While such facts may have been known to the Ministry, there is no reference to them in the application, in the evaluation prepared by the two advisors, or in the resolution itself. Indeed, there is no reference whatsoever to excess capacity in Mexico, or to a likelihood that imports would increase, in the resolution or the underlying recommendation. Thus, we cannot consider such facts in evaluating whether the Ministry properly concluded that there was sufficient evidence to justify initiation in this case."

According to the standard of review the Panel is to evaluate the considerations of the investigating authority at the time it made its decision on the basis of its determinations and the evidence before it. It is not appropriate for the Panel to take into consideration these facts that were allegedly "known" by the Ministry as it is impossible to evaluate what role they played in their decision to initiate, since there is no mention of them in any of the documentation preceding and supporting the initiation.

it follows logically that there was also insufficient evidence of the causal link between the two to justify initiation.

(d) Conclusion

8.58 For the reasons set forth above, we find that the Ministry violated Article 5.3 of the AD Agreement by determining that there was sufficient evidence of dumping, threat of injury, and causal link, to justify the initiation of an investigation.

2. *Sufficiency of the Application - Article 5.2*

8.59 In light of our finding that the Ministry's determination that it had sufficient evidence to justify the initiation of an investigation was inconsistent with Article 5.3, we do not consider it necessary to rule on Mexico's Article 5.2 claims regarding the sufficiency of Cementos Progreso's application.

8.60 We would note, however, that for the purposes of our analysis of claims under Article 5.3, we assumed that information in the application was, in fact, all that was reasonably available to the applicant. We would like to make clear that this assumption has been made purely for the purpose of analysis, and we are not at all convinced that the information presented in the application was all that was reasonably available to the applicant, especially with regard to evidence of threat of injury.

8.61 Article 5.2(iv) of the AD Agreement provides that an application "shall contain such information as is reasonably available to the applicant on ... the effect of the allegedly dumped imports on prices of the like product in the domestic market, and the consequent impact of allegedly dumped imports on the domestic industry". Such information would normally be in the hands of the domestic industry filing an application for anti-dumping relief. This is even more likely to be the case when the company bringing the application is the sole producer of the domestic product, as in this investigation. Of the specific elements for which information is required in Article 5.2(iv), Cementos Progresos's application contained little evidence on the evolution of the volume of the allegedly dumped imports. It might have been reasonable for the investigating authority not to expect the applicant to provide information on the evolution of the volume of the imports, as a private company might not have easy access to the import statistics kept by the national customs authority. However, regarding the other factors in Article 5.2(iv), concerning information on the effect of the allegedly dumped imports on prices of the domestic like product in the domestic market and consequent impact of the imports on the domestic industry, Cementos Progreso merely makes some allegations. These allegations are not supported by evidence, and in most cases are not quantified. Given that this information should be readily available to the sole domestic producer composing the domestic industry producing cement in Guatemala, this information should have been included in the application.

8.62 It is evident to us that the Guatemalan authorities relied on the same evidence that was presented in the application for purposes of the initiation. We have expressed the view that Articles 5.2 and 5.3 contain different obligations. One of the consequences of this difference in obligations is that investigating authorities need not content themselves with the information provided in the application but may gather information on their own in order to meet the standard of sufficient evidence for initiation in Article 5.3. On this issue we are in full agreement with the reasoning and findings expressed in by the *Guatemala-Cement I* panel which made the following comments:

> "7.53 We have concluded that the question whether there is "sufficient evidence" to justify initiation is not answered by a determination that the application contains all the information "reasonably available" to the applicant on the factors specified in Article 5.2 (i) - (iv). This does not, however, mean that investigations may not be initiated in cases where "sufficient evidence" is not "reasonably available" to the applicant. In particular, there is nothing in the Agreement to prevent an investigating authority from seeking evidence and information on its own, that would allow any gaps in the evidence set forth in the application to be filled. We do not suggest that such action by the investigating authority is in any case required by the ADP Agreement. However, if, as in this case, an authority chooses to refrain from such action, the "reasonably available" language in Article 5.2 does not permit the initiation of an investigation based on evidence and information which, while all that is "reasonably available" to the applicant is not, objectively judged, sufficient to justify initiation. Indeed, in this case the applicant requested that the Ministry obtain certain information on import volumes which it was unable to obtain itself. This the Ministry did not do, however, until **after** it had initiated the investigation based on the information in the application."[807]

3. *Simultaneous Examination of the Evidence and Failure to Reject the Application*

(a) Claim under Article 5.7 of the AD Agreement

8.63 Mexico claims that Guatemala violated Article 5.7 of the AD Agreement because, prior to initiation, the Ministry failed to examine the evidence on dumping and injury simultaneously.

8.64 Guatemala argues that Mexico has not discharged its burden of proof as a complainant that there was any violation of Article 5.7. Moreover, Guatemala asserts that the Ministry reviewed the available evidence for both dumping and injury.

8.65 Article 5.7 reads:

> "5.7 The evidence of both dumping and injury shall be considered simultaneously *(a)* in the decision whether or not to initiate an investigation, and *(b)* thereafter, during the course of the investigation, starting on a date not later than the earliest date on which in accordance with the provisions of this Agreement provisional measures may be applied. "

8.66 We understand Mexico to argue that, because the application contained no evidence on injury and inadequate evidence of dumping, there was no evidence of dumping and injury that could be examined simultaneously by the Ministry at the time of initiation. In other words, we understand Mexico to argue that the initiation

[807] *Guatemala - Cement I, supra*, footnote 25, para. 7.53.

of an investigation in the absence of sufficient evidence to justify initiation (contrary to Article 5.3) necessarily constitutes a violation of Article 5.7.

8.67 We do not share the interpretation of Article 5.7 implied in Mexico's argument. We are of the view that Article 5.7 requires the investigating authority to examine the evidence before it on dumping and injury simultaneously, rather than sequentially. We do not consider that the fulfilment of this requirement is conditioned in any way on the substantive nature of that evidence.

8.68 As a result of the nature of its argument, Mexico has not demonstrated that in fact the Ministry failed to examine the evidence on dumping and injury before it simultaneously. We therefore reject Mexico's claim that Guatemala violated Article 5.7 of the AD Agreement.

(b) Claim under Article 5.8

8.69 Mexico also claims that Guatemala violated Article 5.8 by not rejecting the application made by Cementos Progreso and by not refraining from initiating the investigation due to the lack of sufficient evidence of dumping and threat of injury to justify initiation.

8.70 Guatemala argues that Mexico had failed to meet its burden to prove that there was a violation. Guatemala also argues that Article 5.8 only applies after the initiation of an investigation and that according to the applicable standard of review the Panel could not conclude that the investigation was initiated without sufficient evidence. In support of this argument Guatemala referred to the findings in the *Mexico-HFCS* report at para. 7.99.

8.71 The first question that we need to address on this issue regards the applicability of Article 5.8 before the initiation of an investigation. This Article provides in pertinent part:

> "5.8 An application under paragraph 1 shall be rejected and an investigation shall be terminated promptly as soon as the authorities concerned are satisfied that there is not sufficient evidence of either dumping or of injury to justify proceeding with the case."

8.72 We note that Article 5.8 makes specific reference to the rejection of an application as soon as the authorities conclude that there is not sufficient evidence of dumping or injury to justify proceeding with the case. This language on rejection of an application seems to be in contrast with Guatemala's argument that Article 5.8 applies only after initiation. We are of the view that, if the drafters intended that Article 5.8 apply only after initiation, the reference to promptly terminating an investigation would have sufficed. By referring to the rejection of an application Article 5.8 addresses the situation where an application has been received but an investigation has not yet been initiated. That the text of Article 5.8 continues after the quoted section to describe situations in which an initiated investigation should be terminated, does not support Guatemala's argument that the whole of Article 5.8 applies only after the investigation has been initiated. On the contrary, the second sentence of Article 5.8, by specifying that "there shall be immediate termination in cases" confirms that the first sentence of Article 5.8 expressly contemplates its application pre-initiation by including a reference to the rejection of an application. Otherwise, mere reference to the termination of an investigation, as in the second sentence of Article

5.8, would have been all that was needed in the first sentence to make it clear that it applied once an investigation was underway.

8.73 In our view, the findings in *Mexico-HFCS* on this issue do not support the interpretation that Article 5.8 applies only after an investigation has been initiated. Paragraph 7.99 of the panel report in *Mexico-HFCS,* cited by Guatemala as supporting its views, reads:

> "In our view, Article 5.8 does not impose additional substantive obligations beyond those in Article 5.3 on the authority in connection with the initiation of an investigation. That is, if there is sufficient evidence to justify initiation under Article 5.3, there is no violation of Article 5.8 in not rejecting the application. Having determined that the initiation of the investigation was not inconsistent with the requirements of Article 5.3, we further conclude that there was no violation of Article 5.8 of the AD Agreement."[808]

8.74 The panel in *Mexico-HFCS* determined that there had not been a violation of Article 5.3 as there was sufficient evidence to justify initiation. After having made that determination the *Mexico-HFCS* panel proceeded to find that given that there was sufficient evidence to justify initiation under Article 5.3, there was no possible violation of Article 5.8. This in no way detracts from our position that Article 5.8 applies pre-initiation. The Panel in *Mexico - HFCS* would not have even considered the question of whether rejection of the application was warranted if it had not considered that Article 5.8 applies before initiation.

8.75 Having concluded that Article 5.8 applies prior to initiation, we find that the Guatemalan investigating authorities acted inconsistently with their obligations under Article 5.8 in failing to reject the application in this case. The Panel is of the view that under the applicable standard of review no objective and unbiased investigating authority would have found that there was sufficient evidence to initiate and, in consequence, the Guatemalan authorities should have rejected the application.

4. *Notification under Article 5.5*

8.76 Mexico argues that Guatemala did not notify the Government of Mexico before proceeding to initiate the investigation, despite being obliged to do so under Article 5.5 of the Agreement, and that the official notification to the Government of Mexico occurred only on 22 January 1996, 11 days after the publication of the notice of initiation of the investigation on 11 January 1996.

8.77 Mexico asserts that Guatemala acknowledged its failure to notify the Government of Mexico prior to initiating, citing a communication from the Ministry to the Mexican Government, which states:

> "We sincerely regret that your country was not notified before the publication of the resolution for the initiation of the investigation, and we offer our sincere apologies in that regard. This was due to a slip on the part of the persons responsible for effecting the notification, as

[808] *Mexico-HFCS*, *supra*, footnote 34, para. 7.99.

they were not familiar with the provisions applicable to anti-dumping investigation procedures. Once again, please accept our apologies."[809]

8.78 Thus, Mexico claims that Guatemala clearly failed to comply with the requirements of the AD Agreement under Article 5.5, and has admitted doing so prior to this dispute settlement proceeding.

8.79 Guatemala argues that the effective date of initiation of the investigation was not 11 January 1996 as Mexico alleged. Guatemala argues that according to its own Constitution and legislation the Ministry could not have initiated the investigation until the Government of Mexico had been officially notified. Guatemala also asserts in its defence that Mexico acknowledges in its response to the questionnaire that the investigation was not initiated until 22 January 1996.[810]

8.80 Guatemala does not disagree that it was required by the AD Agreement to notify the Government of Mexico before proceeding with the initiation of an investigation, or the timing of the notification. Guatemala's arguments relate to the timing of the initiation of the investigation. Thus, the first question for the Panel to resolve is, what was the actual date of initiation in this case?

8.81 Article 5.5 provides:

> "5.5 The authorities shall avoid, unless a decision has been made to initiate an investigation, any publicizing of the application for the initiation of an investigation. However, after receipt of a properly documented application and before proceeding to initiate an investigation, the authorities shall notify the government of the exporting Member concerned."

8.82 In our view, footnote 1 to the AD Agreement is useful in clarifying what is meant by the term "initiated". Footnote 1 defines the term "initiated" as follows:

> "The term "initiated" as used in this Agreement means the procedural action by which a Member formally commences an investigation as provided in Article 5".

Thus, the date of initiation is the date of the procedural action by which Guatemala formally commenced the investigation. We are of the view that in the case before us the action by which the investigation was formally commenced is the date of publication of the notice of initiation which occurred on 11 January 1996. In this respect, we note that the 15 December 1995 decision of the Director for Economic Integration underlying the Ministry's resolution to initiate the investigation specifically states in paragraph 5 that: "The date of the initiation of the investigation shall be considered to be the date on which such notice is published in the Official Journal".[811] Subsequently the Ministry's 9 January 1996 resolution set forth its decision to "give public notice of said initiation, which shall take effect as from the day on

[809] Annex Mexico-21.

[810] Guatemala also argued that, assuming *arguendo* that it did not notify Mexico before the initiation date of 11 January 1996, this delay in notification did not affect the course of the investigation. Guatemala posits that (a) the alleged delay in notification was not harmful to Mexico (principle of "harmless error"), (b) that Mexico "convalidated" the alleged delay by not objecting immediately after its occurrence, and (c) the alleged delay in notification did not cause nullification or impairment.

[811] Annex Mexico-5.

which the notice is published in the official journal". Furthermore, deadlines for interested parties to respond to the initiation were activated on 11 January 1996 the investigation started running as of the publication of the notice, as the notice published on that date invited interested parties to state their legal interest in the matter within 30 days of the date of publication of that notice, and to submit any supplementary arguments and evidence within that same period.

8.83 The argument that Guatemala could not have initiated the investigation until after it had notified Mexico, pursuant to provisions of its own Constitution and laws, does not affect our conclusion in this regard. In acceding to the WTO, Guatemala undertook to be bound by the rules contained in the AD Agreement, and our mandate is to review Guatemala's compliance with those rules. The fact that the Constitution of Guatemala mandates that the investigating authorities proceed in a way which is consistent with its international obligations, does not validate the actions actually carried out by those authorities if those actions violate Guatemala's commitments under the WTO. Whether Mexico chose not to pursue its rights under Guatemalan law is of no concern to us, as this would not affect its rights under the WTO Agreements. Guatemala also mentions that in some cases Mexico has failed to notify the government of the investigated exporters in a timely fashion under Article 5.5. We are of the view that Mexico's actions regarding notifications is of no relevance to issues before us in this case, which requires us to review the actions of the Guatemalan authorities.[812]

5. *Public Notice of Initiation Claims under Articles 12.1 and 12.1.1*

(a) Claims under Article 12.1

8.84 Mexico claims that Guatemala violated Art. 12.1 by (i) not satisfying itself as to the sufficiency of the evidence before giving notice of the initiation and (ii) not publishing the notice of initiation and notifying Mexico and Cruz Azul when it considered that it was satisfied that there was sufficient evidence for initiation, an event which Mexico argues occurred as early as 15 December 1995. Mexico argued that notice should have been given immediately after 15 December 1995, the date of the report from the Economic Integration Directorate to the Minister containing the recommendation to initiate an investigation, as this constituted the moment when Guatemala had satisfied itself of the sufficiency of the evidence. The public notice of the initiation of the investigation was made on 11 January 1996, following the Minister's decision of 9 January 1996 to initiate.

8.85 Guatemala asserts that the competent authority to decide on the initiation was the Ministry and not the Economic Integration Directorate. The 15 December report issued by the Directorate could have been rejected by the Ministry. Also Guatemala asserts that Art 12.1 does not mandate an immediate notification and that it specifies

[812] As for Guatemala's defences claiming acquiescence and estoppel, harmless error or lack of nullification or impairment of a benefit, these issues are addressed in sections VIII.B.5 and VIII.C.7.

no time periods for the notification to occur but for the mention of "when" the authorities are satisfied.

8.86 We first address Mexico's claim that Guatemala breached Article 12.1 of the AD Agreement by failing to publish a notice of initiation and notify Mexico and Cruz Azul when it was satisfied that there was sufficient evidence of to justify initiation of an investigation. Article 12.1 provides as follows:

> "12.1 When the authorities are satisfied that there is sufficient evidence to justify the initiation of an anti-dumping investigation pursuant to Article 5, the Member or Members the products of which are subject to such investigation and other interested parties known to the investigating authorities to have an interest therein shall be notified and a public notice shall be given.

8.87 In our view, this provision can most reasonably be read to require notification and public notice once a Member has decided to initiate an investigation. This interpretation is confirmed by the fact that the public notice to be provided is a "notice of initiation of an investigation". We can conceive of no logical reason why the AD Agreement would require a Member to publish a notice of the initiation of an investigation **before** the decision had been taken that such an investigation should be initiated.

8.88 We accept that, the report from the Directorate does not constitute the act by which the Government of Guatemala decided to initiate an investigation. In this respect, we note that the Minister had the discretion not to act as recommended in the Directorate's report. Thus, the Government of Guatemala cannot be considered to have decided to initiate an investigation until the Minister has acted on the Directorate's recommendation.[813] Accordingly, the Panel rejects Mexico's claim of a violation of Article 12.1 regarding the timing of the notification and public notice of the initiation of an investigation.

8.89 The Panel now turns to Mexico's claim that Guatemala did not satisfy itself as to the sufficiency of the evidence before giving notice of the initiation. Given the function and context of Article 12.1 in the AD Agreement, we interpret this provision as imposing a procedural obligation on the investigating agency to publish a notice and notify interested parties after it has taken a decision that there is sufficient evidence to proceed with an initiation. The Panel is of the view that Article 12.1 is not concerned with the substance of the decision to initiate an investigation, which is dealt with in Article 5.3. By issuing a public notice of initiation in the case before us, the Guatemalan authorities complied with their procedural obligation under Article 12.1 to notify known interested parties and publish a public notice after they had decided to initiate an investigation. Whether or not Guatemala was justified in initiating an investigation on the basis of the evidence before it is an issue governed by Article 5.3. Therefore the Panel rejects Mexico's claim that Guatemala violated Article 12.1 in failing to satisfy itself as to the sufficiency of the evidence before it.

---

[813] Guatemala specifically asserts in its first submission that "the "authorities" in charge of the investigation were the Ministry, not the Directorate of Economic Integration ... [t]his is a subordinate directorate and therefore the Ministry could have rejected its report of 15 December".

(b) Claim under Article 12.1.1

8.90 Mexico claims that Guatemala's notice of initiation did not meet the standard of "adequate information" because it did not contain adequate information on the basis on which dumping was alleged in the application nor adequate information summarizing the factors on which the allegation of injury, in this case threat of material injury, was based, as required by Article 12.1.1

8.91 Guatemala responds that the public notice as supplemented by the report of the Directorate of Economic Integration of 17 November 1995 is adequate to fulfill the requirements of Article 12.1.1. Since the file was open to the public Guatemala considered that the report from the Economic Integration Directorate was available to Mexico and contained the relevant information to comply with Article 12.1.1.[814]

8.92 Article 12.1.1 provides:

> 12.1.1 A public notice of the initiation of an investigation shall contain, or otherwise make available through a separate report, adequate information on the following:
>
> (i) the name of the exporting country or countries and the product involved;
>
> (ii) the date of initiation of the investigation;
>
> (iii) the basis on which dumping is alleged in the application;
>
> (iv) a summary of the factors on which the allegation of injury is based;
>
> (v) the address to which representations by interested parties should be directed;
>
> (vi) the time-limits allowed to interested parties for making their views known."

8.93 As a threshold matter, we must first consider whether the public notice in and of itself complies with the requirements in 12.1.1. In order to do this it is necessary for the Panel to verify whether all the elements listed in Article 12.1.1 have been included in the public notice. On the first of the factors listed in Article 12.1.1, the notice contains information on the country and the product involved. On the second factor, arguably it could be considered that the date of initiation is the date of the public notice,[815] thus also providing the date for the initiation. Moving on to the third factor, regarding whether the public notice contains the basis on which dumping is alleged in the application, the Panel observes that in section 3 of the initiation notice Guatemala refers to the legal basis for the investigation. However, there is nothing on the factual basis of dumping alleged in the application. The Panel thus finds that the information provided in the public notice is not adequate to fulfill the requirement contained in Article 12.1.1(iii).

---

814 Moreover, Guatemala also asserted that any alleged deficiency in the public notice was a harmless error, was acquiesced to by Mexico and therefore it is estopped to bring this claim, and did not cause Mexico any nullification or impairment of its rights under the AD Agreement.

815 The Panel recalls its findings on the claim brought by Mexico under Article 5.5, para. 8.82.

8.94 Guatemala argues that whatever the insufficiencies of the public notice itself a separate report was provided which satisfies the requirements of Article 12.1.1. Guatemala asserts that the 17 November 1995 technical report of the Directorate recommending the initiation of the investigation constitutes the "separate report" which makes available the information required by Article 12.1.1.

8.95 The issue before us then is whether the public notice of initiation by Guatemala "makes available" through a separate report the information required in Article 12.1.1. There is no reference to a separate report in the public notice of initiation. Under Article 12.1.1, it is the "public notice", and not the Member, that must "make available through a separate report", certain information. We take this to mean that the public notice must at a minimum refer to a separate report. This conclusion is logical in that the separate report is a substitute for certain elements of the public notice and thus should perform a notice function comparable to that of the public notice itself. If there were no reference to a separate report in the public notice, how would the public and the interested parties concerned become aware of its existence? If the public and interested parties do not know of the existence of the report, how can it be considered that the required information was properly made available to them?

8.96 Our view on this issue is confirmed by Footnote 23 of the AD Agreement, which provides:

> "[23] Where authorities provide information and explanations under the provisions of this Article in a separate report, they shall ensure that such report is readily available to the public."

It cannot be said that the separate report was "readily available" to the public, if the public is not informed about where, when and how to have access to this report, leave alone if they were not even publicly informed of its existence. In conclusion, the Panel is of the view that Guatemala's public notice of initiation fails to meet the requirements under Article 12.1.1 by not providing adequate information on the basis on which dumping is alleged in the application, or otherwise making this information available in a separate report.[816]

6. *Failure to Provide the Full Text of the Application in a Timely Manner*

8.97 Mexico claims that Guatemala failed to provide the full text of the application to either the Mexican producer, or the Government of Mexico "in good time, i.e. as soon as the investigation had been initiated" in violation of Article 6.1.3 of the Agreement. Mexico does not state precisely when, if ever, the full text of the application was provided to the Mexican producer, Cruz Azul, and the Government of Mexico.

8.98 Guatemala asserts that Mexico is mistaken as to the facts. It contends that the Ministry sent the full text of the application, together with the notice of initiation of the investigation, to the Government of Mexico on 22 January 1996. Guatemala fur-

[816] As for Guatemala's defences claiming acquiescence and estoppel, harmless error or lack of nullification or impairment of a benefit, these issues are addressed in sections VIII.B.5 and VIII.C.7.

ther asserts that the full text of the application and the notice of initiation of the investigation were sent to Cruz Azul together with the questionnaires, which Guatemala asserts were received on 29 January. Guatemala provides a copy of the courier invoice dated 4 February 1996 for the posting of the documents to Cruz Azul in support of its assertion.[817] In any event, Guatemala argues that it is clear that Cruz Azul received the application and had sufficient opportunity to defend its interests during the course of the investigation, as evidenced by the arguments it submitted to the Guatemalan authorities.[818]

8.99 Mexico responds that, even if Guatemala's assertion that it provided the full text of the application to Cruz Azul on 29 January 1996 was correct, this would still be 18 days after the initiation of the investigation. Moreover, as the courier invoice indicates Guatemala did not send the documents until 4 February 1996, that is 24 days after initiation. Concerning the provision of the application to the Government, Mexico argues that the letter which Guatemala submits as evidence that Mexico received the application on 22 January 1996, does not state that the application was annexed to the letter. In any case, Mexico argues, provision of the application would still have been done 11 days after the initiation.

8.100 Article 6.1.3 provides:

> "6.1.3 As soon as an investigation has been initiated, the authorities shall provide the full text of the written application received under paragraph 1 of Article 5 to the known exporters and to the authorities of the exporting Member and shall make it available, upon request, to other interested parties involved. Due regard shall be paid to the requirement for the protection of confidential information, as provided for in paragraph 5."

8.101 We note that Article 6.1.3 does not specify the number of days within which the text of the application shall be provided. What it does specify is that the text of the application be provided "as soon as" the investigation has been initiated. In this regard, the term "as soon as" conveys a sense of substantial urgency. In fact, the terms "immediately" and "as soon as" are considered to be interchangeable.[819] We do not consider that providing the text of the application 24 or even 18 days after the date of initiation fulfils the requirement of Article 6.1.3 that the text be provided "as soon as an investigation has been initiated."

8.102 We further consider that the timeliness of the provision of the text of the application should be evaluated in the context of its purpose and function. Timely access to the application is important for the exporters to enable preparation of the arguments in defence of their interests before the investigating authorities. Moreover, once the investigation has been initiated the timetable of the investigation commences and the timing for many events in the proceeding are counted from initiation including the 12 or 18 months total for completion of the investigation provide for in

---

[817] Annex Guatemala-20.

[818] Moreover, Guatemala also asserted that any alleged deficiency in the public notice was a harmless error, was acquiesced to by Mexico and therefore it is estopped to bring this claim, and did not cause Mexico any nullification or impairment of its rights under the AD Agreement.

[819] "**Immediately**: Without delay, at once, instantly. B *conj.* at the moment that, as soon as. *The New Shorter Oxford English Dictionary*, Oxford University Press, 1993.

Article 5.10. Since deadlines in the timetable of the investigation are counted from the date of initiation it is critical that the investigating authority provide the text of the application "as soon as an investigation has been initiated", for the exporter to be able to devise a strategy to defend the allegations it is being confronted with. Also, Article 7.3 of the AD Agreement allows a Member to impose provisional measures as early as sixty days after the date of initiation of an investigation. Access to the text of the application is crucial for the exporter to prepare its defence, and even more so if the authorities are likely to consider applying a provisional measure which may come as early as 60 days after initiation.[820]

8.103 With respect to the provision of the application to the Government of Mexico, Guatemala asserts that it provided the application as an annex to a letter addressed to the Mexican Embassy in Guatemala dated 19 January 1996[821] and received 22 January 1996. Mexico in turn asserts that the letter does not prove that the full text of the application was delivered on that date. The text of the letter refers to the fact that an application for an anti-dumping action against cement from Mexico's Cruz Azul has been received by the Ministry of Economy and mentions that the "copy of the pertinent documentation has been annexed". In our view, this reference to the "pertinent documentation" most likely means the application by Cementos Progreso. Mexico has not offered any evidence that would lead us to conclude otherwise. We shall therefore conclude that Guatemala sent the full text of the application on 19 January 1996 and that Mexico received it on 22 January 1996. That is 8 and 11 days respectively after initiation of the investigation.

8.104 Having determined that Guatemala sent the full text of the application at the earliest 8 days after initiation of the investigation. We are of the view that given the nature of the obligation in Article 6.1.3 sending the of the application even 8 days after the initiation of investigation is not adequate to fulfill the requirement that it be done "as soon as an investigation has been initiated". Thus, we find that Guatemala acted inconsistently with its obligation under Article 6.1.3, to provide the full text of the application to Mexico as soon as an investigation was initiated.[822]

7. *Lack of Nullification or Impairment*

8.105 Guatemala maintains that even if the Panel finds violations in the notification under Article 5.5, the insufficient public notice of initiation and the delay in providing the full text of the application, any such violations did not nullify or impair benefits accruing to Mexico under the AD Agreement.

8.106 Mexico responds that if a violation of an obligation has been found there is a presumption of nullification or impairment and Guatemala has simply not provided

[820] On a similar issue the *Korea-Dairy Safeguards* panel found that a 14 day delay on notification to the WTO Safeguards Committee as required by Article 12.1 of the Safeguards Agreement did not satisfy the requirement that the notification be provided "immediately" after initiation. See, *Korea-Dairy safeguards, supra*, footnote 531, para. 7.134.

[821] This letter was provided by Mexico as Annex Mexico-12.

[822] As for Guatemala's defences claiming acquiescence and estoppel, harmless error or lack of nullification or impairment of a benefit, these issues are addressed in sections VIII.B.5 and VIII.C.7.

evidence to rebut the presumption that there was nullification or impairment of Mexico's rights under the WTO Agreements.

8.107 On the Article 5.5 notification, Guatemala argues that it did not take any steps to begin the investigation until Mexico had been notified, and that it granted Cruz Azul a two-month extension to reply to the questionnaire. Thus, a delay in notification under Article 5.5 did not prejudice Mexico's ability to defend its interests nor affect in any other way Mexico's benefits under the Agreement.

8.108 Article 3.8 of the DSU provides guidance with respect to the issue of nullification or impairment. It provides that:

> "In cases where there is an infringement of the obligations assumed under a covered agreement, the action is considered prima facie to constitute a case of nullification or impairment. This means that there is normally a presumption that a breach of the rules has an adverse impact on other Member parties to that covered agreement, and in such cases, it shall be up to the Member against whom the complaint has been brought to rebut the charge".

Thus, there is a presumption that a violation nullified or impaired a benefit accruing to the complaining Member. Article 17 of the AD Agreement entitles a Member to relief when benefits accruing to that Member under the AD Agreement are nullified or impaired." Article 3.8 of the DSU also provides for the possibility that the Member found to have violated a provision may rebut the presumption.

8.109 This is what Guatemala argues that it has rebutted this presumption. Specifically, Guatemala argues that in the case of the Article 5.5 notification it did not initiate the investigation until after Mexico had been notified and that it granted Cruz Azul an extension to respond to the questionnaire and thus Mexico was not impaired in the defence of its interests. We have already found that the initiation date was 11 January 1996 and thus notification under Article 5.5 was not provided until after initiation.[823] There is no way to ascertain what Mexico might have done if it had received a timely notification. The extension of time for response to the questionnaire granted to Cruz Azul has no bearing on the fact that Mexico was not informed in time. Thus, we do not consider that Guatemala has rebutted the presumption of nullification or impairment with respect to violations of Article 5.5.

8.110 Regarding the violations we have found of Article 6.1.3 and 12.1 we have found that there is no specific argumentation from Guatemala as to how it rebutted the presumption of nullification or impairment. Therefore, we conclude that Guatemala has not rebutted the presumption of nullification or impairment in this case.

8.111 Guatemala argues that the Panel should examine Guatemala's acts and decide whether the non-fulfilment of a procedural obligation should be overlooked on the grounds that the omission did not prejudice the rights of Mexico or Cruz Azul. We could find no basis for such a distinction in the DSU, as suggested by Guatemala between substantive and "mere" procedural violations. There is no reason to regard violations of procedural obligations differently than obligation of a substantial nature. Compliance with the complete set of procedural rules relating to anti-dumping investigations, including those concerning notification and enhanced transparency, is

[823] See, para. 8.82.

required. This obligation to comply with all provisions, both procedural and substantive should not be taken lightly if one is not to devoid of all meaning the AD Agreement itself. As detailed in sections 4, 5(b) and 6 above we have found that Guatemala violated Articles 5.5, 6.1.3 and 12.1.1 of the AD Agreement by failing to timely notify Mexico of the decision to initiate an investigation, to timely provide Mexico and Cruz Azul a copy of the application, and to publish an adequate notice of initiation. We consider that a key function of the transparency requirements of the AD Agreement is to ensure that interested parties, including Members, are able to take whatever steps they deem appropriate to defend their interests. Where a required notification is not made in a timely fashion, or the application is not provided in time, or the public notice is inadequate the ability of the interested party to take such steps is vitiated. It is not for us to now speculate on what steps Mexico might have taken had it been timely notified or provided with the application, or had the public notice been adequate, and how Guatemala might have responded to those steps. Thus, while there is a possibility that the investigation would have proceeded in the same manner had Guatemala complied with its transparency obligations, we cannot state with certainty that the course of the investigation would not have been different.[824]

8.112 Thus, the Panel rejects Guatemala's defence that, concerning the violations of Articles 5.5, 6.1.3 and 12.1.1 of the AD Agreement, it has rebutted the presumption of nullification or impairment established in Article 3.8 of the DSU.

D. Alleged Procedural Violations During the Course of the Investigation

8.113 Mexico has raised a number of claims concerning alleged procedural violations committed by the Ministry during the course of its investigation. We shall address each of these claims in turn.

1. The Submission of Evidence

8.114 Mexico has raised claims concerning (a) the alleged failure by the Ministry to set time-limits for the submission of evidence, and (b) the Ministry's treatment of technical accounting evidence submitted by Cruz Azul.

(a) Time-limits for the submission of arguments and evidence

8.115 Mexico claims that the Ministry violated Article 6.1 by failing to set a time-limit for the presentation of arguments and evidence during the final stage of the investigation. Mexico asserts that the Ministry fixed a time-limit for the submission of arguments and evidence for the early part of the investigation (in the public notice of initiation), but failed to do so for the latter stage of the investigation (in the public notice of its preliminary determination).

[824] Our finding on this issue is consistent with the view expressed by the panel in *Guatemala - Cement I*, *supra*, footnote 25, para. 7.42.

8.116 Guatemala asserts that the Ministry did fix specific periods for the presentation of information. For example, Guatemala claims that the Ministry fixed 17 May 1996 as the last date for replying to the original questionnaire, 30 October 1996 for responding to the supplementary questionnaire, and 19 December 1996 for the final arguments.

8.117 We shall begin by examining Mexico's claim under Article 6.1 of the AD Agreement. Article 6.1 provides:

> "All interested parties in an anti-dumping investigation shall be given notice of the information which the authorities require and ample opportunity to present in writing all evidence which they consider relevant in respect of the investigation in question."

8.118 We do not consider it necessary to determine whether, in fact, the Ministry did set periods for the presentation of arguments and evidence during the final stage of the investigation. This is because we find Mexico's claim to be without merit as a matter of law. In our view, Article 6.1 of the AD Agreement does not require investigating authorities to set time-limits for the presentation of arguments and evidence during the final stage of the investigation. The only time-limit provided for in Article 6.1 is that contained in Article 6.1.1, whereby exporters shall be given at least 30 days for replying to questionnaires. Mexico does not allege that Cruz Azul was not provided the 30 days provided for in Article 6.1.1.

8.119 Article 6.1 requires investigating authorities to provide interested parties "ample opportunity" to present in writing certain evidence. Article 6.1 does not explicitly require an investigating authority to set time limits for the submission of arguments and evidence during the final stage of an investigation.[825] Article 6.1 simply requires that interested parties shall have "ample" opportunity to present evidence and "full" opportunity to defend their interests. Interested parties may have such opportunity without the investigating authority setting time limits for the submission of evidence. In other words, these provisions impose substantive obligations, without requiring those obligations to be met through any particular form (except as provided for in sub-paragraphs 1 through 3 of Article 6.1). What counts is whether, in practice, sufficient opportunity was provided, not whether time limits for the submission of evidence were set. Thus, even if the Ministry had failed to set time-limits for the submission of arguments and evidence during the final stage of the investigation, this would not *ipso facto* constitute a violation of Article 6.1 of the AD Agreement.

8.120 Mexico has argued that the Ministry's public notice of initiation granted interested parties 30 days in which to defend their interests, whereas no such time-limit was included in the public notice concerning the imposition of a provisional measure. We would note that Article 12.1.1(vi) explicitly provides that a public notice of the initiation of an investigation shall include adequate information on the "time-limits allowed to interested parties for making their views known". No such obligation is included in Article 12.2.1, concerning the contents of public notices on the imposition of provisional measures. We consider that Article 12.2.1 constitutes use-

[825] This does not, of course, preclude an authority from establishing such limits, so long as the basic requirements (such as "ample opportunity", or 30 days in respect of questionnaire replies) are respected.

ful context when examining Mexico's claim under Article 6.1. In particular, the fact that there is no requirement for investigating authorities to include time-limits for the submission of evidence in the public notice of their preliminary determinations confirms the conclusion set forth in the preceding paragraph.

8.121 Mexico has also raised a claim (ostensibly in respect of the Ministry's failure to establish time-limits) based on the first sentence of Article 6.2 of the AD Agreement, which provides that "[t]hroughout the anti-dumping investigation all interested parties shall have a full opportunity for the defence of their interests...". Upon closer examination of Mexico's Article 6.2 claim, we note that it relates more to the Ministry's rejection of Cruz Azul's technical accounting evidence, than to the Ministry's failure to set time-limits for the submission of evidence and arguments in the latter stages of its investigation. In this regard, we note that Mexico's Article 6.2 claim is summarised in para. 325 of its first written submission to the Panel:

> "The denial of Cruz Azul's right of defence can be seen in the Ministry's rejection of the technical accounting evidence submitted by Cruz Azul on 18 December 1996 and the acceptance of new evidence from Cementos Progreso during the public hearing between the Ministry and the parties. ..."

(b) Refusal of "technical accounting evidence"

8.122 Mexico claims that the Ministry violated Articles 6.1, 6.2, 6.8, and Annex II (5) and (6) of the AD Agreement by rejecting certain technical accounting evidence submitted by Cruz Azul on 18 December 1996, one day before the 19 December 1996 public hearing scheduled by the Ministry. Mexico submits that the technical accounting evidence was prepared by an external accounting firm, to confirm that the information submitted by Cruz Azul during the course of the investigation was complete and taken from Cruz Azul's accounting records.

8.123 Guatemala asserts that the technical accounting evidence was rejected because it was not "verifiable", or "appropriately submitted", within the meaning of Annex II(3). According to Guatemala, the technical accounting evidence was not verifiable because the Ministry was required to cancel the verification visit to Cruz Azul, and it was not appropriately submitted because it was neither requested by the Ministry, nor supplied in a timely fashion. Guatemala asserts that the deadline for the submission of new evidence was 6 December 1996, and that this deadline had therefore expired when the technical accounting evidence was submitted on 18 December 1996. Guatemala argues that the appropriate and timely juncture for submission of the technical accounting evidence would have been the verification visit at Cruz Azul. According to Guatemala, therefore, the Ministry's decision not to accept Cruz Azul's technical accounting evidence was consistent with Article 6.8 and Annex II(3) of the AD Agreement.

8.124 The Ministry's failure to take into account Cruz Azul's technical accounting evidence was clearly linked to the Ministry's cancellation of its verification visit to Cruz Azul. The Ministry stated in its final determination that the technical accounting evidence "could not replace verification".[826] Furthermore, the technical account-

[826] Section B.6, page 14, Annex Mexico-41.

ing evidence was submitted by Cruz Azul in lieu of verification, and would not have been submitted if the Ministry had not cancelled the verification. In our view, we need only address Mexico's claim concerning the Ministry's failure to take into account Cruz Azul's technical accounting evidence, if we find that the Ministry was entitled to cancel its verification visit to Cruz Azul.

8.125 At para. 8.251 below, we state that we do not consider that an objective and impartial investigating authority could properly have found that Cruz Azul significantly impeded its investigation by objecting to the inclusion of conflicted non-governmental experts in its verification team. Accordingly, the Ministry did not act in a reasonable, objective and impartial manner by cancelling its verification visit to Cruz Azul. This is an important consideration for our conclusion that the Ministry violated Article 6.8, read in light of Annex II(3), by having recourse to "best information available" for the purpose of determining normal value. Inherent in this finding is the fact that the Ministry reacted unreasonably to reasonable objections raised by Cruz Azul, in that such reasonable objections did not entitle the Ministry to cancel its verification visit to Cruz Azul. In light of these considerations, we do not consider it necessary to address Mexico's claims regarding the Ministry's treatment of technical accounting evidence submitted by Cruz Azul as a result of the cancellation of the verification visit.

2. *Cruz Azul's Access to Evidence*

8.126 Mexico claims that the Ministry violated Articles 6.1.2, 6.2 and 6.4 of the AD Agreement by (a) refusing Cruz Azul access to the file in November 1996, and (b) failing to promptly provide Cruz Azul with a copy of a submission made by Cementos Progreso on 19 December 1996. Mexico also claims that the Ministry violated Article 6.4 by (c) failing to provide Cruz Azul with copies of the file, and (d) failing to provide Cruz Azul with a full record of the 19 December 1996 public hearing. We shall now examine each of these claims.

(a) Alleged denial of access to the file

8.127 Mexico claims that the Ministry refused Cruz Azul access to the file on 4 November 1996. Mexico has submitted a notarial deed to that effect, in support of its claim.

8.128 Guatemala argues that Cruz Azul was provided access to the file on 4 November 1996. In this regard, Guatemala asserts that interested parties have a constitutional right (under Guatemalan law) to access to the file in question. However, Guatemala could not prove that access to the file was granted, because the Ministry did not keep a record of interested parties' access to the file. Guatemala argues that the fact that Cruz Azul had timely access to the file is demonstrated by its numerous submissions in which it alludes to evidence in the file. Guatemala also argues that the Ministry was never shown a copy of the 4 November 1996 notarial deed.

8.129 Article 6.1.2 of the AD Agreement provides:

> "Subject to the requirement to protect confidential information, evidence presented in writing by one interested party shall be made available promptly to other interested parties participating in the investigation."

8.130 Article 6.4 of the AD Agreement provides:

> "The authorities shall whenever practicable provide timely opportunities for all interested parties to see all information that is relevant to the presentation of their cases, that is not confidential as defined in paragraph 5, and that is used by the authorities in an anti-dumping investigation, and to prepare presentations on the basis of this information."

8.131 Mexico has provided the Panel with a copy of a notarial deed dated 4 November 1996, according to which Cruz Azul was denied access to the file on 4 November 1996. The circumstances of the alleged denial of access to the file are set forth in that notarial deed:

> "*FIRST*: [Cruz Azul's notary] went to the Department of Economic Integration of the Ministry of the Economy, on the third floor of the Ministry building, and requested to see file number one thousand two hundred and eighty one-ninety five (1281-95), and was told by an official from that Department that the file was under the responsibility of Ms. Edith de Molina, an advisor in that Ministry, on the sixth floor. [Cruz Azul's notary] therefore went to the sixth floor and enquired after Ms. Edith de Molina. [Cruz Azul's notary] was received by Ms. Gabriela Montenegro, also an advisor in the Ministry, who confirmed to [him] that the file was indeed under the responsibility of Ms. Edith de Molina, but that she was not currently in Guatemala, having left the country for Mexico. *SECOND*: [Cruz Azul's notary] therefore asked Ms. Gabriela Montenegro to allow [him] to see file one thousand two hundred and eighty one-ninety five (1281-95). [Cruz Azul's notary] was told categorically that that would not be possible, as the only person in the entire Ministry who could permit that was Ms. Edith de Molina, and who was expected back in Guatemala on Thursday the seventh of November of nineteen hundred and ninety six, and that [Cruz Azul's notary] had to make a written request for any information whatsoever concerning the file in question. [Cruz Azul's notary] therefore asked Ms. Montenegro whether, in view of the fact that nobody could show [him] the file on that particular day, [he] could see it on Thursday the seventh of November, when Ms. Edith de Molina was expected to be back in Guatemala. She replied that even then it would not be possible to see the file, as the Ministry first had to evaluate and review the documents in it."

8.132 Thus, it is alleged that the Ministry refused Cruz Azul access to the administrative file because the person responsible for that file was out of the country. It is further alleged that Cruz Azul was told that it could not have access to the file when the responsible person returned to the Ministry, because the Ministry would first have to evaluate and review the documents contained therein.

8.133 Article 6.1.2 of the AD Agreement provides that evidence presented by one interested party shall be "made available promptly" to other interested parties. Article 6.4 provides that an interested party shall have "timely opportunities" to see all information that is relevant to the presentation of its case. On their face, neither Article 6.1.2 nor Article 6.4 necessarily require access to the file. For example, if an investigating authority required each interested party to serve its submissions on all other interested parties, or if the investigating authority itself undertook to provide copies of each interested party's submission to other interested parties, there may be no need for interested parties to have access to the file. If, however, there is no service of evidence by interested parties, or no provision of copies by the investigating authority, access to the file may be the only practical means by which evidence presented by one interested party could be "made available promptly" to other interested parties (consistent with Article 6.1.2), or by which interested parties could have "timely opportunities" to see information relevant to the presentation of their cases (consistent with Article 6.4). Assuming access to the file is the only practical means of complying with Articles 6.1.2 and 6.4, access to the file need not necessarily be unlimited. Nor need the file be made available on demand. Provided access to the file is regular and routine, we consider that the requirements of Articles 6.1.2 and 6.4 would be satisfied.

8.134 There is no evidence to suggest that submissions made to the Ministry by one interested party were "made available promptly" to other interested parties by virtue of intra-party service or the provision of copies by the Ministry.[827] Nor has Guatemala argued that this was the case. Accordingly, if Cruz Azul wanted to review evidence submitted by Cementos Progreso, it would have to have access to the file to do so. In these circumstances, regular and routine access to the file is required by Articles 6.1.2 and 6.4.

8.135 In the factual circumstances set forth in the notarial deed of 4 November 1996, a denial of access on 4 November 1996 because the relevant official is overseas, followed by a denial of access during the following week because the investigating authority is working on the file, and in the absence of any indication as to when access to the file would be granted, would not be consistent with the need to ensure routine and regular access to the file. We are of the view that these circumstances are indicative of a pattern of behaviour which would prevent regular and routine access to the file, and which would fail to ensure that evidence presented by one interested party would be "made available promptly" to other interested parties (consistent with Article 6.1.2), and which would fail to ensure that interested parties have "timely opportunities" to see information relevant to the presentation of their cases (consistent with Article 6.4).

8.136 For all the above reasons, we find that the pattern of behaviour described in the 4 November 1996 notarial deed establishes a *prima facie* case that the Ministry violated Articles 6.1.2 and 6.4 of the AD Agreement by refusing Cruz Azul access to the file on 4 November 1996. In a bid to rebut that *prima facie* case, Guatemala has asserted that access to the file was not refused on that date. However, Guatemala has not been able to adduce any evidence to that effect. Guatemala has not adduced an

[827] At para. 297, Guatemala asserts that "[d]uring the investigation the Ministry provided the interested parties with a copy of the documents in the file". These "documents in the file" would presumably include [non-confidential versions of) submissions made by interested parties. However, Guatemala has adduced no evidence to that effect. Accordingly, we are not persuaded that Guatemala has demonstrated that copies of interested parties' submissions were provided by the Ministry to Cruz Azul. Indeed, had that been the case, we wonder why the Ministry offered copies of the file to interested parties (at their expense) in a communication dated 6 December 1996 (Annex Mexico-36).

affidavit from any Ministry official to the effect that access was granted on 4 November 1996. Similarly, Guatemala has failed to establish that a Cruz Azul representative was granted access to the Ministry building on that date. Guatemala claims that it cannot demonstrate when access to the file was granted, because the Ministry does not keep the appropriate records. In our view, a Member's failure to keep records of who was granted access to the file, and when, provides no basis on which to rebut a *prima facie* case that access was denied on a particular date. Guatemala also seeks to rebut the *prima facie* case by arguing that the fact that Cruz Azul had sufficient access to the file is demonstrated by numerous submissions which refer to evidence in the file. However, the fact that Cruz Azul may have had access to the file on certain occasions does not demonstrate that Cruz Azul had regular and routine access to the file. We do not consider that we are compelled to adopt a different approach simply because Cruz Azul may not have shown the Ministry a copy of the 4 November 1996 notarial deed. The notarial deed is simply a record of fact. Guatemala has adduced no argument why Cruz Azul's record of fact should have been shown to the Ministry.

8.137 At the second substantive meeting with the parties, Guatemala asserted:

> "[i]n order to meet its burden, Mexico must establish a *prima facie* case of inconsistency with a provision of the AD Agreement or GATT 1994 that is within the Panel's terms of reference. In case all the evidence and arguments remain equal, the Panel must give the benefit of the doubt to Guatemala, as the defending party."[828]

This assertion appears to be based on the following statement by the panel in *United States - Sections 301 - 310 of the Trade Act of 1974*:

> "Since, in this case, both parties have submitted extensive facts and arguments in respect of the EC claims, our task will essentially be to balance all evidence on record and decide whether the EC, as party bearing the original burden of proof, has convinced us of the validity of its claims. In case of uncertainty, i.e. in case all the evidence and arguments remain in equipoise, we have to give the benefit of the doubt to the US as defending party."

8.138 We make no finding as to whether or not there may be circumstances in which the benefit of any doubt should go to the defending party if all the evidence and arguments "remain in equipoise", or equal. This is because we do not consider that the evidence and arguments adduced by the parties in the present case are equal. Guatemala has failed to adduce any evidence to the effect that Cruz Azul was granted access to the file on 4 November 1996, or to dispute the other facts described in the notarial deed of that date. Accordingly, there is no "benefit of the doubt" for us to give to Guatemala.

8.139 For these reasons, we find that the pattern of behaviour described in the notarial deed of 4 November 1996 constitutes a violation of Articles 6.1.2 and 6.4 of the AD Agreement.

---

[828] Guatemala's second oral statement, para. 27.

(b) Alleged failure to provide Cruz Azul with a copy of Cementos Progreso's submission of 19 December 1996

8.140 Mexico claims that the Ministry violated Articles 6.1.2 and 6.4 by failing to provide Cruz Azul promptly with a copy of the submission made by Cementos Progreso at the 19 December 1996 public hearing as it was done only on 8 January 1997.

8.141 Guatemala asserts that the Ministry was justified in delaying Cruz Azul's access to Cementos Progreso's submission at the December 1996 public hearing because of the possibility that the submission contained confidential information. Furthermore, Guatemala asserts *inter alia* that any submission prepared by Cruz Azul in response to Cementos Progreso's submission of 19 December 1996 would not have been "practicable", since it would have been submitted too late to be taken into account by the investigating authority (because of the alleged closure of the Ministry's record prior to that date).

(i) Article 6.1.2

8.142 Guatemala does not deny that Cementos Progreso's 19 December 1996 submission was not made available to Cruz Azul until 8 January 1997. Thus, there is no dispute between the parties that the Cementos Progreso submission was not made available to Cruz Azul until 20 days after its submission to the Ministry. In principle, we consider that a 20-day delay is inconsistent with the Ministry's Article 6.1.2 obligation to make this submission available to Cruz Azul "promptly".

8.143 Guatemala asserts that "the Ministry had a valid reason for not giving Cruz Azul immediate access to this document".[829] In particular, Guatemala argues that "it was reasonable for the Ministry to conclude that the lengthy written submission of 19 December prepared by Cementos Progreso would contain confidential information that "ought not to be revealed to Cruz Azul".[830] In this regard, we note that the obligation in Article 6.1.2 is qualified by the words "[s]ubject to the requirement to protect confidential information". In principle, therefore, evidence presented by one interested party need not be made available "promptly" to other interested parties if it is "confidential". However, insofar as confidentiality is concerned, Article 6.1.2 must be read in the context of Article 6.5, which governs the treatment of confidential information. We examine Article 6.5 in detail at paras 8.207 - 8.223 below. We have noted that Article 6.5 reserves special treatment for "confidential" information only "upon good cause shown", and we have determined that the requisite "good cause" must be shown by the interested party which submitted the information at issue. Guatemala has not demonstrated, or even argued, that Cementos Progreso requested confidential treatment for its 19 December 1996 submission, or that "good cause" for confidential treatment was otherwise shown.[831] The Article 6.1.2 proviso regarding

---

829 Guatemala's first written submission, para. 295.

830 Guatemala's first written submission, para. 296.

831 Even if Cementos Progreso had requested confidential treatment, the Ministry should (consistent with 6.5.1) have required it to furnish a non-confidential version thereof which could have been made available to Cruz Azul "promptly", or to provide "a statement of the reasons why [non-confidential] summarization is not possible".

the "requirement to protect confidential information", when read in the context of Article 6.5, cannot be interpreted to allow an investigating authority to delay making available evidence submitted by one interested party to another interested party for 20 days simply because of the possibility - which is unsubstantiated[832] by any request for confidential treatment from the party submitting the evidence - that the evidence contains confidential information. We do not believe that the specific requirement of Article 6.1.2 may be circumvented simply by an investigating authority determining that there is a possibility that the evidence at issue contains confidential information. Such an interpretation could undermine the purpose of Article 6.1.2, since in principle there is a possibility that any evidence could contain confidential information (and therefore not be "made available promptly" to interested parties). Accordingly, we find that the Ministry violated Article 6.1.2 of the AD Agreement by failing to make Cementos Progreso's 19 December 1996 submission available to Cruz Azul until 8 January 1997.

(ii) Article 6.4

8.144 Mexico claims that the Ministry violated Article 6.4 by failing to provide Cruz Azul with the submission presented by Cementos Progreso at the 19 December 1996 public hearing until 8 January 1997, only two weeks before the Ministry's final determination. Guatemala claims that the Ministry was not required to provide Cruz Azul with a copy of Cementos Progreso's submission before 8 January 1997, since - because of the closure of the record before that date - it would not have been "practicable" for Cruz Azul to respond to Cementos Progreso's submission. Guatemala also relies on Article 6.14 of the AD Agreement to argue that the Ministry was not required to delay the conclusion of the investigation in order to allow either party to prepare a rejoinder to the 19 December 1996 final submissions of the other party.

8.145 Since we have already found that the facts giving rise to Mexico's Article 6.4 claim constitute a violation of Article 6.1.2, we do not consider it necessary to consider whether those facts also constitute a violation of Article 6.4.

---

[832] The Cementos Progreso submission at issue was made at a public hearing on 19 December 1996. Guatemala argues that, although the Ministry authorized parties to make submissions in writing, the Ministry had not specified whether such written submissions could contain confidential information or not. According to Guatemala, this justified the Ministry in assuming that the Cementos Progreso submission may contain confidential information. We are not at all convinced by this argument. The instructions issued by the Ministry concerning the public hearing state that "[t]he hearing is being organized for the purpose of receiving the final arguments of the parties, which may submit **a written version thereof**" (emphasis supplied). Thus, any written submission was simply to be a written version of arguments presented orally. Arguments made by a party at a public hearing will presumably not contain confidential information. Similarly, therefore , written versions of arguments presented orally will also not contain information. Thus, to the extent that Cementos Progreso would not have included confidential information in its oral presentation, similarly its written version of that oral presentation also would not have included confidential information. In these circumstances, we fail to see how Cementos Progreso's written submission - which, consistent with the Ministry's instructions, was to be a written version of its oral presentation - could have contained confidential information.

(c) Alleged failure to provide copies of the file

8.146 Mexico claims that the Ministry violated Article 6.4 of the AD Agreement by failing to provide Cruz Azul with two copies of the file.

8.147 In response to a question from the Panel, Guatemala asserts that the relevant copies were not provided because Cruz Azul did not pay the required fee, even though the Ministry's 6 December 1996 communication indicated that copies would be at the expense of the party requesting the copy. In its first written submission, however, Guatemala asserts that "Cruz Azul did not request that a copy of any document be supplied at its expense".[833]

8.148 We note that the Ministry's 6 December 1996 communication stated, *inter alia,* that:

> "2. The technical study issued by this Directorate will record the facts investigated and the evidence available as well as the results of verifications conducted. These documents form part of the file, and **the parties are free to obtain copies at their own expense**." (emphasis supplied)

8.149 On 17 January 1997, Cruz Azul requested that:

> "in keeping with the appropriate legal procedures and **at the expense of my principal**, the latter be issued with two attestations in regard to or certified copies of all the records contained in the above-mentioned file. This request is based on the articles cited and Articles 28 and 29 of the Political Constitution of the Republic of Guatemala. Five copies of the present submission are included." (emphasis supplied)

8.150 Therefore, as a factual matter, we are in no doubt that Cruz Azul requested two copies of the file. Despite Guatemala' assertion to the contrary (see para. 8.147 above), we are also in no doubt that Cruz Azul offered to pay for those copies.

8.151 There are various ways in which an investigating authority could satisfy the Article 6.4 obligation to provide "whenever practicable ... timely opportunities for all interested parties to see all information that is relevant to the presentation of their cases ...". In the present case, the Ministry chose to offer interested parties copies of the file, against payment of a fee. Mexico does not challenge the Ministry's decision to comply with its obligations under the AD Agreement by offering copies of the file against payment of a fee. Rather, Mexico challenges the Ministry's failure to provide the relevant copies, despite Cruz Azul's offer to pay the relevant fee.

8.152 In our view, the Ministry's reaction to Cruz Azul's request of 17 January 1997 did not "provide timely opportunities for all interested parties to see all information that is relevant to the presentation of their cases". The Ministry could have reacted to Cruz Azul's request in a number of ways.[834]

8.153 However, there is nothing before the Panel to suggest that the Ministry responded in any way to Cruz Azul's letter of 17 January 1997. There is no evidence to

---

[833] Guatemala's first written submission, para. 294.

[834] For example, (a) it could have provided the requested copies, and invoiced Cruz Azul for the relevant fee. Alternatively, (b) it could have informed Cruz Azul of the exact fee to be paid, and provided details of the preferred method of payment. There again, (c) it could have arranged for Cruz Azul to collect the copies from the Ministry, and to pay the relevant fee upon collection.

suggest that the Ministry even informed Cruz Azul how much each copy of the file would cost. Guatemala has stated in these proceedings that Cruz Azul would have had to pay the cost of reproducing the file, plus Q 0.30 per page.[835] However, there is no evidence to suggest that the Ministry informed Cruz Azul how much it would cost to reproduce the file, or the number of pages in the file. Since Cruz Azul could not, therefore, have known how much each copy of the file would cost (because it did not know the number of pages in the file), we do not consider that an objective and impartial investigating authority seeking to "provide timely opportunities for all interested parties to see all information that is relevant to the presentation of their cases" would have failed to respond to Cruz Azul's request for two copies simply because - in the words of Guatemala - "Cruz Azul did not pay the required fee".[836] An investigating authority cannot "provide timely opportunities for all interested parties to see all information that is relevant to the presentation of their cases" if it conditions the provision of copies on the payment of a fee without at least informing the requesting party how much the fee would be, or without at least providing the requesting party with the information it would need (*e.g.*, the number of pages in the file) to calculate the fee for itself.

8.154 In these circumstances, we consider that the Ministry did not comply with its Article 6.4 obligation to "provide timely opportunities for all interested parties to see all information that is relevant to the presentation of their cases". Since there is no evidence to suggest that it was not "practicable" for the Ministry to do so, or that the relevant information was not "used" by the Ministry in its investigation, we find that the Ministry violated Article 6.4 of the AD Agreement by failing to provide the two copies of the file requested by Cruz Azul on 17 January 1997.

(d) Alleged failure to provide a full record of the public hearing

8.155 Mexico claims that the Ministry violated Article 6.4 of the AD Agreement by failing to provide Cruz Azul with a complete copy of the Ministry's record of the 19 December 1996 public hearing. Guatemala does not admit that the copy of the record was incomplete. Even if it were incomplete, Guatemala asserts that Cruz Azul could have requested a complete copy as soon as it realized that there had been an omission. Guatemala also argues that Cruz Azul did not bring this matter to the attention of the Ministry during the investigation, and that this matter was only raised in the present WTO dispute settlement proceedings.

8.156 Evidence before us demonstrates that the record of the 19 December 1996 public hearing provided by the Ministry to Cruz Azul was incomplete. Although the sequential numbers stamped on the pages of the document suggest that the document is complete, it is quite clear to us that at least two pages are actually missing from the document. The words at the beginning of page 02737 do not follow on from the phrase at the end of page 02376. This demonstrates that there is at least one page missing between pages 02736 and 02737. Furthermore, page 02737 refers to a sec-

[835] In doing so, Guatemala stated that the amount of the fee is regulated by Article 27(c) of Decree 111-96 of the Congress of the Republic of Guatemala.

[836] Guatemala's response to question 2 from the Panel.

ond point ("SEGUNDO"), without any first point identified in the preceding pages of the document. The first point is presumably cited in the first missing page. There is also at least one page missing between pages 02738 and 02739. Again, the wording at the end of page 02738 and at the beginning of page 02739 does not match. In addition, page 02739 refers to "CUARTO" and "QUINTO", while the third point is not included in the document. This third point is presumably cited in the second missing page.

8.157 Despite the factual accuracy of Mexico's argument, we do not consider that it amounts to a violation of Article 6.4 of the AD Agreement, as Mexico has failed to adduce any evidence that the Ministry's failure to provide a full copy of its record of the public hearing was anything other than inadvertent. Although we consider that an interested party is entitled to see a full version of the investigating authority's record of any public hearing, it is not inconceivable that an investigating authority which chooses to provide interested parties with a copy of the record could inadvertantly fail to provide a complete copy. In our view, such an inadvertent omission on the part of an investigating authority does not constitute a violation of Article 6.4. Although a violation could arise if an investigating authority failed to correct its omission after having been informed of that omission by an interested party, there is no evidence that Cruz Azul informed the Ministry of its omission in the present case.

8.158 In order to avoid any uncertainty, we wish to emphasize that we do not consider that the inadvertent nature of the Ministry's omission renders that omission "harmless", in the sense of being a defence to a violation of Article 6.4 of the AD Agreement (see para. 8.22). Our position is not that there was a violation of Article 6.4, but that such violation should be disregarded because it was "harmless". Rather, our position is that the factual circumstances before us do not amount to a violation. The question of whether or not any violation is "harmless" therefore does not arise.

3. Interested Party's Right to Defend its Interests - Article 6.2

8.159 Mexico claims that the Ministry violated Article 6.2 of the AD Agreement (a) by failing to provide a complete copy of the Ministry's record of the public hearing to Cruz Azul, (b) by failing to grant Cruz Azul access to the file on 4 November 1996, (c) by failing to provide Cruz Azul promptly with a copy of Cementos Progreso's 19 December 1996 submission, (d) by failing to respond to Cruz Azul's 13 November 1996 request for a non-confidential version of evidence submitted by Cementos Progreso, (e) by failing to provide Cruz Azul with a non-confidential version of the information submitted to the Ministry during its verification visit to Cementos Progreso, (f) by extending the period of investigation, (g) by delaying notification of initiation to Cruz Azul and the Government of Mexico; and (h) by failing to furnish the full text of Cementos Progreso's application for initiation.

8.160 Guatemala asserts that the Ministry complied with Article 6.2 of the AD Agreement by affording Cruz Azul and other interested parties the opportunity to examine the information, arguments and evidence presented during the course of the investigation.

8.161 Article 6.2 of the AD Agreement provides in relevant part:

> "Throughout the anti-dumping investigation all interested parties shall have a full opportunity for the defence of their interests..."

8.162 Whereas this provision clearly imposes a general duty on investigating authorities to ensure that interested parties have a full opportunity throughout an anti-dumping investigation for the defence of their interests, it provides no specific guidance as to what steps investigating authorities must take in practice. By contrast, other more specific provisions apply to the facts at hand, in respect of which Mexico has also made claims. Although there may be cases in which a panel will nevertheless need to address claims under Article 6.2, we do not consider it necessary for us to do when we have already made findings concerning the conduct allegedly violating Article 6.2 under other, more specific provisions of the AD Agreement.[837]

8.163 Accordingly, we shall only consider Mexico's claims under Article 6.2 to the extent that we have not made findings regarding the factual situation at issue under another provision of the AD Agreement which specifically addresses that situation.

8.164 For the most part, we have already made findings regarding the factual situations forming the basis of Mexico's Article 6.2 claim under provisions of the AD Agreement which specifically address those factual situations. Thus, we have made findings concerning item (a) under Article 6.4.[838] We have made findings concerning item (b) under Articles 6.1.2 and 6.4.[839] We have made findings concerning item (c) under Articles 6.1.2 and 6.4.[840] We have made findings concerning item (e) under Article 6.5.1.[841] We have made findings concerning item (f) under a number of provisions, including Article 6.2.[842] We have made findings concerning item (g) under Article 12.[843] We have made findings concerning item (h) under Article 6.1.3.[844] It is only the factual situations identified under item (d) which are not the subject of findings under provisions of the AD Agreement which specifically address those situations.[845]

8.165 Mexico's claim under item (d) is based on a document dated 13 November 1996, in which Cruz Azul requested "all the information submitted by CEMENTOS PROGRESO S.A. and other interested parties ...".[846] We are unable to make a finding that Cruz Azul's rights of defence were violated simply on the basis of Cruz Azul's

[837] In this regard, we recall that the Appellate Body stated in *European Communities - Bananas*, *supra*, footnote 80, para. 204, that "[a]lthough Article X:3(a) of the GATT 1994 and Article 1.3 of the *Licensing Agreement* both apply, the Panel, in our view, should have applied the *Licensing Agreement* first, since this agreement deals specifically, and in detail, with the administration of import licensing procedures" Furthermore, the panel in *United States - Anti-Dumping Act of 1916 – Complaint by the European Communities*, *supra*, footnote 14, stated that "[i]t is a general principle of international law that, when applying a body of norms to a given factual situation, one should consider that factual situation under the norm which most specifically addresses it" (footnote deleted).

[838] See paras. 8.155-8.158 above.

[839] See paras. 8.140-8.145 above.

[840] See paras. 8.155-8.158 above.

[841] See paras. 8.209-8.215 below.

[842] See paras. 8.175-8.179 below.

[843] See paras. 8.84-8.96 above.

[844] See paras. 8.97-8.104 above.

[845] Although we have made findings concerning item (f) under Article 6.1 and Annex II(1) of the AD Agreement, we do not consider that those provisions specifically address the extension of the Ministry's period of investigation.

[846] This document was provided by Mexico in Annex Mexico-54.

request for information. It is the Ministry's reaction to Cruz Azul's request which is relevant to determining whether Cruz Azul's rights of defence were violated. However, Mexico has not informed the Panel of how, if at all, the Ministry responded to Cruz Azul's request. We therefore reject Mexico's Article 6.2 claim based on its request for information dated 13 November 1996.

4. The Ministry's Failure to Satisfy Itself as to the Accuracy of Information - Article 6.6 / Annex II(7)

8.166 Mexico claims that the Ministry failed to satisfy itself of the accuracy of the information used by the Ministry in its final determination, contrary to Article 6.6 and Annex II(7) of the AD Agreement. Mexico claims that the Ministry's failure to satisfy itself of the accuracy of the information used to determine normal value violated paragraph 7 of Annex II, since the Ministry failed to act with "special circumspection" with regard to the best information available used as a basis for that determination. Mexico claims that the Ministry's failure to satisfy itself of the accuracy of the information used to determine injury violated Article 6.6, because: (i) the Ministry examined the maximum and minimum amounts of imports during the period of investigation ("POI"), rather than comparing the trend in imports during the POI with the trend in the previous comparable period; (ii) the import data concerning tariff heading 2523.29.00 used by the Ministry includes products other than that under investigation; the import data concerning tariff heading 2523.29.00 includes non-dumped imports from Mexico, and imports from countries other than Mexico.[847]

8.167 With regard to the accuracy of the injury data, Guatemala replies that the Ministry used data supplied by Cruz Azul for calculating the volume of imports. The Ministry therefore did not take into account imports from other countries, or imports of other types of cement not subject to the investigation. With regard to the accuracy of the information used to determine normal value, Guatemala asserts that the Ministry was entitled to use the "best information available", consistent with Article 6.8 of the AD Agreement. As regards that "best information available", Guatemala asserts that the Ministry used four invoices as the basis for its calculations. Furthermore, Mexico did not suggest that those invoices were fraudulent during the course of the Ministry's investigation.

8.168 Article 6.6 of the AD Agreement provides:

> "Except in circumstances provided for in paragraph 8, the authorities shall during the course of an investigation satisfy themselves as to the accuracy of the information supplied by interested parties upon which their findings are based."

8.169 Paragraph 7 of Annex II provides:

> "If the authorities have to base their findings, including those with respect to normal value, on information from a secondary source, including the information supplied in the application for the initiation of the investigation, they should do so with special circumspection. In

[847] Further details concerning this claim were provided in response to Mexico Question 3 from the Panel.

> such cases, the authorities should, where practicable, check the information from other independent sources at their disposal, such as published price lists, official import statistics and customs returns, and from the information obtained from other interested parties during the investigation. It is clear, however, that if an interested party does not cooperate and thus relevant information is being withheld from the authorities, this situation could lead to a result which is less favourable to the party than if the party did cooperate."

8.170 We shall examine Mexico's claims under Annex II(7) and Article 6.6 separately.

(a) Annex II(7)

8.171 Mexico's claim under Annex II(7) concerns the alleged failure by the Ministry to satisfy itself as to the accuracy of certain information used to determine normal value. This claim is based on paragraph 7 of Annex (II), because the information at issue constitutes "best information available", which the Ministry considered itself entitled to use as a result of the cancelled verification visit to Cruz Azul. We find at section E.1 para. 8.251 that the Ministry's recourse to "best information available" was contrary to Article 6.8 of the AD Agreement, read in light of Annex II(3). Since the Ministry was not entitled to rely on the "best information available" in order to make a final determination of normal value, we see no need to examine whether the Ministry did, or did not, exercise "special circumspection" in respect of that information. Even if the Ministry had exercised "special circumspection" in respect of the relevant "best information available", that would not change the fact that the Ministry was not justified in using that "best information available". The issue of whether or not the Ministry exercised the requisite "special circumspection" is therefore moot.

(b) Article 6.6

8.172 In our view, it is important to distinguish between the accuracy of information, and the substantive relevance of such information. Once an investigating authority has determined what information is of substantive relevance to its investigation, Article 6.6 requires the investigating authority to satisfy itself (except when "best information available" is used) that the substantively relevant information is accurate. Thus, Article 6.6 applies once an initial determination has been made that the information is of substantive relevance to the investigation. Article 6.6 provides no guidance in respect of the initial determination of whether information is, or is not, of substantive relevance to the investigation.

8.173 Whereas Mexico purports to raise issues concerning the accuracy of the import data used by the Ministry, we consider that in fact Mexico is simply questioning the substantive relevance of that data. Mexico argues that the Ministry should have used other data, since the data used by the Ministry were not substantively relevant; Mexico does not argue that the data used by the Ministry are factually inaccurate. For example, Mexico does not argue that the Ministry's data concerning the maximum and minimum amounts of imports during the POI are inaccurate; Mexico simply asserts that the Ministry should have used (what Mexico considers to be) more relevant data, *i.e.*, data concerning the import trend in absolute terms or relative to the previous comparable period. Similarly, Mexico does not argue that the import data concerning tariff heading 2523.29.00 was inaccurate; Mexico simply asserts that such data was not substantively relevant, because it included non-dumped imports from Mexico, and imports from countries other than Mexico.

8.174 In focusing on the substantive relevance of injury data used by the Ministry, Mexico has not demonstrated that the Ministry failed to satisfy itself as to the accuracy of that data. We therefore reject Mexico's claim under Article 6.6 of the AD Agreement. Mexico's claims regarding the substantive relevance of the import data relied on by the Ministry are more properly addressed under the relevant substantive provisions of Article 3 of the AD Agreement.

5. *Extension of the Period of Investigation - Articles 6.1, 6.2, Annex II(1)*

8.175 Mexico challenges the Ministry's 4 October 1996 decision to extend the POI from 1 June 1995 - 30 November 1995 to include the period 1 December 1995 - 31 May 1996 as well, because it claims that the extension was not justified in either fact or law. Mexico alleges in particular that Cruz Azul did not know the legal grounds for the extension of the POI, and that the Ministry did not respond to requests for information from Cruz Azul concerning the extension. Mexico claims that, as a result, Cruz Azul was not able to defend its interests in respect of the extension of the POI, contrary to Articles 6.1 and 6.2 of the AD Agreement. Mexico also asserts that the extension of the POI imposed an excessive and unreasonable burden on the exporter. Mexico claims that, since the investigating authority should specify in detail the information required from interested parties "as soon as possible after the initiation of the investigation" (Annex II(1)), investigating authorities are effectively precluded from extending the POI during the course of the investigation. Mexico claims that the extension of the POI during the course of an investigation, and after the imposition of provisional measures, is contrary to the logic of the structure of investigations. Changing the POI between the preliminary and final determinations can completely distort the investigation, because the data used to determine dumping, injury or threat of injury, and causal link in each case will not be the same.

8.176 Guatemala asserts that no provision of the AD Agreement imposes any requirements on the investigating authority with respect to the POI. Guatemala asserts that the investigating authority has absolute discretion regarding the selection of the POI, which it claims will vary from case to case. Concerning Mexico's claim that the extension imposed an excessive and unreasonable burden on Cruz Azul, Guatemala notes that Cruz Azul did not request any extension of the time allowed for responding to the supplementary questionnaire. Guatemala also denies that Annex II(1) of the AD Agreement prevents investigating authorities from extending the POI during the course of the investigation. Guatemala argues that this is an unacceptable proposition, since it would prevent investigating authorities from requesting information in addition to that requested at the time of initiation. Guatemala asserts that such a proposition would render the implementation of Articles 7.4 and 9.1 (lesser duty rule) and 10.2 (post-provisional measure information necessary to determine the effects of imports) more difficult, if not impossible. Guatemala also argues that the AD Agreement recognizes the need to use as much up-to-date information as possible, particularly with respect to threat of injury. Furthermore, Guatemala asserts that the

Ministry notified Cruz Azul of the information requested and granted Cruz Azul ample opportunity to submit in writing all the evidence it considered appropriate.

8.177 We are not persuaded that paragraph 1 of Annex II, or any other provision of the AD Agreement, prevents an investigating authority from extending the POI during the course of an investigation. We agree with Guatemala that there may be a number of circumstances in which the investigating authority will need updated information during the course of its investigation. In this regard, we would also note that the extension of a POI may in certain cases lead to *negative* findings of dumping and/or injury, to the benefit of exporters. The fact that the POI may be extended after the imposition of provisional measures is not necessarily problematic, since even without any extension of the POI there is no guarantee that the factual basis for the preliminary determination will be the same as that of the final determination. The factual basis may change, for example, if a preliminary affirmative determination of injury is made on the basis of data provided by the complainant, and if some (or all) of that data are shown to be erroneous during verification of the domestic industry. Indeed, in such cases differences in the factual bases of the preliminary and final determinations would normally be necessary in order to preserve the integrity of the investigation. Although Annex II(1) provides that interested parties should be informed of the information required by the investigating authority "as soon as possible after the initiation of the investigation", this does not mean that information concerning a particular period of time may only be required if the request for that information is made immediately after initiation. We interpret the first sentence of paragraph 1 of Annex II to mean that any request for specific information should be communicated to interested parties "as soon as possible". Since Mexico has not advanced any argument that it was possible for the Ministry to have requested information concerning the extended POI before it actually did so, we reject Mexico's claim that the Ministry's extension of the POI violated Guatemala's obligations under paragraph 1 of Annex II of the AD Agreement.

8.178 Mexico claims that the Ministry violated Articles 6.1 and 6.2 by extending the POI, because Cruz Azul was not informed of the reasons for the extension, and was not provided with an opportunity to comment on that extension. In addressing Mexico's Article 6.1 claim first, we consider that Mexico's interpretation of that provision is too expansive. The plain language of Article 6.1 merely requires that interested parties be given (1) notice of the information which the authorities require, and (2) ample opportunity to present in writing all evidence which they consider relevant in respect of the investigation. First, we note that Cruz Azul was given two weeks in which to present data concerning the extended POI. Cruz Azul therefore had two weeks' notice of the information required by the Ministry in respect of the extended POI.[848] Second, Mexico has made no claim to the effect that Cruz Azul was prevented from adducing written "evidence" concerning the extended POI. Whereas Mexico claims that Cruz Azul was denied any opportunity to comment on the extension of the POI *per se*, Article 6.1 does not explicitly require the provision of oppor-

[848] We note that Mexico has not alleged that a failure to provide Cruz Azul with at least 30 days to respond to the Ministry's supplementary questionnaire (which required the provision of data for an additional six-month POI) constitutes a violation of Article 6.1.1 of the AD Agreement. That being the case, we shall refrain from making any findings on this matter.

tunities for interested parties to comment on decisions taken by the investigating authority in respect of the information it requires. We therefore reject Mexico's claim that the Ministry's extension of the POI violated Guatemala's obligations under Article 6.1 of the AD Agreement.

8.179 Mexico claims that the Ministry violated Article 6.2 because Cruz Azul was not given any opportunity to comment on Cementos Progreso's request for extension of the POI. There is no evidence before us to suggest that Cruz Azul even knew that Cementos Progreso had requested an extension of the POI. We interpret the first sentence of Article 6.2 of the AD Agreement as a fundamental due process provision. In our view, when a request for an extension of the POI comes from one interested party, due process requires that the investigating authority seeks the views of other interested parties before acting on that request. Failure to respect the requirements of due process would conflict with the requirement to provide interested parties with "a full opportunity for the defence of their interests", consistent with Article 6.2.[849] Clearly, an interested party is not able to defend *its* interests if it is prevented from commenting on requests made by other interested parties in pursuit of *their* interests. In the present case, Cementos Progreso's request for extension of the POI was made on 1 October 1996. The Ministry's decision to extend the POI was made on 4 October 1996, only three days after Cementos Progreso's request. There is no evidence to suggest that the Ministry sought the views of Cruz Azul, or other interested parties, before deciding to extend the POI. Accordingly, we find that by extending the POI pursuant to a request from Cementos Progreso without seeking the views of other interested parties in respect of that request, the Ministry failed to provide Cruz Azul with "a full opportunity for the defence of [its] interests", contrary to Guatemala's obligations under Article 6.2 of the AD Agreement.

6. *Request for Cost Data - Articles 2.1 and 2.2*

8.180 Mexico claims that the Ministry's request for cost data violated Articles 2.1 and 2.2 of the AD Agreement. Mexico asserts that the request for cost data was not justified because Cementos Progreso's application did not contain any allegation that Cruz Azul was selling below cost, because the Ministry had no information from Cruz Azul to suggest that it was selling below cost, and because the Ministry had imposed a provisional measure on the basis of price data (*i.e.*, on the assumption that there were no sales below cost). Mexico asserts that the Ministry was not justified in requesting cost data in order to make adjustments for differences in physical characteristics initially requested by Cruz Azul, because the Ministry had already rejected those adjustments in its preliminary affirmative determination of dumping.

---

[849] We do not consider that the obligation in the first sentence of Article 6.2 is qualified by the second sentence of that provision. Thus, we do not consider that the obligation in the first sentence of Article 6.2 is concerned exclusively with "providing opportunities for all interested parties to meet those parties with adverse interests...". Although the words "[t]o this end" at the beginning of the second sentence suggest that such meetings are one way in which the obligation of the first sentence can be fulfilled, it does not follow that such meetings provide the only means by which the obligation of the first sentence may be fulfilled. If that were the case, there would be no need for the first sentence of Article 6.2.

8.181 Guatemala asserts that Articles 2.1 and 2.2 do not prevent an investigating authority from gathering cost information. Furthermore, Guatemala asserts that cost data was necessary in order to make an allowance for differences in physical characteristics between the cement sold in Mexico and the cement sold in Guatemala, as requested by Cruz Azul.

8.182 Articles 2.1 and 2.2 provide:

> "2.1 For the purpose of this Agreement, a product is to be considered as being dumped, i.e. introduced into the commerce of another country at less than its normal value, if the export price of the product exported from one country to another is less than the comparable price, in the ordinary course of trade, for the like product when destined for consumption in the exporting country.
>
> 2.2 When there are no sales of the like product in the ordinary course of trade in the domestic market of the exporting country or when, because of the particular market situation or the low volume of the sales in the domestic market of the exporting country[850], such sales do not permit a proper comparison, the margin of dumping shall be determined by comparison with a comparable price of the like product when exported to an appropriate third country, provided that this price is representative, or with the cost of production in the country of origin plus a reasonable amount for administrative, selling and general costs and for profits."

8.183 We are not persuaded that the Ministry violated Articles 2.1 and 2.2 of the AD Agreement by requesting cost data from Cruz Azul.[851] Nothing in those provisions prevents an investigating authority from requesting cost information, even if the applicant does not allege sales below cost. We therefore reject Mexico's claim that the Ministry violated Articles 2.1 and 2.2 of the AD Agreement by requesting cost data from Cruz Azul.

---

[850] Sales of the like product destined for consumption in the domestic market of the exporting country shall normally be considered a sufficient quantity for the determination of the normal value if such sales constitute 5 per cent or more of the sales of the product under consideration to the importing Member, provided that a lower ratio should be acceptable where the evidence demonstrates that domestic sales at such lower ratio are nonetheless of sufficient magnitude to provide for a proper comparison.

[851] According to Guatemala, the Ministry made two requests for cost data from Cruz Azul: one in its original questionnaire to exporters, and another in its supplementary questionnaire. Although we agree that cost data was requested in the supplementary questionnaire, there is no evidence that cost data was expressly requested in the original questionnaire. Section C of the original questionnaire makes it clear that an exporter need only complete the section on cost of production if the domestic producers' application alleges sales below cost. Section C also states that exporters will be informed - in a notification accompanying the questionnaire - whether the section on cost of production must be completed. In response to a question, Guatemala informed the Panel that the notification accompanying the original questionnaire to Cruz Azul is missing from its file. Thus, there is no evidence that the Ministry actually requested cost of production data from Cruz Azul. In these circumstances, we consider that Cruz Azul would have been entitled to assume that it did not need to provide cost data in response to the Ministry's original questionnaire.

7. *Verification Visit*

8.184 Mexico claims that the Ministry's verification visit to Cruz Azul was inconsistent with Article 6.7 and Annex I (2), (3), (7) and (8) of the AD Agreement because the Ministry intended to conduct the verification visit with the participation of non-governmental experts with an obvious conflict of interest, because the Ministry sought to proceed with the verification without the express agreement of Cruz Azul to the terms of the verification, because the Ministry failed to notify the Government of Mexico of the participation of non-governmental experts, and because the Ministry sought to verify information that had not been submitted by Cruz Azul.

8.185 Guatemala asserts that Mexico's claims are without foundation. First, Guatemala argues that Article 6.7 is silent on the permissible scope of a verification, and Annex I(7 and 8) does not support Mexico's position. Guatemala asserts that Cruz Azul's failure to provide the cost data requested by the Ministry would have justified the Ministry in immediately applying the "best information available" rule. Instead, Guatemala states that the Ministry acted in good faith, and provided Cruz Azul with one last chance to supply the cost data during the verification. Guatemala notes that Annex I(7) refers to "any further information which needs to be provided", interpreting this to mean that an investigating authority may seek "further information" during the course of an investigation.

8.186 Second, Guatemala asserts that the Ministry notified the Government of Mexico of its intention to include non-governmental experts in its verification team in a letter dated 26 November 1996 (addressed to Cruz Azul, but copied to the Government of Mexico). According to Guatemala, Mexico acknowledged having received a copy of its letter. Guatemala asserts that it was not required to explain the exceptional circumstances which necessitated the inclusion of non-governmental experts, and that in any event Mexico knew that non-governmental experts were required because this was the Ministry's first investigation.

8.187 Third, Guatemala denies that the non-governmental experts had any conflict of interest, because Cruz Azul was not an interested party in any of the US proceedings in which the non-governmental experts at issue had participated. Guatemala also asserts that the conflict-of-interest issue is in any event irrelevant, since Cruz Azul refused to allow any verification of cost data, whether or not the verification team included non-governmental experts.

(a) Inclusion of non-governmental experts with an alleged conflict of interest in the verification team

8.188 Mexico claims that the inclusion of non-governmental experts with an alleged conflict of interest in the Ministry's verification team constitutes a violation of Article 6.7 and Annex I (2), (3), (7) and (8) of the AD Agreement. In a communication dated 31 October 1996, the Ministry informed Cruz Azul of its intention to conduct a verification visit at Cruz Azul from 18 - 22 November 1996. The Ministry's communication informed Cruz Azul of the identities of three non-governmental experts to be included in the verification team, and of the Ministry's intention to verify certain cost and sales data. Cruz Azul initially responded to this communication on 7 November 1996, in which response Cruz Azul requested rescheduling of the verification visit to 2 - 6 December 1996. Subsequently, in a letter dated 25 November 1996, Cruz Azul objected to the participation of two of the three proposed non-governmental experts, whom Cruz Azul considered to have a conflict of interest as a result of their work as representatives of the US domestic cement industry in the context of a US anti-dumping investigation concerning imports of cement from Mexico.

8.189 We find at para. 8.250 below that it was entirely reasonable for Cruz Azul to object to the inclusion in the Ministry's verification team of two non-governmental experts who had a conflict of interest. Although we are of the view that an impartial and objective investigating authority would not include non-governmental experts with a conflict of interest in its verification team, none of the provisions cited by Mexico explicitly prohibit such conduct. Accordingly, we are unable to find that the Ministry violated Article 6.7 and Annex I (2), (3), (7) and (8) of the AD Agreement by including non-governmental experts with a conflict of interest in its verification team.

(b) Alleged failure to notify Mexico of the inclusion of non-governmental experts

8.190 Mexico claims that the Ministry violated paragraph 2 of Annex I of the AD Agreement by failing to notify the Government of Mexico of the inclusion of non-governmental experts in the Ministry's verification team, and of the exceptional circumstances justifying their inclusion.

8.191 Guatemala asserts that the Ministry notified the Government of Mexico of its intention to include non-governmental experts in its verification team in a letter dated 26 November 1996. According to Guatemala, Mexico acknowledged having received a copy of its letter. Guatemala asserts that it was not required to explain the exceptional circumstances which necessitated the inclusion of non-governmental experts, and that in any event Mexico knew that non-governmental experts were required because this was the Ministry's first investigation.

8.192 Paragraph 2 of Annex I of the AD Agreement provides:

> "If in exceptional circumstances it is intended to include non-governmental experts in the investigating team, the firms and the authorities of the exporting Member should be so informed. Such non-governmental experts should be subject to effective sanctions for breach of confidentiality requirements."

8.193 According to this provision, therefore, the Ministry was obligated to inform the Mexican authorities of is intention to include non-governmental experts in the verification team for the Ministry's visit to Cruz Azul. The question before us is whether the Ministry did so.

8.194 The Ministry sent a letter to Cruz Azul on 26 November 1996.[852] The letter informed Cruz Azul of the Ministry's intention to include non-governmental experts in its verification team. The letter even identified those experts by name. The letter ends with the phrase "c.c. Secretaría de Comercio y Fomento Industrial de México" (hereinafter "SECOFI"). In principle, therefore, a copy of the 26 November 1996 letter to Cruz Azul was to have been communicated to SECOFI, and therefore to the Mexican Government. However, Guatemala has not provided any proof that this letter was actually sent, or faxed, to SECOFI. Guatemala asserts that receipt of this

[852] See Annex Guatemala-57.

letter is demonstrated by the first sentence of a letter from a SECOFI official to the Ministry dated 2 December 1996, in which SECOFI refers to the Ministry's notification of a verification visit at Cruz Azul from 3 - December 1996. In response, Mexico asserts that the notification referred to in the 2 December 1996 letter was a separate notification of 26 November 1996 addressed to Mexico's Ambassador to Guatemala (see Annex Mexico-27). We consider that Mexico's assertion is borne out by the reference in Mexico's 2 December 1996 letter to a "notification to the government of Mexico, through its Ambassador in Guatemala". Furthermore, we note that the second paragraph of Mexico's 2 December 1996 letter states that Cruz Azul provided SECOFI with a copy of the letter it received from the Ministry concerning details of the verification and the names of the persons who would perform the verification. Thus, far from confirming that SECOFI was notified by Guatemala's authorities on 26 November 1996 of the participation of non-governmental experts in the Ministry's verification team, Mexico's letter of 2 December 1996 suggests that (1) it only learnt about the participation of non-governmental experts through a copy of the Ministry's 26 November 1996 letter to Cruz Azul, sent to SECOFI by Cruz Azul, and (2) the only letter dated 26 November 1996 that Mexico received from the Ministry was that sent to Mexico's Ambassador to Guatemala, which did not refer to the participation of non-governmental experts in the Ministry's verification team.

8.195 We recall once again that the panel in *United States - Sections 301 - 310 of the Trade Act of 1974* found that:

> "Since, in this case, both parties have submitted extensive facts and arguments in respect of the EC claims, our task will essentially be to balance all evidence on record and decide whether the EC, as party bearing the original burden of proof, has convinced us of the validity of its claims. In case of uncertainty, i.e. in case all the evidence and arguments remain in equipoise, we have to give the benefit of the doubt to the US as defending party."

8.196 In principle, Mexico bears the burden to prove that the Ministry failed to inform it of the inclusion of non-governmental experts in the Ministry's verification team. As a practical matter, this burden is impossible for Mexico to meet: one simply cannot prove that one was not informed of something. Although Mexico cannot establish definitively that it was not informed by the Ministry of the Ministry's intention to include non-governmental experts in its verification team, there is sufficient evidence before us to suggest strongly that it was not so informed. Although an investigating authority should normally be able to demonstrate that it complied with a formal requirement to inform the authorities of another Member, Guatemala has failed to rebut the strong suggestion that it failed to do so. In fact, Guatemala has simply referred to the very letter which suggests strongly that Mexico was *not* notified by Guatemala.[853] In these circumstances, we do not consider that the evidence

[853] The fact that the Mexican authorities knew of the inclusion of non-governmental experts in the Ministry's verification team (by virtue of Cruz Azul sending SECOFI a copy of the 26 November 1996 letter Cruz Azul had received from the Ministry) is not relevant to Mexico's claim. This is because Annex I(2) requires that the authorities of the exporting Member be "informed" of the inclusion of non-governmental experts. In our view, the obligation to "inform" is clearly on the authorities of the investigating Member. Those authorities cannot rely on exporters informing their own

and arguments of the parties "remain in equipoise". Accordingly, we find that the Ministry violated paragraph 2 of Annex I of the AD Agreement by failing to inform the Government of Mexico of the inclusion of non-governmental experts in the Ministry's verification team.[854]

8.197 Mexico also claims that the Ministry violated Annex I(2) by failing to inform Mexico of the exceptional circumstances which justified the inclusion of non-governmental experts in the Ministry's verification team. Guatemala asserts that Annex I(2) did not require the Ministry to inform Mexico of the exceptional circumstances at issue.

8.198 We agree with Guatemala. Whereas paragraph 2 of Annex I requires the exporting Member to be "so informed", the logical conclusion from the structure of that provision is that the exporting Member need only be informed of the intention to include non-governmental experts in the investigating team. If the intention of the drafters had been to impose an obligation on authorities to inform exporting Members of the "exceptional circumstances" at issue, presumably the first sentence of Annex I(2) would have been drafted in a manner that clearly provided for that obligation. We therefore reject Mexico's claim that Guatemala violated Annex I(2) by the Ministry's failure to inform Mexico of the exceptional circumstances justifying the need to include non-governmental experts in the Ministry's verification team.

(c) Scope of the Verification

8.199 Mexico claims that the Ministry violated Article 6.7 and Annex I(7) of the AD Agreement by seeking to verify certain information (concerning the extended period of investigation) not submitted by Cruz Azul in its questionnaire responses. Mexico asserts that the Ministry should have limited itself to verifying the information submitted by Cruz Azul, and obtaining further details concerning this information. According to Mexico, under no circumstances was the Ministry entitled to require or review additional information. Mexico notes that paragraph 7 of Annex I of the AD Agreement provides in relevant part that "the main purpose of the on-the-spot investigation is to verify information provided or to seek further details". According to Mexico, the "further details" referred to in that provision are details concerning information already "provided" in the questionnaire response.

8.200 Guatemala rejects the argument that a verification must be limited to information already submitted by an exporter in its questionnaire response. Guatemala notes that Annex I(7) refers to "any further information which needs to be provided",

---

authorities of the inclusion of non-governmental experts in order to establish compliance with Annex I(2).

[854] Para. 2 of Annex I provides that exporting Members "should" be informed of the inclusion of non-governmental experts in a verification team. It does not provide that exporting Members "shall" be so informed. Although the word "should" is often used colloquially to imply an exhortation, it can also be used "to express a duty [or] obligation" (See The Concise Oxford English Dictionary, Clarendon Press, 1995, page 1283). Since Article 6.7 provides in relevant part that the provisions of Annex I "shall" apply, we see no reason why Annex I (2) should not be interpreted in the mandatory sense. In our view, a hortatory interpretation of the provisions of Annex I would be inconsistent with Article 6.7. Furthermore, Guatemala has not argued that para. 2 of Annex I is merely hortatory. Accordingly, we proceed on the basis that para. 2 of Annex I should be interpreted in a mandatory sense.

interpreting this to mean that an investigating authority may seek "further information" during the course of an investigation.

8.201 In addressing Mexico's claim under Article 6.7 and Annex I(7), we note that Article 6.7 provides that "[t]he procedures described in Annex I shall apply to investigations carried out in the territory of other Members". When examining verification visits scheduled by investigating authorities in the territory of other Members, therefore, it is important to read Article 6.7 and Annex I as a whole.

8.202 We note that Mexico has referred to specific parts of paragraph 7 of Annex I of the AD Agreement. In our view, however, it is important to examine the full text of that provision, which provides:

> "As the main purpose of the on-the-spot investigation is to verify information provided or to obtain further details, it should be carried out after the response to the questionnaire has been received unless the firm agrees to the contrary and the government of the exporting Member is informed by the investigating authorities of the anticipated visit and does not object to it; further, it should be standard practice prior to the visit to advise the firms concerned of the general nature of the information to be verified and of *any further information which needs to be provided*, though this should not preclude requests to be made on the spot for further details to be provided *in the light of information obtained*." (emphasis supplied)

8.203 Although Annex I(7) provides that the "main purpose" of the verification visit is to verify information already provided, or to obtain further details in respect of that information, it also provides that an investigating authority may "prior to the visit ... advise the firms concerned ... of any further information which needs to be provided". Since there would be little point in advising a firm of "further information ... to be provided" in advance of the verification visit if the investigating authority were precluded from examining that "further information" during the visit, we consider that the phrase "further information ... to be provided" refers to information to be provided during the course of the verification. Mexico's view that an investigating authority may only verify information submitted prior to the verification visit is not consistent with this interpretation of Annex I(7).

8.204 In response to a question from the Panel, Mexico argues that the phrase "any further information ... to be provided" refers to accounting information to be provided by the verified company during verification in order to substantiate the information previously supplied to the investigating authority. We note, however, that the phrase does not read "any further accounting information ... to be provided". The term "information" is not qualified in any way by the express wording of Annex I(7), and there are no elements in the context which plead for such qualification.

8.205 Furthermore, we note that the last phrase of Annex I(7) refers to on-the-spot requests for further details to be provided in light of "information obtained". Thus, although it should be "standard practice" to advise firms of additional information to be provided in advance of the verification visit, this does not preclude an investigating authority from requesting "further details" during the course of the investigation, "in light of the information obtained". In our view, the reference to "information obtained" cannot mean the information obtained from the exporter in advance of the verification visit, since (consistent with "standard practice") requests regarding that information should be made prior to the visit, and not during the course of the investigation. Accordingly, the "information obtained" must refer to information obtained during the course of the verification visit, since it is only information obtained during the course of a verification visit which may prompt a request for further details during the course of the verification visit. The last phrase of Annex I(7) therefore confirms our understanding that an investigating authority may seek new information during the course of the verification visit.

8.206 We therefore reject Mexico's claim that the Ministry violated Article 6.7 and paragraph 7 of Annex I of the AD Agreement by seeking to verify information not previously submitted in Cruz Azul's questionnaire responses.

8. *Confidential Treatment - Articles 6.1, 6.2, 6.3, 6.5, 6.5.1 and 6.5.2*

8.207 Mexico claims that the Ministry violated Articles 6.1, 6.2, 6.3, 6.5, 6.5.1 and 6.5.2 of the AD Agreement in according confidential treatment to certain information submitted by Cementos Progreso. Mexico's claims concern (1) information submitted during the verification visit at Cementos Progreso, and (2) information submitted by Cementos Progreso at the 19 December 1996 public hearing.[855]

8.208 Guatemala asserts that, in its handling of the information supplied by Cementos Progreso, the Ministry complied with Articles 6.5.1 and 6.5.2 of the AD Agreement. Guatemala asserts that the documents submitted by Cementos Progreso were clearly of a confidential nature and could not be summarized in accordance with Article 6.5.1. Guatemala understands that it is common practice for investigating authorities in other countries not to require public versions of confidential documents obtained during verification visits.

(a) Information submitted during verification

8.209 First, Mexico claims that the Ministry violated Article 6.5.2 by accepting to provide confidential treatment for certain information submitted during the verification visit at Cementos Progreso, despite Cementos Progreso failing to justify its request for confidential treatment. However, Article 6.5.2 does not require any justification to be provided by the interested party requesting confidential treatment. If any such obligation exists, it derives from Article 6.5, not 6.5.2. Mexico has not based this claim on Article 6.5. Article 6.5.2 speaks only to events when "the authorities find that a request for confidentiality is not warranted". Since there is nothing to suggest that the Ministry found that Cementos Progreso's request for confidentiality of the relevant information was not warranted, Article 6.5.2 would appear not to apply

[855] In its second oral statement to the Panel (paras 32 -35), Mexico claimed that the Ministry violated Article 6.5 of the AD Agreement by handing Mr. Cannistra confidential information submitted by Cruz Azul, without Cruz Azul's permission. This claim was not included in Mexico's request for establishment of this Panel (WT/DS156/2 and WT/DS156/2/Corr.1). The only Article 6.5 claims included in Mexico's request for establishment (at section D.8) concern the Ministry's treatment of "information from Cementos Progreso". There is no reference to information submitted by Cruz Azul. Mexico's claim concerning the confidentiality of information submitted to the Ministry by Cruz Azul therefore falls outside our terms of reference.

in the factual circumstances of this case. We therefore reject Mexico's Article 6.5.2 claim.

8.210 Second, Mexico makes a series of claims under Articles 6.1, 6.2, 6.4, 6.5, 6.5.1 and 6.5.2 of the AD Agreement. Mexico's claims are all based on the fact that either (1) the Ministry failed to require Cementos Progreso to provide non-confidential summaries of information that was "susceptible of summary" (within the meaning of Article 6.5.1), or (2) the Ministry failed to require Cementos Progreso to provide reasons why the information - if it was not "susceptible of summary" - could not be made public.

8.211 Mexico's claims concern the following information submitted by Cementos Progreso during the Ministry's verification visit to that company: technical information on the firm's principal equipment; a contract between Cementos Progreso and F.L. Smith & Co.; and tables used to prepare questionnaires and reconcile the cost structure calculated for production of grey portland cement with the accounting statements. Although Mexico's claim is based in part on an implicit argument that the abovementioned information was "susceptible of summary", Mexico has adduced no evidence to that effect. Mexico has failed to demonstrate how information of the sort enumerated above could be summarized "in sufficient detail to permit a reasonable understanding of the substance" thereof. In our view, information of that sort is not generally capable of summarization "in sufficient detail to permit a reasonable understanding of the substance". In our view, and in the absence of any evidence or argument from Mexico to the contrary, we are not persuaded that an impartial and objective investigating authority could not properly have concluded that the abovementioned information was not "susceptible of summary". For this reason, we reject all of Mexico's claims that are based on Mexico's understanding that the Ministry failed to require Cementos Progreso to provide non-confidential summaries of information that was "susceptible of summary".

8.212 As for Mexico's claims that the Ministry failed to require Cementos Progreso to provide reasons why the information - which was not "susceptible of summary" - could not be made public, we note that Article 6.5.1 provides:

> "The authorities shall require interested parties providing confidential information to furnish non-confidential summaries thereof. These summaries shall be in sufficient detail to permit a reasonable understanding of the substance of the information submitted in confidence. In exceptional circumstances, such parties may indicate that such information is not susceptible of summary. In such exceptional circumstances, a statement of the reasons why summarization is not possible must be provided."

8.213 Thus, Article 6.5.1 generally obliges investigating authorities to require interested parties providing confidential information to furnish non-confidential summaries thereof. However, such non-confidential summaries need not be furnished when, "in exceptional circumstances", the information "is not susceptible of summary". In such cases, "a statement of the reasons why summarization is not possible must be provided". Although Article 6.5.1 does not explicitly provide that "the authorities shall require" interested parties to provide a statement of the reasons why summarization is not possible, any meaningful interpretation of Article 6.5.1 must impose such an obligation on the investigating authorities. It is certainly not possible to conclude that the obligation concerning the need to provide a statement of reasons is an obligation imposed exclusively on the interested party submitting the information, and not the investigating authority, since the AD Agreement is not addressed at interested parties. The AD Agreement imposes obligations on WTO Members and their investigating authorities. Accordingly, in our view Article 6.5.1 imposes an obligation on investigating authorities to require parties that indicate that information is not susceptible of summary to provide a statement of the reasons why summarization is not possible. Guatemala has failed to adduce any evidence that the requisite statement of reasons was provided by Cementos Progreso, or that the Ministry even required Cementos Progreso to provide such a statement of reasons. We therefore find that the Ministry violated Article 6.5.1 of the AD Agreement by failing to require Cementos Progreso to provide a statement of the reasons why summarization of the relevant information was not possible. In making this finding, we attach no importance whatsoever to Guatemala's assertions concerning the alleged treatment of similar information by other WTO Members. Whether or not other WTO Members act in conformity with Article 6.5.1 is of no relevance to the present dispute, which concerns the issue of whether or not the Ministry acted in conformity with that provision.

8.214 Mexico has also made additional claims concerning the need for a statement of the reasons why the information is not susceptible of summary on the basis of Articles 6.1, 6.2, 6.4, 6.5 and 6.5.2 of the AD Agreement. In our view, the need for a statement of the reasons why the information is not susceptible of summary is specifically addressed by Article 6.5.1. It is not specifically addressed by the other provisions cited by Mexico. Accordingly, having made a finding on the basis of Article 6.5.1, we do not consider it necessary to make additional findings on the basis of Articles 6.1, 6.2, 6.4, 6.5 and 6.5.2 of the AD Agreement.

8.215 Finally, and in the alternative, Mexico refers to the possibility that the Ministry accepted a "verbal justification" from Cementos Progreso concerning the need for confidential treatment of the information at issue. Mexico claims that such acceptance constitutes a violation of Articles 6.1, 6.2, 6.3 and 6.4. However, since there is no evidence before us to suggest that any such "verbal justification" was provided, there is no factual basis for any examination of this claim by the Panel.

(b) Information submitted by Cementos Progreso at 19 December 1996 public hearing

8.216 First, Mexico claims that the Ministry violated Articles 6.1, 6.2 and 6.4 of the AD Agreement by failing to allow Cruz Azul "proper access" to the information submitted by Cementos Progreso at the 19 December 1996 public hearing. We recall that we have already addressed this issue in previous sections of our report (see section 2(b)), where we found a violation of Articles 6.1.2 and 6.4 of the AD Agreement. Since we consider these to be the specific provisions of the AD Agreement governing an interested party's right to information submitted by another interested party, we do not consider it necessary to address Mexico's claims under Articles 6.1 and 6.2. These provisions do not specifically address an interested party's right of access to information submitted by another interested party.

8.217 Second, Mexico claims that the Ministry violated Articles 6.5, 6.5.1 and 6.5.2 of the AD Agreement by granting Cementos Progreso's 19 December 1996 submission confidential treatment on its own initiative. We understand Mexico to claim that the Ministry violated Articles 6.5, 6.5.1 and 6.5.2 by providing confidential treatment without "good cause" having been shown by Cementos Progreso.

8.218 Article 6.5 provides:

> "Any information which is by nature confidential (for example, because its disclosure would be of significant competitive advantage to a competitor or because its disclosure would have a significantly adverse effect upon a person supplying the information or upon a person from whom that person acquired the information), or which is provided on a confidential basis by parties to an investigation shall, upon good cause shown, be treated as such by the authorities. Such information shall not be disclosed without specific permission of the party submitting it." (footnote deleted)

8.219 The text of Article 6.5 distinguishes between two types of confidential information: (1) "information which is by nature confidential", and (2) information "which is provided on a confidential basis". Article 6.5 then provides that the provision of confidential treatment is conditional on "good cause" being shown. Logically, one might expect that "good cause" for confidential treatment of information which is "by nature confidential" could be presumed, and that "good cause" need only be shown for information which is *not* "by nature confidential" (but for which confidential treatment is nonetheless sought). It is presumably for this reason that, in rejecting Mexico's claim, Guatemala argues that the relevant information was "clearly of a confidential nature". While we have some sympathy for Guatemala's argument, given the logical appeal of such an interpretation of Article 6.5, we note that Article 6.5 is not drafted in a way which suggests this approach. Instead, the requirement to show "good cause" appears to apply for both types of confidential information, such that even information "which is by nature confidential" cannot be afforded confidential treatment unless "good cause" has been shown.[856]

8.220 In our view, the requisite "good cause" must be shown by the interested party submitting the confidential information at issue. We do not consider that Article 6.5 envisages "good cause" being shown by the investigating authority itself, since - with respect to information that is not "by nature confidential" in particular - the investigating authority may not even know whether or why there is cause to provide confidential treatment.

8.221 As noted in para. 8.143 above, Guatemala has not demonstrated, or even argued, that Cementos Progreso requested confidential treatment for its 19 December 1996 submission, let alone that Cementos Progreso showed "good cause" for confidential treatment of that submission. Accordingly, we find that the Ministry violated Article 6.5 of the AD Agreement by granting Cementos Progreso's 19 December submission confidential treatment on its own initiative. We note that Mexico has also alleged a violation of Articles 6.5.1 and 6.5.2 of the AD Agreement. Since Article 6.5 specifically addresses the issue of whether or not an investigating authority may grant confidential treatment on its own initiative, and since Articles 6.5.1 and 6.5.2

[856] Although we will now consider who must show "good cause", we make no findings as to how "good cause" may be shown in respect of information which is "by nature" confidential.

do not, we do not consider it necessary to address Mexico's claims under the latter provisions of the AD Agreement.

8.222 Third, and in the alternative, Mexico claims that the Ministry violated Articles 6.1, 6.2, 6.3 and 6.4 of the AD Agreement by accepting a "verbal justification" that the information contained in the submission made by Cementos Progreso at the 19 December 1996 public hearing should be considered confidential. As noted above,[857] there is no evidence that any such "verbal justification" was provided in the present case. It is therefore not necessary for us to address this claim.

8.223 At paras 414 - 416 of its first written submission, Mexico also alleges violation of Articles 6.1, 6.2, 6.3, 6.4, 6.5.1 and 6.5.2 on the basis of "the facts mentioned in section V.A.1(e) and (f), V.A.2, V.B, V.C.3, V.D.1, 2, 4, 9 and 10, E.2 and 4". Since Mexico has made absolutely no effort to link those facts with the aforementioned provisions of the AD Agreement, we are in no position to examine these claims.

9. *Essential Facts*

8.224 Mexico claims that the Ministry did not inform Cruz Azul promptly of the "essential facts under consideration" that would be taken into account for the definitive anti-dumping measure, contrary to Articles 6.1, 6.2 and 6.9.

8.225 Guatemala asserts that the "essential facts under consideration" were disclosed to Cruz Azul. Guatemala asserts that, in a notice dated 6 December 1996, interested parties were informed that the Directorate of Economic Integration would make a technical study on the basis of the evidence in the file, and that copies of the file were available. Guatemala therefore argues that the "essential facts" were in the file, to which interested parties had access. In addition, Guatemala claims that the "essential facts" were already disclosed in a detailed report setting out the factual basis for the Ministry's preliminary determination, and that the parties could comment on these "essential facts" at the 19 December 1996 public hearing. Guatemala argues that the Ministry was permitted to proceed expeditiously under Article 6.14, rather than delaying the final determination in order to issue "another description of the essential facts".

8.226 Article 6.9 provides:

> "The authorities shall, before a final determination is made, inform all interested parties of the essential facts under consideration which form the basis for the decision whether to apply definitive measures. Such disclosure should take place in sufficient time for the parties to defend their interests."

8.227 We shall first examine Guatemala's argument that the "essential facts" were disclosed to interested parties in a detailed report setting out the Ministry's preliminary findings. In doing so, we note that Guatemala has sought to draw parallels between this alleged disclosure mechanism and that employed by the United States.[858] We take no view on whether or not the procedure used by the Ministry is similar in any way to that employed by the United States, or whether the US procedure is in

[857] See para. 8.215.

[858] Guatemala's first oral statement, para. 62.

conformity with Article 6.9, since the conformity of the United States' procedure with Article 6.9 of the AD Agreement is not at issue in the present dispute.

8.228 In our view, the alleged disclosure by the Ministry of the "essential facts" forming the basis of the Ministry's preliminary determination does not meet the requirements of Article 6.9. Article 6.9 provides explicitly for disclosure of the "essential facts ... which form the basis for the decision whether to apply *definitive* measures" (emphasis supplied). Disclosure of the "essential facts" forming the basis of a preliminary determination is clearly inadequate in circumstances where the factual basis of the provisional measure is significantly different from the factual basis of the definitive measure. In the present case, the preliminary measure was based on a preliminary determination of *threat* of material injury, whereas the final determination was based on *actual* material injury. Furthermore, the Ministry's preliminary determination (16 August 1996) was based on a POI different from that used for its final determination, since the POI was extended on 4 October 1996. Indeed, Guatemala has cited[859] the United States' assertion that "[i]n the course of an anti-dumping investigation, the bulk of the evidence which forms the basis of the final determination is generally gathered after the preliminary determination".[860] If the bulk of the evidence which forms the basis of the final determination is generally gathered after the preliminary determination, we fail to see how disclosure of the "essential facts" forming the basis of the preliminary determination could amount to disclosure of the "essential facts" forming the basis of the final determination, since the "bulk" of the "essential facts" underlying the final determination would not yet have been gathered. In these circumstances, we do not consider that the Ministry could satisfy the Article 6.9 obligation to "inform all interested parties of the essential facts under consideration which form the basis for the decision whether to apply definitive measures" by providing disclosure of the essential facts forming the basis of its preliminary determination.

8.229 We now turn to Guatemala's argument that the Ministry disclosed the "essential facts" by making copies of the file available to interested parties. We note that an investigating authority's file is likely to contain vast amounts of information, some of which may not be relied on by the investigating authority in making its decision whether to apply definitive measures. For example, the file may contain information submitted by an interested party that was subsequently shown to be inaccurate upon verification. Although that information will remain in the file, it would not form the basis of the investigating authority's decision whether to apply definitive measures. The difficulty for an interested party with access to the file, however, is that it will not know whether particular information in the file forms the basis of the authority's final determination. One purpose of Article 6.9 is to resolve this difficulty for interested parties. This has been acknowledged by Guatemala, which has itself asserted that "[t]he object and purpose of Article 6.9 is to allow exporters a fair opportunity to comment on the important issues in an investigation after the record is closed to new facts".[861] An interested party will not know whether a particular fact is "important" or

---

[859] Guatemala's second oral statement, para. 61.
[860] United States' third party submission, para. 43.
[861] Guatemala's second oral statement, para. 63.

not unless the investigating authority has explicitly identified it as one of the "essential facts" which form the basis of the authority's decision whether to impose definitive measures.

8.230 Furthermore, if the disclosure of "essential facts" under Article 6.9 could be undertaken simply by providing access to all information in the file, there would be little, if any, practical difference between Article 6.9 and Article 6.4. Guatemala is effectively arguing that it complied with Article 6.9 by complying with Article 6.4, *i.e.*, by providing "timely opportunities for interested parties to see all information that is relevant to the presentation of their cases ... and that is used by the authorities ...". We do not accept an interpretation of Article 6.9 that would effectively reduce its substantive requirements to those of Article 6.4. In our view, an investigating authority must do more than simply provide "timely opportunities for interested parties to see all information that is relevant to the presentation of their cases ... and that is used by the authorities ..." in order to "inform all interested parties of the essential facts under consideration which form the basis for the decision whether to apply definitive measures". In light of these considerations, we do not consider that the Ministry could comply with the requirement to "inform all interested parties of the essential facts under consideration which form the basis for the decision whether to apply definitive measures" simply by offering to provide interested parties with copies of all information in the file.

8.231 For the above reasons, we find that the Ministry violated Article 6.9 of the AD Agreement by failing to "inform all interested parties of the essential facts under consideration which form the basis for the decision whether to apply definitive measures".

8.232 Mexico claims that the Ministry's failure to disclose the "essential facts" forming the basis of its final determination also constitutes a violation of Articles 6.1 and 6.2 of the AD Agreement. Article 6.9 is the provision of the AD Agreement which specifically addresses the disclosure of "essential facts". Since we have already found that the Ministry violated the specific obligation provided for in Article 6.9, we do not need to consider whether the Ministry's failure to disclose "essential facts" also constituted a violation of Articles 6.1 and 6.2.

10. Failure to Inform Cruz Azul of Changed Injury Determination

8.233 Mexico claims that the Ministry violated Articles 6.1, 6.2 and 6.9 of the AD Agreement by changing its injury determination from a preliminary determination of *threat* of material injury to a final determination of *actual* material injury during the course of the investigation, without informing Cruz Azul of that change, and without giving Cruz Azul a full and ample opportunity to defend itself. Mexico argues that during the course of the investigation and up until the public hearing which the Ministry held with the parties, i.e. 11 months after the initiation of the investigation, Cruz Azul did not know that the Ministry had changed the examination and determination of threat of material injury. Mexico asserts that Cruz Azul was therefore denied an opportunity to exercise the right of defence given under Article 6.1, 6.2 and 6.9, including the opportunity to provide relevant information and evidence that might have counteracted the determination of injury by the authority.

8.234 According to Guatemala, Mexico is essentially suggesting that an investigating authority must inform the exporter of its intention to base its final determination on threat of injury or material injury in order that the exporter may have an adequate opportunity to defend its interests. Guatemala asserts that there is no support for this argument in the AD Agreement. Article 6.1, 6.2 and 6.9 contain nothing to suggest that an investigating authority must inform an exporter of the legal basis for the final determination prior to notice of that determination being given. According to Guatemala, Article 5 of the AD Agreement itself provides the legal basis for a final determination, in that the final determination may be based either on threat of material injury or actual material injury. Thus, Guatemala asserts that an exporter defending an anti-dumping case knows, through Article 5, that to escape unscathed he must show no threat of injury and no material injury. Guatemala submits that Cruz Azul can only blame itself for having failed to mount a defence for material injury, and that it is significant that Mexico does not identify any particular evidence that Cruz Azul would have supplied if it had known that the Ministry was going to find material injury and not threat of injury. Guatemala argues that Cruz Azul never provided any evidence that it had not been engaged in dumping or that Cementos Progreso had not been adversely affected by the dumped imports, and that Mexico has not informed the Panel that Cruz Azul was not engaged in dumping or that Cementos Progreso was not materially injured. All Mexico's arguments before the panel, like Cruz Azul's complaints to the investigating authority, relate to procedural, not substantive issues. According to Guatemala, however, facts are facts: in August 1996, when the preliminary determination was issued it was clear that Cementos Progreso was being threatened with material injury. By January 1997, when the final determination was issued, the files showed that Cementos Progreso had already been injured.

8.235 Mexico does not question the right of an investigating authority to initiate an investigation and make a preliminary affirmative determination on the basis of threat of material injury, and subsequently issue a final determination on the basis of actual material injury. Rather, we understand Mexico to claim that an investigating authority exercising that right should inform exporters accordingly, and provide them with an opportunity to comment. In other words, an investigating authority should inform interested parties when it changes its injury determination from a preliminary, legal determination of threat of material injury to a final, legal determination of actual material injury.

8.236 In addressing this claim, we reject Guatemala's argument that, in order to "escape unscathed", the onus is on the exporter to demonstrate that it has not caused injury through dumping. The onus is not on the exporter to demonstrate a negative. Rather, the onus is on the investigating authority to demonstrate affirmatively that the exporter has engaged in dumping which has caused injury to the relevant domestic industry. Only if the affirmative case of dumping, injury and causal link is proven may anti-dumping measures be imposed. We also attach no importance to Guatemala's assertion that Mexico has failed to deny before the Panel that Cruz Azul had not dumped, and had not caused injury to Cementos Progreso as a result of such dumping. The issue before us is not whether Cruz Azul engaged in dumping which caused injury to Cementos Progreso. That assertion would involve us in a *de novo* examination of the evidence before the Ministry, which we are not prepared to undertake. Rather, the issue is whether the Ministry, in finding that Cruz Azul had engaged in dumping which caused injury to Cementos Progreso, complied with its various obligations under the AD Agreement.

8.237 We do not consider that an investigating authority need inform interested parties in advance when, having issued a preliminary affirmative determination on the basis of threat of material injury, it subsequently makes a final determination of actual material injury. No provision of the AD Agreement requires an investigating authority to inform interested parties, during the course of the investigation, that it has changed the legal basis for its injury determination. Investigating authorities are instead required to forward to interested parties a public notice, or a separate report, setting forth "in sufficient detail the findings and conclusions reached on all issues of fact and law considered material by the investigating authorities", consistent with Article 12.2 of the AD Agreement. If decisions on issues of law had to be disclosed to interested parties during the course of the investigation, there would be little need for interested parties to receive the notice provided for in Article 12.2. Furthermore, to the extent that there is any difference between the preliminary determination of injury and the final determination of injury, that change will be apparent to interested parties comparing the public notice of the investigating authority's preliminary determination with the public notice of its final determination.

8.238 Mexico's claim is based on Articles 6.1, 6.2 and 6.9 of the AD Agreement. We note that Articles 6.1 and 6.9 impose certain obligations on investigating authorities in respect of "information", "evidence" and "essential facts". However, Mexico's claim does not concern interested parties' right to have access to certain factual information during the course of an investigation. Mexico's claim concerns interested parties' alleged right to be informed of an investigating authority's legal determinations during the course of an investigation. As for Article 6.2, we note that the first sentence of that provision is very general in nature. We are unable to interpret such a general sentence in a way that would impose a specific obligation on investigating authorities to inform interested parties of the legal basis for its final determination on injury during the course of an investigation, when the express wording of Article 12.2 only imposes such a specific obligation on investigating authorities at the end of the investigation.

8.239 We therefore reject Mexico's claim that the Ministry violated Articles 6.1, 6.2 and 6.9 by changing its injury determination from a preliminary determination of threat of material injury to a final determination of actual material injury during the course of the investigation, without informing Cruz Azul of that change.

E. Alleged Violations Concerning the Final Determination

1. Mexico's Claims Concerning the Ministry's Final Determination of Dumping

8.240 Mexico makes a number of allegations concerning the dumping analysis performed by the Ministry in its final determination. Mexico's claims concern the Ministry's calculation of normal value, of the export price, and its comparison of the two. The information used by the Ministry to calculate normal value was the "best information available". Mexico claims that the Ministry's recourse to the "best information available" was inconsistent with Article 6.8 of the AD Agreement. We need only examine Mexico's additional claims regarding normal value and dumping, if the

Ministry's use of the "best information available" was consistent with Article 6.8. We shall therefore examine this issue first.

8.241 Mexico claims that the Ministry's use of "best information available" was not justified in the present case, since Cruz Azul did not deny access to the necessary information, nor significantly impede the Ministry's investigation. Mexico also claims that the Ministry violated paragraphs 3, 5 and 7 of Annex II of the AD Agreement in its handling of the "best information available"

8.242 Guatemala asserts that the Ministry was justified in having recourse to the "best information available" for the purpose of calculating normal value, because of Cruz Azul and Mexico's "refusal to cooperate".[862] In this regard, Guatemala refers to Cruz Azul's refusal to provide cost data, to provide sales data for the period 1 December 1995 - 31 May 1996, and to cooperate during the verification visit.

8.243 Article 6.8 provides:

> "In cases in which any interested party refuses access to, or otherwise does not provide, necessary information within a reasonable period or significantly impedes the investigation, preliminary and final determinations, affirmative or negative, may be made on the basis of the facts available. The provisions of Annex II shall be observed in the application of this paragraph."

8.244 Article 6.8 therefore permits the use of "best information available" if an interested party (1) refuses access to necessary information, (2) otherwise does not provide necessary information, or (3) significantly impedes the investigation.

8.245 Before determining whether the Ministry was justified in having recourse to the "best information available" for the purpose of calculating normal value, we note that Guatemala's justification for the Ministry's use of "best information available" does not correspond to that provided by the Ministry in its final Resolution of 17 January 1997. In that Resolution, the Ministry considered that:

> "the information submitted by the exporter cannot be taken into account when calculating the normal value of the product investigated **because it could not be verified** and the technical accounting evidence submitted by the exporter on 18 December 1996 (confidential information) could not replace verification of the information by the Guatemalan investigating authority, as required by Article 6.6 of the Anti-Dumping Code"[863] (emphasis supplied, footnote omitted).

Thus, the Ministry clearly based its recourse to the "best information available" on its inability to verify the data submitted by Cruz Azul. The Ministry did not, according to its final Resolution, rely on the "best information available" because of Cruz Azul's failure to provide certain sales and cost data, as alleged by Guatemala in these Panel proceedings. Even if the additional factors identified by Guatemala before the Panel could justify the use of "best information available", such *ex post* justification by Guatemala should not form part of our assessment of the conduct of the Ministry leading up to the imposition of the January 1997 definitive anti-dumping measure. The issue before us is whether the Ministry complied with the AD Agreement. In

[862] Guatemala's first written submission, para. 106.

[863] See section B.6, page 14, Annex Mexico-41 (translated).

examining that issue, we shall confine ourselves to the reasoning provided by the Ministry in its determinations. We note that this approach is similar to that adopted by the panel in *Korea - Definitive Safeguard Measure on Imports of Certain Dairy Products*, which ignored explanatory statements made in Korea's first submission to the panel that were not reflected in the Korean authorities' analysis at the time of the investigation.[864]

8.246 Confining ourselves to the reasoning contained in the Ministry's determination, we shall consider whether the Ministry's inability to verify certain data could properly have justified the Ministry's recourse to the "best information available". In the context of Article 6.8, we must consider whether the Ministry could properly have concluded that Cruz Azul "significantly impede[d] the [Ministry's] investigation" by failing to cooperate with the Ministry's verification visit to its premises.

8.247 In a letter dated 31 October 1996, the Ministry informed Cruz Azul that its verification team would include three non-governmental experts, whose names were also included in that letter. In a letter dated 25 November 1996, Cruz Azul raised concerns regarding the inclusion in the verification team of two of the three non-governmental experts identified by the Ministry. These concerns were based on the fact that the two non-governmental experts at issue had represented the US domestic industry in the context of US anti-dumping proceedings concerning imports of cement from Mexico. Cruz Azul provided the Ministry with copies of the Administrative Protection Orders ("APOs") signed by those individuals in the context of those US proceedings.

8.248 In a letter dated 26 November 1996, the Ministry informed Cruz Azul, *inter alia*, that the non-governmental experts had signed an agreement to protect the confidentiality of all confidential information. The Ministry also informed Cruz Azul that it was up to the investigating authority to determine the composition of its verification team, and that the Ministry would have no choice but to base its final determination on the best information available if Cruz Azul refused to cooperate.

8.249 The Ministry's verification team arrived at the offices of Cruz Azul on 3 December 1996. Cruz Azul again claimed that two of the non-governmental experts in the Ministry's verification team had a conflict of interest, referring to their participation in a US anti-dumping investigation against imports of cement from Mexico. Cruz Azul requested that the verification proceed without those two particular non-governmental experts. The Ministry repeated that those experts had signed a confidentiality agreement, and added that Cruz Azul had not been a party to the US anti-dumping proceedings in which the experts had represented the US domestic industry. According to Guatemala, the Ministry therefore had no choice but to inform Cruz Azul and the Mexican Government that their refusal to cooperate would require the Ministry to base its final determination of dumping on the best information available.

8.250 In our view, it was entirely reasonable for Cruz Azul to object to the inclusion in the Ministry's verification team of two non-governmental experts who had represented US cement producers against Mexican cement producers in US anti-dumping proceedings. Although it is true, as argued by Guatemala, that Cruz Azul was not an interested party in those US anti-dumping proceedings, information gleaned by rep-

[864] See *Korea - Dairy Safeguards*, *supra*, footnote 531, para. 7.67.

resentatives of the US domestic industry could be used to Cruz Azul's disadvantage in the Ministry's proceeding against it. We consider it unlikely that individuals who had acted against Mexican cement producers in the context of the US proceeding could completely detach themselves from their previous functions when conducting a verification at Cruz Azul. In particular, there is no guarantee that the role of the two non-governmental experts in the US proceedings (*i.e.*, to assist US domestic producers in their claims against Mexican cement exporters) would not undermine their objectivity and impartiality during the verification visit to Cruz Azul. The fact that steps may have been taken to ensure that the non-governmental experts did not violate the confidentiality of Cruz Azul's data provides no guarantee that their role in the US proceedings would not undermine their objectivity and impartiality during the verification visit to Cruz Azul, since it is possible to be partial and non-objective while preserving confidentiality.

8.251 In light of these considerations, we do not consider that an objective and impartial investigating authority could properly have found that Cruz Azul significantly impeded its investigation by objecting to the inclusion of non-governmental experts with a conflict of interest in its verification team. We do not consider that a failure to cooperate necessarily constitutes significant impediment of an investigation, since in our view the AD Agreement does not require cooperation by interested parties at any cost. Although there are certain consequences (under Article 6.8) for interested parties if they fail to cooperate with an investigating authority, in our view such consequences only arise if the investigating authority itself has acted in a reasonable, objective and impartial manner. In light of the facts of this case, we find that the Ministry did not act in such a manner.

8.252 Furthermore, Annex II(3) provides that all information which is "verifiable", and "appropriately submitted so that it can be used in the investigation without undue difficulties", should be taken into account by the investigating authority when determinations are made. In other words, "best information available" should not be used when information is "verifiable", and when "it can be used in the investigation without undue difficulties". In our view, the information submitted by Cruz Azul was "verifiable". The fact that it was not actually verified as a result of the Ministry's response to reasonable concerns raised by Cruz Azul does not change this. In addition, there is nothing in the Ministry's final determination to suggest that the information submitted by Cruz Azul could not be used in the investigation "without undue difficulties". Since the information was "verifiable", and since the Ministry did not demonstrate that it could not be used "without undue difficulties", Annex II(3) provides strong contextual support for the above conclusion that the Ministry violated Article 6.8 in using the "best information available" as a result of the cancelled verification visit.

8.253 Accordingly, we find that the Ministry violated Article 6.8, read in light of paragraph 3 of Annex II of the AD Agreement, in having recourse to the "best information available" for the purpose of making its final dumping determination.

8.254 The above finding is based on the Ministry's own justification for recourse to the "best information available" (*i.e.*, that the information submitted by Cruz Azul could not be verified). We do not consider it necessary to make findings on the basis of the *ex post* justification provided by Guatemala in these proceedings (*i.e.*, Cruz Azul's failure to provide sales data for the extended POI, and its failure to provide certain cost data). Even if we did so, however, a similar result would likely ensue.

With regard to Cruz Azul's failure to provide sales data for the extended POI, we have found that the Ministry was entitled to extend the POI without informing Cruz Azul of the reasons why it did so. In such circumstances, the Ministry may have been entitled to use the "best information available" for sales data which Cruz Azul failed to submit in respect of the extended POI. However, the Ministry's use of the "best information available" was not restricted to the extended POI. The Ministry also used "best information available" (*i.e.*, two invoices attached to Cementos Progreso's application) concerning the original POI, even though neither the Ministry nor Guatemala has argued that Cruz Azul failed to provide sales data for the original POI. An impartial and objective investigating authority could not properly rely on "best information available" sales data for the original POI, simply on the basis of Cruz Azul's failure to provide sales data for the extended POI. Although we do not consider it necessary to make any finding in this regard, we do not consider that an impartial and objective investigating authority could properly have had recourse to the "best information available" for sales data for the original POI in these circumstances.

8.255 With regard to cost data, we note that the Ministry used "best information available" cost data for the whole POI. However, there is evidence in the record that Cruz Azul submitted cost of production data for its Lagunas plant for the year 1995 (see Annex Mexico-64) in its reply to the Ministry's supplementary questionnaire. The year 1995 covers the original POI, and the first month of the extended POI. Mexico asserts that only the Lagunas plant manufactured cement destined for the Guatemalan market. Guatemala has not disputed that assertion, but has stated that the Ministry required access to cost data from all of Cruz Azul's Mexican production facilities in order to calculate normal value. However, Guatemala has failed to demonstrate that the information could not be used in the investigation "without undue difficulties", within the meaning of Annex II(3) of the AD Agreement. There is no such explanation in the Ministry's January 1997 Resolution. Indeed, the fact that Cruz Azul even submitted this information is not mentioned in the Ministry's final Resolution. It is true that the cost data only covered the original POI and part of the extended POI. Thus, the Ministry may have been entitled to use "best information available" cost data for the remainder of the extended POI. However, the Ministry used "best information available" cost data for the whole POI. As discussed above, failure to provide data for part of the POI cannot justify recourse to "best information available" for the whole POI. Although we do not consider it necessary to make any finding in this regard, we do not consider that an impartial and objective investigating authority could properly have had recourse to the "best information available" to ascertain costs for the whole of the POI in these circumstances.

8.256 In light of our finding that the Ministry's recourse to the "best information available" violated Article 6.8, read in light of paragraph 3 of Annex II, we need not examine Mexico's additional claims concerning the dumping analysis performed by the Ministry.

2. *Mexico's Claims Concerning the Ministry's Final Determination of Injury*

(a) Change of threat of injury to material injury

8.257 Mexico claims that Guatemala's change of its injury finding from a preliminary determination of threat of material injury to a final determination of material injury gave rise to violations of Articles 6, 12 as well as Article 3.

8.258 To the extent that this claim refers to the issue that Guatemala acted inconsistently with Articles 6 in respect of its extension of the period of investigation and a change from a preliminary determination of threat of material injury to a final determination of material injury, we have already addressed these claims *supra* in sections D.5. and D.10.

8.259 To the extent that Mexico claims that the Ministry's injury determinations were not based on positive or sufficient evidence, contrary to Article 3, this matter is addressed in the following sections.

8.260 To the extent that Mexico claims that the notification under Article 12 of imposition of a definitive anti-dumping measure was insufficient, we address this matter at para. 8.291 below.

(b) Volume of dumped imports

8.261 Mexico claims that the evaluation by Guatemala of the volume of dumped imports was not consistent with Article 3.2 of the AD Agreement for a number of reasons. *First,* Mexico asserts that Guatemala confined itself to considering the maximum and minimum volumes imported during the investigation period. *Second,* Guatemala used a data collection period of one year and failed to compare the volume of dumped imports during that period to earlier periods in order to analyse long-term trends in imports. *Third*, Guatemala erroneously determined the volume of imports of grey portland cement from Mexico by including imports of the product under investigation from sources other than Mexico and by including other types of cement not under investigation, for example, grey cement or slow-setting cement, which are imported under the same tariff heading. *In addition,* Mexico argues that Guatemala violated Articles 3.1, 3.2, and 3.5 by failing to take into account certain imports of the product under investigation imported by MATINSA, an importer associated with the petitioner, Cementos Progreso.[865]

8.262 Guatemala asserts that it examined the volume of dumped imports both in absolute and in relative terms. Guatemala found that during the investigation period imports from Cruz Azul increased from 140 tons in June 1995 to 25,079 tons in May 1996, with a maximum in March 1996 (45,859.31 tons). Cruz Azul's share in do-

---

[865] Mexico also asserts that the Ministry did not consider that the change from a threat of material injury to material injury would in any case require an evaluation of the volume of dumped imports in accordance with Article 3.2 of the AD Agreement, as opposed to the analysis of "a significant rate of increase of dumped imports" under Article 3.7(i) carried out in the preliminary determination of threat of material injury. We are of the view that our present task is to consider whether Guatemala's examination of the volume of dumped imports complied with Article whether 3.2, not whether and how it differed from Guatemala's examination of the volume of dumped imports for the purpose of the preliminary determination.

mestic consumption went from one per cent of the Guatemalan market (in June 1995) to 21 per cent of the market (May 1996) with a high of 32 per cent in March. Guatemala argues that it properly examined the rate at which import volumes were increasing as required by Article 3.2. Guatemala asserts that there was no need to evaluate import trends for periods prior to 1995 as there were simply no imports of Cruz Azul cement until June 1995. Guatemala also argues that it took MATINSA's imports into account and concluded that they did not weaken its determination of injury caused by cement imports from Cruz Azul. Guatemala also argues that it did not disregard the existence of other types of cement, imported under tariff heading 2523.29.00. In its analysis, the Ministry only considered imports from Cruz Azul. The Ministry noted that imports from Cruz Azul represented 91 per cent of total imports of grey cement into Guatemala during the investigation period. The Ministry did not assume that all the imports under this tariff heading were from Cruz Azul.

8.263 Articles 3.2 provides that:

> "3.2 With regard to the volume of the dumped imports, the investigating authorities shall consider whether there has been a significant increase in dumped imports, either in absolute terms or relative to production or consumption in the importing Member. With regard to the effect of the dumped imports on prices, the investigating authorities shall consider whether there has been a significant price undercutting by the dumped imports as compared with the price of a like product of the importing Member, or whether the effect of such imports is otherwise to depress prices to a significant degree or prevent price increases, which otherwise would have occurred, to a significant degree. No one or several of these factors can necessarily give decisive guidance."

8.264 We have based our analysis of Guatemala's compliance with Article 3 on the Ministry's resolution imposing the anti-dumping measure and the Extended Report on Injury[866] (hereinafter "Injury Report").

8.265 We first examine Mexico's claim that Guatemala's consideration whether there was a significant increase in dumped imports was inconsistent with Article 3.2 because Guatemala confined itself to considering the maximum and minimum imports during the period of investigation. We note that the Ministry did a month by month examination of the total volume of imports of grey portland cement as well as of the volume of Mexican imports.[867] Although in the text of the resolution Guatemala reported the end to end and highest and lowest point results of their analysis of the volume of dumped imports, it is evident from Table 10 of the Injury Report that the authorities considered the situation during each of the intervening months during the period they chose for data collection. The Panel does not agree with Mexico's assertion that "Guatemala confined itself to maximum and minimum volumes imported during the investigation period". Thus, we do not consider that Guatemala acted inconsistently with Article 3.2 in this respect.

---

[866] Annex Mexico-43.

[867] This can be evidenced in Table 10 of the Ministry's resolution imposing the definitive measure and the extended report on injury.

8.266 We next consider Mexico's claim that Guatemala's consideration whether there was a significant increase in dumped imports was inconsistent with Article 3.2 because Guatemala used a data collection period of one year and failed to compare the volume of dumped imports during that period to earlier periods in order to analyse long-term trends in imports. In this regard, we recall that Guatemala chose a period of data collection of one year from June 1995 to May 1996. A recent recommendation of the Committee on Anti-Dumping Practices calls on Members to use a data collection period of at least three years. This recommendation reflects the common practice of Members.[868] That said, there is no provision in the Agreement which specifies the precise duration of the period of data collection. Thus, it cannot be said *a priori* that the use of a one-year period of data collection would not be consistent with the requirement of Article 3.2 to consider whether there has been a significant increase in the volume of dumped imports in the circumstances of a particular case. In this case, Guatemala argues that the reason for the short period of data collection was that exports by Cruz Azul did not become significant until 1995. The record of the investigation supports this conclusion.[869] Under these circumstances, while a longer data collection period might have been preferable, we are unable to find that the use by Guatemala of a one-year data collection period was inconsistent with Guatemala's obligation under Article 3.2 to consider whether there was a significant increase in dumped imports.

8.267 We next turn to Mexico's argument that Guatemala made an erroneous determination of the volume of imports of grey portland cement from Mexico by including imports from sources other than Mexico, and by including types of cement other than the product under investigation, imported under the same tariff heading. Although we note that Mexico has presented evidence indicating the existence of imports of grey cement from sources other than Mexico and of products other than grey portland cement during the period of investigation.[870] We do not consider that this evidence goes to the question, presented in Mexico's claim, of whether there were any imports other than those of Mexico or of the product under investigations which have been included in the column "Imports from Mexico" in Table 10 of the Injury Report (Annex Mexico-43).[871] The evidence presented by Mexico on this issue does not render the figures included in Table 10 of the Injury Report unreliable. The fact that Mexico has shown that there were imports of grey cement from different sources

---

[868] The recommendation provides that:

> "(c) the period of data collection for injury investigations normally should be at least three years, unless a party from whom data is being gathered has existed for a lesser period, and should include the entirety of the period of data collection for the dumping investigation; " (Recommendation Concerning the Periods of Data Collection for Anti-Dumping Investigations, adopted by the ADP Committee on 5 May 2000, G/ADP/6).

We note that this recommendation is a relevant, but non-binding, indication of the understanding of Members as to appropriate implementation practice regarding the period of data collection for an anti-dumping investigation.

[869] See, Table 10 of the Injury Report.

[870] Annex Mexico-41.

[871] We consider Table 10 of the Injury Report to be the basis for Guatemala's analysis under Article 3.2.

and that there were imports of other types of cement different from the product under investigation, does not show that the Ministry has erred when calculating the total volume of imports of grey portland cement figures that appear in Table 10 of the injury report. Thus, we find that Mexico has failed to make a *prima facie* case that Guatemala's establishment of the facts was improper and violated Article 3.2 by wrongly including as imports grey portland cement from Mexico, imports from sources other than Mexico and imports of other types of cement not under investigation.

8.268 Finally, we turn to Mexico's claim that Guatemala violated Articles 3.1, 3.2, and 3.5 by failing to take into account certain undumped imports of the product under investigation imported by an importer named MATINSA, which is associated with the petitioner, Cementos Progreso. Although Mexico's arguments on this point are unclear, we understand Mexico to be arguing that Guatemala considered MATINSA's imports to be of non-pozzolanic cement which differed from the like domestic product and thus were not taken into consideration during the investigation. Mexico considers however that the product imported by MATINSA was in fact the same product as that under investigation. In Mexico's view, the failure by Guatemala to correctly characterise the imports by MATINSA carried the following consequences (i) the resulting volume of total imports of the product under investigation was lower; (ii) the share of allegedly dumped imports in total imports of the product under investigation was artificially inflated; (iii) the consideration of a faulty and incomplete figure for total imports of the product under investigation yielded a distorted figure for apparent domestic consumption; (iv) because of this incorrect figure for apparent domestic consumption, the relationship between the increase in dumped imports and consumption was ultimately incorrect; (v) by considering that MATINSA's imports did not concern the product under investigation, the investigating authority failed to assess other factors which were injuring the domestic industry at the same time, such as imports that were not sold at dumped prices.

8.269 The consequences listed as number (i) through (iv) above constitute a violation of Article 3.1 and 3.2 in that an exclusion of MATINSA's imports from the figures for domestic consumption of the like product affects the comparison that is made with the figures for volume of dumped imports for purposes of determining that there has been a significant increase in dumped imports relative to domestic consumption in the importing Member.[872] Item (v) above constitutes a violation of Article 3.5 in that this provision establishes:

> "The authorities shall also examine any known factors other than the dumped imports which at the same time are injuring the domestic industry, and the injuries caused by these other factors must not be attributed to the dumped imports. Factors which may be relevant in this

[872] We note that Guatemala establishes that there was both an increase of the dumped imports in absolute terms and also an increase relative to domestic consumption and production (see Injury Report Table 10 and Guatemala's first submission para. 359). Guatemala relied on both of these finding to determine that there was material injury to the domestic industry. So, to the extent that one of the findings on the increased volume of dumped imports was proved to be inappropriate Guatemala's determination under Articles 3.1 and 3.2 would be inconsistent with its obligations.

> respect include, *inter alia*, the volume and prices of imports not sold at dumping prices..."

Imports by MATINSA of grey portland cement would constitute the type of imports which are recognized in the AD Agreement as a possible source of injury different from the dumped imports. Thus, a failure to examine such imports as another known factor causing injury would constitute a violation of Article 3.5. We recognize the merit in Mexico's arguments on this issue and to the extent that Mexico presents us with evidence to support the argument it has succeeded in establishing a *prima facie* case that Guatemala has violated Articles 3.1, 3.2 and 3.5. It would be then for Guatemala to rebut the existence of a violation under Articles 3.1, 3.2 and 3.5. We shall now examine whether it has succeeded in doing so.

8.270 Mexico's argument on this issue relies on two factual predicates. The first is that there were imports by MATINSA during the period of investigation of the subject product. To this effect Mexico has presented evidence that shows that during the period of investigation there were imports by MATINSA classified as grey portland cement and type I pozzolanic cement.[873] Guatemala did not challenge the validity of such evidence.

8.271 The second factual predicate relied on by Mexico is that Guatemala excluded all imports by MATINSA from the total imports of the like product. On this predicate we note that the evidence is unclear and there are several inconsistencies in Guatemala's argumentation. In its final determination,[874] injury report[875] and answer to question 63 from Mexico, Guatemala asserts that imports by MATINSA were not of the like product. In order to clarify this issue the Panel asked Guatemala whether it had included imports by producers other than Cruz Azul in the total volume of Mexican imports shown in Table 10 of the Injury Report. Guatemala failed to directly answer our question and asserts in their answer that:

> "The file of the investigation also confirms that the cement investigated was produced by Cruz Azul. The only evidence in the file that remotely suggests otherwise consists of a few imports by the company MATINSA in 1995. However, these transactions concern type I pozzolanic cement which was not produced by Cruz Azul, and represent only 0.003 per cent of MATINSA's total imports, a negligible amount in comparison to total imports from Cruz Azul (i.e. only 348.5 metric tonnes), as Guatemala explained in its reply to question 61 from Mexico following the second substantive meeting. In its reply to question 63 from Mexico, Guatemala explained that the rest of the cement imported by MATINSA was high-resistance cement type 5,000 PSI which was not under investigation by the Ministry of the Economy."

Thus, Guatemala does not deny that there were imports of the like product by MATINSA during the period of investigation. However, this still leaves the issue of

[873] Annex Mexico-46. This annex consists of a list of import transactions of cement from the official statistics by the Customs Authority of Guatemala.

[874] Final Determination Section E.2 (Annex Mexico-10).

[875] Injury Report p. 3 (Annex Mexico-43).

their treatment for purposes of the injury determination unclear. Guatemala further argues that imports by MATINSA of the product under investigation were insignificant as they represent only 0.003 per cent of MATINSA's total imports.[876] We find that there are inconsistencies in this assertion. First, we note that there is an inconsistency as to the total volume of imports during the period of investigation by MATINSA. Guatemala asserts in answer to question 60 from Mexico that total imports by MATINSA for the period of investigation were 117,223.83 tons, while in the Final Determination the figure for total imports by MATINSA is of 79,426 tons.[877] Second, there is also an inconsistency as to the volume of imports of MATINSA's imports of type I pozzolanic cement. Guatemala asserts that imports of type I pozzolanic cement by MATINSA were 348.5 tons, while the evidence presented by Mexico indicates that these imports were at least 16,766.71 tons during the period of investigation.[878] Third, even assuming that Guatemala's figures for total imports and type I pozzolanic cement imports by MATINSA were correct, there is also an inconsistency as to the calculation of the proportion of imports of type I pozzolanic cement in MATINSA's total imports. Guatemala asserts that imports of type I pozzolanic cement were 0.003 per cent of total imports by MATINSA. Even assuming that the correct figure for total imports by MATINSA was the higher of the two reported (i.e. 117,223.83 tons), the 348.5 tons imports of type I pozzolanic cement by MATINSA would represent 0.297 per cent of total imports by MATINSA not 0.003 per cent as alleged by Guatemala.

8.272 The issue of Guatemala's treatment of MATINSA's imports of the subject merchandise remains obscure. However, In the face of the inconsistencies of Guatemala's argumentation and taking into account the evidence presented by Mexico, we are of the view that Guatemala has failed to rebut the *prima facie* case of violation of Article 3.1, 3.2 and 3.5 established by Mexico. Thus, we find that Guatemala has violated Articles 3.1, 3.2 and 3.5 as explained above in para. 8.269 by wrongly characterizing some imports by MATINSA as not of the like product and failing to take into account these imports in its determination of injury and causality.

(c) Price effects

8.273 Mexico claims that Guatemala did not comply with Article 3.2 of the AD Agreement because in its final affirmative determination of injury it included a series of assertions concerning the price trends without having any elements to uphold its determination. Specifically Mexico argues Guatemala lacked evidence to: i) support a determination that the price of the grey portland cement imported from Mexico undercut the price of domestic grey portland cement manufactured by Cementos Progreso; ii) substantiate a determination that the effect of the imports on the domestic production had led to a significant reduction or prevented an increase, or; iii) support the finding that the alleged dumping, was the cause of any negative effect on domestic prices and not other elements. Mexico argues that this lack of support is evi-

[876] We note that the significance of the imports would be more appropriately measured with respect of the total imports of the subject merchandise, not total imports by MATINSA.

[877] Final Determination, Antecedentes para. 8. (Annex Mexico-10).

[878] Annex Mexico-46.

denced by the fact that Guatemala did not compare the domestic like product prices for the period of investigation with the prices for the previous year to establish that the dumped Mexican imports were causing the price depression.

8.274 Mexico also claims that the Ministry's analysis of the effect on the prices was erroneously done at the regional level only, and not at the national level in violation of Article 3.2. Mexico bases its claim on the statement in the final determination by Guatemala that the difference between the prices actually charged for the domestic product and the ceiling price fixed by the government was greater in the western region of Guatemala bordering with Mexico.

8.275 Guatemala asserts that it examined information on prices at both wholesale and retail level in Guatemala during the investigation period. This examination revealed significant price undercutting by Cruz Azul at both levels. Then it examined whether imports from Cruz Azul were depressing prices or preventing price increases in Guatemala to a significant degree. Among other things, the Ministry found that "(a) imports from Cruz Azul had an immediate and adverse effect on Cementos Progreso's prices; (b) the dumped imports made a greater impact in the area adjacent to the Mexican frontier (especially in the Departments of San Marcos, Quetzaltenango and Retalhuleu) where Cruz Azul concentrated its sales; (c) despite increases in the maximum price for cement established by the government during the investigation period, Cementos Progreso "undertook a significant number of transactions at below the maximum selling price ..."; and (d) if there had been no imports from Cruz Azul, Cementos Progreso "would have been able to sell at the maximum prices established [by the government]".[879] Guatemala also argues that Mexico has not shown, as required by the standard of review applicable, that Guatemala's factual findings were not properly established or were biased. Thus, the Panel has no basis to substitute its interpretation of the facts for that of the Guatemalan authorities.

8.276 We shall first address Mexico's argument that Guatemala lacked the elements to support its conclusion that there had been a negative price effect on the prices for the domestic like product by the dumped imports. We note that Mexico's argument on the lack of support for Guatemala's finding on price effect depends on Mexico's assertion that Guatemala should have done a comparison with the prices that the domestic industry charged for a period prior to the period of investigation. We have already found that Guatemala did not violate the AD Agreement in establishing a period of data collection of injury of only one year,[880] and consequently it was not obliged to review data outside that period. Moreover, Guatemala submitted evidence[881] that was part of the record of the investigation, and that supports the determination that: i) prices for the domestic industry declined after the Mexican imports entered the market, configuring a situation of price depression; ii) that those prices declined to a level below the maximum price authorized by the Government, and; iii) that although the maximum price increased at the end of the period the domestic producer could not increase its prices accordingly, configuring a situation of price

[879] Injury Report p. 18-20 (Annex Mexico-43).

[880] See para. 8.266 *supra*.

[881] Annex Guatemala-68.

suppression.[882] Based on the evidence of declining prices and inability to achieve established price levels, coinciding with imports at lower prices we find that an objective and unbiased investigating authority could have properly concluded that the dumped imports were having a negative effect on the prices of the domestic industry. Moreover, Mexico did not adduce any evidence to convince us otherwise. Thus, we reject Mexico's claim of an improper and unsupported Article 3.2 analysis by Guatemala.

8.277 We shall now address Mexico's argument that Guatemala improperly conducted a regional evaluation of the effect the dumped imports had on the prices of the domestic like product. The mere fact that Guatemala mentions that the greatest differential between the government fixed ceiling price and the actual price was felt in the Departments of San Marcos, Quetzaltenango and Retalhuleu does not, in our view, mean that the analysis was limited to these regions alone, to the exclusion of Guatemala as a whole. In fact, the mention that these were the departments with the greatest differential indicates to us that other departments were analysed. Moreover, there is only one producer of cement in Guatemala, thus, even if the negative effect of the dumped imports on the prices of the domestic like product was only evidenced in the region bordering Mexico, this could still be viewed as causing injury to Cementos Progreso. Based on these considerations we find that Guatemala acted in accordance with its obligation under Article 3.2 to conduct an examination of the effect the dumped imports had on the domestic industry. Therefore, we reject Mexico's claim of violation of Article 3.2 on the basis of an improper regional injury evaluation.

(d) Impact on the domestic industry

8.278 Mexico claims that Guatemala made an incorrect determination of the alleged impact of the dumped imports on sales of grey portland cement by the domestic industry. Among other arguments Mexico asserts that Guatemala has failed to consider whether the domestic industry experienced a decline in their returns on investment and a negative effect on their ability to raise capital.

8.279 Other arguments by Mexico with respect to the adequacy of the examination of the impact of the imports on the domestic industry include Guatemala's failure to consider the potential decline in the factors listed in Article 3.4, as well as, inconsistent and inappropriate comparisons by Guatemala between data pertaining to the period of investigation and data outside the period of investigation.

8.280 Guatemala asserts that it based its final determination on positive evidence and an objective examination of, *inter alia*, the consequent impact of Cruz Azul imports on the domestic industry, in accordance with Article 3.1 and 3.4 of the Anti-Dumping Agreement. Guatemala states that the Ministry's examination revealed that, among other things, Cruz Azul imports had caused:

---

[882] Guatemala presented evidence indicating that before the arrival of the imports prices were to the level of the maximum price. We are of the view that as this price is calculated on the basis of costs and inflation it constitutes a reasonable benchmark to establish the price at which the domestic producer of cement in Guatemala could have expected to increase its prices but for the competition from the dumped imports.

(i) Cementos Progreso's sales to decline by 14 per cent between the first quarter of 1995 and the first quarter of 1996. This decline coincided with Cruz Azul's entry into the market;

(ii) Cementos Progreso to lose customers;

(iii) domestic cement production to a decline of 14 per cent between the first quarter of 1995 and the first quarter of 1996. This reduction began when Cruz Azul started importing cement into Guatemala;

(iv) a decline of between 20 and 30 per cent in Cementos Progreso's share of the domestic market;

(v) a decline in Cementos Progreso's capacity to utilise both clinker and finished cement;

(vi) a 12 per cent fall in domestic utilization of cement grinding capacity and a 16 per cent fall in domestic utilization of clinker production capacity;

(vii) Cementos Progreso to experience negative cash flow during the first months of 1996;

(viii) Cementos Progreso to postpone investment plans to modernize its plant and increase its production capacity; and

(ix) Cementos Progreso to accumulate excessive inventories as from August 1995.

8.281 Guatemala also argues that the issue before this Panel is whether the establishment of the facts by the investigating authority was "proper" and whether its evaluation of those facts was "unbiased and objective". Guatemala asserts that Mexico has not shown Guatemala to have violated any of these standards.

8.282 Article 3.4 provides:

> "3.4 The examination of the impact of the dumped imports on the domestic industry concerned shall include an evaluation of all relevant economic factors and indices having a bearing on the state of the industry, including actual and potential decline in sales, profits, output, market share, productivity, return on investments, or utilization of capacity; factors affecting domestic prices; the magnitude of the margin of dumping; actual and potential negative effects on cash flow, inventories, employment, wages, growth, ability to raise capital or investments. This list is not exhaustive, nor can one or several of these factors necessarily give decisive guidance."

8.283 Before turning to Guatemala's analysis with respect to the factors in Article 3.4 we would like to outline what is the task before us in this review. We note that Article 3.4 lists a series of factors which it characterizes as relevant in an examination of whether the dumped imports had an impact on the domestic industry. It also mentions that the list is non exhaustive, in other words, there may also be other factors which although not listed may give guidance on the state of the industry. We also note that Article 3.4 provides that the examination "shall include" all relevant economic factors and indices having a bearing on the state of the industry and specifies that among those factors which are considered relevant are those which listed therein. Thus, it is essential, in order to satisfy the requirements in Article 3.4, to examine each of the factors listed in that provision. In our view Article 3.4 establishes a rebuttable presumption that those factors listed are relevant in giving guidance on whether the dumped imports have had an effect on the domestic industry. It is only after consideration of the listed factors that the investigating authority may dismiss some of them as not being relevant for the particular industry, thus in effect rebutting the presumption established in Article 3.4. We are also of the view that the consideration of the factors in Article 3.4 must be apparent in the determination so the Panel may assess whether the authority acted in accordance with Article 3.4 at the time of the investigation.

8.284 Our interpretation is supported by other panels which have expressed similar views. For example the panel in *Mexico - HFCS* determined:

> "In our view, this language makes it clear that the listed factors in Article 3.4 must be considered in all cases. There may be other relevant economic factors in the circumstances of a particular case, consideration of which would also be required. In a threat of injury case, for instance, the AD Agreement itself establishes that consideration of the Article 3.7 factors is also required. But consideration of the Article 3.4 factors is required in every case, even though such consideration may lead the investigating authority to conclude that a particular factor is not probative in the circumstances of a particular industry or a particular case, and therefore is not relevant to the actual determination. Moreover, the consideration of each of the Article 3.4 factors must be apparent in the final determination of the investigating authority."[883] (Footnote omitted)[884]

8.285 As a first step in our examination of Guatemala's analysis of the impact of the dumped imports on the domestic industry, we must evaluate whether all the factors listed in Article 3.4 have been considered. In this regard, we note that Mexico argues that Guatemala has failed to consider whether the domestic industry's experienced a decline in return on investment and a negative effect on their ability to raise capital. Paragraph 4.9 of Guatemala's final determination, contains some discussion concerning investment and the risks to investors for the period of investigation. How-

---

[883] *Mexico - HFCS, supra*, footnote 34, para. 7.128.

[884] In the context of a safeguard investigation the *Korea - Dairy Safeguard* panel when considering Article 4.2 of the Agreement on Safeguards, which is very similar to Article 3.4 of the AD Agreement, made the following remarks:

> "among 'all relevant factors' that the investigating authorities 'shall evaluate', the consideration of the factors listed is always relevant and therefore required, even though the authority may later dismiss some of them as not having a bearing on the situation of that industry". (*Korea-Dairy Safeguard, supra*, footnote 531, para. 7.55. *See also Argentina-Footwear Safeguard, supra*, footnote 697, para. 8.123.)

That panel also noted that in reviewing the serious injury determination made by the Korean authorities, its task was to examine:

> "whether at the time of the determination all factors listed in Article 4.2 were appropriately considered; whether the Korean authorities explained how each factor considered supports (or detracts from) a finding of serious injury; and whether valid reasons have been put forward for dismissing a considered factor as not being relevant to the serious injury determination in this case". *Korea-Dairy Safeguard, supra*, footnote 531, para. 7.55.)

ever, this paragraph is just a discussion of the operative balance of Cementos Progreso and does not pertain to the specific factors of return on investment and ability to raise capital. With respect to factors of return on investments and ability to raise capital, we can find no indication in the determination that Guatemala considered these factors in the injury determination. Thus, we find that Guatemala has acted inconsistently with Article 3.4 in its examination of the impact of the dumped imports on the domestic industry, by failing to examine all relevant factors listed in Article 3.4.

8.286 Having found that Guatemala acted inconsistently with its obligations under Article 3.4 in failing to consider all of the relevant factors, we are of the view that it is neither necessary nor appropriate for us to further examine the rest of the arguments put forward by Mexico with respect to the adequacy of the consideration of each of the factors in Article 3.4.

3. *Mexico's Claims Concerning the Ministry's Final Determination of the Existence of a Causal Link Between the Dumped Imports and the Injury to the Domestic Industry.*

8.287 Mexico claims that Guatemala could not have demonstrated the existence of a causal link in compliance with Article 3.5, for the following reasons. First, the investigating authority did not evaluate the alleged impact of the imports investigated on the value and volume of sales, pressure on selling prices, deterioration in the financial situation, market share and employment, as required by Article 3.4 of the AD Agreement. Neither did it make statistically valid comparisons to allow it to undertake an objective examination of the effect of the imports allegedly dumped, as required by Article 3.1 of the AD Agreement. Second, in the final determination, the Ministry recognized that the fixing of a maximum selling price was a disadvantage for the domestic industry in comparison with products imported from any country, but failed to consider fully the injury that may have been caused by this other factor. Third, the Ministry did not evaluate the impact that a commitment by Cementos Progreso to sell the product investigated to the Guatemalan State at a price lower than the selling price to the public might have had on the status of the domestic industry.

8.288 Mexico also claims that the Ministry was not able to establish a causal relationship between the imports of grey portland cement and the alleged injury to the domestic industry because it had not properly determined the existence of material injury.

8.289 In our examination concerning the Ministry's evaluation of the volume of the dumped imports we found that Guatemala acted in violation of Article 3.5 by failing to consider other factors known to the investigating authority which may also be a cause of injury.[885] In light of that finding, we are of the view that it is neither necessary nor appropriate for us to further consider Mexico's claims concerning a violation of Article 3.5.

---

[885] See, *supra* para. 8.272.

4. *Claims by Mexico Concerning the Public Notice of Imposition of a Definitive Anti-Dumping Measure*

8.290 Mexico claims that the public notice of conclusion of the investigation, which contained the final affirmative determination on the imposition of definitive anti-dumping duties, published in the *Diario Oficial de Centro América* of 30 January 1997[886] did not comply with the requirements in Article 12.2 and 12.2.2 of the AD Agreement because it did not contain all the relevant information on the issues of fact and law nor did it include sufficiently detailed explanations of the reasons that led the Ministry to impose the definitive anti-dumping measure nor several of its determinations.

8.291 We are of view that the issue of Guatemala's' compliance with the transparency obligations deriving from its decision to impose definitive anti-dumping measures on imports of cement from Mexico would only be relevant if the decision to impose the measure itself had been consistent with the AD Agreement. Therefore, having found that Guatemala infringed the substantive provisions of the AD Agreement in their decision to impose an anti-dumping measure in this case, we consider that it is not necessary for us to rule on whether Guatemala complied with its transparency obligations under Article 12.2 and 12.2.2 with respect to the imposition of a measure already found not to be consistent with Guatemala's WTO obligations.

5. *Claims by Mexico Regarding the Definitive Measure's Inconsistency with Articles 1, 9 and 18 of the AD Agreement and Article VI of GATT 1994*

8.292 Throughout this dispute Mexico has claimed that Guatemala did not make a valid determination of dumping or injury and also failed to demonstrate a causal relationship between them, as required by Articles 2 and 3 of the AD Agreement. Mexico has also claimed that Guatemala violated Articles 5, 6, 7 and 12 when initiating the investigation and during its course.[887] Therefore, Mexico claims that Guatemala has also violated Articles 1, 9 and 18 of the AD Agreement and Article VI of GATT 1994, in so far as:

(a) Guatemala decided to establish definitive anti-dumping duties on grey portland cement from the Mexican firm Cruz Azul without having duly complied with all the requirements for their establishment prescribed by Article 9.1 of the AD Agreement;

(b) the application of the definitive anti-dumping measure without a valid determination of dumping injury and causal relationship between the two, is contrary to the provisions of Article VI of the GATT 1994 and in turn constitutes a violation of Article 1 and 18 of the AD Agreement.

8.293 Guatemala argues that Article 9.1 does not relate to and in no way incorporates the substantive requirements for the imposition of definitive anti-dumping duties contained in other provisions of the AD Agreement. With respect to claims of

---

886 Annex Mexico-11.

887 These claims the Panel has resolved *supra* in other sections of this report.

violations of Articles 1, and 18 of the AD Agreement and Article VI of the GATT 1994, Guatemala responds that these claims are based on the violation of other articles in the AD Agreement. Since Guatemala maintains that its investigation complied with all the rules in the AD Agreement, therefore, Guatemala asserts these claims lack merit.

8.294 Article 1 and Article 9.1 read:

> "1. An anti-dumping measure shall be applied only under the circumstances provided for in Article VI of GATT 1994 and pursuant to investigations initiated and conducted in accordance with the provisions of this Agreement. The following provisions govern the application of Article VI of GATT 1994 in so far as action is taken under anti-dumping legislation or regulations" (Footnote omitted)
>
> "9.1 The decision whether or not to impose an anti-dumping duty in cases where all requirements for the imposition have been fulfilled, and the decision whether the amount of the anti-dumping duty to be imposed shall be the full margin of dumping or less, are decisions to be made by the authorities of the importing Member. It is desirable that the imposition be permissive in the territory of all Members, and that the duty be less than the margin if such lesser duty would be adequate to remove the injury to the domestic industry.

8.295 Although Mexico does not specify exactly which provisions of Article 18 are pertinent to their claim, we believe that as it has been formulated, it can only refer to Article 18.1. This provisions reads:

> "18.1 No specific action against dumping of exports from another Member can be taken except in accordance with the provisions of GATT 1994, as interpreted by this Agreement."

8.296 We note that Mexico's claims under Articles 1, 9 and 18 of the AD Agreement, and Article VI of GATT 1994, are dependent claims, in the sense that they depend entirely on findings that Guatemala has violated other provisions of the AD Agreement. There would be no basis to Mexico's claims under Articles 1, 9 and 18 of the AD Agreement, and Article VI of GATT 1994, if Guatemala were not found to have violated other provisions of the AD Agreement. In light of the dependent nature of Mexico's claims under Articles 1, 9 and 18 of the AD Agreement, and Article VI of GATT 1994, we see no useful purpose to deciding them. In particular, deciding such dependent claims will provide no additional guidance as to the steps to be undertaken by Guatemala in order to implement our recommendation regarding the violations on which they are dependent.

F. Claims by Mexico Concerning the Provisional Anti-Dumping Measure

8.297 Mexico has made various claims concerning Guatemala's imposition of a provisional measure, specifically Mexico argues that :

(i) Guatemala was in breach of its obligations: under Article 7.1 of the AD Agreement, to give Cruz Azul an adequate opportunity to comment on the information provided to the Ministry in reply to a questionnaire it received; and, under Article 2.4 of the AD Agreement, to request from Cruz Azul additional information in order to clarify inaccuracies in Cruz Azul's reply to its questionnaire and to make a fair comparison between normal value and export price.

(ii) Guatemala's investigating authority never satisfied itself that the volume of sales on the Mexican domestic market of cement like that exported to Guatemala was of a sufficient magnitude to provide for proper comparison with the export price, thus violating Article 2.2 of the AD Agreement.

(iii) Guatemala's provisional anti-dumping measure was based on an affirmative determination of threat of injury derived from an inadequate and insufficient analysis of the factors in Article 3.7, as well as of the factors in Article 3.2, 3.4 and 3.5.

(iv) Guatemala violated Article 12.2.1 of the AD Agreement which sets out the requirements to be met by parties in their public notices of preliminary determinations.

8.298 We note that in response to a question from the Panel, Mexico confirms that it has not requested any recommendation from the Panel concerning the provisional measure *per se*.[888] We also note that Mexico's claims concerning the provisional measure are made in the context of the provisional measure as "an action preceding the definitive anti-dumping measure",[889] and those claims are made as a challenge to the definitive measure. Mexico therefore requests a ruling concerning the definitive measure, on the basis of claims regarding the provisional measure. At most, Mexico's claims concerning the provisional measure could only result in a ruling with respect to part of the definitive measure insofar as it relates to retrospective collection of the provisional measure (i.e., where it is mandated that the "provisional anti-dumping duties collected would remain in favor of the treasury"[890]). Since we have already made findings that give rise to a recommendation concerning the totality of the definitive measure,[891] we do not consider it necessary to further address claims (i.e. concerning the provisional measure) that could only result in a ruling concerning only part of the definitive measure. Accordingly, we do not consider it necessary to address Mexico's claims regarding the consistency of Guatemala's provisional measure with the provisions of the AD Agreement.

IX. CONCLUSIONS AND RECOMMENDATION

9.1 In light of the findings above, we conclude that Guatemala's initiation of an investigation, the conduct of the investigation and imposition of a definitive measure on imports of grey portland cement from Mexico's Cruz Azul is inconsistent with the requirements in the AD Agreement in that:

(a) Guatemala's determination that there was sufficient evidence of dumping and threat of injury to initiate an investigation, is inconsistent with Article 5.3 of the AD Agreement

[888] Oral response provided at the second meeting of the panel with the parties.
[889] Mexico oral statement at the first meeting of the Panel with the parties, Para.39.
[890] Guatemala's Final Determination, (Annex Mexico-10).
[891] See sections VIII.E.1 and VIII.E.2 above.

(b) Guatemala's determination that there was sufficient evidence of dumping and threat of injury to initiate an investigation and consequent failure to reject the application for anti-dumping duties by Cementos Progreso is inconsistent with Article 5.8 of the AD Agreement.

(c) Guatemala's failure to timely notify Mexico under Article 5.5 of the AD Agreement is inconsistent with that provision.

(d) Guatemala's failure to meet the requirements for a public notice of the initiation of an investigation is inconsistent with Article 12.1.1 of the AD Agreement.

(e) Guatemala's failure to timely provide the full text of the application to Mexico and Cruz Azul is inconsistent with Article 6.1.3 of the AD Agreement.

(f) Guatemala's failure to grant Mexico access to the file of the investigation is inconsistent with Articles 6.1.2 and 6.4 of the AD Agreement.

(g) Guatemala's failure to timely make Cementos Progreso's 19 December 1996 submission available to Cruz Azul until 8 January 1997 is inconsistent with Article 6.1.2 of the AD Agreement.

(h) Guatemala's failure to provide two copies of the file of the investigation as requested by Cruz Azul is inconsistent with Article 6.1.2 of the AD Agreement.

(i) Guatemala's extension of the period of investigation requested by Cementos Progreso without providing Cruz Azul with a full opportunity for the defence of its interest is inconsistent with Article 6.2 of the AD Agreement.

(j) Guatemala's failure to inform Mexico of the inclusion of non-governmental experts in the verification team is inconsistent with paragraph 2 of Annex I of the AD Agreement.

(k) Guatemala's failure to require Cementos Progreso's to provide a statement of the reasons why summarization of the information submitted during verification was not possible is inconsistent with Article 6.5.1 of the AD Agreement.

(l) Guatemala's decision to grant Cementos Progreso's 19 December submission confidential treatment on its own initiative is inconsistent with Article 6.5 of the AD Agreement.

(m) Guatemala's failure to "inform all interested parties of the essential facts under consideration which form the basis for the decision whether to apply definitive measures" is inconsistent with Article 6.9 of the AD Agreement.

(n) Guatemala's recourse to "best information available" for the purpose of making its final dumping determination is inconsistent with Article 6.8 of the AD Agreement.

(o) Guatemala's failure to take into account imports by MATINSA in its determination of injury and causality is inconsistent with Articles 3.1, 3.2 and 3.5 of the AD Agreement.

(p) Guatemala's failure to evaluate all relevant factors for the examination of the impact of the allegedly dumped imports on the domestic industry is inconsistent with Article 3.4.

9.2 Under Article 3.8 of the DSU, in cases where there is infringement of the obligations assumed under a covered agreement, the action is considered *prima facie* to constitute a case of nullification or impairment of benefits under that agreement. Guatemala has argued before us that the violations it committed under Articles 5.5, 6.1.3 and 12.1 did not cause nullification and impairment to Mexico. We have addressed this issue in section VIII.C.7 of this report and found that Guatemala failed to rebut the presumption of nullification or impairment in Article 3.8. As for the rest of the violations incurred by Guatemala, we conclude that to the extent that Guatemala has acted inconsistently with the provisions of the AD Agreement, as described in paragraph 9.1 *supra*, it has nullified or impaired the benefits accruing to the Mexico under that agreement.

9.3 The Panel recommends that the Dispute Settlement Body request Guatemala to bring its measures into conformity with its obligations under the WTO Agreement.

9.4 Mexico requests us to make certain specific suggestions on ways in which Guatemala could implement the Panel's recommendation. Specifically, Mexico asks us to suggest that Guatemala "revoke the anti-dumping measure adopted against imports of Mexican cement and refund the anti-dumping duties collected" pursuant to that measure.[892]

9.5 In considering Mexico's request, we first recall that Article 19.1 of the DSU provides in relevant part that:

> "When a Panel or the Appellate Body concludes that a measure is inconsistent with a covered agreement, it shall recommend that the Member concerned [footnote omitted] bring the measure into conformity with that agreement.[footnote omitted]. In addition to its recommendations, the panel or Appellate Body *may suggest ways in which the Member concerned could implement the recommendations*".(emphasis added).

Therefore, by virtue of Article 19.1 of the DSU, panels have discretion ("may") to suggest ways in which a Member could implement the above recommendation. Clearly, however, a panel is not required to make a suggestion should it not deem it appropriate to do so.

9.6 We have determined that Guatemala has acted inconsistently with its obligations under the AD Agreement in its imposition of anti-dumping duties on imports of grey portland cement from Mexico. We have found these violations to be of a fundamental nature and pervasive. Indeed, in general terms we have found that:

(a) An unbiased and objective investigating authority could not properly have determined, based on the evidence and information available at the time of initiation, that there was sufficient evidence to justify initiation of the anti-dumping investigation;

[892] Mexico first submission, p. 101.

(b) Guatemala conducted the anti-dumping investigation in a manner inconsistent with its obligations under various provisions of the AD Agreement;

(c) An unbiased and objective investigating authority could not properly have determined that the imports under investigation were being dumped, that the domestic producer of cement in Guatemala was being injured and that the imports were the cause of that injury.

In light of the nature and extent of the violations in this case, we do not perceive how Guatemala could properly implement our recommendation without revoking the anti-dumping measure at issue in this dispute. Accordingly, we suggest that Guatemala revoke its anti-dumping measure on imports of grey portland cement from Mexico.

9.7 In respect of Mexico's request that we suggest that Guatemala refund the anti-dumping duties collected, we note that Guatemala has now maintained a WTO-inconsistent anti-dumping measure in place for a period of three and a half years. Thus, we fully understand Mexico's desire to see the anti-dumping duties repaid and consider that repayment might be justifiable in circumstances such as these. We recall however that suggestions under Article 19.1 relate to ways in which a Member could implement a recommendation to bring a measure into conformity with a covered agreement. Mexico's request raises important systemic issues regarding the nature of the actions necessary to implement a recommendation under Article 19.1 of the DSU, issues which have not been fully explored in this dispute. Thus, we decline Mexico's request to suggest that Guatemala refund the anti-dumping duties collected.

9 780521 828574